# For-Profit Enterprise in Health Care

Committee on Implications of For-Profit
Enterprise in Health Care

INSTITUTE OF MEDICINE

Bradford H. Gray, Ph.D., *editor*

NATIONAL ACADEMY PRESS
Washington, D.C.   1986

National Academy Press • 2101 Constitution Avenue, NW • Washington, DC 20418

NOTICE: The project that is the subject of this report was approved by the Governing Board of the National Research Council, whose members are drawn from the councils of the National Academy of Sciences, the National Academy of Engineering, and the Institute of Medicine. The members of the committee responsible for the report were chosen for their special competences and with regard for appropriate balance.

This report has been reviewed by a group other than the authors according to the procedures approved by a Report Review Committee consisting of members of the National Academy of Sciences, the National Academy of Engineering, and the Institute of Medicine.

The Institute of Medicine was chartered in 1970 by the National Academy of Sciences to enlist distinguished members of the appropriate professions in the examination of policy matters pertaining to the health of the public. In this, the Institute acts under both the Academy's 1863 congressional charter responsibility to be an adviser to the federal government and its own initiative in identifying issues of medical care, research, and education.

**Library of Congress Cataloging in Publication Data**

For-profit enterprise in health care.
  Bibliography: p.
  Includes index.
  1. Medical economics. 2. Health facilities,
Proprietary. 3. Medical corporations. I. Institute
of Medicine (U.S.). Committee on Implications of For-
Profit Enterprise in Health Care. [DNLM: 1. Health
Facilities—United States. WX 27 AA1 F6]
RA410.5.F67    1986    362.1'1'0681    86-854

ISBN 0-309-03643-7

First Printing, May 1986
Second Printing, July 1987

Printed in the United States of America

# Committee on Implications
# of For-Profit Enterprise in Health Care

WALTER J. McNERNEY, M.H.A.
(Chairman)
Herman Smith Professor of Hospital
and Health Services Management,
J. L. Kellogg Graduate School of
Management, Northwestern University,
Evanston, Illinois

KARL D. BAYS, M.B.A.
Chairman, Baxter Travenol
Laboratories, Inc., Deerfield, Illinois

JOHN C. BEDROSIAN, LL.B
Senior Executive Vice President,
National Medical Enterprises, Inc., Los
Angeles, California

ROGER J. BULGER, M.D.
President, University of Texas Health
Science Center at Houston

ALEXANDER M. CAPRON, LL.B
Topping Professor of Law, Medicine,
and Public Policy, University of
Southern California, Los Angeles

ROBERT A. DERZON, M.B.A.
Vice President, Lewin and Associates,
Inc., San Francisco, California

ELIOT FREIDSON, Ph.D.
Professor of Sociology, New York
University, New York City

JOHN K. KITTREDGE
Executive Vice President, The
Prudential Insurance Company of
America, Newark, New Jersey

ALAN I. LEVENSON, M.D.
Professor and Head, Department of
Psychiatry, University of Arizona
College of Medicine, Tucson

JOHN H. MOXLEY III, M.D.
Senior Vice President, American
Medical International, Inc., Beverly
Hills, California

STANLEY R. NELSON, M.H.A.
President, Henry Ford Health
Corporation, Troy, Michigan

KENNETH A. PLATT, M.D.
Westminster Medical Center,
Westminster, Colorado

UWE E. REINHARDT, Ph.D.
Professor of Economics and Public
Affairs, Woodrow Wilson School of
Public and International Affairs,
Princeton University, Princeton,
New Jersey

ARNOLD S. RELMAN, M.D.
Editor, *The New England Journal of
Medicine*, Boston, Massachusetts

STEVEN A. SCHROEDER, M.D.
Professor of Medicine and Chief,
Division of General Internal Medicine,
University of California, San Francisco

STEPHEN M. SHORTELL, Ph.D.
A. C. Buehler Professor of Hospital and
Health Services Management and
Professor of Organizational Behavior,
J. L. Kellogg Graduate School of

# Contents

# Part II
# PAPERS ON FOR-PROFIT ENTERPRISE IN HEALTH CARE

# Preface

*For-Profit Enterprise in Health Care* was stimulated by concerns among members of the Institute of Medicine (IOM) and others that health services—already heavily dependent on monetary transactions through prepayment and insurance—will become excessively commercialized, with growing ownership by stockholders. The issues closely associated with these concerns are examined in depth in this report, against a background of such broad public policy challenges as how to balance social justice and efficiency and to what degree regulation or competition can be relied on to strike the proper balance.

In my view, this report makes clear that *type of ownership* is an important variable affecting the *entire* health care system—delivery and financing institutions alike. And I believe that it will become even more important as competition among health institutions increases and services are paid for increasingly on a prospective or incentive basis. Indeed, it is an issue that will require close attention by regulators and informed buyers in both the public and private sectors. In this context, special attention must be given systemwide to such key outcomes as cost, access, quality, and equity, as well as to the viability of research and educational programs.

With regard to the broad public policy challenges, opinions differ as to the degree to which the market can be trusted to allocate limited resources; but in my view, there can be little doubt that the market alone cannot be trusted and that it must be buttressed by enlightened public policy beyond what is seen today and by a clearer commitment to excellence among professionals.

In a sense, little is new for those who have watched the health field evolve for the past forty years. The same underlying public issues enlivened the debates when, for instance, Medicare (1965), Medicaid (1965), and the National Health Planning and Resources Development Act of 1974 were enacted. But today, these issues are seen across a broader spectrum as market forces have been unleashed in such commercial areas as banking and transportation—as well as in education and welfare—by a federal government that sees greater use of the private sector and the sale of government assets as an effective, philosophically right way to reduce budget deficits. This may be viewed, alternately, as pruning the excesses of the Great Society or as dismantling the New Deal legacy. At the grass roots level, we may be seeing a new conception of what is properly public or private in mature markets and what is taxable.

In recent months, a series of incidents have arisen that suggest we are undergoing a major reappraisal of our health institutions. For example, the House Ways and Means Committee has acted to strip the nation's 85 Blue Cross and Blue Shield plans of their tax-exempt status, a matter still being debated in Congress; proposals to reduce or eliminate tax-exempt debt financing for hospitals are being seriously considered; five major not-for-profit teaching hospitals in New York City recently signed a preliminary agreement with Maxicare Health Plans, Inc., to plan the city's first for-profit health maintenance organization; and the Utah Supreme Court created a test that not-for-profit hospitals in the state must pass to gain exemption from county property taxes.

The context within which this report is issued is clearly undergoing remarkable change, and many of the underlying changes in values are having a substantive impact on services well beyond the health field. The question of ownership of health institutions per se is timely and of major consequence because it has refocused our attention on effectiveness after a period of preoccupation with cost containment; on our commitment to the underserved; and on the fundamental significance of education and research.

The study was a challenge. The facts bearing on the issues are limited, and, in a health care system in which rapid change is pervasive, differences in institutions of different ownership are blurring. Thus, the study committee had to exercise considerable judgment in framing the issues and the conclusions. It was helped significantly by a valuable group of commissioned research papers, three case studies, and a public meeting at which testimony was received from many knowledgeable individuals speaking either on their own behalf or on behalf of their organizations. Furthermore, the study committee, by design, offered diverse skills, experiences, and points of view. Members varied widely in terms of their orientation to the changes that have been taking place in the health care system, their willingness to accept nonquantitative evidence as valid, and their beliefs about the likely course of events (for example, whether investor-owned institutions will achieve dominant market position or peak short of this). These differences enriched and enlivened the committee process, but nevertheless, a high degree of general agreement was reached. It should be noted that a statement, termed "supplementary" by committee members who signed it, appears at the end of the report, adding emphasis or different interpretations to some of the points made therein.

In our examination of the characteristics and influences of investor versus not-for-profit ownership, it is tempting to focus on the potential results of further investor-owned initiatives. In my view, we should be equally concerned with the responses of the not-for-profit institutions to these initiatives, as well as to a maturing, inherently more competitive market in general. It is tempting to overlook the crucial role of government in all of this. Without enlightened public policy, the private sector cannot function effectively. Problems such as we face with the underserved, for example, cannot be resolved on a community-wide basis absent adequate protection for the poor and selective regulation bearing on the quality of the services they receive. If this report were to avert our attention from this fundamental fact, it would have failed. The committee's concerns with public policy deserve careful note.

Similarly, because most available data have been derived from institutions, principally hospitals, it is possible to overlook important committee observations and recommendations on the practicing physician, who in many ways sets the tone for all sectors and who, in a competitive environment, faces an increasing number of potential conflicts between his or her fiduciary responsibilities to the patient and more entrepreneurial opportunities. Concerns expressed in this regard certainly need to be addressed.

Finally, the report should be viewed as a benchmark and not the final answer to the issues addressed. Its essence lies in an illumination of the issues, not in their resolution. As the health field matures and grows more slowly and as territory becomes more precious, increased competition will put many of the quality and service issues to test against a background of new institutions and relationships where our experience is limited. Given the speed of change in the environment and our unprecedented state of flux—extraordinary in institutional terms—we must accent accountability and fully support vigilant monitoring of important outcomes involving costs, quality, access, and equity.

Any report of this complexity demands a highly skilled staff, and, characteristic of the Institute of Medicine's ability to attract first-rate scholarship, the staff work was indeed exceptional. I particularly want to thank Bradford H. Gray, who headed a fine team and who personally deserves credit for most of the organization and composition of a report that is by far the most comprehensive and insightful on the subject to date. Also, I should like to thank the members of the committee, all of whom expressed themselves openly and honestly throughout the study, and gave clear leadership to the staff. Because of the strength of the committee, the report should serve as an excellent resource of lasting value on an issue that, almost like no other, touches raw nerves in a field that is undergoing a major and troubling transition.

WALTER J. McNERNEY, *Chairman*
Committee on Implications of
For-Profit Enterprise
in Health Care

# Acknowledgments

The contributions of many individuals and organizations to the committee's work deserve acknowledgment.

Major support for the study was provided by the Andrew W. Mellon and John A. Hartford Foundations of New York City; The Medical Trust, one of several charitable trusts established over the past thirty years by members of the Pew Family of Philadelphia; and the National Research Council (NRC) Fund. The NRC Fund is a pool of private, discretionary, nonfederal funds that is used to support a program of Academy-initiated studies of national issues in which science and technology figure significantly. The NRC fund consists of contributions from: a consortium of private foundations including the Carnegie Corporation of New York, the Charles E. Culpeper Foundation, the William and Flora Hewlett Foundation, the John D. and Catherine T. MacArthur Foundation, the Andrew W. Mellon Foundation, the Rockefeller Foundation, and the Alfred P. Sloan Foundation; the Academy Industry Program, which seeks annual contributions from companies that are concerned with the health of U.S. science and technology and with public policy issues with technological content; and the National Academy of Sciences and the National Academy of Engineering endowments.

Supplemental financial assistance for the study was received from various health care corporations, nonprofit hospital organizations, and investment and accounting firms. These sponsors were American Medical International, Inc.; Arthur Andersen & Co.; Associated Health Systems (which has since merged with United Healthcare Systems, Inc., to become American Healthcare Systems); Charter Medical Corporation; Community Psychiatric Centers; Ernst & Whinney; Hospital Corporation of America; Humana, Inc.; Kidder, Peabody & Co.; Multihospital Mutual Insurance, Ltd.; United Healthcare Systems, Inc.; and Voluntary Hospitals of America, Inc.

Less-direct support was provided by several organizations. The James Irvine Foundation of San Francisco provided financial support to the Health Services Research Foundation for a study done at the committee's request by Robert Pattison, whose paper appears herein. The University of Texas Health Science Center at Houston provided support for the paper on ethics and for-profit health care by Dan

Brock and Allen Buchanan. The American Medical Association added several questions of interest to the study committee to one of its periodic surveys of physicians. These and other data were analyzed in the paper prepared for the committee by Robert Musacchio, Stephen Zuckerman, Lynn E. Jensen, and Larry Freshnock. Costs associated with the data analyses and papers prepared for the committee by staff members of the Joint Commission on Accreditation of Hospitals and the American Hospital Association's Hospital Research and Educational Trust were borne in total or in part by those organizations. Merlin K. DuVal, M.D., now president of the American Healthcare Institute, and Thomas Frist, Jr., M.D., Chief Executive Officer of the Hospital Corporation of America, were instrumental in obtaining financial support for the committee's work from the not-for-profit and for-profit health care sectors.

The committee is particularly grateful to all of the authors who prepared the papers appearing in this volume. It also wishes to thank the many researchers who shared unpublished work with the committee, including Frank Sloan, Diane Rowland, Karen Davis, Deborah Freund, Mark Hiller, Burton Weisbrod, Mark Schlesinger, Jeffrey Alexander, Michael Morrisey, Stephen Shortell, Geri Dallek, Ruth Hanft, Richard Egdahl, Howard Veit, and Michael Watt and colleagues at Lewin and Associates. Frost and Sullivan, Inc., of New York, provided several of its major industry analyses, and Douglas Sherlock of Salomon Brothers, Seth Shaw of Shearson Lehman/American Express, and Gerald Bisbee of Kidder, Peabody provided their periodic published evaluations of the investor-owned health care sector. The AHA's Center for Hospital Data, directed by Peter Kralovec, responded quickly and expertly to numerous requests for data.

The committee also expresses appreciation to four individuals who shared their expertise with it at a special meeting at Airlie House, Virginia, in 1984: Paul Ellwood of Interstudy, Henry Hansmann of Yale Law School, Clark Havighurst of Duke University, and Burton Weisbrod of the University of Wisconsin. Many other individuals provided valuable data and/or consultation to the staff, including Jack Hadley and Judith Feder of the Georgetown University Center for Health Policy; Helen Darling of the Government Research Corporation; Alan Sager of Boston University School of Public Health; Michael Watt of Lewin and Associates; Samuel Mitchell of the Federation of American Hospitals; Steven Renn, The Johns Hopkins University; Ross Mullner, Steven Wood, and Deborah Freko Reczynski of the American Hospital Association; Philip Held of The Urban Institute; Brian Kinkead of Moody's Municipal Department; Donald Cohodes of Blue Cross; B. J. Anderson of the American Medical Association; Jeffrey L. Fiedler of the AFL-CIO Food and Beverage Trades Department; Penelope Roeder of American Medical International; Peaches Blank of the Hospital Alliance of Tennessee; Lacy Maddox of the North Carolina Center for Public Policy Research; Brian Sperry and Karen Greider, then of the Texas Task Force on Indigent Health Care; Kristie Zamrazil of the Texas Hospital Association; George Annas of Boston University Law School; Howard Newman of Memel, Jacobs, Pierno and Gersh; Robert Halper of O'Connor and Hannan; Myron Straf of the National Research Council's Committee on National

Statistics; Phyllis Virgil and James Smith of the Hospital Corporation of America; Michael Stoto of Harvard School of Public Health; and Richard Knapp of the American Association of Medical Colleges. Judith Miller Jones's inclusion of the committee's staff in programs organized by the National Health Policy Forum was consistently valuable.

The committee staff and committee members who served as site visitors—Jessica Townsend, Bradford Gray, Rosemary Stevens, Carleton Evans, Steven Schroeder, Katharine Sommers, Alan Levenson, and Daniel Wikler—express particular appreciation to everyone who shared their time and knowledge in the committee's three case studies of communities and hospitals.

The committee is most grateful to all of the individuals and organizations who made presentations at the committee's public meeting on March 15, 1984, and to Margaret A. McManus, who prepared an excellent summary of the meeting. The committee received testimony from the following:

Quentin D. Young, President, Health and Medicine Policy Research Group, Chicago, Illinois
James E. Bryan, medical journalist
Toby Edelman, Board Member, National Citizens' Coalition for Nursing Home Reform
Paul R. Willging, Executive Vice President, National Council of Health Centers
Ran Coble, Executive Director, North Carolina Center for Public Policy Research, Inc.
Edward E. Berger, Director of Planning and Project Development, National Medical Care, Inc.
Ruth Watson Lubic, General Director, Maternity Center Association
Cecil G. Sheps, American Public Health Association
Joseph C. Hutts, Jr., President, Hospital Corporation of America, West
Robert M. Heyssel, Chairman, Association of American Medical Colleges
Duira Ward, Board Member, National Home Caring Council
Adele S. Hebb, President, Community Home Health Services of Philadelphia
James F. Doherty, Executive Director, Group Health Association of America
James Roberts, Executive Director, National Association of Freestanding Emergency Centers
J. Alexander McMahon, President, American Hospital Association
Judith G. Waxman, Managing Attorney, East Coast Office, National Health Law Program, Inc.
William S. Hoffman, Acting Director, Social Security Department, United Auto Workers International Union
Frank S. Swain, Chief Counsel for Advocacy, U.S. Small Business Administration
Robert E. McGarrah, Jr., Director for Public Policy, American Federation of State, County, and Municipal Employees
Stuart Wesbury, Jr., President, American College of Hospital Administrators
Linda B. Miller, Executive Director, Volunteer Trustees of Not-for-Profit Hospitals
Michael D. Bromberg, Executive Director, Federation of American Hospitals

James F. Davis, Vice Speaker, House of Delegates, American Medical Association
Donald Arnwine, President, Voluntary Hospitals of America (written testimony)
Leslye E. Orloff, National Women's Health Network (written testimony)

Finally, the contributions of the report's authors should be acknowledged. The study director, Bradford H. Gray, was the primary author of the report. Jessica Townsend drafted the chapters on changes in the ownership and control of health services (Chapter 2), the costs of care (Chapter 4), and access to care (Chapter 5), in addition to planning the site visits and writing the paper on the case studies that is included in this volume. Sunny Yoder revised the first draft of the education and research chapter (Chapter 7) and prepared the appendix to Chapter 1. Committee member Uwe Reinhardt did much of the writing for Chapter 3, on financial capital. Elizabeth Hoy, a research assistant, prepared several tables based on American Hospital Association data and collaborated on the paper on the growth of the six major hospital management companies that is published herein.

# Introduction to the Volume

The growth of for-profit enterprise in health care has become a passionately debated phenomenon. Investor-owned companies, which have come about in just the past 20 years, have made a business of providing health services and achieved great size and diversity. The proliferation of these companies is but one manifestation of a broad trend toward more openly entrepreneurial activities in health care. A wave of such activities involving physicians is also taking place, and the changing relationship between physicians and institutions may have important implications for the doctor-patient relationship. Both fearful and hopeful expectations have been expressed for these developments, but their policy implications have not heretofore been systematically examined.

Ordinarily, in our predominantly capitalist society, it would be deemed odd to inquire into the implications of making a business of providing services or of making money from such a business. However, the services discussed here help people to keep or regain their health and can affect, at minimum, whether they are able to pursue their life goals, and, at maximum, whether they live or die. Many people see health care as the sort of public good that should be the right of all citizens, but this view has never prevailed in public policy.

Traditionally, health services have been provided primarily by not-for-profit institutions and by professions whose codes of ethics disdained commercial practices and a commercial image. Until recently, health care was seldom thought of in terms of business or investment; medical institutions typically were regarded as charitable or community service organizations.

A change in that outlook has taken place for several reasons. Scientific and technological advances that have made cure and rehabilitation a more likely outcome have also made health care a more plausible "product" that organizations can sell. The development of a flexible, open-ended system of health insurance, although incomplete, allowed most Americans to choose services from a wide array of providers and organizations. Revenues from services provided have become the primary source of income for health care institutions. And costs of health care have risen to almost 11 percent of the gross national product.

Although proprietary organizations have long existed in health care, their history is largely irrelevant in today's discussions of for-profit enterprise in health care for two reasons. First, many of the profit-making organizations, such as pharmaceutical and hospital supply companies, have not been directly involved in patient care, at least until recently. Second, health care organizations such as the original proprietary hospitals (which constituted 40 percent of hospitals in the 1920s) were typically small, independent, and locally owned, usually by physicians as extensions of their medical practices. Often such hospitals were a community's only place for treatment of patients who could not be cared for at home. However, there was not a "for-profit sector" as a factor for consideration in health policy matters on the national scene. The archetypal hospital was voluntary or governmental.

Today's for-profit health care companies are a new type of organization in health care. They were established explicitly as business ventures, in response to government programs (and private insurance plans) that made money available for providing health care services. Many of these companies are publicly held and thus responsible to stockholders. Company ownership of multiple institutions often means that ownership is no longer local. Some of the health care organizations—both investor owned and the not-for-profit systems that have grown in tandem—have exhibited growth trends that have led some observers to speculate that most health care in the United States could be controlled by as few as 20-30 organizations by the end of the century.

## ORIGINS OF THIS INQUIRY

In June 1981, the Institute of Medicine (IOM) invited a diverse group of people for a one-day workshop to identify and discuss issues raised by a topic of growing controversy: "Trends in For-profit Health Care." Although a very broad range of perspectives was represented, most of the discussion focused on four issues: (1) ethical problems raised by physician involvement in for-profit enterprises that provide health services, (2) the effects of such involvement on professional autonomy and power, (3) the behavior or performance (for example, cost, efficiency, quality, and types of patients served) of institutions with different types of ownership, and (4) the effects of for-profit trends on medical education and research. There was broad agreement that the growth of for-profit enterprise was a very important development, that the issues raised were poorly defined, and that the available data were inadequate for a sound assessment of the issues.

The Institute was encouraged by workshop participants to examine the topic further, and in subsequent discussions the outline for a study was developed. It was decided that the Institute would appoint a committee to examine professional issues raised by for-profit health care, including questions of physician conflict of interest, professional autonomy, and trust in the physician-patient relationship.

This relatively narrow scope was suggested in part because few studies were available that compared the behavior of the new investor-owned institutions with their not-for-profit counterparts. It was felt that several years of work by health services researchers at institutions around the country would be required to develop the body of empirical research that would be needed by an IOM study committee concerned with issues of comparative organizational behavior. Meanwhile the Institute should examine the professional issues.

During the following year a proposal was prepared, funds were sought and obtained, a series of background papers were commissioned and published as *The New Health Care for Profit* (Washington, D.C.: National Academy Press, 1983), and a study committee was appointed.

At the committee's first meeting in July 1983 the questions and issues to be addressed in the study were broadened well beyond a focus on professional issues. The committee had a strong sense that the behavior of investor-owned health care organizations demanded examination. As a result, much of this report is concerned with the comparative behavior of health care organizations under different types of ownership and control. Furthermore, it was becoming apparent that a research literature was developing rapidly and that much more research could be conducted that would utilize existing data. Eventually, a substantial group of research papers was stimulated by the committee's activities and is published as Part II of this volume.

## FOCUS OF THIS STUDY

This study attempts to understand the provision of health care by investor-owned organizations and to illuminate the issues that are involved. It focuses primarily on the development of the newer forms of investor-owned health care providers, with attention to other types of organizations (including physicians' office practices; public and not-for-profit health care organizations; and traditional, independent proprietary hospitals and nursing homes) for purposes of comparison and contrast. It does not examine other commercial enterprises in the health field, such as insurers, suppliers, and pharmaceutical and equipment manufacturers, except as these enterprises have diversified into the provision of services. The intent is to understand what, if anything, is new and significant about the provision of health care by investor-owned health care organizations.

Because expansion of investor-owned chains of health care facilities involves two elements—investor ownership and multi-institutional arrangements—efforts have been made whenever data permit to compare independent and chain institutions, both for-profit and not-for-profit. The distinction between independent and chain institutions is examined in part because of the possible implications for institutional governance if the institution is owned by a larger organization whose home office is elsewhere. In addition, the hospitals of investor-owned companies are different from independent proprietary hospitals on several other important grounds. For one, their growth mirrors the decline in the number of proprietary hospitals. They also differ in terms of accountability of management to stockholders, who typically have no contact with the hospital, and in terms of the sources of capital to which they have access. Whether such differences translate into behavioral differences is an empirical question that is examined in this report whenever relevant data are available.

Although this report attempts to illuminate the implications of the growth of for-profit provision of health services in general, its emphasis is on hospitals. This is partly because most available data comparing for-profit and not-for-profit providers pertain to hospitals. Time and space limitations were factors as well. However, the report's emphasis also derives from the fact that different types of health services providers—nursing homes, home health agencies, dialysis centers, ambulatory surgery centers, psychiatric hospitals, urgent care centers, and so forth—each have their own particular characteristics and issues. Data from such types of providers are cited where available and relevant, but no systematic attempt has been made to address issues that are specific to any type of provider other than hospitals.

## THE COMPLICATIONS OF CHANGE

Any serious consideration of the implications of for-profit trends in health care must contend with the ubiquity and rapidity of change throughout today's health care environment. Public policy in the last decade has shifted from the goals embodied in the passage of the Medicare and Medicaid programs—to enhance access to care—and from the incentives embodied in cost-based and charge-based reimbursement for services provided. Such incentives in the 1960s and 1970s rewarded the provision of additional services, stimulated the development of new technologies and the growth of health care expenditures, and helped to ensure institutional survival and the growth of the health care economy as a whole. In contrast, public policy during the 1980s has emphasized competition, organizational innovation, and control of the costs and use of medical services.

Medicare's so-called prospective payment system* fundamentally changed hospitals' incentives by paying prospectively set rates per case, rather than reimbursing for expenses incurred in the care of a patient. Other payers are seeking to reduce their costs through a wide variety of mechanisms—for example, by more cost-sharing by beneficiaries, by establishing second opinion and pre-admission screening programs, by creating other incentives for beneficiaries to use low-cost providers, by negotiating discounts from providers, and by entering into health maintenance organizations (HMO) or preferred provider arrangements that include controls on utilization of services.

Some sectors of health care now have the appearance of a maturing market: excess beds and physicians in some areas, leveling or falling demand for hospital beds, the growth of one provider coming more and more at the expense of another, increased attention to market share, segmentation of the market, and shake-outs of unsuccessful competitors. Remarkable changes have begun to take place in the use of hospitals as admission rates and lengths of stay have declined rapidly in recent years. Patient visits per physician show a similar pattern of decline as the number

---

*The term "prospective payment" is conventionally used to refer to the payment system that Medicare instituted in 1983 to pay hospitals according to prospectively set rates per case. Although the committee recognizes that what transpires prospectively is the setting of rates, not the making of payments, it bows to convention and uses the term "prospective payment" to refer to the new system.

of physicians in practice has increased rapidly. The Federal Trade Commission has become active in health care by discouraging regulations and practices it deems anticompetitive, even if done in the name of preserving professionalism or controlling costs.

The changing environment is putting pressure on all parties, and the rapidity of their responses constantly outpaces our ability to document them adequately. For example, because of inevitable lags in the availability of data, the committee had access to very little systematic information about how health care organizations of different types of ownership are responding to the new economic incentives in health care. In a period of rapid change, available numbers always describe a reality that has changed. The committee's response to this problem has been not only to report on various pieces of factual information, but also to interpret those facts in light of our current theoretical understanding of the nature of for-profit, not-for-profit, and public organizations and in light of our understanding of the changing environmental constraints that health care institutions face.

## SOURCES OF INFORMATION

This report of an IOM study committee, whose members were selected for both diversity and expertise, synthesizes information from several sources:

1. Committee discussions and deliberations over nine meetings between July 1983 and June 1985;

2. A public meeting on March 15, 1984,* at which testimony was received from 23 witnesses (named in the section on acknowledgments);

3. Case studies based on site visits in three small cities with populations between 50,000 and 150,000 in which hospitals owned by for-profit and not-for-profit multi-institutional systems could be studied in the same environment;

4. Original research studies, literature reviews, and scholarly papers conducted or prepared for the IOM study committee by independent researchers. These papers are published after the committee's report, in Part II of this volume.

Much additional information was obtained from the published literature and, as the acknowledgments section notes, from unpublished studies, data from trade sources and regulatory agencies, and discussions between the staff and those people who are involved in the developments examined in this report.

## THE PRODUCTS OF THIS INQUIRY

The results of the study committee's activities take two forms: the committee report itself and a group of 15 papers—most of which convey original research—that were prepared at the committee's request or as part of its work. Although

---

*Some copies of a summary of this hearing are available from the Office of Information, Institute of Medicine, 2101 Constitution Avenue, NW, Washington, DC 20418.

designated members of the committee reviewed the papers, they reflect the views of the authors, not of the committee.

These papers are published in the second part of this volume. They include literature reviews on ownership differences among hospitals and nursing homes, an analysis of the ethics of for-profit health care, and new empirical studies on the growth of the hospital management companies and the impact of their acquisitions, on ownership differences in hospital governance and control and in the cost and quality of hospital care, on physicians' experiences with different types of hospitals, and on the operation of different types of hospitals in the same market. This group of papers constitutes a very substantial addition to the empirical literature on for-profit versus not-for-profit health care and was used by the committee in its deliberations.

The committee report itself makes up the first half of this volume and is organized as follows:

Chapter 1 introduces the topic and sets forth the value conflicts that underlie most of the concerns about the growth of for-profit enterprise in health care. It also contains an appendix by Sunny G. Yoder that summarizes economic theories regarding the behavior of for-profit and not-for-profit organizations.

Chapter 2 documents the various trends that are part of the organizational transformation taking place in health care: the growth of investor ownership, of multi-institutional arrangements, of new types of health care organizations that provide ambulatory services, of vertically integrated organizations, and of for-profit/not-for-profit hybrids.

Chapter 3 examines the issue of access to capital, a factor that underlies many changes taking place in health care. It also contains an appendix by Professor Uwe Reinhardt on the cost of equity capital.

Chapters 4 through 7 examine the comparative performance of for-profit and not-for-profit health care organizations in four key areas: cost, quality, providing access to care, and involvement in education and research.

Chapters 8 and 9 examine how changes taking place in health care affect the fiduciary aspects of the role of the physician, either by their becoming involved in entrepreneurial activities or by changing their involvement in institutional decisions that may affect patient care.

Chapter 10 summarizes the conclusions from the earlier chapters and offers the committee's analysis of the issues raised by empirical and theoretical inquiries.

**CONCLUSION**

In many ways, as committee member Rosemary Stevens noted, the topic of this inquiry is a lens that brings into often troubling focus many fundamental problems and issues in the health care system:

● How to provide access to medical care for those who are unable to pay
● How to regard the occurrence and likely further development of a multi-tiered or multiclass health care system

• How to control health care costs under cost-based and charge-based methods of payment, a problem whose "solution" via administered prices and price competition raises its own set of questions about health care quality and institutional survival

• How to create incentives that serve patients' interests but that do not reward either inefficiency or greed

• How to obtain the potential benefits of multi-institutional arrangements while keeping local identity and sensitivity in our health care institutions

• How to sustain or encourage responsiveness to noneconomic values (altruism, service, caring, science-based rather than demand-based services) when capital for all types of health care institutions (both for-profit and not-for-profit) comes from lenders and investors of equity

• How to support professional education in the health care field (particularly graduate medical education)

• How to avoid increasing conflict of interest in the physician's role

• How to ensure an appropriate dynamic balance between market forces and community interests in health care

These problems were not created by the emergence or growth of a significant investor-owned sector in health services in the 1970s and 1980s, and their solution will require attention to much more than the for-profit sector. Yet the existence of a vigorous and growing investor-owned sector in health care raises many questions of public policy, the implications of which are not yet fully understood. This report, bringing together the available data on comparisons between for-profit and not-for-profit institutions in recent years and examining changes in the role of the physician, is a beginning—a baseline for ongoing debates and future explorations.

BRADFORD H. GRAY, *Study Director*
Committee on Implications of
For-Profit Enterprise in Health Care

# Part I
# COMMITTEE REPORT

# 1 Profits and Health Care: An Introduction to the Issues

Few changes in the organization of health care in the United States have stimulated more interest and alarm than the rise of a new form of entrepreneurism—investor-owned, for-profit organizations that provide health services as a business.[1] Although proprietary health care organizations are not new, publicly traded health care companies that own multiple facilities have appeared only in the past 20 years. With their rapid growth and diversification they have become increasingly visible and influential. In many ways they represent a challenge to established interests, practices, values, and ideals.

The revenues of businesses that provide health services for profit have been estimated at 20 to 25 percent of the nation's expenditures on personal health services (Relman, 1980), which would amount to $70 to $90 billion dollars today. Investor-owned health service businesses range from large companies (such as Hospital Corporation of America, Beverly Enterprises, and Humana, Inc.) that own or operate hundreds of hospitals, nursing homes, and other facilities to independent institutions owned by local investors. In mid-1985 the stock of 34 investor-owned companies that provide health care was publicly traded (*Modern Healthcare*, 1985:173). Some of these companies concentrate on a particular type of facility or service, such as hospitals, nursing

homes, psychiatric hospitals, health maintenance organizations (HMOs), alcoholism and drug abuse treatment, rehabilitation, home health care, urgent care, or medical offices. Others are diversified into a variety of health care and related services. In addition, several large companies whose primary lines of business are not in the delivery of health services have established or acquired health services subsidiaries.[2] Many other proprietary or for-profit health care organizations are not publicly traded. Some of these are subsidiaries of not-for-profit hospitals and hospital chains; others are owned by local investors, many of whom, anecdotes suggest, are physicians. (Growth trends among health care organizations are examined in detail in Chapter 2.)

Although ours is a predominantly capitalistic society, there has long been concern about the possible adverse or pernicious effects of profit motivations in health care (Veatch, 1983; Steinwald and Neuhauser, 1970:830-834; see also Shaw, 1911). Conflicting opinions about for-profit health care mirror common views of the profit motive and market-driven behavior. Thus, various positive benefits of the investor-owned model are often cited: that it provides new impetus for innovation, more responsiveness to the needs and desires of patients and physicians, sounder approaches to management, and an important source of new capital for health services. On the other hand, some observers see for-profit health care organizations as antithetical to the traditional mission and values of health care institutions, as a threat to the autonomy and ideals of the medical profession, and as destructive of implicit social arrangements by which medical care has often been provided to people who could not pay for it and by which teaching and research have been indirectly supported. Others are skeptical about these fears or are dubious about the extent to which health care institutions and professionals actually embody the ideals that they enunciate. Some view physicians as a type of businessperson and see nothing wrong in making money from health care. Others identify the problems not in the behavior of providers but in terms of (1) inflationary economic incentives in the way that health care is paid for (a factor that has been undergoing rapid change), (2) the lack of competition among health care providers (also rapidly changing), and (3) failures of public policy, particularly regarding people who lack insurance coverage and who are not eligible for public programs. Thus, the debate about for-profit health care touches upon most issues of health care policy in the United States.

## QUESTIONS EXAMINED IN THIS REPORT

In preparing this report the committee focused on the following major questions in seeking to illuminate for-profit health care and the issues associated with it:

1. How extensive is the trend toward for-profit health care and what factors underlie it?

2. What are the implications of the growth of investor ownership of health care institutions on the costs and quality of health care, on access to care for those who are unable to pay, and on the funding and conduct of medical education and research? In other words, does the for-profit form's sup-

posed greater responsiveness to economic incentives lead to systematic differences from not-for-profit and governmental institutions in the kinds of patients that are served, the kinds of services that are offered to communities, the efficiency[3] with which services are provided, the prices that are charged for services, or the quality of services?

3. Are changes taking place in physicians' relationships with health care institutions that will alter the traditional fiduciary aspects of the profession and the public trust that has been vested in it?

4. What are the public policy implications of the committee's analysis of these questions?

## THE DIVERSE OWNERSHIP OF AMERICAN HEALTH CARE ORGANIZATIONS

In our highly decentralized and pluralistic health care system, health care is provided by a mixture of for-profit, secular and religious not-for-profit, and public institutions, some of which are independent and some of which are a part of multi-institutional systems. Different types of ownership typify different types of institutions. Nursing homes have long been predominantly proprietary, for-profit institutions. Acute care general hospitals are typically private, not-for-profit institutions. Among certain specialized types of institutions (e.g., psychiatric and tuberculosis hospitals) governmental ownership was typical, because of the public health and safety concerns that led to their creation. (Changing patterns of ownership and control of different types of institutions are described in Chapter 2.)

Increasingly, institutions of different ownership types and with ostensibly different rationales and missions now operate side by side. In a sharpening competitive environment, some observers see decreasing ownership-related differences in institutional behavior. Still, certain values, beliefs, and labels remain associated with governmental (last resort, inefficient but equitable), not-for-profit (voluntarism, charity, community), and for-profit (efficient, innovative but self-interested) organizations. However much these may be historical myths, they are very powerful ideas in American society (Stevens, 1982). Their reality transcends their history, although they have roots in history as well as in economic theory.

Deeply felt issues have long surrounded questions of ownership in health care and the proper role of government. There have always been advocates of a publicly controlled health care system, who argue that health care is a basic service or public good that should be provided for by government. Almost all industrialized countries have adopted some such approach. In the United States, however, a mixture of private and public insurance and control has always prevailed, with private ownership predominating. This pattern is rooted in history, the development and subsequent importance of local institutions, the generally high level of public satisfaction with a mostly private health care system, American distrust of big government, and the widespread perception that public institutions produce "bureaucratic arrogance, high costs, and inefficiency" (Drucker, 1984:21). Public institutions have frequently, if not always willingly, been cast in the role of provider of last resort, even though many of these institutions have been aggressively seeking a broader clientele.

Today, most governmental spending on health care is for payments to private physicians (and other health professionals) and private institutions (both for-profit and not-for-profit) for services rendered to individual beneficiaries of public programs and not for appropriations to governmental institutions. As a result of history and past public policy, then, the debate about for-profit health care is not about private versus public control of medical institutions but is instead largely about the differences between (and relative virtues of) two types of private institutions—not-for-profit and for-profit.

## THE FOR-PROFIT/NOT-FOR-PROFIT DISTINCTION

Among general hospitals the not-for-profit, voluntary institutions have long been predominant. The first hospitals served exclusively as charitable or public organizations for the sick and destitute who had nowhere else to go, but today's not-for-profit hospitals have diverse origins in the missions of both religious and secular charitable organizations and the actions of civic-minded citizens seeking to improve their communities.

For-profit (or investor-owned) institutions have been distinguished from not-for-profit institutions on a variety of aspects, many of which are summarized in Table 1.1. These distinctions suggest why differences in institutional behavior are often assumed to exist and whence are derived the hypotheses in the empirical literature (examined later in this report) on the comparative behavior of for-profit and not-for-profit institutions.

Theory for predicting the behavior of not-for-profit institutions is still in a relatively undeveloped state (Weisbrod, 1981; Hansmann, 1980; Easley and O'Hara, 1983), and divergent theories exist about for-profit organizations (see, for example, Williamson, 1981). Economic theories of for-profit and not-for-profit organizations are summarized in an appendix to this chapter. It should be noted, however, that two contradictory beliefs are frequently heard regarding the comparative behavior of for-profit and not-for-profit health care organizations.

One belief is that the economic incentives faced by those who control the organization are so different in for-profit and not-for-profit institutions that the two types of organizations can be expected to behave quite differently from each other. (People who hold this view differ in which type of organization

**TABLE 1.1**   Common Distinctions Between For-profit and Not-for-profit Organizations

| For-profit | Not-for-profit |
|---|---|
| Corporations owned by investors | Corporations without owners or owned by "members" |
| Can distribute some proportion of profits (net revenues less expenses) to owners | Cannot distribute surplus (net revenues less expenses) to those who control the organization |
| Pay property, sales, income taxes | Generally exempt from taxes |
| Sources of capital include<br>  a. Equity capital from investors<br>  b. Debt<br>  c. Retained earnings (including depreciation and deferred taxes)<br>  d. Return-on-equity payments from third-party payers (e.g., Medicare) | Sources of capital include<br>  a. Charitable contributions<br>  b. Debt<br>  c. Retained earnings (including depreciation)<br>  d. Govermental grants |
| Management ultimately accountable to stockholders | Management accountable to voluntary, often self-perpetuating boards |
| *Purpose:* Has legal obligation to enhance the wealth of shareholders within the boundaries of law; does so by providing services | *Purpose:* Has legal obligation to fulfill a stated mission (provide services, teaching, research, etc.); must maintain economic viability to do so |
| Revenues derived from sale of services | Revenues derived from sale of services and from charitable contributions |
| *Mission:* Usually stated in terms of growth, efficiency, and quality | *Mission:* Often stated in terms of charity, quality, and community service, but may also pursue growth |
| Mission and structure can result in more streamlined decision making and implementation of major decisions | Mission and diverse constituencies often complicate decision making and implementation |

they see as appropriate in health care.) The other belief is that for-profit and not-for-profit organizations are not necessarily very different from each other. Some economic theorists suggest that many not-for-profit hospitals, particularly the community (as opposed to the university) variety, are through one device or another, essentially run to further the economic interests of physicians (Pauly, 1980; Pauly and Redisch, 1973; Clark, 1980). As Sloan (forthcoming) notes, "to the extent this is so, the voluntary hospital is only a profit-seeking hospital in disguise, and there is no reason to expect it to behave much differently." However, it is not necessary to accept this hospital-as-physician-cartel view to argue that for-profit and not-for-profit organizations that exist in a similar economic and competitive environment will behave similarly in many respects. Many observers point to examples to support the argument that there is little, if anything,

that "the for-profits" are doing that cannot also be found among "the not-for-profits." The argument then turns to whether the behavior in question is more common in one or the other sector and to whether not-for-profit organizations are being forced by competition to behave in ways that are in some sense aberrant to the not-for-profit form.

Much empirical evidence on the comparative behavior of for-profit and not-for-profit health care organizations is examined in this report. This chapter examines historical and organizational differences, as well as some factors that may attenuate the different behavioral tendencies of for-profit and not-for-profit health care organizations.

### Investor Ownership

The purpose of investor-owned corporations in general is to make money for investors—to preserve and enhance the economic value of the invested capital. This purpose is built into the corporate governance structure. An investor-owned corporation is ultimately governed by its owners (stockholders), who elect the board of directors. The stockholders accepted the risk of purchasing stock in the expectation of gaining an economic return that is larger than would be available through nonequity forms of investment, such as the purchase of bonds. Profits for stockholders come in the form of dividends and appreciation in the value of their investment. Large blocks of stock are owned by institutional investors (mutual funds, financial institutions, pension funds, labor union trust funds) and are thus controlled by individuals who themselves are accountable for their investment decisions, who closely monitor companies' performance, and whose decisions to sell can affect a stock's price (transactions involving 10,000 or more shares are not unusual institutional trades) (Blumstein, 1984).

The board of directors makes broad policy decisions and employs the top management (the officers) of the corporation.[4] In health care and other fields, top officials of the corporation not only serve on the board but also have significant holdings of the corporation's stock. The dividends that they and other stockholders receive and the value of their holdings depend on the corporation's earnings. In addition to the accountability and incentives that investor ownership present for management, other profitability incentives also exist. First, many companies explicitly tie large incentives for management to the company's economic performance; for top executives, such incentives (in cash, stock, or other forms) often run into the hundreds of thousands or even many millions of dollars.[5] Second, and more important, for a publicly traded company the value of its stock and, hence, its ability to raise additional capital is a function of the company's past and projected earnings (see Chapter 3). Thus, it is understandable that

companies devote careful attention to the Wall Street analysts whose recommendations influence the market's valuation of their stock (Siegrist, 1983).

None of these characteristics determine what strategies a company might pursue (whether it is interested in short-term profits or long-term growth; whether it wants specialization or diversification; whether and how much it centralizes decision making; whether it seeks to base its reputation on unsurpassed quality or on providing good value for the money, etc.). Nor do they determine how a company defines its social responsibilities; for example, many companies, including some health care corporations, have established departments or foundations to make charitable contributions. This is not behavior that bespeaks single-minded commitment to short-term profit maximization, although in the long term it can be presumed that hard economic criteria ordinarily guide American business behavior.

Since Adam Smith, the fulcrum of economic theory about for-profit organizations is the objective of profit maximization. More recent alternative theories of the corporation recognize the role of managers (as distinct from owners), whose primary objective may pertain to status or security, for example, rather than maximizing profits. Similar goals may animate management in not-for-profit organizations. Some theorists suggest that whereas the status of management in for-profit organizations rests substantially on profitability, managerial prestige in the not-for-profit organization rests much more on the size and reputation (e.g., for quality) of the institution.

## Not-for-profit Organizations

Although state laws under which not-for-profit organizations are incorporated vary in their requirements, a not-for-profit corporation is barred by its charter from "distributing its net earnings, if any, to individuals who exercise control over it, such as members, officers, directors, or trustees" (Hansmann, 1980:838).[6] This key characteristic is referred to as the "nondistribution requirement," and a variety of managerial and organizational behaviors are thought to follow from it. On the one hand it is seen as providing some assurance of quality and proper performance to consumers who lack the knowledge or information with which to monitor performance adequately. Thus, Hansmann suggests that not-for-profit organizations are a response to contract failure in circumstances that make contracts between consumers and suppliers impractical to write or too costly to monitor. On the other hand the nondistribution constraint is sometimes alleged to cause indifference to consumers and inattention to efficiency, except where resources are tight.

Despite their label, not-for-profit organizations are not prohibited from earning profits (usually called "surpluses") from their operations; however, these surpluses generally must be devoted to the further financing and production of the services that the organization was formed to provide. There is debate about whether not-for-profit organizations should be restricted to certain traditional charitable purposes (Hansmann, 1980:839; U.S. Small Business Administration, 1983), but the provision of medical care and the conduct of teaching and research, are clearly qualifying purposes.

Related to, but distinct from, the question of not-for-profit status is the availability to not-for-profit organizations, under certain conditions, of exemptions from federal income taxes (under Section 501(c)(3) of the Internal Revenue Code) and from state and local income, property, and sales taxes. Since many not-for-profit organizations own valuable property and earn healthy surpluses, these are significant advantages.

Not-for-profit organizations can be distinguished from each other by two attributes: their control and their financing. "Membership" or "mutual" not-for-profit organizations (such as country clubs or professional associations) are controlled by the organization's patrons or members, who elect the board of directors (Hansmann, 1980:841; Horty and Mulholland, 1983:20). "Nonmembership" not-for-profit organizations are controlled by a self-perpetuating board, which is a common pattern among not-for-profit nursing homes and hospitals. On the financing side, not-for-profit organizations can be distinguished according to the degree to which they derive their income from donations or from charges for the services they provide.[7] The not-for-profit organization that derives its income primarily from charges for services is largely a creature of the post-World War II period, when the growth of private and public third-party payment programs effectively monetized health care (Ginzberg, 1984).

Many statements have been made over the years about the goals and ideals that not-for-profit health care organizations (and their boards) should pursue—they should be responsive to community health care needs, they should be responsible and efficient custodians of the resources entrusted to them, they should provide service to all who need it without regard to ability to pay, and so forth. Over the years certain criticisms have been recurrent—that administrators and trustees (1) are insufficiently critical of physicians' requests for new equipment and facilities, (2) are motivated not by trying to meet all of the community's medical needs but by a growth imperative stemming from the desire for prestige and power, and (3) are not interested enough in sound management, in part because the nondistribution requirement prevents their sharing any surplus that might be created and because association with independent hospitals tends to tie administrators to a particular community rather than to put them on the career ladder of a larger organization.

Trustees have tended to come from the economic and professional elites of the community, not from among people for whom inability to pay was commonplace. These factors are alleged by some to have led trustees and ambitious administrators to concentrate surpluses on salaries and staff (thereby making not-for-profit organizations inherently inefficient, according to a common criticism) and on new services, facilities, and equipment, regardless of whether an objective community need existed. Indeed, some observers have seen not-for-profit hospitals' tendency toward excessive investment in unneeded facilities and equipment as jeopardizing their economic soundness (Vladeck, 1976). The purpose here is not to assess the validity of old criticisms or the extent to which not-for-profit organizations conform to some set of ideals, but only to emphasize the lack of agreement in the field about their motivating principle.

### Problems with the For-profit/ Not-for-profit Distinction

The clarity of the distinction between for-profit and not-for-profit health care providers is muddied by several factors. First, differences in sources of capital have sharply diminished, as is discussed in Chapter 3. Historically, charitable donations and governmental grants were the major sources of capital and important sources of revenue for not-for-profit hospitals. However, the revenues of not-for-profit hospitals have increasingly come from billing for the services they provide and now, with the rising capital intensity of health care, the relative decline of charity, the rapid inflation in the 1960s and 1970s, and the end of the government's Hill-Burton program, leave capital requirements to be met mostly from retained earnings and debt. These also are the primary sources of capital for for-profit institutions.

Second, although investor-equity capital puts constant economic pressure on the managers of investor-owned enterprises, economic pressure is not peculiar to the for-profit sector. Thus, it is not surprising that many observers see similarities in the behavior of for-profit and not-for-profit hospitals. Both types have been forming multiinstitutional arrangements in the hopes of gaining economies of scale and greater access to capital, aggressively marketing and vertically integrating (e.g., through the acquisition of primary care centers and long-term-care facilities) to increase control of patient flow and market share, and paying more heed to the vigor of the bottom line by heightening cost control and limiting uncompensated care.

Third, not-for-profit organizations can and do make profits (usually termed a "surplus") in the customary accounting sense of the term. Indeed, in 1984 the average total net margin (the percent of revenues retained after expenses) of U.S. hospitals, most of which are not-for-profit, was 6.2 percent (American Hospital Association, 1985). The ability of any organization to survive requires that it generate revenues beyond those necessary to cover operating expenses, not only because of the need for working capital but also because the equipment and renovations needed to keep an institution up-to-date and acceptable to doctors and patients require new infusions of capital.

Fourth, ends and means can displace each other at various levels of any organization. Providing services might be the way that the for-profit health care organization makes money; but for many people in such an organization, providing services becomes the purpose of their work, rather than making money for stockholders. Conversely, within a not-for-profit organization there are officials whose responsibilities are primarily financial and who evaluate organizational options, strategies, and policies primarily in terms of their effect on the organization's bottom line.

Fifth, it is simplistic to conclude that because the for-profit company's purpose is to make profits it will strive for short-term profit maximization at every opportunity, if only because of the likely impact on its public image and the importance of that image for its long-term profitability. The extent to which companies provide uncompensated care to patients who are unable to pay, engage in educational and training activities, and devote resources to research and development are all empirical questions, not matters of definition.

Sixth, various forms of not-for-profit/for-profit hybrids have become widespread among hospitals in recent years. These include (a) for-profit subsidiaries set up for a variety of purposes by many not-for-profit institutions; (b) not-for-profit (and public) hospitals that have entered into contracts with for-profit companies for management of the entire institution or for providing specific services (e.g., coverage of the emergency room); (c) joint ventures for a wide variety of purposes between not-for-profit hospitals and members of their staffs, between not-for-profit hospitals and for-profit hospitals (or hospital companies), and between for-profit multihospital systems and not-for-profit multihospital systems; and (d) for-profit alliances (such as Voluntary Hospitals of America, American Healthcare Systems, SunHealth) that are owned by, and provide services to, not-for-profit hospitals or multihospital systems. Such hybridization is described in more detail in Chapter 2. Although the amount of hybridization that has come from the other direction is smaller, some for-profit health care organizations have set up foundations that receive and dispense donated monies. Some of these are set up at the local hospital level to receive charitable contributions, particularly from former patients and their families, that are used for such purposes as building a chapel. Investor-owned companies make charitable contributions (e.g., to colleges and universities, art galleries, and other cultural centers) that are typical of the giving programs of other corporations in the United States, and some health care companies have set up foundations for this purpose with substantial gifts of company stock.

Seventh, the requirements for incorporation as a not-for-profit organization are not stringent in many states. In some states a not-for-profit organization can be established "for any lawful purpose" (Horty and Mulholland, 1983). Among certain types of health care providers, such as home health care agencies, owner-operated, not-for-profit organizations are sometimes difficult to distinguish from their for-profit competitors by any criterion other than the former's exemptions from paying corporate taxes.

Eighth, even the not-for-profit's prohibition against distribution of profits has begun to break down as legal ways are discovered whereby not-for-profit organizations can develop incentive compensation arrangements for management and staff that are essentially profit-sharing plans.

Ninth, access to tax-exempt financing is not the sole province of not-for-profit organizations. Under certain circumstances for-profit companies can gain access to tax-exempt debt financing through industrial revenue bonds and through construction and lease-back arrangements.

Finally, it must be recognized that a variety of other factors can affect the behavior of health care organizations and may attenuate ownership-related differences. Strong values are associated with health care, and certain types of institutional behavior can result in strong negative publicity. Health care institutions all operate within a web of statutory and case law and regulations. These laws and regulations determine whether an institution may open, who may practice medicine, eligibility for governmental programs, governance and medical staff responsibilities, liability for negligence, restrictions on the "corporate practice of medicine," and so forth. The larger economic or marketplace environment also places constraints on institutions and affects their ability to do many things, such as raise prices, cross-subsidize care of uninsured patients, or offer specialized services. Also, a major constraint on many institutions is that their ability to attract patients depends on physicians, who have traditionally been relatively independent of the institution and whose first ethical responsibility is to the patient. This factor is discussed in more detail later in this chapter.

Notwithstanding the many factors that can be cited that blur the borders between for-profit (or investor-owned) and not-for-profit health care organizations, most distinctions in Table 1.1 between institutions owned by an investor-owned company and institutions owned by not-for-profit corporations still hold. The question that remains is whether the type of ownership and control of institutions makes a difference. That question is the subject of much of this report.

## THE VALUE QUESTION

Although a large portion of this report is devoted to comparisons and contrasts in the behavior of institutions with different types of ownership, the argument about for-profit health care is as much about values as it is about facts. A deep division about values underlies and inevitably affects all discussions of the behavior and implications of the growth of investor-owned health care.[8]

The depth of feeling about this topic is only partly a reaction to perceived threats to the institutions that people believe in or attacks on the legitimacy of enterprises to which people have devoted their energies. Another cause has to do with value conflicts and beliefs about the nature of health care itself, the place of health care in society, the role of health care providers, the relationship between professionals and patients, and about whether it is legitimate to make profits from the misfortunes of the ill.

The value questions about health care can be discussed under two broad categories— health care as an economic good and health care as a social good. One view emphasizes the attributes that health care shares with other goods and services that are offered and purchased in the marketplace. The second identifies and emphasizes the characteristics

that distinguish medical care from commercial services. In the next sections these two views, which emphasize different aspects of the same set of activities that we know as health care, are described in more detail. They are stated as polar extremes, although most observers probably accept the validity of some aspects of both sets. (An interesting set of contrasting views held by members of the committee can be seen in correspondence between committee members Uwe Reinhardt and Arnold Relman in Part II of this volume.)

### Health Care as Economic Good

The view, oversimplified here, that personal health care (in contrast to public health measures) is much like other consumer goods also implies that marketplace forces and the operation-for-profit motive are largely beneficial. Furthermore, because there is evidence that medical institutions and physicians respond to economic incentives (as everyone else does), it seems realistic to view health care in these terms. This view does not deny that government plays an essential role in making these market forces work. Indeed, because of the cost, unpredictability of individual need, and importance of health care, many adherents of this view believe government should fund care for those who cannot otherwise obtain it. The breadth of coverage of governmental, as well as private, insurance programs determines the extent to which market forces can produce the anticipated beneficial results. Governmental involvement does not deny that other market factors and competitive forces should be allowed to operate, although the form of that involvement determines the extent of the competition. For example, if beneficiaries of governmental programs could receive care only at governmental hospitals, the role of market forces would be minimal.

In this view, competition and market forces (rather than central planning or "command and control regulation") are seen as producing the best outcome for all—a system that is responsive to consumers, in which the producer of inferior services will be punished and the hard test of the bottom line will restrain capital expenditures for equipment and facilities if demand is lacking. Such a system should lead to maximum efficiency in the production of services, except in perverse circumstances where revenues are based on reimbursement for costs, thereby creating incentives to increase expenses rather than to control them. In this view government's roles are (1) to facilitate participation in the market by people whose resources would otherwise preclude their doing so (i.e., to pay for all or part of services for the indigent) and (2) to pay and regulate in ways that will foster competition and, perhaps, appropriate care. Some forms of regulation, including some aspects of professional and institutional self-regulation, are opposed as being antithetical to competition; other forms may be necessary to maintain fair competition.

As with markets generally, the best outcome from this viewpoint is expected if the players, making free and independent choices, all pursue their own interests. The market will shape the configuration of services that are made available. If some payers are willing or able to pay for more amenities or services than are other payers, a multi-tier system will result. Similarly, the market (not "regulators" or "planners") should decide whether institutions should attempt to provide all services to all segments of the community or should specialize or pursue a particular segment of the market for health services.

In extolling the market, this view emphasizes the purchaser's role (and the incentives created by purchasers) in disciplining or shaping the system. Thus, providers will focus their attention on factors that can be judged by patients (availability, accessibility, amenities, courtesy) and by physicians (because they make so many of the key decisions). As payers become more aggressive,

attention will increasingly be focused on factors that payers can monitor (cost, convenience, patterns of care, and quality-related measures of outcomes, such as readmission or mortality rates). Patients (or payers) that uncritically assume that health care providers will subordinate their own interests to the patient's interests are vulnerable to exploitation, no matter what ideals the provider may state. In this view, entrepreneurism and competition are essential and proven elements in our free enterprise system, and the burden of argument lies with those who contend that they are inappropriate in health care.

## Health Care as Social Good

A contrasting set of views opposes the idea that health care is properly seen as an economic good that is appropriately bought, sold, and disciplined by competitive forces in a marketplace. This view holds that health professionals and institutions should pursue the goals or ideals of applying biomedical science on behalf of patients and to meet community needs, whether or not it is profitable to do so. Although the proper pursuit of such goals may often produce behavior that the market will reward, the behavior is not so motivated. This view holds that health care should be seen as a "social good," a conception that was more obviously applicable when infectious disease made an individual's misfortune a threat to his or her neighbors (Stevens, 1985) and in an era when many people were dependent either on charity or public facilities (in distinction to public programs) for their medical care.

In this view, health care is a community service to which words such as caring and compassion and charity should apply—words that connote the family and the church, where the functions of caring for the sick once resided. The response to disease and disability should stem not from the fact that a market is created from peoples' misfortunes but from a humane response to their needs. The ideal is that the needs of the sick and unfortunate should be met by persons who, as a philosopher expressed it, are acting out of love rather than out of the expectation of gain (Braybrooke, 1983).

The idea that everyone's interest would ultimately be best served if everyone pursued self-interest is alien to this view, which holds that health professionals and institutions should put patients' interests ahead of self-interest (although it may be "good business" to behave thusly). In this view it is quite appropriate to expect health care institutions and professionals to provide care to patients who are unable to pay. Ideally, perhaps, the funds required for such care should be raised by government through taxes; however, in the absence of such support, the institution's role is to provide needed service and to make up the resulting deficits however it can, including cross-subsidization from paying patients. Prices should be set to enable institutions to remain financially viable, not at whatever level the market might sustain.

The business orientation that is seen as a concomitant of for-profit health care also is regarded as a threat to the very ethos of health care. Among the fears that health care will become a business are that a multi-tier system will become more inescapable and more socially acceptable,[9] and that providers will come to feel no shame in refusing to serve those who cannot pay, in declining to offer or provide needed services that cannot generate an acceptable economic return, in setting prices as high as the market will allow and doing whatever is necessary to maximize income, and in aggressively marketing services that may be unrelated to basic health needs but that generate profits (e.g., cosmetic surgery).[10] It is thus feared that the move toward for-profit health care will affect the moral or ethical climate of health care.

This view also emphasizes the limitations of competition and market forces, arguing that such forces do not properly adjust for many key elements of health care. These elements include the great knowledge imbalance between providers and recipients of medical services; the inability of the patient to judge much more than superficial aspects of quality; the essential fiduciary role required of the physician; the necessity of third-party payment because of the unpredictability and cost of medical expenses, but which substantially reduces the patient's price sensitivity and attenuates market restraints on prices; the importance of a community-wide perspective on the need for services, particularly of high-cost, low-utilization services such as 24-hour emergency room coverage, burn treatment units, and neonatal intensive care units; the fact that there are people who need care who cannot afford it; and the fact that individuals' needs for care are unpredictable and tend to be inversely related to ability to pay.

Adherents of the "social good" view also frequently point to some perverse effects of the marketplace—its stimulus to provide unnecessary services; its tendency to offer only those services from which, and to serve only those patients from whom, money can be made either directly or indirectly; its eagerness to duplicate services without respect for community "need" if doing so serves competitive advantages;[11] its alleged willingness to shade on aspects of quality when detection by customers is unlikely, as can happen in medical care; its emphasis on amenities, which are seen as the equivalent of packaging in other areas of merchandising. Critics see amenities as unrelated to quality in a basic functional sense, but as having the potential to become the basis of competition, thereby drawing the consumer's dollars away from the necessities and tempting the provider to substitute the improvement of amenities for more expensive and genuine improvements in the quality of services.

A source of concern about the rise of investor-owned health facilities is the belief that they behave differently from not-for-profit organizations. As Douglas (1983) writes, "while the nonprofit producer, like its for-profit counterpart, may have the capacity to raise prices and cut quality, it has nowhere the same incentive since those in charge are barred from taking home the profit." (The theoretical conceptions that underlie predictions of different behavior by for-profit and not-for-profit organizations are discussed in more detail in the Appendix at the end of this chapter.)

Although the two views of health care acknowledge the key role of the physician in the operation of the system, the social view emphasizes the fiduciary aspects of that role rather than the physician as entrepreneur or as customer, the object of the hospital's marketing efforts. The physician is seen as the translator of biomedical knowledge into practice, as the patient's agent, as motivated to identify needs and to do what is required, not to identify demand and satisfy it. It is felt that these key aspects of the physician's role can best be pursued in settings where profit is not the primary goal. A largely unexamined sense of compatibility has existed between the ideals of professionalism and the not-for-profit form for health care organizations such as hospitals (Steinwald and Neuhauser, 1970; Majones, 1984). As Starr (1982:23) put the argument,

> The contradiction between professionalism and the rule of the market is long-standing and unavoidable. Medicine and other professions have historically distinguished themselves from business and trade by claiming to be above the market and pure commercialism. In justifying the public's trust, professionals have set higher standards of conduct for themselves than the minimal rules governing the marketplace and maintained that they can be judged under those standards by each other, not by laymen. . . . [The] shift from clients to colleagues in the orientation of work, which professionalism demands, represents a clear departure from the normal role of the market.

In discussions of ideals that run counter to economic incentives, the question inevitably arises of the extent to which the behavior of physicians or health care institutions has actually conformed to ideals of altruism, service, and science (Relman and Reinhardt, 1986). Skeptics point to several facts: the rise in physician fees and income that followed the shift from their depending for income on the means of their patients to their drawing on funds from third-party payers who reimbursed under the "usual, customary, and reasonable" approach (Roe, 1981); widespread and long-standing variations in medical care (*Health Affairs*, 1984); the tendency of volume of services to increase when they are covered by insurance (Aday et al., 1980); low levels of hospitalization and surgery when fee-for-service incentives are not present (Luft, 1981; Bunker 1970); patterns of acquisition and use of laboratory and diagnostic testing equipment in physicians' offices (Schroeder and Showstack, 1978); widespread physician unwillingness to accept Medicare as full payment for their services (AMA, 1985); and the struggles of legal services attorneys to force not-for-profit hospitals to care for more indigent patients (see *Clearinghouse Review*, 1969-present). Clearly, the highest ideals of medicine are not always fully realized in any sector of the health care system. Jonsen (1983) has noted that medical practice always involves a tension between altruism and self-interest. Ideals, even if imperfectly realized, may affect where the balance is struck, as may the way care is organized and paid for.

### Economic Good Versus Social Good

The contrasting views of health care as economic good and as social good involve a complex mix of values, assumptions, beliefs, and assertions. They underlie debates about many questions of health policy, such as community rating versus experience rating in health insurance and whether bad debts and charity care should be treated as allowable costs under cost-based reimbursement, whether market forces or health planning organizations should shape the configuration of available services, whether hospitals that care for a disproportionate share of the poor should be especially rewarded, and whether hospital rates and revenues should be regulated. These contrasting views certainly underlie the debate about for-profit or corporate trends in health care. Recognition of the value issues may offer clarification when differences of opinion arise; it also may help to temper expectations about the amount of agreement that can be reached in the examination of the "facts" about a controversial topic.

In health research and policy, relatively little attention has been given to means by which altruism rather than self-interest is stimulated in health professionals. Can incentives be designed to reward providers for pursuing self-interest in a way that also is in the best interests of patients (and that does not waste health care dollars on inefficiency or unnecessary care)? Or is such perfection of incentives an unrealistic goal, making it essential to the ideals of health care that providers respond to values of charity and altruism, as well as to anxiety about peer approval and legal liability? That is still another form of the issue posed by the growth of for-profit health care.

## Relationship of Physicians to Health Care Organizations

The framework for the committee's examination of the relationship between physicians and organizations rests on two premises. First, the committee believes that physicians have substantial fiduciary responsibilities toward their patients, meaning that the physician has an ethical and often a legal obligation to act in the patient's best interests. The arrangements between physicians and institutions must be considered in light of the physician's fiduciary responsibilities.

The question of the physician's fiduciary responsibilities inevitably leads to questions of the economic arrangements in medical practice and of the compatibility of professional responsibilities and the not-for-profit organization. This is the subject of Chapter 8. Fears that physicians might exploit the vulnerabilities of patients for pecuniary gain are not new. Indeed, a conflict of interest of sorts is present and manifest in any situation in which the potential provider of a service is asked to define whether it is needed. The problem of conflict of interest becomes more difficult to control when it is not understood by the recipient of services, and when the economic return for providing the advice is relatively small in proportion to the return for providing the service that is recommended.

Conflict of interest is also created when physicians make substantial capital outlays for high-cost technologies; the need to have such an investment pay off must be a motivating force in stimulating the use of these technologies, along with a desire to close the income gap with high-income specialists. Thus, there has long been concern about physicians creating a conflict of interest by establishing organizations (pharmacies, diagnostic centers, hospitals) external to their practice and then making patient-care decisions that can affect the economic well-being of the organization, a concern that can be extended to the doctor's office when tests are ordered using the doctor's own X-ray, laboratory, electrocardiograph, or other equipment. Notwithstanding that multiple conflicts of interest can be identified in health care, proprietary activities involving physicians appear to be increasing and have created special concerns about conflict of interest and its impact on trust in the doctor-patient relationship.

Second, the committee believes that physicians' responsibilities to patients require that they play a role in monitoring and assuring the quality of care in medical organizations to which they refer or admit patients. Although this role frequently has been inadequately realized and although institutions (and their boards and administration) share this responsibility, the committee has focused on the physician's role in this regard, because of the concern with fiduciary responsibilities and because organizational changes are taking place that could alter significantly the balance of power and influence within medical institutions. Changes that reduce the physician's ability to shift patients to other institutions could have that effect, as could changes that reduce the physician's voice on decision-making bodies. Many current developments— the growth of HMOs, preferred provider arrangements, and joint ventures, not to mention the growing supply of physicians— could reduce physicians' freedom to shift patients away from an institution that the physician finds unsatisfactory. And trends such as the growth of multi-institutional arrangements and the growth of for-profit organizations could alter physicians' roles in institutional management and governance. These issues are examined in Chapter 9.

## NOTES

[1] The terms "for-profit," "investor-owned," and "proprietary" are all used in this report to refer to organizations that are owned by individuals and corporations (such as institutional investors) to whom profits are distributed. Such organizations stand in contrast to organizations that are incorporated under state laws as nonprofit or not-for-profit organizations. (The defining characteristics of both types of organizations are discussed later in this chapter.) Terms within each set are not used in a consistent fashion in the literature. Nevertheless, the committee sees some differences in connotation among the terms and has attempted to use terminology appropriately and consistently as follows.

The term "proprietary" is used to connote the traditional independent owner-operated institution (for example, hospital, nursing home, or home health agency). The term "investor-owned" is used to connote companies (rather than institutions) that have a substantial number of stockholders. The term "for-profit" encompasses both. (A drawback of the term "for-profit" is that it seems to define organizations in terms of assumed behavior—that is, that such organizations will seek to maximize profit, because by definition that is their purpose. However, the committee sees organi-

zational behavior not as a matter for definition but as a topic to be investigated empirically.)

On the other side, the committee prefers the term "not-for-profit" over the term "nonprofit," both because the term "not-for-profit" conveys a direct contrast with the term "for-profit" and because the term "nonprofit" often is incorrectly interpreted to mean that the organization has (or should have) no surplus of revenues over expenses. That is again an empirical question, not a matter of definition.

Both for-profit and not-for-profit types of ownership stand in contrast to "public" or "government" ownership. Most health care institutions in the United States are private, not public, and the debate about for-profit versus not-for-profit ownership of health care institutions should not be misconstrued as a debate about public versus private ownership. Except where explicitly noted, the public or government-owned institutions referred to in this report are owned by state or local governments, not the federal government.

[2] For example, the merging health care supply companies, Baxter Travenol and American Hospital Supply Corporation, both have home care subsidiaries; several insurance companies (e.g., Prudential, John Hancock, Aetna, CIGNA) have HMO subsidiaries; the Owens-Illinois glass company bought nursing homes and hospitals; W. R. Grace and Co. has acquired National Medical Care, the hemodialysis company, and McDonnell Douglas owns more than half interest in an HMO company called Sanus.

[3] The term "efficiency" appears in the report because for-profit organizations are commonly alleged to be more efficient than public or not-for-profit organizations. However it should be recognized that because "efficiency" refers to the comparative cost at which a given good or service is produced, it can be properly studied only when there is a high degree of standardization of the good or service being produced. This condition seldom holds in studies of health care costs. Data tend to be available only on such measures as expenses per day or per case. Whether differences in such measures indicate differences in efficiency or are due to differences in the service being produced is, unfortunately, generally conjectural.

[4] Of course, in addition to such boards and top management, centrally managed multi-institutional systems, whether for-profit or not-for-profit, typically also have separate boards and management at the local institutional level. The amount of local authority over institutional affairs is variable.

[5] Stock options are a form of long-term compensation characteristic of growth-oriented companies, because they are a method of rewarding employees (usually executives) for company growth and they sometimes substitute for higher salaries, thereby increasing the amount of corporate earnings that can be devoted to growth. The price at which the option to purchase a

given amount of the stock is offered to an employee is often only slightly below the current market value. The option, which is typically for a period of years, becomes valuable when the value of the stock increases. Old stock options with a growth company such as Humana are extremely valuable when exercised, since "a share of stock bought for $4 in 1974 is now worth $403.20" according to *Business Week* (1985:79), which explains how the 1984 compensation of Humana, Inc. board chairman David Jones included $17,394 million in stock options.

[6]Public institutions share some of the characteristics of not-for-profits (most important, the restrictions on distributing surpluses to the individuals controlling the organization, although in the case of public institutions, surpluses commonly are returned to the public treasury), but have several key differences: They are owned not by a state-chartered corporation but by government itself (federal, state, or local); they are directly or indirectly under control of elected officials; a significant portion of their operating budgets and capital needs often comes in the form of direct governmental appropriations; and their responsibilities often explicitly include providing care to patients without insurance or the ability to pay for care.

[7]Hansmann has labeled these two types as donative and commercial not-for-profits, respectively.

[8]The concerns and arguments about the appropriateness of markets as the mode of distribution of health services parallel more general arguments about market societies that go back more than two centuries. As Hirschman (1982) has shown, there is a very old debate about whether self-interest can replace love and charity as the basis of a well-ordered society and whether values such as trust are generated or eroded by the incentives and practices of the market. Thinkers such as David Hume and Adam Smith saw the growth of commercialism as enhancing such virtues as "industriousness and assiduity (the opposite of indolence), frugality, punctuality, and, most important perhaps for a market society, probity," and would create as a by-product "a more 'polished' human type—more honest, reliable, orderly and disciplined, as well as more friendly and helpful, ever ready to find solutions to conflicts and a middle ground for opposed opinions" (Hirschman, 1982:1465). The opposing thesis, among both Marxist and conservative thinkers, was that the emergence of a capitalist society fundamentally undermined the proper moral foundations of society—that religiously based virtues (truth, trust, acceptance, restraint, obligation, and cooperation) would be threatened or destroyed by market society's pursuit of individual self-interest rather than the general interest (Hirschman, 1982; Hirsch, 1976).

[9]Multiple tiers in health care are, of course, not new and are particularly exemplified by the split between public and private institutions. Multiple tiers also have existed within institutions (See Duff and Hollingshead, 1968), although this has been diminished substantially by governmental funding programs, particularly Medicare and Medicaid.

[10]To illustrate this ethos, *Forbes Magazine* noted with approval Republic Health's strategies for maximizing profits by identifying surgical procedures that can be "done quickly, often in a few hours, without lots of nurses, tests, meals or general care" and marketing them to the public "just as hotels market cut rate weekends." The article noted that in one of this company's hospitals, with a 25 percent occupancy rate, sales on elective surgery were offered. The hospital accepted whatever Medicare was willing to pay and charged the patient no deductible. Without raising occupancy, 1,800 more patients were treated at the hospital in 1984 than in 1983. "Result: the hospital made $3 million pretax in 1984" (Tietelman, 1985).

[11]Willingness to duplicate services without respect to need is, of course, in no way peculiar to the for-profit sector, as the experience of the past 20 years (including the history of the health planning program and the growth of surplus beds) clearly shows. Competitive impulses of a slightly different nature (e.g., for prestige) were undoubtedly in part responsible.

## REFERENCES

Aday, LuAnn, Ronald Anderson, and Gretchen V. Fleming (1980) *Health Care in the U.S.: Equitable for Whom?* Beverly Hills, Calif.: Sage.

American Hospital Association (1985) 1984 Hospital Cost and Utilization Trends. *Economic Trends* 1(Spring).

American Medical Association (1985) Medicare Assignment: Recent Trends and Participation Rates. *SMS Report* 4(February).

Blumstein, Michael (1984) How Institutions Rule the Market. *New York Times* (November 25): Section 3.

Braybrooke, David (1983) *Ethics in the World of Business.* Totowa, N.J.: Rowman and Allanheld.

Bunker, John (1970) Surgical Manpower: A Comparison of Operations and Surgeons in the United States and in England and Wales. *The New England Journal of Medicine* 282:135-144.

*Business Week* (1985) Executive Pay: Who Made the Most (May 6):78-79.

Clark, Robert C. (1980) Does the Nonprofit Form Fit the Hospital Industry? *Harvard Law Review* 93(May):1416-1489.

*Clearinghouse Review* (1969-present) Chicago, Ill.: National Clearinghouse for Legal Services.

Douglas, James (1983) *Why Charity? The Case for a Third Sector.* Beverly Hills, Calif.: Sage.

Drucker, Peter F. (1984) Beyond the Bell Breakup. *The Public Interest* 77(Fall):3-27.

Duff, Raymond S., and A. B. Hollingshead (1968) *Sickness and Society.* New York: Harper and Row.

Easley, David, and Maureen O'Hara (1983) The Economic Role of the Nonprofit Firm. *Bell Journal of Economics* 14(Autumn):531-538.

Ginzberg, Eli (1984) The Monetarization of Medical Care. *The New England Journal of Medicine* 310(May 3):1162-1165.

Hansmann, Henry B. (1980) The Role of Nonprofit Enterprise. *Yale Law Journal* 89(April):835-901.

*Health Affairs* (1984) Special issue on "Variations in Medical Practice." 3(Summer).

Hirsch, Fred (1976) *Social Limits to Growth.* Cambridge, Mass.: Harvard University Press.

Hirschman, Albert O. (1982) Rival Interpretations of Market Society: Civilizing, Destructive, or Feeble? *Journal of Economic Literature* 20(December):1463-1484.

Horty, John F., and Daniel Mulholland III (1983) Legal Differences Between Investor-Owned and Nonprofit Health Care Institutions. Pp. 17-34 in Bradford H. Gray (ed.) *The New Health Care for Profit.* Washington, D.C.: National Academy Press.

Jonsen, Albert (1983) Watching the Doctor. *The New England Journal of Medicine* 308(June 23):1531-1535.

Luft, Harold S. (1981) *Health Maintenance Organizations: Dimensions of Performance.* New York: Wiley.

Majones, Giandomenico (1984) Professionalism and Nonprofit Organizations. *Journal of Health Politics, Policy and Law* 8(Winter):639-659.

*Modern Healthcare* (1985) 15(June 7).

Pauly, Mark (1980) *Doctors and Their Workshops.* Chicago, Ill.: University of Chicago Press.

Pauly, Mark, and Michael Redisch (1973) The Notfor-Profit Hospital as a Physicians' Cooperative. *American Economic Review* 63(March):87-99.

Relman, Arnold S. (1980) The New Medical-Industrial Complex. *The New England Journal of Medicine* 303(October 23):963-969.

Relman, Arnold S., and Uwe Reinhardt (1986) An Exchange on For-Profit Health Care. This volume.

Roe, Benson B. (1981) The UCR Boondoggle: A Death Knell for Private Practice? *The New England Journal of Medicine* 305(July 2):41-45.

Schroeder, Steven A., and Jonathan A. Showstack (1978) Financial Incentives to Perform Medical Procedures and Laboratory Tests. *Medical Care* 12 (August):709-713.

Shaw, Bernard (1911) *The Doctor's Dilemma.* New York: Brentano's.

Siegrist, Richard B., Jr. (1983) Wall Street and the For-Profit Hospital Management Companies. Pp. 35-50 in Bradford H. Gray (ed.) *The New Health Care for Profit.* Washington, D.C.: National Academy Press.

Sloan, Frank A. (Forthcoming) Property Rights in the Hospital Industry. In H. E. Frech III (ed.), *Health Care Policy.*

Starr, Paul (1982) *The Social Transformation of American Medicine* New York: Basic Books.

Steinwald, Bruce, and Duncan Neuhauser (1970) The Role of the Proprietary Hospital. *Law and Contemporary Problems* 35(Autumn):817-838.

Stevens, Rosemary (1982) A Poor Sort of Memory: Voluntary Hospitals and Government Before the Depression. *Milbank Memorial Fund Quarterly* 60:551-584.

Stevens, Rosemary (1985) The Historical Perspective [on The New Entrepreneurialism in Health Care]. *Bulletin of the New York Academy of Medicine* 61(January-February):54-59.

Tietelman, Robert (1985) Selective Surgery. *Forbes* (April 22):75-76.

U.S. Small Business Administration (1983) *Unfair Competition by Nonprofit Organizations with Small Business: An Issue for the 1980s.* Washington, D.C.: U.S. Small Business Administration.

Veatch, Robert M. (1983) Ethical Dilemmas of For-Profit Enterprise in Health Care. Pp. 125-152 in Bradford H. Gray (ed.), *The New Health Care for Profit.* Washington, D.C.: National Academy Press.

Vladeck, Bruce (1976) Why Nonprofits Go Broke. *The Public Interest* 42(Winter):86-101.

Weisbrod, Burton A. (1981) The Limitations of Competition: A Skeptical View. Pp. 40-51 in *Competition-Regulation and the HMO: Impact on Hospitals and Physicians*, 23rd Annual George Bugbee Symposium on Hospital Affairs. Chicago, Ill.: University of Chicago Graduate School of Business.

Williamson, Oliver E. (1981) The Modern Corporation: Origins, Evolution, Attributes. *Journal of Economic Literature* 19(December):1537-1568.

# APPENDIX TO CHAPTER 1

# Economic Theories of For-Profit and Not-for-Profit Organizations

## Sunny G. Yoder

This appendix considers, from a theoretical perspective, the rationale for the existence of private, for-profit; private, not-for-profit; and governmental production of goods and services. It describes the different objectives that economic theory suggests are pursued by organizations in each sector and considers the implications for the behavior of health care providers—primarily hospitals—of these objectives. Because it is the nature of theory to abstract from the complexities of everyday reality, the emphasis here is on the basic elements that theoretically distinguish the three sectors.[1]

### ECONOMIC RATIONALE FOR THE THREE SECTORS

The standard for comparison among models of economic production and distribution is the private, for-profit firm in a market economy. The simple competitive model is based on the presence in an industry of many firms acting to maximize their profits and many individual consumers acting to maximize their welfare (utility). If there are a sufficient number of firms in the industry so that no one firm can affect the market price, if firms can enter and exit the industry readily, and if consumers have enough information to make informed decisions, then prices serve as accurate signals of firms' willingness to produce and consumers' willingness to buy. In the equilibrium state the prices are such that the quantity and mix of goods and services being produced are just the quantity and mix that consumers want to buy. Because new firms can enter the industry and compete away excess profits, production is carried out in the least costly manner, given feasible production technology. As a consequence, resources are used in a way that sacrifices the least amount of alternative production. In addition to directing resources

into their most productive uses, the competitive market model has the result that consumers attain their highest possible levels of economic satisfaction, given their preferences and incomes.

Why, then, does an economy include governmental production or not-for-profit, private production? What are the comparative advantages of these sectors, and what variables determine which services are produced by which sector?

According to economic theory, the government produces services (and sometimes goods) that the private, for-profit sector either does not produce or that it produces in smaller quantities than society desires (Samuelson, 1967:46-463; Musgrave and Musgrave, 1973:5). National defense, law and order, fire protection, administration of justice and of contracts, parks, and basic research are services that benefit the community. However, since people can receive the benefits of such services without paying for them, they are unlikely to be produced by profit-making firms. Too, the private, for-profit market will tend to underproduce goods and services for which one person's consumption also benefits another. One person's fire protection, for example, also protects his neighbors' houses; one child's vaccination against measles also protects his schoolmates. There is neither a means to exclude the neighbors or schoolmates from the benefits nor to charge them for their share.

Governments also may produce some services for people who, if they had to pay a private provider, would go without. Thus, another important rationale for governmental production is redistribution of income in instances when society judges that the distribution of income and wealth resulting from the private market alone is unsatisfactory. Direct transfers (e.g., Aid to Families with Dependent Children) are one form of redistribution; direct provision of services such as health and education is another. Government also can finance the private production of such services or can purchase them on behalf of some members of society.

The theoretical rationale for governmental production, in summary, stems from two sources: the failure of the profit-maximizing private market to supply goods that society values, but that benefit consumers collectively rather than individually (another excellent example from Samuelson is lighthouses); and the need to assure that all citizens have access to certain basic goods and services.[2]

What is the rationale for not-for-profit production, then, if the for-profit market generally achieves a high level of social welfare and the government provides compensation when the market fails? A not-for-profit organization gives up "the right to accumulate a monetary residual which then can be distributed to its owners for personal consumption. Instead, all not-for-profit organizations' resources must be used internally . . ." (James, 1982:1). In this respect they differ from for-profit firms. On the other hand, not-for-profit organizations do not have the government's right to raise funds through compulsory taxation, but must depend on some combination of (1) selling their product or products at price levels sufficient to cover their costs and (2) obtaining revenues from voluntary donations of money, goods, and services. Many not-for-profit organizations do both.

Provided that an organization agrees to the nondistribution constraint (and, in most states, has "reasonable" operating costs), state and federal laws accord it special status. It is generally exempt from taxes[3] and also receives favored status under most federal legislation. The principles on which this special treatment is founded are not clearly formulated (Hansmann, 1980); however, since not-for-profit organizations existed before these government-conferred advantages, this favored status would not appear to be causative.

A number of theories attempt to explain the existence of not-for-profit organizations. One is that the not-for-profit organization is optimal when information regarding the quality or quantity of service is asymmetric

in favor of the seller (Hansmann, 1980; Easley and O'Hara, 1983; Bays 1983). When consumers are at an informational disadvantage, the market may not provide sufficient discipline to prevent a for-profit producer from marketing inferior services at excessive prices—a welfare loss for consumers and, by extension, for society. In such a case consumers are better served by a not-for-profit producer. Although it, too, could cut quality or raise prices, according to this theory its managers have little incentive to do so, because they are prohibited from sharing in any excess profits.

Complex personal services such as health care are especially at issue:

Often the complexity of these services, their nonstandard character, and the circumstances under which they are provided make it difficult for the consumer to determine whether the services are performed adequately. Thus, the patron has an incentive to seek some constraints on the organizations' behavior beyond those he is able to impose by direct, private contract. (Hansmann, 1980:862)

According to this theory, then, not-for-profit firms would be dominant in markets in which the quality of the product is difficult to monitor, because the preferences of consumers for the ostensible protection of the not-for-profit form would make it difficult or impossible for for-profit producers to remain in the market. However, we observe the continued existence of both forms in the nursing home and daycare industries, where presumably information asymmetry exists and where transferring to a different provider is difficult (James and Rose-Ackerman, Forthcoming). Other goods and services for which quality is difficult to ascertain are produced almost entirely by for-profit firms; examples are legal and medical services, personal computers, and used cars (Ben-Ner, 1983; James and Rose-Ackerman, Forthcoming). In higher education, where public and not-for-profit production predominates, considerable information is available about the "selectivity, student/faculty ratios, faculty credentials, and alumni of colleges and universities . . ." (James and Rose-Ackerman, Forthcoming). On empirical grounds, then, it appears that information asymmetry alone does not explain the presence of not-for-profit organizations.

An alternative theory is proposed by Ben-Ner (1983), who theorizes that the not-for-profit organization emerges in response to consumers' desire for control. According to his model, consumers may choose to establish their own organization in preference to taking their chances in the marketplace. A group of parents might start its own day-care center, for example. The not-for-profit firm (e.g., the consumer-run, not-for-profit cooperative) is theorized to dominate when the consumers' principal objective is to maintain high quality. The nondistribution constraint reduces the tendency by managers of such organizations to misrepresent or produce lower quality. (Ben-Ner does not discuss another alternative available to consumers, which is to form coalitions to reduce or remove information asymmetry by sharing information, seeking expert advice, or conducting research.)

Weisbrod (1977, 1980) characterizes not-for-profit organizations as responses to failures by government rather than failures by the private market. According to this theory, government responds to society's average demand for public services, conveyed through its collective-choice mechanisms. This average, however, underrepresents those members of society who have a very high demand for governmental services, as well as those whose tastes differ from the average. A private school, for example, can be a means for citizens to meet their demand for higher quality or to meet their special religious, linguistic, or other preferences. Thus, this model suggests that not-for-profit organizations arise to meet the heterogeneous demands of consumers for public and quasi-public services that are not fully met by the government's standardized output.

A somewhat different model proposes that the government delegate the production of certain public or quasi-public goods to not-for-profits rather than producing them itself (James and Rose-Ackerman, Forthcoming). According to this model, private production may offer the advantage of lower costs, because private firms can charge fees to cover some of their costs (e.g., tuition, hospital charges) and can avoid legally imposed wage rates and procurement practices that raise production costs for the government. Not-for-profit organizations also offer the potential for receiving donations of money and in-kind services that is not offered by for-profit firms. "Contracting out," as well as more subtle forms of delegation therefore give the government a degree of flexibility, as well as the possibility of reduced cost. The subsidy or grant to a not-for-profit organization is often used by government when it desires to purchase intangible services for which it is difficult to measure the quid pro quo. Too, policymakers may wish to provide more differentiated services, but may be bureaucratically unable to do so except by subsidizing private organizations.

Thus, economic theory offers several explanations for why some goods and services are produced by not-for-profit firms. The theory suggests that not-for-profit production may exist as a response to consumers' need for protection when the good or service cannot be observed or its quality accurately evaluated, as a response to differential demand for public or quasi-public goods when government has difficulty providing other than standardized output, as a means for government's achieving lower-cost production of certain public goods, or for a combination of these reasons. The rationale for the existence of not-for-profit firms, however, does not answer other important questions such as, what decision rules characterize the use of economic resources by these firms? In particular, how do their decisions about what to produce, and in what quantities, differ from the decisions of for-profit firms? Theories addressing these questions are reviewed in the following section.

## MODELS OF THE BEHAVIOR OF FOR-PROFIT AND NOT-FOR-PROFIT ORGANIZATIONS

Traditional economic theory treats the management structure and decision-making process as a black box. The firm is characterized by an objective function that represents either a single decision maker or the result of interactions (and the resolution of any conflicts) among stockholders, trustees, and managers. The basic model hypothesizes that, irrespective of how decisions are made, the firm's objective is to maximize profits. More recent theories of the for-profit firm, discussed below, take greater cognizance of the role of managers and the possibility that profit maximization may not be their sole or even their primary objective.

Economic theories of the behavior of not-for-profit firms generally ascribe to them objectives other than profit (i.e., net revenue) maximization (Davis, 1972; James and Rose-Ackerman, Forthcoming). In the simplest not-for-profit model the objective is to maximize output. If the not-for-profit organization produces a single product, such as day care, receives all its revenues from the sale of that product, and has the same cost structure as a for-profit producer, in the short run the not-for-profit firm will produce more of the product than the profit-maximizing firm, but at a higher cost. However, if there are no barriers to prevent new firms (either not-for-profit or for-profit) from entering the industry, over the long run their entry will cause the industry to become as efficient as if it were entirely populated by profit-maximizing producers.

This picture becomes more complicated, however, in the more relevant case in which a not-for-profit firm receives unrestricted donations and produces more than one product. Whether the not-for-profit firm's long-run output is greater or lesser than that of the for-profit firm under these conditions—which are characteristic of not-for-profit hospitals and private educational institutions—will depend on the objectives of managers. If not-for-profit managers and their donors desire to produce higher levels of some or all of their outputs (serving greater numbers of people, for example), these levels will be obtained at the expense of efficiency in comparison with the profit-maximizing firm in a competitive industry. As discussed below, however, the hospital industry has substantial entry barriers and other characteristics that cause it to differ from the purely competitive model.

The fact that a not-for-profit firm's managers do not share in any surplus resulting from efficiency and the fact that they usually have access to donated revenues not tied to specific production are offered as positive reasons for the existence of not-for-profit organizations. These characteristics also may have potential negative effects. For instance, whereas stockholders can exercise control of managers of for-profit firms, or, in extreme cases, takeovers via the capital market can perform the role of selecting managers who maximize profits through efficient production, such mechanisms are not available in the not-for-profit arena. The attenuation of "property rights" (managers' rights to any residual earnings or capital gains) in the case of not-for-profits can encourage "shirking," choice of inefficient inputs, and production of a nonoptimal mix of outputs (James and Rose-Ackerman, Forthcoming; Sloan, Forthcoming). Managers of not-for-profit organizations may accord themselves high salaries, "perks" such as plush offices, or lavish expense accounts; they also may choose an inefficient production technology (e.g., greater use of high-technology capital than is optimal from an efficiency standpoint).[4] In the latter case, the not-for-profit firm will operate well short of maximum efficiency in the short run. Lee's (1971) model of the not-for-profit hospital, for example, suggests that it will acquire sophisticated equipment and highly trained personnel beyond the point required for production in order to enhance the prestige of the organization and, by extension, its managers. The ability of a not-for-profit hospital to continue to operate in this manner should be limited by the extent to which for-profit firms can enter the market and drive down the price through competition, but the availability of donations can cushion the not-for-profit manager from the pressures of competition.

Models of not-for-profit organizations often include the objective of maximizing quality (Newhouse, 1970); however, the effect of this objective on consumer welfare is ambiguous. If not-for-profits produce higher quality and charge higher fees (prices) to cover the added costs, then consumers can infer quality from the fees, and those consumers who desire higher quality and are willing to pay the additional cost can choose to do so. If, however, the higher quality is paid for out of donations, fees may be the same for both high-quality and low-quality providers. In this case other sorting methods will be utilized, such as waiting lists in the case of high-quality not-for-profit nursing homes or day-care centers.

In the case of not-for-profit organizations that have multiple outputs (e.g., the various clinical services of a hospital, as well as education and research), the not-for-profit organization is hypothesized to engage in cross-subsidization. The profit-maximizing firm theoretically will not do so, because its optimal strategy is to produce each product line to the point where marginal costs and marginal revenues are equal. The manager of a not-for-profit organization, however, may pursue the goal of producing outputs that he values (e.g., high-quality or esoteric medical care as suggested by Newhouse) by producing other outputs that he does not particularly value but that generate a surplus. The surplus then can be used to subsidize the valued outputs. The sale of gifts and T-shirts to subsidize the exhibits and research activities of the Metropolitan Museum and the Smithsonian Institution is one example. The provision of well-reimbursed ancillary services to subsidize a coronary care unit is another. As with preferred inputs, however, the ability of not-for-profit managers to engage in cross-subsidization over time is limited to the extent that new firms may enter and compete away the profits on the products that are providing the subsidies. Thus, not-for-profits' continued discretion over the production of desired outputs over time requires barriers to entry, donations, or both. This discretionary behavior by managers does not necessarily coincide with the preferences of donors or with maximum social welfare.

The presence of entry barriers and asymmetric information suggests that profit-maximizing firms may not operate efficiently in industries such as hospital care and education. However, there also is a question of whether pure profit maximization is the sole objective of private firms in this (or indeed any) industry. Alternative models have been suggested that give greater weight than does the traditional model to the preferences of managers. Baumol (1967), for example, develops a model that characterizes the firm as maximizing total revenues, subject to the constraint that stockholders receive a sufficient return to make the firm's securities attractive in the capital market. Such a firm will behave, according to the theory, very similarly to a not-for-profit firm. Also similarly, this type of behavior can be sustained

only if there are entry barriers.

Another model, from Williamson (1981), suggests that managers of for-profit firms prefer certain expenditures to others because they contribute to the managers' status and security. This model is analogous to the input-preference model of not-for-profit behavior discussed previously. However, as distinct from Baumol's model, Williamson's model gives a greater weight to profits, because they permit the firm to expand, which also provides prestige to the manager. Both models predict that the firm will favor certain factors of production and will produce some outputs beyond profit-maximizing levels, behaviors that also are attributed to the not-for-profit firm and that imply nonefficient production.

## WHY FOR-PROFIT HOSPITALS MAY BE INEFFICIENT

This review of the theoretical literature comparing the behavior of not-for-profit with for-profit enterprises suggests that for-profit organization results in greater efficiency (i.e., least-cost production) under very specific circumstances: profit maximization as the overriding objective, no substantial barriers to entry, observable output. These circumstances do not appear to typify the hospital industry. Hospital managers may well have preferences and objectives that differ from profit maximization, including the enhancement of their organization's prestige; the provision of specific services that further this or other goals; the provision of charitable care, teaching, or research; and the improvement of their own professional status. Also, this is an industry in which there are substantial entry barriers. The capital requirements to start a hospital are large. Too, certificate-of-need regulations greatly constrain the ability of firms to enter the hospital industry. Hospital services are extremely complex, and most consumers have little or no direct experience for evaluating them, nor do they always have the opportunity to obtain information from others before seeking these services. Thus, information asymmetry with its potential market failure is likely to be present for many hospital services. However, the issue of information asymmetry depends crucially on the role of the physician. If, as Hansmann suggests, the physician acts as the patient's knowledgeable agent with respect to assessing the quality of hospital services, the hospital is faced with a powerful constraint on its ability either to cheat on quality or to produce services on which consumers and their physicians place little value. If, on the other hand, physicians dominate hospital decision making and direct it toward maximizing their own incomes, as Pauly and Redisch (1973) and others have suggested, the quantity and mix of services produced would be that which satisfies the preferences of physicians rather than the preferences of consumers or managers.

The nature of hospital services and the characteristics of the hospital industry pose the question of whether for-profit production will achieve the optimal levels of efficiency and consumer satisfaction that the competitive market model predicts. Thus, while the nonprofit organization appears to compare unfavorably with the competitive ideal, this standard of comparison probably is inappropriate in the hospital industry. For-profit hospitals, because of entry barriers, information asymmetry, and the ambiguity of the physician's role as the consumer's agent, may not be presumed to produce the quantity and quality of services desired by society at an efficient price. At the same time, economic theory suggests that there also may be reasons why not-for-profit hospitals do not behave in socially optimal ways. Even though managers of not-for-profits cannot receive directly a share of any monetary surplus, the presence of donations and entry barriers and the absence of stockholder pressures may allow them considerable leeway to use resources and to produce services according to their own preferences. These preferences may or may not be consistent with those of society.

This discussion has not addressed the crucial issue of how services are to be distributed. According to standard economic theory, the profit-maximizing firm in a competitive economy sells its product at the market price to anyone who wants to buy at that price and who can afford it. Thus, the competitive market distributes goods and services in accord with the existing income distribution. If society prefers that hospital services be distrib-

uted more equitably, and if managers of not-for-profit hospitals share society's preferences, then these hospitals may be superior to for-profit hospitals when judged in terms of societal well-being.

## NOTES

[1] A fourth sector, households, principally engages in selling its labor services to one of the other sectors and using its earnings to purchase goods and services. Household production for the most part consists of home maintenance and repair, care of children and infirm adults, food preparation, and the like, activities that are not generally monetized.

[2] Defining the standards of such access and devising mechanisms to ensure it are central problems in all societies, of course. The efficiency-equity dilemma has been explored by Okun (1975).

[3] In the case of certain not-for-profits—religious, educational, health, scientific, cultural, and social service organizations—donor contributions also are tax deductible. Others, chiefly membership groups such as social clubs, fraternal organizations, and labor unions, are tax-exempt but donations are not (Rudney, 1981).

[4] The legal requirement that a nonprofit organization's costs must be reasonable is intended to deter such behavior.

## REFERENCES

Baumol, W. J. (1967) *Business Behavior, Value and Growth.* New York: Harcourt, Brace, and World.

Bays, Carson W. (1983) Why Most Private Hospitals Are Nonprofit. *Journal of Policy Analysis and Management* 2(3):366-385.

Ben-Ner, Avner (1983) Nonprofit Organizations: Why Do They Exist in Market Economies? Working Paper No. 51. Program on Non-profit Organizations, Yale University.

Davis, Karen (1972) Economic Theories of Behavior in Nonprofit, Private Hospitals. *Journal of Economics and Business* 24(2):1-13.

Easley, David, and Maureen O'Hara (1983) The Economic Role of the Nonprofit Firm. *The Bell Journal of Economics* 14(2):531-538.

Hansmann, Henry B. (1980) The Role of Nonprofit Enterprise. *The Yale Law Journal* 89(5):835-901.

James, Estelle (1982) Production, Consumption and Cross-Subsidization in Non-profit Organizations. Working Paper No. 30. Program on Non-profit Organizations, Yale University.

James, Estelle, and Susan Rose-Ackerman (Forthcoming) The Nonprofit Enterprise in Market Economies. In M. Montias and J. Kornai (eds.) *Economic Systems.*

Lee, Maw Lin (1971) A Conspicuous Production Theory of Hospital Behavior. *Southern Economic Journal* 28(1):48-58.

Musgrave, Richard A., and Peggy B. Musgrave (1973) *Public Finance in Theory and Practice*. New York: McGraw-Hill.

Newhouse, Joseph P. (1970) Toward a Theory of Nonprofit Institutions: An Economic Model of a Hospital. *American Economic Review* 60(1):64-74.

Okun, Arthur M. (1975) *Equality and Efficiency: The Big Tradeoff*. Washington, D.C.: The Brookings Institution.

Pauly, Mark, and Michael Redisch (1973) The Not-for-Profit Hospital as a Physicians' Cooperative. *American Economic Review* 63(1):87-99.

Rudney, Gabriel (1981) A Quantitative Profile of the Nonprofit Sector. Working Paper No. 40. Program on Non-profit Organizations, Yale University.

Samuelson, Paul A. (1967) *Economics*. 7th ed. New York: McGraw-Hill.

Sloan, Frank A. (Forthcoming) Property Rights in the Hospital Industry. In H. E. Frech III (ed.), *Health Care Policy*.

Weisbrod, Burton A. (1977) *The Voluntary Nonprofit Sector: An Economic Analysis*. Lexington, Mass.: Lexington Books.

Weisbrod, Burton A. (1980) Private Goods, Collective Goods: The Role of the Nonprofit Sector. Pp. 139-177 in Kenneth W. Clarkson and Donald L. Martin (eds.) *The Economics of Nonproprietary Organizations*. Greenwich, Conn.: JAI Press.

Williamson, Oliver E. (1981) The Modern Corporation: Origins, Evolution, Attributes. *Journal of Economic Literature* 19(December):1537-1568.

# 2 Changes in the Ownership, Control, and Configuration of Health Care Services

Elements of change have been filtering through the ownership and configuration of health care organizations over the past two decades. Although the emergence of investor-owned hospital chains has been an important part of this change, there also has been substantial growth in multi-institutional arrangements among not-for-profit hospitals and a surge of investor ownership and multi-institutional arrangements among most kinds of health care organizations— psychiatric hospitals, nursing homes, health maintenance organizations, home health agencies, and various types of ambulatory care centers.

Distinctions between organizational types have begun to break down. Hybrid organizations have evolved that combine for-profit and not-for-profit components. Hospitals and multihospital systems have moved into other types of health services (primary care centers; ambulatory surgery, diagnostic, and rehabilitation centers; nursing homes; and home health services). Hospital companies, like health maintenance organizations, have begun to combine an insurance function with the provision of services.

Many of these developments—such as the emergence and growth of investor-owned hospital companies—were spurred by the rather sudden availability of money that accompanied the general rise of third-party payments and the specific passage of the

Medicare and Medicaid legislation in 1965. Federal dollars also were the driving force behind the expansion of, and for-profit interest in, the nursing home field (primarily funded by Medicaid) and hemodialysis (funded by Medicare's End-Stage Renal Disease Program). Some developments also were shaped by the bias toward hospital care that long characterized third-party payment programs and, more recently, by efforts to provide incentives for less-expensive forms of care, such as ambulatory surgery. The organizational configuration of the health care system has also been deeply affected by the fundamental changes in the sources of financial capital for health care, in particular the substitution of debt and equity capital from private investors for capital from government and philanthropy, as described in Chapter 3. As hospitals have become more dependent on borrowing, the greater borrowing power of multi-institutional systems has spurred the development of such systems. The need to gain access to lower-cost capital also generated alliances of not-for-profit systems and independent hospitals that are hybrids of not-for-profit and for-profit. The alliances raise equity capital, guarantee debt, and seek economies of scale.

Some organizational developments were stimulated by regulatory programs that squeezed only part of the system. For example, after the government required that hospitals obtain approval for expansions or for acquisition of costly technology, investors took the opportunity to initiate services, such as computed tomographic (CT) scanning, outside of hospitals, where the regulations did not apply.

The growth of multi-institutional systems, which widen the pool of administrative and managerial expertise on which individual institutions can draw, was undoubtedly stimulated in part by the difficulties of individual institutions in coping with an increasingly complex regulatory and reimbursement environment.

Other developments, such as a recent wave of hospital expansion into nursing homes, and home and psychiatric care, can be attributed to the changed economic incentives resulting from Medicare's shift from cost-based reimbursement to a fixed, per-case payment. Many other changes have resulted from developments in the private sector— particularly the efforts of employers to reduce the cost of their health benefit programs through devices ranging from employee cost-sharing to contractual arrangements with low-bidding providers.

The remainder of this chapter describes the organizational changes that have become a pervasive trend in health care. The growth of for-profit enterprise and of multi-institutional arrangements among different types of health care providers is examined, as well as some of the trends that are blurring the distinctions between types of health care organizations. Much of the movement described is toward larger organizations that provide an increasingly broad range of services.

Many of the numbers reported in this chapter should be regarded only as general indications of trends, because the rate of change is so rapid, definitions of what is being counted are not always precise (because of new and changing organizational forms), and the only available data are often from trade associations and sources.

## HOSPITALS

For-profit hospitals and multi-institutional health care organizations, the latter usually religious or governmental, have long been in existence. What is new are the rise of investor-owned hospital companies that own dozens of hospitals and the proliferation of multi-institutional arrangements among not-for-profit hospitals. Compared with independent hospitals, these systems are better able to fill capital needs, to engage in political maneuvering, and to maintain a body of managerial and specialized staff expertise. As summarized by one observer, multi-institutional organizations are the result of strategies "designed to provide sufficient strength to cope with the environment, to acquire scarce and valued resources, to allow organizational stability, to achieve organizational purposes, to enable growth and/ or survival, and to enhance the organization's competitive market position" (Zuckerman, 1983). Thus, multihospital systems have been created and developed on both the for-profit side—where the large companies have gained much attention—and among not-for-profit organizations.

### Investor-Owned Hospital Systems

For-profit hospitals are not new. Indeed, in the early 1900s more than half of the hospitals in the United States were proprietary. However, the proprietary share shrank thereafter (Steinwald and Neuhauser, 1970), and since 1970 the for-profit proportion has remained relatively stable at around 13 percent. The makeup of that 13 percent share, however, has been anything but stable, as independent proprietaries have become less common and companies owning and managing chains of hospitals and other health care institutions have grown rapidly. Most of today's largest companies were founded as recently as the last 20 years.

Table 2.1 shows steady growth in the

**TABLE 2.1**  Investor-Owned Hospitals and Beds: Number and Percentage of U.S. Nonfederal Short-Term General and Other Special Hospitals, 1975–1984

|      | Investor-Owned Hospitals[a] | Percent of U.S. Hospitals[b] | Investor-Owned Beds[a] | Percent of U.S. Beds[b] |
|------|------|------|------|------|
| 1975 | 378 | 6.3 | 51,230 | 5.3 |
| 1976 | 396 | 6.6 | 54,744 | 5.7 |
| 1977 | 420 | 7.0 | 58,357 | 5.9 |
| 1978 | 437 | 7.4 | 61,499 | 6.2 |
| 1979 | 464 | 7.8 | 66,039 | 6.7 |
| 1980 | 531 | 9.0 | 74,012 | 7.5 |
| 1981 | 580 | 9.9 | 79,002 | 7.8 |
| 1982 | 682 | 11.6 | 90,328 | 8.9 |
| 1983 | 767 | 13.1 | 99,958 | 9.8 |
| 1984 | 878 | NA | 113,122 | NA |

[a]Community, psychiatric, and specialty hospitals owned by corporations that own or manage three or more hospitals.

[b]Nonfederal short-term general and other special hospitals.

SOURCES: Calculated from data from: Federation of American Hospitals: *Directory of Investor-Owned Hospitals and Management Companies, 1975; Statistical Profile of the Investor-Owned Hospital Industry, 1979 and 1980; Statistical Profile of the Investor-Owned Industry, 1983; 1985 Directory, Investor-Owned Hospitals and Hospital Management Companies.* American Hospital Association, *Hospital Statistics,* 1984 edition.

number of investor-owned hospitals and in the proportion of the nation's hospitals and beds represented by investor-owned corporations.[1] Since 1975, investor-owners have added 500 hospitals and nearly 62,000 beds, more than doubling their holdings of hospitals and beds. In addition, 354 hospitals were managed by investor-owned companies in 1984 (Federation of American Hospitals, 1984). Conversely, the number of independent for-profit hospitals declined between 1975 and 1984 at almost the same rate as the number of investor-owned hospitals grew. Independent for-profit hospitals numbered 682 in 1975 and 303 in 1984 (Federation of American Hospitals, 1980 and 1984). This reduction is accounted for in part by closures and in part by purchase by investor-owned systems.

Purchase or lease of formerly independent for-profit hospitals has been a source of growth for investor-owned systems. The six largest companies, which in 1984 owned 58 percent of investor-owned hospitals, have bought or leased 436 acute care hospitals (80 percent of the short-term hospitals they have owned) since their inception.[2] Of these 436, 33 percent were formerly for-profit independent hospitals and 45 percent were for-profit chain-owned. The remaining 20 percent were not-for-profit or public hospitals, the majority of which were bought in the 1980s. Construction of new hospitals accounted for 20 percent of the growth of the six companies' short-term hospital holdings (Hoy and Gray, 1986).

## Not-for-profit Hospital Systems

The formation of not-for-profit hospital systems predates that of investor-owned systems. Such "systems," defined broadly to include affiliation or mutual support, have existed for more than 50 years, beginning mostly among hospitals of religious organizations (Keenan, 1981). Some historical data on today's not-for-profit systems are available from an American Hospital Association survey of systems in existence in 1980 (Table 2.2). Religious systems were predominant among systems that existed in 1940. By the 1980s, secular systems represented close to 40 percent of the 981 hospitals owned, leased, or sponsored by not-for-profit systems. An additional 215 hospitals were managed by not-for-profit systems in 1983.

## COMPARISONS OF INVESTOR-OWNED AND NOT-FOR-PROFIT SYSTEMS

Since the inception in the 1960s of investor-owned hospital systems, their rate of growth has exceeded that of not-for-profit systems. By 1983, the total number of hospitals owned by investor-owned corporations still fell somewhat short of the number owned by not-for-profit systems, and the number of beds in investor-owned systems was substantially less than half the number in not-for-profit systems (see Table 2.3). This difference results in part from the small average size of investor-owned hospitals. The investor-owned systems differed from the far more numerous not-for-profit systems in

other ways. The investor-owned systems were, on average, substantially larger than the not-for-profit systems in terms of owned hospitals or beds. Hospital Corporation of America, the largest investor-owned system, owned or leased 178 and managed 167 hospitals in 1984. It vastly exceeded the size of the largest not-for-profit system, Adventist Health Systems, with 60 owned or leased and 15 managed hospitals (*Modern Healthcare*, 1985b). (Two much larger organizations of not-for-profit hospitals—Voluntary Hospitals of America and American Healthcare Systems—are not generally classified as multihospital systems because they are owned by their member hospitals, rather than vice versa.) And nearly 70 percent of investor-owned hospitals were operated (owned, leased, or managed) by the four largest companies, while the four largest not-for-profit systems operated only 15 percent of not-for-profit system hospitals (Johnson, 1985). High concentration in a few large organizations characterizes the investor-owned sector much more than the not-for-profit sector.

Investor-owned systems have shown clearer location preferences than have not-

**TABLE 2.2** Number of Hospitals and Beds[a] in Religious and Secular Not-for-profit Multihospital Systems, 1940–1983

| | Religious | | Secular | | Total | |
|---|---|---|---|---|---|---|
| | Hospitals | Beds | Hospitals | Beds | Hospitals | Beds |
| 1940 | 183 | NA | 35 | NA | 218 | NA |
| 1950 | 211 | NA | 50 | NA | 261 | NA |
| 1960 | 242 | NA | 89 | NA | 331 | NA |
| 1970 | 283 | NA | 189 | NA | 472 | NA |
| 1980 | 600 | 153,000 | 364 | 85,000 | 964 | 238,000 |
| 1983 | 598 | 157,000 | 383 | 85,000 | 981 | 242,000 |

NOTE: 1940–1970 data are from responses to a special 1980 survey of multihospital systems. 1980 and 1983 data are from current surveys. 1980 and 1983 data are published as 1981 and 1985 data, respectively, in the original source, but pertain to the years shown in the table (Elworth Taylor, American Hospital Association, Chicago, Illinois, personal communication, 1985).

[a]Leased, owned, and sponsored.

SOURCE: American Hospital Association, *Data Book on Multihospital Systems 1980–1981; Data Book on Multihospital Systems, 1980–1985.*

**TABLE 2.3**  Comparative Information About Not-for-profit and
Investor-Owned Systems, 1983

|  | Investor-Owned Systems[a] | Not-for-profit Systems[b] |
|---|---|---|
| Number of systems | 41 | 212 |
| Number of hospitals in systems | 767 | 981 |
| Number of beds in systems | 100,000 | 242,000 |
| Average number of beds per hospital | 130 | 247 |
| Average number of hospitals per system | 18.7 | 4.6 |
| Average number of beds per system | 2,439 | 1,141 |

[a]Systems that own or manage three or more hospitals. Data pertain to owned facilities.

[b]Systems that own, lease, sponsor, and manage. An additional seven systems only manage. Data pertain to owned, leased, and sponsored facilities.

SOURCES: American Hospital Association, *Data Book on Multihospital Systems, 1980–1985;* Federation of American Hospitals, calculated from data from *Statistical Profile of the Investor-Owned Hospital Industry, 1983.*

for-profit systems. The hospitals they own are concentrated in the "sun belt" states; 46 percent of all investor-owned hospitals were located in Texas, California, and Florida in 1984 (Federation of American Hospitals, 1984). Table 2.4 shows what this preference has meant in terms of investor ownership of hospitals in individual states. In no state do investor-owned hospitals represent more than 50 percent of all nonfederal short-term general and other special hospitals, but they have more than 30 percent of such hospitals in seven states.

The investor-owned market share has grown most rapidly in states with the greatest increases in per capita income and population, with widespread insurance coverage, and where for-profit hospitals already had a relatively large market share of beds. Assuming that income and insurance coverage are associated with demand for hospital services, investor-owners have exhibited standard market behavior by seeking to establish themselves in areas of growing demand (Mullner and Hadley, 1984). Investor-owned hospitals are also more likely than are not-for-profit systems to be located in suburban areas and less likely to be in rate-setting states. Investor-owners often selected areas

in which Blue Cross pays hospital charges (Watt et al., 1986). Given the greater geographic selectivity of investor-owned systems, it is not surprising that not-for-profit systems more closely approximated the national distribution of hospitals among regions than did investor-owned systems in 1983 (Table 2.5).

Investor-owned hospital systems have also shown selectivity in the size of the hospitals they acquired or constructed. As Table 2.6 shows, they own few of the nation's smallest hospitals, which are frequently rural, and few of the largest, most complex hospitals, which generally are teaching hospitals, although there are signs of change in the latter area (see Chapter 7).

**Psychiatric Hospitals**

Half of all psychiatric hospitals (297 of 586) were government-owned in 1983 (American Hospital Association, 1984), but in the private sector, investor ownership has become a major presence. In mid-1985 the records of the National Association of Private Psychiatric Hospitals (NAPPH) indicated that 52 percent of the 224 member hospitals were affiliated with investor-owned systems, 19

**TABLE 2.4** Investor-Owned Hospitals as a Percentage of Nonfederal Short-Term General and Other Special Hospitals by State[a]

| State | Percentage | State | Percentage |
|---|---|---|---|
| Alabama | 29 | Nebraska | 1 |
| Alaska | 11 | Nevada | 50 |
| Arizona | 12 | New Hampshire | 7 |
| Arkansas | 16 | New Jersey | 3 |
| California | 31 | New Mexico | 10 |
| Colorado | 10 | New York | 0 |
| Connecticut | 2 | North Carolina | 18 |
| Delaware | 13 | North Dakota | 0 |
| District of Columbia | 8 | Ohio | 1 |
| Florida | 44 | Oklahoma | 9 |
| Georgia | 29 | Oregon | 13 |
| Hawaii | 5 | Pennsylvania | 4 |
| Idaho | 6 | Puerto Rico | 5 |
| Illinois | 5 | Rhode Island | 0 |
| Indiana | 10 | South Carolina | 21 |
| Iowa | 1 | South Dakota | 4 |
| Kansas | 3 | Tennessee | 38 |
| Kentucky | 23 | Texas | 32 |
| Louisiana | 31 | Utah | 20 |
| Maine | 7 | Vermont | 0 |
| Maryland | 4 | Virginia | 31 |
| Massachusetts | 3 | Washington | 9 |
| Michigan | 2 | West Virginia | 8 |
| Mississippi | 4 | Wisconsin | 1 |
| Missouri | 12 | Wyoming | 11 |
| Montana | 2 | | |

[a]Investor-owned is defined as owned by a corporation that owns or manages three or more hospitals; includes psychiatric and other speciality hospitals

SOURCES: Calculated from data from American Hospital Association (1984); Federation of American Hospitals (1984).

percent were independent for-profit hospitals, and the remainder were not-for-profit facilities (Robert L. Thomas, National Association of Private Psychiatric Hospitals, Washington, D.C., personal communication, 1985).[3]

The growth of investor-owned psychiatric hospital systems shows both similarities to and differences from the growth of investor-owned hospital systems. Similarities include rapid growth, a high degree of concentration in a few companies, absorption of some multihospital systems by other multihospital systems, and a decrease in the independent for-profit sector. Differences include a far greater market penetration by investor-owned systems and the absence of a significant market presence of not-for-profit systems. (Not-for-profit hospital systems have exhibited only a small interest in the psychiatric hospital market, an estimated eight systems owning a total of nine psychiatric hospitals (Fackelman, 1985a).) During the late 1960s nearly half of all private psychiatric hospitals were for-profit and for the most part were independently owned by individuals or small groups of psychiatrists. Today, chain ownership is more prevalent than individual ownership among the for-profits (Levenson, in press).

**TABLE 2.5**   Regional Distribution of System-Owned Community Hospitals and Beds, Investor-Owned, Not-for-profit, and All U.S. Hospitals, 1983

|  | Hospitals | | | Beds | | |
|---|---|---|---|---|---|---|
| Region | I-O | NFP Systems | Total U.S. | I-O | NFP Systems | Total U.S. |
| New England | 0.5% | 2.8% | 5.3% | 0.3% | 2.7% | 5.9% |
| Middle Atlantic | 1.4 | 9.2 | 11.4 | 1.4 | 10.4 | 18.4 |
| South Atlantic | 25.5 | 11.4 | 14.6 | 30.6 | 11.5 | 16.2 |
| E-N Central | 2.3 | 19.6 | 15.5 | 2.4 | 25.7 | 18.3 |
| E-S Central | 17.3 | 5.3 | 8.0 | 15.2 | 5.0 | 6.9 |
| W-N Central | 2.5 | 16.4 | 13.0 | 2.5 | 13.4 | 9.3 |
| W-S Central | 25.7 | 9.4 | 14.0 | 24.8 | 10.5 | 10.5 |
| Mountain | 4.4 | 10.9 | 6.1 | 4.7 | 7.6 | 3.9 |
| Pacific | 20.4 | 15.0 | 12.1 | 18.1 | 13.2 | 10.6 |
| Total | 100.0 | 100.0 | 100.0 | 100.0 | 100.0 | 100.0 |

SOURCE: Compiled from data provided by Peter Kralovec, Hospital Data Center, American Hospital Association, Chicago, Ill., 1985.

**TABLE 2.6**   Distribution of System-Owned Community Hospitals by Size and Type of Ownership, 1983

| Beds | I-O Chain (N = 515) | NFP Chain (N = 1,100) | All Hospitals (N = 5,783) |
|---|---|---|---|
| 6- 24 | 0.6% | 2.5% | 3.9% |
| 25- 99 | 7.2 | 12.4 | 17.0 |
| 50- 99 | 29.3 | 18.3 | 24.5 |
| 100-199 | 41.2 | 23.6 | 23.9 |
| 200-299 | 15.5 | 16.3 | 12.5 |
| 300-399 | 3.9 | 10.6 | 7.6 |
| 400-499 | 1.9 | 7.6 | 4.7 |
| 500+ | 0.4 | 8.7 | 5.9 |
| Total | 100.0 | 100.0 | 100.0 |

SOURCE: Compiled from data provided by Peter Kralovec, Hospital Data Center, American Hospital Association, Chicago, Ill., 1985.

The concentration of ownership within the investor-owned sector is indicated by four corporations owning 66 percent of the investor-owned, NAPPH-affiliated psychiatric hospitals in 1985. Three of the four are primarily hospital chains—Hospital Corporation of America, National Medical Enterprises, and Charter Medical. The fourth is Community Psychiatric Centers, which owns no acute care hospitals. This concentration has emerged in large part through the acquisition of the smaller chains by larger chains.[4]

## NURSING HOMES

For-profit ownership has long been predominant among nursing homes.[5] Before the 1930s, people in need of long-term care outside their homes were admitted to private charitable homes. Demographic changes, the availability of funding through the Social Security Act of 1935, subsequent amendments to the act, and the enactment of Medicaid and Medicare stimulated the growth in nursing homes. The number of facilities increased from 1,200 in 1939 to nearly 15,000 in 1969, while the United States population increased approximately 50 percent. Much of the growth in nursing homes was in the proprietary sector, which by 1969 had 64.5 percent of nursing home beds (U.S. National Center for Health Statistics, 1984). During the 1970s the growth in the total number of nursing homes slowed, but the proprietary sector share continued to increase. By 1980, 81 percent of the 17,700 nursing homes and 69 percent of the 1.5 million beds were proprietary.

Information about the market share of investor-owned nursing homes is made up of approximations. One estimate suggests that between 1979 and 1982 the major investor-owned chains increased their control (owned, leased, and managed) of nursing home beds by 50 percent to more than 200,000 beds, representing roughly 17 percent of all nursing home beds.

In the investor-owned sector, ownership is concentrated in relatively few corporations. In 1984 the largest system, Beverly Enterprises, operated 950 homes. The three largest systems (Beverly Enterprises, Hillhaven—a subsidiary of National Medical Enterprises, and ARA Living Centers) together operated approximately 1,500 homes comprising about 70 percent of the investor-owned nursing homes identified by *Modern Healthcare* (Punch, 1985).

Multi-institutional system growth among not-for-profit nursing homes has lagged substantially behind the investor-owned sector. Investor-owned nursing home systems operated six times as many nursing home beds as were operated by not-for-profit systems in 1984.

Multihospital systems are rapidly increasing their nursing home operations; in 1984 they operated 365 freestanding nursing homes (an increase of 17 percent over a year earlier), of which 127 were operated by investor-owned systems (Punch, 1985).

## HEALTH MAINTENANCE ORGANIZATIONS

Health maintenance organizations (HMOs) were the first of what is a growing and more varied type of organization that combines the provision of health services with an insurance function. An HMO plan provides comprehensive health care for a set monthly premium paid to the plan; thus, the plan's income for each member's care is fixed regardless of utilization, and the plan is the risk carrier.[6] An HMO can take many forms. The two basic types are the group model,

in which the plan hires or contracts with a limited number of physicians to provide care at a central location, and the individual practice model in which the plan contracts with physicians who operate out of their offices. In some plans physicians receive a bonus or share in the profits derived from controlling expenses.

The first HMO dates back to 1929 when the Ross-Loos Health Plan was organized to provide care for the employees of the Los Angeles water department. During the 1930s and 1940s the precursors of HMOs were established—Kaiser Permanente, Group Health Cooperative of Puget Sound, Group Health Association of Washington, and the Health Insurance Plan of Greater New York. But it was not until the 1970s that the HMO concept became widely known and adopted. The federal government stimulated HMO growth with passage of The Health Maintenance Organization Act of 1973, which required employers to offer local qualified HMOs as an insurance option and provided grants and loans to HMOs to cover development and initial operating deficits. In 1981 these funds were terminated, but federal encouragement of HMOs has continued through promotional efforts to generate private investment.

Table 2.7 shows the growth of HMOs from 1970 to 1985 and the recent acceleration in growth, but does not indicate some important changes that occurred within the HMO sector. Until about 10 years ago for-profit HMOs were a rarity (*Hospitals*, 1984). By 1985 there were 136 for-profit plans with almost 3 million enrollees representing roughly 35 percent of all HMO plans and close to 26 percent of enrollees (InterStudy, 1985). Some of the for-profit plans converted from not-for-profit status; others were established as for-profits.

In 1983 the first stock of a publicly traded HMO company was issued. The first to go public was U.S. Health Care Systems, formerly not-for-profit, which raised $25 million in stock offerings. Another former not-

TABLE 2.7  Growth of Health Maintenance Organizations, Number of Plans
and Enrollees, 1970–1985

|          |      | Plans | Enrollees (millions) |
|----------|------|-------|----------------------|
| January  | 1970 | 26    | 2.9                  |
|          | 1972 | 39    | 3.5                  |
|          | 1974 | 142   | 5.3                  |
| June     | 1976 | 175   | 6.0                  |
|          | 1978 | 198   | 7.3                  |
|          | 1980 | 236   | 9.1                  |
|          | 1982 | 265   | 10.8                 |
|          | 1984 | 306   | 15.1                 |
|          | 1985 | 393   | 18.9                 |

SOURCES: Office of Health Maintenance Organizations, U.S. Department of Health and Human Services, Rockville, Md.; InterStudy, National HMO
Census, 1982, 1984, 1985, Excelsior, Minn.

for-profit, Maxicare Health Plans, raised $16
million on the stock market, and Health
America raised $20 million (Washington Re-
port on Medicine and Health, 1984a). HMO
stock issues received favorable reports from
Wall Street analysts, quickly followed by eager reception from the buying public. By
1984, seven HMO corporations had entered
the stock market; all but two were multistate
organizations.

Multistate organizations are networks of
HMO plans linked by ownership or management operating in two or more states.
There were six such organizations in 1978.
In 1983, 14 multistate organizations owned
or managed 81 plans that enrolled 7.1 million people—52 percent of all HMO enrollment.[7] The largest by far was not-for-
profit Kaiser Foundation Health Plan, Inc.,
with 4.4 million enrollees. For-profit CIGNA
with 663,000 enrollees and PruCare with
338,000 enrollees were ranked second and
third; both are owned by insurance companies. Fourth- and fifth-ranked Maxicare
Health Plans, Inc., and United Healthcare
Corporation have publicly traded stock, as
have three other national firms (Baker et al.,
1984).

Investment analysts expect the move toward more and larger multistate HMO firms
to continue, using terms such as "land rush
mentality" to describe publicly traded HMO
firms' efforts to manage, acquire, or start
new plans.[8] Projections of continued rapid
growth in HMO enrollment are commonplace and recognize the potential importance of changes that open up the Medicare
market to HMOs, which the trade associations anticipate will bring an estimated 20
percent of elderly people into HMOs (Group
Health Association of America, 1984).

Most observers agree that HMOs—be they
independent physicians' associations or
closed-group models—have become an accepted way of delivering health care at a
savings. The need to gain access to capital
to tap the expanding HMO market has led
some HMOs to change to for-profit status,
in addition to those that started that way.
As Iglehart (1984) points out, signs that for-
profit organizations will become more important in the HMO arena already exist. So
too are signs that a shake-out of weak competitors will take place in locales where intense competition has developed among
multiple HMOs.

## HOME CARE

Home care services comprise a broad and
increasing range of services provided by
several different types of personnel affiliated
with thousands of home health agencies.
Types of care include skilled nursing, occupational speech and physical therapy,
meals, homemaker services, respiratory
therapy, and intravenous therapy. Employees include nurses, home health aides,
homemakers, and specialists in specific
therapies. The organizations that employ
these personnel and supply these services
are varied. For some, home care is the only
line of business. Others combine temporary
staffing (nurse and clerical) with home care.
Some are affiliated with pharmaceutical
manufacturers, some with nursing homes,

**TABLE 2.8** Medicare-Certified Participating Home Health Agencies, 1978 to 1984

|                        | 1978  | 1980  | 1982  | 1984  |
| ---------------------- | ----- | ----- | ----- | ----- |
| Visiting Nurse Association | 502   | 515   | 517   | 525   |
| Government             | 1,272 | 1,260 | 1,211 | 1,226 |
| Hospital-based         | 316   | 359   | 507   | 894   |
| Proprietary            | 145   | 186   | 628   | 1,569 |
| Private nonprofit      | NA    | 484   | 619   | 756   |
| Other                  | 488   | 119   | 157   | 277   |
| Total                  | 2,723 | 2,923 | 3,639 | 5,247 |

SOURCE: Health Care Financing Administration, Health Standards and Quality Bureau, Office of Survey and Certification, Baltimore, Md.

some with hospitals, and some with large national hospital corporations.

Because of the fragmented and diverse nature of the home care market, no reliable source of aggregate data is available. Medicare assembles data covering agencies licensed as Medicare providers, but these data undoubtedly understate the number of home care providers.

The dynamic growth in the number of these Medicare-certified agencies (almost doubling between 1978 and 1984) and the growth of the for-profit sector are particularly striking trends (Table 2.8). Much of this growth predated the likely increased demand for home care that Medicare's prospective payment methods for hospitalized patients will encourage. The striking increase in for-profit agencies (from 186 to 628) between 1980 and 1982 was caused by a change in Medicare reimbursement legislation. Before the Omnibus Reconciliation Act of 1980, for-profits could not get certification in states not having a home health agency licensure law. The removal of this restriction opened up more than 20 states to for-profit home health agencies (Frost and Sullivan, Inc., 1982).

Medicare expenditures on home health care reached $2 billion in 1984. Using a broader definition that would include durable equipment and consumables, a private

market research firm estimated the home health market to be $4.9 billion, growing to $9.4 billion by 1990 (*Modern Healthcare,* 1985a).

There are many new providers in the home health care field, apart from the growing number of independent for-profit operations. For instance, major medical supply companies such as Abbott Laboratories and Baxter Travenol Laboratories are offering home care services in conjunction with their new, high-technology home care products. The nursing home subsidiary of National Medical Enterprises provided home care in 21 locations in 1984, and Beverly Enterprises, a large nursing home chain, had 134 home care units in 1984. Hospital Corporation of America and American Medical International both entered the home care field in 1984 (Kuntz, 1984; Fackelman, 1985b).

The degree of ownership concentration is difficult to estimate. Knowledgeable observers list such investor-owned companies as Upjohn Health Care Services, Personnel Pool of America, Beverly Enterprises, and Quality Care, Inc., as the largest home care providers. The only multihospital system listed among leading providers of home health care in 1984 was National Medical Enterprises' National Medical Home Care Inc. (Fackelman, 1985b).

### NEW TYPES OF PROVIDERS

For-profit organizations have been prominent in the newer settings for health care, such as freestanding ambulatory surgery centers and freestanding primary care centers. Both types were started by entrepreneurial physicians to compete with hospitals and physicians. Now such ambulatory facilities are increasingly being created by, or coming under the control of, hospitals and multihospital systems, both investor-owned and not-for-profit.

Ambulatory surgery—sometimes called one-day surgery, same-day surgery, or in-out surgery—consists of surgical procedures

**TABLE 2.9**  Number of Freestanding Surgery Centers and Surgical Operations, 1970–1990

|  | Number of Centers | Number of Operations |
|---|---|---|
| 1970 | 3 | 6,700 |
| 1975 | 41 | 20,000 |
| 1980 | 128 | 33,300 |
| 1985[a] | 428 | 743,400 |
| 1990[a] | 832 | 1,932,700 |

[a]Estimated.

SOURCE: Compiled from data in Henderson (1985:148).

performed without an overnight stay in a hospital. Freestanding ambulatory surgery centers have, on average, three operating rooms and perform nearly 2,000 surgical procedures annually—most often gynecological surgery (Henderson, 1985). Hospitals also are heavily involved in ambulatory surgery. In 1983 nearly 90 percent of community hospitals had outpatient departments equipped for such procedures (Demkovich, 1983).

Several factors have stimulated the growth of ambulatory surgery: technological advances such as fast-acting anesthetics and new surgical methods, cost containment concerns, the expansion of insurance coverage for outpatient surgery, and the preferences of consumers. The first such center opened in 1967, but failed because of lack of physician and reimbursement support. Three years later three centers opened. Growth was slow through the mid-1970s, but by 1980, 128 ambulatory surgery centers were counted nationally. A private market research firm estimates that 114 new freestanding surgery centers will become operational in 1985, for a total of 428 such facilities (see Table 2.9) (Henderson, 1985).

More than 90 percent of freestanding surgery centers are for-profit enterprises, even when operated by not-for-profit hospitals (Bernard Kerschner, President, Freestanding Ambulatory Surgery Association, Dal-

las, Texas, personal communication, 1985). Freestanding surgery centers affiliated with hospitals (which excludes outpatient surgery programs operated on the hospital campus) constitute 7 percent of all freestanding surgery centers (Henderson, 1985); independently owned (nonchain) surgery centers make up 65 percent. Some formerly independent surgery centers have been acquired by corporations, and today, through construction and acquisition, corporations owning more than one center hold 28 percent of all freestanding surgery centers. The corporate sector, with 150 surgery centers open or under development, is composed of 10 firms (Henderson, 1985). More than one-third of corporate centers are owned by one company—Medical Care International, which was formed in 1984 by the merger of Medical 21 and Surgicare Inc. Medical Care International's 56 centers performed 13 percent of all surgeries in freestanding centers during 1984.

Future growth of freestanding surgery centers is uncertain. Although a private market research firm predicts double the number of such centers over the next five years (Henderson, 1985), aggressive competition by hospitals is a limiting factor, and freestanding surgery centers without hospital affiliation could decrease as hospitals develop their own centers and buy existing centers.

### Freestanding Primary Care Centers

Freestanding "primary care" (or "urgent care") centers have proliferated during the last decade. Urgent care centers generally operate as a private physician's office (in terms of licensure) and provide 12 or more hours of service per day, 365 days a year.[9] Appointments are not needed, waiting times are short, charges are usually lower than hospital emergency room charges, and the centers often are located in shopping malls or high-population areas.

The earliest centers were generally owned

**TABLE 2.10** Growth of Freestanding Urgent Care Centers, 1982–1990

| Year | Number of Centers |
| --- | --- |
| 1982 | 600 |
| 1983 | 1,200 |
| 1984 | 2,300 |
| 1985[a] | 3,000 |
| 1990[a] | 5,500 |

[a]Estimated.

SOURCE: National Association for Ambulatory Care (1985).

by physicians. Today they are increasingly owned wholly or in part by hospitals or hospital chains, and they now typically style themselves as urgent care or primary care centers rather than emergency centers, their original appellation. The name change is in part a response to the criticism that patients in need of emergency care, such as victims of major trauma or patients suffering heart attacks, would inappropriately seek care in "emergency" centers, which generally are not equipped or staffed to handle such cases, rather than in hospitals. In part the change in name is to emphasize the type of care they do provide—treatment for minor medical problems and injuries, immunizations, and preemployment physicals. The centers once were staffed by emergency and family-practice physicians, but today specialty physicians such as pediatricians and orthopedists are also employed, and the range of services has been expanded to encompass many primary care activities.

The first freestanding "emergicenter" opened in 1973. Growth has been rapid (see Table 2.10). By mid-1985, 2,600 centers were operational and another 400 were expected to be functional by the end of the year. However, the short period of extraordinary growth, when the numbers doubled each year, may be over. Trade sources expect that the number of urgent care centers will increase by fewer than 100 percent between 1985 and 1990 (National Association for Ambulatory Care, 1985).

The growth of this new practice form has its roots in several causes. Initially, entrepreneurially inclined physicians identified a service that was attractive to consumers from a standpoint of cost and convenience. The growing physician surplus has made traditional solo practice more risky and difficult and salaried positions in organized settings more attractive. Hospitals (and hospital companies) became involved in the operation of urgent care centers either as a competitive response or to secure a flow of patients into the hospital.

The ownership of the urgent care centers that exist today has been the subject of conflicting estimates. One study found that physicians own 73 percent of centers, hospitals own 7 percent, and corporations that are controlled by neither hospitals nor physicians own the rest; another estimate puts hospital ownership or affiliation of urgent care centers at 25 percent (Washington Report on Medicine and Health, 1984b). A survey of almost 4,000 nonfederal physicians in 1983 found that half who provided care at urgent care centers said the center was owned by a not-for-profit hospital (American Medical Association, 1983). Of the 455 centers that responded to a National Association for Ambulatory Care (1985) survey, almost 40 percent were physician-owned and 42 percent were nonphysician corporations. The latter group was identified as a growing group, and a change from the physician-owned, for-profit centers that were characteristic of the early years.

There are also reports of for-profit chain ownership. *Modern Healthcare* identified 44 chains (excluding multihospital systems) that operated a total of 260 freestanding urgent or primary care centers in 1984. These chains were generally small; only eight chains operated 10 or more centers. The largest chain, Doctor's Officenters, with 51 centers, was acquired by Humana at the end of 1984. Humana already operated centers under the MedFirst name and, with a total of 144 centers, is the largest operator of freestanding urgent or primary care centers in the country (Wallace, 1985). Thus, this rapidly growing health care sector remains highly fragmented in terms of ownership, and for-profit status is likely to remain dominant because even the centers operated by not-for-profit hospitals are after for-profit enterprises.

## Other Services

For-profit ownership is prominent among freestanding dialysis centers. It is now nearly two decades since dialysis emerged from its experimental state and more than a decade since the Medicare program started to pay for it. Although a market for dialysis services existed before the introduction of Medicare coverage in 1972 (National Medical Care, the oldest for-profit dialysis provider, was formed in 1968), it was small.

With the advent of Medicare coverage the dialysis market began its rapid expansion. Medicare enrollment grew from 18,000 in 1974 to 78,479 at the end of 1984. Medicare expenditures for dialysis grew from $229 million in 1974 to $1.6 billion by 1984, and the number of facilities providing dialysis rose from 606 in 1973 to 1,290 at the end of 1984 (Committee on Government Operations, 1982; Health Care Financing Administration, personal communication, 1985; Gibson and McMullan, 1984). In 1973 only 11 percent (66 of 606) of all dialysis centers were freestanding. The remainder were hospital units or hospital satellites. As the Medicare End-Stage Renal Disease Program increased its enrollment, the major growth in dialysis suppliers was in freestanding units. In 1984, 52 percent (668 of 1,290) of dialysis facilities were freestanding, and 79 percent of freestanding units were proprietary. Overall, 42 percent of renal facilities were proprietary in 1983 (compared with 30 percent in 1980), almost all of them freestanding centers (Table 2.11)

*Modern Healthcare* identified nine chains that operated dialysis centers in 1984, of

which three were not-for-profit. The two largest chains were for-profit: National Medical Care Inc. (recently bought by W. R. Grace, a large chemical and natural resources conglomerate) is overwhelmingly the largest, with 178 centers treating 14,000 patients in 1984—nearly 18 percent of the Medicare dialysis population. Second-ranked Community Dialysis Centers, Inc., is a wholly owned subsidiary of Community Psychiatric Centers, with 47 centers. Third-ranked was not-for-profit Dialysis Clinics Inc., with 27 centers. Most of the major chains have shown substantial growth during the past eight years, and with certificate-of-need laws being relaxed in some states and the number of dialysis patients expected to grow by between 5 and 11 percent next year, dialysis is seen as a steady-growth field (Richman, 1985).

For-profit enterprises are also involved in other new forms of care once provided on a not-for-profit basis. Cardiac rehabilitation, physical rehabilitation, and diagnostic imaging are among the services that for-profit organizations are finding new ways to develop—often in freestanding facilities. For-profit examples include C. P. Rehab, which owns cardiac rehabilitation centers; Rehab Hospital Services; Vari-Care Inc., a nursing home company that has established rehabilitation programs; and Diagnostic Centers Inc., a subsidiary of Omnimedical, designed to set up diagnostic radiology centers throughout the United States. For-profit companies are opening other new services in new settings. There are no data concerning the range or extent of this movement, but it includes sports medicine, obesity clinics, executive health services, and wellness programs. Some of these services are provided on a freestanding for-profit basis, but others are provided by not-for-profit and for-profit hospitals, and some are being developed by for-profit and not-for-profit hospital systems.

For-profit activity has also begun in two somewhat surprising areas: hospice care and

TABLE 2.11   Number of Medicare-Certified End-Stage Renal Disease Providers by Type of Ownership and Type of Facility, 1980–1984

| | 1980 | | 1982 | | 1984 | |
|---|---|---|---|---|---|---|
| | Number | Percent | Number | Percent | Number | Percent |
| All facilities | 1,703 | 100.0 | 1,218 | 100.0 | 1,290 | 100.0 |
| Proprietary | 323 | 30.1 | 437 | 35.1 | 544 | 42.2 |
| Hospital-based | 23 | 2.1 | 14 | 1.8 | 15 | 1.2 |
| Freestanding | 300 | 28.0 | 423 | 33.3 | 529 | 41.0 |
| Not-for-profit | 750 | 69.9 | 781 | 64.9 | 746 | 57.8 |
| Hospital-based | 620 | 57.8 | 677 | 56.9 | 607 | 47.0 |
| Freestanding | 130 | 12.1 | 104 | 8.5 | 139 | 10.8 |

SOURCES: Gibson and McMullan (1984); Health Care Financing Administration, personal communication, 1985.

birthing centers. In 1984, Hospice Care, Inc., started with $5 million in capital from two investment houses, announced plans to manage 12-15 new hospices around the country (*Health Policy Week*, 1984). In another move that put a previously not-for-profit service into the for-profit field, Health Resources Corporation, Inc., acquired a consulting company that is developing birthing centers as joint ventures with obstetricians. Also, a for-profit hospital chain and a number of venture capital companies have attended workshops on birthing centers (Lubic, 1984). Such interest could translate into for-profit birthing centers.

## VERTICAL INTEGRATION AND DIVERSIFICATION

The previous discussion suggests that hospitals have increasingly become involved in nonhospital activities. Movement to encompass other levels of care is commonly called vertical integration, because it entails care that often precedes or follows hospitalization (e.g., primary care; after-hospital care in the patient's home, nursing home, and other sites; and other services). Diversification refers to selling of other services such as contract management or the addition of nonhealth businesses. Vertical integration and diversification can protect organizations from uncertain flows of inpatient revenues

by generating new revenue sources. Vertical integration can help control the flow of patients and dollars into hospitals, thereby capturing patients, dollars, and growth opportunities that might be lost to competing providers or because of reimbursement restrictions.

Vertical integration is increasing at the multihospital system level, with corporations acquiring or developing divisions for nonhospital functions. Vertical integration is also occurring at the local level with independent hospitals branching into nonhospital activities. At the overlap between financing and services delivery, systems and independent hospitals are diversifying into HMOs and preferred provider arrangements.

These changes are responses to changes in the health care environment. Individual hospitals as well as members of multihospital systems are vulnerable to pressures that are causing their occupancy rates to drop. Cheaper, more convenient ambulatory services are keeping some patients away. Prospective payment is reducing the length of stay. Cost-sharing insurance contracts are causing patients to reduce their out-of-pocket expenses by seeking lower-cost forms of care and by cutting hospital stays. By expanding into outpatient services, systems and hospitals receive revenues that might otherwise go elsewhere; they also create feeder services for their hospitals. By expanding into after-hospital care (nursing homes, home care, etc.), hospitals can discharge patients as soon as is medically reasonable, thus minimizing the cost incurred under the hospital DRG (diagnostic-related group) while the patient continues to be revenue-producing in the home care or nursing home setting. By expanding into psychiatric care, hospitals can serve patients for whom payment is generally not under prospectively set rates.

A 1981 study noted that vertical integration was more common in not-for-profit than for-profit systems because of the former's greater emphasis on providing comprehensive services in a locality. Regarding diversification, the study noted that not-for-profit had moved more into selling management services while for-profits were more into contracts for ancillary services (Derzon et al., 1981).

The extent of vertical integration is not well documented, but there is anecdotal evidence that it is an increasing phenomenon among systems and independent hospitals. At the system level (for-profit and not-for-profit), *Modern Healthcare* (1985b) identified the following in 1984:

- 27 multihospital systems operating one or more psychiatric hospitals
- 98 multihospital systems operating one or more nursing homes
- 27 multihospital systems operating one or more lifecare centers
- 15 multihospital systems operating one or more HMOs
- 1,322 freestanding facilities (surgery, urgent care, diagnostic, wellness, rehab centers, etc.) operated by multihospital systems.

The major for-profit multihospital corporations remain, however, engaged mostly in providing acute hospital care. Of the major corporations, National Medical Enterprises is most diversified, deriving only about half of its operating revenues from general hospital and primary care services (National

Medical Enterprises, Inc., 1984). At the other end of the spectrum is the Hospital Corporation of America, whose 360 owned and managed general hospitals and 27 psychiatric hospitals provided 95 percent of its revenues in 1984 (Hospital Corporation of America, 1985), a picture that seems certain to change.

The eight largest investor-owned hospital corporations combined present an interesting picture of vertical integration. In 1983 they owned and operated the following (Federation of American Hospitals, Hospital Management Company Facilities by Line of Business, unpublished data, 1984):

- 426 acute care hospitals
- 102 psychiatric hospitals
- 234 hospital management contracts
- 163 medical office buildings
- 89 ambulatory care centers
- 34 substance abuse/alcohol centers
- 272 long-term-care units
- 38 home health agencies
- 62 dialysis centers
- 32 clinics
- 103 pharmacies
- 3 radiology units
- 2 medical laboratories
- 1 freestanding diagnostic center.

Although some investor-owned corporations have had a degree of apparent vertical integration at the system level for some time, this has not necessarily affected patient flow into and out of their local hospitals. Patient flow is affected not merely by ownership of nonhospital services but also by close physical location and coordination of services. There are indications, however, that some investor-owned corporations are moving toward closer integration of services, a development that fixed-payment systems encourage. For example, National Medical Enterprises has initiated the building of medical "campuses," with many components of a continuum of care located together (Washington Report on Medicine and Health, 1983). Humana's MedFirst urgent care centers, originally built away from Humana hospitals, are now being constructed within their hospital service areas to act as feeders for inpatient care. HCA is building psychiatric "pavilions" on their own hospital grounds.

Among not-for-profit hospitals and systems, some vertical integration and diversification efforts have been facilitated by membership in alliances such as American Healthcare Systems and Voluntary Hospitals of America. The latter has developed a design for ambulatory surgery centers to reduce construction and operating costs for its members and has created VHA Health Ventures—to help members vertically integrate, and Voluntary Health Enterprises—to give members engaged in diversification activities access to equity markets (Voluntary Hospitals of America, undated).

Hospital systems are also increasingly integrating provider and financing functions (by means of HMOs, preferred provider arrangements, or other insurance vehicles) in the hope of generating revenues and of capturing patient populations for their hospitals. Humana led the investor-owned industry with its HumanaCare Plus program, under which Humana assumes the actuarial risk for emloyees' health benefit plans, guaranteeing employers a fixed health care premium cost for one year and limited increases of no more than the increase in the Consumer Price Index for three years. Patients can choose their physicians, but are penalized for use of non-Humana hospitals by heavy out-of-pocket expenses. Similar or related developments can be seen at the other major investor-owned hospital chains through the development of preferred provider arrangements, acquisition of HMOs, purchase of insurance companies, and so forth (*Modern Healthcare*, 1985c; Hospital Corporation of America, 1984). Such activities are not confined to the investor-owned sector. For example, the Health Central Corporation owns an insurance company, St. Joseph Health System has purchased an HMO, and

Adventist Health System North is conducting a joint venture with a for-profit HMO (Washington Report on Medicine and Health, 1985).

The assumption of risk by hospitals and hospital chains is of major potential importance because of the departures from the traditional incentives under which hospitals operate and because of the increases it entails in the size and scope of health care organizations.

## FOR-PROFIT/NOT-FOR-PROFIT HYBRIDS

The discussion thus far has been couched in terms of not-for-profit as contrasted with for-profit organizations. Although this is an important distinction, the lines between the two types of organizations cross at numerous points, and at the crossover points new types of hybrid organizations are emerging. For the purposes of this section they are grouped into management contract arrangements, hybrids that emerge from corporate restructuring, alliances formed to help independent voluntary hospitals reap the benefits of multi-institutional arrangements, and joint ventures. The hybrids are often examples of diversification.

In general, the new, complex hybrid organizations are designed to bring to one sector some of the advantages of the other. Hybridization may become increasingly important as competitive pressures grow and access to resources such as capital and personnel become crucial to maintaining or increasing market share.

The most familiar of these crossover points occurs in contract management. According to *Modern Healthcare*, 76 multihospital systems had contracts to manage 537 hospitals in 1984. Investor-owned systems managed 137 not-for-profit hospitals, but not-for-profit systems managed only 1 for-profit hospital. Public hospitals managed under contract numbered 288, of which 53 percent were under investor-owned management (Johnson, 1985). Contract management of independent hospitals by systems brings the management concepts, skills, and systems of the multi-institutional sector to troubled hospitals, while more or less preserving the goals and autonomy of the employing hospital.

A closer linkage of for-profit and not-for-profit forms is seen in the establishment of for-profit subsidiaries by not-for-profit hospital corporations. The mechanism usually used to accomplish this is corporate restructuring, described as "the conversion of a not-for-profit hospital operating corporation into a multiple-corporation system or a network of related corporations for strategic purposes" (Bryant, 1981). Corporate restructuring involves the unbundling of services into separate organizations under an umbrella parent organization. Not-for-profit corporations can create for-profit companies under the not-for-profit umbrella. Corporate restructuring has been used for a number of reasons. One frequently cited reason is to enable hospitals to diversify into both health and nonhealth areas, thus increasing revenue flows. Another is to gain access to equity markets. Hospitals have built parking lots and physician offices, sold services to physicians and other hospitals, and invested in housing for the elderly, supermarkets, and many other activities.

There are no data available on the number of not-for-profit hospital corporations with for-profit subsidiaries, but examples are legion. One is Roanoke Memorial Hospital Association, which operates for-profit subsidiaries that include a collection agency, a long-term-care center, an air ambulance service, and widely dispersed real estate operations (Kidwell, 1983). Another is not-for-profit Lutheran General Hospital in Illinois, which runs for-profit Parkside Medical Services Corporation, a consulting and management company that also owns or manages freestanding alcohol treatment centers and performs numerous other functions (LaViolette, 1983).

Multi-institutional systems can also be hybrids. Not-for-profit Intermountain Health Care Inc. operates five for-profit subsidiaries that include insurance, shared services, and professional services businesses. One subsidiary, Golden Valley Care Unit, takes the notion of hybridization a step beyond the creation of for-profit subsidiaries into joint for-profit, not-for-profit ownership. This subsidiary is a "behavioral medicine hospital" owned jointly with CompCare, a major investor-owned company (Gray, 1985). Intermountain also has a joint venture with the Hospital Corporation of America for operation (and ultimate replacement) of two hospitals in one community.

Memorial Care Systems in Texas, a multi-institutional not-for-profit system, has been described as "a labyrinth of companies." It controls a not-for-profit subsidiary that acts as the parent's investment arm. This subsidiary formed for-profit Health Ventures, offering shares to physicians who are members of Memorial Health Net Providers, another subsidiary of Memorial Care Systems. Holders of Health Ventures preferred stock can convert to common stock if the company goes public, as intended. Other activities of Memorial Care Systems' subsidiaries include third-party claims administration, a real estate company, and developing and managing surgery and urgent care centers (Tatge, 1984a). These for-profit/not-for-profit hybrids permit diversification to control local markets, to achieve new revenue sources outside of core inpatient care activities, and to raise capital. The effect on institutional behavior has received little study.

Another example of a hybrid is designed to bring to independent not-for-profit hospitals some of the advantages of membership in a multihospital system without sacrificing institutional autonomy. Voluntary Hospitals of America Inc. (VHA) is a for-profit company whose member shareholders include more than 70 large not-for-profit hospitals and medical centers. VHA's companies and subsidiaries (all for-profit) provide members and affiliates with management services, and access to capital, and engage in their own entrepreneurial activities. The complex structure of VHA includes VHA Management Services (a subsidiary that developed VHA Regional Healthcare Partnerships), which sells services to members and affiliates. Voluntary Health Enterprises (VHE) is a holding company created by VHA and a New York financial services company. VHE privately sold $11 million in common stock to finance a number of activities, including a VHE subsidiary that offers consulting and equity investment in ambulatory surgery centers. Behavioral Medical Care is a joint venture of VHE with Comprehensive Care Corporation which operates alcohol treatment centers and provides related consulting and staffing services. American Health Capital, Inc., formed in conjunction with the Mellon Bank, is a subsidiary of VHA that, with its subsidiaries, helps members meet capital needs and offers real estate development and a syndication. Other services available from VHA include physician recruitment and a telecommunications network (Tatge, 1984b; Voluntary Hospitals of America, undated). In short, VHA offers member hospitals a wide array of services that members of multi-institutional systems often receive from their home office management.

A total of 31 not-for-profit multihospital systems have become shareholders in a similar sort of alliance, American Healthcare Systems (AHS). AHS is a for-profit corporation with divisions for centralized purchasing and shared services, the development of new businesses, and access to capital through multihospital bond issues and stock offerings. AHS describes its purpose as "to improve the competitive and economic position of our shareholders." To do that, it says, "we treat the business of health care like a business. We run lean, we manage tough and we retain control of community health at the local level" (American Healthcare Systems, undated).

One further example of emerging hybrids is joint ventures between for-profit and not-for-profit entities. For example, a for-profit surgery center chain, Medical Care International, is engaged in a joint venture with Mission Services Corp. (operated by the Daughters of Charity, St. Vincent de Paul) to develop and construct freestanding ambulatory surgery centers.

A 1984 American Hospital Association survey of hospitals regarding 10 types of joint ventures found that 12 percent of hospitals had such ventures. The most frequently reported type was for preferred provider organizations. Hospitals in large cities were most likely to engage in joint ventures, suggesting that competition plays an important role (Morrisey and Brooks, 1985).

## CONCLUSIONS

Several major shifts are taking place simultaneously in the ownership, control, and configuration of health care organizations. Initiation of some of these changes took place in for-profit organizations; others in not-for-profit. Some changes were direct responses to government actions; some were stimulated by other factors.

From the many organizational responses to the change in environment, some general trends can be identified. First, there is a tendency toward consolidation of health care providers into larger organizations. This is seen in the emergence of the large investor-owned and the smaller not-for-profit multi-institutional organizations, and it is seen in the emergence of chains of varying size in almost every provider field, from primary care centers to nursing homes, and from dialysis centers to HMOs. The degree of concentration varies among different types of providers, but in most cases the largest chains are for-profit.

A second trend is the development of new services or traditional services in new settings, often led by entrepreneurial physicians. (Issues of control and conflict of interest of physician involvement in for-profit enterprise are examined in Chapters 8 and 9.) A subsequent stage of development of these services occurred as hospitals entered new fields to protect their own interests and to ensure a flow of patients and revenues into their facilities.

The spread of hospital control to nonhospital activities exemplifies a third trend—vertical integration and diversification of hospitals and multihospital organizations. This, like the combining of insurance and provider functions, has occurred as hospitals have recognized that inpatient care services have become a less-reliable revenue source, with prospective payment reducing occupancy rates, competition cutting prices, and outpatient services drawing patients away from inpatient services.

Finally, a pervasive trend is the increasing for-profit presence in almost all forms of health care. In some, such as nursing homes and freestanding surgery centers, for-profits are the dominant form. In others, such as dialysis and home care, for-profit is a very substantial presence. An adjunct to the proliferation of for-profit activity is the creation of not-for-profit/for-profit hybrids, which bring to the not-for-profit form the advantages of the for-profit form (particularly access to equity capital) and which may be regarded as the not-for-profit way of circumventing some of the disadvantages of the not-for-profit status.

## NOTES

[1]The number of investor-owned hospitals as reported by the Federation of American Hospitals (the trade association of investor-owned hospitals) exceeds the number reported by the American Hospital Association. Each organization collects its own data, and the reasons for the discrepancies are not known.

[2]The six companies are Hospital Corporation of America, Humana, American Medical International, National Medical Enterprises, Republic Health Corporation, and Charter Medical.

[3]The membership of the National Association of Private Psychiatric Hospitals excludes hospitals whose main business is substance abuse, hospitals that are not ac-

credited by the Joint Committee on Accreditation of Hospitals (JCAH), and hospitals whose patients are not admitted by a physician.

[4]Hospital Corporation of America acquired the majority of its psychiatric hospitals through the purchase of Hospital Affiliates International in 1981. National Medical Enterprises acquired almost all of its psychiatric hospitals when it bought Psychiatric Institutes of America in 1982 (Levenson, 1983).

[5]The following discussion of nursing homes is derived from Hawes and Phillips (1986).

[6]Several new organizational forms that combine provider and insurance functions are proliferating. Hospitals are providing or purchasing insurance capability, and preferred provider organizations are bringing together purchasers (employers and insurers) with sellers (hospitals and doctors) in negotiated arrangements where the price of care for groups is agreed upon. The key elements of these organizations include a contract between payers and providers and the need for utilization control to gain control of expenses.

[7]Blue Cross/Blue Shield HMOs are excluded from the count of national firms because they do not operate as a centralized system. In 1983 these HMOs accounted for 11 percent of all HMO enrollees and 20 percent of all plans.

[8]Multistate HMO firms enable employers active in more than one state to contract with a single, centralized HMO entity—an important advantage in a sector in which the vast majority of contracts are employer-related. Other advantages of the multistate network firm include possible economies of scale and access to the lower-cost capital available to larger organizations.

[9]In some states there are moves to bring primary care centers under certificate-of-need review and to develop licensing standards. Three states require licensure of the centers if the name or advertising claims to provide emergency care. Five states are expanding certificate-of-need programs to include primary care centers.

## REFERENCES

American Healthcare Systems (undated) *The Positive Alternative for Not-For-Profit Hospitals*. San Diego, Calif.: American Healthcare Systems.

American Hospital Association (1984) *Hospital Statistics*. 1984 Edition. Chicago, Ill.: American Hospital Association.

American Medical Association (1983) Changing Medical Practice Arrangements. *SMS Report* 2(November).

Baker, Noel, Jeanne McGee, and Maureen Shadle (1984) *HMO Status Report 1982-1983*. Excelsior, Minn.: InterStudy.

Bryant, Edward L., Jr. (1981) The Financial Exchange. *Trustee* 34(November):11-12.

Committee on Government Operations (1982) *Management of the End-Stage Renal Disease Program*. House Report No. 97-918. Washington, D.C.: U.S. Government Printing Office.

Demkovich, Linda E. (1983) AMA, Government Officials Skeptical of "Convenience Medicine" Facilities. *National Journal* 15 (November 26):2470-2473.

Derzon, Robert, Lawrence S. Lewin, and J. Michael Watt (1981) Not-for-profit Chains Share in Multihospital System Boom. *Hospitals* 55(May 16):65-71.

Fackelman, Kathy A. (1985a) Number of Beds Rises as Demand Increases. *Modern Healthcare* 15(June 7):120-123.

Fackelman, Kathy A. (1985b) Top Firms Guarded Market Share in '84. *Modern Healthcare* 15(June 7):160-161.

Federation of American Hospitals (1980) *1981 Directory of Investor-Owned Hospitals and Hospital Management Companies*. Little Rock, Ark.: Federation of American Hospitals.

Federation of American Hospitals (1984) *1985 Directory, Investor-Owned Hospitals and Hospital Management Companies*. Little Rock, Ark.: Federation of American Hospitals.

Frost and Sullivan, Inc. (1982) *Home Health and Hospital Temporary Staffing*. New York: Frost and Sullivan, Inc.

Gibson, David, and Michael McMullan (1984) End-stage Renal Disease: A Profile of Facilities Furnishing Treatment. *Health Care Financing Review* 6(Winter):87-90.

Gray, Bradford H. (1985) Overview: Origins and Trends [of the New Entrepreneurialism in Health Care]. *Bulletin of the New York Academy of Sciences* 61(Jan-Feb):7-22.

Group Health Association of America (1984) 40 Million HMO Enrollees by 1990 Says Study. *Group Health News* 25(November):3-4.

Hawes, Catherine, and Charles D. Phillips (1986) The Changing Structure of the Nursing Home Industry and the Impact of Ownership on Quality, Cost, and Access. This volume.

*Health Policy Week* (1984) For-profit Hospice Stirs Controversy. February 6.

Henderson, John (1985) Surgery Centers May Double: Consultant. *Modern Healthcare* 15(June 7):148-150.

Hospital Corporation of America (1984) *Annual Report*. Nashville, Tenn.: Hospital Corporation of America.

Hospital Corporation of America (1985) Form 10-K for year ending December 31, 1984 (filed with the Securities and Exchange Commission in Washington, D.C.). Nashville, Tenn.: Hospital Corporation of America.

*Hospitals* (1984) Investor-owneds Enter Not-for-profits' Bastion. 58(April 16):100-101.

Hoy, Elizabeth W., and Bradford H. Gray (1986) Trends in the Growth of the Major Investor-Owned Hospital Companies. This volume.

Iglehart, John K. (1984) HMOs (For-Profit and Not-For-Profit) on the Move. *The New England Journal of Medicine* 310(May 3):1203-1208.

InterStudy (1985) *HMO Summary, 1985*. Excelsior, Minn.: InterStudy.

Johnson, Donald E. (1985) Investor-owned Chains Continue Expansion, 1985 Survey Shows. *Modern Healthcare* 15(June 7):75-90.

Keenan, Carol (1981) Not-for-profit Systems Position Themselves to Meet Upcoming Challenges. *Hospitals* 55(September 1):77-80.

Kidwell, Roland (1983) RMH: A Growing Concern. *Roanoke Times and World News* (May 8):A-15.

Kuntz, Esther Fritz (1984) For-profits Adding Home Healthcare to Aid Bottom Lines. *Modern Healthcare* 14(May 15):168-184.

LaViolette, Suzanne (1983) Parkside Is 'for-profit' in Name Only. *Modern Healthcare* 13(October):34-35.

Levenson, Alan I. (1983) Issues Surrounding the Ownership of Private Psychiatric Hospitals by Investor-Owned Hospital Chains. *Hospital and Community Psychiatry* 36(December):1127-1131.

Levenson, Alan I. (In press) The For-Profit Movement. In S. Sharfstein and A. Beigel (eds.) *Prospective Payment and Psychiatric Practice*. Washington, D.C.: American Psychiatric Press.

Lubic, Ruth Watson (1984) Presentation by the General Director, The Maternity Association, New York, before the Institute of Medicine's Committee on the Implications of For-profit Enterprise in Health Care, March 15, Washington, D.C.

*Modern Healthcare* (1985a) Home Healthcare Sales Will Hit $9.4 Billion by 1990—Study. 15(May 24):86.

*Modern Healthcare* (1985b) Multi-unit Providers, 15(June 7):75-160.

*Modern Healthcare* (1985c) NME Introduces MediGap to Fend Off HMO Competition. 15(May 29):100.

Morrisey, Michael A., and Deal Chandler Brooks (1985) Hospital-physician Joint Ventures: Who's Doing What. *Hospitals* 59(May 1):74-78.

Mullner, Ross, and Jack Hadley (1984) Interstate Variations in the Growth of Chain-owned Proprietary Hospitals, 1973-1982. *Inquiry* 21(Summer):144-151.

National Association for Ambulatory Care (1985) *FEC Factor II*. Dallas, Tex.: National Association for Ambulatory Care.

National Medical Enterprises, Inc. (1984) *Annual Report 1984*. Los Angeles, Calif.: National Medical Enterprises, Inc.

Punch, Linda (1985) Investor-owned Chains Lead Increase in Beds. *Modern Healthcare* 15(June 7):126-136.

Richman, Dan (1985) Most Chains Report More Patients, Profit. *Modern Healthcare* 15(June 7):158-159.

Steinwald, Bruce, and Duncan Neuhauser (1970) The Role of the Proprietary Hospital. *Law and Contemporary Problems* 35(Autumn):817-838.

Tatge, Mark (1984a) Memorial Sells Stock to Physicians and Shelters Earnings from Taxes. *Modern Healthcare* 14(May 1):104-106.

Tatge, Mark (1984b) Stock Deal Finances VHA Firms. *Modern Healthcare* 14(June):147-148.

U.S. National Center for Health Statistics (1984) Trends in Nursing and Related Care Homes and Hospitals. *Vital and Health Statistics*, Series 14, No. 30, DHHS Pub. No. (PHS)84-1825. Washington, D.C.: U.S. Government Printing Office.

Voluntary Hospitals of America (undated) *The Future of America's Health Care*. Dallas, Tex.: Voluntary Hospitals of America.

Wallace, Cynthia (1985) Ambulatory Care Facilities Multiply. *Modern Healthcare* 15(June 7):142-146.

Washington Report on Medicine and Health (1983) Vertical Integration: One Response to DRGs. *Perspectives*, September 26. Published as a supplement to *Medicine and Health*. Washington, D.C.: McGraw-Hill.

Washington Report on Medicine and Health (1984a) Integration, Conversion Mark HMO Growth. *Perspectives*, April 23. Published as a supplement to *Medicine and Health*, Washington, D.C.: McGraw-Hill.

Washington Report on Medicine and Health (1984b) DRGs Boost the Emergicenter Boom. *Perspectives*, March 26. Published as a supplement to *Medicine and Health*, Washington, D.C.: McGraw-Hill.

Washington Report on Medicine and Health (1985) Provider-based Insurance. *Perspectives*, April 1. Published as a supplement to *Medicine and Health*. Washington, D.C.: McGraw-Hill.

Watt, J. Michael, Steven C. Renn, James S. Hahn, Robert A. Derzon, and Carl J. Schramm (1986) The Effects of Ownership and Multihospital System Membership on Hospital Functional Strategies and Economic Performance. This volume.

Zuckerman, Howard S. (1983) Industrial Rationalization of a Cottage Industry: Multi-Institutional Hospital Systems. *Annals of the American Academy of Political and Social Sciences* 468(July):216-230.

# 3 Financial Capital and Health Care Growth Trends

First on most lists of factors explaining the growth of investor ownership and multi-institutional systems is "access to capital." Although capital costs represent a relatively small proportion of health care costs (on average, approximately 7 percent of hospital costs under the Medicare program), capital expenditures (for example, for new technologies) often translate into higher operating costs. Access to capital by health care institutions is crucial not only to their own future but to the future shape and configuration of the health care system itself. Access to capital is also integral to the topic of this report, because it is affected (by definition and in practice) by whether institutions are for-profit, not-for-profit, or government owned. It is also a topic about which there are many misconceptions.

The purpose of this chapter is to explain the nature and importance of capital, to discuss the factors that affect institutions' access to capital and the cost of that capital, and to identify the costs that are associated with the use of different sources of capital. Although the committee did not get into the details of policy options regarding capital,[1] it did examine some of the implications of the for-profit/not-for-profit distinction for capital policy in health care.

## WHAT IS CAPITAL?

Like any form of organized economic activity, health care organizations need financial capital to carry out their functions.[2] Before an organization can provide services or undertake a new program, it must use financial capital to purchase or rent space, equipment, supplies, labor, and so forth—that is, to prepay for certain inputs used in the production of health services. Normally, these prepayments are expected to be recovered eventually through cash revenues earned by rendering health services or, in the case of some public or not-for-profit institutions, from nonoperating revenues (e.g., charitable contributions, governmental appropriations, income of subsidiary organizations).

At any point in time, the dollar amounts of the unrecovered prepayments are listed as "assets" on the organization's statement of financial position (or balance sheet). Tables 3.1 and 3.2 show the balance sheets of two health care organizations—a not-for-profit HMO (the Harvard Community Health Plan) and an investor-owned hospital company (Humana, Inc.). As the figures show, a health care provider's assets include not only real capital assets such as movable and fixed equipment, land, and buildings but also

---

Portions of this chapter are based on material prepared by committee member Uwe Reinhardt, Ph.D., who also prepared the analysis of the cost of equity capital that is appended to this chapter.

47

**TABLE 3.1**  Harvard Community Health Plan, Inc., Balance Sheet, September 30, 1984

| | |
|---|---:|
| *Assets (cumulative uses of funds)* | |
| Current Assets | |
|   Cash and equivalents | $ 22,742,810 |
|   Investments, at cost—quoted market price of | |
|     $8,591,000 | 8,743,152 |
|   Accounts receivable | |
|     Member premiums, less collection allowances of | |
|       $414,000 | 2,876,677 |
|     Grants | 80,457 |
|     Estimated contractual settlements with hospitals | 722,790 |
|     Other, less collection allowances of $455,000 | 1,255,271 |
|   Supplies inventory | 765,624 |
|   Prepaid expenses | 1,116,130 |
|   Total current assets | 38,302,911 |
| Long-Lived Assets | |
|   Land, buildings, and equipment, less accumulated | |
|     depreciation | 59,506,139 |
|   Funds held by trustee | 15,303,907 |
|   Bond issue costs | 3,764,405 |
|   Other | 2,076,127 |
|   Total long-lived assets | 80,650,578 |
| Total Assets (total uses of funds) | $118,953,489 |
| | |
| *Liabilities and Fund Balances (cumulative sources of funds)* | |
| Current Liabilities | |
|   Accounts payable and accrued expenses | $ 10,178,124 |
|   Amounts payable to HCHP Fndn., Inc., net | 279,237 |
|   Accrued claims payable—hospitals and physicians | 11,997,683 |
|   Unearned premium revenue and advance payments | 2,106,509 |
|   Unearned grant revenues | 176,485 |
|   Current installments of long-term debt | 206,636 |
|   Total current liabilities | 24,944,674 |
| Construction Costs Payable, from trusteed funds | 5,090,405 |
| Long-Term Debt, less current installments | 63,528,205 |
| Fund Balances | |
|   Operating funds | 15,912,155 |
|   Utilization reserve | 9,478,050 |
|   Operating and board-designed fund balances | 25,390,205 |
| Total Liabilities and Fund Balance (total sources of | |
|   funds) | $118,953,489 |

SOURCE: Adapted from Harvard Community Health Plan, Inc. (1984).

supplies, certain financial assets (cash, marketable securities, and accounts receivable), and any other form of prepayment such as prepaid interest and rent. Assets for which recovery of the prepayment through earned revenues is expected within a year are usually grouped under the heading of "current assets" or working-capital assets. Prepayments expected to be recovered through revenues earned over a longer span of time are referred to as fixed or long-lived assets. The latter consist mainly of equipment, structures, and land owned by the organization and represent a substantial (but far from the total) amount of the total financing that an organization needs in order to operate.[3]

Access to financial capital is essential to

any health care organization that would respond to changes in its community, acquire new technologies and replace old equipment, renovate or replace deteriorated facilities, offer new programs or new services, or make changes to improve productivity or enhance quality. Much attention has been given to the aggregate future needs for financial capital among hospitals. Estimates of such needs in the 1980s vary widely, depending on assumptions, from $100 billion to nearly $260 billion (ICF Incorporated, 1983; Cohen and Keene, 1984:24-26). Assessments of the ability of health care organizations to raise needed capital vary as well.

Clearly, with overall hospital occupancy at 66 percent, there are many areas of the country in which the supply of hospital beds is excessive. However, even if a significant

**TABLE 3.2** Humana, Inc., Consolidated Balance Sheet, August 31, 1984

| | |
|---|---|
| *Assets (cumulative uses of funds)* | |
| Current Assets | |
|     Cash and cash equivalents | $   260,954 |
|     Accounts receivable less allowance for loss of | |
|       $59,215 | 257,675 |
|     Inventories | 45,249 |
|     Other current assets | 41,428 |
|     Total current assets | 605,306 |
| Property Equipment, at cost | |
|     Land | 165,413 |
|     Buildings | 1,228,701 |
|     Equipment | 681,756 |
|     Construction in progress (estimated cost to complete | |
|       and equip after August 31, 1984: $246,000) | 160,079 |
|     Subtotal | 2,235,949 |
|     Accumulated depreciation | 452,641 |
| | 1,783,308 |
| Other Assets | 189,233 |
| Total Assets (total uses of funds) | $2,577,847 |
| | |
| *Liabilities and Stockholders' Equity* | |
| Current Liabilities | |
|     Trade accounts payable | $     88,323 |
|     Salaries, wages, and other compensation | 52,292 |
|     Other accrued expenses | 97,936 |
|     Income taxes | 59,956 |
|     Long-term debt due within one year | 53,720 |
|     Total current liabilities | 352,227 |
| Long-Term Debt | 1,286,526 |
| Deferred Credits and Other Liabilities | 195,909 |
| Common Stockholders' Equity | |
|     Common stock, 16-2/3¢ par; authorized 200,000 | |
|       shares; issued and outstanding 96,848,643 | 16,141 |
|     Capital in excess of par value | 219,218 |
|     Translation adjustments | (19,340) |
|     Retained earnings | 527,166 |
| | 743,185 |
| Total Liabilities and Owners' Equity (total sources of | |
|   funds) | $2,577,847 |

SOURCE: Adapted from Humana, Inc. (1984).

number of hospitals should close, there are many purposes for which other health care institutions will have substantial needs for capital funds in the future. Debt must be retired. Facilities and equipment must be kept current and in good repair. Some hospitals (or portions thereof) will need to be reconfigured; alternative sites will have to be developed for long-term care and ambulatory care; and other steps will be necessary if hospitals are to become more comprehensive health care organizations. Also, certain areas of the country have rapid population growth, and new facilities or expansions of existing hospitals may be needed.

Thus, health care institutions have and will continue to have substantial capital needs, and access to capital translates directly into institutional ability to grow and even to survive. Differences among health care sectors in their access to capital will shape the future makeup of the health care system.

### SOURCES OF CAPITAL FUNDS FOR HEALTH CARE PROVIDERS

Financing for the current and long-lived assets owned by a health care provider can be obtained from the following sources:

- philanthropy (or an endowment set up from philanthropic funds received in the past)
- grants or other appropriated money from government
- funds accumulated from past operations
- the sale of short-term and long-term debt instruments
- the sale of ownership certificates (stock).

One other source available in some instances is funds from the sale of assets already owned.

Thus, whether an institution has access to financial capital depends on at least one of three things: whether it can attract philanthropy (a source that as a practical matter is not available to for-profit institutions);

whether it can obtain governmental grants or appropriations, which were a major source of capital for not-for-profit hospitals during the Hill-Burton era from the late 1940s until the 1970s, but are available now only to government-owned hospitals (federal, state, or local); or whether it has earnings (or potential earnings). Earnings are not only an important source of capital, they are also crucial to an organization's ability to secure funds through borrowing or through selling shares.

Funds accumulated from business operations are, in principle, a source of financial capital that is available to any ongoing organization, regardless of ownership type. Such funds are created when an organization's annual cash revenues exceed its corresponding annual cash expenses. Tables 3.3 and 3.4 show statements that detail the sources of funds accumulated during 1984 by the Harvard Community Health Plan and Humana, Inc. These so-called flow-of-funds statements also indicate how the funds were used in 1984. Funds accumulated from operations are shown in the first few lines of each statement, although they are labeled differently.

The cash revenues of investor-owned hospitals include return-on-equity payments from Medicare (and certain other third-party payers), a source of funds that is not available to the not-for-profit sector.[4] The rationale of such separate return-on-equity payments is closely linked to cost-based reimbursement methods, which are now being phased out by Medicare. Interest expenses (that is, payments to lenders) have been a reimbursable expense, but dividend payments to investors were not so treated, either in accounting or in reimbursement rules. Yet, as is discussed later in this chapter, suppliers of equity financing—the shareholders—supply these funds in the expectation that they will earn an appropriate rate of return on their investments. The willingness of the investors to provide such funds depends, at minimum, on their being able to expect a return on their investment

**TABLE 3.3** Harvard Community Health Plan, Inc.—Statement of Sources and Uses of Cash and Marketable Securities for the Fiscal Year Ended December 31, 1984

| | | |
|---|---:|---|
| *Sources of Funds* | | |
| From Operations | | |
| Excess of revenues over expenses as reported | $ 7,975,239 | |
| Add back: Reported expenses that did not require an outlay of funds (depreciation and amortization) | 3,602,698 | $11,577,937 (16%) |
| From External Sources | | |
| Trade credit | 4,813,751 | |
| Advances on as yet unearned grant revenue | 35,500 | |
| Proceeds from sale of long-term bonds | 49,035,000 | 58,974,656 (84%) |
| Increase in long-term construction costs payable | 5,090,405 | |
| Total Sources of Funds in 1984 | | $70,552,593 (100%) |
| | | |
| *Uses of Funds* | | |
| Investments in Assets | | |
| Increases in inventories, accounts receivable and prepaid expenses | $ 2,351,806 | |
| Increases in land, buildings, equipment | 33,558,891 | $51,804,850 (73%) |
| Increase in other assets | 617,280 | |
| Increase in funds held by trustees | 15,276,873 | |
| Repayment of Debt | | |
| Decrease in accounts payable | 421,126 | |
| Repayment of long-term debt | 5,209,148 | 5,630,274 (8%) |
| Other | | |
| Bond issue cash | 3,913,718 | |
| Decrease in unearned premiums | 42,833 | 3,956,551 (6%) |
| Net Increase in Cash and Marketable Securities | | 9,160,918 (13%) |
| Total Uses of Funds in 1984 | | $70,552,593 (100%) |

SOURCE: Adapted from Harvard Community Health Plan, Inc. (1984).

that would be equivalent to or higher than the earnings they sacrificed by supplying their funds to the hospital sector rather than, say, to the food or electronics industries. While such a return is not properly portrayed as an entitlement, it must in fact be paid if the hospital sector hopes to continue to procure funds on this basis. If investor-owned hospitals were reimbursed strictly on a cost basis, without this allowance for the cost of equity financing, then the suppliers of such funds would not earn any return and that source of funds would dry up. However, under a prospective rate-setting system, as with a charge-based system, the opportunity exists for institutions to generate funds in excess of costs.

Prior to 1982, Medicare's return-on-equity allowance for investor-owned hospitals was set at 1.5 times the rate of return earned by Medicare's Hospital Insurance Trust Fund on its investments. Legislation passed in 1982 reduced the amount of return-on-equity payments to the same rate as the trust fund. However, return on equity remains a significant source of capital, amounting to an estimated $200 million in 1984, about 7 percent of Medicare capital payments to hospitals and 38-40 percent of Medicare capital payments to investor-owned hospitals.[5] With the phasing out of cost-based reimbursement, the rationale for separate return-on-equity payments to investor-owned facilities becomes much less clear. The question will undoubtedly be addressed in legislation on how Medicare should pay capital expenses in the future, a topic examined later in this chapter.

**TABLE 3.4**  Humana, Inc., Consolidated Statement of Sources and Uses of Cash for the Year Ended August 31, 1984 (in thousands of dollars)

| | | |
|---|---|---|
| *Sources of Cash* | | |
| From Operations | | |
| Net income, as reported to shareholders | $193,341 | |
| Add back: reported expenses that did not require an outlay of cash in 1984 | | |
| Depreciation | 120,560 | $346,930  (41%) |
| Deferred income taxes | 7,404 | |
| Increase in allowance for professional liability risk | 22,032 | |
| Other | 3,593 | |
| From External Sources | | |
| Increases in short-term debt | 50,626 | |
| Increases in long-term debt | 358,811 | |
| Issuance of common stock | 9,695 | 419,132  (49%) |
| Sale of Properties and Investments | | 58,187  (7%) |
| Other Sources | | 20,124  (3%) |
| Total Sources of Cash in 1984 | | $844,373 (100%) |
| | | |
| *Uses of Cash* | | |
| Investments in Assets | | |
| Increases in current assets | $ 72,841 | |
| Increases in property and equipment | 445,741 | $542,148  (64%) |
| Increases in investment in subsidiaries | 23,566 | |
| Reductions in Debt | | |
| Repayment of short-term debt | 2,890 | |
| Repayment of long-term debt | 137,067 | 139,957  (17%) |
| Redemption of Preferred Stock | | 62,277  (7%) |
| Payment of Cash Dividend | | 60,217  (7%) |
| Other Uses of Cash | | 28,868  (3%) |
| Increase in Cash Balance | | 10,906  (2%) |
| Total Uses of Cash in 1984 | | $844,373 (100%) |

SOURCE: Adapted from Humana, Inc. (1984).

In addition to recoveries of earlier expenditures through revenues for depreciation and amortization expenses, for-profit entities commonly subtract from the income they report to shareholders certain income tax expenses that did not occasion an outflow of funds during the fiscal year covered by the report.

The cash revenues of both for-profit and not-for-profit (as well as public) institutions also include funds that represent the recovery of earlier cash outlays that have been carried as "assets" on the provider's balance sheet. These recoveries—the most common of which are "depreciation and amortization"—are shown on the income statement as expenses and are deducted from revenues to arrive at what for-profit entities call "net profits" and what not-for-profit entities refer to as "excess of revenues over expenses"—the proverbial bottom line in either case. It follows that the net profits or excess revenues shown in annual reports tend to understate significantly the funds a hospital earns from operations in any given year. To eliminate the distortion, a properly executed flow-of-funds statement therefore adds back to reported income these noncash expenses (see Figures 3.3 and 3.4).

The current tax code provides one other source of working capital for for-profit organizations in the form of investment incentives, which allow companies to recover their investment costs more quickly by deferring a portion of their corporate income taxes. Table 3.5 shows corporate taxes paid by the four largest investor-owned hospital companies in relationship to several different financial measures. The percentage of taxes that are deferred (and that are therefore available as working capital) vary, depending primarily on the investment patterns of the companies. Because Humana has not been investing heavily in new facilities, its taxes paid in 1983 were at 77 percent of the statutory rate, and deferred taxes provided only a minor source of working capital ($7.4 million of almost $800 million of funds provided), as Table 3.4 shows. Deferred taxes were a more important source of funds for other companies, however. NME paid taxes at the rate of only 29 percent of the statutory rate in 1983 (Table 3.5), and deferred taxes constituted almost 8 percent of NME's new working capital in 1984 (National Medical Enterprises, 1984).

In reporting the sources of "funds from operations" in its flow-of-funds statement,

**TABLE 3.5** Income Tax Obligations and Payments of Four Investor-Owned Health Care Corporations, Fiscal Year Ending 1983 (in thousands of dollars)

| | AMI | Humana | HCA | NME | |
|---|---|---|---|---|---|
| Gross revenues | $2,217,862 | $2,298,608 | $3,917,057 | $2,148,000 | |
| Net income before taxes | 233,441 | 288,782 | 391,718 | 170,000 | |
| Statutory tax obligation[a] | 107,383 | 132,840 | 180,190 | 78,200 | |
| Provision for income tax[b] | 104,100 | 128,133 | 148,500 | 75,000 | |
| Currently payable income tax[c] | | | | | |
| Federal | 40,700 | 92,128 | 73,167 | 18,000 | |
| State | 7,400 | 10,280 | 14,466 | 5,000 | |
| | | | | | *Average* |
| Tax actually paid as % of gross revenue | 2.2 | 4.4 | 2.2 | 1.1 | 2.5[d] |
| Tax actually paid as % of net income | 20.6 | 35.5 | 22.3 | 13.5 | 24.1 |
| Tax actually paid as % of statutory rate | 44.8 | 77.1 | 48.6 | 29.4 | 52.4 |
| Tax actually paid as % of provision for taxes shown in annual report to shareholders | 46.2 | 80.0 | 58.9 | 30.7 | 57.3 |

[a]Calculated simply as 46 percent of the net income figure reported to shareholders. The effective tax rate (i.e., the actual tax obligation for federal corporate income taxes) has been slightly less because of the adjustments for amortization of investment tax credits, credit for state and local taxes paid, and so forth. According to the Federation of American Hospitals, the effective tax rate for the six largest investor-owned hospital companies in 1983 averaged 42.2 percent (Samuel Mitchell, Director of Research, Federation of American Hospitals, personal communication, 1985).

[b]The tax liability actually reported to shareholders in the annual report (net of investment tax credit and state tax credit).

[c]The taxes actually paid. These taxes are based on taxable income as reported to the Internal Revenue Service (IRS). Such taxable income usually deviates significantly from taxable income as reported to shareholders. Typically the income figure reported to the IRS has been lower than that reported to shareholders.

[d]The Federation of American Hospitals reports that local property taxes for all for-profit general hospitals (chain and independent) totaled $99 million in 1983, a figure equivalent to 0.7 percent of gross patient revenues (Samuel Mitchell, personal communication, 1985). If this average is applicable to the four companies included in the table, the amount of taxes actually paid as a percentage of gross revenues would increase to 3.2 percent.

SOURCE: Data prepared from company financial reports by Steven C. Renn of the Johns Hopkins University Center for Hospital Finance and Management (1985).

the firm must adjust the reported net profit figure shown in that statement as follows:

• For those years in which taxes reported to shareholders (T) are higher than those actually paid (X), the difference (T − X) must be added back to book income as a reported expense not requiring the payment of cash.

• For those years in which taxes reported to shareholders (T) are below those actually paid (X), the difference (T − X) must be subtracted from reported net income as a cash outflow not booked as an expense in deriving the income figure.

In the literature and in the debate on for-profit hospitals, deferred taxes are often viewed as a "source of funds," an "interest-free loan from the government." The manner in which accountants treat this item in the flow-of-funds statement reinforces that interpretation. The example in Note 6 should make clear that this interpretation is based on a strong implicit assumption, namely, that the proper tax the firm ought to pay in a given year is the amount it reported as an allowance for taxes in its report to stockholders. With that assumption as a baseline, "deferred taxes" might be viewed as an interest-free loan. For a firm whose investment outlays on depreciable assets grow from year to year, clearly the balance outstanding on these interest-free government loans would grow over time, because in any given year more tax would be deferred than repaid.

On the other hand, one could take the view that through its legislative representatives, the people have amended the social contract between society and for-profit corporations and defined as the tax properly payable that amount calculated under the accelerated cost recovery (ACRS) depreciation system. After all, if that is not the proper tax, why legislate it? With ACRS taxes as the proper baseline, the item "deferred tax liability" is not really a source of funds and certainly is not an interest-free government loan. The item appears on the firm's balance sheet only because accountants prefer to report smooth, straight-line depreciation and income tax figures to their shareholders, which gives rise to an accounting discrepancy between taxes reported to shareholders and taxes already paid. Indeed, the item could be made to disappear from the firm's balance sheet and flow-of-funds statement by the simple expedient of reporting to shareholders the same depreciation and tax figures that are required by law.

One additional point emerges from the preceding discussion. In any discussion on the income taxes paid by for-profit corporations, a clear distinction must always be made between the taxes these corporations show as having been paid in their annual reports to stockholders and the taxes they actually did pay. Otherwise the wrong impression may be conveyed. In this connection, the reader is referred once more to Table 3.5.

Thus, in any given year the "profits" reported by for-profit providers, or the analogous "excess of revenues over expenses" reported by not-for-profit providers, understate the investable funds made available through operations. That amount includes the year's amortization of depreciable assets on the balance sheet and, for for-profits, deferred taxes.

### Trends in Sources of Financial Capital

Although no comprehensive source of data on sources of capital funds is available, data on funding for hospital construction provide a substantial part of the picture. As Table 3.6 and Figure 3.1 show, a remarkable change in sources of capital for hospital construction has taken place since the late 1960s. Philanthropy and governmental grants and appropriations have declined markedly as a source of funds for hospital construction, and by the early 1980s, debt (a form of investor financing) accounted for 70 percent of such funds. Table 3.6 and Figure 3.1 actually un-

**TABLE 3.6** Trends in Funding for Hospital Construction, 1973–1981 (percent of total funding)[a]

|  | 1968 | 1973 | 1978 | 1981 |
|---|---|---|---|---|
| Governmental grants and appropriations | 23 | 21 | 16 | 12 |
| Philanthropy | 21 | 10 | 6 | 4 |
| Hospital reserves | 16 | 15 | 17 | 15 |
| Debt | 38 | 54 | 61 | 69 |

[a]Reserves include past surpluses, funded depreciation, proceeds from sales of replaced assets and, for investor-owned facilities, equity paid in by investors.

SOURCE: AHA Survey of Sources of Funding for Hospital Construction (Charhut, 1984).

derstate the trend, because they include data on all construction that was under way in the years shown. If attention is confined to projects begun in 1981, the pattern is even more dramatic: debt was the source of 76 percent of the funding, and philanthropy and governmental grants and appropriations combined accounted for less than 8 percent (Metz, 1983).

Approximately 80 percent of the debt financing in 1981 was through tax-exempt bonds, with taxable public offerings (4 percent), government-sponsored lending programs (4 percent), mortgages with commercial banks (5 percent), and private placements (6 percent) accounting for the remainder (Metz, 1983). A small irony in the financing of hospital construction is that for-profit lenders (e.g., banks, insurance companies, investment companies) are attracted to the tax-exempt debt of not-for-profit hospitals (the lower interest rates on such bonds are compensated for by taxes not having to be paid on the income), while the taxable debt of the investor-owned companies is more attractive to tax-exempt entities (e.g., pension funds).

Private financing of hospital capital through the hospital's own revenues and through investor financing (debt or equity) parallels the ownership of hospitals in the United States, which also is predominantly private. However, it should not be forgotten that this pattern of ownership and financing is unique among industrialized nations (see Table 3.7 for a summary of hospital ownership and financing in several countries) and that our heavy reliance on investor financing has undeniable social and economic consequences. It may, for example, lead to more expensively equipped hospitals. If, however, government does not wish to use its tax revenues

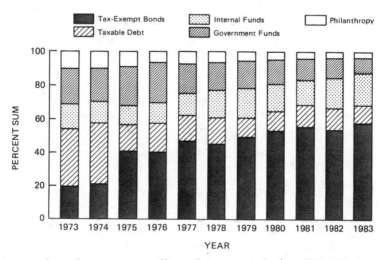

**FIGURE 3.1** Sources of capital as percentages of hospital construction funding, 1973-1983. Source: Cohodes and Kinkead (1984).

**TABLE 3.7**  A Synopsis of Hospital Financing in Selected Countries

| Country | Ownership of Hospitals | Basis of Reimbursement for— | | Role of Health-Sector Planning |
| --- | --- | --- | --- | --- |
| | | Capital Costs | Operating Costs | |
| Canada | Hospitals are predominantly owned by lay boards of trustees or by communities | Separate capital budgets are granted upon specific approval of proposed investments by the provincial governments | Annual prospective global budgets controlled by the provincial governments | The hospital sector is subject to planning by the provincial government. The capacity of the system is fully determined by the provincial governments. |
| United Kingdom | Hospitals are owned by the central government's National Health Service | Separate capital budgets are controlled by the central government through its National Health Service | Annual prospective global budgets controlled by the National Health Service (i.e., the central government) | The central government's National Health Service develops the nation's health plan on the basis of consultation with local health officers and local governments. Because the National Health Service owns all but the few private hospitals, the central government fully determines the capacity of the hospital system. |
| France | About 70% of all hospital beds are publicly owned (mainly by local governments); the rest are privately owned | Capital costs are recovered in part through amortization allowances in the per diems and charges; the balance of costs is financed through subsidies from the central and local governments | Prospective per diems and prospectively set charges for particular services; these per diems and charges are government controlled | The hospital sector is subject to regional and national planning. The central government, through its health plan, determines the capacity of the hospital system. |
| Netherlands | Hospitals are owned by local communities or lay boards of trustees | Until 1983, the per diems included amortization of capital costs; since 1983, hospitals are reimbursed for capital costs via separately controlled line items in the budget | Until 1983, by negotiated per diems and charges; since 1984, by annual global budgets. The system is still in a state of transition | Construction of facilities and acquisition of major medical equipment requires a government-issued license, which is issued on the basis of regional and national health-sector planning. |
| Sweden | Hospitals are owned and operated by local community councils | Community-financed, by means of specific appropriations voted by the community councils | Annual budgets controlled by the local community councils | The capacity of the hospital sector is planned and controlled at the community level. |

**TABLE 3.7** *Continued*

| Country | Ownership of Hospitals | Basis of Reimbursement for— | | Role of Health-Sector Planning |
|---------|------------------------|-----------------------------|---|-------------------------------|
| | | Capital Costs | Operating Costs | |
| Finland | Hospitals are owned and operated by local communities | Specific appropriations; financed in part by the communities and in part by central government subsidy | Annual budgets determined by a system of national health planning and ultimately controlled by central government | There is no formal national health plan. There is a system of national health planning ultimately controlled by the central government. A system of central-government subsidies effectively controls the capacity of the hospital system. |
| West Germany | Hospitals are owned by local communities, by religious foundations, or by private individuals (usually physicans) | Financed by the federal and state governments through lump sum grants (for short-lived equipment) or upon specific application (for structures or long-lived equipment) | Prospective, hospital-specific, all-inclusive per diems negotiated between the hospital and regional associations of sickness funds; these rates are subject to approval by the state governments | Capital investments are approved and financed by the state governments on the basis of statewide hospital planning. The state governments therefore control the capacity of the hospital system. |

SOURCE: Reinhardt (1984:25A).

to supply financial capital to the health care sector, as appears to be the case, Americans must realize that the health care sector will increasingly conform to the performance expectations of the financial markets, which are interested in the rendering of services to humankind only insofar as such services yield cash revenues. Whether for-profit and not-for-profit health care organizations will respond to these pressures in the same way is an empirical question to which much of this report is devoted. The questions that we will address here are how similar are they in their sources of financial capital, and what is the significance of their differences in this regard.

## Relationship of Ownership to Sources of Capital

Although it might be expected that government-owned health care organizations would obtain financial capital from tax revenues, that not-for-profit organizations would obtain capital from philanthropy, and that for-profit organizations would obtain capital from investors, the picture is more complicated. The type of ownership of health care organizations does have important implications for the sources of capital to which they have access, but data from hospitals show that all types are heavily dependent on cash reserves and debt. Figures 3.2, 3.3, and 3.4 show sources of financial capital for construction of hospitals by different ownership types. Philanthropy has become a very small part of the picture and is largely confined to not-for-profit and public hospitals. Governmental capital grants are a part of the picture only for public institutions. In both not-for-profit and for-profit institutions, retained earnings are a major source of capital (this makes up a substantial portion of the

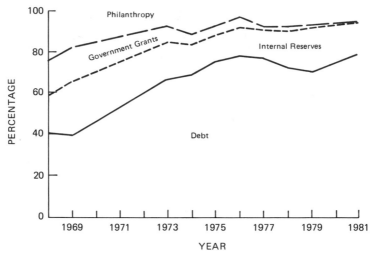

**FIGURE 3.2** Sources of capital as a percentage of construction funding—voluntary hospitals. Source: Kinkead (1984). Data are from American Hospital Association's Construction Survey for various years. Values for 1970, 1971, and 1972 have been interpolated from data from 1969 and 1973.

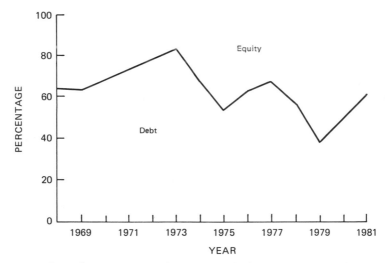

**FIGURE 3.3** Sources of capital as a percentage of construction funding—investor-owned hospitals. Source: Kinkead (1984). Data are from American Hospital Association's Construction Survey for various years. Values for 1970, 1971, and 1972 have been interpolated from data from 1969 and 1973.

sector labeled "equity" in Figure 3.3). For-profit institutions have one additional source of capital beyond the sources available to not-for-profit institutions—the equity capital from investors.

Several reasons for the trends in debt financing can be identified, in addition to the obvious factor—the end of the Hill-Burton program's governmental grants. Many of the factors involve governmental policies (Co-

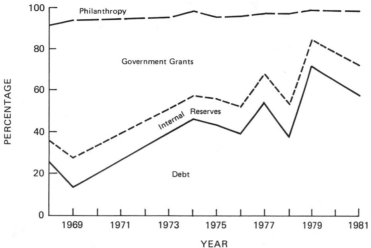

FIGURE 3.4   Sources of capital as a percentage of construction funding—public hospitals. Source: Kinkead (1984). Data are from American Hospital Association's Construction Survey for various years. Values for 1970, 1971, and 1972 have been interpolated from data from 1969 and 1973.

hodes and Kinkead, 1984). The Hill-Burton program itself included loan and interest subsidy programs, and the Federal Housing Administration's so-called 242 program provides mortgage insurance for both investor-owned and not-for-profit hospitals. More generally, the increasing comprehensiveness of third-party coverage greatly increased the likelihood that hospitals could break even or earn a surplus. Recognition of capital costs by Medicare—as in the earlier Blue Cross Association/American Hospital Association *Principles of Payment for Hospital Care* (1963) that was the basis for subsequent public and private cost-based, third-party payments—was of key importance. Reimbursing for interest expenses provided incentives to use debt as a source of funds (taking money out of an endowment was not reimbursable), and reimbursing for depreciation expenses helped hospitals to build internal reserves that could be used as leverage in the capital market. (However, inflation and technological change meant that depreciation schedules based on original cost did not provide sufficient funding for replacement—another reason that hospitals needed to borrow, even if they had funded

depreciation.) Tax-exempt debt has become the single largest source of financial capital for hospitals. Tax-exempt bonds opened up a market for small issues and made it easier to secure loans, because pledges of earnings could be used instead of the assets that commercial banks had generally required.

## THE COSTS OF CAPITAL

Substantial costs are incurred not only in obtaining equity and debt financing, but also in obtaining governmental or philanthropic grants and contributions.[7] Debt requires (and equity investments usually require) that periodic payments of interest (or dividends) be made. To all sources of capital are attached certain expectations of performance; however, the expectations tied to various sources of capital differ in some very significant ways.

### Philanthropy and Governmental Grants

The expectations attached to philanthropic and governmental grants are to varying degrees explicit and detailed. The most general expectation, however, is that the recipient institution will not act as a profit-maximizing entity. Indeed, one way of looking at the costs of governmental or philanthropic grants is in terms of deviation from the profit-maximizing model—for example, rendering care to indigent patients at no cost or at a price that is lower than a theoretically profit-maximizing price. Seen in this light, funds from governmental or philanthropic grants can be very expensive to an institution, such as the so-called community service and free-care obligations that were attached to the use of Hill-Burton funds. On the other hand, however, these sources of funds enable (or require) institutions to conform to some extent with the traditional social missions of health care institutions, that is, as community, charitable, teaching, or research institutions. The marked decline in the relative magnitude of these sources of capital financing helps to explain today's uncertainty and debate about the proper mission of health care institutions.

### Debt Financing

If funds are advanced in the form of debt instruments, they can be thought of as being "rented" for a specified period at a specified annual rate called interest. The specifics of the rental contract are spelled out in great detail in a bond indenture, which stipulates not only the interest rate and date of maturity on which the funds must be returned to their owners (the creditors) but also sets forth numerous additional constraints on behavior the borrowing entity must obey, lest there be foreclosure or other penalities (Wilson et al., 1982).[8] Such constraints have prompted concern that the generation of cash to pay interest and to repay debt will become the hospital's first obligation, making not-for-profit hospitals with financial obligations to bondholders little different from investor-owned hospitals similarly responsible to shareholders (Wilson et al., 1982:1428).

Both the availability and the terms of debt

financing depend substantially on formal assessments of creditworthiness by lenders and, when bonds are the vehicle, by rating agencies (Moody's or Standard and Poor's). Key factors include hospital location, hospital market share, the ability and skills of management, the reimbursement and regulatory environment of the state, and financial performance (Cohodes and Kinkead, 1984). Too much bad debt (above 5 percent) and too much dependency on nonoperating income (e.g., income from philanthropy, governmental appropriations, or endowments) are negative factors. Thus, one of the consequences of American hospitals' dependency on private sources of capital is that providing uncompensated care will likely harm their ability to gain access to capital.

The growing dependence on bonded indebtedness also signals an important change in the relationship between medical institutions (of all ownership types) and the communities in which they are located (Schlesinger, 1985). First, the money comes from (and the accompanying accountability is to) sources outside the community. The relationship that was established between hospital and community via fund-raising drives (e.g., to match Hill-Burton funds) has been greatly attenuated in many communities.

Second, because management depth and diversified sources of revenue reduce risk, multi-institutional systems (and their component institutions) have greater access to capital than do independent institutions (Booz, Allen & Hamilton, 1982; Hernandez and Henkel, 1982). This is true for both for-profit and not-for-profit multi-institutional systems. The advantage of multi-institutional systems can be measured in terms of their bond ratings (all other things being equal, the higher the bond rating, the lower the cost of capital), as is shown in Table 3.8. The financial market's preference for the debt of multi-institutional systems, as opposed to the debt of independent institutions, is a key factor in the growth of multi-institutional

**TABLE 3.8** Comparative Distribution of Health Care Borrowers by Rating Category, 1978–1981

| Rating Category | Single-Facility Providers (%) | Multihospital Systems (%) |
|---|---|---|
| Nonrated | 8 | 3 |
| BBB (+/−) | 16 | 8 |
| A− | 23 | 5 |
| A | 35 | 23 |
| A+ | 16 | 38 |
| AA (+/−) | 2 | 23 |

SOURCE: Kidder, Peabody & Co., Health Finance Group, Hospital Database (Hernandez and Henkel, 1982). Reprinted by permission from *Hospitals* 56(5), March 1, 1982. Copyright 1982, American Hospital Publishing, Inc.

arrangements. Whether the benefits of the options made possible by systems' access to capital outweigh the loss of local control that characterizes multi-institutional systems is subject to debate. It is clear, however, that some types of decisions migrate away from the local level when an institution becomes part of a multi-institutional arrangement. (For more on this subject see Chapter 9.) The relationship between this trend and the reliance on private capital is also clear.

## Equity Financing

The controversy over the role that equity financing plays in directing the flow of resources into the health care sector has been fueled by a widespread lack of understanding of the legal and financial characteristics of this type of financing. Because of the importance of misconceptions about equity capital, the nature and cost of equity financing are discussed briefly here and in greater detail in the Appendix to this chapter.

It is widely believed that the earnings retained by a corporation are a costless source of funds and that financing procured by the issue of new stock certificates is cheap relative to debt financing. This inference appears to be based on the relatively low dividend yield (defined as the ratio of dividends per share to market price) on corporate stocks. In 1984, for example, Humana, Inc., paid its shareholders a dividend of $0.575 per share, which amounts to about 29 percent of its reported earnings per share for that year. The market price per share of Humana stock during 1984 fluctuated between $25.50 and $33.00. Dividends per share thus amounted to only about 2 percent of the average market price per share during that year. In the same year, the weighted average interest rate on all of Humana's long-term debt was 12 percent, or about 6.5 percent on an after-tax basis. From these numbers one might easily infer that debt financing constituted a much more expensive source of funds from Humana's viewpoint than did equity financing—about three times as expensive, to be exact.

There is the further thought, occasionally encountered in the debate on this issue, that the ability to print and sell common-stock certificates endows investor-owned hospitals with a money pump. Spokesmen for investor-owned hospitals contribute to that impression. As reported in the *American Medical News*, for example, at a June 1985 conference a senior vice president of the Hospital Corporation of America gave "a striking explanation of how a for-profit hospital company can raise huge amounts of capital almost instantly. Say, for example, a for-profit chain produces $1 million in earnings. If the company's stock is selling at a price-to-earnings ratio of 12-1, the company can issue new stock and gain $12 million in new equity capital. With that $12 million in new equity, the company can go to the debt market and borrow another $12 million. The result is that the for-profit firm can leverage initial earnings of $1 million into $25 million of capital. The nonprofit hospital, by comparison, cannot sell stock. It can use its $1 million earnings to borrow another $1 million—for $2 million of capital" (Lefton, 1985:37). The clear implication of this pronouncement is that investor-owned hospitals possess a special kind of magic in the markets for financial capital—something approximating the legendary money pump.

How valid are these impressions? Is equity capital really as cheap as the preceding example would suggest? And do investor-owned hospitals really possess a money pump, as this senior vice president's illustration implies? Students of corporation finance will answer both questions in the negative. Responsibly utilized, equity financing is typically more expensive than is debt financing. Furthermore, equity financing would be a money pump only if analysts in the financial markets were unbelievably incompetent. The major advantages of equity financing lie in its flexibility and in the additional sources of financing that it makes available, not in its cost or its supposed availability just for the asking. A detailed discussion of equity financing will be found in the Appendix to this chapter.

## THE LEVEL PLAYING FIELD ARGUMENT

Arguments about policy issues regarding for-profit and not-for-profit health care organizations frequently refer to the levelness of the playing field on which such organizations compete. Generally, it is alleged that either for-profit or not-for-profit organizations have been given an unfair competitive advantage by governmental policies, and it is implied that fairness in this regard should be an important goal of health policy. Much of this debate is concerned with issues of capital financing.

Thus, critics of for-profit providers have argued that access to equity financing gives them a decided advantage over not-for-profit providers, who cannot issue common stock. As discussed earlier, it is often alleged that the ability to print and sell common-stock certificates endows for-profit providers with the ability to print money. The analysis presented in the Appendix to this chapter shows

that this view of investor-equity capital as essentially costless is quite wrong. However, access to any unique and important source of capital is a significant advantage, an advantage that is enhanced by the additional borrowing power that such access makes possible. Another advantage enjoyed by the for-profit sector is the receipt of "return-on-equity" payments as a reimbursable capital cost from Medicare and some other third-party payers.

The for-profit sector also benefits from tax provisions (investment tax credits, accelerated cost recovery) that are designed to encourage investment and that allow deferral of corporate income taxes. Thus, as shown in Table 3.5, corporate taxes paid by the four largest investor-owned hospital companies in 1984 averaged 52 percent of the basic corporate tax rate, and the companies varied widely (from 29 percent to 77 percent) in this regard.

On the other hand, spokesmen for for-profit providers point out certain advantages enjoyed by not-for-profit health care providers. First is their ability to procure funds through the sale of tax-exempt bonds. Although for-profit health care organizations have in some limited circumstances procured financing through tax-exempt bonds—particularly industrial development bonds—this device is largely available to the not-for-profit sector. The monetary advantage of such financing depends on the spread between the interest rates that institutions have to pay to sell tax-exempt debt and the rate they would otherwise have to pay (an interest cost that has of late saved them 20-40 percent, depending on the length of time before the bond matures). As a tax expenditure, tax-exempt bonds represented a government subsidy of $1.065 billion for not-for-profit health care institutions in 1984 (Executive Office of the President, 1985). Of course, from the government's broader standpoint, the availability of tax-exempt financing reduced hospitals' capital expenses, almost half of which were directly passed through to governmental programs such as Medicare.

A second advantage is the ability of not-for-profit organizations to attract funds through philanthropy; a third is their exemption from income and property taxes,[9] an advantage that is reduced somewhat by provisions that allow for-profit organizations to defer certain taxes.

Although the imagery of a level playing field in a competitive environment has superficial appeal, it does not appear to be a sensible goal for public policy. Part of the difficulty lies in devising a practical definition of a level playing field.

First, a level playing field between for-profit and not-for-profit health care organizations would require that competitors procure resource inputs, including financial capital, in the same markets and on the same terms (i.e., at the same prices for given quantities). However, by definition, policy, and practice, there are significant differences in this regard. Also, a level playing field would require, inter alia, similar incentives and burdens in the tax code. Again, the departure from this condition is virtually definitional. A level playing field would presumably require that both forms of providers sell their outputs in the same market, to identical sets of potential patients, on identical terms. But data on geographic locations suffice to show that, although there are many examples of direct competition in the same market, there are many locales and areas of the country that are served only by public and not-for-profit hospitals (Watt et al., 1986; see also Chapter 2 of this report). A level playing field would presumably require that competitors be expected by society and permitted by law to pursue the same objective or set of objectives. Whether this condition generally holds between for-profit and not-for-profit hospitals is, at the very least, debatable; there continue to be many not-for-profit (and public) hospitals that

clearly pursue missions that have little to do with profitability.

The conditions that would level the playing field are stringent, and they involve more than one dimension. If all but one of the conditions are met, it could be meaningful to assess what the implications of that one violation would be for the level playing field. One could even suggest policy actions to level the field. If, however, more than one condition is violated, that assessment becomes very complex and, inevitably, judgmental. Each form has advantages that are incommensurate with the other's advantages.

Second, there are more pressing policy concerns than whether the advantages and disadvantages of the two forms balance each other. The question of what is expected of institutions in exchange for the benefits of tax exemptions is important of itself, on its own terms. Similarly, the question of what to do to assure the survival of institutions that genuinely provide services that would otherwise have to be provided by the government is also important on its own terms. Likewise, the question of whether tax-exempt bond funding should continue to be available to not-for-profit hospitals is best considered in terms of the impact on the ability of these institutions to fulfill or continue a mission of community service and quality health care. In neither case is the answer illuminated in any important way by level playing field arguments.

Third, there is no particular reason why the goal of policy should be equivalence in treatment by the government rather than a substantive goal—such as to assure that services of acceptable quality are available to all who need them.

The major circumstance in which questions of a level playing field might gain importance is if the advantages and disadvantages conveyed on the different forms affected their ability to survive. If governmental policy were such that the existence of well-run hospitals of one type or another were threatened because of that policy, that would be a matter of concern. As discussed in the concluding chapter of this report, this committee believes that at this time a significant degree of diversity in ownership of health care institutions has positive aspects.

## POLICY ISSUES REGARDING CAPITAL

Two major policy issues are of immediate importance. The first concerns how capital costs will be paid by Medicare now that it has begun to pay all other costs on a per-case basis. The second concerns the continued availability of tax-free bond funding. The committee's discussions of these very complex issues led to several general conclusions.

First, the committee concluded that it is essential that Medicare continue to meet its obligations of paying for the cost of procuring capital for health care. Although the low occupancy rates among hospitals certainly support an argument that there is surplus capacity in the system, many of the changes that are needed in health care will require additional infusions of capital into the health care sector. Among these changes are the emergence of new technologies, new types of services, and types of care that are in short supply in selective areas (home care, extended care, alcohol treatment, rehabilitation services, and so forth).

The committee agrees that the method by which capital expenses have traditionally been paid by Medicare must be changed, so that capital costs are included in the prospectively set DRG rates. Under a prospective payment system the committee sees no justification for differential payments (e.g., for return on equity) on the basis of for-profit or not-for-profit status.

The change in methods of paying for capital should not be the occasion, however, to starve institutions. Among other effects, such a policy would be likely to change signifi-

cantly the current balance between the for-profit and not-for-profit sectors. Some evidence presented in Chapter 4 and Chapter 5 suggests that for-profit providers respond more closely to economic incentives, implying that their response to such circumstances might be to reduce services more quickly, to introduce more differential pricing (particularly in multi-institutional systems that have institutions in different markets), and to take other steps to protect and enhance their capital. The committee is concerned that not-for-profit institutions might be more likely to avoid hard choices that are seen as inconsistent with their mission (such as reducing indigent care) by spending reserves that are needed to fund future capital improvements, thereby significantly weakening themselves in an increasingly competitive environment. The alternative of institutions' abandoning traditional missions would be equally unfortunate.

If in view of the widespread excess capacity in the hospital sector the government decides to constrain the flow of funds that allow capital formation in this sector, mechanisms should be created for establishing exceptions in situations of merit (e.g., tertiary care institutions with high costs for technology and specialized personnel, vital training centers committed to health professional education, institutions with a high indigent care burden, and so forth).

Finally, regarding tax-exempt bonds, it must be recognized that in recent years this has been a key source of outside capital for the not-for-profit sector and that it provides a vehicle for making capital available to many institutions that otherwise would have no chance to obtain it (Cohodes and Kinkead, 1984). Furthermore, some institutions in the not-for-profit sector might in desperation be tempted to change to for-profit or simply to sell out to investor-owned companies. Thus, governmental policy in this area affects not only governmental revenues—the term in which the debate is often framed—but it also affects the balance between the for-profit and not-for-profit sectors. It would be very unwise to do away with such an important mechanism without much greater study of the possible impact on the for-profit/not-for-profit composition of the hospital sector. The committee strongly believes in the importance of a not-for-profit sector in health care, and that it is imperative that tax-exempt financing be maintained. However, it would be appropriate to review the requirements of eligibility for tax-exempt debt to make more certain that institutions that obtain approval for tax-exempt bonds will serve a public purpose regarding those unable to pay, services that are not profitable, and education and research.

## CONCLUSION

The much misunderstood topic of capital is key to the future for-profit/not-for-profit composition of health care. Although a level playing field is itself not an important goal for health policy, eliminating not-for-profit access to tax-exempt funding could have a devastating effect on that particular sector. Changes are needed in Medicare policies for paying for expenses, including the past practice of paying for-profit institutions a separate return-on-equity payment. Because of foreseeable changes in different sectors' access to capital, significant changes in the overall composition of health care could result inadvertently from federal policies, a factor that should be included with other capital-related policy questions to be considered.

## NOTES

[1]Recent reports on capital include the American Hospital Association's *Report of the Special Committee on Equity of Payment for Not-for-Profit and Investor-Owned Hospitals* (1983), the American Health Planning Association's *Report of the Commission on Capital Policy* (1984), the Healthcare Financial Management Association's "Proposed Method of Medicare Payment for Hospital Capital-Related Costs" (1983), The Na-

tional Committee for Quality Health Care's "Proposed Method for Incorporating Capital-Related Costs Within the Medicare Prospective Payment System" (1984), and a series of very useful reports and studies by consulting firms and scholars done for the Office of the Assistant Secretary for Planning and Evaluation, DHHS, in 1983 and 1984.

[2]The term "financial capital" stands in distinction to "physical capital"—which refers to facilities, equipment, and other physical assets that are acquired through the use of financial capital—and "human capital," the employees who make the organization work and in whom the organization has invested.

[3]Laypersons not familiar with either accounting or corporation finance frequently think only of equipment, structures, and land when they speak of "capital." However, a firm's capital includes the sum total of the monetary value of all of its assets, both current and long-lived. In 1984, for example, the current assets of the Harvard Community Health Plan accounted for 32 percent of its total asset base; the corresponding figure for Humana, Inc., was 23 percent.

[4]Arguments have been made in recent years that not-for-profit institutions have the same need for return-on-equity payments as do for-profit institutions and that Medicare's movement to a prospective pricing system removes any justification for differences in payments based on differences in type of ownership. (See HFMA, 1980; AHA, 1983; and Conrad, 1984). For the history of the return-on-equity issue, see Somers and Somers (1967), Feder (1977) and Kinkead (1984).

[5]The estimate of $200 million in return-on-equity payments was provided to the committee in personal communications from Randy Teach of the Office of the Assistant Secretary, DHHS, July 10, 1985, and from Samuel Mitchell, director of research at the Federation of American Hospitals, July 1985. Mr. Mitchell provided the estimate of return-on-equity's percentage of Medicare capital to investor-owned hospitals, based on FAH survey data that showed depreciation and interest expenses totaling $881 million in 1983 (FAH, 1983), and the estimate that Medicare payments constituted approximately 36-38 percent of payments to investor-owned hospitals.

[6]To illustrate, suppose that, at the beginning of fiscal 1983, a firm had purchased for $1 million an asset with an estimated use-life of five years and a zero salvage value at the end of that use-life. In its reports to shareholders the firm would probably deduct from revenues straight-line depreciation expenses equal to $1 million/5 years, or $200,000 per year in fiscal years 1983-1987. Furthermore, in its reports to shareholders it would show that it had paid income taxes on the net income calculated with these flat, straight-line depreciation figures.

Under the accelerated cost recovery system (ACRS) legislated in 1981, however, the firm actually would be able to depreciate the asset over only three years for purposes of calculating taxable income to be reported to the Internal Revenue Service (IRS). The annual tax-deductible depreciation expense would be $250,000 for 1983, $380,000 for 1984, and $370,000 for 1985. During these three years, then, the taxes the firm showed as having been paid in its report to shareholders would exceed the taxes it actually paid. This divergence gives rise to the so-called "deferred income taxes due" shown as a liability on the firm's balance sheet. Accountants treat this expense as a liability because in years 1986 and 1987 the firm would still book $200,000 a year in depreciation expenses in its report to shareholders, but would book no depreciation expense at all (on this asset) in calculating its taxable income for the IRS. In other words, other things being equal, the firm would report lower income taxes to its shareholders in 1986 and 1987 than it actually paid during those years.

[7]For example, a recent survey by the National Association for Hospital Development of its members (individuals with fund-raising responsibilities in hospitals) found that the hospitals surveyed had budgeted 0.9 percent of their overall budgets for development purposes and that they were planning to devote 1.4 percent of their budgets to this purpose in 1985 (AAFRC, 1985).

[8]These constraints typically include appointing a trustee (usually a bank) to monitor economic performance and to take appropriate actions on behalf of the bondholders, including taking possession of the hospital on behalf of the bondholders in the event of default; agreeing to set rates and charges to provide sufficient income for debt service; agreeing to maintain the corporate existence of the hospital and to give the trustee veto power over any substantial disposition of assets or any merger with another institution; and operating the institution to meet various indicators of financial performance and status (e.g., debt-to-equity ratios).

[9]Data published by the American Hospital Association (1984) show the total revenues of community not-for-profit hospitals in 1983 to be $89,462,795 and total expenses to be $85,637,108. Had this income of $3,825,787 been taxed at the average effective tax rate for the six largest investor-owned hospital companies (42.2 percent), their federal income tax liability would have been just over $1.6 billion; had they been taxed at the rate actually paid by the four largest investor-owned firms (24.1 percent; see Table 3.5), they would have had to pay $922 million. In either case, the exemption from federal income taxes was very valuable to the not-for-profit hospital sector.

### REFERENCES

American Association of Fund Raising Counsel, Inc. (AAFRC) (1985) *Giving USA: A Compilation of Facts and Trends on American Philanthropy for the Year 1984.* New York: American Association of Fund Raising Counsel, Inc.

American Hospital Association (1983) *Report of the Special Committee on Equity of Payment for Not-for-Profit and Investor-Owned Hospitals.* Chicago, Ill.: American Hospital Association.

American Hospital Association (1984) *Hospital Solutions—1984.* Chicago, Ill.: American Hospital Association.

Booz, Allen & Hamilton (1982) Historical Linkages Between Selected Hospital Characteristics and Bond Ratings. Appendix to *Report of the Special Committee on Equity of Payment for Not-for-Profit and Investor-Owned Hospitals.* Chicago, Ill.: American Hospital Association.

Charhut, Maureen M. (1984) Trends in Hospital Philanthropy. *Hospitals* 58(March 16):70-74.

Cohen, Harold A., and Jack C. Keane (1984) Approaches to Setting the Level of Payment. Hospital Capital Finance Background Paper prepared for Assistant Secretary for Planning and Evaluation, DHHS. Washington, D.C.: Department of Health and Human Services.

Cohodes, Donald R., and Brian M. Kinkead (1984) *Hospital Capital Formation in the 1980s.* Baltimore, Md.: Johns Hopkins University Press.

Conrad, Douglas A. (1984) Return on Equity to Not-for-profit Hospitals: Theory and Implementation. *Health Services Research* 19(April):41-63.

Executive Office of the President, Office of Management and Budget (1985) Budget of the United States Government, FY 1986. Special Analysis G, Tax-Expenditures, Table G-2 (Revenue Loss Estimates for Tax Expenditures by Functions), p. G-46.

Feder, Judith M. (1977) *Medicare: The Politics of Federal Hospital Insurance.* Lexington, Mass.: D. C. Heath.

Federation of American Hospitals (1983) *Statistical Profile of the Investor-Owned Hospital Industry, 1983.* Washington, D.C.: Federation of American Hospitals.

Harvard Community Health Plan, Inc. (1984) *Annual Report.* Boston, Mass.

Hernandez, Michael D., and Arthur J. Henkel (1982) Need for Capital May Squeeze Freestanding Institutions into Multi-institutional Arrangements. *Hospitals* 56(March 1):75-77.

Hospital Financial Management Association (1980) Hospital Financial Management Association Principles and Practices Board, Statement 3. *Hospital Financial Management* 34:50-59.

Humana, Inc. (1984) *Annual Report.* Louisville, Ky.

ICF Incorporated (1983) *Assessment of Recent Estimates of Hospital Capital Requirements.* Contract study done for Assistant Secretary for Planning and Evaluation, DHHS. Washington, D.C.: ICF Incorporated.

Kinkead, Brian (1984) Historical Trends in Hospital Capital Investment. Report prepared for the Assistant

Secretary for Planning and Evaluation, DHHS. Washington, D.C.: Department of Health and Human Services.

Lefton, Doug (1985) Will For-Profit Hospital Chains Swallow Up Nonprofit Sector? *American Medical News* (June 18/July 5):1, 35, 37.

Metz, Maureen (1983) Trends in Sources of Capital in the Hospital Industry. Appendix D to the *Report of the Special Committee on Equity of Payment for Not-for-Profit and Investor-Owned Hospitals*. Chicago, Ill.: American Hospital Association.

National Medical Enterprises (1984) *Annual Report*. Los Angeles, Calif.

Reinhardt, Uwe (1984) *Financing the Hospital: The Experience Abroad*. Washington, D.C.: Department of Health and Human Services.

Schlesinger, Mark J. (1985) Review of Cohodes and Kinkead, *Hospital Capital Formation in the 1980s. The New England Journal of Medicine* 312:323.

Somers, Herman M., and Anne R. Somers (1967) *Medicare and the Hospitals: Issues and Prospects*. Washington, D.C.: The Brookings Institution, 1967.

Watt, J. Michael, Steven C. Renn, James S. Hahn, Robert A. Derzon, and Carl J. Schramm (1986) The Effects of Ownership and Multihospital System Membership on Hospital Functional Strategies and Economic Performance. This volume.

Wilson, Glenn, Cecil Sheps, and Thomas R. Oliver (1982) Effects of Hospital Revenue Bonds on Hospital Planning and Revenue. *The New England Journal of Medicine* 307(December 2):1426-1430.

# APPENDIX TO CHAPTER 3

# The Nature of Equity Financing

## Uwe Reinhardt

Equity financing is a topic about which misconceptions exist, such as the belief that equity capital is a cheap and plentiful source of funds. Although access to equity capital has significant advantages, these advantages are less than often supposed. These points become clear if the topic is examined carefully.

To understand the nature of equity financing, it is best to think of an investor-owned firm as a separate entity with a life of its own, apart from that of its owners—the shareholders. From that perspective the owners then become just another source of financial capital. They are individuals or institutions willing to supply the firm with funds against what one might call a veritable "hope-and-prayer" paper, the common-stock certificate.

A debt instrument typically obliges the firm to pay coupon interest at stated intervals and to redeem the instrument, at face value, at a specified date of maturity. Failure on the part of the firm to meet these commitments invokes the risk of foreclosure by the holders of the debt instrument. By contrast a common-stock certificate merely promises its holder that cash dividends may be paid at certain intervals *if* there are sufficient earnings to finance these dividends and *if* management and the owners'

elected representatives—the firm's board of directors—decide to pay such dividends. Furthermore, there is no promise whatsoever to repay the shareholders' original investment in the stock certificate at any time other than at liquidation of the firm, and even then the investor is promised only a pro rata share in whatever is left over after all of the firm's assets have been sold and all of its creditors have been paid.

From the perspective of a shareholder the purchase of a firm's common-stock certificate is thus truly an act of faith in the integrity of the firm's management. As the daily drama surrounding corporate takeovers amply demonstrates, management makes light of this act of faith at its own peril. It may well be true that in years past—prior to the 1970s—the ownership of American corporations was so diffuse that corporate managements could ride roughshod over their firms' shareholders. In the meantime, however, an ever-increasing proportion of corporate stock is being held by large institutional investors, including the managers of pension funds. These institutional investors are under strong pressure from their clients to produce high rates of return on the funds entrusted to them. They transmit this pressure explicitly to the corporations whose stock they hold, and they have shown no hesitation to throw managements that have disappointed them to the mercies of corporate raiders.

In soliciting funds from potential investors against newly issued common-stock certificates, the firm's management must convince these investors that their investment will ultimately earn a rate of return that compensates them for (a) the returns forgone by exchanging their funds against the stock certificates rather than by investing them in gilt-edged corporate or government bonds and (b) the uncertainty inherent in the acquisition of the "hope-and-prayer" certificates. The sum of these two components—the opportunity cost of funds and the risk premium—is referred to in the literature as the cost of equity financing. It is the minimum rate of return that the firm must achieve for its shareholders to keep the latter whole, so to speak. The nature of this cost can be illustrated with the aid of a few stylized illustrations.

Suppose the ABC Corporation sold newly issued common-stock certificates to investors, with the implied or explicitly stated promise (made by way of an accompanying prospectus) to pay holders of the certificates an annual cash dividend of $6 per share for the indefinite future. For the moment it is convenient to assume that this dividend exhausts the firm's net after-tax income, that is, that the firm does not retain any income at all. If investors could earn an annual rate of return of, say, 10 percent on relatively safe corporate or government bonds, they probably would require an expected annual rate of return of at least 15 percent against ABC Corporation's common-stock certificates. Thus, they would pay ABC $40 at most for such a certificate, since an annual return of $6 is exactly 15 percent of $40. The price of $40 per share can also be referred to as the present, discounted value of the future dividend stream, which is calculated as the sum

$$P = \frac{\$6.00}{1.15} + \frac{\$6.00}{1.15^2}$$
$$+ \frac{\$6.00}{1.15^3} + \cdots \frac{\$6.00}{1.15^n}$$
$$= \frac{\$6.00}{0.15}$$
$$= \$40.00 \qquad (3.1)$$

If management strives to live up to the promises it made when first marketing the stock issue, it must earn sufficient revenues to cover all production costs (such as wages and the cost of raw materials, energy, and other inputs), all interest on debt, and all taxes and still leave a sufficiently large residual to finance the payment of an annual cash dividend of $6 per share to shareholders. Although modern accounting rules would define the $6 as part of corporate "profits," from this firm's perspective that dividend actually can be viewed as a cost of procuring the equity funds that sustain the corporation's activities. The annual dividend is a cost of financing in this sense. It is the analogue of interest on debt. In our example this cost of equity financing can be expressed as $6 per year per $40 of equity financing, or, simply, as 15 percent per year. By contrast, if the firm had raised $40 of financing by selling newly issued bonds that pay bondholders an annual coupon-interest rate of, say, 10 percent, and if the firm faced a profit tax of 46 percent, then its annual after-tax cost of debt financing would be only $(1 - 0.46)(0.10)\$40 = \$2.16$ per $40 of debt financing, or 5.4 percent per year. Clearly, then, from the firm's point of view, the cost of debt financing would be much lower than the cost of equity financing. On an after-tax basis it would be only about one-third as high (precisely the opposite of the erroneous conclusion reached in Chapter 3 in connection with the financing of Humana, Inc.).

What would happen if the hypothetical ABC Corporation ultimately failed to deliver the promised dividend of $6 per share? Could it do so with impunity? Suppose, for example, that shortly after the sale of the new stock issue an apologetic management of the ABC Corporation issued a revised dividend forecast of only $4.50 per share for the indefinite future. Under the revised forecast, investors seeking to earn at least 15 percent per year on investments of this kind would then pay only $30 per share of the company's stock. Investors who originally bought the stock at $40 per share would suffer a capital loss of $10 per share upon reselling the shares. If they held on to the stock, they would be earning, ex post, only $4.50 or 11.25 percent per year on their original investment of $40 per share.

It may be interjected at this point that the

relative cheapness of equity financing lies precisely in management's ability to breach with impunity—that is, without the threat of legal sanction—the implicit promises made when stock was originally sold. While the original investors' opportunity and desired risk premium may well have been 15 percent, it may be argued, the firm's cost of equity financing ex post was only 11.25 percent. In fact, if management had wished to do so, it could have reduced ABC Corporation's cost of equity financing to zero simply by paying no dividends at all. How valid is that argument?

If the persons active in the financial markets had no memory at all, a strategy of optimistic projections and dismal performance ex post might, indeed, lower a corporation's cost of equity financing permanently. The financial markets, alas, do have a memory. In the present example, the firm obviously could sell additional shares of stock only at $30 per share, and perhaps not even at that much lower a price. Having been disappointed once, investors would be apt to increase the risk premium demanded on investments in ABC stock. Their minimum required rate of return might be revised upward from 15 percent to, say, 17 percent per year. Where previously investors were willing to pay the firm $6.67 per dollar of projected dividend ($1/0.15), they would now be willing to pay only $5.88 ($1/0.17), or $26.47 for a share promising a dividend of $4.50 per year. Shareholders suffering the implied capital loss might be disappointed enough to support any proxy fight seeking to oust the incumbent management. In short, while a firm does have the legal leeway to reduce its cost of equity financing ex post once or twice, this is not a viable, long-run strategy of financial management.

So far it has been assumed that the ABC Corporation pays out all of the firm's net income in dividends. What if the firm retained some of these earnings? Would that constitute a costless source of funds from its point of view?

Suppose, specifically, that in 1985 the firm's board of directors decided not to pay any dividend and to retain the entire $6 of earnings per share in the firm's activities. The firm's shareholders might go along with that decision if they were promised additional dividends in the future. Abstracting from the taxation of dividends, it can be shown that management

would keep the shareholders whole—that is, it would maintain the market price per share— if the earnings retained in the firm were invested in assets yielding an annual return of at least 15 percent. In other words, responsibly used, a firm's retained earnings are not a costless source of funds. In principle such earnings belong to shareholders. If they are retained in the firm, shareholders bear opportunity costs—the returns they could have achieved had the retained earnings been paid to them in the form of dividends and had these dividend proceeds then been reinvested elsewhere. Although the taxation of dividends and the cost of issuing new stock certificates complicates matters somewhat in practice, at this level of the discussion it is best to think of the cost of a firm's retained earnings as equivalent to the cost of equity financing procured by the sale of new stock certificates.

All of the preceding illustrations have assumed flat annual dividends of either $6 or $4.50 in perpetuity. In reality such a projection would be rare. More typically, corporations project and potential investors assume that dividends per share will grow over time. ABC Corporation had led investors to expect not a flat annual cash dividend of $6, but a dividend stream growing at a steady annual growth rate of, say, 5 percent, with the first dividend payable one year hence projected at $4 per share. In this case potential investors would expect a dividend of $4.20 in the second year, $4.41 in the third, $4.63 in the fourth, and so on. The maximum price they would pay for one share of stock would, as before, be calculated as the present, discounted value of this perpetually growing dividend stream. If investors sought, as before, to earn an annual rate of return of 15 percent on their investment in this stock, then the present value of the projected perpetually growing dividend stream can be shown to reduce to the simple expression

$$P = \frac{\$4}{0.15 - 0.05}$$
$$= \$40 \qquad (3.2)$$

As before, the firm's after-tax cost of equity capital would be 15 percent. By itself the change in the time path of future cash dividends would not alter the firm's cost of equity capital (unless, of course, the change affected the risk potential that investors attribute to the stock and thus the risk premium that they demand of investments in that stock).

The model of the perpetually growing projected dividend stream can be used to illustrate the role of growth in the valuation of common stock. Let $P$ denote the current market price paid at the end of the current period, $D$ the dividend per share expected to be paid at the end of the current period, $g$ the growth rate per period in dividends per share, and $r$ the minimum rate of return investors consider acceptable for this type of investment. Then, as before, we can express the current market price per share of the stock as

$$P = \frac{D}{r - g} \qquad (3.3)$$

Suppose one knew the current market price $(P)$, the first-period dividend $(D)$, and the required rate of return $(r)$. Then one could solve this expression for the expected growth rate $(g)$ implicit in these numbers as follows:

$$g = r - \frac{D}{P} \qquad (3.4)$$

It has been shown in Chapter 3 that in 1984 Humana, Inc., paid its shareholders a dividend yield $(D/P)$ of 2 percent per year. If one assumes that investors in Humana stock will wish to earn an annual rate of return of at least 15 percent then, according to the model, they must be expecting annual dividends per share to grow at a rate of at least $(r - D/P)$ or $(0.15 - 0.02) = 0.13$ or 13 percent per year. Although the constant, perpetual-growth model used in this illustration may be only an approximation of the algorithm actually used by investors to value Humana stock, the general proposition implicit in the illustration is nevertheless valid: A corporation's shareholders will accept a low current dividend yield only if they are convinced that dividends per share will grow commensurately rapidly in the future. This proposition does not imply that an investor-owned hospital chain must pursue a high-growth policy to survive in the financial markets. Such a firm could, after all, adopt a policy of low growth and high-dividend yield. But it does mean that a hospital chain with a low current dividend yield clearly has committed itself to a high-growth strategy. This conclusion is the basis for the quite valid observation that the nation's investor-owned hospital chains appear to be driven by the imperative of growth in earnings per share.

Finally, it may be thought that the preceding conclusions were forced by the highly unrealistic assumption that investors evaluate investments in common stock on an infinite investment horizon. Most investments in stock, it may be argued, are made in contemplation of the finite investment horizon of a few years, in which case it is not the expected future dividends but the expected future capital gains from a resale of the stock that drive its current market value. Would a finite investment horizon alter the insights illustrated above? They would not.

Suppose, for the sake of simplicity, that a potential investor in ABC Corporation stock had an investment horizon of one year. If $P_1$ were the price per share at which the investor now expects to be able to resell the stock one year hence, $D$ the expected first-year dividend, and $r$ the rate of return the investor wishes to earn on this investment, then the current market price $(P_0)$ that investor would be willing to pay per share of the stock would be

$$P_0 = \frac{P_1 + D}{1 + r} \qquad (3.5)$$

How would investors formulate their expectation of the future resale price $P_1$? Presumably, they would put themselves into the shoes of investors who would contemplate purchasing the stock one year hence. The latter could be expected to follow the same algorithm currently being followed by investors, with all of the variables pushed one year further into the future. By simple extension, an entire succession of such investors would eventually convert the finite-horizon model into one with an infinite stream of future dividends. In other words, the current market price of a common stock can be viewed as ultimately nothing more than the discounted present value of an infinite future dividend stream.

The one-period model can also be used to illustrate the interplay between dividend yield and capital gains. From the expression for the current price per share $(P_0)$ we can obtain the following expression for the investor's expected annual rate of return:

$$r = \frac{D + (P_1 - P_0)}{P_0}$$

$$= \underbrace{\frac{D}{P_0}}_{\substack{dividend \\ yield}} + \underbrace{\frac{(P_1 - P_0)}{P_0}}_{\substack{capital \\ gain}} \qquad (3.6)$$

Clearly, this expected rate of return is merely the sum of the expected dividend yield and the expected capital gain from the investment in the stock. The two forms of return are substitutes for one another. The expected capital gain, however, is strictly a function of expected future dividends, as mentioned above. If there is to be a capital gain, future dividends per share must be expected to grow, which is, of course, a repetition of our earlier proposition that a corporation paying only a modest current dividend yield has implicitly committed itself to a high-growth strategy, and failure to achieve ultimately the appropriate growth rate will disappoint shareholders.

These insights may be used to reexamine the previously cited (p. 61) assertion that an investor-owned hospital chain could easily translate $1 million of current annual earnings into $25 million of additional financing, while a not-for-profit hospital could leverage such an earnings figure into at most $2 million of additional financing. Such a statement betrays either ignorance of financial markets or, if it were valid, an astounding ignorance among analysts in the financial markets.

In the illustration cited earlier, the $25 million of additional financing would consist of $12 million additional debt, $12 million procured by issuing additional common-stock certificates, and $1 million of retained earnings, the assumption being that not a penny of the $1 million in earnings would be paid out in dividends. Presumably, the suppliers of these funds would expect the usual "rentals" in return for parting with their money. These "rentals" would consist of the annual coupon interest on the new debt and the returns (dividend yield and capital gains) that would have to be achieved for the suppliers of the additional $13 million in equity capital.

If the hospital chain's pretax cost of the debt financing were, say, 12 percent per year, then on an after-tax basis the $12 million additional debt would imply additional coupon interest of $1.44 million. Additional pretax net income would have to be available to finance this expense. Furthermore, at some fixed date in the future, the $12 million of debt would have to be repaid. That repayment would not be a charge against income, but the cash would have to be available at the date of maturity.[1]

In addition to the extra net income that would be required to service the $12 million of additional debt, additional future earnings would be required to compensate the suppliers of the additional $13 million in equity financing. If we assume that the hospital chain's shareholders would be satisfied with a relatively modest annual rate of return of 15 percent of their funds, then the firm would have to achieve additional after-tax earnings of $1.95 million per year to keep shareholders whole. To provide that level of return through dividends would require pretax earnings of $3.61 million, if the chain's profit tax rate were 46 percent. (If it were intended to provide the return mainly through capital gains, then future dividends would have to be commensurately higher.)

Altogether, then, the additional $25 million in financing would require additional annual pretax net income of about $5.7 million per year or an after-tax net income of close to $3 million per year. The average profit margin (net after-tax income as a percentage of revenue) tends to be below 10 percent in the for-profit hospital industry. But even if one used a profit margin as high as 10 percent, an additional $30 million or more in extra annual revenues would have to be yielded by the additional $25 million of assets that were financed with the assumed infusion of capital. Such revenues might well be attainable with the new assets, but the hospital chain would have to convince the financial markets of such a forecast. To simply point to the additional $1 million in current earnings that have come, after all, from assets already in place and financed with funds raised earlier would never convince any financial analyst worthy of that title. Furthermore, if a not-for-profit chain could convince financial analysts that it, too, could translate an additional $25 million of capital into additional annual net profits of $5.7 million or so, then that not-for-profit chain, too, would be able to procure much more than the alleged $2 million in the financial markets. In short, the spokesman for the investor-owned hospital industry quoted in Chapter 3 errs rather remarkably with his illustration. He has succumbed to the myth of price-earnings-ratio magic. The nation's financial markets are not perfect, but they are surely not as gullible as that spokesman seems to surmise.

The major conclusions from this discussion of equity financing may be distilled into the following propositions:

1. From the perspective of the firm as an entity, equity financing is just another source of financing requiring the firm to earn sufficient revenues to reward the suppliers of such funds for parting with their money.

2. The reward the firm must offer the suppliers of equity funds must be sufficiently high to compensate the suppliers for the opportunity cost of parting with their funds and for the risk they assume by accepting the relative uncertain stream of rewards implicit in common-stock certificates. This minimally required level of reward is the firm's cost of equity capital.

3. Because of the uncertainty inherent in the rewards to holders of common stock, the cost of that financing typically is much higher than the cost of debt financing, at least at normal debt-to-equity ratios.

4. From the firm's perspective, the major advantage of equity financing lies in the flexibility it offers management to phase the reward stream paid to shareholders over time. Under a debt contract the reward stream is rigidly fixed and legally enforceable. Under the common-stock contract the firm (with the approval of its board of directors) can trade off reward payments at one time for higher reward payments later on.

5. In an environment dominated by institutional investors in the role of shareholders, a firm's management cannot breach with impunity the promises made explicitly or implicitly to shareholders.

6. In conducting their affairs many investor-owned hospital chains appear to have chosen low current dividend yields in exchange for an implicit promise of rapid growth in future earnings per share and dividends. Com-

panies could, for example, pay dividends that approximate prevailing interest rates. This growth imperative is a deliberate managerial choice, but not, in principle, a necessary condition for survival in the for-profit hospital market.

7. The much vaunted ability of investor-owned chains to parlay current earnings into high multiples of additional financing is an exaggeration based on a misperception of the financial community.

There is the added insight that the "profits" reported by investor-owned business firms tend to be widely misunderstood. To illustrate this point, let us assume that a corporation has assets of $1 billion, that $400 million of these assets have been financed with debt at an average pretax interest rate of 12 percent per year, and that the rest of the financing has come from shareholders through original contributions of funds or through retained earnings. If that firm earned an average of $0.25 of pretax net operating income for every dollar of assets it deploys, then its income statement for a given year could be cast as that shown in Table 3-A.1

From the firm's net operating income of $250 million, there would be deducted, first, its annual coupon interest of $48 million. The remainder would be the firm's taxable income. If the firm did not avail itself of any tax loop-

**TABLE 3-A.1**  Income Statement for a Hypothetical Business Corporation, Fiscal Year 19xx (millions of dollars)

| | |
|---|---:|
| Sales revenue | $ 1,250. |
|    Less operating expenses | (1,000.) |
| Equals operating profit | $  250. |
|    Less interest on debt (12% on     $400) | (  48.) |
| Equals taxable net income | $  202. |
|    Less income taxes (46%) | (  93.) |
| Equals net income available to     shareholders[a] | $  109. |
|    Less costs of equity financing     (15% of $600) | (  90.) |
| Equals profit[b] | $   19. |

[a]The accountant's definition of "profits."
[b]The economist's definition of "profits."

holes or deferrals, and if it faced a profit tax rate of 46 percent, its after-tax net income would be $109 million. This amount would be available for distribution to shareholders or retention in the firm on behalf of shareholders. Under modern accounting practices the entire $109 million would be reported as the firm's "profits."

In textbooks and writings, economists differ sharply with accountants on this point. As is shown in Table 3-A.1, economists would define "profits" as the residual after deduction of the cost of equity capital from reported book profits. If it is assumed, as before, that shareholders minimally require a rate of return of 15 percent per year on funds entrusted to the firm under the common-stock contract, then the economists measure of "profits" would be only $19 million, not $109 million. In other words, economists define as profits only the windfall gain over and above the shareholders' required return. The latter—$90 million in the present example—is treated simply as part of the firm's cost of doing business.

## NOTE

[1]At the conceptual level, one can visualize the required accumulation of cash as follows. Presumably the firm used the additional $12 million of debt financing to acquire $12 million of income-yielding assets. To calculate the income from these assets, the firm would annually deduct an allowed depreciation expense based on the value of the underlying assets. The annual depreciation expense would not require a cash outlay in the year for which it is recognized. Rather, one can think of this expense as a form of earmarking cash revenues either for replacing the underlying assets when they are worn out or for repaying the debt that financed them. In other words, we imagine the firm to have deposited the cash revenues "earmarked" through depreciation expense in a fund designated for the repayment of debt. That repayment, then, will not be a further charge against future income. It was charged to income over time in the form of depreciation expense.

# 4 Investor Ownership and the Costs of Medical Care

What is the effect of investor ownership on health care costs? Some observers believe that the rise in investor-owned health care organizations exacerbates the cost problem—that investor-owned organizations will exploit inadequacies in whatever system is used to pay for care; that cost increases will result from the need to attain consistent earnings growth to maintain the price of their stock; and that it is costly to pay dividends, taxes, and the salaries that business executives expect from the revenues they generate.

Others, however, expect investor ownership to help alleviate the cost problem, particularly if payment systems reward restraints on expenses. Several factors are cited: the motivation and clarity of purpose that come with the for-profit form; economies of scale that result from multi-institutional arrangements; flexibility of the corporate form that permits rapid response to changing conditions; advantages in developing a repository of managerial skills because greater financial incentives and more extensive career paths can be offered; and cost advantages that can flow from careful decisions regarding markets to be targeted (location, services offered, types of patients sought). (See the Appendix to Chapter 1 for a summary of economic theories about the behavior of for-profit and not-for-profit organizations.)

The contradictory speculations indicate a need to define different types of cost, to identify the nature of various parties' concerns about cost, and to examine the available evidence.

This chapter defines different types of cost and reviews evidence on ownership-related differences in hospital costs. The impact on the cost of acquisition of hospitals by for-profit chains is discussed next, followed by a review of what is known about cost differences that relate to the ownership of other types of health care facilities, such as nursing homes and freestanding ambulatory care centers. The chapter closes with the committee's conclusions.

## DEFINITION AND MEASUREMENT OF COSTS—AND WHO IS CONCERNED

Costs can be categorized according to who incurs them. First, providers of health care incur operating costs—including capital costs—in producing goods or services. They purchase resources, including plant and equipment. They also incur costs for the supplies and personnel required to provide patient care. For purposes of clarity we will call these costs "expenses."

Second, the purchasers of health care pay a price for the care they buy. For some payers this price is based on the hospital's charges (or a discount therefrom); for some, the price is based on reimbursement for allowable expenses incurred. In either case the price

74

paid becomes cost to purchasers and revenue to providers. We will call costs to the purchasers of health care "price."

Accordingly, two types of questions arise regarding cost and type of ownership. The first is concerned with ownership-related differences in expenses per unit of output. The second is concerned with ownership-related differences in the price that purchasers pay for similar services.

The two questions are of interest to different groups. Economists, who are concerned with efficiency, are interested in the relationship of ownership type to expense per unit of output. Some theorize that the not-for-profit organization's prohibition on distribution of profits leads to an emphasis on other goals, which are not conducive to efficient operations. For example, it is argued that administrators of not-for-profit hospitals seek added prestige for their hospitals by increasing the range of services, equipment, and personnel, which results in an expansion of services without adequate regard for their need or likely use (Lee, 1971). It is commonly believed that the economic discipline that is assumed to accompany the more singular purpose of for-profit organizations helps them to avoid such pitfalls and, hence, to operate more efficiently.

Purchasers of care are more interested in price than in productive efficiency, especially since the move away from cost-based reimbursement by Medicare and most Blue Cross plans. Questions of relative efficiency are of little interest unless they translate into lower prices. Until recently, charge-paying purchasers have been generally inattentive to price differences among hospitals, in part because higher hospital prices could be passed along in higher premiums and because patients and the physicians who ordered services were substantially insulated from price differences because of third-party payments. Thus, keeping strict control of expenses was often not a necessity for hospitals. This picture is of course changing rapidly. Medicare's prospective payment system

and the emergence of much more price competition are putting pressure on both expenses and price. Providers who can offer services for lower prices now stand to gain market share. Questions of quality will likely become more salient.

Measurement and comparisons of hospital expenses and revenues are complicated by hospitals' being "multiproduct firms." A firm with one standard product devotes all expenses to the production of that product, making it relatively simple to calculate the cost per item. But hospitals have numerous "products," including many types of inpatient services, outpatient services, ancillary services, and, at some hospitals, educational and nonpatient care services. Even if the discussion is limited to inpatient services, these can be measured as admissions, days of care, and caring for patients with specific diagnoses. Comparisons remain difficult even after a unit of comparison has been selected. For instance, a day of care in one hospital may differ from a day of care in another hospital in terms of services provided and their frequency and quality. Severity of illness of patients with the same diagnosis can vary widely. Another problem is that calculations of expense per unit of output are influenced by the method used to allocate indirect costs (such as administration, laundry, capital costs, etc.) to revenue departments.[1] Although payers who paid on the basis of incurred costs all specified indirect cost-allocation methods, there nevertheless was considerable leeway for hospital managers to manipulate allocation to maximize revenues. In addition, if a hospital was part of a multi-institutional system, some indirect expenses could be allocated either to a hospital or to other entities (such as the home office), depending on the incentives in reimbursement rules. Thus, several variations in cost-allocation processes can make expense comparisons among institutions imprecise, even for a well-defined service such as a brain scan.

Price comparisons are further complicated by differences in the extent to which hospitals provide uncompensated care. Although cost-based purchasers pay on the basis of expenses incurred in the care of their covered patients, others pay what the hospital charges. Such charges must be set at a level that covers the institutions' expenses in caring for patients who either pay less than their share of expenses or pay nothing. Thus the price for charge payers and certain cost payers includes a subsidy to patients who cannot or do not pay for the full costs of their care.[2] Differences among institutions in the amounts of uncompensated care that they provide are thus likely to affect their charges, unless the institution has access to nonpatient care revenues with which to subsidize uncompensated care. For those concerned with the price of care for particular groups—for instance, a privately insured employee group—such price and cost shifting and resultant price differences are important.

Finally, it is important to recognize that all available studies are of hospitals operating under economic incentives and constraints that existed prior to the introduction of Medicare prospective payment.[3] Although these studies describe expenses, prices, and margins under one set of incentives, comparative data are not yet available to indicate how different types of hospitals have responded to the new incentives. However, early data show that growth in hospital expenses has slowed significantly.

## STUDIES OF HOSPITAL EXPENSE AND PRICING

Many studies examine the relationship between type of hospital ownership and expenses, prices, and profitability. The committee focused on recent studies that examine investor-owned chain hospitals, rather than for-profit hospitals in general. The ideal comparisons of independent and chain hospitals, both for-profit and not-for-profit, are not always possible from available data and

published studies. Only such data would allow differences due to ownership type to be distinguished clearly from differences associated with membership in a multi-institutional system.

Few available studies compare the two types of systems. However, the authors of one national study that did make this comparison note, "The clear pattern that emerges from the study is that in 1980 there were much greater similarities among hospitals of the same ownership type (for-profit or not-for-profit) than among hospitals of the same organizational type (multi-hospital system or freestanding) . . . . Clearly in 1980 the strategies and performance of for-profit and not-for-profit multi-hospital system hospitals had not converged as some observers believe they have today" (Watt et al., 1986a).

### Expenses

According to popular belief and economic theory (see the Appendix to Chapter 1), for-profit organizations produce services less expensively. Indeed, the assumed expense disadvantage of not-for-profit hospitals has prompted serious doubt about public policies that are believed to encourage the not-for-profit mode (Clark, 1980). Studies examined by the committee show the postulated for-profit advantage in expenses to be a myth.

Table 4.1 summarizes eight studies that analyzed hospital expenses as they relate to ownership. The methods, data sources and dates, and geographic scope of the studies varied considerably. As might be expected, therefore, results were not entirely consistent; however, the weight of the evidence and the overall direction is clear: not-for-profit hospitals controlled their expenses more effectively than did for-profit hospitals of the same general size. (All studies excluded large teaching hospitals from their analyses.)

Five of the studies compared the expenses per day in for-profit and not-for-profit hospitals, making more or less rigorous attempts to control for institutional size and geographic location. On this measure, for-profit chain hospitals had higher expenses than not-for-profit hospitals in four of the five studies. The range was from 3 percent lower in a Florida study to 10 percent higher in a national study. In another national study the difference was not statistically significant.

Seven of the studies compared expenses per case (sometimes measured as "per admission" or "per discharge." For-profit hospitals' expenses were again found to be higher than not-for-profit hospitals in six of the seven studies. The range was from 4 percent lower (again in the Florida study) to 8 percent higher in one of the two national studies. On this measure, the differences were not statistically significant in two of the seven studies; however, the two studies with the largest number of observations found for-profits to have statistically significant higher costs. Studies that examined both per-day and per-case expenses generally found the not-for-profit advantage to be larger on the former measure, largely because of shorter average lengths of stay in for-profit hospitals.[4]

The pattern of differences in expenses notwithstanding, two studies—one national (1974-1980) and one in California (1977-1981)—showed no major difference in the average annual rate of increase in expenses per discharge between for-profit chain hospitals and not-for-profit hospitals (Coelen, 1986; Pattison, 1986). During this period of rising hospital expenses, for-profit chain hospitals constrained expenses no better and no worse than not-for-profit hospitals.[5]

One reason for the for-profits' expense disadvantage can be found in rates of occupancy. Unit expenses (expenses per case or per day) are affected by the hospital's occupancy rates, owing to the number of cases to which fixed expenses must be allocated. In 1983, when overall hospital occupancy was 73 percent, for-profit chain and for-profit independent hospitals had occu-

pancy rates of 62 and 64 percent, respectively, lower than the 74 and 75 percent occupancy rates of not-for-profit chain and independent hospitals (Peter Kralovec, Hospital Data Center, American Hospital Association, 1985, unpublished data).[6]

One study estimated that each additional percentage point of occupancy reduces operating expenses by $2.00 per case, total patient care expenses by about $2.50 per case, and general and administrative expenses by about $3.00 per case (Watt et al., 1986b). Thus, according to this study the 1983 12-percent difference in average occupancy rate between for-profit and not-for-profit chain hospitals accounts for $25.56 in operating expenses per case. This represents only 1.5 percent of the $1,712.88 average operating expenses per case in for-profit chain hospitals. However, it accounts for almost one-third of the $78.72 difference in average operating expenses per case between for-profit chain and not-for-profit chain hospitals.

Because of the large size of for-profit chain hospital organizations, economies of scale might be expected to occur in some areas. Investor-owned hospitals might be expected to have lower administrative expenses because of their profit orientation and their economies of scale. But both national and California data show that investor-owned hospitals operate with higher administrative expenses than their not-for-profit counterparts (Pattison and Katz, 1983; Pattison, 1986; Watt et al., 1986a). Earlier caveats concerning different ways of allocating overhead costs in hospitals are particularly applicable to chain organizations. Such organizations have some flexibility in spreading corporate overhead expenses across hospitals. Under cost-based reimbursement it was advantageous to allocate as many expenses as were allowable to the central office so that they could be reallocated to the hospitals with the greatest Medicare loads. These costs became the prices to government payers.

**TABLE 4.1** Summary of Study Findings Concerning Hospital Expenses

| Study | Controls | Data Sources | Measure | Findings |
|---|---|---|---|---|
| Lewin et al. (1981) | 53 matched pairs of hospitals | 1978 Medicare Cost Reports, California, Florida, Texas | Total operating cost per adjusted patient day and total inpatient care cost per inpatient day | For-profit chain hospitals 8 percent higher than independent not-for-profit hospitals |
| | | | Inpatient care costs per admission | No significant difference |
| Sloan and Vraciu (1983) | Included only nonteaching hospitals under 400 beds | Data reported to Florida Hospital Cost Containment Board | Operating expenses per adjusted day | For-profit chain hospitals 3 percent lower than not-for-profit hospitals[a] |
| | | | Operating expenses per adjusted admission | For-profit chain hospitals 4 percent lower than not-for-profit hospitals[a] |
| Pattison and Katz (1983) | Large teaching, Kaiser, rural, specialty and tertiary care hospitals excluded; proxy case-mix measure used | 280 hospitals in California; data reported to the California Health Facilities Commission, 1980 | Total operating expenses per patient day | For-profit chain hospitals 6 percent higher than private not-for-profit hospitals |
| | | | Operating expenses per admission | For-profit chain hospitals 2 percent higher than private not-for-profit hospitals |
| Becker and Sloan (1985) | Numerous controls including case mix, teaching status, size, area characteristics; regression analysis | 2,231 community hospitals; AHA Reimbursement Survey & Annual Survey of Hospitals, 1979 | Cost per adjusted patient day | For-profit chain hospitals 10 percent higher than chain not-for-profit hospitals |
| | | | Cost per adjusted admission | For-profit chain hospitals 8 percent higher than chain not-for-profit hospitals |

| Study | Comments | Data source | Measure | Findings |
|---|---|---|---|---|
| Pattison (1986) | Included only short-term 76- to 230-bed hospitals | Over 230 hospitals in California; data reported to the California Health Facilities Commission, 1977-1978, 1979-1980, 1981-1982 | Operating expenses per adjusted discharge | For-profit chain hospitals 4-7 percent higher than voluntary hospitals (1977-1981) |
| Watt et al. (1986a) | 80 matched pairs of hospitals, adjusted for case-mix differences | Medicare Cost Reports, 1980 AHA Annual Survey of Hospitals | Cost per adjusted admission and cost per adjusted day (including capital and education costs) | For-profit chain hospitals higher than not-for-profit hospitals, but difference not statistically significant |
| Watt et al. (1986b) | Regression analyses, length of chain affiliation, competition and regulation, case mix, input costs, capacity, utilization, medical education | 561 general acute care hospitals, 1980 Medicare Cost Reports, AHA Annual Survey of Hospitals, and other sources | Total operating and patient care expenses per case | For-profit chain hospitals higher than the not-for-profit chain hospitals, but the difference not statistically significant |
| Coelen (1986) | Regression analysis, geographic location, bed size, case mix | Medicare Cost Reports, AHA Annual Surveys, and others, 1975-1981 | Total expenses per adjusted discharge | For-profit chain hospitals 4 percent higher than not-for-profit chain hospitals; independent for-profit lowest; differences statistically significant |

[a] The findings of lower expenses in for-profit chain than in not-for-profit hospitals in Florida were confirmed by Lewin et al. (1983).

Economies of scale resulting from bulk purchasing might also be expected to lower expenses of investor-owned chains for drugs and supplies. However, Watt et al. (1986a) found higher aggregate expenses for drugs and supplies sold to patients in for-profit chain hospitals than in not-for-profit hospitals on a per-day basis. If savings in the purchase price had been realized there, they were absorbed by the use of more chargeable items per day in for-profit than not-for-profit hospitals (Pattison and Katz, 1983).

Personnel constitute a major hospital expense. Data from studies of 1978 and 1980 showed that for-profit chain hospitals employed fewer full-time equivalent staff per adjusted average daily census than did not-for-profit hospitals.[7] However, the for-profit hospitals paid higher salaries and benefits per employee, which largely eroded any difference that might have shown up in lower total personnel expenses (Watt et al., 1986a).[8]

Capital costs are incurred in the purchase, construction, and improvement of plant and the purchase of major equipment. For-profit chain hospitals operated with significantly higher capital costs relative to operating costs than did not-for-profit hospitals (Anderson and Ginsberg, 1983; Watt et al., 1986a,b). This is due in part to the younger accounting age of for-profit chain facilities than not-for-profit facilities, but it is not known how much accounting age reflects the newer facilities or the timing of acquisitions. Nor is it known how much capital costs reflect the cost of acquisitions rather than expenditures to improve plant or equipment. Also not known is the extent to which acquisitions represent the rescue of hospitals in danger of closure or needing renovation and the extent to which construction represents the addition of unnecessary capacity.

### Prices

How do the prices paid by purchasers of care compare at for-profit and not-for-profit hospitals? Studies have examined two aspects of price—overall price to payers and strategies used by hospitals, such as markup and patient selection.

Table 4.2 arrays six studies of price differentials between for-profit chain hospitals and not-for-profit hospitals. The studies consistently found that prices of for-profit chain hospitals were substantially higher than the prices of not-for-profit hospitals—chain or independent. The price-per-day differential for charge payers ranged from 23 to 29 percent higher in for-profit chain than not-for-profit hospitals; for cost payers, from 11 to 13 percent. Although smaller, the per-case differential was still substantial, ranging from 17 to 24 percent for charge payers and from 8 to 15 percent for cost payers such as Medicare. Across both types of payers the differences in the average price realized by the hospitals (net patient revenues) ranged from 12 to 14 percent; when measured per admission, to about 17 percent on a per-day basis. Because investor-owned companies own less than 10 percent of the nation's hospital beds, these differences in price are the equivalent of less than half of one percent of the nation's hospital cost.[9]

It can be argued that the price paid by a community for hospital care should include nonoperating revenues provided to not-for-profit (and public) hospitals from philanthropy and grants, and that adjustments should be made for the net difference between tax subsidies to not-for-profit hospitals and taxes paid by the for-profits. Philanthropy and grants can be viewed as a price paid by the community for care and, thus, as an economic cost to the community. It can also be argued that tax payments are returned to public coffers and therefore represent a reduction in net price to the community. Several studies attempted to make these complex adjustments (Table 4.3).

All of the studies began with net patient service revenue—the average price measure described above—and made additional adjustments. Lewin et al. (1981), using 1978 data, removed an estimated income tax figure from the for-profit hospitals' average. Sloan and Vraciu (1983) performed the same adjustment using different data that included a more explicit measure of taxes (but not a higher income tax rate). Finally, Watt et al. (1986a) widened the adjustment to standardize for differences in public subsidies and contributions received by not-for-profit hospitals in 1980. Sloan and Vraciu's results from Florida, which show little remaining price difference after removing taxes, stand in contrast to the other two studies, which cover more states and show a residual difference of about 10 percent. While the latter difference is large, the authors were unable to estimate its statistical significance. Watt et al. (1986a) point out that taxes paid by the for-profit group accounted for less than half the difference in price per day between the for-profit and not-for-profit hospitals.

These calculations of "community" cost have been criticized on the grounds that taxes accrued to the nation, not to the local community, and that only a small portion of tax money is spent on health. Furthermore, the studies measured accrued, not paid, taxes. For growing organizations, taxes paid are lower than taxes accrued (see Chapter 3; see also Lewin et al., 1983; Conger, 1983). Finally, the studies make no adjustments for differences between types of hospitals in the costs of capital, especially the subsidy represented by greater access to tax-exempt bonds by not-for-profit hospitals.

The studies reviewed to this point have used average hospital revenues per case as a measure of price. A small study by Blue Cross/Blue Shield of North Carolina (1983) took a different approach. This study compared payment claims of six for-profit chain hospitals with similar-sized not-for-profit hospitals for three frequently performed procedures (hysterectomy, cholecystectomy, and normal deliveries) in 1981 and 1982. Charges at for-profit chain hospitals were higher (ranging from 6 to 58 percent) than those at not-for-profit hospitals, with the exception of one for-profit chain hospital's charges for normal deliveries—which were 10 percent lower than the comparison hospital's. Comparison of the for-profit chain hospitals with other hospitals in the same communities showed a near-perfect pattern of higher charges by the former.

**MARKUP**

Given the findings of equal or higher expenses and considerably higher prices in for-profit chain hospitals, there is likely to be a difference in the markup by hospitals of different ownership types. The most visible component of hospital price is routine daily service—the basic room rate. Because this component is likely to be the most price sensitive, many hospitals try to keep routine service prices close to expenses, or even accept a loss, recouping profits on ancillary services—for which demand is generated once the patient is in the hospital (e.g., diagnostic tests). This strategy appears to have been pursued more vigorously by for-profit than not-for-profit hospitals, although it is followed by both.

Four studies using data from different sources and years all show that routine daily room services were priced at or below expenses by all types of hospitals (Lewin et al., 1981; Watt et al., 1986a; Pattison and Katz, 1983; State of Florida Hospital Cost Containment Board, 1984).[10] However, ancillary services appeared to be marked up to be highly profitable. In Florida in 1982, the markup for ancillary services at for-profit hospitals was 121 percent; at state hospitals, 88 percent; and at not-for-profit hospitals, 74 percent (State of Florida Hospital Cost Containment Board, 1984). California data indicate that all ownership types earned income on clinical laboratories, central service and supplies, pharmacy, and inhalation therapy, but in each case for-profit chain hospitals made a greater profit than not-for-profit or public hospitals (Pattison and Katz,

82

**TABLE 4.2** Summary of Study Findings Concerning Hospital Price

| Study | Controls | Data Sources | Measure | Findings |
|---|---|---|---|---|
| Lewin et al. (1981) | 53 matched pairs of hospitals | 1978 Medicare Cost Reports, California, Florida, Texas | Price per inpatient day for charge payers (total inpatient charges per patient day) | For-profit chain hospitals 23 percent higher than not-for-profit hospitals |
| | | | Price per inpatient admission for charge payers | For-profit chain hospitals 17 percent higher than not-for-profit hospitals |
| | | | Price per inpatient day for cost payers (inpatient allowable costs, plus return on equity for for-profit hospitals) | For-profit chain hospitals 13 percent higher than not-for-profit hospitals |
| | | | Price per admission for cost payers | For-profit chain hospitals 8 percent higher than not-for-profit hospitals |
| Pattison and Katz (1983) | Large teaching, rural, specialty, Kaiser, and tertiary care hospitals excluded | 280 hospitals in California; data reported to the California Health Facilities Commission, 1980 | Total inpatient charges per patient day | For-profit chain hospitals 29 percent higher than not-for-profit hospitals |
| | | | Total inpatient charges per admission | For-profit chain hospitals 24 percent higher than not-for-profit hospitals |
| Pattison (1986) | Included only short-term 76- to 230-bed hospitals | Over 230 hospitals in California; data reported to the California Health Facilities Commission, 1977-1978, 1979-1980, 1981-1982 | Gross patient charges per adjusted discharge (equivalent to inpatient charges per patient admission) | For-profit chain hospitals 18-23 percent higher than not-for-profits in 1977-1981 period |
| | | | Net patient revenue per adjusted discharge (weighted average of prices to charge payers and price to cost payers—actual average price realized by hospital) | For-profit chain hospitals 12-14 percent higher than not-for-profits in 1977-1981 period |

| Study | Methodology | Data source | Variable | Result |
|---|---|---|---|---|
| Watt et al. (1986a) | 80 matched pairs of hospitals, adjusted for case-mix differences | Medicare Cost Reports, 1980; AHA Annual Survey of Hospitals, 1980; Office for Civil Rights Survey of Hospitals, 1980 | Price per patient day for charge payers | For-profit chain hospitals 24 percent higher than not-for-profit hospitals |
| | | | Price per inpatient admission for charge payers | For-profit chain hospitals 22 percent higher than not-for-profit hospitals |
| | | | Price per inpatient day for cost payers | For-profit chain hospitals 11 percent higher than not-for-profit hospitals |
| | | | Price per inpatient admission for cost payers | For-profit chain hospitals 8 percent higher than not-for-profit hospitals |
| | | | Net patient revenue per adjusted day | For-profit chain hospitals 17 percent higher than not-for-profit hospitals |
| Watt et al. (1986b) | Regression analyses, length of chain affiliation, competition and regulation case mix, input cost levels, capacity, utilization, medical education | 561 general acute care hospitals, 1980 Medicare Cost Reports, AHA Annual Survey, and other sources | Price per admission for charge payers (total patient care revenues per adjusted admission) | For-profit chain hospitals 21 percent higher than not-for-profit chain hospitals |
| | | | Net patient revenues per adjusted admission (weighted average of prices to charge payers and price to cost payers—actual average charges realized by hospital) | For-profit chain hospitals 12 percent higher than not-for-profit chain hospitals |
| Coelen (1986) | Regression analysis; geographic location, bed size, case mix; teaching hospitals excluded | Medicare Cost Reports, and others, 1975-1981 | Medicare charge per case | For-profit chain hospitals 15 percent higher than not-for-profit chain hospitals. |

**TABLE 4.3**  Summary of Study Findings Concerning "Net Community Cost"

| Study | Controls | Data Sources | Measure | Findings |
|---|---|---|---|---|
| Lewin et al. (1981) | 53 matched pairs of hospitals | 1978 Medicare Cost Reports, California, Florida, Texas | Net patient service revenue less taxes per adjusted day | For-profit chain hospitals 18 percent higher than not-for-profit hospitals before tax adjustment; 12 percent higher after tax adjustment[a] |
| Sloan and Vraciu (1983) | Nonteaching hospitals under 400 beds | Data reported to Florida State Cost Containment Board | Net operating funds per adjusted patient day[b] Net operating funds per adjusted admission[b] | For-profit chain hospitals 2 percent higher than not-for-profit hospitals Difference not statistically significant |
| Watt et al. (1986a) | 80 matched pairs of hospitals, adjusted for case-mix differences | Medicare Cost Reports, 1980; AHA Annual Survey of Hospitals, 1980; Office for Civil Rights Survey of Hospitals, 1980 | Net patient service revenue standardized for differences in accrued taxes, public subsidies, and contributions income, per adjusted day | For-profit hospitals 17 percent higher than not-for-profit hospitals before adjustment; 10 percent higher after adjustment[a] |

[a]Methodological difficulties in calculating the measures precluded estimation of statistical significance. The 18 percent difference in net patient revenues in the 1981 study and the 17 percent difference in the 1986 study were statistically significant ($p < .01$).

[b]Net operating funds are defined as net operating revenues (net of contractual allowances and unpaid accounts) minus income taxes.

1983). Furthermore, ancillary services that were profitable were used with greater frequency per patient day and per admission in for-profit chain hospitals than in not-for-profit hospitals. However, ancillary services that broke even or lost money were used at similar rates in for-profit chain and not-for-profit hospitals. In California, ancillary services contributed a higher proportion of total revenues in for-profit chain than in not-for-profit hospitals in 1982 (69 percent compared with 63 percent), and this differential occurred after a period of years in which hospitals of all types of ownership shifted more inpatient charges to ancillary services (Pattison, 1986). In another study that used national data, differences in pricing or use of ancillary services, or both, resulted in significant differences in ancillary service charges per case: in for-profit chains, charges were almost 34 percent higher and in not-for-profit chains, a little over 5 percent higher than independent not-for-profit hospitals (Coelen, 1986).

The studies reviewed so far measure markup on individual components of patient care. Watt et al. (1986b) took a broader measure—gross patient care markup, defined as total patient charges divided by total operating costs—and found that for-profit chain hospitals averaged 14.2 percentage points higher than not-for-profit chain hospitals.

## PROFITABILITY

Comparing the surpluses or profits of not-for-profit and for-profit hospitals is complicated by several issues: (1) whether pretax or after-tax profits should be examined for the for-profits and, if after-tax numbers are to be used, whether the pretax profits should be reduced by the amount of taxes that are accrued or by the amount actually paid (see Table 3.5); (2) whether hospitals' nonpatient care income should be included (for-profit hospitals have much less, as is discussed in Chapter 5); (3) which measure should be used (net margins, return on assets, return on equity); (4) whether per hospital numbers regarding profitability are meaningful for large companies that have diverse sources of revenues and expenses and that can allocate certain overhead expenses in many different ways; and (5) whether it is more valid to look at the comparative profitability of statistically controlled samples of hospitals or of entire sectors (for-profit and not-for-profit).

The answer to the questions of whether for-profit or not-for-profit hospitals are more or less profitable, and what the size of the difference in profitability is between the sectors, depends to some degree on how these questions are answered. Statistically controlled studies show, with one exception, that for-profit chain hospitals are more profitable than not-for-profit hospitals, regardless of whether profitability is measured before or after taxes are paid by for-profits, and whether nonpatient care revenues are excluded or included (Lewin et al., 1981; Sloan and Vraciu, 1983; Watt et al., 1986a and b; Coelen, 1986). Studies that calculate more than one measure of profitability show that the difference between for-profit and not-for-profit hospitals is largest for margin on patient care revenues. The difference for margin on total revenues is smaller owing to the higher nonpatient care revenues received by not-for-profit hospitals. The smallest difference between for-profit and not-

for-profit hospitals is in after-tax margins on total net revenues. For example, Lewin et al. (1981), looking at matched pairs of hospitals in three states, found a 9.2 percentage point difference in margin on net patient service revenues (6.5 percent for for-profit chains and $-2.7$ percent for not-for-profit hospitals). Because nonpatient care revenues added $7.60 per day to not-for-profit revenues, and only $2.48 per day to the revenues of for-profit chain hospitals, the difference in margin on total net income was reduced to 6.3 percentage points (7.6 percent compared with 1.3 percent). Finally, the after-tax margin on total net income was just 2.4 percentage points higher for the for-profit chain hospitals than the not-for-profit hospitals (3.7 percent compared with 1.3 percent). Other examples of similar findings, but of different magnitudes, include Coelen's (1986) national study, which found that the margin on patient revenue was 6.1 percentage points higher for for-profit chain hospitals than not-for-profit chain hospitals. The for-profit chain hospitals' margin on total revenue (which reflected a mixture of pretax and after-tax net income figures) was 2.4 percentage points higher. Both differences were found to be statistically significant.

A second national study, which used a random sample of hospitals and regression analysis (Watt et al., 1986b), found that for-profit chain hospitals achieved greater profitability than not-for-profit chain hospitals when measured by total markup (total revenue divided by total expense), return on assets (total net income divided by assets), and return on equity (net income divided by owner's equity or fund balance)—a difference of 12.8, 5.5, and 34 percent higher, respectively. Again, all differences were found to be statistically significant.

One study that did not find the for-profit sector to be more profitable (Sloan and Vraciu, 1983) used data from Florida hospitals in 1980. Using regression analysis to control for bed size, location, payer mix, and other factors, the authors found no statistically significant difference in after-tax margins on total revenues between Florida's for-profit chain and not-for-profit hospitals. The raw data showed not-for-profit hospitals to be slightly more profitable than for-profit hospitals.

As studies show, nonpatient care revenues and taxes paid have a substantial impact on the bottom line of both not-for-profit and for-profit hospitals. Comparing the profitability of hospitals by measures other than margin on total net (after-tax) revenues omits an important source of revenue for not-for-profit hospitals, and an important deduction from revenues of for-profit hospitals. Although for some purposes it is important to compare levels of profitability achieved through patient services, such a measure does not indicate the financial health or future viability of hospitals. Indeed, national figures indicate that the average U.S. hospital had a negative margin on patient care service until the 1980s, although this is to some degree an artifact of the tendency of many not-for-profit and public hospitals to expend any surpluses as fast as they were achieved. Positive total net margins were achieved only through the contribution of nonpatient care revenues (see Table 5.1, Chapter 5).

The studies reviewed have all used controls to try to ensure that the hospitals being compared are similar in characteristics—such as size, location, and teaching status—that are expected to affect profitability. Thus, the studies' finding that for-profit hospitals are more profitable than not-for-profit hospitals (even when margin on after-tax total net income is the measure) is based on similar not-for-profit and for-profit hospitals. But for-profit and not-for-profit hospitals are not similar in all ways. For-profit hospitals, for example, are more often located in sun-belt states, are smaller than not-for-profit hospitals, and are virtually never teaching hospitals. National, uncontrolled data that compare for-profit (chain and independent)

TABLE 4.4    Total Net Margin of U.S. Community and For-profit Acute Care General Hospitals, 1980-1984

| Year | United States | For-profit |
|------|---------------|------------|
| 1980 | 4.6 | 3.9 |
| 1981 | 4.7 | 4.4 |
| 1982 | 5.1 | 5.1 |
| 1983 | 5.1 | 4.2 |
| 1984 | 6.2 | 4.8 |

SOURCES: Office of Public Policy Analysis, American Hospital Association, Chicago, Ill.; Federation of American Hospitals, *Statistical Profile of the Investor-Owned Hospital Industry*, 1979 and 1980, 1981, 1983, and personal communication, Samuel Mitchell, Director of Research, Federation of American Hospitals, 1985. For-profit figures are after taxes.

with all U.S. community hospitals (including for-profit and not-for-profit hospitals and nonfederal public hospitals), show that the for-profit group as a whole has not been more profitable than the average U.S. hospital in terms of total net margin. Indeed, in four of the past five years, the for-profit hospitals have been less profitable; in one year, profitability was equal (see Table 4.4). Furthermore, during the period covered by the studies reviewed, for-profit hospitals and the companies that own them did not on average generate high profit margins when compared to other industries. Average profit margins for two-thirds of American industries exceeded margins for the hospital sector (The Value Line Investment Survey, 1981 and 1982, cited in Sloan and Vraciu, 1983).

In sum, the studies reviewed show that for-profit chain hospitals have been more profitable than similar not-for-profit hospitals, but not-for-profit hospitals as a group have been less profitable than the average hospital. Thus, a for-profit chain hospital of the same size, in the same location, and similar in other aspects to a not-for-profit hospital is likely to achieve higher margins. The reverse is true for the average for-profit hospital, compared with the average community hospital.

## COSTS AND ACQUISITION OF HOSPITALS

The growth of for-profit chains through acquisition (and, to a lesser extent, through construction) has led to two concerns about impact on cost. The first, particularly among third-party payers who pay charges, pertains to the for-profit sector's willingness to price "aggressively" (i.e., to charge more). The second concern stems from the capital costs associated with an acquisition, which can be passed on to charge payers, as well as to cost payers, who have included capital costs (interest, depreciation, and, for for-profits, return on equity) as a reimbursable expense under cost-based reimbursement (and currently as a "pass through" under prospective payment). Until recently, acquisitions also put in place a new and higher depreciation schedule (based on the price paid for a facility), which was reimbursed as an expense and thereby contributed important cash flow.

A General Accounting Office (GAO) report on the costs associated with Hospital Corporation of America's 1981 acquisition of Hospital Affiliates International found a first-year net capital cost increase of $55.2 million from the acquisition of the 54 Hospital Affiliates hospitals—$62.5 million from interest, $8.4 million from depreciation, minus $15.7 million in savings from a reduction in home office costs. GAO calculated Medicare cost increases at only two of the acquired hospitals, and estimated them to be nearly $600,000 in the year following acquisition (U.S. General Accounting Office, 1983).[11] The GAO report did not conclusively answer the question of the magnitude of the increase in hospital prices that results from hospital mergers and acquisitions. However, the fact that very substantial increases in reimbursable expenses could result from an acquisition, even with no change in the services being provided, led Congress to change the law that permitted an acquiring company to revalue the assets it acquired for purposes of being reimbursed for depreciation expenses under Medicare.

Three studies shed light on the changes made by new owners after an acquisition. One study grouped hospitals by length of ownership by a chain, noting that average expenses were lower in hospitals that had longer affiliations with a for-profit multihospital system than in those with a shorter affiliation. They found support for a hypothesis that companies acquire poorly managed hospitals and improve their efficiency (Becker and Sloan, 1985). Two studies conducted for the committee described some characteristics of acquired hospitals and analyzed changes in the years immediately following acquisition. Pattison (1986) studied nine California hospitals acquired by for-profit systems between fiscal years 1977-1978 and 1981-1982. The study showed evidence that the hospitals were initially in financial trouble and that the change in ownership generated some dramatic operating changes. At the beginning of the period the hospitals showed an after-tax loss of $1.38 per patient day, which was changed to a $23.70 after-tax profit per patient day about two-and-a-half years after acquisition—a profit level below that of other for-profit chain hospitals, but substantially higher than that of comparison for-profit hospitals that remained independent.

Apparently, some of the increase in profitability was achieved by initiating operating-cost efficiencies. In 1978, expenses per day were $12 higher in for-profit hospitals that were later acquired than in those hospitals that remained independent. By 1982, expenses per day were $15 lower in the acquired than in the still independent for-profit hospitals. However, occupancy showed only a slight improvement, rising from 48 to 50 percent, while inpatient charges per day rose 89 percent—only slightly more than the 86 percent increase in the unacquired for-profit hospitals. Thus, profitability improvements in the acquired hospitals evolved partly through tight control of expenses relative to charges. Capital costs per day increased from $11 to $55, partly because of additional debt, which increased from $7,800 to $57,700 per bed. This striking increase of over 600 percent should be put in context. For-profit hospitals that remained independent more than doubled their debt per bed to $24,000, while hospitals that were already part of investor-owned chains increased their debt per bed only 60 percent, to $39,000 (Pattison, 1986).

A detailed description of 15 hospitals bought by for-profit chains in Florida between 1979 and 1981 (Brown and Klosterman, 1986) confirms the California finding of low profit levels before acquisition: their pre-acquisition after-tax margin was below that of unacquired hospitals, although their pretax operating margin was higher than that of unacquired hospitals. The data also suggest that potential for improvement in the control of expense existed, because pre-acquisition operating expenses per adjusted admission were roughly 10 percent higher than in unacquired hospitals.

Profitability after acquisition varied. Three years after acquisition by for-profit chains, 2 of the 15 Florida hospitals were operating in the red. One-third of the acquired hospitals achieved margins comparable to other for-profit hospitals in the state, and almost half had margins higher than unacquired hospitals. During the three years after acquisition, the previously independent hospitals acquired by for-profit chains improved their margins to become more profitable than the average unacquired hospital. This was not true of acquired hospitals formerly in for-profit chains. Despite high operating expenses before takeover, such expenses per adjusted admission increased at a faster rate after acquisition by for-profit chains than did operating expenses in unacquired hospitals. Gross and net revenues per adjusted admission and ancillary revenues per adjusted admission generally increased at a higher rate in hospitals acquired by for-profit chains than in unacquired hospitals—again despite

high pre-acquisition levels. These data suggest that any improvements in profitability were achieved not through tight control of expenses but rather through higher prices. Another strategy to enhance profitability after acquisition—reductions in uncompensated care—is discussed in Chapter 5.

The data from Florida and California suggest that acquisitions by for-profit chains had the effect of increasing the cost of care. Increases in charges in acquired California hospitals were only slightly above those of unacquired for-profit hospitals. In contrast, in Florida some hospitals acquired by for-profit chains showed substantially larger increases in revenue per adjusted admission than hospitals whose ownership did not change. For hospitals that belonged to for-profit chains before acquisition, the rate of increase in net revenues per adjusted admission was significantly higher than the rate of increase in other hospitals. Since financially troubled hospitals seem to be common acquisition candidates, it is possible that in the absence of a change in ownership, the former owners might have had to either raise prices to improve the financial standing of the hospitals or close the hospitals.

## NURSING HOME COSTS

Nursing homes provide a striking contrast to hospitals and their cost-based/charge-based system of reimbursement. Nursing homes operate with a payment system that has not changed fundamentally in recent years. Also, the nursing home business—unlike the hospital business—is marked by constraints on growth, imposed by regulation and by limited competition caused by high occupancy rates and lack of alternatives for long-term care.

Nursing home care is generally charged on a per diem basis. Medicaid accounts for roughly half of all nursing home revenues. States vary in the way the Medicaid payment is determined, but typically, the per diem rate is cost-based within the limits of the state-imposed cap. The cap can apply to operating or capital expenses, or both. There are no limits on charges to private-pay patients, except in Minnesota, where nursing homes cannot charge private-pay patients more than the Medicaid rate.[12] Estimates of the price differential between Medicaid and private pay hover around the 18-20 percent mark (Lawrence Lane, unpublished data prepared for the Institute of Medicine Committee on Nursing Home Regulation, 1984).

An extensive review of the literature on nursing homes was conducted for the committee (Hawes and Phillips, 1986). Most available studies of nursing home expenses and prices fail to distinguish investor-owned chain from independent proprietary nursing homes. The usual comparison is between not-for-profit and for-profit ownership. Very few studies use national data, or control for severity of illness or quality of care.

Empirical studies generally show significantly higher reported per-patient-day expenses in not-for-profit than in for-profit nursing homes (Hawes and Phillips, 1986). Studies that control for factors that affect expenses, such as location, patient case mix, intensity, and some proxies for quality, show that an expense differential exists, but the magnitude is smaller than found in studies lacking controls. A study of Illinois nursing homes in 1976, notable for its controls for patient mix, facility size, occupancy rate, and other variables, found that for-profit facilities were more efficient, providing a given level of care at lower cost to the facility, but there was no difference in cost to payers (Koetting, 1980). There are tentative indications that for-profit nursing homes achieve expense savings through lower patient care expenditures, but spend more on property-associated costs (Caswell and Cleverly, 1978, cited in Hawes and Phillips, 1986). However, lower for-profit expenses do not translate into lower charges. The few studies that focus on charges show no or small differences between the two types of ownership (Hawes and Phillips, 1986).

Findings of lower expenses in for-profit nursing homes was confirmed by a study that used a four-way classification to investigate the effects of ownership and affiliation of selected efficiency measures (Hiller and Sugarman, 1984). A sample of approximately 1,100 nursing homes was drawn from the 1977 National Nursing Home Survey. Chain for-profit homes had the lowest average cost, operating cost, and nursing cost per resident day, followed by for-profit independent nursing homes (see Table 4.4). However, regression analysis suggested that lower for-profit average and nursing costs were due to such factors as occupancy rates and location, not ownership or chain affiliation. Finally, the data in Table 4.5 show chain for-profit nursing homes to have the highest before-tax profit per resident day after inclusion of nonpatient care revenues. Independent not-for-profit nursing homes had a negative bottom line. For both for-profit and not-for-profit homes, chain-affiliated facilities were substantially more profitable than independent facilities. Regression analysis suggested that ownership accounts for only a small (3 percent) part of the differences among ownership groups in this measure of profit.

In an effort to differentiate more finely among ownership groups than did earlier studies, Hawes and Phillips (1986) analyzed data from private not-for-profit nursing homes that participated in the Ohio Medicaid program in 1977 and three types of for-profit nursing homes: those owned by individuals operating 3 or fewer homes; intrastate chains, usually of 4 to 10 homes; and interstate, publicly held chains. Not-for-profit homes were found to operate with expenses higher by $6 to $8 per patient day than the average for-profit homes, and interstate chains had expenses of $1.50 higher per patient day than the other two for-profit forms. A similar pattern (Table 4.6) was found in expenditures for direct patient care (nursing, social services, supplies, etc.). Administrative and general service expenses are items for which

TABLE 4.5 Selected Nursing Home Cost and Profit Measures by Ownership and Affiliation, National Nursing Home Survey, 1977

| | For-profit | | Not-for-profit | |
| Measure | Chain | Independent | Chain | Independent |
|---|---|---|---|---|
| Net profit (before tax) per resident day | $ 1.00 | $ 0.19 | $ 0.32 | $ −0.66 |
| Average cost per resident day[a] | 22.38 | 31.43 | 40.50 | 37.38 |
| Operating cost per resident day[b] | 4.67 | 7.52 | 9.87 | 8.18 |
| Nursing cost per resident day | 7.25 | 10.14 | 13.71 | 12.06 |

[a]Includes all costs (including operating, labor, and fixed).
[b]Operating cost includes the cost of food, drugs, and services such as laundry or nursing services purchased from outside sources. Excluded are labor costs (payroll) and fixed costs of capital expenses and rent.

SOURCE: Hiller and Sugarman (1984).

chain operators might be expected to show economies of scale, and Table 4.6 shows that interstate chains in Ohio had the lowest expenses per patient day for these two categories. However, the costs of ownership (interest, depreciation, and rent payments) are lower for not-for-profit than for all types of for-profit nursing homes. Controlling for such factors as location, certification, and quality (by proxy measures), the differences among ownership types are reduced, but remain significant.

The higher for-profit ownership expenses could be due in part to acquisitions and selling of nursing homes to take advantage of tax and reimbursement benefits. Capital payments for depreciation, interest, and a return on equity are generally reimbursed by public programs, particularly Medicaid. The 1981 tax provisions on accelerated cost recovery also spur acquisition activity. However, some states have moved to slow acquisition activity by limiting reimbursement for capital and interest costs. As in the hospital industry, chain growth in nursing homes has been achieved mainly through acquisi-

TABLE 4.6 Comparison of Average Nursing Home Expenditures per Patient Day in Major Cost Centers, State of Ohio, 1977

| | Type of Ownership | | | |
| Cost Center | For-profit Individual Ownership (N = 382) | For-profit Intrastate Chain (N = 78) | For-profit Interstate Chain (N = 32) | Not-for-profit (N = 87) |
|---|---|---|---|---|
| General services costs | 2.47 | 2.44 | 2.04 | 3.27 |
| Ownership or rent | 3.12 | 3.12 | 3.10 | 2.69 |
| Patient care costs | 9.05 | 8.90 | 9.52 | 13.16 |
| Administrative costs | 2.73 | 2.90 | 2.53 | 3.17 |

SOURCE: Hawes and Phillips (1986).

tion—partly because construction has been limited by states, constraining the expansion of the supply of nursing homes through certificate-of-need restrictions, and partly because inflation of building costs has made acquisition cheaper than construction. Although payment by Medicaid is frequently inadequate, the nursing home market continues to attract for-profit enterprises that generate sufficient total revenue to provide an adequate return on investment.

In sum, for-profit nursing homes, operating with reimbursement that has similarities to the Medicare prospective payment system being implemented for hospitals but lacking the competition that hospitals are now confronting, operate with lower expenses but with similar charges than not-for-profit nursing homes. Lower for-profit expenses are in some cases the result of lower patient care expenditures, and there is some evidence that chain operations are more efficient in the provision of general and administrative services. Limited evidence from Ohio suggests that interstate chain homes operate with expenses that are substantially lower than not-for-profit homes, but somewhat higher than other for-profit homes. Despite low Medicaid reimbursement levels, profitability is sufficiently high to attract for-profit providers to the nursing home business in many states.

## OTHER FOR-PROFIT PROVIDERS

Although there is no literature available on the comparative cost of freestanding for-profit and not-for-profit urgent care centers, surgery centers, imaging centers, and the like—indeed, there are little data available on the extent of not-for-profit ownership of such centers—the growth of freestanding centers represents a dynamic entrepreneurial trend in American health care. It undoubtedly has important cost implications, although these may shed little light on the comparative behavior of for-profit and not-

for-profit institutions. Both for-profit and not-for-profit hospitals and investor-owned companies have established new ambulatory care centers, but it is not known whether the practice is more common among not-for-profit than among for-profit organizations. Many of the centers established by not-for-profit organizations are set up as for-profit subsidiaries.

Some of the new types of ambulatory care centers are based on innovations. The innovations can be in marketing, such as primary care centers' convenient hours and location or lack of an appointment requirement. Other innovations, particularly in ambulatory surgery centers, involve new technologies and new ways of providing services. Through such innovations and through various means of reducing overhead, including specialization, selection of particular types of patients, and limiting hours of service, many new types of ambulatory care centers are able to charge less for services than do the hospitals with which they compete, a finding documented in several studies reviewed by Ermann and Gabel (1986). There are also many anecdotes of hospitals lowering their charges to compete with freestanding centers.

Many innovations in various types of ambulatory care centers have undoubtedly led to significant unit-cost savings to many payers and greater convenience for many patients. The competitive responses they have stimulated on the part of hospitals may also help control certain health care costs. Whether the thousands of freestanding centers that now exist represent a net reduction in health care costs is much less certain, however, because they constitute additional capital investment and because existing institutions that lose patients to the centers must spread their overhead over fewer cases. Also, if existing institutions lose revenues from services on which they can make money, they may be less able to provide unprofitable services and uncompensated care. These are matters that deserve scrutiny as the cost implications of freestanding centers are assessed.

## MONITORING COST TRENDS

Almost all the analyses of expenses and prices reported here were based on data collected in an environment that differs significantly from that in which hospitals and physicians find themselves today. Much of the data in this report provides an important baseline, but continued and expanded data collection and monitoring of expenses and prices are essential. The move away from cost-based reimbursement; the rapid growth of preferred provider organizations, health maintenance organizations, and many new forms of ambulatory care; and the expansion of home care all indicate that major changes are taking place in the way medical care is organized and paid for in the United States. These changes, which alter many of the economic incentives to providers and create a competitive environment, are likely to affect provider behavior with respect to prices, control of expenses, and in many other ways. Dramatic changes are occurring and seem likely to continue.

Data systems to monitor operating and capital expenses and prices will need to be sensitive to subtle changes in the hospital product as well as to changes in national health care expenditures, in providers' uses of resources, and in expenses and prices for different payers and different population groups. Moreover, to determine savings and/or cost shifting in the health care system as a whole, the various new types of nonhospital providers should be monitored. In light of the findings from the studies reviewed in this chapter that suggest a greater responsiveness of for-profit providers to economic incentives, it is important to track differences between not-for-profit and for-profit providers as the new incentives take hold. Multi-institutional systems, also separated into for-profit and not-for-profit, should be monitored to determine the relationships between ownership and system membership.

The major sources of data today include Medicare costs reports, which are the only existing source of national hospital expense information; some very valuable state reporting systems; and regular surveys by organizations such as the American Hospital Association. No sources were identified for data on national nursing home expenses.

The committee believes that Medicare cost reports provide valuable information and should be maintained even as cost-based reimbursement is phased out. The committee would also like to see other states adopt hospital reporting systems uniform with those already in place in some states. States should develop similar kinds of uniform reporting systems to monitor operating and capital expenses and prices in nursing homes and other out-of-hospital facilities.

Until quite recently, most analyses of hospital expenses were conducted without reference to case mix or case severity, which affect the costs of care. Medicare's case-mix index, a measure of costliness of cases treated by a hospital relative to the average of all Medicare patients, is for hospitals only and is based on Medicare program data. It is the only national source of case-mix information. The Prospective Payment Assessment Commission (ProPAC) is working to refine and improve the index. The commission has not yet decided on how it will respond to the needs of non-Medicare private and public payers who are beginning to use the system for their own purposes (Prospective Payment Assessment Commission, 1985). The committee emphasizes the need for continued improvement of case-mix and case-severity measures, and the use of such measures in studies of expenses and prices.

The committee is aware that much useful data is being collected by insurers, employers, providers, and other organizations concerned with the price of health care. However, for reasons of confidentiality and competitive position, such organizations have been reluctant to make their data publicly available. The committee believes that with the proper assurance of confidentiality and the removal of individual identifiers, valuable information could be released. The committee urges those in control of relevant data to work with agencies, such as the National Center for Health Statistics, to arrange for increased release of information.

## CONCLUSIONS

The evidence reviewed in this chapter reveals several patterns in the cost-related behavior of for-profit and not-for-profit institutions. First, studies of hospital costs that control for size (and in some cases for case mix and other factors) show for-profit hospitals to have slightly higher expenses than not-for-profit institutions—ranging from a statistically insignificant level to 8-10 percent higher—when payment is based on costs incurred.

Second, studies (again, controlling for size and sometimes other variables) show that for-profit institutions charge more per stay than not-for-profit institutions—ranging from 8 percent for cost payers to 24 percent for charge payers. Using the difference in for-profit chain and not-for-profit chain prices found in a national study, for-profit chains' high prices added approximately $470 million, or less than 1 percent to the nation's bill for hospital care. If for-profit chain hospitals increase their share of the hospital market and maintain the price differential, the price impact will increase.

Third, controlled studies comparing the profitability of for-profit chains and not-for-profit hospitals show that for-profit chains have achieved higher levels of profitability before and after taxes. They are also less likely than not-for-profit hospitals to have losses on patient revenues and more likely to have high margins on patient revenues. Nonoperating revenues such as charitable contributions and investment income are important sources of revenues for not-for-profit hospitals, contributing substantially to their overall margins. But national, uncontrolled data show that for-profit hospitals have lower (after-tax) margins on total net revenues than the average U.S. hospital.

Fourth, data from nursing homes suggest that when payment levels are fixed on a per diem basis, for-profit institutions restrict expenses more than not-for-profit institutions, which have lower margins, obtain revenues from philanthropy, and have more charge-paying patients. The cost savings are obtained on patient care expenses, not on capital or administrative expenses.

These findings support the broad conclusion that for-profit institutions respond more precisely to economic incentives than do not-for-profit institutions. (The for-profit hospitals' shorter lengths of stay and their lower occupancy rates are inconsistent with this broad interpretation.) Under circumstances in which it is economically rewarding to charge more (e.g., when payers pay charges and when there is little price competition), for-profit institutions have charged more. Under circumstances that reward investment, they have invested more. Under circumstances in which it has been economically rewarding to have higher expenses, even if allowable expenses are sharply defined, expenses of the for-profits have been slightly higher. Under circumstances where prices are fixed, such as nursing homes, their expenses have been lower. Economic rewards that derive from revaluation of assets and increased reimbursement may also explain why changes of ownership have occurred rather frequently among for-profit hospitals and nursing homes.

In addition to comparisons of costs associated with different types of ownership, the question of the effect of for-profit health services on the nation's health care costs also deserves comment. Two areas of heavy for-profit influence—nursing homes and dialysis treatment—are characterized by fixed-payment methods that provide strong incentives to limit expenses per unit of service (per day or per dialysis treatment). In other areas of for-profit growth, including both ambulatory care centers of various sorts and health maintenance organizations, new entrepreneurial organizations have been competing on the basis of price, services, and convenience. As noted earlier, the emergence of ambulatory care centers may have resulted in many reductions in unit price and cost to payers, although the increased capacity these centers represent may well have increased national health care costs.

A comparison of expenses and charges on a per-day or per-case basis, however, does not adequately answer the question of impact on total community costs of hospital services. It can be argued that the true costs of care to communities must take account of government grants and charitable contributions received by not-for-profit facilities and taxes paid for for-profit facilities. The few studies that make these complex and difficult-to-quantify adjustments suggest that for-profit hospital care is more expensive, but less so than indicated by simpler measures of prices and cost.

Comparisons of hospital charges and expenses also overlook the fact that the for-profit sector has made substantial capital investments in the modernization and construction of health care institutions and the acquisition of financially weak institutions that in some cases might otherwise have perished. In this regard, an important historical question about the impact of the for-profit sector on the nation's health care costs is not whether their investments in health care have increased costs but whether the capacity that has resulted from their investment is a net gain. This is partly an issue of values about the operation of markets and the objectivity of community health care needs. However, occupancy rates in hospitals in early 1985, at 66 percent nationally, suggest overbedding, and the investor-owned chains, with occupancy rates of 10-12 percent less than the national average, have

more unused capacity than the average hospital. Only the future will reveal whether the costs of unused capacity will be absorbed by communities or by the hospitals themselves.

Although some predict that for-profit health care organizations will lead the way toward lower-cost care now that economic incentives reward such behavior, this should not be regarded as a forgone conclusion. Their expenses and prices have been higher in the past; they have high ongoing capital expenses because of past acquisition activities; their average lengths of stay are already shorter; they have lower occupancy rates across which to spread fixed costs; they have less access to nonpatient care revenues; and they must not only earn a profit to stay viable but they must also pay taxes on these profits (as well as on their property.) The strategies they (and not-for-profit hospitals) adopt will undoubtedly affect the shape and configuration of our health care system, the provision of at least some services to those patients who are unable to pay, and perhaps the quality of care.

## NOTES

[1]Cost allocation is an accounting technique that is used to spread the common overhead expenses of an institution (e.g., the administrator's salary, insurance) among its revenue-producing departments. This requires identifying outputs, defining expenses to be allocated, and establishing rules for allocating expenses to outputs (Yoder, 1980).

[2]Some cost payers allowed some costs of bad debts and charity care in their calculation of reimbursable costs. Medicare so treated the bad debts of only its beneficiaries (incurred when deductibles and co-payments were not paid), not of other patients. Some cost-based Blue Cross plans treat charity care as an allowable expense, and in some areas in which Blue Cross pays charges less a discount, payment includes a factor for bad debt and charity care incurred by all patients in the hospital.

[3]Under retroactive cost-based reimbursement, hospitals were paid on the basis of the cost of providing a service; thus, the greater the expenditure, the greater the reimbursement. Cost-based reimbursement contained few restraints on the provision of costly services

and virtually no restraints on capital spending. On the contrary, expenditures on plant and equipment could be recaptured more swiftly by higher utilization, as well as through depreciation and other capital payments. However, some restraints were imposed by disallowance of certain costs, by limits on costs per day, by utilization controls by professional services review organizations, and by capital controls under certificate of need. By paying a flat rate per diagnosis, the DRG approach severs the direct link between expenses and reimbursement and reverses the incentive for greater intensity of services in particular cases. A hospital with expenses that exceed the payment rate will lose money, and a hospital with expenses below the payment rate will earn income. Thus, new incentives exist to provide cost-effective care.

[4] In 1983 the average length of stay in for-profit chain hospitals was 6.4 days, compared with 6.7 days in for-profit independent and public state and local hospitals, 7.2 days in not-for-profit chain hospitals, 7.4 days in not-for-profit independent hospitals. One reason for the relatively shorter length of stay in for-profit chain hospitals might be that they treat less sick patients, which would presumably be shown by a lower Medicare case-mix index; regional factors may also play a role, since hospitals on the West Coast have a substantially shorter length of stay than East Coast hospitals. Indeed, two studies have found that after adjusting for differences in case mix, location, and other factors, differences in length of stay among ownership types virtually disappear (Coelen, 1986; Freund et al., 1985). Watt et al. (1986b), however, in their multiple regression analysis of national data, found that for-profit chain hospitals had only slightly lower Medicare case-mix indices than did not-for-profit chain hospitals (0.999 compared with 1.017).

[5] One study (Ashby, 1982) showed more rapid growth of expenses in for-profit than not-for-profit hospitals between 1973 and 1978, but this study does not distinguish investor-owned from proprietary for-profit hospitals.

[6] This differential was sustained as overall occupancy rates dropped to 66 percent in early 1985. The major for-profit chains had occupancy rates ranging from 55 percent at Hospital Corporation of American to 43 percent at Republic Health Corporation (Tatge, 1985a). Some not-for-profit multihospital systems were running closer to the national average—three of five listed in one recent report had occupancy rates between 60 and 64 percent, although one was 45 percent (Tatge, 1985b).

[7] Adjusted daily census, adjusted patient day, and adjusted admissions reflect inpatient care adjusted to reflect the volume of outpatient care provided.

[8] Data provided to the committee by the American Hospital Association show investor-owned chain hospitals had lower labor expenses per adjusted patient day than did not-for-profit hospitals in three out of four regions of the United States and for the United States as a whole ($183.49 versus $212.31 in 1983). However, because of the absence of controls for hospital size or range of services, it cannot be determined if these factors, rather than type of ownership, are responsible for the difference.

[9] Data supplied to the committee by the American Hospital Association show 2,544,000 admissions in for-profit hospitals in 1983. Watt et al. (1986b) found net patient care revenues adjusted per admission at investor-owned hospitals to average $184.55 more than the similar figure for not-for-profit chain hospitals and $137.94 more than independent not-for-profit hospitals. Thus, the difference is equivalent to $351-$469 million of the nation's total hospital expenditures of more than $100 billion.

[10] A problem of cost allocation should be noted with respect to routine daily service. Under Medicare cost-based reimbursement, it was advantageous to allocate expenses to routine daily service up to a set limit, beyond which payment was not made. The advantage occurred because Medicare paid hospitals the average cost for all patients for the routine daily service component of care, and, until 1982 paid hospitals an additional "nursing differential" payment on the assumption that Medicare patients required more nursing care than the average patient. However, the average cost for Medicare patients, who tend to have long stays, may actually have been lower than the average cost for other patients.

[11] Hospital Corporation of America challenged several of GAO's findings and noted some omissions in the analysis—particularly that GAO omitted that Medicare's share of the $55 million cost increase was only about $8 million. Furthermore, over $135 million in one-time federal capital gains tax liabilities were incurred, which more than offset Medicare's total future cost increase (James P. Smith, Hospital Corporation of America, Washington, D.C., personal communication, 1984).

[12] For a discussion of differences in Medicaid nursing home reimbursement policies and incentives among states, see Holahan (1983). Some changes in reimbursement methods are being considered, and some are being implemented. Medicare, which pays only 2 percent of nursing home costs, is considering moving to resource utilization groups—similar in concept to Medicare's hospital prospective payment system. Some state Medicaid programs are using or considering reimbursement systems that recognize differences in case mix.

### REFERENCES

American Hospital Association (1985) *Economic Trends* 1(Summer):4.

Anderson, Gerard F., and Paul B. Ginsberg (1983) Prospective Capital Payments to Hospitals. *Health Affairs* 2(Fall):53-63.

Ashby, John L., Jr. (1982) An Analysis of Hospital Costs by Cost Center, 1971 through 1978. *Health Care Financing Review* 4(September):37-53.

Becker, Edmund R., and Frank A. Sloan (1985) Hospital Ownership and Performance. *Economic Inquiry* 23(January):21-36.

Blue Cross/Blue Shield of North Carolina (1983) Proprietary Hospitals. Charges to BCBSNC Subscribers. Durham, N.C: Blue Cross/Blue Shield of North Carolina.

Brown, Kathryn J., and Richard E. Klosterman (1986) Hospital Acquisitions and Their Effects: Florida, 1979-1982. This volume.

Clark, Robert (1980) Does the Nonprofit Form Fit the Hospital Industry? *Harvard Law Review* 93(May):1417-1489.

Coelen, Craig G. (1986) Hospital Ownership and Comparative Hospital Costs. This volume.

Conger, J. N. (1983) Letter to the Editor. *Health Affairs* 2(Fall):138-141.

Ermann, Dan, and Jon Gabel (1986) Investor-Owned Multihospital Systems: A Synthesis of Research Findings. This volume.

Freund, Deborah, et al. (1985) Analysis of Lengths-of-Stay Differences Between Investor-Owned and Voluntary Hospitals. *Inquiry* 22(Spring):33-44.

Hawes, Catherine, and Charles D. Phillips (1986) The Changing Structure of the Nursing Home Industry and the Impact of Ownership on Quality, Cost, and Access. This volume.

Hiller, Marc D., and David B. Sugarman (1984) Private Nursing Homes in the U.S.: Effects of Ownership and Affiliation. Unpublished paper. University of New Hampshire, Durham, N.H.

Holahan, John (1983) State Rate Setting and the Effects on Nursing Home Costs. Working Paper 3172-05. Washington, D.C.: Urban Institute.

Koetting, M. (1980) *Nursing Home Organization and Efficiency*. Lexington, Mass.: Lexington Books.

Lee, Maw Lin (1971) A Conspicuous Production Theory of Hospital Behavior. *Southern Economics Journal* 28(July):48-58.

Lewin, Lawrence S., Robert A. Derzon, and Rhea Margulies (1981) Investor-owneds and Nonprofits Differ in Economic Performance. *Hospitals* 55(July 1):52-58.

Lewin, Lawrence S., Robert A. Derzon, and J. Michael Watt (1983) Letter to the Editor. *Health Affairs* 2(Fall):134-137.

Pattison, Robert V. (1986) Response to Financial Incentives Among Investor-Owned and Not-for-Profit Hospitals: An Analysis Based on California Data, 1978-1982. This volume.

Pattison, Robert V., and Hallie M. Katz (1983) Investor-Owned and Not-for-Profit Hospitals. *The New England Journal of Medicine* 309(Aug. 11): 347-353.

Prospective Payment Assessment Commission (1985) *Report and Recommendations to The Secretary, U.S. Department of Health and Human Services*. Washington, D.C.: U.S. Government Printing Office.

Sloan, Frank A., and Robert A. Vraciu (1983) Investor-Owned and Not-For-Profit Hospitals: Addressing Some Issues. *Health Affairs* 2(Spring):25-37.

State of Florida Hospital Cost Containment Board (1984) *Annual Report 1983-1984*. Tallahasse: State of Florida Hospital Cost Containment Board.

Tatge, Mark (1985a) For-profits' Inpatient Occupancy Drops in Quarter; Outpatient Visits Are Rising. *Modern Healthcare* 15(May 10):23.

Tatge, Mark (1985b) Occupancy Rate Declines Level Off While Outpatient Visits Continue to Climb. *Modern Healthcare* 15(May 10):94.

U.S. General Accounting Office (1983) Hospital Mergers Increase Medicare and Medicaid Payments for Capital Costs. (GAO/HRD 84-10). Washington, D.C.: U.S. General Accounting Office.

Watt, J. Michael, Robert A. Derzon, Steven C. Renn, and Carl J. Schramm (1986a) The Comparative Economic Performance of Investor-owned Chain and Not-for-profit Hospitals. *The New England Journal of Medicine* 314(January 9):89-96.

Watt, J. Michael, Steven C. Renn, James S. Hahn, Robert A. Derzon, and Carl J. Schramm (1986b) The Effects of Ownership and Multihospital System Membership on Hospital Functional Strategies and Economic Performance. This volume.

Yoder, Sunny G. (1980) Financing Graduate Medical Education. Pp. 107-147 in *Graduate Medical Education Present and Prospective. A Call for Action*. New York: Josiah Macy, Jr., Foundation.

# 5 Access to Care and Investor-Owned Providers

Probably the most commonly expressed concern about the emergence and growth of investor-owned health care organizations is the belief that their pursuit of profitability goals will limit or preclude them from serving patients who are unable to pay or from offering needed services that cannot be provided at a profit. Implicit in this concern is the value premise—which some dispute and which is not typical of business—that health care institutions (whether for-profit or not-for-profit) have certain social responsibilities to meet individual and community needs, even needs that cannot be met profitably. Implicit also is the assumption that for-profit and not-for-profit institutions will behave differently in this regard.

Behind these concerns lies one of the most serious problems in our patchwork system of financing health care: the 35 million people who lack adequate private health insurance coverage and who are not eligible for public programs, particularly Medicare and Medicaid.[1] The care of these and many underinsured people is now largely dependent on the ability and willingness of health care institutions and individual physicians to provide uncompensated care.

Although this chapter is primarily concerned with questions of access in economically unrewarding circumstances, it should be recognized at the outset that the overall impact of for-profit providers on access to care includes their effect on access to care for people who can pay. Such access has undoubtedly been enhanced by for-profit providers purchasing facilities that are in financial trouble and that might otherwise have closed, renovating and modernizing facilities and attracting new physicians as a result, investing in new services and facilities where there is demand, and responding to patients' desires for convenient hours and locations. For-profit providers also pay taxes, which are used for such purposes as policymakers may determine. Although some tax money finances care for the indigent, plainly most federal tax revenues are used for other purposes.

This chapter deals with four negative allegations regarding the behavior of for-profit providers: that they will not serve those who cannot pay; that their ability to attract paying patients will make it increasingly difficult for other type institutions to care for those who cannot pay; that they will offer only profitable services, regardless of the community's need for other services; and that they will be more likely to close hospitals that fail to achieve economic goals. The questions of whether the traditional expectation that health care institutions contribute to the care of those unable to pay is the proper mechanism for solving access problems, and whether for-profit and not-for-profit providers should be expected to contribute equally are discussed later in this chapter.

## THE PROBLEM OF CARE FOR THOSE UNABLE TO PAY

A basic paradox or ambivalence in American health policy is that despite the absence of a public commitment to the availability of financing to assure access to health care for all who need it, a widespread expectation exists that hospitals will provide needed care for the millions of Americans who are unable to pay part or all of their medical bills. The expectation that hospitals will do what needs to be done and will find a way to pay for it is no doubt a residue of the history of hospitals as public or charitable institutions. Hospitals provide a substantial, if inadequate, amount of uncompensated care. Although there are wide variations among hospitals, uncompensated care (the sum of charity care and bad debts) amounted to 5.4 percent of the gross revenues of the average U.S. hospital in 1983, a total of $7.8 billion (American Hospital Association, 1985). Nevertheless, in a 1982 national survey, 15 percent of uninsured families reported that they had not obtained needed medical care during the previous year, and 4 percent reported that they had been refused care for financial reasons (Robert Wood Johnson Foundation, 1983).

To what extent, if any, does the for-profit presence exacerbate these problems? A full answer to this question would require data on the number of persons who needed services but lacked the means to pay (1) who didn't believe they could obtain services so did not try, (2) who sought care but were turned away, (3) who were given emergency care and transferred to another institution; or (4) who were cared for with the provider (hospital, nursing home, HMO, ambulatory care center, etc.) absorbing the costs in full or in part. Unfortunately, such data are largely lacking. Existing evidence is limited mostly to hospitals. Even then, it is limited to (1)

survey data on the number of uninsured people treated and (2) the dollar value of uncompensated care provided. Furthermore, the measure "uncompensated care" (charity care and bad debt as a percentage of revenues) includes the uncollected charges from people who were admitted as paying patients but whose insurance did not cover full costs, and from people who were known at the time of admission to be unable to pay. In short, available data are fragmentary and are, at best, suggestive of the true extent to which people who are unable to pay are served.

The legal responsibilities of institutions toward people who are unable to pay for their care vary, but are generally limited. Case law, accreditation requirements, and some state statutes require treatment of patients in immediately life-threatening circumstances, but this is very different from extending the full resources of a hospital to all who need care. Many public hospitals are legally obligated to care for all residents in their area. Some voluntary hospitals are supposed to provide a set amount of free care annually because of earlier receipt of Hill-Burton construction funds, but the amount of care required is limited and applies to a decreasing number of hospitals. Obligations to provide free care as a condition of the tax-exempt status of not-for-profit institutions have largely disappeared insofar as federal income taxes are concerned,[2] although a 1985 Utah Supreme Court decision tied hospital exemptions from local property taxes to several criteria, including provision of charity care. Other not-for-profit hospitals that are not statutorily responsible for caring for the needy of the community nevertheless see maintaining an "open door" as a fundamental value.

### The Financing of Uncompensated Care

Institutions that provide uncompensated care and unprofitable services must recover the costs elsewhere. The choices are few.

The costs can be subsidized out of revenues from paying patients, a practice that has been facilitated by third-party payers who pay hospital charges set high enough to allow such subsidization. (Bad debts for non-Medicare patients were never an allowable cost under Medicare's cost-based reimbursement rules.) However, private third-party payers (including self-insuring companies) are becoming much less willing to pay for costs incurred in the care of patients that they do not insure. Changes in the reimbursement environment—most notably in the growth of negotiated rates and price competition—are making cross-subsidization increasingly problematic. As these changes continue to happen, institutions that provide uncompensated care will increasingly have to finance such care in one of two ways—by cannibalizing themselves (using money that should go for future capital needs, deferring maintenance, cutting costs excessively, having operating deficits) or by raising money from nonpatient care sources.

Obtaining nonpatient revenues has long been essential to the sound operation of hospitals. Indeed, until recent years, the average U.S. hospital would have had a negative margin (i.e., more expenses than revenues) if it had not obtained revenues from sources other than patient care, as Table 5.1 shows. Sources of nonpatient revenues include governmental appropriations; charitable contributions; interest; and income from gift shops, parking facilities, and other subsidiary organizations. As Table 5.2 shows, the magnitude of nonpatient revenues varies across hospital types, comprising 15 percent of the total revenues of public hospitals in 1983, 5 percent of the total revenues of not-for-profit hospitals, and less than 2 percent of the total revenues of for-profit hospitals. Governmental grants and appropriations are available mainly to public hospitals. Charitable contributions are available to not-for-profit and public institutions, but now are less than 1 percent of hospital revenues.

Nevertheless, because of past public pol-

**TABLE 5.1** Revenue Margins for U.S. Community Hospitals, 1963-1984

| Year | Net Patient Margins | Total Net Margin |
|------|---------------------|------------------|
| 1963 | −6.0% | 2.5% |
| 1964 | −4.8 | 3.0 |
| 1965 | −5.1 | 2.3 |
| 1966 | −3.8 | 3.7 |
| 1967 | −4.6 | 2.6 |
| 1968 | −3.0 | 3.2 |
| 1969 | −3.9 | 2.4 |
| 1970 | −3.4 | 2.1 |
| 1971 | −3.2 | 2.3 |
| 1972 | −3.7 | 1.8 |
| 1973 | −4.4 | 1.2 |
| 1974 | −3.7 | 2.1 |
| 1975 | −3.0 | 2.3 |
| 1976 | −1.5 | 3.1 |
| 1977 | −0.6 | 3.5 |
| 1978 | −0.8 | 3.6 |
| 1979 | −0.6 | 3.9 |
| 1980 | 0.3 | 4.6 |
| 1981 | 0.2 | 4.7 |
| 1982 | 0.7 | 5.1 |
| 1983 | 1.0 | 5.1 |
| 1984 | 2.0 | 6.2 |

SOURCE: National Hospital Panel Survey, copyright 1985 by the American Hospital Association.

icies—particularly the public sector's unwillingness to use tax revenues to finance care for those who are unable to pay—access to medical care for millions of people depends on the policies, practices, and resources of health care providers. It is in this context that concern about the behavior of for-profit organizations has developed.

## THE PROVIDERS OF UNCOMPENSATED CARE

In assessing the relationship between type of ownership and service to patients who are unable to pay, the committee examined national data and data from five states in which for-profit hospitals have a relatively large market share. All data sources show that public hospitals provide a disproportionately large amount of uncompensated care

**TABLE 5.2**   Sources of Revenue, Community Hospitals by
Ownership, 1983 (millions of dollars)

|  | Not-for-profit | | For-profit | | State/Local Government | |
|---|---|---|---|---|---|---|
|  | $ | % | $ | % | $ | % |
| Total net revenue | 89,632.6 | 100.0 | 10,231.2 | 100.0 | 22,050.4 | 100.0 |
| Net patient revenue | 84,955.3 | 94.8 | 10,070.5 | 98.4 | 18,813.8 | 85.3 |
| Other operating |  |  |  |  |  |  |
|   revenue | 2,623.5 | 2.9 | 124.8 | 1.2 | 2,402.5 | 10.9 |
|   Tax appropriations | 53.1 | a | — | 0.0 | 1,931.9 | 8.8 |
|   Other | 2,570.4 | 2.9 | 124.8 | 1.2 | 470.6 | 2.1 |
| Nonoperating |  |  |  |  |  |  |
|   revenue | 2,053.8 | 2.3 | 35.9 | 0.4 | 834.1 | 3.8 |
|   Contributions | 370.9 | 0.4 | 1.1 | a | 220.5 | 1.0 |
|   Grants | 160.8 | 0.2 | — | 0.0 | 92.2 | 0.4 |
|   Interest | 1,155.4 | 1.3 | 12.6 | 0.1 | 212.0 | 1.0 |
|   Other | 366.7 | 0.4 | 22.2 | 0.2 | 309.5 | 1.4 |

[a]Less than 0.1 percent.

SOURCE: Peter Kralovec, Hospital Data Center, American Hospital Association, unpublished data, 1985.

relative to their gross patient revenues. But since the data are generally not adjusted to reflect the governmental appropriations that such institutions receive, data from public hospitals are not strictly comparable to private institutions. A similar point pertains to comparisons of for-profit and not-for-profit hospitals: to the extent that not-for-profit hospitals receive more nonpatient care revenues (via philanthropy, governmental grants, or other sources) than do for-profit hospitals, provision of uncompensated care requires less subsidization from patient care revenues.

The most recent national data on who provides uncompensated care come from two sources: a 1981 survey conducted by the Office for Civil Rights (OCR) in the Department of Health and Human Services, and annual American Hospital Association (AHA) surveys of hospitals in 1982 and 1983. These national data show some differences between for-profit and not-for-profit hospitals.

**OCR Data**

The OCR survey sought data from all hospitals on admissions of uninsured patients during two weeks in 1981 (Rowland, 1984).[3] Table 5.3 displays data on uninsured admissions as a proportion of total admissions in each type of hospital. Public hospitals accepted the greatest burden of uninsured patients—16.8 percent of their admissions—followed by not-for-profit hospitals (including teaching hospitals) with 7.9 percent, and for-profit hospitals with 6 percent.

Analysis of variations within ownership groups shows a consistent picture (Table 5.4). A slightly higher percentage of not-for-profit than for-profit hospitals (4.1 percent versus 3.1 percent) reported that more than 25 percent of the patients they admitted were uninsured. (The comparable number for public hospitals was 10.7 percent.) Conversely, a higher percentage of for-profit than not-for-profit hospitals (58.6 percent versus 44.5 percent) reported that less than 5 percent of the patients they admitted were uninsured. Since data are so often reduced to

**TABLE 5.3**   Inpatient Admissions by Source of Payment and Type of Hospital Ownership, United States, 1981 (millions of admissions)

| Type of Hospital | Total | | Uninsured | | Medicaid | | Medicare | | Private and Other | |
|---|---|---|---|---|---|---|---|---|---|---|
| | Number | % | Number | % | Number | % | Number | % | Number | % |
| For-profit | 3.4 | 100.0 | 0.2 | 6.0 | 0.3 | 8.7 | 1.0 | 30.7 | 1.9 | 54.6 |
| Not-for-profit | 27.2 | 100.0 | 2.1 | 7.9 | 2.5 | 9.4 | 7.8 | 28.5 | 14.7 | 54.2 |
| Public | 7.6 | 100.0 | 1.3 | 16.8 | 0.9 | 11.9 | 2.0 | 27.0 | 3.4 | 44.3 |
| Total | 38.2 | 100.0 | 3.6 | 9.5 | 3.7 | 9.8 | 10.9 | 28.5 | 20.0 | 52.2 |

NOTE: Columns and rows may not add to totals due to rounding. The number of admissions is an annual number projected from data for a 2-week period in January 1981.

SOURCE: Office for Civil Rights, DHHS. Data reported in Rowland (1984).

averages, these data on variability within categories are notable.

On one measure, the OCR data showed no difference between for-profit and not-for-profit hospitals: 22 percent of emergency room visits were accounted for by uninsured patients in both types of hospitals. (The figure for public hospitals was 34 percent.) However, on another measure, for-profit hospitals saw relatively fewer emergency room patients than did not-for-profit hospitals: 1.4 versus 1.8 emergency room visits per hospital admission (Rowland, 1984).

In sum, for-profit and not-for-profit hospitals differ somewhat in the care of the vulnerable category of uninsured people, although the difference is relatively small. Furthermore, the fact that 6 percent of the patients admitted to for-profit hospitals are uninsured does not conform to the stereo-

type. Methodological questions arise because of the magnitude of the effort that was required of responding institutions and because of the limited (2-week) sampling period. Nevertheless, the OCR data are based on a very large sample (almost 5,800 hospitals) because they were collected as part of mandatory civil rights compliance efforts. No other source of national data exists on hospital services to uninsured patients, a plausible proxy for patients who are unable to pay for care.

**AHA Data**

The American Hospital Association's annual survey of hospitals includes information on bad debt and charity care as a percentage of hospital charges (i.e., the amount hospitals charge for the services provided over

**TABLE 5.4**   Hospitals with a High or Low Volume of Uninsured Admissions, by Type of Ownership, United States, 1981

| Type of Hospital | Number of Hospitals | Hospitals with Less Than 5 Percent Uninsured Admissions (%) | Hospitals with More Than 25 Percent Uninsured Admissions (%) |
|---|---|---|---|
| For-profit | 732 | 58.6 | 3.1 |
| Not-for-profit | 3,324 | 44.5 | 4.1 |
| Public | 1,641 | 29.8 | 10.7 |
| All hospitals | 5,697 | 42.1 | 5.8 |

SOURCE: Office for Civil Rights, DHHS. Data reported in Rowland (1984).

a period of time, in contrast to the amount they collect).[4] The data are self-reported and are subject to bias because of low response rates, particularly on financial items. The 1982 data reported below are based on a 40 percent response rate; the nonresponse problem was greater among the for-profits than not-for-profits. The use of bad debt and charity dollars as a measure of uncompensated care itself presents problems. Although conceptually distinct and reported separately by hospitals, it is recognized that bad debt and charity care are neither generally nor consistently distinguished from each other for hospital accounting purposes. The distinction is probably made mostly by hospitals that have a positive reason to do so—for example, to demonstrate that they are meeting Hill-Burton "free care" obligations or to maximize reimbursement from those Blue Cross plans that include charity care (but not bad debt) as a reimbursable cost. Thus, although "bad debt and charity as a percentage of charges" reflects the vigor of debt-collection efforts, as well as willingness to serve patients who cannot pay, it is the most widely used measure of uncompensated care, and the AHA annual survey is the only national data source.

Data from the 1983 AHA survey (Table 5.5) show uncompensated care as 4.2 percent of the gross patient revenues in not-for-profit hospitals, but only 3.1 percent in for-profit hospitals (differences that are remarkably similar to the OCR data). (Both contrast sharply with public hospitals.) The 1982 AHA survey showed no clear difference between for-profits and not-for-profits (Table 5.5). In metropolitan areas, not-for-profit hospitals provided slightly more uncompensated care than did for-profit hospitals; the opposite was true in nonmetropolitan areas. (No breakdown of independent and chain hospitals was available.) A regression analysis that included such variables as size, region, and teaching status, showed no statistically significant difference between not-for-profit and for-profit

**TABLE 5.5** Uncompensated Care as a Percentage of Charges, by Ownership and Location, United States, 1982 and 1983

| Type of Hospital | Metropolitan Areas,[a] 1982 | Non-metropolitan Areas,[a] 1982 | U.S.,[b] 1983 |
|---|---|---|---|
| For-profit | 3.0 | 4.2 | 3.1[c] |
| Not-for-profit | 3.7 | 4.0 | 4.2 |
|   Teaching | (4.6) | | |
|   Nonteaching | (3.6) | | |
| Government | 8.6 | 5.3 | 11.5 |
|   Teaching | (15.0) | | |
|   Nonteaching | (7.2) | | |
| Total | 4.4 | 4.5 | |

[a]Sloan et al. (1986).
[b]American Hospital Association. News Release, February 6, 1985.
[c]The Federation of American Hospitals, the association of for-profit hospitals, reported on the basis of its own survey that its members' deductions from gross revenue for charity and bad debt averaged 4.4 percent in 1983 (Federation of American Hospitals, no date).

hospitals (Sloan et al. 1986); however, this analysis also controlled for "payer mix," a variable that appears to be closely associated with some types of uncompensated care (i.e., self-pay patients). Nevertheless, the lack of a clear difference between for-profit and not-for-profit hospitals in 1982 is apparent. Overall, the national data from AHA surveys provide weak support for the hypothesis that for-profit hospitals do less than not-for-profit hospitals to meet the needs of patients who are unable to pay.

### State Data

Data from several states show a different picture. The committee sought data on uncompensated care in states where for-profit chain hospitals are an important presence. Data were obtained for five such states—California, Florida, Tennessee, Virginia, and Texas. The Texas data are from a special survey (response rate 80 percent) conducted by the Texas Hospital Association (1985) in connection with the activities of a state commission on the indigent care problem (Kent Stevens, Texas Hospital Association, personal communication, 1985). Data from the other four states are from state agencies to which hospitals are required to submit data. Except for the California data (which included only hospitals with 76-250 beds), these state data do not control for size, rural-urban differences, or teaching status. The data also do not indicate the presence or absence of nearby public providers—another factor that can influence the provision of uncompensated care in private hospitals.[5]

Table 5.6 shows bad debt and charity care as a percent of gross revenues in these five states. In California, which had a well-functioning system of public hospitals during the study years, the data show no difference between for-profit and not-for-profit hospitals. A different picture is seen in the other four states, where because of the characteristics of the Medicaid programs and the demographic makeup of the states, hospitals of all types provide higher levels of uncompensated care than is typical nationally. In Florida, Tennessee, Virginia, and Texas, for-profit hospitals have substantially lower bad debt and charity care deductions from gross revenues than do not-for-profit hospitals. Not-for-profit hospitals provide from 50 to over 150 percent more uncompensated care as a percentage of revenues in these states. Table 5.6 also shows that in the two states where data distinguish between chain and independent hospitals—Tennessee and California—the chain for-profit hospitals have lower charity care and bad debt rates than do independent for-profits.

These data and the data showing differences between metropolitan and nonmetropolitan areas indicate that location plays a role in the amount of uncompensated care that hospitals provide. Since poor people and nonwhite people are more likely than others to be uninsured and unable to pay for care, some would expect for-profit hospitals to avoid counties with relatively high poverty or nonwhite populations. A national

**TABLE 5.6** Hospital Uncompensated Care as Percentage of Gross Patient Revenues, Various States, 1981-1983

| Type of Ownership | California[a] 1981-1982 | Florida[b] 1982 | Tennessee[c] 1983 | Texas[d] 1983 | Virginia[e] 1982 |
|---|---|---|---|---|---|
| Public | 7 | 12.1 | 18.7 | 32.4 | 21.5 |
| Not-for-profit chain | 2 | 6.6 | 9.0 | 6.5 | 5.5 |
| Not-for-profit independent | | | 8.7 | | |
| Investor-owned chain | 2 | 3.8 | 3.4 | 3.5 | 3.5 |
| Proprietary (independent) | 3 | | 4.6 | | |

[a]Robert V. Pattison (1986) Response to Financial Incentives Among Investor-Owned and Not-for-profit Hospitals: An Analysis Based on California Data, 1978-1982. This volume.

[b]State of Florida (1984) Hospital Cost Containment Board, 1983-1984 Annual Report. Tallahassee, Fla.

[c]State of Tennessee, Department of Health and Environment, Nashville, Tenn. Unpulished data.

[d]Texas Hospital Association, Survey of Uncompensated Care in Hospitals, published in "THA Statement of Fair Share Formula for Financing Care for the Medically Indigent, 1985."

[e]Virginia Health Services Cost Review Commission, Richmond, Va. Unpublished data.

study showed that this was not the case at the county level (Watt et al., 1986). More for-profit hospitals located in counties with slightly higher rates of poverty and non-white populations than did not-for-profit hospitals, but the differences were not statistically significant when controlled for census regions. On the other hand, for-profit hospitals—chain and independent—are more likely to be located outside of central cities than their not-for-profit counterparts, many of which of course made location decisions during an earlier period.

## REDUCING UNCOMPENSATED CARE

Numerous strategies are available to both for-profit and not-for-profit hospitals that seek to minimize provision of uncompensated care. Transferring or "dumping" undesired patients has received considerable attention in the media. No available data indicate whether for-profit or not-for-profit hospitals are more likely to transfer patients for "economic reasons," or the extent to which health or lives are being endangered by such practices. However, there are concerns that in the face of a changing payment system and price competition, both for-profit and not-for-profit hospitals are increasingly "dumping" unwanted patients. There are also fears that "dumping" will create serious financial stress on recipient hospitals. Chicago's Cook County Hospital reportedly receives 6,000 inpatients per year from Chicago's private hospitals and an estimated 25,000-75,000 outpatients, all described as "dumped" (Schiff, 1985). One major public hospital, Parkland Memorial Hospital in Dallas, whose budget had been strained by transfers of out-of-county indigent patients for whom the hospital is not legally responsible, has instituted a "hot-line" to be used by referring hospitals. This is an attempt to ensure that medically unstable patients receive treatment before transfer and that "economic" reasons are not the only reason for transfer. Taking action to deflect uninsured patients

is not unique to that hospital. In 1981 and 1982 alone, 15 percent of all hospitals adopted explicit limits on the amount of charity care they would provide. (Sloan et al., 1986).

Case studies conducted by the committee in three cities where for-profit chain, not-for-profit chain, independent not-for-profit, and public hospitals competed, showed that all types of hospitals have intentionally or unintentionally taken steps that can diminish their chances of providing indigent care (Townsend, 1986). The location of a hospital in relation to low-income populations and to other hospitals can heavily influence whether patients who are unable to pay will seek access, a factor that affected the siting decision of an investor-owned hospital in one of the cities. Other actions taken by for-profit, not-for-profit, or public hospitals in just these three cities include

• locating in neighborhoods with well-insured populations (for-profit and not-for-profit);

• having an emergency room that is not equipped for trauma, so that such cases (which produce disproportionate numbers of bad debts) are taken elsewhere by ambulance drivers (for-profit);

• refusing admission of uninsured patients and referring them to a public hospital, sometimes as much as two hours away (this strategy was sometimes defeated by uninsured pregnant women, who would wait in the parking lot until they were in late stages of labor before entering the emergency room) (for-profit and not-for-profit);

• deciding not to provide (for-profit) or to stop providing (not-for-profit) obstetric services—a service that often produces disproportionate numbers of bad debts;

• screening for financial status before admitting and admitting only urgent cases, which are then transferred to a public hospital after stabilization (for-profit and not-for-profit);

• requiring preadmission deposits (for-profit and not-for-profit).

The case studies also showed that the most dramatic action taken to reduce uncompensated care was the public hospital that closed its emergency room so it could shift uninsured patients to two nearby religiously affiliated hospitals. This example shows that hospitals of all types may act to reduce the amount of uncompensated care that they provide.

This brief list of strategies used by hospitals to deflect nonpaying patients suggests that it is difficult to avoid providing some uncompensated care. Case law, some state statutes, and accreditation standards all hold hospitals responsible for providing services in medical emergencies (although it is often not clear what constitutes an emergency or what services are required). The case studies showed several other reasons why hospitals would accept some level of uncompensated care as the price of doing business. Maintenance of good medical staff relations may sometimes require hospitals to allow physicians to admit a few patients who lack means to pay. Also, some services that attract indigent patients may also draw enough paying patients to result in a net revenue gain. Moreover, it may not be possible to reduce bad debt below a certain minimum in any service industry that cannot operate on a cash-and-carry basis. Data on bad debts do not by themselves reveal how assiduously institutions tried to minimize the provision of uncompensated care.

### The Impact of For-profit Acquisition

The acquisition (and construction) activities of investor-owned hospital companies could, in theory, have both positive and negative impacts on access to care. The positive hypothesis, largely undocumented, is that their investments may at minimum make services more convenient to the people they serve. The growth of investor-owned hospitals in areas of relatively high population growth supports this idea, their relatively low hospital occupancy rates notwithstand-

ing. Anecdotes suggest that some acquisitions may have prevented the closure of hospitals, a notion supported by data showing that hospitals purchased by for-profit chains in California were unprofitable prior to acquisition (Pattison, 1986). However, in few cases are for-profit hospitals the only source of care available to populations; fewer than a dozen of the 365 hospitals on the Health Care Financing Administration's list of "sole community hospitals" are for-profit.[6]

The negative hypothesis is that acquisitions by investor-owned companies will reduce the amount of services provided to patients who are unable to pay. Two studies conducted for the committee, which examined data on small numbers of hospitals before and after acquisition,[7] provide some support for this concern. One study describes for-profit chain acquisitions between 1979 and 1981 in Florida; the other examines acquisitions in California between 1977 and 1981 (Brown and Klosterman, 1986; Pattison, 1986). Because most acquired hospitals were previously for-profit, the changes observed cannot be attributed to a change from not-for-profit to for-profit ownership but, rather, to changes in goals and strategies.[8]

At hospitals purchased by investor-owned corporations in Florida, the percentage of total patient revenues for charity care and bad debt declined between 14 and 35 percent in three years, while hospitals that had not changed ownership showed an average 5 percent increase in the same measure of uncompensated care (Brown and Klosterman, 1986). In California, hospitals acquired by for-profit chains reportedly reduced bad debt from 2.7 percent to 0.2 percent of charges within four years of acquisition (Pattison, 1986). At least some of the reduction in uncompensated care may result from initiation of more effective collection procedures by the new owners.

This evidence on reduced uncompensated care after hospital acquisitions by investor-owned companies is based on a small number of cases and a problematic measure (bad debt and charity care as a percentage of gross patient revenues). Yet, there may be reason for concern, particularly because acquisitions in the 1980s began to include more public and not-for-profit hospitals than in earlier years (Hoy and Gray, 1986). Some protective mechanisms are available for communities that fear a reduction in indigent care after an investor-owned purchase of a hospital, some protective mechanisms are available, particularly if a local government hospital is bought. For instance, the money paid for the hospital may be placed in a fund devoted to payment for indigent care, the purchase agreement may require provision of some amount of charity care, or a buy-back clause may be inserted in the purchase agreement that will enable the local authority to regain control of the hospital if it is not satisfied with the administration of the facility.

## Cross-Subsidies and Uncompensated Care

Although some hospitals have significant nonpatient care revenue sources (Table 5.2), revenues from paying patients are key to the economic health of many institutions that provide substantial amounts of uncompensated care. Hadley et al. (1982) found that in 1980, one-third of the hospitals providing a high volume of care to poor people (i.e., with more than 24 percent of charges going to Medicaid, charity care, and bad debt) were financially "stressed," having deficits on operating and total accounts. Among hospitals that provided high amounts of uncompensated care, the main factor imposing financial stress was a relative lack of revenues from charge-paying, commercially insured patients from which to subsidize uncompensated care.

A frequently stated concern is that the success of for-profit hospitals in attracting paying patients could erode the ability of other hospitals in their communities to sub-

sidize indigent care. However, it is obvious that any hospital that attracts paying patients and serves few indigent patients could have this effect on hospitals that attempt to cross-subsidize indigent care.[9] Although these problems and concerns are very real, the committee found no systematic data on the impact of investor-owned hospitals on other hospitals that cross-subsidize uncompensated care.[10]

### Other For-profit Providers

Perhaps a more serious threat to the ability of institutions to cross-subsidize uncompensated care is in the growth of freestanding alternative sites that provide such services as urgent care, certain surgical procedures, radiological procedures, and the like. These centers tend to be for-profit, whether they are owned by physicians, investor-owned corporations, or not-for-profit hospitals. The services are usually designed to offer more convenient locations and hours, and lower charges than those found at traditional sites, such as hospitals and physicians' offices. Thus, they undoubtedly enhance access in some respects. However, although systematic data are not available, it appears that many—perhaps most—of the new alternative sites provide little uncompensated care; typically, cash, credit card, or evidence of workmen's compensation eligibility is demanded at the time of service.

Such freestanding providers attract paying patients needing those services on which many hospitals have generated surpluses that could be used to make up losses on uncompensated care. Thus, although the new providers may improve access to care for certain segments of the population, the segment that experiences major financial barriers—the poor and uninsured—could be hurt if hospitals respond to the revenue loss by reducing uncompensated care. While systematic documentation is lacking on this effect, the emergence of freestanding providers is clearly one of several factors making it more difficult for hospitals to cross-subsidize uncompensated care.

## Types of Services in Various Hospitals

It is widely agreed that hospitals lose money on some types of services either because of difficulty in charging patients for full costs (services that are infrequently used may present this problem) or because the service attracts an unusually large proportion of uninsured patients. It has frequently been alleged that for-profit institutions are more likely than not-for-profits to confine their operations to profitable services, which either deprives the community of access to certain services or throws an extra burden on institutions that do offer the services. Thus, the committee sought information on which services are unprofitable for institutions and which services for-profit institutions tend to offer or not to offer. Data are more readily available on the latter question.

### Which Hospital Services Lose Money?

Unfortunately, only scattered and unsatisfactory data are available in answer to this question. Several types of services have been identified for which at least some hospitals are less likely to receive full payment. In one tertiary care institution, services that utilize low- or mid-level technology were more likely to be uncompensated than were such procedures as coronary bypass, hip replacement, and peripheral vascular surgery, perhaps because it was both feasible and important to obtain assurance of payment before such elective surgery was performed. National Discharge Survey data show that maternity and accident cases are heavily represented among "self-pay" patients, which are a primary source of bad debts (Sloan et al., 1986). Estimates derived from the Census Bureau's 1984 Current Population Survey show that 25 percent of women in the prime childbearing years of 18-24—when 40

percent of births occur—had no health insurance (Gold and Kenney, 1985). At Vanderbilt Hospital, a regional neonatal care center, the treatment of newborns accounted for 27 percent of the entire institution's uncompensated charges (Sloan et al., 1986). More inferential evidence comes from regression analysis of national data, which show that margins per case (revenues less expenses) for an entire institution are negatively related to the volume of births therein (Watt et al., 1986).

Such data suggest why obstetrical services (along with emergency rooms, to which come trauma victims, who are often uninsured are often identified as services that generate disproportionate amounts of uncompensated care. This is undoubtedly true at some institutions, but not all of them. Depending on a variety of factors having to do with controlling bad debt and with stimulating other services (emergency rooms being a major source of admissions), obstetrical services and emergency departments can contribute to an institution's bottom line. For example, analyses of hospital operating statements suggest that public hospitals and large not-for-profit teaching hospitals in major metropolitan areas suffer large outpatient clinic losses and often admit unfinanced patients for essential inpatient services. In contrast, not-for-profit and investor-owned hospitals in economically advantaged areas usually earn surpluses on outpatient diagnostic and treatment services. Similarly, whether obstetrics is a money-losing service depends on such factors as institutional location and admitting policies. It is significant that in some cities, well-publicized amenities (champagne and gourmet meals) are used to attract obstetrical patients (well-financed ones, presumably) and that one of the most profitable of the investor-owned hospital companies, Humana, Inc., owns several women's hospitals. Furthermore, with the trend toward vertical integration and institutional marketing of a complete array of services, there may be serious competitive disadvantages in being unable to provide basic services.

In sum, the committee was unable to find satisfactory information about how often (and under what circumstances) it is a net financial drain on an institution to offer particular services. However, although obstetrics and emergency services may sometimes provide economic rewards to an institution, it is known that these services (or at least some aspects of these services—e.g., having an emergency room open in the early morning hours) are often money losers.

### For-profit/Not-for-profit Differences in Services

At the committee's request the American Hospital Association's Hospital Data Center provided 1983 data showing how the facilities and services reported on the AHA's annual survey were distributed in hospitals of different size and ownership types. The validity of such data are often questioned, because hospitals may exaggerate their services and because a report that a hospital has a given service reveals nothing about how often it is used. Nevertheless, the AHA is the only source of national data on what services and facilities hospitals offer. The 1983 data appear in Table 5.A.1, which is appended to this chapter.

With data presented on 42 services, 5 sizes of hospitals, and 5 types of ownership, the results of the comparisons are not easily described. However, several points can be made regarding the services offered by investor-owned chain hospitals.

First, focusing on the modal-size category (100-199 beds) and larger institutions, there is a set of basic services that virtually all hospitals offer and that differ little between investor-owned chain hospitals and not-for-profit hospitals—emergency rooms, postoperative recovery rooms, respiratory therapy, physical therapy, pharmacies. Most investor-owned chain and not-for-profit hospitals also have blood banks, histopathology laboratories, and diagnostic radiation services.

However, there is a large group of services that are more commonly offered in not-for-profit hospitals (chain and independent) than in investor-owned chain hospitals and very few that are more common in investor-owned chain than not-for-profit hospitals. Not-for-profits are more likely to have an outpatient department, premature nursery, dental services, hospice care, home care, hospital auxiliary, health promotion services, family planning services, various types of psychiatric services, radiation therapy, radioisotope implants, and therapeutic radioisotopes. (Some of these differences may change, in the view of some, because changing payment incentives may stimulate the availability of outpatient and home health services among all types of hospitals.) More commonly available in investor-owned chain hospitals are abortion services and patient representatives; among smaller hospitals, investor-owned facilities are more likely than not-for-profit institutions to offer podiatric services, ultrasound, CT scanners, and diagnostic radioisotopes.

The data also show a pattern of more services being offered by investor-owned chain hospitals than by independent proprietary hospitals, suggesting that the growth of the investor-owned hospital companies may have increased the availability of a broader range of services at the hospitals they acquired.

In sum, the AHA data provide some evidence of a narrower range of services in investor-owned hospitals, compared with not-for-profit hospitals. However, the data do not permit judgment on either of two crucial items. First, although some of the services that are found less frequently in for-profit hospitals seem unlikely to be money-makers (e.g., health promotion services, hospital auxiliaries), the extent to which the greater breadth of services provided by not-for-profit institutions includes money-losing services that must be cross-subsidized from other services is not clear. Second, the data do not show the extent to which services not offered by hospitals are essential (or even important) services that are not otherwise available in the community.

Regarding the narrower topic of emergency services and obstetrical services, few inferences can be drawn. Almost all hospitals in the AHA survey reportedly having emergency services, and the difference between investor-owned and not-for-profit hospitals is only a few percentage points. (Differences in having outpatient departments were slightly larger.) A study of Florida nonteaching hospitals with fewer than 400 beds showed that investor-owned hospitals were slightly more likely than not-for-profit hospitals to have an emergency room (80 percent versus 72.5 percent) (Sloan and Vraciu, 1983). It is likely that institutional variations in what their emergency services actually consist of and what screening procedures are used before services are provided are more important than the presence or absence of an emergency room in determining the extent to which a facility provides access, particularly to people who are unable to pay.

The committee found no sources of data on for-profit/not-for-profit differences in hospitals having obstetrical services.[11] But national data show that for-profit hospitals (both chain and independent) have significantly fewer births as a percentage of admissions than do not-for-profit hospitals (Watt et al., 1986). The AHA data, as well as data from Florida, which show that premature nurseries are much less common in investor-owned than in not-for-profit hospitals (Sloan and Vraciu, 1983), are also suggestive.[12] However, no means are available to determine whether this pattern reflects a strategy to minimize uncompensated care or the decision (by hospitals or planning agencies) not to offer services that are already being amply met in communities.

## Closing of Hospitals

Still another access-related concern about the growth of investor-owned hospital companies is whether they may be less willing than not-for-profit organizations to sustain a money-losing hospital or one that fails to attain economic goals. Although the closure of a hospital in a region with substantial excess capacity is not necessarily a tragedy, the closure of hospitals on which large numbers of uninsured patients depend or which are the only source of care in a given locale could jeopardize access to care.

Because the management of investor-owned companies is responsible to shareholders to make profitable use of invested capital, and because not-for-profit hospitals have a long history of losing money on operations, a differential willingness to close money-losing facilities may seem self-evident. However, the survival of a not-for-profit (or public) hospital that persistently loses money on patient care services depends on its ability to obtain nonpatient revenues. Clearly, some are more successful than others. Nor is it evident that an investor-owned company would readily walk away from a money-losing facility in which it had made a substantial investment without carefully evaluating the options that might be available. In short, the topic of hospital closure and type of ownership is a complex empirical (as well as theoretical) issue.

Studies of hospital closures show that for-profit hospitals are disproportionately likely to close (Sloan et al., 1986; Mullner et al., 1982). However, the long historical decline in the number of independent, proprietary for-profit hospitals and the growth of investor-owned chains during the past 15-20 years suggest that it is the former that have been closing, not the latter. To assess this possibility, the committee obtained data on all 540 hospitals that had ever been acquired or constructed by the six largest investor-owned companies[13] (which owned two-thirds of all investor-owned hospitals in 1984) (Hoy and Gray, 1986). Of the 540 hospitals, 12 (2.2 percent) had been closed (a number that does not include hospitals that were replaced). In most cases, the closure of a hospital was associated with the addition of beds at another facility, the construction of a new facility that replaced two others, or the conversion of a facility into a different type of facility. Very few hospitals were simply closed.[14]

In short, to date investor-owned hospitals have not shown a propensity to close. Indeed, in view of the likelihood that some of the hospitals they have acquired had been in serious financial trouble (Pattison, 1986), and in view of the overall low occupancy rates among investor-owned hospitals (Peter Kralovec, Hospital Data Center, American Hospital Association, unpublished data, 1985) a more plausible criticism, ironically, is that they have contributed to the nation's surplus bed capacity.

The available information pertains to a time when most hospitals experienced relatively little trouble in maintaining economic viability. If increasing competition, declining occupancy rates, new governmental regulations, or a major economic recession erode hospital margins generally, it becomes increasingly likely that some hospitals of all ownership types will become financial liabilities. Some observers predict the closure of as many as 20 percent of the nation's hospital beds in the next 5-10 years. More serious (and plausible) than concerns about investor-owned hospitals closing is the likelihood that some of the hospitals that are the most vulnerable to closure are the ones that are performing a vital role in serving uninsured populations. If that is the case, as studies of financially distressed hospitals suggest, strong public policies are needed to mitigate the growing crisis created by an uninsured population of almost 35 million people in an increasingly competitive health care system.

## ACCESS TO NURSING HOMES

Whereas the major concerns regarding hospital care pertain to uninsured patients, a major access concern of nursing homes involves low-income patients covered by the federal/state Medicaid program. Between people who are Medicaid-eligible when they enter a nursing home and "private-pay" patients who deplete their resources until they become eligible for Medicaid, the Medicaid program has become the largest source of payment for nursing home care. However, because Medicaid payment rates are often substantially lower than the rates other patients pay, nursing homes tend to prefer private-pay patients. The incentive to select non-Medicaid patients is illustrated by 1983-1984 data showing that nursing home return-on-equity in California declined as Medicaid utilization increased (Hawes and Phillips, 1986). A second major access issue involves "heavy-care" patients (e.g., with multiple medical problems) for whom payment (e.g., under Medicaid) is set on a per-diem basis, but whose care is costly.[15]

Nursing home operators often have the option of being selective in admissions and of charging private-pay patients more than Medicaid patients. This is because the demand for nursing home beds greatly exceeds the supply in many states and because adequate alternatives do not often exist for people in need of long-term care or assistance. Thus, nursing homes usually have high occupancy rates and often have waiting lists, enabling operators to select private-pay or "light-care" individuals over less-remunerative patients. Methods used by for-profit and not-for-profit nursing homes to select the most financially advantageous patients include separate waiting lists for private-pay and Medicaid patients, discharging private-pay patients to hospitals when their financial resources are gone, holding vacant beds open until a private-pay patient becomes available, requiring large pre-admission "contributions," and selecting "light-care" Medicaid patients certified to be in need of skilled nursing care.[16]

Regarding ownership and access issues in nursing homes, among which for-profit ownership predominates, for-profit homes appear to serve a disproportionately large number of Medicaid patients. Although studies at the local and state levels are somewhat inconsistent,[17] the most recent national data, from the 1977 National Nursing Home Survey, show that the percentage of Medicaid patients in for-profit nursing homes was substantially larger than in not-for-profit homes (Table 5.7). (The data do not differentiate between chain and independent homes.) Although economic incentives can discourage admission of "heavy-care" patients, and although such patients do not always receive the specialized care they need, the committee found no studies that compare the behavior of for-profit and not-for-profit nursing homes with regard to "heavy-care" patients.

## ISSUES AND RECOMMENDATIONS

### The Measurement of Care to Patients Unable to Pay

"Uncompensated care" (deductions from gross revenues for bad debt and charity care) is a seriously flawed measure of either institutional performance or the extent to which the needs of those who are unable to pay are being met. (The number of uninsured patients served is a better measure, but it is less widely available.) To say that a hospital has a given percentage of bad debt does not reveal precisely whether it has been acting with generosity or whether it has been lax or ineffective in trying to collect payment. Furthermore, "uncompensated care" is not a measure of an institution's real costs in providing such care, but only of what revenues would have been gained if payment had been received. Finally, expressed as a percentage of gross patient revenues, "uncompensated care" does not reflect any nonpatient care revenues that may be obtained to subsidize uncompensated care. Nevertheless, uncompensated care as a percentage of gross revenues is the most commonly used measure of institutions' service to patients who are unable to pay. It is useful for comparisons across categories, but it should not be taken as a true measure of the extent to which human needs are being met. And, because not all persons seek needed care, uncompensated care (or number of uninsured patients served) is at best a partial proxy for the full unfinanced needs of the population.

**TABLE 5.7** Payment Source for Nursing Home Residents by Type of Facility Ownership, 1977 (number and percent of residents)

| Payment Source | Proprietary | | Not-for-profit | | Government | |
|---|---|---|---|---|---|---|
| | Number | % | Number | % | Number | % |
| Private-pay | 333,400 | 37.5 | 130,200 | 46.2 | 37,300 | 28.2 |
| Medicaid/Medicare skilled care | 178,400 | 20.1 | 52,100 | 18.5 | 30,200 | 22.8 |
| Medicaid intermediate care | 263,300 | 29.6 | 60,300 | 21.4 | 39,100 | 29.5 |
| Other | 113,700 | 12.8 | 39,200 | 13.9 | 25,900 | 19.5 |
| Total | 888,800 | 100.0 | 281,800 | 100.0 | 132,500 | 100.0 |

SOURCE: National Center for Health Statistics (1979).

## The Need for Better Information

Clearly, there is a need for better information about the extent to which hospitals and other health care institutions are admitting and treating patients who are unable to pay or are providing services that are unprofitable, about changes in the provision of uncompensated care, and about why these changes are occurring. The committee's ability to draw conclusions about the effect of investor-owned providers on access to care has been limited by the nature of available data. However, much of the data that has been summarized in this chapter can provide a baseline against which changes among providers of all types can be compared.

Accordingly, *the committee recommends the monitoring and study of the following topics and issues:*

• The number of people unable to pay for care who (1) needed care but did not try to obtain it and (2) tried to obtain care but were refused for financial reasons.

• The amount of uncompensated care, both absolutely and relative to gross revenues, provided by hospitals of different ownership types. This will enable policymakers and others to monitor changes across all types of hospitals and differences among types of hospitals, which may change over time. Controlling for size of hospital, location, and teaching status will help ensure that factors known to affect uncompensated care are accounted for. Breaking out data by whether hospitals are sole providers or are located near a public hospital will help in assessing the impact on access of differences among hospitals in the amount of uncompensated care provided.

• The types of services and the amount of each type of service provided by hospitals of different ownership. Local-level studies and controls on whether alternative providers of care will help show whether absence of a service in a particular hospital represents deprivation for a community.

• The provision of care to the poor and medically indigent in other service settings, such as nursing homes, ambulatory surgery centers, dialysis centers, birthing centers, and outpatient diagnostic centers.

• Before-and-after studies of acquisitions of hospitals by for-profit and not-for-profit hospital systems, to examine changes in the provision of uncompensated care and the number and types of services provided.

• An evaluation of the effects of state and local governmental programs that were designed to increase the resources available to those unable to pay for care. These studies should examine the extent to which differences in the mix of hospital ownership (state by state) affect the kinds of programs adopted, the ways in which the programs are implemented, and their eventual effects.

Such information will be of growing importance as competitive conditions make it more difficult for institutions to finance important activities. State health planning agencies, and the 141 local health planning agencies that still exist, can play an important role in obtaining and publicizing information about problems of access to health care.[18]

## The Obligations of Health Care Institutions

What are the social, moral, or legal obligations of hospitals and other health care organizations to serve people who need care, but who lack the ability to pay? From whence might such an obligation derive, and what is its extent (e.g., to emergency situations only or to more than that)? A full analysis of such questions is beyond the scope of this study. However, it is important to keep in mind why the questions arise and to consider their implications for the for-profit/not-for-profit distinction.

The questions arise partly because the care of millions of uninsured and underinsured people may depend on the willingness of institutions to provide services for which they may not get paid. The question of institutional obligation to provide care to those who cannot pay (or to provide services that lose money) is, thus, also a question of whether institutions are obligated to raise funds for this purpose. Historically, many health care institutions were given or accepted such an obligation, and it has been part of the traditional ethos of many hospitals, particularly not-for-profit and public institutions. However, these institutions also had access to nonpatient revenues—governmental grants and appropriations, charitable contributions, and the like. The availability of these crucially important sources of revenue has dramatically diminished in proportion to need,[19] and institutions have long had to subsidize the care of some patients with revenues derived from charge-paying patients. Their ability to do this depends on the number of such patients that they serve and the impunity with which they can raise prices for the services they provide.

The committee, like the President's Commission for the Study of Ethical Problems in Medicine and Biomedical and Behavioral Research (1983) and many other bodies before it, believes that ensuring an adequate level of health care is a societal obligation (for which provisions can be made in both the public and private sectors) and that government should, and eventually must, make provisions to assure care for those whom the private sector fails.

However, the committee also believes that government's failure to make such provisions does not relieve health care institutions of their moral obligation to help care for those who are unable to pay. The committee believes that in the absence of full governmental funding of health care for all those who are unable to pay, health care institutions should be expected to do whatever they can to care for needy members of their communities. At minimum, health care institutions, because of the peculiar vulner-

ability of people who need medical care but lack resources to pay and because of the traditional values that have been attached to providing health care, are morally obligated—and should be legally obligated—to provide medical care in situations of emergency. (The definition of emergency and the extent of care that must be provided are slippery issues. See, for example, Relman, 1985; Annas, 1985.) Beyond this, the amount of such care that should be provided depends on various factors, including need in the community and the ability of the institution to provide uncompensated care without imprudent financial strain.

## The Issue of Tax Status

A question that arises is whether taxpaying and tax-exempt institutions have the same or different moral or legal obligations to provide uncompensated care in other than emergency situations. Although the committee had insufficient discussion on which to base strong recommendations, the matter of taxes and tax exemptions merits much additional consideration and discussion in health care. Several issues are discussed below.

*The Question of "Fair Share."* Our "system" of health care for the uninsured has consisted of undefined, unorganized, and uncoordinated institutional and professional contributions, financed largely by the shifting of costs onto insured patients. It is, accordingly, difficult even in theory to provide a standard for determining whether a particular hospital has done its "fair share" of charity care or, indeed, whether the notion of "fair share" makes sense (Brock and Buchanan, 1986). We can examine comparative performance data, as this report has, but these data alone do not lead to conclusions about whether hospitals have satisfied their obligations, if indeed such obligations exist. All we know for certain is that without governmental assistance, many people will not get adequate medical care unless enough hospitals provide a substantial amount of uncompensated care.

*Obligations Attached to Tax Exemptions.* In the committee's view some social obligations or expectations should be attached to an institution's tax-exempt status. At the local level, as the Supreme Court of the State of Utah recently held, it is legitimate for local governments—recognizing the extent to which exemptions from property taxes entail a taxpayer subsidy of a health care institution—to evaluate what benefits are received in exchange and to act accordingly (*Utah County v. Intermountain Health Care, Inc.*, 1985). The more health care institutions behave as a commercial enterprise might be expected to behave—for example, in not obtaining or dispensing charity care—the more problematic is the justification for property tax exemptions. Similar reasoning can be applied to federal exemptions from corporate income taxes. However, it should be remembered that the social obligation of a not-for-profit institution can be discharged in many ways (which includes offering unprofitable services and engaging in inadequately funded educational activities and unsponsored research); providing significant amounts of uncompensated care is but one.

*Obligations of For-profit Institutions.* Do for-profit hospitals have a lesser responsibility to provide uncompensated care than other kinds of hospitals? The answer depends on values and points of view. From the standpoint of an indigent patient in need of care, but ineligible for publicly funded care, an argument that the local hospital has paid its taxes and thereby has discharged its social obligations would clearly be of little comfort.

From the standpoint of a taxpaying health care organization, the argument that its taxes at least partly discharge its social obligations is more telling. Since the taxpaying (i.e., for-

profit) institution is not afforded the benefits of a tax exemption, the argument goes, it should not be saddled with the obligations that attach thereto.

Empirically, the question of whether for-profits accept as great a burden in taxes and charity care as not-for-profits accept in charity care alone is not answered simply. The tax data needed to make an exact comparison are not easily available, but a rough estimate can be made. In 1983 the four largest investor-owned multihospital companies (Hospital Corporation of America, Humana, National Medical Enterprises, and American Medical International) paid on average 2.5 percent of gross revenues in income taxes[20] (Steven C. Renn, The Center for Hospital Finance and Management, The Johns Hopkins University, personal communication, 1985). If their level of uncompensated care is reflected in the for-profit average reported by the AHA for 1983—3.1 percent of gross revenues, as shown in Table 5.6—the sum of income taxes and uncompensated care (5.6 percent of gross revenues) exceeded the 4.1 percent of gross revenues that not-for-profit hospitals accounted for as uncompensated care. Accepting the argument that taxes are in some sense equivalent to uncompensated care, and making the somewhat problematic assumption that not-for-profit hospitals are doing their fair share, these four companies together can claim to have done their "fair share," if such average figures are meaningful given the highly variable nature of local uncompensated care problems and of the resources available to meet them.

In sharp contrast is the point of view that payment of taxes is irrelevant to a health care institution's purpose and obligations. From this viewpoint, social policy should insist that hospitals be public service institutions. Whether they choose to operate as not-for-profit or for-profit enterprises, hospitals should be made to serve public needs. There is no fundamental right to public support in the operation of a hospital for private ends—whether those ends are to generate profits, create employment, or engage in educational and research activities. From this point of view, the public can, and should, set some conditions to guarantee access to the services it needs. Community support, whether financial or otherwise, should be contingent on performance in the public interest. This includes, of necessity, some activities that are not profit maximizing. Whether those who wish to operate the hospitals under these conditions want to organize themselves on a for-profit or a not-for-profit basis is a matter of secondary interest. If hospitals can make a profit while performing their functions to the community's satisfaction, however that might be expressed, everyone comes out ahead; but there is no special reason to excuse any such institution from public service.

Although the conflicting positions just discussed cannot be fully reconciled, the committee holds that all health care institutions have social obligations that flow from the needs of the communities that they serve and the ethical traditions of health care. However, taxing authorities that grant tax exemptions are entitled to expect not-for-profit organizations to continue, within reasonable limits, to provide some form of service in exchange for the tax exemptions, whether that service be providing uncompensated care, offering unprofitable services, sponsoring educational or research activities, or offering care at reduced prices. The feasibility of institutions' generating the revenues required to provide all needed care to uninsured and underinsured patients is becoming increasingly doubtful.

## The Government's Obligation for Uninsured Patients

Notwithstanding the committee's belief that institutions have an obligation to do whatever they can to meet the health care needs of people who are unable to pay, it is increasingly clear that new ways of providing financial support and encouragement for providing uncompensated care are needed.

Cross-subsidization at the institutional level has never been a satisfactory or adequate method of meeting the health care needs of uninsured people. People often do not obtain needed care, and institutions that provide large amounts of uncompensated care tend to become financially distressed (Hadley et al., 1982; Kelly and O'Brien, 1983). Furthermore, it is apparent that institutions will find it increasingly difficult to cross-subsidize indigent care. Providers are under increasing pressure from third-party payers to compete on price. Institutions in such circumstances—probably only a small number today, but likely many more in the future—risk their very survival if they engage in behavior that makes them noncompetitive on price. This being the case, in the absence of governmental intervention, the likelihood is that care for those who are unable to pay will be increasingly jeopardized.

The committee did find some evidence that hospitals of all types are attempting to diminish their uncompensated care burden. Although it is likely that some hospitals are decreasing their uncompensated care load because of financial necessity, the committee is concerned that others are reacting not to financial stress, but rather to a change in the ethos of health care. Maturation of the health care market has made growth more difficult; efforts by purchasers of care to control costs are beginning to make competition a way of life; and health care increasingly is becoming commercialized. These developments may be eroding the charitable attitude that has characterized many hospitals. Notions of responsibility for community health needs and acceptance of charitable activities as an inherent part of the provision of health care services may be disappearing. These changes in the spirit of health care may allow uncompensated care burdens to be reduced without fear of public or professional opprobrium.

Federal action to solve access problems

for the poor is not imminent, but there is an encouraging and growing movement among state and local governments to enhance access to care for people who lack a source of funds. A variety of financing mechanisms are possible;[21] evaluation of efforts now under way at the state level is needed. How states choose to approach the problems of financing care for those who are unable to pay will depend on political circumstances, and the access problems will have to be identified. In the committee's view, providing medical care to the nation's 35 million uninsured people is a challenge that should be very high on the nation's public policy agenda.

## CONCLUSION

The major access issue in the United States concerns patients who are unable to pay for care and who are dependent on the willingness of hospitals to provide services. Two measures of such willingness were examined in this chapter: admissions of uninsured patients to hospitals and provision of uncompensated care by hospitals. The performance of not-for-profit hospitals was more favorable on both measures, although when measured as percentages of total admissions or total revenues, the national differences were not large. Small percentage differences, however, can translate into large numbers of patients, particularly if institutions that provide comparatively small amounts of uncompensated care comprise a relatively large proportion of the market. Data from four of five states about which the committee obtained data showed that not-for-profit hospitals provided two or three times as much uncompensated care, on average, than did for-profit hospitals. (Both types provided less such care than did public hospitals.) Because revenues from paying patients are key to the ability of many institutions to provide uncompensated care, and because the amount of revenue needed depends on the amount of uncompensated care provided,

the for-profit presence in such circumstances may make it more difficult for other hospitals to provide uncompensated care.

Freestanding ambulatory care centers (which tend to be for-profit) have a similar effect. However, little direct evidence is available on the question of how some institutions impact on other institutions. The question of whether for-profit hospitals eschew nonprofitable services also could not be answered satisfactorily. Although larger percentages of many services are offered in not-for-profit than for-profit hospitals of similar size, satisfactory evidence is not available on which services are unprofitable.

In the view of the committee, traditional values of health care institutions remain important, meaning that health care institutions should do whatever they can to meet the needs of uninsured patients. The committee also concluded that tax-exempt institutions should be reasonably expected to accept a heavier responsibility for actions that depart from profit-maximizing behavior.

Finally, the committee concluded that the problem of access for uninsured patients cannot be dealt with adequately by health care institutions, and that the expectation that they will do so is a major public policy failure. A variety of options are available to address this problem, but as our health care system becomes more competitive and price sensitive, the resulting impact on uninsured patients is a major problem that should no longer be ignored.

### NOTES

[1]Estimates of the number of people who are unable to pay for medical care vary. National sample surveys in 1977 and 1982 showed that approximately 9 percent of the population—almost 20 million people—had neither health insurance nor eligibility for public programs, and as many as 9 percent of the insured population reported having been without insurance at some time during the previous year (Farley, 1985a; Robert Wood Johnson Foundation, 1983). More recent estimates of the uninsured population range as high as 15 percent

of the population or 35 million people (Katherine Swartz, The Urban Institute, personal communication, 1985; U.S. Bureau of the Census, 1985). In addition, there are millions of underinsured people, whose limited insurance puts them at substantial risk of having out-of-pocket expenses upwards of 10 percent of their total income. The best data on this topic, the government's 1977 National Medical Care Expenditure Survey, found that depending on the definition used, from 5 to 18 percent of the population under age 65 was underinsured (Farley, 1985b).

[2] A 1956 Internal Revenue Code Ruling held that for tax-exemption purposes, not-for-profit hospitals had to accommodate patients who were unable to pay, to the extent of their financial abilities. By 1983 that requirement had been dropped, as had another requirement for the operation of a full-time emergency department open to all patients, without financial prerequisites. A 1983 Internal Revenue Code Ruling (83-157) held that a hospital could maintain its tax exempt status in the absence of an emergency room if a state planning authority had determined that an emergency department would duplicate existing services. In that event, however, the hospital must—as community service—accept Medicaid and Medicare patients, reinvest surplus revenue into capital improvements or health services, maintain an open medical staff, and appoint a governing board representative of the composition of the area (Bernstein, 1984). Other legal obligations flow from state and local interventions to ensure that hospitals offer some care for poor people. For example, under Texas law, hospital districts are responsible for their "needy," and public district and county hospitals are responsible for the "indigent sick." Furthermore, the Texas Property Tax Code states that to be tax-exempt, hospitals must be organized to perform a charitable purpose, generally by providing medical care without regard to the ability of the beneficiaries to pay. The only requirement that applies to for-profit as well as not-for-profit hospitals in Texas is an obligation to provide emergency care in life- or limb-threatening circumstances.

[3] Uninsured is defined as self-pay, reduced pay, Hill-Burton, or no charge.

[4] Although bad debt and charity are conceptually different, the way they are accounted for and reported by hospitals is influenced less by conceptual distinctions than by reimbursement rules, Hill-Burton obligations, and other factors. Thus, the two figures have been combined in the committee's analyses reported herein. Deductions from revenue for bad debt and charity care exaggerate the cost to institutions of providing uncompensated care, because such cost is measured in terms of charges for services rather than the marginal cost of providing the services.

[5] For example, the Hospital Corporation of America (HCA) reports that uncompensated care amounts to 3 percent of revenues in areas of Kentucky where public facilities exist, but is 4.8 percent of revenues in areas where the HCA hospital is a sole provider (Vraciu and Virgil, 1986).

[6] Only 11 for-profit hospitals listed in the Federation of American Hospital's 1985 directory appear among the 365 hospitals on the Health Care Financing Administration's (HCFA's) list of sole community hospitals as of July 17, 1985. Two of these institutions were independent. It should be noted that the HCFA definition of sole community provider is partly designed to minimize the number of such institutions, and that people in a larger number of communities may view their own hospital as the only one that is reasonably convenient and available.

[7] No data are available describing changes that occur when hospitals are acquired by not-for-profit multihospital systems.

[8] Hoy and Gray (1986) found that 80 percent of the hospitals owned by the largest six investor-owned hospital companies were either acquired from previous for-profit owners or were newly constructed. Acquisition of public or not-for-profit hospitals has become more common in recent years.

[9] A design for a systematic study was recently explored by Jack Hadley and Judith Feder of the Georgetown University Center for Health Policy Studies. Their approach was to use data from American Hospital Association surveys between 1977 and 1981 and to focus on hospitals' (1) deductions from gross revenues for charity care and bad debt and (2) revenue from privately insured patients. The study was to focus on trends of these measures before and after the entry into a community of an investor-owned hospital or an existing hospital becoming part of an investor-owned or not-for-profit multihospital system. Unfortunately, the data proved to be inadequate, and the study could not be done.

[10] Case examples illuminate the dynamics of such interactions among the hospitals in a service area. One such case study is the Public Broadcasting System's "Crisis at General Hospital," which describes the forced reduction in uncompensated care at a public hospital—Tampa General Hospital in Florida, owing to the hospital's loss of revenue-producing patients to for-profit and not-for-profit hospitals.

The committee's case studies (Townsend, 1986) also show what the loss of substantial numbers of paying patients can mean to hospitals committed to providing care to the poor and uninsured of their communities. Two of the case studies were conducted in cities that had particularly difficult indigent care problems. In both cities religiously affiliated hospitals that made serious efforts to provide uncompensated care had been affected by the construction of investor-owned hospitals that provided very modest amounts of uncompensated care. In one case the investor-owned hospital had only moderate success in drawing patients away from the existing two hospitals. Although the stronger of the existing hospitals felt relatively little impact from the addition of a new hospital (and continued its provision of uncompensated care and construction and renovation projects while maintaining a healthy surplus), the weaker existing hospital developed a deficit and closed its obstetrical unit because of lack of paying maternity cases. Whether these changes were due to competition from the investor-owned hospital or to other factors was not clear. However, the key role of surplus revenues to cross-subsidize uncompensated care is well illustrated by the contrast between the two hospitals.

The second case study illustrated more clearly how a new investor-owned hospital, if successful at drawing paying patients, can affect the existing providers. In this case two well-established religious hospitals experienced substantial census declines after an investor-owned hospital opened. The hospitals suffered a period of financial and management stress while rebuilding the census—an effort helped by a growing local population. Continued cross-subsidization of uncompensated care was undoubtedly helped by the existing hospitals raising their prices substantially, bringing them more closely in line with the new investor-owned hospital. Such options will become less feasible if more price competition develops.

[11]There are many reasons other than profitability why an institution might not offer obstetrical services. It hardly makes sense for all hospitals to offer obstetrical services, particularly with birth rates having declined. Furthermore, because a significant portion of investor-owned hospitals are new facilities constructed after the implementation of health planning and certificate-of-need programs, some investor-owned hospitals may not have been allowed to offer obstetrical services because of the availability of such services at other hospitals.

[12]This comparison does not indicate the size of premature nurseries. Some hospitals may have very small premature nurseries for temporary care of babies prior to transfer.

[13]The six chains are Hospital Corporation of America; Humana, Inc.; American Medical International, Inc.; National Medical Enterprises; Charter Medical Corporation; and Republic Health Corporation.

[14]Lending support to the interpretation that it is the proprietary, rather than the investor-owned, for-profit hospitals that account for most for-profit hospital closures is the fact that while Sloan et al. (1986) found that 50 "for-profit" hospitals had closed during the period 1980-1982, Hoy and Gray (1986) found that only two hospitals owned by the six largest investor-owned hospital chains had closed during that period.

[15]Nursing homes are generally paid a per-diem rate, regardless of the cost of caring for individual patients. A few states have attempted to improve access for heavy-care patients by paying a higher rate for patients needing more intensive care, but in general there is a disincentive to admit heavy-care patients. In Illinois, where "points" are awarded for a patient's disabilities, there are fears that nursing homes have "gamed" the system by making patients appear to be more sick than they really are.

[16]Some states have acted to discourage such schemes. For example, Minnesota prohibits charging higher rates to private-pay patients. Massachusetts prohibits the refusal of a Medicaid patient when a bed is available. Connecticut requires admission on a first-come, first-served basis.

[17]For example, a study in Washington State found no difference by ownership type in the use of nursing homes by Medicaid patients (Winn, 1974), while a study in the Cleveland metropolitan area showed that for-profit homes served a higher proportion of Medicaid patients than did not-for-profit homes (Brooks and Hoffman, 1978).

[18]Health planning agencies, established under the National Health Planning and Resources Development Act of 1974, have in the past done important work in assessing the adequacy of access to care at the state and local levels. Although these agencies have undergone severe funding cuts, all states have a planning agency today and 141 local agencies still exist (Terry Shannon, Director of Field Services and Private Sector Programs, American Health Planning Association, personal communication, 1985). In principle, planning agencies at the state and local levels are well situated to provide important forums of discussion and information collection and dissemination regarding issues of access to care.

[19]Table 5.2 shows that contributions amount to 0.4 percent of the revenues of not-for-profit hospitals and 1.0 percent of the revenues of public hospitals. However, even these numbers can be misleading. A recent American Hospital Association (unpublished data, 1983) survey of sources of working capital found that only 42 percent of responding hospitals reportedly received philanthropic support and that the median amount of support for these hospitals was $43,700. (The mean amount was more than $700,000. The wide gap between mean and median is due to the influence of very large philanthropic contributions received by a relatively few institutions. Thus, the median provides a better indicator of what the typical institution might have received.) An earlier American Hospital Association (1979) survey showed that 71 percent of the respondents received charitable donations—the mean amount was just over $200,000. (Unfortunately, no median figure was available.) Neither of the above surveys shows the amount of philanthropy available for general operating purposes, which is where money to subsidize uncompensated care would presumably come from. However, a 1984 survey conducted by the National

Association for Hospital Development suggests that only a small amount of the charitable contributions received by hospitals is available for general operating purposes (AAFRC, 1985). The Association's 1,500 individual members at 1,200 hospitals (presumably the bulk of institutions that have an organized fund-raising apparatus) reported that they had raised just over $1 billion in 1984, and that 12.7 percent of this money, a mean of $108,000 per institution, was for general operating purposes. (Funds for construction and renovation comprise 25 percent of the total; spending for equipment, 17 percent; and research and education, 9 percent.) Given that the average hospital's total net revenues in 1983 were in excess of $21 million (American Hospital Association, 1984)—and the hospitals that had formal fund-raising activities were presumably larger than the average—charitable contributions for general operating purposes averaged less than 1 percent of hospital operating revenues. Given the fact that relatively few hospitals benefit from very large charitable contributions, charity for general operating purposes would appear to be less than 1 percent of revenues at most institutions, a conclusion that is supported less inferentially by Table 5.2.

[20]There was substantial variation among the four companies—from 1.1 percent for National Medical Enterprises to 4.4 percent for Humana. For-profit hospitals pay property taxes in addition to income tax. It is not known how much property tax is paid, although an industry source estimates it at roughly 20 percent of income taxes (Samuel Mitchell, Federation of American Hospitals, personal communication, 1985). This would inflate the tax burden above the figures shown in Table 3.7 in Chapter 3.

[21]Actions that can be taken to enhance access to care for disadvantaged people (some of which are being considered or are being acted on in various states) include creating a funding pool with which hospital care can be financed. A pool can be created by taxing all hospitals, or only those hospitals that fail to provide a specified amount of uncompensated care. Florida has established a pool through a contribution from state general revenues and an assessment on the net operating revenues of hospitals. Tying a hospital's assessment to the amount of uncompensated care provided reduces the incentive to "dump" patients, as do proposals requiring hospitals to devote a specified percentage of revenues to indigent care.

Some states (including Maryland, New Jersey, and Massachusetts), with all-payer rate setting, include charity or bad debt allowances in payments to hospitals. Other states create funding pools through a tax on health insurance premiums or by earmarking certain portions of general sales or other taxes. States have the option of using pooled money to finance care for all "medically needy" people or of targeting funds for especially vulnerable populations. Florida may use its funds to provide care for specific groups that are not covered by Medicaid.

Groups can also be targeted through direct governmental payments to certain teaching hospitals or governmental hospitals (Colorado, Virginia, North Carolina) or through an expansion of state Medicaid programs. In 1984, South Carolina extended Medicaid coverage to low-income pregnant women, regardless of marital status, and to children under 18, regardless of the marital status of their parents. Some states developed insurance programs to cover "catastrophic" episodes of sickness, unemployed people, and those unable to obtain conventional insurance. Finally, to spread the burden of uncompensated care more evenly among providers, licensure or certificates of need could be contingent on providing certain amounts of uncompensated care. Each approach differs in terms of who pays (e.g., hospitals, insurers, taxpayers), who benefits (e.g., people with specific medical needs such as pregnancy care, groups defined by income, groups defined by gaps in insurance), and the incentive to providers (e.g., to provide care for targeted groups, to provide uncompensated care generally, or reduce "dumping").

In seeking to reduce the number of people who are unable to find care, an option that might be considered is the use of tax credits or waivers to encourage for-profit health care institutions to provide more care to people who are unable to pay or to provide services that may be needed in a community, but that cannot be provided profitably. The use of the federal tax law to encourage private corporations to act in a way that advances some important public policy goal is hardly unprecedented, and local taxes are frequently waived or adjusted to encourage corporations to locate in a given area. However, little attention has been given to the possible use of taxing power to encourage institutions to meet public purposes.

## REFERENCES

American Association of Fund Raising Counsel, Inc. (AAFRC) (1985) *Giving USA: A Compilation of Facts and Trends on American Philanthropy for the Year 1984.* New York: American Association of Fund Raising Counsel, Inc.

American Hospital Association (1984) *Hospital Statistics.* Chicago, Ill.: American Hospital Association.

American Hospital Association (1985) *Economic Trends* 1.

Annas, George J. (1985) Adam Smith in the Emergency Room. *Hastings Center Report* 15(August):16-18.

Bernstein, Arthur H. (1984) Guidelines Issued for Preserving Tax-exempt Status. *Hospitals* 58(May 1):102.

Brock, Dan W., and Allen Buchanan (1986) Ethical Issues in For-Profit Health Care. This volume.

Brooks, Charles H., and John H. Hoffman (1978)

Type of Ownership and Medicaid Use of Nursing Care Beds. *Journal of Community Health* 3(Spring):236-244.

Brown, Kathryn J., and Richard E. Klosterman (1986) Hospital Acquisitions and Their Effects: Florida, 1979-1982. This volume.

Farley, Pamela J. (1985a) *Private Insurance and Public Programs: Coverage of Health Services.* Data Preview 20, National Health Care Expenditures Study. Rockville, Md.: National Center for Health Services Research and Health Care Technology.

Farley, Pamela J. (1985b) Who Are the Under-insured? *Milbank Memorial Fund Quarterly* 63(Summer):476-503.

Feder, Judith, Jack Hadley, and Ross Mullner (1983) *Poor People and Poor Hospitals: Implications for Public Policy.* Working Paper 3179-06. Washington, D.C.: Urban Institute.

Federation of American Hospitals (no date) *Statistical Profile of the Investor-Owned Hospital Industry 1983.* Washington, D.C.: Federation of American Hospitals.

Gold, Rachel B., and Asta M. Kenney (1985) Paying for Maternity Care. *Family Planning Perspectives* 17(May/June):103-110.

Hadley, Jack, Ross M. Mullner, and Judith Feder (1982) The Financially Distressed Hospital. *The New England Journal of Medicine* 307(November 11):1283-1287.

Hawes, Catherine, and Charles D. Phillips (1986) The Changing Structure of the Nursing Home Industry and the Impact of Ownership on Quality, Cost, and Access. This volume.

Hoy, Elizabeth, and Bradford H. Gray (1986) Trends in the Growth of the Major Investor-Owned Hospital Companies. This volume.

Kelly, Joyce V., and John J. O'Brien (1983) Characteristics of Financially Distressed Hospitals Cost and Utilization Project. Research Note 3. Rockville, Md.: National Center for Health Services Research.

Mullner, Ross M., Calvin S. Byre, Paul Levy, and Joseph D. Kubal (1982) Closure Among U.S. Community Hospitals, 1976-1980: A Descriptive and a Predictive Model. *Medical Care* 20(July):699-709.

National Center for Health Statistics (1979) *The National Nursing Home Survey: 1977 Summary for the United States.* Vital and Health Statistics, Series 13, No. 43. Washington, D.C.: U.S. Government Printing Office.

Pattison, Robert V. (1986) Response to Financial Incentives Among Investor-Owned and Not-for-Profit Hospitals: An Analysis Based on California Data, 1978-1982. This volume.

President's Commission for the Study of Ethical Problems in Medicine and Biomedical and Behavioral Research (1983) *Securing Access to Health Care. Vol. 1: Report.* Washington, D.C.: U.S. Government Printing Office.

Relman, Arnold S. (1985) Economic Considerations in Emergency Care: What Are Hospitals For? *The New England Journal of Medicine* 312(February 7):372-373.

Robert Wood Johnson Foundation (1983) *Updated Report on Access to Health Care for the American People.* Princeton, N.J.: The Robert Wood Johnson Foundation.

Rowland, Diane (1984) Hospital Care for the Uninsured: An Analysis of the Role of Proprietary Hospitals. Paper prepared for the Annual Meeting of the American Public Health Association, Anaheim, California.

Schiff, Gordon (1985) Letter to the Editor. *The New England Journal of Medicine* 312(June 6):1522.

Sloan, Frank A., Joseph Valvona, and Ross Mullner (1986) Identifying the Issues: A Statistical Profile. In Frank A. Sloan, James F. Blumstein, and James M. Perrin (eds.) *Uncompensated Hospital Care: Rights and Responsibilities.* Baltimore, Md.: Johns Hopkins University Press.

Sloan, Frank A., and Robert A. Vraciu (1983) Investor-Owned and Not-For-Profit Hospitals: Addressing Some Issues. *Health Affairs* 2(Spring):25-37.

Texas Hospital Association (1985) Table from a THA Survey of Uncompensated Care in Hospitals, published with "THA Statement of Fair Share Formula for Financing Care for the Medically Indigent."

Townsend, Jessica (1986) Hospitals and Their Communities: A Report of Three Case Studies. This volume.

U.S. Bureau of the Census (1985) *Economic Characteristics of Households in the United States: Fourth Quarter 1983.* Current Population Reports, P-70-83-4. Washington, D.C.: U.S. Government Printing Office.

Vraciu, Robert A., and Phyllis M. Virgil (1986) The Impact of Investor-Owned Hospitals on Access to Health Care. Paper presented at the Hirsch Symposium, The George Washington University, and published in Warren Greenberg and Richard M. F. Southby (eds.) *For-Profit Hospitals: Access, Quality, Teaching, Research.* Columbus, Ohio: Battelle Press.

Watt, J. Michael, Steven C. Renn, James S. Hahn, Robert A. Derzon, and Carl J. Schramm (1986) The Effects of Ownership and Multihospital System Membership on Hospital Functional Strategies and Economic Performance. This volume.

Winn, Sharon (1974) Analysis of Selected Characteristics of a Matched Sample of Nonprofit and Proprietary Nursing Homes in the State of Washington. *Medical Care* 12(March):221-228.

# APPENDIX TO CHAPTER 5

# Data on Hospital Services and Facilities

**TABLE 5.A.1**  Percent of Hospitals with Various Services and Facilities, by Type of Ownership and Selected Bed Size Categories, 1983

| Bed Size | Investor-Owned Chain (N = 440) | Proprietary (N = 172) | Not-for-profit Chain (N = 1,083) | Not-for-profit Independent (N = 2,165) | State and Local Government (N = 1,540) |
|---|---|---|---|---|---|
| | | *Specialized Services* | | | |
| Premature nursery | | | | | |
| 25- 49 | 6.5 | 5.3 | 1.5 | 3.4 | 3.8 |
| 50- 99 | 6.3 | 5.4 | 11.2 | 13.5 | 11.2 |
| 100-199 | 13.6 | 2.8 | 29.0 | 26.0 | 27.0 |
| 200-299 | 23.5 | 22.2 | 40.3 | 46.5 | 55.6 |
| 300-499 | 28.0 | * | 63.0 | 66.3 | 68.1 |
| Ambulatory surgery services | | | | | |
| 25- 49 | 67.7 | 66.7 | 78.0 | 76.5 | 69.9 |
| 50- 99 | 88.3 | 81.1 | 87.3 | 88.1 | 80.0 |
| 100-199 | 94.6 | 86.1 | 96.4 | 93.5 | 87.4 |
| 200-299 | 97.1 | 88.9 | 100.0 | 98.5 | 98.0 |
| 300-499 | 100.0 | * | 99.0 | 97.3 | 93.6 |
| Dental services | | | | | |
| 25- 49 | 32.3 | 24.6 | 31.8 | 34.9 | 23.3 |
| 50- 99 | 32.0 | 21.6 | 37.1 | 41.5 | 33.7 |
| 100-199 | 40.2 | 41.7 | 48.8 | 52.2 | 52.9 |
| 200-299 | 45.6 | 27.8 | 54.0 | 67.1 | 58.6 |
| 300-499 | 40.0 | * | 67.0 | 72.0 | 80.9 |
| Podiatric services | | | | | |
| 25- 49 | 51.6 | 17.5 | 19.7 | 25.2 | 12.0 |
| 50- 99 | 40.6 | 35.1 | 31.5 | 32.1 | 19.0 |
| 100-199 | 34.2 | 55.6 | 32.1 | 44.4 | 28.1 |
| 200-299 | 41.2 | 27.8 | 43.2 | 47.1 | 46.5 |
| 300-499 | 20.0 | * | 46.5 | 47.2 | 40.4 |
| Abortion services | | | | | |
| 25- 49 | 22.6 | 8.8 | 10.6 | 9.7 | 10.1 |
| 50- 99 | 19.5 | 27.0 | 10.7 | 19.5 | 12.5 |
| 100-199 | 28.8 | 30.6 | 22.2 | 28.9 | 20.5 |
| 200-299 | 47.1 | 33.3 | 16.5 | 43.5 | 47.5 |
| 300-499 | 60.0 | * | 20.5 | 55.5 | 60.6 |
| Hospice | | | | | |
| 25- 49 | 0.0 | 0.0 | 0.8 | 2.1 | 3.3 |
| 50- 99 | 0.8 | 2.7 | 7.1 | 5.7 | 2.9 |
| 100-199 | 1.6 | 0.0 | 13.9 | 11.3 | 5.0 |
| 200-299 | 1.5 | 0.0 | 13.1 | 17.9 | 8.1 |
| 300-499 | 0.0 | * | 30.5 | 18.9 | 9.6 |

*(Continued)*

**TABLE 5.A.1** *Continued*

| Bed Size | Investor-Owned Chain (N = 440) | Proprietary (N = 172) | Not-for-profit Chain (N = 1,083) | Not-for-profit Independent (N = 2,165) | State and Local Government (N = 1,540) |
|---|---|---|---|---|---|
| *Community Services* | | | | | |
| Emergency department | | | | | |
| 25- 49 | 83.9 | 77.2 | 90.2 | 89.1 | 95.1 |
| 50- 99 | 91.4 | 75.7 | 93.4 | 90.6 | 97.8 |
| 100-199 | 94.6 | 72.2 | 96.0 | 93.7 | 97.1 |
| 200-299 | 92.6 | 100.0 | 99.4 | 95.9 | 98.0 |
| 300-499 | 96.0 | * | 99.5 | 98.9 | 93.6 |
| Outpatient department | | | | | |
| 25- 49 | 12.9 | 24.6 | 28.8 | 39.1 | 24.9 |
| 50- 99 | 29.7 | 29.7 | 36.5 | 36.9 | 27.4 |
| 100-199 | 36.4 | 33.3 | 47.6 | 45.5 | 36.3 |
| 200-299 | 48.5 | 50.0 | 57.4 | 62.4 | 55.6 |
| 300-499 | 64.0 | * | 76.0 | 72.5 | 69.1 |
| Home care program | | | | | |
| 25- 49 | 6.5 | 7.0 | 15.2 | 8.4 | 8.2 |
| 50- 99 | 7.8 | 2.7 | 11.7 | 9.6 | 8.2 |
| 100-199 | 11.4 | 5.6 | 19.8 | 13.6 | 13.3 |
| 200-299 | 13.2 | 11.1 | 16.5 | 20.6 | 13.1 |
| 300-499 | 8.0 | * | 30.0 | 27.5 | 13.8 |
| Volunteer services department | | | | | |
| 25- 49 | 25.8 | 17.5 | 38.6 | 37.4 | 25.6 |
| 50- 99 | 70.3 | 37.8 | 62.4 | 55.0 | 49.1 |
| 100-199 | 74.5 | 69.4 | 85.3 | 79.4 | 65.5 |
| 200-299 | 89.7 | 72.2 | 91.5 | 90.3 | 82.8 |
| 300-499 | 100.0 | * | 99.5 | 97.0 | 92.6 |
| Patient representative | | | | | |
| 25- 49 | 16.1 | 22.8 | 27.3 | 25.6 | 18.8 |
| 59- 99 | 57.0 | 45.9 | 41.6 | 39.7 | 31.7 |
| 100-199 | 64.7 | 55.6 | 59.9 | 51.1 | 47.1 |
| 200-299 | 72.1 | 66.7 | 65.9 | 62.4 | 64.6 |
| 300-499 | 88.0 | * | 73.5 | 69.8 | 69.1 |
| Social work services | | | | | |
| 25- 49 | 64.5 | 29.8 | 45.5 | 51.3 | 32.5 |
| 50- 99 | 84.4 | 73.0 | 78.7 | 78.7 | 63.4 |
| 100-199 | 89.7 | 86.1 | 95.6 | 91.6 | 88.1 |
| 200-299 | 92.9 | 94.4 | 98.9 | 97.9 | 93.9 |
| 300-499 | 88.0 | * | 99.5 | 99.5 | 95.7 |
| Hospital auxiliary | | | | | |
| 25- 49 | 61.3 | 38.6 | 82.6 | 78.6 | 71.8 |
| 59- 99 | 63.3 | 45.9 | 88.8 | 86.9 | 86.7 |
| 100-199 | 74.5 | 47.2 | 89.7 | 91.4 | 87.1 |
| 200-299 | 64.7 | 44.4 | 92.6 | 94.1 | 92.9 |
| 300-499 | 56.0 | * | 95.0 | 97.3 | 86.2 |
| Health promotion | | | | | |
| 25- 49 | 6.5 | 12.3 | 17.4 | 23.1 | 16.7 |
| 50- 99 | 30.5 | 13.5 | 36.5 | 27.8 | 18.2 |
| 100-199 | 36.4 | 30.6 | 54.8 | 45.3 | 28.1 |
| 200-299 | 38.2 | 16.7 | 58.5 | 59.4 | 41.4 |
| 300-499 | 52.0 | * | 73.5 | 69.3 | 48.9 |

**TABLE 5.A.1** *Continued*

| Bed Size | Investor-Owned Chain (N = 440) | Proprietary (N = 172) | Not-for-profit Chain (N = 1,083) | Not-for-profit Independent (N = 2,165) | State and Local Government (N = 1,540) |
|---|---|---|---|---|---|
| Family planning services | | | | | |
| 25- 49 | 3.2 | 3.5 | 3.0 | 5.9 | 1.9 |
| 50- 99 | 3.1 | 2.7 | 5.6 | 3.9 | 2.0 |
| 100-199 | 1.6 | 8.3 | 7.9 | 5.6 | 3.6 |
| 200-299 | 0.0 | 0.0 | 14.8 | 15.6 | 12.1 |
| 300-499 | 0.0 | * | 31.0 | 22.9 | 34.0 |
| *Capital-Intensive Therapies* | | | | | |
| Open-heart surgery facility | | | | | |
| 25- 49 | 3.2 | 0.0 | 0.0 | 0.0 | 0.0 |
| 50- 99 | 0.8 | 0.0 | 0.0 | 0.2 | 0.2 |
| 100-199 | 4.3 | 2.8 | 4.4 | 4.5 | 0.4 |
| 200-299 | 16.2 | 5.6 | 18.8 | 8.8 | 12.1 |
| 300-499 | 32.0 | * | 41.0 | 27.0 | 42.6 |
| Hemodialysis | | | | | |
| 25- 49 | 3.2 | 0.0 | 0.8 | 0.0 | 0.7 |
| 50- 99 | 6.3 | 16.2 | 6.1 | 3.4 | 3.7 |
| 100-199 | 25.0 | 19.4 | 20.6 | 14.2 | 11.2 |
| 200-299 | 50.0 | 11.1 | 51.1 | 39.1 | 46.5 |
| 300-499 | 26.0 | * | 63.5 | 67.1 | 67.0 |
| Organ transplant | | | | | |
| 25- 49 | 3.2 | 0.0 | 1.5 | 0.8 | 0.7 |
| 50- 99 | 2.3 | 0.0 | 0.5 | 0.5 | 0.2 |
| 100-199 | 1.6 | 2.8 | 2.4 | 3.4 | 0.4 |
| 200-299 | 2.9 | 0.0 | 8.5 | 2.6 | 4.0 |
| 300-499 | 0.0 | * | 5.5 | 9.2 | 19.1 |
| CT scanner | | | | | |
| 25- 49 | 0.0 | 3.5 | 2.3 | 2.9 | 0.9 |
| 50- 99 | 23.4 | 21.6 | 10.2 | 11.9 | 8.4 |
| 100-199 | 53.8 | 33.3 | 39.3 | 34.2 | 25.9 |
| 200-299 | 73.5 | 66.7 | 75.6 | 70.9 | 72.7 |
| 300-499 | 92.0 | * | 92.0 | 92.2 | 86.2 |
| X-ray radiation therapy | | | | | |
| 25- 49 | 0.0 | 3.5 | 0.0 | 1.7 | 0.9 |
| 50- 99 | 0.8 | 0.0 | 3.0 | 0.5 | 2.0 |
| 100-199 | 7.6 | 2.8 | 11.5 | 10.4 | 6.8 |
| 200-299 | 11.8 | 16.7 | 26.7 | 27.1 | 36.4 |
| 300-499 | 24.0 | * | 52.0 | 51.8 | 55.3 |
| Megavoltage radiation therapy | | | | | |
| 25- 49 | 0.0 | 0.0 | 0.0 | 0.4 | 0.2 |
| 50- 99 | 0.0 | 0.0 | 1.5 | 0.5 | 1.4 |
| 100-199 | 5.4 | 2.8 | 8.7 | 8.2 | 5.8 |
| 200-299 | 7.4 | 16.7 | 23.3 | 23.8 | 31.3 |
| 300-499 | 24.0 | * | 51.0 | 49.6 | 51.1 |
| Radioactive implants | | | | | |
| 25- 49 | 6.5 | 0.0 | 0.8 | 0.8 | 0.5 |
| 50- 99 | 4.7 | 5.4 | 4.1 | 3.9 | 3.1 |
| 100-199 | 14.7 | 11.1 | 25.8 | 13.6 | 12.2 |
| 200-299 | 32.4 | 33.3 | 39.2 | 35.3 | 39.4 |
| 300-499 | 48.0 | * | 67.0 | 62.8 | 68.1 |

*(Continued)*

**TABLE 5.A.1**   *Continued*

| Bed Size | Investor-Owned Chain (N = 440) | Proprietary (N = 172) | Not-for-profit Chain (N = 1,083) | Not-for-profit Independent (N = 2,165) | State and Local Government (N = 1,540) |
|---|---|---|---|---|---|
| Therapeutic radioisotope facility | | | | | |
| 25- 49 | 3.2 | 0.0 | 0.8 | 1.3 | 0.7 |
| 50- 99 | 1.6 | 2.7 | 4.1 | 2.3 | 2.9 |
| 100-199 | 12.5 | 8.3 | 24.6 | 15.8 | 14.0 |
| 200-299 | 32.4 | 38.9 | 41.5 | 39.7 | 52.5 |
| 300-499 | 40.0 | * | 68.5 | 66.8 | 69.1 |

*Labor-Intensive Therapies*

| Bed Size | Investor-Owned Chain | Proprietary | Not-for-profit Chain | Not-for-profit Independent | State and Local Government |
|---|---|---|---|---|---|
| Psychiatric partial hospitalization program | | | | | |
| 25- 49 | 0.0 | 0.0 | 0.8 | 2.1 | 3.3 |
| 50- 99 | 2.3 | 2.7 | 3.0 | 4.6 | 3.3 |
| 100-199 | 3.8 | 5.6 | 9.5 | 10.9 | 6.1 |
| 200-299 | 4.4 | 5.6 | 10.2 | 15.9 | 18.2 |
| 300-499 | 8.0 | * | 28.0 | 21.3 | 29.8 |
| Psychiatric outpatient services | | | | | |
| 25- 49 | 0.0 | 0.0 | 0.8 | 5.0 | 3.3 |
| 50- 99 | 1.6 | 0.0 | 4.1 | 3.7 | 2.9 |
| 100-199 | 4.3 | 11.1 | 10.7 | 12.5 | 7.2 |
| 200-299 | 2.9 | 11.1 | 19.9 | 24.7 | 15.2 |
| 300-499 | 0.0 | * | 40.0 | 33.2 | 48.9 |
| Psychiatric emergency services | | | | | |
| 25- 49 | 0.0 | 8.8 | 7.6 | 8.4 | 8.9 |
| 50- 99 | 7.8 | 10.8 | 9.6 | 14.2 | 11.7 |
| 100-199 | 15.2 | 22.2 | 36.1 | 31.7 | 21.2 |
| 200-299 | 23.5 | 22.2 | 50.0 | 50.6 | 53.5 |
| 300-499 | 40.0 | * | 61.0 | 59.8 | 70.2 |
| Psychiatric foster and/or home care program | | | | | |
| 25- 49 | 0.0 | 0.0 | 0.0 | 0.0 | 0.0 |
| 50- 99 | 0.0 | 0.0 | 0.0 | 0.2 | 0.2 |
| 100-199 | 0.5 | 0.0 | 0.0 | 1.4 | 0.4 |
| 200-299 | 0.0 | 0.0 | 2.8 | 1.2 | 0.0 |
| 300-499 | 0.0 | * | 3.5 | 4.0 | 3.2 |
| Psychiatric consultation and education services | | | | | |
| 25- 49 | 3.2 | 5.3 | 1.5 | 7.1 | 5.2 |
| 50- 99 | 7.8 | 10.8 | 7.1 | 11.0 | 5.5 |
| 100-199 | 14.1 | 19.4 | 25.4 | 23.5 | 10.4 |
| 200-299 | 22.1 | 22.2 | 33.5 | 37.6 | 33.3 |
| 300-499 | 28.0 | * | 54.5 | 51.5 | 58.5 |
| Clinical psychology services | | | | | |
| 25- 49 | 3.2 | 0.0 | 6.8 | 8.4 | 6.8 |
| 50- 99 | 9.4 | 13.5 | 13.7 | 16.5 | 6.5 |
| 100-199 | 18.5 | 30.6 | 27.0 | 24.4 | 14.0 |
| 200-299 | 25.0 | 16.7 | 38.6 | 40.3 | 45.5 |
| 300-499 | 16.0 | * | 59.5 | 52.3 | 63.8 |
| Substance abuse/rehabilitation | | | | | |
| 25- 49 | 3.2 | 3.5 | 1.5 | 7.1 | 3.8 |
| 50- 99 | 3.1 | 5.4 | 5.1 | 8.3 | 3.7 |
| 100-199 | 8.7 | 19.4 | 19.4 | 11.1 | 7.2 |
| 200-299 | 11.8 | 11.1 | 13.6 | 20.6 | 13.1 |
| 300-499 | 0.0 | * | 32.0 | 27.8 | 23.4 |

**TABLE 5.A.1** *Continued*

| Bed Size | Investor-Owned Chain (N = 440) | Proprietary (N = 172) | Not-for-profit Chain (N = 1,083) | Not-for-profit Independent (N = 2,165) | State and Local Government (N = 1,540) |
|---|---|---|---|---|---|
| Genetic counseling | | | | | |
| 25- 49 | 0.0 | 1.8 | 0.8 | 0.8 | 0.9 |
| 50- 99 | 1.6 | 0.0 | 2.0 | 1.8 | 0.6 |
| 100-199 | 1.6 | 5.6 | 5.2 | 5.6 | 3.2 |
| 200-299 | 1.5 | 5.6 | 5.1 | 10.0 | 10.1 |
| 300-499 | 0.0 | * | 12.0 | 18.1 | 27.7 |
| Occupational therapy services | | | | | |
| 25- 49 | 6.5 | 1.8 | 15.2 | 15.1 | 9.2 |
| 50- 99 | 14.8 | 10.8 | 18.8 | 21.6 | 10.2 |
| 100-199 | 28.3 | 27.8 | 45.6 | 38.0 | 20.9 |
| 200-299 | 50.0 | 38.9 | 64.2 | 60.6 | 54.5 |
| 300-499 | 64.0 | * | 84.5 | 78.1 | 77.7 |
| Speech pathology | | | | | |
| 25- 49 | 19.4 | 5.3 | 13.6 | 17.2 | 12.7 |
| 50- 99 | 21.9 | 10.8 | 25.9 | 31.2 | 18.8 |
| 100-199 | 31.0 | 30.6 | 50.8 | 44.8 | 33.5 |
| 200-299 | 38.2 | 44.4 | 58.0 | 66.2 | 44.4 |
| 300-499 | 40.0 | * | 76.5 | 73.6 | 68.1 |
| Rehabilitation outpatient services | | | | | |
| 25- 49 | 9.7 | 3.5 | 12.1 | 15.5 | 7.8 |
| 50- 99 | 12.5 | 16.2 | 23.4 | 23.6 | 11.9 |
| 100-199 | 25.0 | 19.4 | 38.5 | 31.2 | 21.9 |
| 200-299 | 42.6 | 44.4 | 54.5 | 58.5 | 45.5 |
| 300-499 | 56.0 | * | 70.0 | 69.0 | 60.6 |
| Respiratory therapy services | | | | | |
| 25- 49 | 90.3 | 82.5 | 88.6 | 77.3 | 80.5 |
| 50- 99 | 94.5 | 81.1 | 89.8 | 92.2 | 89.6 |
| 100-199 | 98.4 | 97.2 | 97.2 | 96.6 | 94.2 |
| 200-299 | 100.0 | 100.0 | 100.0 | 99.7 | 99.0 |
| 300-499 | 100.0 | * | 100.0 | 99.7 | 96.8 |
| Physical therapy services | | | | | |
| 25- 49 | 80.6 | 52.6 | 75.8 | 80.7 | 66.4 |
| 50- 99 | 89.1 | 89.2 | 90.4 | 93.3 | 84.0 |
| 100-199 | 95.7 | 97.2 | 96.4 | 95.9 | 90.3 |
| 200-299 | 95.6 | 100.0 | 97.7 | 98.2 | 98.0 |
| 300-499 | 96.0 | * | 100.0 | 99.2 | 98.9 |
| *Ancillaries* | | | | | |
| Pharmacy | | | | | |
| 25- 49 | 96.8 | 89.5 | 84.8 | 85.7 | 86.4 |
| 50- 99 | 96.1 | 94.6 | 95.4 | 95.9 | 95.1 |
| 100-199 | 98.4 | 91.7 | 98.0 | 98.7 | 98.9 |
| 200-299 | 100.0 | 100.0 | 100.0 | 100.0 | 99.0 |
| 300-499 | 100.0 | * | 100.0 | 99.7 | 100.0 |
| Ultrasound | | | | | |
| 25- 49 | 45.2 | 50.9 | 49.2 | 43.7 | 46.6 |
| 50- 99 | 80.5 | 64.9 | 64.5 | 66.5 | 73.4 |
| 100-199 | 96.2 | 83.3 | 89.3 | 88.0 | 85.6 |
| 200-299 | 95.6 | 100.0 | 97.7 | 97.6 | 96.0 |
| 300-499 | 100.0 | * | 100.0 | 98.1 | 95.7 |

*(Continued)*

**TABLE 5.A.1** *Continued*

| Bed Size | Investor-Owned Chain (N = 440) | Proprietary (N = 172) | Not-for-profit Chain (N = 1,083) | Not-for-profit Independent (N = 2,165) | State and Local Government (N = 1,540) |
|---|---|---|---|---|---|
| Histopathology laboratory | | | | | |
| 25- 49 | 35.5 | 35.1 | 22.7 | 27.3 | 22.1 |
| 50- 99 | 53.9 | 51.4 | 43.1 | 50.9 | 37.0 |
| 100-199 | 83.7 | 83.3 | 83.3 | 83.3 | 72.3 |
| 200-299 | 98.5 | 94.4 | 96.0 | 95.0 | 96.0 |
| 300-499 | 96.0 | * | 99.5 | 98.1 | 97.9 |
| Cardiac catheterization | | | | | |
| 25- 49 | 0.0 | 0.0 | 0.0 | 0.4 | 0.2 |
| 50- 99 | 0.8 | 2.7 | 1.0 | 0.7 | 0.4 |
| 100-199 | 10.3 | 8.3 | 7.9 | 7.0 | 2.5 |
| 200-299 | 29.4 | 22.2 | 28.4 | 21.5 | 29.3 |
| 300-499 | 52.0 | * | 56.5 | 44.5 | 60.6 |
| Blood bank | | | | | |
| 25- 49 | 58.1 | 56.1 | 53.8 | 57.1 | 51.1 |
| 50- 99 | 71.1 | 62.2 | 66.0 | 63.5 | 65.0 |
| 100-199 | 73.9 | 77.8 | 76.2 | 76.0 | 76.3 |
| 200-299 | 83.8 | 88.9 | 87.5 | 87.4 | 83.8 |
| 300-499 | 96.0 | * | 88.0 | 89.5 | 83.0 |
| Diagnostic radioisotope facility | | | | | |
| 25- 49 | 29.0 | 43.9 | 24.2 | 26.9 | 21.6 |
| 50- 99 | 71.1 | 48.6 | 45.2 | 51.8 | 49.9 |
| 100-199 | 85.9 | 63.9 | 81.0 | 81.9 | 69.1 |
| 200-299 | 92.6 | 88.9 | 97.2 | 93.2 | 94.9 |
| 300-499 | 96.0 | * | 99.0 | 97.6 | 95.7 |
| | *Total Hospitals Reporting* | | | | |
| 6- 24 | 3 | 19 | 30 | 49 | 91 |
| 25- 49 | 31 | 57 | 132 | 238 | 425 |
| 50- 99 | 128 | 37 | 197 | 436 | 489 |
| 100-199 | 184 | 36 | 252 | 558 | 278 |
| 200-299 | 68 | 18 | 176 | 340 | 99 |
| 300-399 | 17 | 2 | 117 | 232 | 61 |
| 400-499 | 8 | 3 | 83 | 139 | 33 |
| 500+ | 1 | — | 96 | 173 | 64 |
| TOTAL | 440 | 172 | 1,083 | 2,165 | 1,540 |

*Too few cases reporting to determine percentages.

SOURCE: Compiled from data provided by Hospital Data Center, American Hospital Association, Chicago, Illinois, 1985.

# 6 Quality of Care

The growth of for-profit health care has prompted concern and speculation about the quality of care.[1] Some observers are doubtful that the increasingly visible investor-owned companies would risk their capital investments, reputations, and the possibility of tighter regulation by deciding to cut corners on quality. Nevertheless, problems could develop if the upper management of an organization emphasizes economic performance or efficiency to such an extent that subordinates make decisions that reduce quality, even if that is not intended. Some concern about the quality of care rests on the assumption that for-profit organizations are more likely than not-for-profit organizations to judge the performance of managers on narrow economic grounds, thereby inducing them to take steps that could negatively affect quality. On the other hand, clearly no general assumption is warranted that goals of high quality are inconsistent with goals of profitability in an organization. The question of the relationship between for-profit status and quality of care is empirical, not definitional. This chapter examines the limited data now available.

## QUALITY OF HOSPITAL CARE

Approaches to the appraisal of health care quality generally fall into three broad categories: evaluation of structure, evaluation of process, and evaluation of outcome or end results (Donabedian, 1969:2). Structural indicators include not only physical aspects of facilities and equipment, but also characteristics of the organization and qualifications of its health professionals. Process measures pertain to the activities of health professionals in the care of patients. Outcome measures may be stated in terms of health or in terms of patient or family satisfaction. Quality indicators vary in their comprehensiveness, their importance, their face validity, and their availability in existing data sources.

Evidence regarding the relationship between hospital ownership and quality of care is fragmentary and limited. Ideally, the committee would have liked to examine patient outcome data from carefully matched for-profit and not-for-profit settings, as well as from chain and independent institutions, in order to draw inferences about quality. Unfortunately, the committee had access only to studies using statistical controls and structure and process quality measures, such as hospital accreditation, board certification rates of staff physicians, and perceptions of physicians and hospital board chairmen, as well as some aggregate but nondefinitive pooled outcome data.

## Accreditation

Probably the most elemental single indicator of the overall quality of care is voluntary accreditation by the Joint Commission on Accreditation of Hospitals (JCAH). Accreditation is based on the evaluation of reports by site visit teams who assess institutional compliance with more than 2,200 separate standards. Although experts agree that accreditation addresses quality, the process also has its limitations. It is based heavily on structural indicators, although some process indicators are also included. Furthermore, accreditation represents a kind of threshold or minimum baseline, and because of its global nature it does not capture many important differences among institutions. Not all institutions seek accreditation; attitudes about the importance of accreditation vary in different parts of the country.

The American Hospital Association, in its annual survey of hospitals, collects data on whether hospitals are accredited. A second source of data on JCAH accreditation is from a paper prepared for the committee by Gary Gaumer (1986), using data that had been compiled for a study of state hospital rate-setting programs. The sample of hospitals included all short-term hospitals in 15 states that have prospective payment programs plus a 25 percent random sample of all other U.S. short-term hospitals. Information about full, two-year accreditation and provisional, one-year accreditation was obtained by Gaumer directly from JCAH. Finally, in response to a request from the committee, JCAH itself prepared an analysis of the outcomes of one year's accreditation visits to independent and chain for-profit and not-for-profit hospitals (Longo et al., 1986). This analysis focused not only on accreditation itself but also on "contingencies" attached by JCAH in its approval of an institution's compliance with particular JCAH standards.

Table 6.1 shows that the highest percentage of accreditation is found among hospitals in investor-owned systems, while the lowest rates are found among the independent investor-owned hospitals and among hospitals owned by state or local governments. There is virtually no difference between investor-owned and not-for-profit chain hospitals. Since much of the past growth of investor-owned chains has been through acquisition of independent for-profit hospitals, the growth of investor-owned systems likely has resulted in the accreditation of a number of hospitals that were not previously accredited.

Table 6.2 shows the results of the JCAH staff's own analysis, which is consistent with the AHA and Gaumer data shown in Table 6.1. Using data from accreditation visits conducted during the fiscal year ending May 31, 1983, the hospitals that were part of investor-owned chains were most likely to be accredited (and to be accredited without contingencies) and least likely to have failed to pass accreditation. Differences between these investor-owned and not-for profit hospitals were very small and again were in striking contrast to independent for-profit hospitals.

## Qualifications of Medical Staff

There is some evidence that investor-owned hospitals are less selective in approving physicians for staff privileges.[2] In a paper prepared for the committee, Morrisey et al. (1986) report data on the percentage of physician-applicants approved in 1981 for privileges in various hospital groupings. They found that hospitals in investor-owned systems approved 89.8 percent of applicants, compared with 81.4 percent in freestanding hospitals (for-profit and not-for-profit combined), 86.8 percent in religiously affiliated system hospitals, 81.4 percent in other not-for-profit systems, and 76.4 percent in contract-managed hospitals. (However, the differences among hospitals from investor-owned, religious, and not-for-profit systems were not statistically significant.)

Regarding board certification of staff phy-

**TABLE 6.1** Rates of JCAH Accreditation, by Type of Hospital, 1983

| Accreditation Status | Investor-Owned Chain (%) | For-profit Independent (%) | Not-for-profit Chain (%) | Not-for-profit Independent (%) | State and Local Government (%) |
|---|---|---|---|---|---|
| Accredited, AHA data, 1983[a] | 91 | 52 | 87 | 83 | 59 |
| Full (2-year) accreditation, 1981[b] | 79 | 50 | 74 | 55 | |
| Average full accreditation, 1974-1981[b] | 69 | 42 | 69 | 54 | |
| Average provisional accreditation, 1974-1981[b] | 10 | 10 | 14 | 12 | |

[a]Peter Kralovec, Hospital Data Center, American Hospital Association, 1985.
[b]JCAH data. Gaumer (1986:Table 10).

sicians,[3] Morrisey et al. (1986) found no statistically significant differences between investor-owned system hospitals and other types of hospitals in their requirements that at least some specialists be board certified, with approximately 30 percent of the hospitals having such requirements. "Proprietary" hospitals (a term that was used to include both chain and independent for-profit hospitals) have more board-certified medical staff per 100 beds than do "nonproprietary" hospitals (28.8 versus 24.6) (American Medical Association, 1984). However, this is because on average they have more physicians on their medical staffs (49.8 versus 37.3). These data, from the 1982 AHA annual survey,

show higher rates of board certification among physicians in nonproprietary hospitals than in proprietary hospitals (66 percent versus 58 percent); this is also true of the specialty groupings compared—general/family practice (41 percent versus 37 percent), medical specialties (68 percent versus 60 percent), surgical specialties (73 percent versus 64 percent), and hospital-based specialties (78 percent versus 69 percent) (American Medical Association, 1984).

These same data, however, were analyzed in a paper prepared for the committee, and it was found that when chain hospitals are separated from independent institutions, the rates of board certification of staff physicians

**TABLE 6.2** Results of JCAH Accreditation Visits for Fiscal Year Ending May 31, 1983

| | Accreditation Outcome | | |
|---|---|---|---|
| | Accredited Without Contingencies (%) | Accredited with Contingencies (%) | Not Accredited (%) |
| System/investor-owned | 48.1 | 51.3 | 0.6 |
| System/not-for-profit | 43.2 | 55.9 | 1.0 |
| Independent/for-profit | 46.4 | 51.8 | 1.8 |
| Independent/not-for-profit | 36.5 | 62.4 | 1.1 |

SOURCE: Longo et al. (1986).

vary little across types of hospitals (Morrisey et al., 1986). The lowest rates of board certification of staff physicians (58 percent) were found in publicly owned system hospitals and in contract-managed hospitals; the highest rates (65 percent) were reported for hospitals in religious systems and in other not-for-profit systems; the rates for hospitals in investor-owned systems and freestanding hospitals of all types were in an intermediate position (61 percent). In a multivariate analysis, only public hospitals were statistically different (lower) from other types of hospitals.

In another paper prepared for the committee (Musacchio et al., 1986), data from a 1984 American Medical Association survey of physicians show that the lowest rates of board certification were among physicians whose primary hospital was owned by an investor-owned system (61.4 percent) and the highest rates were among physicians practicing primarily in not-for-profit hospitals (almost 69 percent), with physicians associated with public hospitals in an intermediate position; however, these differences were not statistically significant. At the committee's request, a table was prepared to display accreditation rates among several specialties. Table 6.3 shows a puzzling and inconsistent pattern: The for-profit chain hospitals show comparatively high rates of board certification among the medical specialties and comparatively low rates among the surgical specialties, including OB/GYN. However, the difference between for-profit and not-for-profit system hospitals was not statistically significant.

### Nursing Personnel

If data on the relationship between physicians and quality are sparse, evidence relating quality of care to nursing services is even more meagre. The only available proxy measures are numbers of nursing personnel per patient. Table 6.4 displays data from the 1983 AHA annual survey of hospitals and

shows no important differences between investor-owned chain hospitals and not-for-profit hospitals, although both independent for-profit hospitals and state and local government hospitals had lower levels of registered nurses.

### Physicians' Evaluations

At the committee's request, the American Medical Association asked the physicians responding to its 1984 core survey to compare their primary hospital with other hospitals that they might be familiar with on four dimensions: the adequacy of nursing support, the responsiveness of the hospital's administration, the level of patient satisfaction, and the adequacy of technical resources and equipment (Musacchio et al., 1986). These data are perceptual in nature, and since they pertain to the hospital where physicians admit most of their patients, the possibility of favorable biases cannot be dismissed. Still, these evaluations from a national probability sample of approximately 3,200 responding physicians are subject to a different set of biases that result from studies based on data provided voluntarily by institutions. No comparable source of data has previously existed.

As shown in Table 6.5, when responses to the four questions are averaged, differences among physicians in not-for-profit and for-profit system hospitals and independent hospitals are small; they are very favorable in comparison to the responses of physicians whose primary hospital is owned by state/local governments. (Because independent for-profit hospitals are typically owned by physicians, that category possibly includes some evaluations from owners and therefore is not included in this chapter's tables; statistics for these tables appear in Musacchio et al., 1986.)

The averages displayed in Table 6.5 conceal some interesting differences in physician evaluations on the four dimensions studied. Table 6.6 shows physician evalua-

**TABLE 6.3**   Percent of Physicians That Are Board Certified, by Hospital Ownership Status and Selected Specialty Breakdown, 1984

| Physicians' Specialties | Multihospital Systems | | | Independent | | |
|---|---|---|---|---|---|---|
| | State and Local Government | Private Not-for-profit | For-profit | State and Local Government | Private Not-for-profit | For-profit |
| All physicians | 68.7 | 68.6 | 61.4 | 63.8 | 68.7 | 63.0 |
| General/family practitioners | 33.3 | 43.3 | 40.8 | 53.9 | 43.1 | 18.8 |
| Medical specialty | 66.7 | 67.3 | 75.0 | 65.0 | 70.3 | 54.6 |
| Surgical specialty other than OB/GYN | 73.9 | 82.1 | 69.6 | 73.3 | 78.8 | 82.4 |
| OB/GYN | 81.1 | 69.8 | 59.1 | 75.0 | 72.3 | — |
| Other[a] | 75.9 | 70.1 | 67.2 | 63.2 | 70.0 | 73.9 |

[a]Psychiatrists, radiologists, anesthesiologists, and pathologists.

NOTE: This breakdown showing the percentage of board-certified physicians by specialty and hospital type is statistically significant (chi-square = 111.316 with 45 degrees of freedom). Chi-square tests of significance show no difference between not-for-profit and for-profit multihospital systems when all five specialty groups were considered or when only medical, surgical, and OB/GYN were considered.

SOURCE: Musacchio et al. (1986).

tions of how nursing, hospital administration, patient satisfaction, and technical equipment in their primary hospital compares with other hospitals. The perception of greater administrative responsiveness at investor-owned hospitals is particularly striking; also noteworthy are the less-favorable evaluations given to for-profit chain hospitals than to not-for-profit hospitals on the other three dimensions: nursing support, patient satisfaction, and technical resources and equipment.

Data from another national AMA survey conducted in 1984 show that 32 percent of physicians believed that not-for-profit hos-pitals provide better quality of care than do for-profit hospitals, while only 5 percent believed the opposite to be true (Musacchio et al., 1986:Table 11). (The remainder of physicians believed there is no difference or they had no opinion.) Interestingly, of the physicians who had some staff privileges at a for-profit hospital (and data are not available on whether proprietary or investor-owned hospitals are involved), 24 percent believed that not-for-profits provide better quality of care, and 8 percent believed that for-profits provided better care. Musacchio et al. (1986) attribute this difference, at least in part, to the fact that most physicians who

**TABLE 6.4**   Nursing Personnel per 100 Adjusted Census, Short-Term General and Other Special Hospitals, 1983

| | Investor-Owned Chain | For-profit Independent | Not-for-profit Chain | Not-for-profit Independent | State and Local Government |
|---|---|---|---|---|---|
| RNs/100 patients | 82 | 70 | 84 | 83 | 71 |
| LPNs/100 patients | 32 | 28 | 26 | 25 | 30 |

SOURCE: Peter Kralovec, Hospital Data Center, American Hospital Association, 1985.

**TABLE 6.5**   Physicans' Average Evaluation of Their Primary Hospital on Four Dimensions, 1984[a]

| Primary Hospital Is— | Type of Primary Hospital | | | | |
| | Investor-Owned Chain (%) | Not-for-profit Chain (%) | Not-for-profit Independent (%) | Nonfederal Government Chain (%) | Nonfederal Government Independent (%) |
| --- | --- | --- | --- | --- | --- |
| Better | 53.1 | 55.4 | 55.4 | 31.0 | 47.6 |
| Same | 41.6 | 40.3 | 39.1 | 44.1 | 34.8 |
| Worse | 5.3 | 4.4 | 5.6 | 25.0 | 17.0 |

[a]Physicians were asked to compare their primary hospital to other hospitals with which they were familiar on four dimensions: (1) adequacy of nursing support, (2) responsiveness of the hospital administration, (3) level of patient satisfaction, and (4) technical resources and equipment. Numbers in the table are averages across these four dimensions.

SOURCE: American Medical Association, 1984 Socioeconomic Monitoring System Core Survey. Calculated from Table 11 in Musacchio et al. (1986).

perceive a difference in the amount of clinical discretion allowed physicians believe that physicians, have less discretion at for-profit hospitals. Implications for quality are quite unclear.

### Board Chairman Evaluations

Another source of perceptions comes from a survey of hospital governing board chairmen that was conducted by Arthur Young for the American Hospital Association's *Trustee Magazine* in 1983 (Arthur Young, 1983). Table 6.7 shows responses on which board responsibilities were "very important" and which responsibilities were being performed "excellently." Although these are hardly direct or objective measures of institutional quality, the responses of chairmen show some are interesting contrasts in the different types of institutions. In comparison with board chairmen from not-for-profit hospitals, board chairmen from investor-owned hospitals reported comparatively low levels of board involvement in financial and management issues (such decisions are

**TABLE 6.6**   Percent of Physicians Evaluating Their Primary Hospital as Better or Worse Than Other Hospitals with Which They Were Familiar, 1984

| Dimension | | Type of Primary Hospital | | | | |
| | | Investor-Owned Chain (%) | Not-for-profit Chain (%) | Not-for-profit Independent (%) | Nonfederal Government Chain (%) | Nonfederal Government Independent (%) |
| --- | --- | --- | --- | --- | --- | --- |
| Nursing support | Better | 48.2 | 59.7 | 56.3 | 29.0 | 50.0 |
| | Worse | 5.1 | 2.0 | 3.5 | 11.8 | 7.9 |
| Responsiveness of the hospital administration | Better | 60.2 | 47.3 | 46.8 | 29.7 | 43.5 |
| | Worse | 7.0 | 10.2 | 11.3 | 25.3 | 41.8 |
| Level of patient satisfaction | Better | 51.5 | 56.6 | 57.6 | 31.9 | 45.7 |
| | Worse | 4.6 | 1.7 | 2.8 | 14.3 | 6.7 |
| Technical resources and equipment | Better | 52.5 | 57.8 | 60.9 | 33.3 | 51.4 |
| | Worse | 4.5 | 3.8 | 4.6 | 48.4 | 11.8 |

SOURCE: American Medical Association, 1984 Socioeconomic Monitoring System Core Survey; Musacchio et al. (1986).

**TABLE 6.7** Perceptions of Hospital Governing Board Chairmen of Their Own Board's Activities, by Type of Hospital (percent of chairmen giving each response)

| | Investor-Owned (%) | Religious (%) | Other Not-for-profit (%) | Government (%) | Total (%) |
|---|---|---|---|---|---|
| *Which board responsibilities are viewed as "very important"?* | | | | | |
| Ensure integrity of operations | 88 | 78 | 81 | 75 | 80 |
| Perform strategic planning | 31 | 48 | 43 | 33 | 42 |
| Monitor CEO | 28 | 45 | 42 | 39 | 41 |
| Monitor financial reporting | 22 | 39 | 42 | 46 | 41 |
| Ensure competitive position | 33 | 31 | 28 | 29 | 29 |
| Ensure quality patient care | 84 | 83 | 84 | 83 | 84 |
| Ensure standards are met | 71 | 59 | 56 | 60 | 58 |
| Monitor legal liability | 38 | 29 | 28 | 29 | 29 |
| Approve medical staff | 47 | 44 | 32 | 37 | 36 |
| *Which board responsibilities are being performed "excellently"?* | | | | | |
| Ensure integrity of operations | 52 | 50 | 54 | 51 | 53 |
| Perform strategic planning | 14 | 22 | 22 | 18 | 21 |
| Monitor CEO | 21 | 24 | 21 | 24 | 22 |
| Monitor financial reporting | 17 | 41 | 42 | 38 | 40 |
| Ensure competitive position | 24 | 15 | 16 | 20 | 17 |
| Ensure quality patient care | 64 | 52 | 49 | 57 | 52 |
| Ensure standards are met | 57 | 39 | 35 | 39 | 38 |
| Monitor legal liability | 36 | 23 | 23 | 22 | 23 |
| Approve medical staff | 40 | 34 | 25 | 28 | 28 |

SOURCE: *The Hospital Governing Board Chairman*: Profile and Opinions: A National Study by *Trustee Magazine* and Arthur Young (1983).

often made at the regional or corporate level in multi-institutional systems) and as much or more concern with issues that bear on quality. This may reflect another finding from the same survey—43 percent of the board chairmen in investor-owned hospitals were physicians, compared with 2-3 percent of chairmen at government, religious, and other not-for-profit hospitals.

Because several studies have provided evidence that greater medical staff participation in governing is associated with higher-quality hospital care (Neuhauser, 1971; Shortell et al., 1976; Shortell and LoGerfo, 1981; Flood et al., 1982; Scott et al., 1979), it is worth noting that investor-owned hospitals have particularly high levels of physician participation in hospital governing (Alexander et al., 1986; Arthur Young, 1983).

These data are discussed at greater length in Chapter 9.

**Outcome Measures**

Of all the possible measures of quality of care, outcomes are the most important. Ideally, comparisons of quality in for-profit and not-for-profit settings would include standardized case-fatality ratios; rates of such events as intra- and postoperative complications, wound infections, and drug reactions; and unnecessary care. Unfortunately, few such comparisons exist.

The only major attempt at examining the relationship between patient outcomes and investor ownership of hospitals was done for the committee by Gaumer (1986). He examined postoperative mortality (during the hospital stay and within 180 days of discharge) and 90-day post-discharge readmission rates among Medicare patients who had undergone one of eight types of elective surgery between 1974 and 1981.[4] Gaumer concluded that hospital ownership was not a "strong or consistent influence on post-operative mortality rates," in that significant differences that were found were "not propagated across all procedures categories." For example, proprietary status was associated with lower in-hospital mortality in several cases, but chain affiliation was sometimes associated with higher mortality, and the data on mortality within 180 days after discharge tended to be the reverse of findings for in-hospital mortality. Chain affiliates tended to have higher 90-day readmission rates. Conceding that his study had not been a conclusive test of the quality-of-care question, Gaumer noted the methodological problems that are involved in studying institutional differences in relatively rare events (such as mortality from elective surgery). Even though several years' data from a 25 percent sample of U.S. hospitals were used, only differences larger than 10-12 percent would have been detected by this analysis. However, no pattern of large and persistent ownership differences could be detected for the serious, postsurgical outcomes that Gaumer studied.

The possibility that the profit-seeking orientation might lead to more unnecessary surgery at for-profit hospitals could not be examined directly, but some data are available on Caesarean sections. Although high rates of elective Caesarean sections are considered by some as an indication of excessive surgery, the great professional debate about indicators for elective Caesarean sections makes it difficult to place too much reliance on such rates as a measure of excessive surgery. However, data from the National Hospital Discharge Survey show Caesarean section rates to be higher in "proprietary" hospitals than in governmental hospitals in all four areas of the country examined and

higher than voluntary not-for-profit hospitals in three of four areas of the country, as is shown in Table 6.8 (Placek et al., 1983). These data do not distinguish chain from independent hospitals, unfortunately, nor do they control for possible variations in patient characteristics. The analysis of primary Caesarean section rates in California by Williams and Chen (1983) fails to show significant differences by ownership category. These data are also shown in Table 6.8.

## QUALITY OF CARE IN NURSING HOMES

Other than hospitals, nursing homes are the only type of health care providers about which there is literature linking quality-of-care concerns and types of ownership. Although the committee did not focus its attention heavily on nursing homes, because of time and budget constraints and because the problem of nursing home regulation is the subject of another Institute of Medicine study (1986), it did commission an extensive review of the nursing home literature (Hawes and Phillips, 1986).

There are important similarities and differences between hospitals and nursing homes in the United States. Both have early histories as charitable institutions and both have been significantly affected by governmental policies. Since the passage of the Medicare and Medicaid programs in 1965,[5] both hospitals and nursing homes have witnessed a substantial decline in locally owned proprietary facilities and the development and rapid growth of investor-owned companies that own and manage large numbers of facilities. However, in contrast to hospitals, where the not-for-profit sector has long predominated (and is still more than 80 percent of the total), more than 75 percent of America's nursing homes are proprietary.

Another important difference between the hospital and long-term-care sectors is that while the investor-owned hospital companies developed during an era of generous

**TABLE 6.8**  Caesarean Section Rates for Nonfederal Short-Stay Hospitals, by Hospital Ownership

|  | For-profit | Not-for-profit | Government |
|---|---|---|---|
| United States—1981 (% of births) | 22.0 | 18.5 | 15.4 |
| Northeast | 25.5 | 20.4 | 14.9 |
| North Central | 30.4 | 15.9 | 14.5 |
| South | 18.9 | 15.8 | 20.4 |
| West | 22.5 | 17.4 | 15.5 |
| Primary Ceasarean sections, California—1978-1980 |  |  |  |
| Observed rate (% of births) | 12.4 | 13.3 | 12.5[a] |
| Expected rate[b] | 11.4 | 12.4 | 11.9 |
| Standardized ratio | 108.8 | 107.9 | 105.2 |

[a]"District" hospitals only.

[b]Expected rate based on risk factors such as maternal age; parity; infant's sex, race, and birthweight; and type of presentation (e.g., breech).

SOURCE: U.S. data: Placek et al. (1983:862); California data: Williams and Chen (1983:865).

funding (Medicare's cost-based reimbursement, with most other third-party payers paying charges), prospectively set rates have characterized much of the financing of nursing home care. Thus, hospitals have had fewer financial incentives which might have led them to consider cost reductions that had quality-of-care implications; reductions in nursing home expenses have long translated much more directly into profits, because revenues were substantially based on fixed rates, rather than reimbursement for costs incurred. As Beverly Enterprises Chairman Robert Van Tuyle noted in 1982, because Beverly would serve 60,000,000 meals that year, "every penny saved per meal translates into $600,000" (*Los Angeles Times*, May 25, 1982).

The presence and influence of medical personnel, particularly physicians, who play an important agency role in hospitals but not in nursing homes—is another difference with important implications. As physician-oriented institutions, hospitals have a long history of genuine self-regulatory activity; nursing home quality has long been seen primarily as a problem of governmental regulation, not of self-regulation. The relatively minor role of physicians in nursing homes

also contributes to the comparatively limited role of market forces in the long-term-care sector. Whereas most American hospitals have long had surplus capacity and have vigorously competed for the loyalty of physicians who controlled the flow of patients, nursing home beds in most parts of the country are in very short supply, and physicians tend not to be involved in the referral process or in the day-to-day care of nursing home residents. Because of their physical and mental disabilities and social isolation, and owing to the scarce financial resources of Medicaid patients, many nursing home residents are less able than hospitalized patients to look out for their own interests or to have advocates to do so.

In other words, economic incentives in support of quality of care are less apparent in nursing homes than in hospitals. Except for the relatively few nursing homes whose facilities and prices are aimed at a wealthy clientele, the primary incentives that operate in favor of quality are based either on ethics and community or religious values or on avoidance of regulatory problems. And, nursing home regulation has generally concentrated enforcement on building and fire safety standards rather than on health and patient care standards. All of these factors help to explain the pattern of scandal in the history of American nursing homes, as well as the frequently expressed concern about providers whose motivation lies in economics rather than "religious responsibility or fraternal solidarity" (Vladeck, 1980:126).

Regarding quality of care and type of nursing home ownership, two major limitations of much of the available literature should be noted (Hawes and Phillips, 1986). First, as with hospitals, most studies use resource measures rather than outcome measures and, as such, are subject to methodological dispute and difference of interpretation. Second, and more unfortunate for a study that is oriented toward understanding implications for the future, most studies lump together as "proprietaries" the independent "mom-and-pop" nursing homes that have been on the decline since the very different investor-owned chain facilities have appeared and have been rapidly growing.[6]

To broadly summarize available evidence, most studies on quality (or surrogate measures) of nursing home care tend to favor the not-for-profit mode of organization. This finding holds up across a wide range of measures—amount of patient care staff, expenditures on food, complaints to state regulatory agencies, nonconformity with regulatory requirements, and, in one study, on the following outcome measures: care planning, quarterly review of patients, room conditions, and quality of living environment (Lee, 1984). These studies are summarized in some detail by Hawes and Phillips (1986), who conclude that "the preponderance of evidence suggests the superiority of not-for-profits—particularly of the church-related not-for-profits." Similar conclusions, and an important caveat about variations, were also reached by Vladeck in his book, *Unloving Care.*

. . . on the average, voluntary facilities are somewhat better than proprietary ones. The worst nursing homes are almost exclusively proprietary. But in the middle ranges, there is substantial overlap. The best way to visualize the difference might be to conceive of the range of quality in each of the two types of nursing homes as a quasi-normal distribution. . . . The two distributions overlap markedly, with the mean for the voluntaries slightly higher than the mean for proprietaries, and with the voluntaries having a shorter low-quality tail (Vladeck, 1980:123).

However, Hawes and Phillips also note that most studies have been flawed in one way or another, and "that the lumping together of various types of not-for-profits (government, church-related, and private) and of independent and chain for-profits may obscure some significant differences in performance." A particular problem in making quality comparisons across the for-profit/not-for-profit line is that not-for-profit nursing homes may have, on average, higher revenues than for-profits. For example, Hawes and Phillips cite Texas data showing that not-for-profits have 19 percent higher revenues (as well as 31 percent higher expenditures) than for-profits. Not-for-profits have a higher percentage of non-Medicaid patients, who in most states pay higher charges than patients covered by the state Medicaid program. Many not-for-profit facilities also benefit from subsidies from their sponsoring organizations (e.g., church or synagogue) or from other sources.

## Hospitals, Nursing Homes, and Quality

Although the limitations of existing studies must be acknowledged, it is clear that there are some differences associated with type of ownership of nursing homes that do not appear among hospitals. The reasons for this are not fully clear, but their implications are important.

If the relatively favorable comparisons of quality between for-profit and not-for-profit hospitals are due to factors that are associated with the growth of investor-owned chains, then the continued growth of the for-profit nursing home chains may lead to improvement in nursing home quality. The analysis by Hawes and Phillips (1986) does suggest that, as was the case with hospitals, the replacement of small proprietary nursing homes by better-financed and better-managed investor-owned chain nursing homes has frequently improved quality.

However, the difference between hospitals and nursing homes could be due to other factors, such as the greater presence and influence of physicians in hospitals (as well as other health professionals), who feel a responsibility to act as agent or advocate for their patient. It is important to consider why physicians do not play a similar role in nursing homes. Is it a lack of patient need, a lack of money to pay for physician services, or a lack of physician interest in the kinds of problems that are presented by residents of long-term-care facilities in contrast to the more acute and dramatic cases seen in the hospital? The most likely answer is the last. A second question to be considered is how the agency aspect of the physicians' role in the hospital setting may be affected by the entrepreneurial trends that are taking place in health care. This issue is discussed in Chapters 8 and 9 of this report.

Another possible explanation of the difference between hospitals and nursing homes is the lack of competitive conditions among nursing homes—because of the tight supply of beds. If so, differences between hospitals and nursing homes will persist so long as the hospital world is relatively competitive (including competition on the basis of quality as well as price) in comparison with the nursing home market.

Still another possible explanation of the difference in the relative performance of for-profits and not-for-profits in nursing homes and hospitals is the stringent financial constraints under which nursing homes operate, which are a reflection of societal values and public policy decisions. If constrained resources do play a role, quality problems could increase in investor-owned hospitals (or, perhaps, in all hospitals in which bottom-line considerations are important) under Medicare's prospective payment and increasing financial constraints. In any event, there is a need for improved monitoring of quality-related patient care outcomes. The possibility that financial goals may supplant quality of care—at least under some circumstances—must be recognized, although some reassurance comes from studies of quality of care in HMOs (Luft, 1981).

Although quality care clearly requires a certain level of funding, research has yet to establish a clear relationship between the level at which long-term care is funded and the quality of care that institutions provide. Unless a change takes place in the cultural values that afford high prestige and funding for hospitals and low prestige and, frequently, meager funding for long-term care, the unfortunate contrast between hospitals and nursing homes may remain.

## QUALITY OF CARE AND THE NEED FOR MONITORING

Assurance of health care quality has long relied heavily on professional and institutional self-regulatory mechanisms and on monitoring efforts focusing primarily on structural and procedural measures—staffing patterns, requirements for obtaining staff privileges, existence of certain facilities and procedures, and the operation of institutional quality assurance systems. However, as our health care system becomes more competitive and as effects of economic incentives gain recognition, it is becoming more apparent that there is a need to supplement self-regulatory mechanisms and structural indicators of quality with more ongoing monitoring mechanisms that focus on utilization patterns and outcome measures. For Medicare, professional review organizations (PROs) have been assigned this responsibility. Because of concerns about cost control, as well as about quality, insurance companies and large employers are showing increased interest in monitoring patterns of care provided to beneficiaries.

The task is not confined to hospital care. For various reasons, continued expansion of the outpatient and long-term-care sectors seems inevitable. Quality-of-care concerns will increase as these sectors expand and for-profit participation accelerates. These quality-of-care concerns will culminate in a demand for quality monitoring in all settings and under all financing mechanisms.

Data systems already exist or are being developed that will allow monitoring of such things as

- Caesarean section rates
- wound infection rates after surgery
- nosocomial infections
- readmission rates
- complication rates
- fatality rates (with adjustments for diagnoses and severity)
- functional status of nursing home patients
- health status measures in geographic areas.

Because the results of one institution's quality problems may turn up at another institution's door, focusing on events that take place within the walls of particular institutions is not adequate. Thus, it is highly desirable that the monitoring of quality of care be done by organizations that have access to information about the total health care utilization experience of a population. Data systems are needed that allow linkage of patients' experiences in one institution with subsequent utilization of other institutions; for example, to establish the rates of hospitalization among patients who had undergone a particular surgical procedure in various institutions within the previous six months. For the foreseeable future, the data systems that have the most potential value in monitoring the health care experience of defined populations are connected with payers, including large employers. Several statewide data systems look promising, but they face formidable problems in moving beyond a focus on particular insti-

tutions and types of institutions to a focus on populations.

## CONCLUSION

Evidence now available does not support the fear that for-profit health care is incompatible with quality of care, nor the belief that public ownership might provide some assurance of quality. Among hospitals, most available (although rudimentary) measures show that investor-owned hospitals are similar in quality to not-for-profit hospitals, and on some measures they are better. Investor-owned hospitals also appear superior to the type of hospitals they have substantially replaced—independent proprietary hospitals.

However, as with many other topics in this report, the past may not predict the future. Some sources of support for quality care are changing as hospitals find ways to market around physicians (e.g., by selling health care plans directly to employers) and as payment methods are changed to reward institutions for finding ways to cut costs. Although there are many differences from hospitals, evidence from nursing homes is not reassuring regarding how investor-owned institutions will behave if profits require that quality be traded off against cost. Entrepreneurial trends that are stimulating the growth of diagnosis and treatment in various types of freestanding centers and through home care organizations,[7] also raise concerns about quality, particularly since quality assurance mechanisms and standards are less well developed outside of hospitals.

For these reasons, *the committee concludes that the monitoring of health care quality, and the research required to increase the sophistication of such monitoring, should be major items on the nation's health policy agenda.*[8] (The need for more resources devoted to long-term care by the public and private sectors is also apparent, but is a subject for another study.) A worthwhile goal is the development of quality assurance systems that would make their results available to the public, although safeguards are needed to avoid unwarranted harm to individual and institutional reputations (e.g., mortality rates for excellent surgeons or institutions would be misleading when their referrals include disproportionate numbers of complicated cases). The publicly funded PRO system is a place where this can begin, although the PRO program (and its PSRO ancestor) has relied to some degree on voluntary participation by physicians, who reflect the long-standing resistance among providers against public disclosure of the results of review activities (Institute of Medicine, 1981).

The possibility of public disclosure of the results of privately funded quality assurance activities is limited by several factors. The Joint Commission for Accreditation of Hospitals is a voluntary organization, funded and controlled by providers who have strong historical attachments to self-regulatory mechanisms in which confidentiality is a hallmark. Also, payers and large employers have little incentive to make public the results of their utilization review and quality assurance activities.

However, if providers fail to respond to information developed through these still embryonic monitoring activities, the threat of public disclosure will undoubtedly come into play. The possibility must also be recognized that institutions that have high standards of care and that are proud of the outcomes of the care they provide may find public relations advantages in making known such facts as how their surgical mortality or readmission rates compare with other institutions' rates.

In sum, if market forces are given increasingly free reign in health care and if cost containment pressures increase, both the interests of patients and the continuing debate over public policy in health care will require an increasing need to monitor the quality of care. Quality should be monitored in all settings, regardless of type of ownership. Although lack of uniform standards for

reporting outcomes other than death make the monitoring of outcomes more difficult, research, standard development, and monitoring of other outcomes—infection rates, readmission rates, complication rates, changes in functional status of nursing home patients—are clearly needed. To assess broader changes in the health care system—not only the growth of the for-profit sector, but also of multi-institutional arrangements, new freestanding centers, and vertically integrated organizations, the monitoring of national and regional health status measures is essential. Important health status indices include infant and maternal mortality, mortality of children, and death from potentially controllable diseases (e.g., diabetes and such infectious diseases as tuberculosis).

Formidable methodological, bureaucratic, and political problems are raised by the idea of more monitoring of, and public accountability about, the performance of health care organizations. Yet, the multiple changes taking place in the organization and ethos of health care, as well as in the regulatory and economic environment, should place the monitoring of the performance of health institutions and of the health status of the population high on the public policy agenda and on the agenda of organizations (such as third-party payers) that are in a position to monitor key aspects of institutions' performances.

## NOTES

[1]The theoretical relationship between quality and for-profit/not-for-profit status is complex. Some of the concern about for-profits and quality may result from the sense that the orientation of for-profit organizations is toward markets and marketing, although a marketing orientation increasingly pervades both for-profit and not-for-profit health care. Excessive attention to market factors could affect aspects of quality either positively or negatively. Weisbrod and Schlesinger (1983) observe that in fields characterized by "asymmetric information" (e.g., the seller knows much more than the buyer), a potential for misrepresentation exists in the form of promises to deliver one level of quality while actually delivering lower, less costly, quality.

When it is difficult for the purchaser to write and enforce contract contingencies against such misrepresentation, consumers seek protective mechanisms such as governmental regulation or devices to limit market entry of providers who are thought likely to exploit their informational superiority. Weisbrod and Schlesinger hypothesize that proprietary firms are more likely than not-for-profit or public firms to take advantage of an informational superiority. Medical care is a classic example of a service characterized by asymmetric information (Arrow, 1963). However, Weisbrod and Schlesinger (1983) also recognize that patients (or, presumably, their physician-agents) are aware of some aspects of institutional performance, such as the responsiveness of floor nurses, while other aspects are more difficult or costly to monitor. Thus, they hypothesize that proprietary firms will perform as well as or better than not-for-profit firms on "outputs" that can be monitored by consumers, but that they will perform worse than not-for-profit firms on "outputs" that the consumer cannot readily monitor.

The premise that for-profit organizations have greater sensitivity toward markets also suggests that in competitive markets proprietary firms will perform as well as or better than not-for-profit firms, but in noncompetitive situations, such as when all facilities are near capacity or when a community has only one provider, they will perform worse than would a not-for-profit institution in similar circumstances.

[2]There are also differences between for-profit and not-for-profit hospitals regarding the specialty composition of their medical staff (Musacchio et al., 1986), with for-profit hospitals having fewer internists and more general/family practitioners. Interpretation of this specialty composition in terms of quality must be tempered by several considerations. First, the relationship between specialty composition of staff and institutional quality of care has not been demonstrated. Second, no data are available regarding restrictions on hospital privileges of general/family practitioners (or other specialties) in different types of hospitals. Third, the not-for-profit percentages undoubtedly reflect, in part, that many large teaching hospitals are in this category. In this regard, it is important to note that the data come from a survey of physicians, not of institutions. Because the probability that a particular hospital's staff physicians would appear in the sample is related to the size of its medical staff, the not-for-profit category reflects the influence of very large institutions, of which virtually none are for-profit. Finally, the specialty composition of for-profit hospitals is very similar to public hospitals.

[3]Board certification is generally accepted by the medical profession as an indicator of competency at a given time in a professional career. As with all indicators, it must be kept in perspective when judging the overall quality-of-care questions raised in this study.

Board certification is conveyed by the 23 specialty boards upon candidates who have completed an accredited training program and then passed a certifying examination.

[4]Williams (1979) reports another outcome study, which found that "for-profit" hospital status had a very small, but significant, relationship to perinatal mortality in California. Unfortunately, the data were for 1960-1973, a period that preceded most of the substantial growth of the modern investor-owned hospital companies.

[5]However, whereas the federal Medicare program is the most important source of dollars for hospitals, it is the state/federal Medicaid program that has become the single most important financier of nursing home care.

[6]A notable exception in a literature that generally does not distinguish between chain and independent proprietary nursing homes are two studies that focused on the single largest nursing home company: "Beverly Enterprises Patient Care Record" and "Beverly Enterprises in Michigan: A Case Study of Corporate Takeover of Health Care Resources." These studies, which were done in 1983 by the Food and Beverage Trades Department of the AFL-CIO and two other AFL-CIO affiliates, both suggest a disturbing pattern of quality-of-care problems in Beverly Enterprises nursing homes with respect to complaints of patient abuse and violations of state regulations. However, because these reports were prepared as part of an innovative "corporate campaign" strategy (English, 1985) to exert pressure on Beverly Enterprises to come to the bargaining table with the unions, the fairness and accuracy of these studies' findings are open to question. Because the committee did not have the time and resources to make its own assessment of the catalog of charges raised by the union against Beverly Enterprises, it chose not to use the information in these reports.

[7]Quality of care in ambulatory care settings has not been examined in this chapter because of the absence of studies in which for-profit/not-for-profit comparisons are made. The few existing studies of ambulatory surgery centers are confined to the experience of particular centers. Some studies with quality implications regarding for-profit and not-for-profit hemodialysis centers do exist; however, because of the specialized aspects of that technology and of Medicaid's End Stage Renal Disease Program, the committee decided not to review these studies.

[8]Researchers at the Rand Corporation have published a very valuable and detailed research agenda for monitoring the effects of Medicare's prospective payment system on the quality of care (Lohr et al., 1985). Virtually all of the ideas in the Rand report could be usefully applied to studies of ownership-related differences in the quality of care.

## REFERENCES

Alexander, Jeffrey A., Michael A. Morrisey, and Stephen M. Shortell (1986) Physician Participation in the Administration and Governance of System and Freestanding Hospitals: A Comparison by Type of Ownership. This volume.

American Medical Association (1984) *SMS Report* 3(June).

Arrow, Kenneth (1963) Uncertainty and the Welfare Economics of Medical Care. *American Economic Review* 53(December):941-973.

Arthur Young (1983) *The Hospital Governing Board Chairman.* Los Angeles: Arthur Young.

Donabedian, Avedis (1969) *A Guide to Medical Care Administration. Vol II: Medical Care Appraisal—Quality and Utilization.* Washington, D.C.: American Public Health Association.

English, Carey W. (1985) When Unions Turn Tables on the Bosses. *U.S.News & World Report* (February 4):69-70.

Flood, A. B., W. R. Scott, W. Ewy, and W. H. Forrest, Jr. (1982) Effectiveness in Professional Organizations: The Impact of Surgeons and Surgical Staff Organization on the Quality of Care in Hospitals. *Health Services Research* 17(Winter):341-366.

Gaumer, Gary (1986) Medicare Patient Outcomes and Hospital Organizational Mission. This volume.

Hawes, Catherine, and Charles D. Phillips (1986) The Changing Structure of the Nursing Home Industry and the Impact of Ownership on Quality, Cost, and Access. This volume.

Institute of Medicine (1981) *Access to Medical Review Data.* Washington, D.C.: National Academy Press.

Institute of Medicine (1986) *Improving the Quality of Care in Nursing Homes.* Washington, D.C.: National Academy Press.

Lee, Y. S. (1984) Nursing Homes and Quality of Health Care: The First Year Result of an Outcome-Oriented Survey. *Journal of Health and Human Resources Administration* 7(Summer):32-60.

Lohr, Kathleen N., et al. (1985) *Impact of Medicare Prospective Payment on the Quality of Medical Care: A Research Agenda.* Santa Monica, Calif.: Rand Corporation.

Longo, Daniel R., Gary A. Chase, Lynn A. Ahlgren, James S. Roberts, and Carol S. Weisman (1986) Compliance of Multihospital Systems with Standards of the Joint Commission on Accreditation of Hospitals. This volume.

Luft, Harold (1981) *Health Maintenance Organization: Dimensions of Performance.* New York: Wiley.

Morrisey, Michael A., Jeffrey A. Alexander, and Stephen M. Shortell (1986) Medical Staff Size, Hospital Privileges, and Compensation Arrangements: A Comparison of System Hospitals. This volume.

Musacchio, Robert A., Stephen Zuckerman, Lynn E. Jensen, and Larry Freshnock (1986) Hospital Ownership and the Practice of Medicine: Evidence from the Physician's Perspective. This volume.

Neuhauser, Duncan (1971) *The Relationship Between Administrative Activities and Hospital Performance.* Research Series No. 28. Chicago, Ill.: University of Chicago Center for Health Administrative Studies.

Placek, Paul L., Selma Taffel, and Mary Moien (1983) Caesarean Section Delivery Rates: United States, 1981. *American Journal of Public Health* 73(August):861-862.

Scott, W. Richard, Ann M. Flood, and Wayne Ewy (1979) Organizational Determinants of Services, Quality, and Cost of Care in Hospitals. *Milbank Memorial Fund Quarterly* 57(Spring):234-264.

Shortell, Stephen M., and James P. LoGerfo (1981) Hospital Medical Staff Organization and Quality of Care: Results for Myocardial Infarction and Appendectomy. *Medical Care* 19(October):1041.

Shortell, Stephen M., Selwyn W. Becker, and Duncan Neuhauser (1976) The Effects of Management Practices on Hospital Efficiency and Quality of Care. Pp. 90-107 in Stephen M. Shortell and Montague Brown (eds.), *Organizational Research in Hospitals.* Chicago, Ill.: Blue Cross Associations.

Vladeck, Bruce (1980) *Unloving Care.* New York: Basic Books.

Weisbrod, Burton A., and Mark Schlesinger (1983) Public, Private, Nonprofit Ownership and the Response to Asymmetric Information: The Case of Nursing Homes. Discussion Paper #209. Madison: University of Wisconsin Center for Health Economics and Law.

Williams, Ronald L. (1979) Measuring the Effectiveness of Perinatal Medical Care. *Medical Care* 17(February):95-110.

Williams, Ronald L., and Peter M. Chen (1983) Controlling the Rise in Caesarean Section Rates by the Dissemination of Information from Vital Records. *American Journal of Public Health* 73(August):863-867.

# 7 Implications for Education and Research

Investor-owned hospitals have not been known for their participation in the education of health professionals or in research. The growth of investor-owned hospital chains has come primarily through the acquisition of independent proprietary hospitals, which tended to be small and to have no relationships with educational institutions. Until recently, investor-owned companies showed little interest in acquiring teaching hospitals, and not-for-profit and public teaching hospitals had little reason to consider a change of ownership. American Hospital Association data show that as recently as 1983 (see Table 7.1) only 2 percent of the hospitals in investor-owned chains and 2 percent of the independent investor-owned hospitals had medical residency programs,[1] and none had a nursing school. The average number of medical residents per bed was much lower in for-profit hospitals, irrespective of size, than in not-for-profit and governmental hospitals (Table 7.2). Also, because of their size, orientation, and lack of medical school affiliations, for-profit hospitals have not been sites for research, nor have they had physician-researchers on their medical staffs. Only since December 1981 have U.S. Public Health Service regulations included provisions that make for-profit organizations eligible to receive research grants from the National Institutes of Health, the nation's

TABLE 7.1  Percentage of Short-Term General Hospitals with Educational Affiliations, by Ownership, 1983

| Bed Size | Investor-Owned Chain (%) | Proprietary (%) | Not-for-profit Chain (%) | Not-for-profit Independent (%) | State and Local Government (%) |
|---|---|---|---|---|---|
| Residency program | 2 | 2 | 26 | 22 | 10 |
| Medical school affiliated | 2 | 2 | 25 | 21 | 9 |
| Professional nursing school | 0 | 0 | 7 | 8 | 1 |
| Council of Teaching Hospitals | 0 | 0 | 6 | 9 | 5 |

SOURCE: Hospital Data Center, American Hospital Association, 1985.

**TABLE 7.2** Average Number* of Residents and Trainees per Community Hospital, by Ownership and Size, 1983

| Bed Size | Investor-Owned Chain (%) | Proprietary (%) | Not-for-profit Chain (%) | Not-for-profit Independent (%) | State and Local Government (%) |
|---|---|---|---|---|---|
| 6- 24 | 0.33 | 0 | 0 | 0.02 | 0 |
| 25- 49 | 0 | 0.16 | 0.14 | 0.25 | 0.01 |
| 50- 99 | 0.15 | 0.10 | 0.38 | 0.43 | 0.16 |
| 100-199 | 0.18 | 0.15 | 1.88 | 2.63 | 1.51 |
| 200-299 | 0.89 | 1.33 | 3.66 | 6.75 | 10.15 |
| 300-399 | 2.60 | 0.50 | 8.85 | 16.53 | 48.14 |
| 400-499 | 1.50 | 0.67 | 29.37 | 36.62 | 92.56 |
| 500-599 | 14.00 | 0 | 64.86 | 122.44 | 195.80 |
| All hospitals | 0.44 | 0.23 | 9.97 | 15.48 | 12.19 |

*Full-time equivalents.

SOURCE: Hospital Data Center, American Hospital Association, 1985.

largest supporter of biomedical research—although, of course, there are many other sources of research support.

Investor-owned hospitals and their parent companies have been criticized for their lack of involvement in education and research on two grounds: for avoiding those costly but important activities on which the future of health care depends (and which activities have never been fully self-supporting), and for allegedly attracting away patients on which some teaching hospitals depended to be able to cross-subsidize educational activities and unsponsored research. These charges raise many of the same issues examined in Chapter 5 (on access to care, particularly of uninsured patients), but satisfactory documentation is lacking about most key points, other than the for-profits' lack of involvement in education and research.

However, these issues and the premises and assumptions that they reflect are to some extent being replaced by new concerns. Since the outset of this study, investor-owned hospital companies have greatly increased their involvement in education and research by acquiring, leasing, or entering into management contracts with hospitals that have long-standing affiliations with medical schools and

traditions of significant involvement in education and research. Less visibly, investor-owned chains have begun to support research within their own institutions and also by outside investigators.

Little information is available yet with which to assess the impact of these changes. At this juncture it is possible only to describe how investor-owned firms are becoming involved in education and research and to suggest some reasons for this involvement, to speculate about future developments, and to raise potential areas of difficulty that should be monitored.

## TEACHING HOSPITALS AND INVESTOR-OWNED HOSPITAL COMPANIES

Because of their size, multiple functions, diverse sources of funding, and relationships with other institutions, major teaching hospitals are exceedingly complex institutions. The functions of teaching hospitals have been described in capsule form by the Association of American Medical Colleges (1984b) as follows:

In addition to the basic hospital services of primary and secondary inpatient care, teaching hospitals provide the bulk of the nation's tertiary care for the most seriously ill; regionalized special care and stand-by services; clinical training of physicians and other health care personnel; access to medical services for disproportionate numbers of the poor and medically indigent; and the development and testing of new diagnostic and treatment services.

Teaching hospitals are, of course, the sites for graduate medical education (residency) programs and for the clinical component of undergraduate education in medicine, nursing, pharmacy, and the allied health professions. Although most support for health professional education comes through health professional schools, hospital funds have been an important source of support for graduate medical education by providing space for instruction, by paying the salaries of residents and directors of graduate medical education programs, and, in some cases, by paying medical faculty to supervise and teach residents.

The funds for this support come from hospital general revenues, most of which are derived from patient care. Third-party payers for health care traditionally have gone along with this practice on the grounds that the presence of educational programs increases the quality of care and that patients, employers, and payers have a stake in the continued adequate supply of health manpower.

In addition to transmitting knowledge to the health professionals being trained therein, these institutions do much to shape the values and attitudes of these health professionals regarding the place of science in medical practice, the value of clinical experience, and the nature of professional responsibility. A major concern that has been voiced about the ownership or operation of teaching hospitals by investor-owned firms is that the ethos of these unique institutions will be changed.

Since the decline and disappearance of proprietary medical schools in the late nine-

teenth and early twentieth centuries, clinical teaching activities have taken place almost exclusively in public or not-for-profit institutions. The modern experience with for-profit companies with teaching hospitals goes back only a few years. Through the 1970s—the first decade of its existence—Tulane Hospital in New Orleans was managed by Hospital Affiliates International. Hospital Corporation of America (HCA) has been managing the hospital of the College of Medicine and Dentistry of New Jersey since late 1982 and more recently has contracted for management of the University of Mississippi Hospital. However, only in the past two years have the first leases and acquisitions of teaching hospitals by investor-owned companies begun to take place. Recent developments include

- Humana's lease of the new teaching hospital at the University of Louisville (now known as Humana Hospital University)
- American Medical International's (AMI) acquisition of St. Joseph Hospital, a 539-bed teaching and tertiary care hospital of Creighton University
- the proposed construction and lease by the Forum Group of Indianapolis (a company whose acute care and psychiatric facilities have more recently been acquired by Hospital Corporation of America) of a psychiatric hospital at the University of South Florida
- HCA's recent agreements to purchase Wesley Medical Center in Wichita, Kansas, and Methodist Hospital in Oklahoma City, Oklahoma
- AMI's agreement to purchase Presbyterian-St. Luke's Hospital in Denver, Colorado
- National Medical Enterprises' agreement with the University of Southern California to build a teaching hospital
- AMI's joint venture with the George Washington University for ownership of the GWU Health Plan (an HMO)
- an agreement for a joint venture be-

tween Vanderbilt University and HCA for construction and management of a psychiatric hospital

● discussion about the sale or lease of several other teaching hospitals, including the George Washington University Hospital.[2]

The interest of investor-owned hospital companies in owning or leasing teaching hospitals has attracted the most discussion, and no small amount of controversy (the major example being Massachusetts General Hospital's proposed and aborted sale to HCA of McLean Hospital, a Harvard University teaching hospital). However, smaller agreements about specific services such as magnetic resonance imaging, psychiatric services, and outpatient surgical centers are proliferating rapidly.

A variety of motivations have led to the discussions and negotiations between major teaching hospitals and investor-owned firms. These are summarized in Table 7.3. Each instance in which an investor-owned company has entered into the ownership or management of a major teaching hospital has had its own unique circumstances and has culminated in a unique arrangement;

undoubtedly the mix of motives also is unique.

## Concerns About For-profit Involvement in Education

As is true of the debate about for-profit health care generally, much of the concern is about broad questions of values, about what is the right or wrong way to run a hospital or to prepare tomorrow's physicians. The proposed or actual takeover of a major teaching hospital by an investor-owned company has, in each case, been a visible, controversial event. In particular, medical school faculties, who serve as the medical staff of these hospitals, have viewed such changes in ownership or management as threats to traditional values, missions, operating procedures, and power relationships within the hospital and between it and other components of academic health centers. More specifically, faculty physicians have been concerned that in the interests of satisfying their investors, these companies sooner or later will institute changes to

● reduce faculty control over undergraduate and graduate medical education

TABLE 7.3  Motivations for Negotiations Between Investor-Owned Health Care Companies and Teaching Hospitals

| Motives for Teaching Hospitals and Their Parent Institutions | Motives for Investor-Owned Companies |
|---|---|
| To obtain the capital needed for future renovation, acquisition of equipment, etc., without adding to hospital cost base | To respond to criticism that they have avoided their social responsibility by not supporting education and research |
| To gain greater cost-effectiveness from advantages in management, scale, and bottom-line discipline and freedom from civil service or university personnel, procurement, and contracting systems | To achieve greater legitimacy, prestige, and visibility |
| To gain access to new sources of revenues through referral networks, marketing skills, and emphasis on patient care | To achieve profits from individual teaching institutions or from regional networks of hospitals and other health care providers that include these hospitals |
| To reduce some governance problems, and reduce diffusion of the decision-making process | To gain access to the capability for technology assessment and other research activities |
| | To provide expert consultations for physicians at company-owned nontertiary care institutions |
| | To gain access to a pool of physician trainees for possible future recruitment |

- reduce the institutional priority given to education and research
- narrow the patient mix needed for teaching and research
- change the values transmitted to health professional students
- lessen institutional commitment to the community (including indigent care)
- threaten academic freedom through pressure to control faculty appointments or to influence the size and nature of the education and research programs
- reduce funds that are supporting faculty for their supervision of residents, service on hospital committees or as service chiefs, or other education-related activities.

The sale of a facility can also mean relinquishing control over such major future possibilities as the resale or closure of the facility.

On the other hand, some opportunities may be involved beyond the factors (such as access to capital) that motivate the hospital to explore relationships with for-profit organizations. It can be argued, for example, that it is valuable to expose the health professional in training for health care delivery in an environment where concern for the bottom line perhaps weighs more heavily than in traditional settings; to provide experience with the type of large-scale organizations that some observers see as constituting the future of health care; or, perhaps, to increase student access to community hospitals, nursing homes, and freestanding ambulatory care centers that companies own.

It is as yet impossible to assess the extent to which the potential positive and negative outcomes will come to pass. There are several reasons for this.

First, instances of the takeover of a teaching hospital by an investor-owned company are so recent that there is very little experience on which to base an assessment. The number of cases is too small to permit statistical study, and not enough time has passed for careful case studies, although such case studies would be of great value.

Second, in response to financial pressures, many changes are taking place in teaching hospitals that would undoubtedly occur even if investor-owned companies did not exist. The advent of hospital prospective payment, aggressive cost-containment activities by employers and third-party payers, the establishment of PPOs, and so forth, are causing reduced hospital admissions, shortened lengths of stay, and increased pressure for greater cost-effectiveness. Federal support for education and research has declined, as has state support.

Teaching hospitals have not been impervious to these pressures. Their responses, some of which have been dramatic, include

- establishing for-profit subsidiaries
- changing governance structures, for instance, becoming independent of the university
- changing management styles and admissions policies
- reducing the autonomy within the institution of those whose primary concerns are educational
- joining multi-institutional arrangements.

Thus, the status quo is unlikely to be maintained, even at institutions that do not become involved with an investor-owned company. Isolating the effects of ownership changes in the presence of so many other forces for change will be difficult at best.

Third, teaching hospitals are a very diverse lot. Something that might represent a significant change in one institution may not be a change at all in another. Teaching is not the highest priority at all teaching hospitals. Although teaching hospitals as a whole carry a disproportionate burden of uncompensated care, not all teaching hospitals do so, and not all teaching hospitals support unfunded clinical research (Hanft, 1986). Teaching hospitals have a wide range of case mixes, and they vary in the extent of their involvement with education; in the nature and extent of their university/medical school ties; in their type of ownership (some are private, some are public and receive state appropriations); in their size; and so forth. Thus, there is no one "standard model" teaching hospital against which to measure changes introduced by a management contract or the sale or lease of institutions.

Fourth, the goals of providing teaching and research may not be inconsistent with the long-term corporate goals of investor-owned firms. Conversely, medical schools and academic health centers are not without entrepreneurial interests and endeavors. Faculty group practices, for example, have for many years been an important source of funds for medical schools. By 1983, income from medical service represented from one-fourth to one-half of medical school revenues (Petersdorf, 1985). This means a considerable shift in emphasis from teaching and research toward practice. As one medical school dean recently described matters,

Most faculty of medicine are, to a progressively greater extent, engaged in practice or in its administration. More and more hours of the faculty are spent in the operating room, the consulting room, or the clinic, and more and more chairmen and deans are investing their time in the administration of practice plans and in conferring with lawyers and accountants (Petersdorf, 1985:2546).

Fifth, the arrangements by which investor-owned companies have become involved with teaching hospitals vary considerably. Specific safeguards can be built into contractual agreements. The details of the agreement may be at least as important as involvement with an investor-owned firm. Crucial issues include

• whether the agreement is a lease or a sale
• how the medical school, the company, and other interested parties (e.g., the community) will be represented on the board
• the relative authority of the hospital board and the company regarding such matters as medical staff composition and governance, mix of services provided, purchase

of major equipment, hospital staffing (particularly nursing), allocation of space, and admission policies
• the nature of provisions, if any, for ending the relationship (Are there buy-back provisions? How are they invoked?)
• provisions for continuing historical missions (e.g., a formula—perhaps based on percentage of revenues—fixing a continuing financial commitment to teaching, research, or uncompensated care)
• whether the hospital or university shares in profits.

What will happen in the joining of corporate medicine and educational medicine depends to some extent on such details in agreements between companies and institutions, as well as on the reasons why the parties are interested in the relationship. Hospital interest seems to stem primarily from a need for capital and, to a lesser extent, from a need to reduce or eliminate operating deficits. Also, the boards of some institutions may wish to improve their position in an increasingly difficult and competitive environment (or to extricate themselves and the capital for which they are trustees from this environment). The explanation of the companies' interest is more speculative, but it nonetheless will have a great deal of impact on the way the acquired hospitals are operated. The particular combination of motivations that underlie the interest of investor-owned companies in teaching hospitals will doubtless have much to do with which of the predicted benefits and problems come to pass.

The fact that the number of major teaching hospitals is small enough to facilitate communication and sharing of information has two important implications. First, corporate reputations are at stake to an unusual degree. Second, institutions can learn from each other's experiences in a way that seldom has happened among the smaller, more isolated institutions that have been acquired over the years by investor-owned companies. It is also likely that the experiences of the first few teaching hospitals to be acquired may not be good predictors for the long run, because of their visibility, and because of the interest of the investor-owned companies in achieving legitimacy and avoiding negative reports (and the hospitals in having made sound decisions). Both the terms that can be reached between the companies and the hospitals (or their owners) and the consequences of involvement of investor ownership in teaching hospitals may be different in the future. In Egdahl's (1986) terms, early acquisitions (and, presumably, prestigious institutions that are acquired later) may have a kind of "flagship" status in the companies and, as such, may be tolerated as "prestige loss leaders."

### Research

The growing involvement in research by investor-owned health care companies now takes several forms. As has been discussed, these corporations have begun to purchase or lease hospitals in which research is done. In addition to the examples of teaching hospitals already discussed, at least one example of a nonteaching hospital can be cited (Humana Hospital Audubon, home of the Humana Heart Institute). Corporations also enter agreements with researchers, or companies such as pharmaceutical manufacturers, enabling them to use the health care companies' multiple facilities or data bases for research purposes. Some corporations have also begun to provide support for research and development activities. Humana's pledge to provide resources for support of its Heart Institute and Dr. William DeVries's artificial heart implant program is well known. Humana and HCA (through a company-established foundation) have made substantial grants for biomedical research (e.g., a Humana grant of $320,000 to Vanderbilt University School of Medicine). HCA has made several grants (to Har-

vard University, the University of Minnesota, the University of Pennsylvania, Vanderbilt University, Washington University, Northwestern University, and the University of Wisconsin) for health services research, and several companies have cooperated in organizational studies of multi-institutional systems. A chair in law, medicine, and public policy was created at the University of Southern California by an endowment from National Medical Enterprises. Other health services research and technology assessment are conducted in the corporation either for internal management purposes or to make information public about the company and its activities.

These developments are mostly very recent and have yet to be systematically studied. Some are typical of corporate philanthropic activities; others are peculiar to the circumstance of acquiring an institution where research is conducted. Although the conduct or support of research is generally recognized as a public good, there are a number of concerns about the research involvement of health care companies, including the acquisition of institutions where research is conducted.

First is the concern that unsponsored research may be curtailed at acquired institutions. Although most biomedical research studies receive outside support (from the National Institutes of Health, the pharmaceutical industry, or other sources), some unsponsored research is conducted at many institutions. The extent and quality of such research is largely undocumented, but teaching hospitals traditionally have allowed medical investigators access to their patients and patient records and have provided small amounts of resources to facilitate studies. Much of the research that is supported is preliminary work that can lead to a full-fledged research proposal, for which outside funding can be obtained. However, because it may not contribute to (and may, in fact, detract from) the bottom line, it is feared that unsponsored research is vulnerable in a change to for-profit ownership.

Second, there is concern that investor-owned hospitals may limit access by outside researchers. Although there have been exceptions, health care institutions generally have been very open to study. A degree of openness to responsible research has been a part of the public accountability of health care institutions. The world of business is generally not so open, and, as competitive conditions increase, health care institutions generally are becoming less open. It is important to note, however, that a number of examples can be cited in which an investor-owned hospital company has cooperated with requests from outside researchers for access to, or information about, the company or institutions that it operates.

Third, some checks and balances against excesses done in the name of research may not be present when the same institution that owns patient care institutions also has commercial interests in research that involves patients as subjects. An example is provided by Humana's commitment to the artificial heart program in one of its hospitals and its ownership of stock in Symbion, the company that makes the Jarvik-7 artificial heart. Perhaps because of the danger that Humana's investment in the artificial heart might conflict with its responsibilities to patients in its hospitals, Humana reported in its 1984 *Annual Report* that it is selling its Symbion stock, although Humana's executives continue to own stock, and one sits on the Symbion board. Similar issues would have arisen had the proposed merger taken place between HCA and the American Hospital Supply Company, the manufacturer of many devices used in patient care (e.g., artificial valves for hearts). If research on new drugs, devices, or procedures is contemplated in hospitals owned or managed by companies with a commercial interest in the particular drugs, devices, or procedures, the need for some additional safeguards beyond local institutional review boards may deserve consideration by the appropriate regulatory agencies (e.g., the Food and Drug Administration).

Fourth, the possibility of changes in the operation of the norms of science at research/health care institutions operated by for-profit firms gives rise to concern. The linkage of health services research and commercial interests in a field that is highly sensitive to public policy may make it more important than ever for the consumer of research to be wary. However, this linkage is hardly peculiar to the for-profit setting. It is also possible that large, well-financed companies may seek competitive advantage in the conduct of proprietary research whose fruits are not shared outside of the company, although a return to nineteenth century proprietary therapeutic practices does not now seem likely.

## CONCLUSION

Investor-owned companies have only begun to have substantial involvement in education and research within the time span of this study. The most visible and controversial form of involvement has been the purchase, lease, or management of teaching hospitals, but these firms have also begun to engage in research internally and to fund research by academic investigators. The committee believes that experience is now too limited to allow an informed evaluation of the consequences of such arrangements. Because there are so many unique aspects of each institution and each agreement, it may be a long time indeed before general conclusions can be drawn. Careful case studies by disinterested investigators, as well as evaluations by interested parties (AAMC, companies, medical schools, etc.), should be conducted to maximize what can be learned from these early examples.

Corporate involvement with teaching hospitals comes at a time when there is a great deal of pressure by society to reduce the cost of health care, and, of particular relevance here, to stop paying for health services at levels that enable hospitals to subsidize education and research. The indirect education support enacted with prospective payment for the Medicare program has been a target for reduction or elimination, and teaching hospitals are facing greater and greater difficulty in competing for patients with lower-cost hospitals. Teaching hospitals, whether for-profit or not-for-profit, are going to have to face some hard choices. There seems little doubt that many teaching hospitals will take actions to reduce their level of involvement in research and education (as they are reducing their level of indigent care), to find new revenues to support these programs, or both.

Teaching hospitals and large companies are complex organizations with multiple objectives, a primary one being continued existence and a niche in the community. Because of their complexity and the complexity of the changes taking place, the evaluation of change will be very difficult. Also, because of the formidable amounts of capital required, the complexity of the institutions and their long traditions, and their questionable profitability, the committee does not expect to see a large number of teaching hospitals coming under the control of investor-owned companies in the near future, although more limited relationships, involving specialized facilities or programs, may continue to proliferate.

## NOTES

[1] More than 1,150 U.S. hospitals have affiliations with medical schools (American Hospital Association, 1984); 424 hospitals were members of the Council of Teaching Hospitals (COTH) in 1984, membership that requires, among other things, four major residency programs and close affiliation with a medical school. Depending on definitions, there are between 100 and 175 "major" teaching hospitals in the United States (Hanft, 1986). Sixty-four hospitals have common ownership with a medical school (Association of American Medical Colleges, 1984a:5). The hospitals comprising the Council

of Teaching Hospitals are disproportionately large (more than half have at least 500 beds), and they are found in disproportionate numbers in a few states (39 percent of the COTH members are located in the northeast region of the country) (Association of American Medical Colleges, 1982).

[2] At least 12 other teaching facilities are now managed by investor-owned corporations. For a list and discussion of how interested parties view the issues raised by investor-related academic health centers, see Goldsmith (1985).

## REFERENCES

American Hospital Association (1984) *Hospital Statistics*. Chicago, Ill.: American Hospital Association.

Association of American Medical Colleges (1982) *A Description of Teaching Hospital Characteristics*. Washington, D.C.: Association of American Medical Colleges.

Association of American Medical Colleges (1984a) New Challenges for the Council of Teaching Hospitals and the Department of Teaching Hospitals: A Discussion Paper. Washington, D.C.: Association of American Medical Colleges.

Association of American Medical Colleges (1984b) Statement on Financing Undergraduate and Graduate Medical Education, presented to the Subcommittee on Health, U.S. Senate, Committee on Finance, October 1, 1984. Published in *Background Information and Selected Readings, Prepared for the Committee on Financing Graduate Medical Education* (revised, November 1984). Washington, D.C.: Association of American Medical Colleges.

Egdahl, Richard G. (1986) A Perspective on the Involvement of For-Profit Hospital Chains with Teaching and Research Institutions. Paper prepared for the 1984 Harold and Jane Hirsh Symposium, The George Washington University, and published in Warren Greenberg and Richard McK. F. Southby (eds.), *For-Profit Hospitals: Access, Quality, Teaching, Research*. Columbus, Ohio: Battelle Press.

Goldsmith, Marcia F. (1985) Investor-related Academic Health Centers: An "Uncertain Courtship"? *Journal of the American Medical Association* 253(June 7):304-307.

Hanft, Ruth (1986) For Profit Hospitals: The Implications for Teaching and Research. Paper prepared for the 1984 Harold and Jane Hirsh Symposium, The George Washington University, and published in Warren Greenberg and Richard McK. F. Southby (eds.), *For-Profit Hospitals: Access, Quality, Teaching, Research*. Columbus, Ohio: Battelle Press.

Petersdorf, Robert G. (1985) Current and Future Directions for Hospital and Physician Reimbursement: Effect on the Academic Medical Center. *Journal of the American Medical Association* 253(May 3):2543-2548.

# 8 Physicians and Entrepreneurism in Health Care

The effects on patients of the profound changes taking place in the ownership and control of health care institutions may be lessened to the extent that patient care decisions remain with physicians. In the past, physicians have been relatively independent of institutions and, as an ideal, have been ethically bound to put a patient's interests ahead of the physician's own self-interest and the institution's economic interests. This chapter examines the implications of the powerful entrepreneurial and competitive forces that are in many ways the result of governmental policy and that are coming to pervade health care (1) as they involve physicians who practice within for-profit organizations, (2) as objects of institutional marketing[1] or cost-control efforts in which economic incentives are used, and (3) as entrepreneurs who assume the economic risk of investing in health care businesses outside of their own practices. What effects will these changes have on physicians' core ethical and legal obligation: primary fidelity to the interests of their patients? This obligation requires physicians to fulfill a role often described as "fiduciary" (Miller, 1983), because it has long been clear that the physician's own economic self-interest can conflict with the best interests of patients.

The fiduciary aspects of a physician's role are premised on the special nature of health care: that its need arises when the person is vulnerable and dependent, that the choices to be made may involve arcane knowledge and high stakes, and that only someone who is not perceived to be acting primarily out of self-interest can enjoy the trust on which success depends. The need for physicians to act as fiduciaries was increased, according to the traditional analysis, by the rise of health insurance, which insulated patients from many of the direct economic consequences of medical care and hence reinforced the willingness of "consumers" of health care to leave decisions regarding consumption of services to the "sellers," namely, physicians.

Of course, the physician's ethical position is not merely a matter of altruistic ideals; it has also been in the profession's enlightened self-interest for physicians to believe in a way that would justify society's willingness to defer to the self-regulation of the profession and to protect its privileges and autonomy. Public trust in the professional integrity of physicians has also been reflected in numerous other advisory and decision-making roles that are assigned to physicians and that, in many cases, are based as much on assumptions of the high moral character and objectivity of physicians as on technical expertise. Thus, physicians certify people as fit parents (e.g., in decisions about artificial insemination), as fit for civil society (under civil commitment laws), as eligible for benefits under disability programs, and so forth.

Some tempering of the imagery of the powerful physician and powerless patient seems warranted today in light of such factors as the increasing sophistication of patients and increased recognition of patients' rights in medical decision making (President's Commission, 1982). Nevertheless, the "fiduciary/advocate" role remains at the heart of the relationship between health care professionals and patients. It is also integral to the relationship between the profession itself and a society that continues to rely on the integrity of the medical profession in a multitude of ways.

There are two essential senses in which physicians have fiduciary responsibilities to their patients. The first, examined in this chapter, is in the application of professional expertise to particular patient care decisions about whether to hospitalize, operate, prescribe, test, discharge, or refer. Such decisions should not be based on the economic interests of the professional who is making the decision or is giving professional advice. The second area of fiduciary responsibility, examined in Chapter 9, is in assuring patients that other professionals or organizations to which the physician entrusts or refers them are worthy of their trust.

## ECONOMIC INCENTIVES AND ETHICAL OBLIGATIONS

The expression of the physician's ethical obligations to the patient has long been seen as subject to influence by economic and organizational arrangements. It is significant, for example, that powerful defenses and successful critiques of the traditional fee-for-service payment system have been stated in such terms. Professionally generated codes of ethics, most notably those of the American Medical Association, long held that departures from fee-for-service arrangements between independent physicians and indi-

vidual patients held potential for dividing or diluting physicians' loyalties. A philosopher recently stated the argument thusly:

Those who wish to eliminate fee for service may overlook the fact that the physician-patient relationship is one of deep intimacy and trust. The patient's monetary power, large or small, is the symbol attesting to the fact that the physician is the agent of the patient. Surprisingly, "unholy mammon" more adequately protects the fiduciary-covenant relationship of physician and patient than if the former is salaried by a company, the military or the government (Benjamin, 1981:64).

Under the influence of earlier versions of this argument, the language of ethics was used in arguments against many practices that have subsequently gained wide and even universal acceptance—including third-party payment, salaried practice, and prepaid health care.

Yet, fee-for-service has also been criticized for the incentives it provides physicians to serve their own economic interests. It has long been observed that a kind of conflict of interest is present whenever the person who is consulted about the need for services is also the most likely provider (for a separate fee) of the services that are recommended (Shaw, 1911). Fee-for-service incentives encourage provision of marginally necessary or even unnecessary services and the substitution of more generously compensated for less well compensated services. This was not widely seen as a problem when most physicians were primary care providers (who had to "live with" the results of their treatment and referrals) and when physicians had relatively few tests and procedures to offer. The growth of technological sophistication and subspecialization has resulted in increased concern about the incentives of fee-for-service medicine, particularly when linked with the widespread and generous insurance programs that have been developed over the past few decades, which give both physicians and patients the feeling that the physicians' choices have no economic impact on patients.

The incentives present in fee-for-service health care are neither new nor concealed, and they are probably understood by most patients. Large numbers of Americans retain a preference for arrangements (epitomized by fee-for-service) that preserve their freedom to select or to change their own physicians. The criticisms and defenses of the private, fee-for-service mode of organizing health care are well known and need not be rehearsed further here, except to note that certain criticisms (about stimulating unnecessary services) and defenses (about stimulating responsiveness to patients' needs and desires) both rest on the belief that economic rewards affect physician behavior.

However, recent years have seen a growth in public policies and private initiative methods to eliminate or attenuate the effects of the incentives inherent in the fee-for-service mode of organizing health care: HMOs, prospective rate setting, programs that encourage or require a second opinion prior to surgery or screening prior to hospitalization, various utilization review programs, and so forth. Of course, alternatives to fee-for-service payment create their own incentives, possibly encouraging undertreatment of patients and failing to encourage productivity.

All compensation systems—from fee-for-service to capitation or salary—present some undesirable incentives for providing too many services, or too few. No system will work without some degree of integrity, decency, and ethical commitment on the part of professionals. Inevitably, we must presume some underlying professionalism that will constrain the operation of unadulterated self-interest. The question is not to find a set of incentives that is beyond criticism, but to seek arrangements that encourage the physician to function as a professional, in the highest sense of that term. Certain changes that are occurring in our increasingly entrepreneurial health care system could undermine patients' trust in their physicians and society's trust in the medical profession. For those who believe that the professionalism of the physician is an essential element in ensuring the quality of health care and the responsiveness of institutions to the best interests of patients, an important question is whether that professionalism will be undermined by the increasingly entrepreneurial health care market in which physicians play a major part.

## INVESTMENTS AND INCENTIVE ARRANGEMENTS

If the fiduciary aspects of professionalism are indeed vulnerable to changes in the physicians' economic incentives, significant changes in physicians' economic arrangements with health care organizations could shift the balance on which the fiduciary role rests, possibly leading to excesses in the pursuit of self-interest by physicians or in the pursuit of economic goals (at the expense of quality) by health care organizations. Certain entrepreneurial and competitive developments in health care are creating situations that raise old and new questions about the organizational and economic arrangements that may affect the probability that the physician's behavior will embody the ethical ideal of primary fidelity to the patient's interest. In particular, physicians' investments in health care organizations and bonus incentive arrangements designed to influence physicians' decisions in organizations in which they practice may have the potential to bias physician decision making in ways that may not serve patients' interests.[2]

These two types of arrangements involve economic rewards that are affected by patient care decisions, although separate from the income derived directly from the services provided by the physician. Until recent years, this would have run afoul of a provision in the AMA's ethical principles that held that "a physician should limit the source of his professional income to medical services actually rendered by him . . . to his patients." However, this provision has been dropped, perhaps because it was becoming common for physicians to derive income from testing done on their own laboratory or X-ray equipment and from services provided by nurses, nurse-practitioners, and other health professionals whom they employ. Today, opportunities for physicians to generate personal income from services that they do not themselves provide are taking on new dimensions and scale.

## Physicians' Investments in Health Care

Investments by physicians in health care organizations are not new and have never been limited to their own office practices, although little systematic information is available on the nature and extent of such entrepreneurial activities. Nevertheless, it must have been relatively common in the past, because it was addressed by and found acceptable by the largest professional association, the American Medical Association, whose ethical standards have long permitted physician ownership of pharmacies, hospitals, nursing homes, and laboratories.[3] Undoubtedly such investments were sometimes motivated by the promise of economic returns and sometimes by the physicians' intent to meet the community's need for facilities or services that would not have been available without such investment.

One form of physician investment that had potential for influencing patient care decisions seems to have declined over the years: the direct ownership of hospitals by physicians. The first surveys of hospitals in the 1920s showed more than 40 percent of general hospitals to be for-profit (White, 1982). In many cases the proprietors of these small hospitals (an average of just over 30 beds) were physicians (Starr, 1982:165, 219). By the mid-1960s, these independent proprietary hospitals had declined to only 15 percent of all general hospitals; their further

decline since then has been a by-product of the growth of investor-owned hospital companies, whose early growth came largely from acquiring such hospitals. Indeed, of the hospitals acquired separately (that is, not acquired via the acquisition of a chain of hospitals) by the four major hospital management companies up to 1984, 60 percent were of the independent proprietary type that were commonly owned by physicians (Hoy and Gray, 1986). Such acquisitions did not always eliminate physician ownership, because hospital management companies sometimes traded shares of their stock for the hospitals they were acquiring. However, in these cases the ownership interest that remained with physicians was substantially diluted (i.e., in a large company rather than in a particular hospital). Physician ownership was eliminated completely in the many hospitals that were sold for cash. Thus, the growth of investor-owned hospital companies at least initially reduced the potential conflict of interest that occurs when physicians own the facilities to which they admit patients.

However, the decline of hospital ownership by physicians appears to be an exception to a very different entrepreneurial trend. Although documentation of ownership is sparse, many observers have noted a rapid growth in recent years in many new types of entrepreneurial activities by physicians. In addition to older forms of investment in hospitals, pharmacies, and laboratory and X-ray equipment (often in their own offices), physicians are major investors in many new types of freestanding or noninstitutional health care centers that have come into being in recent years and that aggressively market their services.[4] A 1982 report to the Federal Trade Commission listed 29 types of centers, including abortion services, birthing centers, alcohol and drug abuse treatment centers, occupational health centers, house call services, home health care services, emergency room contract management services, freestanding urgent care centers, cardiopulmonary testing services, genetic counseling programs, freestanding surgery centers, freestanding dialysis centers, optometric services, retail dental offices, baldness clinics, respiratory therapy services, parenteral nutrition services, optometric centers, podiatry centers, and sports medicine centers (Trauner et al., 1982). This list could easily be extended.

Much of this entrepreneurial activity appears to be for laudable purposes—to make certain surgical, diagnostic, and other services available in less-expensive settings; to increase the convenience of services to patients; to provide capital that sometimes would otherwise not be available. However, purposes must be distinguished from the details of economic arrangements and the incentives they create.

These freestanding centers are created under a wide variety of arrangements, depending on tax laws, state laws on the corporate practice of medicine, and various local circumstances. Physicians are the sole investors in many of these enterprises, some of which are virtually indistinguishable from physicians' office practices and some of which are distinguished only by a catchy name or extended hours. Some new enterprises are joint ventures between physicians and hospitals or other health care organizations (Morrisey and Brooks, 1985). Although no systematic data exist, many of these joint ventures involve not-for-profit hospitals, with the joint venture typically established through a for-profit subsidiary. Some centers are franchise or turnkey operations in which investor-owned organizations (some of which are publicly traded companies) build a facility (such as a radiologic imaging center or a cataract surgery center) and take local physician-investors as minority partners. Some of these physician investors may operate the facility and practice therein, and some may, by design, be likely referral physicians (Wallace, 1984; Holoweiko, 1984:123).

Several diverse causes may underlie the apparent surge in physicians' making new kinds of investments either in expensive technologies for their own practices or in new types of health care organizations outside of their own practices. Contributing factors include the following:

• Incentives created by regulatory programs (such as certificate of need) that have applied to hospitals but not to doctors' practices, thereby encouraging the purchase or leasing of expensive technologies (e.g., CT scanners) by physicians and the growth of freestanding centers built around these technologies

• The tendency of payment mechanisms to value technology-intensive care over other services, making it more profitable for physicians to spend time on technological procedures (Schroeder, 1985)

• Incentives created by third-party payers for shifting services from inpatient to less expensive outpatient settings

• Changes in technology that made some services (e.g., cataract surgery) more feasible on an outpatient basis

• The increasing economic complexity of medical practice, making it more important for physicians to operate in a businesslike, economically calculating fashion

• Tax law changes and sophisticated tax advisers, which have undoubtedly stimulated physicians' interest in certain investments

• The removal, under pressure from the Federal Trade Commission, of many restrictions on truthful advertising in the professions

• State laws against the corporate practice of medicine that have given physicians an advantage over other entrepreneurs in establishing certain kinds of facilities[5]

• Economic pressures resulting from the growing supply of physicians, which have undoubtedly stimulated interest in new sources of income and in organizations over which physicians, as owners, can have substantial control

• Competitive conditions that make health

care institutions more concerned with market share and that stimulate interest in joint ventures

• The general increase of physician experience in practicing medicine in organizations larger than the solo practices that were once typical.

With such a large and complex group of possible stimuli, entrepreneurism among physicians is a movement of considerable force. Finally, by making open entrepreneurism by physicians less unusual, the growth of physician entrepreneurism may itself have stimulated more such activity.

### Incentive Bonus Arrangements

The possibility for secondary gain from patient care decisions also arises from bonus arrangements established by health care institutions to encourage staff physicians to make treatment decisions that are favorable to the institution's financial interests (Capron and Gray, 1984; Tatge, 1984a; Adams and Klein, 1985). Such arrangements have been advanced as one possible solution to a problem created by Medicare's adoption of a prospective payment system for hospitals but not for physicians.[6] Under cost-based reimbursement, hospitals and physicians were both rewarded for the provision of additional services, a situation that is generally acknowledged to have contributed to the rapid growth of health care expenditures. However, Medicare's change to rates set on a prospective per-case basis for hospitals, but not for physicians, gave hospitals an incentive to reduce expenses, but left unchanged the economic incentives for physicians—who order the tests and decide when the patient is ready for discharge. Concern quickly developed among hospitals about their economic vulnerability to the consequences of physicians' decisions.

Hospitals have responded in several ways. Most have developed or purchased data systems to enable monitoring of physicians'

patterns of care and identification of those physicians whose practice patterns (such as long lengths of stay or high rates of ordering tests) might cause the hospital to lose money on their Medicare patients. Beyond this, hospitals' strategies differ. Some hospitals decided to rely on educational efforts and appeals to physicians' loyalties and concern for the well-being of the hospital. At an unknown number of hospitals, physicians' admitting privileges may be at stake. Two-thirds of the physicians in a 1984 AMA survey reported that their hospital had set guidelines to reduce patients' lengths of stay; approximately 40 percent of these physicians said that their hospital had tried to reduce the number of diagnostic tests ordered, and approximately 30 percent said their hospital had attempted to reduce the number of treatment procedures prescribed (American Medical Association, 1984b). (Proprietary hospitals were less likely than nonproprietary hospitals to have taken these actions, but the differences were small.)

An alternative or complementary strategy adopted by an unknown number of hospitals and other types of providers (such as HMOs) is to give physicians a direct economic stake in the well-being of the institution by setting up arrangements that re-align the physicians' economic incentives with the institution's economic incentives (Iglehart, 1984; Sandrick, 1984; Goldsmith, 1982; Richards, 1984). This can be done by giving or selling physicians an equity interest in the organization so they share in profits as owners (*Modern Healthcare*, 1984; Simler, 1985), or by creating a new entity—often a joint venture between a hospital and some or all of its medical staff—through which both expense and income dollars flow (Ellwood, 1983a,b; Tatge, 1984b; Shortell, 1984). Many joint ventures have the additional purposes of emphasizing cooperation with key physicians, maintaining or enhancing a hospital's market share, or improving community access to care (Sachs, 1983; Strum, 1984; Shortell et al., 1984).

Incentive bonus arrangements have been utilized as an alternative to such equity arrangements.[7] What is involved is the creation of a pool of money and a formula for sharing it. Whether (and how much) money goes into the pool depends on whether the institution makes money or loses money under its fixed-rate reimbursement. The possible formulas for sharing it are many, including payments made equally among all staff physicians, in proportion to number of patients admitted, in proportion to contribution to the pool, and so forth.

The implementation of such incentive bonus arrangements has been impeded by unresolved questions about whether a nonprofit institution's tax-exempt status might be jeopardized by such an arrangement and whether such arrangements might violate Medicare and Medicaid fraud and abuse laws (Tatge, 1984a; Wallace, 1985; Elmquist, 1985; Adams and Klein, 1985). Thus, it is not known how successful they will be in encouraging physician behavior that serves the interests of the institution. Nor is anything systematic known about the positive or negative effects on patients that might result.

### THE PROBLEM: ISSUES AND OPTIONS

Several arguments can be offered in favor of physicians' economic linkages with health care organizations that are outside of their own practices and that provide them with secondary sources of income from their own patient care decisions. First, it has been argued that physicians can better exercise leverage on behalf of patients and on behalf of quality in organizations in which they have an ownership interest (Guidotti, 1984). Available evidence allows no test of this argument. (The general topic of physician influence on institutions is explored in Chapter 9.) Second, in an environment in which cost containment has high priority (reflected in the growth of prospective payment and other methods that reward provision of services at less cost) and in which there is reason to

believe that many services that have been provided in the past have been of marginal value at best, arrangements that increase physicians' sensitivity to the economic consequences of their decisions are not necessarily suspect and could even be beneficial. Incentives that encourage the provision of fewer hospitalizations, shorter lengths of stay, or fewer tests may not be harmful to patients and may indeed be beneficial in many cases. (Of course, not all new arrangements reward reduced use of services. For example, giving primary care physicians an economic interest in an ambulatory surgery facility or a diagnostic imaging center could stimulate the provision of unnecessary services.)

Third, and more fundamentally, it can be argued that the more competitive health care environment of the future will make it increasingly necessary to bridge the historical gap between institutions (such as hospitals) and the independent physicians who practice therein and whose patient care decisions generate income and expenses for the institution. Arrangements that allow institutions and their medical staffs to organize as a single unit—for example, with regard to competing on price for the business of particular employers or payers—may provide health care organizations with competitive advantages unless payers or patients come to see these arrangements as not working in their interests. Joint ventures and other economic arrangements that make partners of hospitals and medical staffs are perhaps the most common formal arrangements by which this may be accomplished, although alternatives by which hospitals build loyalty and induce cooperation by making themselves more valuable to their medical staffs also exist (Goldsmith, 1982).

### The Problem

There is a potentially beneficial side to increased physician awareness of the economic consequences of their patient care decisions or recommendations. However, the committee is concerned about two possible negative effects arrangements, whereby physicians gain secondary income from their patient care decisions through investments in organizations that provide the services that they recommend or through incentive bonus arrangements with an institution in which they provide care. The primary concern is the unnecessary creation of conflicts of interest that may detract from the appearance or the fact that the physician is primarily concerned with the patient's interest, and that this conflict of interest may create patient distrust and produce undue, harmful effects on physicians' patient care decisions.

Some committee members had an additional concern about the effects of bonus incentives and physician investments, namely, that the credibility and moral standing of the medical profession itself might be harmed, and the distinction between professionals and businessmen might be further eroded. In addition to making it increasingly difficult for patients to trust a physician's advice, physicians' statements on scientific and policy questions in society might more often be dismissed as self-serving. Some of these concerns are similar to concerns raised earlier about bonus incentive arrangements in HMOs. Such arrangements were criticized as similar to split fees, kickbacks, rebates, and bribes; as constituting payments to physicians for services they provide to a third party rather than to the patient; and as "perverting the doctor-patient relationship into an article of commerce" (Geist, 1974:1304).

### The Evidence

Empirical studies do not yet exist on the impact on patient care decisions of the new forms of physician entrepreneurism or of incentive bonus plans for DRG patients. However, studies on laboratory and X-ray use show a direct relationship between physician ownership and utilization.[8] A study of

the use of X-ray by physicians caring for aged persons under a medical assistance program in California in 1965 showed that nonradiologists who provided "direct X-ray services" to patients (i.e., using their own equipment) used diagnostic X-ray on almost twice as many patients as did physicians who referred patients to radiologists for X-ray work (Childs and Hunter, 1972). A 1983 study by HCFA's Region V offices found that average per-patient reimbursement was 34 percent higher in laboratories in which primary physicians had an ownership interest than in "non-practice-related laboratories," because of higher prices (perhaps because it was not necessary to compete for business) and higher utilization levels. The HCFA study also cited a 1981 study by Blue Cross/Blue Shield of Michigan, which found that practice-related laboratories averaged 14.16 services per patient, as compared with 9.94 services per patient in nonpractice-related laboratories. Similarly, a small study of six laboratories by the Michigan Medical Services Administration found that patients referred by physicians who had ownership interest in the laboratories had 41 percent more tests ordered than did patients referred by nonowners (State of Michigan, 1981).

Survey evidence also shows that the rate of laboratory test ordering by physicians was higher for physicians who did tests "in house" than for physicians who referred their testing out; among those who referred their tests out, rates of testing were higher among physicians who purchased tests and billed patients than among physicians who referred their patients to laboratories that billed patients directly (Danzon et al., 1984). Clearly, as the analysis by Schroeder and Showstack (1978) suggested, physician ownership of testing and laboratory equipment can substantially increase their income.[9] The proliferation of such testing and the level at which it has been reimbursed are a partial explanation of the finding that physicians' incomes have risen faster than fees for their own services[10] (Redisch, 1978; Juba and Sulvetta, 1985). Studies have also shown physicians to change the volume of services provided to patients in response to price controls or changes in payment levels (Holahan and Scanlon, 1978; Rice, 1984).

It is also well known that prepaid group plans (e.g., HMOs) have substantially lower (an average of 35 percent) rates of hospital use than other plans, and that plans in which physicians are paid salaries have lower rates of hospital use than do plans that pay physicians on a fee-for-service basis (Luft, 1981:388). Also suggestive of the influence of economic factors on physician decision making is the rapid change in patterns of hospital use that has accompanied changes in economic incentives in recent years—particularly increased cost-sharing by patients and the onset of Medicare's prospective payment system. Although these changes do not affect physicians' incentives directly, lengths of stay in hospitals have declined for several years. The Health Care Financing Administration (1985) reported that the average number of days per Medicare bill for all short-stay hospitals declined from 9.3 days in fiscal year 1983 to 7.4 days in fiscal 1984 under the prospective payment system (PPS). Data from the AHA's National Hospital Panel Survey show that the decline in length of stay began well before PPS was implemented, and that the sharp decline among patients age 65 and over (from 10.4 days in the first quarter of 1981 to 8.8 days in the third quarter of 1984) has also been accompanied by a smaller decline in the lengths of stay for those below age 65 who, of course, are not covered by PPS (from 5.9 to 5.6 days during the same period) (Freko, 1985).

This evidence itself is adequate to confirm the common sense conclusion that investments and economic arrangements that reward physicians financially for making certain patient care decisions (e.g., ordering lab tests) will bias physicians in favor of making such decisions, although little data are available to demonstrate whether particular patients

benefit. Although specific effects of the newer and emerging types of arrangements have yet to be studied, the committee believes that serious concern about these arrangements is warranted. The committee's specific conclusions and recommendations are presented after an analysis of the types of policy options that are available.

## Policy Options

The problem of investments or incentive arrangements that enable physicians to derive secondary income from their patient care decisions can be approached through three types of policies: (1) policies to require disclosure of such arrangements, (2) policies aimed at eliminating or minimizing the economic benefits that might be obtained from such arrangements, or (3) policies that would discourage or forbid such arrangements.

### Disclosure

There is general agreement that the fiduciary aspects of the physician's role require at minimum that at least certain conflicts of interest be disclosed to patients or to referring physicians or to third-party payers. For example, disclosure to patients of physicians' financial interest in facilities to which referrals are made is an element of American Medical Association policy on conflict of interest (American Medical Association, 1984a:14; 1984c), and HCFA's "program integrity" regulations require disclosure to HCFA of information about the ownership and control of home health agencies (45 CFR Sec. 420.201). Disagreements arise about what should be viewed as a conflict of interest. Is ownership in an independent clinical laboratory any more of a conflict of interest than ownership of laboratory equipment in a physician's own practice? Is ownership of a few hundred shares of stock in the multinational hospital company that owns the local hospital a conflict of interest? Obviously, clear distinctions are difficult to draw.

There is also disagreement about the form disclosure should take and when it should be made. Doubt is also expressed about patients' ability to make use of knowledge about physicians' ownership interest in such facilities as laboratories or pharmacies. However, even when individual patients are unable to make effective use of disclosures about economic linkages, such information could be used to guide some of the review and emerging monitoring activities of third-party payers, professional review organizations, employers, organized consumer groups, and local health care coalitions. Such organizations may also find themselves in a position to define and demand such disclosures.

### Curbing Benefits from Economic Linkages

Several possible approaches fall into this category, including

● Development of payment systems (e.g., capitation, salaries, or low levels of reimbursement for certain procedures) that minimize the incentives for self-dealing or self-referral. For example, changes in reimbursement rules in recent years have reduced the amount of profit that can be built into the markup of laboratory tests for Medicare patients.

● Third-party payers could establish rules against paying for certain services that are provided by the person who orders or recommends the services. Such rules are obviously less practical for surgeons (whose practices require that they make recommendations about the need for their own services) than for primary care physicians who refer patients to surgical centers in which they have an ownership interest or for physicians who order diagnostic testing or home health services from organizations in which they have an ownership interest. An example of such a rule is the Medicare regulations that forbid physicians from certifying that a patient needs home health services if the physician has a significant ownership interest in the home health agency (at least 5 percent of the agency's assets) or a significant contractual relationship with it (i.e., business transactions involving at least $25,000 or 5 percent of the agency's operating expenses for the year) (45 CFR Sec. 405.170).

● Third-party payers can establish rules against paying for the wholesaling and retailing of testing, as in Bailey's suggestion regarding the overuse of laboratory testing: "moving the physician out of the financial transaction in testing—via direct billing laws—is the only workable means of discouraging testing based on economic incentives" (Bailey, 1979). Such rules would not be unprecedented. In Canada's Ontario province, for example, the physician who bills (and is paid) is the one who does the testing, not the physician who orders the testing. In the United States the Federal Deficit Reduction Act of 1984 restricted physicians from marking up the price of tests sent to outside laboratories, although this is believed to have strongly stimulated the acquisition and use of laboratory equipment in physicians' offices (Gallivan, 1985).

● Pre-admission certification and second opinion programs, already used in many areas for some expensive procedures, such as major surgery.

● Utilization review and peer review programs, such as HCFA's professional review organization (PRO) program and the review activities of other third-party payers.

● Maximum return-on-equity arrangements could be formulated by HCFA and major third-party payers for the total fees collected by a physician per year for use of laboratory equipment in the physician's office, to eliminate incentive for overuse of such equipment.

## Rules Forbidding Certain Conflicts of Interest

Practicality precludes attempts to eliminate all conflict of interest from professional practice. However, certain types of arrangements have been or could be forbidden under rules certifying organizations eligible to treat patients or receive reimbursement, state medical practice acts, or the standards of professional organizations.

The Medicare and Medicaid antifraud and abuse law prohibits the offering, solicitation, payment, or receipt of "any remuneration (including any kickback, bribe, or rebate) directly or indirectly, overtly or covertly, in cash or in kind" in return for referring (or to induce a referral) of any individual to receive service for which payment will be made under the Medicare or Medicaid law (Sections 1877(b) and 1909(b) of the Social Security Act). Uncertainty now exists about the applicability of the current Medicare fraud and abuse laws to bonus incentive arrangements. To the extent that such bonuses might induce physicians to admit their patients to a particular hospital, the law seems applicable. To the extent that such bonuses encourage physicians to reduce utilization of ancillary services and to shorten patients' lengths of stay, bonuses seem consistent with the intention of the Medicare prospective payment system, although not necessarily consistent with the patient's interests. Some health lawyers have called for changes or clarification of the law, noting its breadth and vagueness, urging removal of criminal penalties, and suggesting that it be specified that the law is intended to discourage provision of unnecessary medical services (Adams and Klein, 1985). However, the possibility that bonus incentives will confuse the physicians' fiduciary responsibilities and divide their loyalties should also be considered.

There seems to be less uncertainty about the application of this fraud and abuse statute to the mode of distribution of profits from joint ventures. The fraud and abuse law is seen as prohibiting the distribution of profits according to the amount of business generated through referrals, but not prohibiting the distribution of profits according to percentage of ownership of the venture (American Hospital Association, 1985).

State medical practice laws, which make "unprofessional conduct" grounds for revocation or suspension of physicians' licenses, could provide another means of controlling conduct, but the lack of agreement among professional codes of ethics about the acceptability of the alleged conflicts of interest in this area renders state laws of little actual usefulness. The American College of Physicians' code of ethics, for example, holds that:

The physician should avoid any business arrangement that might, because of personal gain, influence his decisions in patient care. Activities of physicians relating to the business aspects of his own or his group's practice should be guided by the principle that such activities be intended for the reasonable support of that practice and for the effective provision of quality care for patients (American College of Physicians, 1984:21).[11]

A very different standard was adopted by the American Medical Association's House of Delegates in December 1984: "Physician ownership interest in a commercial venture with the potential for abuse is not in itself unethical." The AMA standard does call for certain precautions including, at minimum, disclosure to patients and, at maximum, making alternative arrangements for care of the patient (American Medical Association, 1984c).[12]

### THE COMMITTEE'S VIEW

The committee strongly affirms that physicians have, and should continue to feel, fiduciary or agency responsibilities toward their patients. Trust is an important, often essential aspect of the physician-patient relationship, and patients' trust in the fidelity of their physicians to the patients' interest, like patient confidence in the physicians' skills, must be warranted. Various forms of physician linkages to medical entrepreneurial activities threaten the basis of that trust by creating new and powerful conflicts of interest. Only if one believes that medical training renders physicians impervious to the effects of economic incentives or that patients can adequately cope with physicians' conflicts of interest can one be indifferent to economic conflicts of interests resulting from physicians' investments.

Although there is a paucity of data on the effects of these arrangements on medical decision making, the committee believes bonus incentive arrangements and physician investments could pose greater problems for physicians' fiduciary role under several conditions:[13]

● The more direct the link between the physician's patient care decisions and the rewards of the incentive bonus arrangement or investment. (One hospital company's practice of sharing operating room revenues with surgeons is an example of a very direct link between decisions and payoffs; arrangements in which revenues are shared with large groups of physicians, who make distributions to individual physicians in equal shares is an example in which the relationship between a patient care decision and the benefit is rather remote.)

● The greater the economic rewards at stake, both in absolute terms and as a percentage of the physician's regular practice income.

● When the economic rewards from the incentive arrangement or investment derive not from the physician's own professional services but from the services of other professionals or other organizations to whom a referral is made.

● When physicians whose patient care decisions affect their incentive arrangements or investments are relatively insulated from the consequences of those decisions for the patients involved. (For ex-

ample, when a physician who has no continuing relationship with a patient makes a referral to another organization in which he or she has an ownership interest but where others assume responsibility for care.)

● When the physician's investment is primarily motivated by, and makes sense in terms of, pursuit of economic gain rather than by improvement in the quality of the physician's own practice.

● When the investments or incentives are not understood by patients, making it impossible for them to protect themselves from any negative consequences, for example, by seeking care from someone who does not have the same conflict of interest.

Because the forms of physician investments, joint ventures, and incentive arrangements are so varied and because developments are taking place so rapidly and under such varied circumstances, simple rules and guidelines regarding economic conflicts of interest are difficult to state. The committee divided the terrain into three categories, for purposes of recommendations. To some extent, the market will discipline arrangements that lead to inappropriate care, particularly if there are disclosure standards and if monitoring systems focused on outcome (as well as process) measures are further developed and agressively used.

**1. Investments in equipment or personnel in a physician's practice.**

**As a general rule, the committee recommends use of physician compensation systems that break the link between the decisions physicians make in treating their patients and the rate of return they earn on investments in their medical practice.**

Technical equipment of varying degrees of complexity and cost and support personnel with different types of skills and expertise are integral to any setting in which medical care is provided. They provide essential information and services and often provide convenience to both doctor and patient. The capital outlays and ongoing expenditures that they entail must, of course, be recovered if the enterprise is to remain viable. However, charges for the use of equipment and the services of ancillary personnel can provide physicians with significant income beyond the income generated through charges for their own services, expertise, skill, and time. Whether this is so depends on the level of charges and volume of use, a matter that is directly affected by the physician's patient care decisions. The larger the capital costs that must be recovered and the larger the margin between expenses and charges, the greater the incentive to make a self-dealing patient care decision.

However, the possibility of undue economic influence on medical decision-making is involved as is the operation of medical practices for the benefit and convenience of patients. In the committee's view, this issue is best addressed by payment incentives rather than through proscriptive rules. Alternative approaches should be explored, particularly for costs above some threshold. They might include paying set charges for certain kinds of patient care visits (say, a "major comprehensive visit") rather than paying separately for the use of items of equipment; paying only for the recovery of capital costs for certain expensive equipment (that is, de-coupling payment from level of usage); development of capitation or prepayment approaches that include a fixed percentage for capital expenditures.

**2. Physicians' investments in facilities to which referrals are made.**

It should be regarded as unethical and unacceptable for physicians to have ownership interests in health care facilities to which they make referrals or to receive payments for making referrals. In the absence of prohibitions on such arrangements that reward physicians for writing prescriptions, making referrals, and ordering tests, it is essential that disclosure standards be developed to make certain that patients, referring physicians, and third-party payers are aware that the conflict of interest exists so that they can respond appropriately.

The trend toward arrangements whereby physicians are given an economic inducement to make particular referral decisions is to be deplored and should be rejected in strong terms by professional associations, in state medical practice laws, and in conditions of reimbursement of third-party payers.[14] These inducements include, but are not limited to, arrangements where physicians are given or sold an ownership share in a facility to which they make referrals. Such arrangements are inconsistent with the physician's fiduciary responsibility to patients, and they are inconsistent with the ethical and moral stance that society is entitled to expect of the medical profession. Although some such arrangements (such as physician ownership of pharmacies) are not new and have perhaps even attained a modicum of respectability through familiarity, they have also in all probability been responsible for cynicism and distrust on the part of some patients.

The practice of physicians referring patients to facilities in which they have economic interest has long been debated. Recent data from a national survey of physicians shows that two-thirds believed it was a conflict of interest for physicians to refer patients to a hospital or other clinical facility in which they have an ownership interest (Musacchio et al., 1986). The proliferation of new types of facilities and economic arrangements needs more attention from the medical profession and in public policy. The committee's statement is intended to stimulate debate. The committee recognizes that its general statement about conflict of interest in physician investment may be problematic under circumstances that it did not contemplate—for example, referrals within group practices or within HMOs. There may also be examples of joint ventures in which physicians' capital is an essential element and which are designed to provide cost-effective care under local control and accountability. It may be possible to build sufficient disclosure and organizational accountability to patients to minimize the conflict-of-interest danger. However, the committee does not believe the problem is adequately dealt with by guidelines stating that so long as there is disclosure and patients are not exploited by inappropriate utilization, physicians can enter into any lawful contractual relationship. Such exhoratory guidelines provide no standard against which to measure the acceptability of an arrangement. The committee believes that the starting point for policy on this issue should be that physicians should not have an economic stake in making one referral rather than another. That is the end sought by the committee's recommendation.

Examples can be cited where the relationship between the referral decision and the economic return is minuscule, as when physicians own a few shares of stock in the hospital company that owns the hospital to which they admit their patients. The cumulative weight of all of the physician's admissions in a whole year would perhaps have only a nominal impact on the physician's equity interest in the company. Nevertheless, the committee believes it unwise for physicians to own such shares because of the principle stated above.

Investments by physicians in companies to which they do not refer patients do not raise the primary concern of this chapter: the creation of conflicts of interest that are inconsistent with physicians' fiduciary responsibilities toward their patients. However, many committee members believe that public trust in, and the moral authority of, the medical profession in general will be eroded if physicians treat medicine not only as a profession but also as a field of investment opportunity. Thus, they believe that the reputation and credibility of the medical profession would be enhanced by general

physician avoidance of investments in investor-owned health care companies, as well as in companies that manufacture and sell products used in medical care.

First, the committee believes that the highest values and ideals that should guide the work of the health professional are inconsistent with physicians viewing the field of health care as an arena of investment opportunities. Second, although this is hardly a new concern, the more that spokespersons for the values and concerns of health and medical care are seen as speaking from a position of economic self-interest, the less seriously those concerns will be taken by policymakers and by the public.

The committee's concerns and ideals may sound naive and even precious to those who are already convinced that health professionals and institutions are, first and foremost, pursuers of their own economic self-interest, and they may sound unnecessary to those who believe that physicians are able to maintain objectivity about all things medical, no matter how their pocketbooks might be affected. The committee, however, does not accept either of these views. It believes that it is in the interests of both the health care of the American people and of the medical profession itself for physicians to be as free of economic conflict of interest as possible. If members of the medical profession invest their money in the 90 percent of the economy outside of health care, they can speak with more moral authority on health matters.

### 3. Incentive bonus plans in health facilities and HMOs.

**Bonus incentive plans under which physicians receive a share in surplus revenues generated by an organization in which they practice pose a danger to the physicians' obligation of primary fidelity to the patients' interests, except when patients are a party to the agreements. In the absence of prohibitions on incentive bonus arrangements, it is essential that disclosure standards be developed to make certain that patients, referring**

**physicians, and third-party payers are aware that the conflict of interest exists so that they can act accordingly.**

Bonus incentives (like some other arrangements, such as joint ventures) have been proposed as a way to get medical staff members more interested in cost containment or in marketing (generating new business). One of the smaller investor-owned hospital companies proposed sharing operating room revenues with surgeons who use the facility and another has proposed a profit-sharing plan based on splitting surplus revenues, if any, derived in the care of Medicare patients for whom revenues are fixed under the DRG prospective payment systems (*American Medical News*, 1985). While these arrangements are now so unusual as to be newsworthy, they could become common if they are not objected to firmly. When bonus incentives are offered to physicians by the organizations in which they work or by third-party payers, even if done as an antidote to the established incentives of fee-for-service, such incentive plans place the physician in an unnecessary and unacceptable conflict of interest. Indeed, they appear to be designed to do so.

The circumstance under which incentive bonuses might be acceptable is if patients were a party to the agreement. That is, the closer the agreement approximates a circumstance in which a group of patients themselves agree to the inclusion of economic incentives in the provision of a defined set of services for a negotiated price, the less such incentives contravene the ethical obligations of the physician toward the patient. Thus, it would be one matter if patients, who had alternative sources of care, were to agree to an HMO contract that included a provision that incentive bonuses were to be included in physicians' compensation arrangements. It would be quite another matter if a hospital offered incentive bonuses to physicians for the care of Medicare patients, who not only were not a party to the agreement but who would often be

without alternative sources of care at the time they need services. Under such circumstances, putting patients on notice that such incentive bonuses are being used in the hospital would not alter the fundamental breech of the physician's ethical obligation to the patient.

The committee is concerned about incentive arrangements that are designed to influence physician behavior. It recognizes that there may be some circumstances in which its recommendation may apply poorly, if at all—for example, in the compensation of hospital-based physicians or salaried physicians (for whom "bonuses" in the form of salary increases could hardly be ruled out). However, the committee supports efforts by professional associations, third-party payers, and regulatory authorities to identify and address situations in which economic incentives are being offered that are inimicable to the patient's interests.

## CONCLUSION

The fiduciary/advocate role of physicians has been, and remains, an important restraint on self-interested actions by professionals and needs continued, explicit endorsement from professional organizations, educators, and public bodies. It is in the interest of the health care professions as well as society to have confidence and trust in physicians' fidelity to patients. While some conflicts of interest are inherent in long-established aspects of our health care system (e.g., the traditional fee-for-service, piecework system in which the same physician frequently acts both as advisor and provider of the service), it is desirable that conflicts of interest be avoided when possible. Developments discussed in this chapter also reinforce the importance of surveillance of inappropriate use of health services, including at ambulatory sites, as recommended in Chapter 6.

## NOTES

[1]To illustrate, a 1985 newsletter directed to hospital administrators advises as follows:

> Too many doctors treat "marketing" as a dirty word. Don't let them get away with it. Be direct. Ask doctors how they plan to send their kids to college. Share marketing data. Offer names of doctors who can use their services. . . . TIP. Just one busy surgeon means $1.5 million per year for the average hospital. One busy internist $750,000. One busy Ob/gyn $600,000. A busy GP? $500,000. (*Health Care Competition Week*, August 1985).

[2]In the view of some, the organizational form of health care institutions may itself affect the professional performance of physicians who practice therein. Some of the distrust of for-profit health care organizations undoubtedly has such a basis, as does the belief that the not-for-profit mode of organizing hospitals is in many ways particularly compatible with the ideals of medical professionalism (Majones, 1984). There is, of course, a more skeptical view: that the not-for-profit form served to allow income maximization by the physicians that practiced therein (Pauly and Redisch, 1973; Feldstein, 1979:191-196).

[3]However, as Veatch (1983:130) notes, until the 1980 revision in the AMA code of ethics, it was held unethical for physicians to profit in proportion to the work they referred to such facilities. The AMA code continues to hold that it is unethical for "the physician to place his own financial interest above the welfare of his patients" (American Medical Association, 1984a:14).

[4]Some data on physician ownership of laboratories comes from a 1983 study by HCFA's Region V offices, which found that 75 percent of laboratory testing in 1981 was done by independent laboratories (the remainder being done directly in physicians' offices), and that one-fourth of the 535 certified independent laboratories in the region were owned entirely or partially by physicians involved in primary care; such "practice-related" ownership increased to 42 percent among the 85 laboratories that were certified in the most recent period studied (the 9 months ending July 30, 1982) (Health Care Financing Administration, 1983). Fragmentary information on physician ownership of free-standing primary care or emergency centers came from a 1983 AMA survey of physicians. Of the only 9 percent of physicians who provided care in such a facility, 13 percent said their facility was physician owned (AMA, 1984e:18).

[5]The American Medical Association's Office of General Counsel now identifies only three states (Texas, Colorado, and California) that have effective laws against the corporate practice of medicine (B. J. Anderson, personal communication, June 24, 1985). Rosoff's recent analysis of the corporate practice of medicine doc-

trine notes that most states still have laws prohibiting the practice of medicine by a lay corporation, but that the enforcement of these laws has declined because of exceptions that developed in the employment of residents and interns, because of an exception built into the 1973 Federal HMO act, and because of the development and growth since the 1960s of professional corporations. Nonetheless, Rosoff contends that "state laws against corporate practice pose a significant threat to innovation in health care practice. They are 'legal landmines,' remnants of an old and nearly forgotten war, half-buried on a field fast being built up with new forms of health care organizations. Occasionally, usually at the instigation of those who resist the change now taking place, one is detonated, with distressing results" (Rosoff, 1984:4). Although concluding that the doctrine is outmoded and deserves reconsideration, Rosoff warns against wholly scrapping it, because "some concerns regarding lay involvement in medical decisionmaking are valid" (Rosoff, 1984:5).

[6]Interestingly, the incentives of Medicare's prospective payment system may stimulate a reduction in another type of incentive compensation agreement between hospitals and physicians—the compensation of hospital-based physicians (radiologists, pathologists, anesthesiologists). Under prospectively set, per-case rates, ancillary services become a cost to the institution rather than the revenue source they were under cost reimbursement. Whereas incentive compensation methods (such as percentage of the department's gross or net revenues) have been common among hospital-based physicians in the past (Steinwald, 1983), an increase in salaried compensation (or equivalent contractual arrangements) can be expected. In any event, from the standpoint of the fiduciary theory, incentive compensation of these categories of physicians is of little concern since they seldom act in an advisory capacity for patients.

[7]Although such bonus systems for physicians have never been common, they have existed for some time, sometimes in subtle forms. Documentation is sketchy, but arrangements have been reported whereby hospitals provide physicians with office space or other services (such as billing or recordkeeping), with the cost to physicians dependent on their admission patterns at the hospital. Arrangements whereby hospitals offer income guarantees to recruit physicians to communities can contain tacit or implicit expectations of repayment in the form of use of the hospital. Moreover, incentive bonus plans have been a feature of some HMOs for years (Somers, 1971:84-85), although the most comprehensive available summary of research on HMOs mentions no systematic studies of the effects of physician incentive plans in HMOs (Luft, 1981). However, a Kaiser Permanente official was quoted years ago as saying that Kaiser's incentive compensation arrangements with physicians had had no "significant effect on

utilization experience" (Palmer, 1971:85). Recently, Mark Blumberg, M.D., Director of Special Studies of the Kaiser Foundation Health Plan, indicated again that although some Kaiser regions use bonus systems and some do not, there appear to be no associated regional variations in utilization (personal communication, April 26, 1985). However, no formal studies have been done. Furthermore, it is not known whether the apparent lack of impact is due to the amounts that are involved, to the structure of the bonus (e.g., that it is tied to the experience of a group of physicians, not to individual physicians' experience), to the fact that a healthy organizational bottom line will show up in future salaries even without a formal bonus system, or to some other factor.

[8] Data showing associations should not be confused with causal data. For example, high use of X-rays by physicians who own their own equipment may be due to the economic incentives of ownership or due to the propensity of high users of X-ray to want to have their own equipment.

[9] It should be noted, however, that ownership itself is not the only route for generating income via testing. Profits can also be generated by physicians when they bill third parties for testing that they purchase from independent laboratories. The HCFA study cited in the text found that 72.5 percent of Medicare (Part B) and Medicaid payments for laboratory testing was paid directly to physicians rather than to laboratories, although 75 percent of the testing was being done in independent laboratories (Health Care Financing Administration, 1983). The average payment to physicians was approximately 250 percent above their cost.

[10] Redisch provides an estimate of the magnitude of this phenomenon by noting that, between 1955 and 1971, physician income rose by 7.2 percent per year, while fees rose by only 4.4 percent per year, and the average hours per week and weeks per year that physicians practiced actually fell slightly. "The maintenance of this high rate of income growth under these conditions was accomplished by increasing physician productivity through dramatic increases in nonphysician resource intensity of medical care" (Redisch, 1978). The role of payment systems' rewards for the use of high technology can be seen in changes in the relative income of practitioners in different specialties (Schroeder, 1985).

[11] A similar approach has long been a tenant of Britain's Royal College of Physicians, having been adopted in 1922:

> It is undesirable that any Fellow or Member of the College should have any financial interest (whether direct or indirect) in any Company or Institution having for its object the treatment of disease for profit, other than the receipt by him from such Company or Institution of (1) a fixed salary, or (2) fees, for such services as he may render to such Company or Institution in his

capacity of medical practitioner (Royal College of Physicians, 1959:49)

Similar is Relman's call for the medical profession to "declare as an article of its ethical code that doctors should derive income in health care only from their professional services and not from any kind of entrepreneurial interest in the health care industry" (Relman, 1983:16).

[12] The entire language of the statement on physician investments that was adopted by the AMA House of Delegates in December 1984 is as follows:

> Physician ownership interest in a commercial venture with the potential for abuse is not in itself unethical. Physicians are free to enter lawful contractual relationships, including the acquisition of ownership interests in health facilities or equipment or pharmaceuticals. However, the potential conflict of interest must be addressed by the following:
>
> 1. The physician has an affirmative ethical obligation to disclose to the patient or referring colleagues his or her ownership interest in the facility or therapy prior to utilization.
> 2. The physician may not exploit the patient in any way, as by inappropriate or unnecessary utilization.
> 3. The physician's activities must be in strict conformance with the law.
> 4. The patient should have free choice either to use the physician's proprietary facility or therapy or to seek the needed medical services elsewhere.
> 5. When a physician's commercial interest conflicts so greatly with the patient's interest as to be incompatible, the physician should make alternative arrangements for the care of the patient.

Regarding incentive bonus arrangements whereby physicians would share surpluses (or losses) generated by hospitals under Medicare diagnosis-related groups (DRG), the recommendation adopted by the AMA Council of Delegates was much less tolerant:

> The AMA has long held as a policy that physicians are not entitled to derive a profit which results directly or indirectly from services delivered by other health care providers who are not their employees or agents. Thus, the physician is not entitled to derive a profit which results from services provided by the hospital under DRG payments (American Medical Association, 1984d).

[13] There can be little doubt that making an investment creates financial and psychological pressure to derive a return; in subtle or obvious ways, incentives generally tend to bias decision making in ways that reward the decision maker (Luft, 1983). However, not all investments are alike. Distinctions can be made between investments in training, investments in es-

tablishing a practice, and investments designed to produce an economic return from sources other than the physician's professional practice. The physician entering practice who must pay back loans of $25,000 for debts incurred in medical education surely has an incentive to make decisions that are economically rewarding, as does the physician who has had to make a large capital outlay to establish or buy into a practice. So long as health care is primarily in the private sector, such pressures on physicians seem inherent in the practice of medicine; another mode of organizing care would present a different set of pressures and incentives (Mechanic, 1974a; 1974b:288; Glaser, 1970). Some pressures can be balanced by other factors, such as professional values, continuing relationships with patients, concern about the opinions of peers, although there is some evidence that the influence of these factors is less than is often suggested (Freidson, 1974).

[14]There may, however, be exceptional circumstances in which the meaning and motivation of such investments cast them in a different light. For example, in some isolated rural areas, the scarcity of capital and expertise may leave few alternatives to physician investment if certain facilities and services are to be made available. General prohibitions on such investment should make allowances for these exceptional circumstances.

# REFERENCES

Adams, Cary M., and Lynne S. Klein (1985) Medicare and Medicaid Anti-Fraud and Abuse Law: The Need for Legislative Change. *HealthSpan* 2(January):19-24.

American College of Physicians (1984) *Ethics Manual*. Philadelphia, Pa.: American College of Physicians.

American Hospital Association (1985) Medicare-Medicaid Anti-fraud and Abuse Amendments: Application to Hospital Activities Under the Medicare Prospective Payment System (Office of Legal and Regulatory Affairs, Legal Memorandum, Number Two) Chicago, Ill.: American Hospital Association.

American Medical Association (1984a) *Current Opinions of the Judicial Council of the American Medical Association—1984*. Chicago, Ill.: American Medical Association.

American Medical Association (1984b) *SMS Report* 3(August).

American Medical Association (1984c) Judicial Council Report C: Conflict of Interest—Guidelines (Adopted by the AMA House of Delegates, December 1984).

American Medical Association (1984d) Judicial Council Report D: Ethical Implications of Hospital-Physician Risk-Sharing Arrangements under DRGs (Adopted by the AMA House of Delegates, December 1984).

American Medical Association (1984e) *Socioeconomic Characteristics of Medical Practice, 1984*. Chicago, Ill.: American Medical Association.

*American Medical News* (1985) Kickback Plan by Hospital Hit (June 28/July 5):1,34.

Bailey, R. M. (1979) *Clinical Laboratories and the Practice of Medicine*. Berkeley, Calif.: McCutchan.

Benjamin, Walter W. (1981) A Reflection on Physician Rights and the Medical Common Good. *Linacre Quarterly* (February):62-72.

Capron, Alexander Morgan, and Bradford H. Gray (1984) Between You and Your Doctor. *Wall Street Journal* (February 6).

Childs, Alfred W., and E. Diane Hunter (1972) Non-Medical Factors Affecting Use of Diagnostic X-ray by Physicians. *Medical Care* 10(July-August):323-335.

Danzon, Patricia Munch, Willard G. Manning, Jr., and M. Susan Marquis (1984) Factors Affecting Laboratory Test Use and Prices. *Health Care Financing Review* 5(Summer):23-32.

Ellwood, Paul (1983a) *The MESH Method for Helping Doctors and Hospitals Work Together*. Excelsior, Minn: InterStudy.

Ellwood, Paul (1983b) When MDs Meet DRGs. *Hospitals* 57(December 16):62-66.

Elmquist, Marion (1985) Incentive Plan Can Add Doctors to Savings Team. *Modern Healthcare* 15(January 4):24.

Feldstein, Paul J. (1979) *Health Care Economics*. New York: Wiley.

Freidson, Eliot (1974) *Doctoring Together: A Study of Professional Social Control*. New York: Elsevier.

Freko, Deborah (1985) Admissions Drop Again, Cost per Case Up. *Hospitals* 59(February 1):35-38.

Gallivan, Mary (1985) Physician Offices Invade Clinical Laboratory Market. *Hospitals* 59(October 16):84-94.

Geist, Robert W. (1974) Incentive Bonuses in Prepayment Plans. *The New England Journal of Medicine* 291(December 12):1304-1306.

Glaser, William A. (1970) *Paying the Doctor: Systems of Remuneration and Their Effects*. Baltimore, Md.: Johns Hopkins University Press.

Goldsmith, Jeff (1982) *Can Hospitals Survive? The New Competitive Health Care Market*. Homewood, Ill.: Dow Jones-Irwin.

Guidotti, Tee L. (1984) Limiting MD Investment in Health Field Ill-Advised. *American Medical News* (September 14):31.

Health Care Financing Administration (1983) Diagnostic Clinical Laboratory Services in Region V (#2-05-2004-11). Mimeograph.

Health Care Financing Administration (1985) HCFA Background Paper [on Medicare Prospective Payment System Monitoring Activities] (January).

Holahan, John, and William Scanlon (1978) *Price Controls, Physician Fees and Physician Incomes from*

*Medicare and Medicaid.* Washington, D.C.: Urban Institute.

Holoweiko, Mark (1984) Doctor Entrepreneurs: Are They Hurting the Profession? *Medical Economics* (August 20):116-133.

Hoy, Elizabeth W., and Bradford H. Gray (1986) Trends in the Growth of the Major Investor-Owned Hospital Companies. This volume.

Iglehart, John K. (1984) Report of the Ninth Duke University Medical Center Private Sector Conference. *The New England Journal of Medicine* 311(July 19):204-208.

Juba, David, and M. Sulvetta (1985) *A Decomposition of Medicare Part B Payment for Physicians' Services.* Washington, D.C.: Urban Institute.

Luft, Harold S. (1981) *Health Maintenance Organizations: Dimensions of Performance.* New York: Wiley.

Luft, Harold S. (1983) Economic Incentives and Clinical Decisions. Pp. 103-123 in Bradford H. Gray, ed., *The New Health Care for Profit.* Washington, D.C.: National Academy Press.

Majones, Giandomenico (1984) Professionalism and Nonprofit Organizations. *Journal of Health Politics, Policy and Law.* 8(Winter):630-659.

Mechanic, David (1974a) Patient Behavior and the Organization of Medical Care. Pp. 67-87 in Laurence R. Tancredi, ed. *Ethics of Health Care.* Washington, D.C.: National Academy of Sciences.

Mechanic, David (1974b) *Politics, Medicine, and Social Science.* New York: Wiley.

Miller, Frances H. (1983) Secondary Income from Recommended Treatment: Should Fiduciary Principles Constrain Physician Behavior? Pp. 153-169 in Bradford H. Gray, ed. *The New Health Care for Profit.* Washington, D.C.: National Academy Press.

*Modern Healthcare* (1984) Mayo Subsidiary Selling Equity to Hospitals, Doctors as It Sets Up Labs. 14(June):106.

Morrisey, Michael A., and Deal C. Brooks (1985) Hospital-Physician Joint Ventures: Who's Done What? *Hospitals* 59(May 1):74-78.

Musacchio, Robert A., Stephen Zuckerman, Lynn E. Jensen, and Larry Freshnock (1986) Hospital Ownership and the Practice of Medicine: Evidence from the Physician's Perspective. This volume.

Palmer, Walter K. (1971) Finances and Planning. Pp. 71-87 in Anne R. Sommers, ed. *The Kaiser-Permannte Medical Care Program.* New York: The Commonwealth Fund.

Pauly, Mark, and Michael Redisch (1973) The Not-For-Profit Hospital as a Physicians' Cooperative. *American Economic Review* 63(March):87-99.

President's Commission for the Study of Ethical Problems in Medicine and Biomedical and Behavioral Research (1982) *Making Health Care Decisions.* Washington, D.C.: U.S. Government Printing Office.

Redisch, Michael A. (1978) Physician Involvement

in Hospital Decision Making. Pp. 217-243 in Michael Zubkoff, Ira E. Raskin, and Ruth S. Hanft, eds. *Hospital Cost Containment: Selected Notes for Future Policy.* New York: Prodist.

Relman, Arnold S. (1983) The Future of Medical Practice. *Health Affairs* 2(Summer):5-19.

Rice, Thomas (1984) Physician-Judicial Demand for Medical Care: New Evidence from the Medicare Program. Pp. 129-160 in R. Scheffler and L. Rossiter, eds. *Advances in Health Economics and Health Services Research.* Vol. 5. Greenwich, Conn: JAI Press.

Richards, Glenn (1984) How Do Joint Ventures Affect Relations with Physicians? *Hospitals* 58(December 1):68-74.

Rosoff, Arnold J. (1984) The "Corporate Practice of Medicine" Doctrine: Has Its Time Passed? Supplement to *Health Law Digest* 12(December).

Royal College of Physicians (1959) *The Charter and By-Laws of the Royal College of Physicians of London and the Acts of Parliament Especially Relating Thereto.* London: Harrison and Sons.

Sachs, Michael (1983) Help Your Physician "Brokers" Make Profits. *Modern Healthcare* 13(April):86.

Sandrick, Karen (1984) Medical Staff-Administration Relations under PPS. *Hospitals* 58(April 16):79-82.

Schroeder, Steven A. (1985) The Making of a Medical Generalist. *Health Affairs* 4(Summer):26-46.

Schroeder, Steven A., and Jonathan A. Showstack (1978) Financial Incentives to Perform Medial Procedures and Laboratory Tests: Illustrative Models of Office Practice. *Medical Care* 16:289-298.

Shaw, Bernard (1911) *The Doctor's Dilemma, Getting Married, and the Shewing-up of Blanco Posnet.* New York: Brentano's.

Shortell, Stephen M. (1984) 10 Guidelines for Success of Hospital-Physician Partnerships. *Modern Healthcare* 14(August 1):132-136.

Shortell, Stephen M., Thomas M. Wickizer, and John R. C. Wheeler (1984) *Hospital-Physician Joint Ventures: Results and Lessons from a National Demonstration in Primary Care.* Ann Arbor, Mich: Health Administrative Press.

Simler, Shelia (1985) Development Company Plans to Use Joint Ventures to Build Surgicenters *Modern Healthcare* 15(January 4:22.

Somers, Anne R. (ed.) (1971) *The Kaiser-Permanente Medical Care Program.* New York: The Commonwealth Fund.

Starr, Paul (1982) *The Social Transformation of American Medicine,* New York: Basic Books.

State of Michigan (1981) Utilization of Medicaid Laboratory Services by Physicians with/without Ownership Interest in Clinical Laboratories: A Comparative Analysis of Six Selected Laboratories. State of Michigan Department of Social Services, Medicaid Monitoring Section.

Steinwald, Bruce (1983) Compensation of Hospital-

Based Physicians. *Health Services Research* 18 (Spring):17-47.

Strum, Arthur C., Jr. (1984) Selling the Medical Staff and Hospital as a Package. *Hospitals* 58(May 16):98-101.

Tatge, Mark (1984a) Illinois Hospital Awaits IRS Ruling on Prototype Physician Inventive Plan. *Modern Healthcare* 14(June):23-24.

Tatge, Mark (1984b) Physicians, Rochester, NY, Hospital Enter Joint Venture to Protect Market. *Modern Healthcare* 14(December):26.

Trauner, Joan B., Harold S. Luft, and Joy O. Robinson (1982) *Entrepreneurial Trends in Health Care Delivery: The Development of Retail Dentistry and Freestanding Ambulatory Services.* San Francisco, Calif.:

Institute for Health Policy Studies, University of California.

Veatch, Robert M. (1983) Ethical Dilemmas of For-Profit Enterprise in Health Care. Pp. 125-152 in Bradford H. Gray, ed. *The New Health Care for Profit.* Washington, D.C.: National Academy Press.

Wallace, Cynthia (1984) Investors Cool on Hospital Companies While Interest in Alternatives Heats Up. *Modern Healthcare* 14(July):120-121.

Wallace, Cynthia (1985) Hospitals' Joint Ventures, Incentive Plans May Violate Fraud, Abuse Laws. *Modern Healthcare* 15(January 4):23-24.

White, William D. (1982) The American Hospital Industry Since 1900: A Short History. *Advances in Health Economics and Health Services Research* 3:143-170.

# 9 The Changing Nature of Physician Influence in Medical Institutions

Do such major developments as the rise of investor ownership, the growth of multi-institutional systems (in which many important decisions are not made at the local level), and growing competitiveness in health care affect the ability of physicians (and other patient care staff) to influence standards of care in institutions where they admit, treat, or refer patients? This chapter examines two means by which such influence takes place—through the physician's ability to alter referral or admitting patterns and through mechanisms by which physicians, nurses, and other patient care staff participate in decisions that shape institutional policies or operations.

## DECISION MAKING IN HOSPITALS

In medical institutions, decisions about patient care and administrative matters or institutional policies are not independent of each other (Shortell, 1983). Cumulatively, physicians' decisions to admit or discharge patients and to order particular services affect many matters typically defined as "administrative." Because the amount of discretion and judgment that are a defining characteristic of professional work make it impossible for anyone else to organize and supervise in a detailed way the performance of professionals, control over their work in organizations is typically exerted via the

power to allocate resources (Freidson, forthcoming). (In addition, anecdotes suggest that hospital privileges are increasingly being used as a mechanism of control.) Although physicians are responsible for patient care decisions, institutional management and resource allocation decisions made by administrators, managers, or trustees have profound implications for patient care. Such decisions determine or influence, for example, what equipment is available, what services are offered, how heavily and by whom various floors are staffed, what management information system is used and for what purposes, what kinds of utilization review and pre-admission screening the institution uses, and so forth. It is hardly surprising that conflict between medical and administrative authority structures is a ubiquitous theme in the literature on the "negotiated order" of hospitals.[1]

The need for institutions to control expenses is by now a cliche. Some actions for which an economic justification can be offered may also improve quality of care. However, some ways of saving money could reduce levels of quality either in minor ways (e.g., by reducing amenities) or in ways that could put certain patients at increased risk.

When views conflict about matters that affect patient care, the resulting decision reflects the relative power and persuasiveness of those who have a stake in the institution.

The perspectives of those who are concerned with some particular aspect of the institution's functioning—the staffing of a particular floor or the availability of a particular piece of equipment—and those who are concerned with the overall economic status of the institution are both legitimate, but are sometimes at odds with each other. On matters that involve some trade-off of cost and quality considerations (e.g., the amount of nursing attention that will be available to patients in an intensive care unit; when to replace a deteriorating piece of equipment), an institution's actions will in some sense reflect the relative influence of those for whom control or reduction of costs is a high priority and those for whom the maximization of quality (or other professional values, such as the physician's autonomy) is a high priority.

Several factors are increasing the power of institutional managers. These include (1) an increasingly competitive and complex environment, (2) the rise of professionally managed multi-institutional systems (and the consequent migration of many decisions from the local to the system level), (3) the rise among health care institutions of a "bottom-line" orientation, (4) the development of payment systems that put hospitals at risk for the economic consequences of physicians' patient care decisions, (5) an apparent increase in medical institutions gaining direct control by employing physicians or entering into contractual relationships with physicians that are little different from an employer-employee relationship, and (6) the development both of data systems that enable institutions to monitor closely physicians' patterns of care and of the will (stemming from economic pressure) to intervene when a physician's practice pattern causes the institution to lose money. These powerful institutional forces provide both the means and the motivation for an ascendancy of administrative power (Starr, 1983:420-449). Finally, at some institutions the threat that dissatisfied physicians might

take their patients elsewhere is declining, for reasons discussed in this chapter.

Whether changes in the relative power of administrators (or, as they are increasingly called in health care institutions, managers) and physicians is a prospect to be resisted or welcomed as overdue depends on one's perspective. The past high degree of physician influence has been used for a variety of sometimes controversial purposes. However, it has undoubtedly contributed to the quality of care in health care institutions, while also greatly complicating the job of the administrator, contributing to the inflation of hospital costs, and inhibiting many financing and delivery innovations in health care. While observers might disagree about the desirability of a shift in the balance of power in medical institutions, there can be little disagreement that physicians, with their knowledge and fiduciary responsibilities to patients, should continue to have significant influence.

## PHYSICIANS' RESPONSIBILITY FOR QUALITY

Chapter 8 examined how physician investments and institutional incentive arrangements could affect the fiduciary aspects of the physician's role, which requires that patient care decisions be made in the interest of the individual patient. In the view of this committee, physicians' fiduciary responsibility extends to ensuring that other professionals or organizations to which the physician refers patients are worthy of their trust. This includes responsibility for the quality of the care in hospitals or other institutions to which their patients are admitted (indeed, hospital medical staffs have formal responsibilities in this regard), organizations to which referrals for radiological work are made or to which laboratory samples are sent for analysis, and specialists to whom referrals for consultation are made.

Although there have been many manifestations of the medical profession's concern with quality over the years, the assertion of special physician responsibility for the quality of care requires qualification on three points. First, like all actors in all organizations, physicians have a variety of concerns and motivations. The pressures that physicians place on institutions in the name of quality of care can be genuine, but they are sometimes motivated by a desire to enhance prestige, increase convenience, further professional rivalries, protect or enhance their economic position, and so forth. It is neither surprising nor inappropriate that physicians' desires for new equipment or services or for additional personnel are sometimes treated skeptically. Second, to assert that physicians have responsibility for quality is not to contend that physicians have a monopoly on concern, knowledge, or responsibility about such matters. Such concerns are an important part of the values of nursing and of other health professions. Furthermore, quality standards must be a major concern of trustees and administrators, because of their sense of personal responsibility and because it could hardly be to a medical institution's advantage (economic or otherwise) to have questions raised about its quality of care. Furthermore, several court decisions (beginning with the Darling decision in 1965) held institutions responsible for the quality and appropriateness of care provided by the "independent" physicians on their staffs. Third, the involvement of referring physicians is clearly not the only mechanism for maintaining standards in a hospital. Many other factors are involved including accreditation mechanisms, outside utilization review (including professional review organizations), the threat of legal liability in the event of untoward events, and, at least in some multi-institutional systems, organized quality assurance activities (often centered around the problem of risk management) and physician advisory councils at the system level.

Nevertheless, in the committee's view, the physicians' position of trust and exper-

tise make it essential that they be in a position to influence standards of care. In a substantial number of cases the physician makes the determination of which hospital will be used or to where a referral will be made. Patients who follow their advice on these matters undoubtedly assume that their physician would not admit or refer them to an institution unless he or she had confidence in the quality of care. Furthermore, because of training and access to what is going on behind the scenes, physicians are uniquely situated to make such judgments on behalf of their patients.

Physicians' responsibilities for quality in the institutions to which they refer or admit patients may be exercised in two primary ways. The first is through involvement in activities that assure that quality is adequate. The formal responsibilities of hospital medical staffs, or designated members of medical staffs, for institutional quality of care is well recognized (Scott, 1982; JCAH, 1984). Some evidence exists that greater physician participation in hospital decision making and more highly structured medical staffs are positively associated with higher quality of care (Flood and Scott, 1978; Palmer and Reilly, 1979; Shortell and LoGerfo, 1981; Shortell, 1983:91).

The second source of physician influence over quality stems from their economic importance as the source of admissions and their power to change referral patterns or to admit patients to different institutions. The committee's case studies of physician-hospital relationships in small cities with several hospitals brought to light several examples of physicians using the threat or the fact of a shift in admitting patterns to convince a hospital administrator to increase the number of nurses on certain floors, to improve the quality of personnel in an intensive care unit, or to purchase certain specialized equipment. While these examples are suggestive, the literature tells little about how often and under what circumstances physicians change their referral or admission patterns or seek privileges in a different institution. Furthermore, little is known about how often such changes occur in response to concerns about standards or quality of care or how often other factors (e.g., economics) are involved.[2]

The two methods of exercising influence on behalf of quality of care concerns can be referred to, in Hirshman's terms, as "exit" and "voice" (Hirshman, 1970). This chapter suggests that several forces may result in a decline in the availability of the exit mechanism, and it examines what is known about the operation of voice mechanisms in institutions with different types of ownership.

### The Potential Decline of Exit Mechanisms as a Source of Influence

Although patients receive the care that is provided in health care institutions, the traditional customer of these institutions has been the physician, who made the decision of whether hospitalization was needed and to what hospital a patient should be referred or admitted. (This is less true of nursing homes, however, where case workers and hospital discharge planners make placement decisions for a large number of patients, half of whom have no close living relatives (Hawes and Phillips, 1986).[3] An important source of the physician's power and influence has been the ability to send patients elsewhere.

Although attending to patients in more than one institution presents physicians with significant transaction costs, the average physician has privileges at 2.1 hospitals (Musacchio et al., 1986). Having privileges at several hospitals makes plain the possibility of a change in admitting patterns. Thus, the emergence of various types of freestanding treatment centers has undoubtedly enhanced the exit option in some situations. However, more than one-third of the physicians practicing in the United States have privileges at only one hospital (Musacchio et al., 1986). Many of these are undoubtedly in single-hospital communities, where the

exit option does not exist; for example, the Hospital Corporation of America estimated that 20 percent of their hospitals in 1983 were the only hospital in the county (Phyllis Virgil, Hospital Corporation of America, personal communication, March 15, 1985).

However, the increasing supply of physicians, the growth of alternative delivery systems that control physicians' access to patients, and the predicted decline in the number of hospitals (as a result of heightened competitive conditions in the industry) are all factors that increase pressure on physicians to cast their lot with a particular institution either directly (e.g., via a joint venture) or indirectly (through joining an HMO or PPO).

Competition for market control is producing various arrangements that effectively bind physicians to particular hospitals, thereby constraining or eliminating the exit option. Several approaches now exist.

- Hiring physicians in a staff capacity, either as employees or as contractors. More than one-fourth (27.6 percent) of hospitals in 1982 had at least one physician or dentist on the payroll (Michael A. Morrisey, personal communication, March 20, 1985), and almost one in five physicians received direct payments from a hospital in 1984 (AMA, 1984). Such arrangements have been most common in the hospital-based specialties (pathology, radiology, anesthesiology), but are likely to increase among all specialties with the growth of alternative delivery systems (HMOs, PPOs) and with the growth of various types of ambulatory care centers. State medical practice laws' prohibitions against corporate practice of medicine have effectively precluded much hiring of physicians by investor-owned companies. However, these laws are coming to be viewed as obsolete (Rosoff, 1984). Furthermore, various types of contractual arrangements are proliferating and can be the equivalent of an employment arrangement in tying physicians to particular institutions.[4]

- Leasing arrangements within hospitals

or in neighboring medical office buildings, and the provision by the hospital of various services (recordkeeping, billing, appointments, etc.) useful to the physician's office practice. Data from a 1984 AMA survey show 7.3 percent of physicians to have a leasing arrangement with a hospital (AMA, 1984).

• The establishment by hospitals, often in conjunction with certain physicians, of freestanding urgent care or ambulatory care centers that link the physician and hospital either by joint ownership or by the fact that the physicians who staff the centers work for the hospital on salary or under contract.

• Rapid growth is taking place in various other types of joint ventures, preferred provider arrangements, and health maintenance organizations that tie physicians to particular institutions.

• Closure of medical staffs. A 1982 AMA survey found that more than 90 percent of physicians believed that their hospital already had sufficient medical staff, and 17 percent of physicians reported that a hospital at which they had admitting privileges had departments or clinical services that were closed to appointments of new, qualified medical practitioners (AMA, 1982). This is an area of likely future conflict. Hospitals seeking to increase admissions would presumably not favor the closing of the medical staff, and there are legal (e.g., antitrust) problems in doing so. However, the function of granting hospital privileges resides with the medical staff, and the growing supply of physicians can be expected to increase medical staff resistance to granting of privileges to physicians not already on staff. If closure of medical staffs becomes more widespread, this would reduce the possibility that physicians dissatisfied with patient care at one institution could seek privileges elsewhere.

• Another tying arrangement, which appears to be developing rapidly, involves agreements between hospitals (or hospital chains) and large employers, whereby employees' health benefit plans give them monetary incentives to obtain their care from particular hospitals and, therefore, from the physicians who have access to those hospitals (Tatge and Wallace, 1985; Waldholz, 1985). Thus, in a reversal of traditional arrangements, hospitals are increasingly gaining influence over physicians' access to patients.

If the feasibility of individual physicians shifting their admitting patterns is indeed diminishing, as the committee believes, then other methods of balancing medical concerns with the institution's administrative or economic concerns become more important. However, it should be noted that groups of physicians—such as independent practice associations, incorporated medical staffs, or large group practices—are increasingly dealing with hospitals; the economic importance of such groups may increase the potency of the exit option. Indeed, dissatisfaction with existing hospitals by a substantial number of physicians or a large group practice was a key factor in the construction of new hospitals by investor-owned companies in two of the committee's case studies. The primary alternative to the exit option is assuring that physicians (and other health care personnel) have an effective voice in the operation of institutions.

## The Growing Importance of Physicians' Voice as an Influence on Institutions

Decision making in health institutions involves many actors: trustees, administrators, independent physicians, hospital-based physicians, and, increasingly, nurses. Students of organizations long saw hospitals as professionally dominated, "doctors' workshops" nominally governed by a board of trustees. "As physicians began to conduct an increasing proportion of their practice in hospitals after the turn of the century, the predominant mode of professional care—independent, entrepreneurial, fee-for-service practice—was simply extended into the hospital" (Scott, 1982:217). However, as hospitals became more technological, capital-intensive, and complex institutions with growing specializations and differentiation of personnel, administrative or managerial functions became more important. Hospitals came to be described as having two lines of authority—clinical and administrative—or as having a demand division (the medical staff) and a supply division (the administrative staff) (Smith, 1955; Harris, 1977). Today's analysts increasingly note that competitive pressures are leading to more interdependence between administrators and physicians in the control of health care organizations, resulting in what Scott (1982) calls "conjoint professional organizations" or what Shortell (1983) calls the "shared authority model."[5]

However, professional dominance and shared authority are not the only possible models for managing organizations in which professionals work. Scott (1982:223) notes other models in which "professional participants are clearly subordinated to an administrative framework," as in secondary schools, engineering firms, and accounting firms. The question is whether such models may come into health care and, if so, with what consequences. Such questions are no longer far-fetched. There are reasons to expect continuing growth of ever larger and more economically powerful health care organizations, as well as growing economic dependency of physicians and dentists on these organizations either because they are employees or because their access to patients depends on a contractual relationship with the institution.

### Investor-Owned Health Care and the Mechanisms of Exit and Voice

Most data about exit and voice mechanisms in health institutions pertain to hospitals. (Little comparative data of any relevance exist about other types of health care organizations, although it is generally acknowledged that physician involvement in any aspect of the operation of nursing homes is very limited.) Although hospitals from investor-owned systems are the primary hospital of only about 10-15 percent of physicians who have hospital privileges (AMA, 1983; Musacchio et al., 1986), the growth of centrally managed multi-institutional hospital systems, particularly investor-owned systems, has raised fears about how medical concerns might be weighed against economic or management concerns therein, because of the combined factors of a "bottom line" orientation and the shift away from local control.

However, such evidence as is available suggests that exit and voice options are particularly available at for-profit hospitals. Regarding exit, whereas the average physician has privileges at 2.1 hospitals, physicians practicing in for-profit hospitals have privileges at an average of 2.7 hospitals, according to an AMA survey of physicians (Musacchio et al., 1986:Table 6). The AMA data also show that whereas 37 percent of all physicians have privileges at only one hospital, this is true for only 27 percent of physicians whose primary hospital is for-profit. Finally, for-profit hospitals have particularly low levels of salaried physicians; American Hospital Association data show an average of 0.28 physicians or dentists on the payroll of investor-owned system hospitals in 1982, compared with 6-8 physicians and dentists in freestanding or nonprofit system hospitals and 80 in hospitals that are part of publicly owned systems (Morrisey et al., 1986: Table 10).[6]

Thus, on the few dimensions on which data exist, exit options now appear to be more available for physicians practicing at for-profit hospitals than at other hospitals. Although no systematic data are available about the newer arrangements that may make the exit more difficult, the large investor-owned hospital companies have taken the lead among hospitals in developing insurance arrangements that give patients (and therefore, indirectly, their physicians) economic incentives to use their hospitals (Tatge and Wallace, 1985).

Although few data are available, exit options may now be more limited for physicians in nonhospital settings—particularly in the various types of ambulatory care settings and in HMOs—where salary and contractual arrangements, reinforced by the growing supply of physicians, may effectively tie physicians to the setting.

Regarding voice, there are many other mechanisms by which physician influence might be expressed—in the form of a full-time medical director, full- or part-time department chairmen, participation in management committee meetings, and so forth. Notwithstanding the importance of such mechanisms, most available data pertain to the narrower topic of board representation in hospitals. AHA data show physician representation on hospital boards to have been increasing, in general—from 67 percent in 1973 to 98 percent in 1982 (Noie et al., 1983). Physicians having voting power on hospital boards went from 54 percent of hospitals in 1963 to "almost all" in 1983.

How do investor-owned hospitals compare with other hospitals regarding physician representation on boards? Available evidence suffers from the difficulty of making comparisons between independent hospitals and hospitals that are part of systems, because membership on a hospital's governing board is usually a less-powerful position in a centrally managed multihospital system than it is in an independent hospital. Hospital boards in multihospital systems share authority with (or yield authority to) a corporate board on a wide variety of issues. Nonetheless, investor-owned systems now appear not to be the most centralized in this regard.[7] Comparisons of physician influence in independent and system hospitals is further complicated by the fact that a number of multihospital systems have physician ad-

visory boards at the corporate level that provide advice on new technologies, joint ventures, and patient care concerns. The evidence on voice, most of which comes from surveys of the composition and structure of governance bodies in institutions of different types, should be viewed with the foregoing caveats in mind.

● A 1982 AHA survey showed investor-owned chain hospitals to have more physicians on their boards (an average of 3.83) than did hospitals in religious chains (1.76), other nonprofit chains (2.13), and freestanding hospitals (1.86). All of these differences were statistically significant (Alexander et al., 1986).

● AHA data also showed investor-owned chain hospitals were the most likely to have physicians as voting members (in 91 percent of hospitals compared with 78 percent of religious chain hospitals, 71 percent of other nonprofit hospitals, and 67 percent of freestanding hospitals (Alexander et al., 1986).

● A 1982 survey of hospital governing board chairmen showed that while only 5 percent of hospital board chairmen were physicians, in investor-owned hospitals 43 percent of chairmen were physicians (Arthur Young, 1983).

● In the same survey, governing board chairmen reports of "very strong" board influence on "hospital medical affairs" were more common in investor-owned than in other types of hospitals, while reports of "very strong" board influence on such management issues as compensation of management, mergers, capital expenditures, and so forth, were particularly low in investor-owned hospitals, presumably because these topics are the prerogative of corporate management (Arthur Young, 1983).

● In an AMA survey in which physicians were asked to evaluate the hospital at which they admitted most of their patients, physicians in investor-owned hospitals were particularly likely to report their hospital administration as being "responsive" to physician concerns (Musacchio et al., 1986:Table 11).

Obviously, membership on boards may mean different things and may serve different purposes—as a device for marketing, as a medium for communication, and as a genuine means for sharing power. Although board members traditionally served important fund-raising functions, this is not the case in investor-owned hospitals. Yet little is known about the strategies at work in structuring the boards in multi-hospital systems in general and in investor-owned hospitals in particular. In their case studies the committee's site visitors heard of instances in which physicians used their membership on the boards of investor-owned chain hospitals to advance concerns about standards of care in the institution, but it is also evident that membership on a board could be used as a device by which the company transmits its views.

Although information on the operation of voice mechanisms in hospitals is limited, only speculation is possible about voice mechanisms in most other settings of investor-owned health care. In instances in which contractual arrangements exist between institutions and groups of physicians—up to and including the entire medical staff—the relative balance of power may well make for effective voice mechanisms. In new types of ambulatory care centers, where it appears that individual physicians are increasingly being hired on salary or contract—frequently in situations in which physicians are hiring other physicians—mechanisms of voice may now be in a relatively undeveloped state.

## CONCLUSION

The committee holds that physicians, in order to fulfill their obligations to patients, have responsibilities to patients for the standards of care in health care organizations to which they refer or admit them. This re-

sponsibility may be carried forth better in the settings in which the physician treats patients rather than in settings in which the physician has only a referral relationship. While recognizing that those responsible for institutional governance and management also have an interest in and responsibility for standards of care, the committee has examined implications of the changing structure of American health care for two broad classes of mechanisms by which such responsibilities might be carried out by physicians—by changing referral or admitting patterns (exit options) or by participation in institutional governance (voice options). A change appears to be taking place in the existing balance of power in medical institutions that may affect both types of options. Although greater accountability by trustees and administrators is desirable, the committee believes that there have been positive aspects to circumstances in which institutions were concerned with retaining the loyalty (and the patients) of physicians who felt a fiduciary responsibility toward their patients.

Although the growth of investor-owned health care organizations may appear, theoretically, to contribute to a possible imbalance of patient care concerns versus economic and managerial concerns, the data examined in this chapter on exit and voice mechanisms do not show these mechanisms to be in decline at investor-owned hospitals.

Several factors may change the balance of power in medical institutions. These factors include the growth of increasingly large and powerful multi-institutional systems, enhanced direct administrative power over professionals who are in increasingly plentiful supply, and the rise of other arrangements that effectively tie physicians to institutions. Furthermore, hospitals, like HMOs, are developing ways to "market around" physicians, by selling health care plans to large employers and by establishing feeder systems of urgent care or primary care centers. Thus, physicians may face a decline in their ability to change referral or admission patterns. This suggests that mechanisms to give physicians (and other patient care personnel) an effective voice in decisions that have implications for patient care concerns will be of growing importance, if patient care concerns are to be effectively advocated in the face of growing economic pressure and managerial power.

If physicians indeed find themselves increasingly tied to particular institutions, any lack of confidence on their part in the means by which their concerns are made known should lead to further exploration of mechanisms by which collective pressure might be brought. Changes that diminish physicians' traditional sources of influence will likely produce interest in new means of exercising power.[8] The most likely models for these means may be found in such developments as contractual relationships between groups of physicians and health care providers (hospitals or HMOs), in the incorporation of medical staffs, or in the development of other physician corporations that negotiate with hospitals. As the size of health care organizations increases, they may find themselves dealing with increasingly large groups of physicians. How these groups blend their fiduciary responsibilities with their economic concerns is an important question for the future of health care (Shortell, 1985).

*The committee, therefore, urges professional associations of the health occupations to develop their own criteria for appropriate modes of organizing effective participation of practitioners in monitoring and sustaining the quality of care in the various new forms of health care delivery and of discouraging excessive restriction of their voice in such issues.* Because of health professionals' knowledge, strategic location, and, ideally, their patient-centered ethos, their collective responsibilities on behalf of the interests of patients and of quality of care are increasing with the growing scale and competitiveness of health services organi-

zations in the United States. If the professional power and influence that can be used in the interests of patients is used instead for economic protection or for retarding needed change, a key source of leadership will have been lost for better assuring the tempering of economic and administrative pressure on quality of care and on the fiduciary role of physicians and other professionals.

## NOTES

[1] As Anderson and Gevitz note, "Administrators who try to contain costs . . . are commonly perceived by physicians as impediments to progress and good medical care, while they in turn are likely to view their physicians as extravagant and unmindful spenders" (Anderson and Gevitz, 1983:311).

[2] Physicians' referral or admission patterns are undoubtedly affected by many factors other than concerns about quality—convenience, prestige, habit, collegial relationships, or availability of facilities or equipment (Shortell, 1973). It is generally accepted that hospitals, for example, have competed for the loyalty of physicians by acquiring the latest technological innovations and offering the broadest feasible range of services (Finkler, 1983; Vladeck, 1976).

[3] Hawes and Phillips note that hospital discharge planners "labor under a set of incentives in which locating an empty bed—in any facility that will accept the patient—is the highest priority" (Hawes and Phillips, 1986).

[4] A description of many of the varieties of contractual arrangements between physicians and institutions can be found in the American Society of Internal Medicine's "Contracting Guidelines for Internists" (ASIM, 1984). Other organizations, such as the American Medical Association, have also provided advice for their memberships on such matters.

[5] Interestingly, in a study of one hospital conducted more than 20 years ago, Perrow (1963) described a progression through four stages of control: trustee domination, which had roots in the charity tradition; medical domination, which resulted from the quantity and complexity of medical knowledge; administrative challenge, resulting from the increased need for sound management; and multiple leadership, which resulted from the power struggle among trustees, the medical staff, and administration, and which Perrow found to be ineffective in terms of long-range planning, thereby identifying one factor that stimulated the growth of multi-institutional systems.

[6] Employment of physicians (or equivalent contractual arrangements) may be much more common in for-

profit (and not-for-profit) settings outside of hospitals. The issues this raises are undoubtedly important, but are outside the scope of this study.

[7]A 1982 American Hospital Association survey of multihospital systems found that the corporate board had responsibility (sometimes shared with the local hospital board) for many issues that are handled at the local level by independent hospitals. The following is a list of decision-making areas and the percentage of corporate boards that assumed responsibility for the decision: appointment of the hospital CEO (58 percent of corporate boards took responsibility); transfer of assets (81 percent); purchase of assets valued greater than $100,000 (76 percent); change in hospital bylaws (80 percent); medical staff privileges (41 percent); operating budgets (73 percent); capital budgets (76 percent); formulation of hospital strategies and long-range plans (59 percent); service additions or deletions at hospital (44 percent); hospital CEO performance evaluation (39 percent); appointment of local board members (66 percent) (Alexander and Schroer, 1984). However, contrary to the researchers' hypotheses, the study showed that secular not-for-profit systems, rather than proprietary systems, showed the "strongest, most consistent relationship to centralization" (Alexander and Fennell, 1985). On the other hand, proprietary systems were generally more centralized than Catholic systems, and were particularly centralized regarding CEO accountability and provision of support services to local hospitals.

[8]Indeed, there is a budding interest in some quarters in unionization activities by physicians, although this seems to be largely motivated by economic, rather than patient care concerns (Marcus, 1984). Under current labor law, attending physicians' status as independent practitioners rather than employees constitutes a significant barrier to unionization (Freidson, forthcoming: Chapter 7). Although the number of employed physicians is growing, recent National Labor Relations Board cases have interpreted physicians to be managers, rather than employees, because physicians sit on various administrative committees within health institutions. On this basis, one recent court decision defined full-time physicians as part of management and part-time physicians as employees with rights to protection under the National Labor Relations Board Act. The industrial model of employer-employee relations that is built into U.S. labor laws at present does not recognize the special position of professionals either as employees or as private contractors who deal as individuals with increasingly large and powerful organizations.

## REFERENCES

Alexander, Jeffrey A., and Mary L. Fennell (1985) Power and Decision Making in Multidivisionalized Forms: The Case of Multihospital Systems. Unpublished Paper. Chicago, Ill.: Hospital Research and Educational Trust.

Alexander, Jeffrey A., Michael A. Morrisey, and Stephen M. Shortell (1986) Physician Participation in the Administration and Governance of System and Free-standing Hospitals: A Comparison by Type of Ownership. This volume.

Alexander, Jeffrey A., and Kathryn A. Schroer (1984) Governance in Multihospital Systems: An Assessment of Decision-making Responsibility. Unpublished Paper. Chicago, Ill.: Hospital Research and Educational Trust.

American Medical Association (1982) SMS Report 1(December).

American Medical Association (1983) SMS Report 2(November).

American Medical Association (1984) SMS Report 3(September).

American Society of Internal Medicine (1984) Contracting Guidelines for Internists. Washington, D.C.: American Society of Internal Medicine.

Anderson, Odin W., and Norman Gevitz (1983) The General Hospital: A Social and Historical Perspective. Chapter 13 in David Mechanic (ed.), Handbook of Health, Health Care, and the Health Professions. New York: Free Press.

Arthur Young and Co. (1983) The Hospital Governing Board Chairman. Los Angeles: Arthur Young.

Finkler, Steven A. (1983) The Hospital as a Sales-Maximizing Entity. Health Services Research 18(Summer):117-133.

Flood, Ann B., and W. Richard Scott (1978) Professional Power and Professional Effectiveness: The Power of the Surgical Staff and the Quality of Surgical Care in Hospitals. Journal of Health and Social Behavior 19(September):240

Freidson, Eliot (Forthcoming) Professional Power: A Study of the Institutionalization of Formal Knowledge. Chicago. Ill.: University of Chicago Press.

Harris, Jeffrey E. (1977) The Internal Organization of Hospitals: Some Economic Implications. Bell Journal of Economics 8(Autumn):467-482.

Hawes, Catherine, and Charles D. Phillips (1986) The Changing Structure of the Nursing Home Industry and the Impact of Ownership on Quality, Cost and Access. This volume.

Hirshman, Albert (1970) Exit, Voice, and Loyalty. Cambridge, Mass.: Harvard University Press.

Joint Commission on Accreditation of Hospitals (1984) Accreditation Manual for Hospitals. Chicago, Ill.: Joint Commission on Accreditation of Hospitals.

Marcus, Sanford (1984) Trade Unionism for Doctors: An Idea Whose Time Has Come. The New England Journal of Medicine 311(December 6):1508-1511.

Morrisey, Michael A., Jeffrey A. Alexander, and Stephen M. Shortell (1986) Medical Staff Size, Hospital

Privileges, and Compensation Arrangements: A Comparison of System Hospitals. This volume.

Musacchio, Robert A., Stephen Zuckerman, Lynn E. Jensen, and Larry Freshnock (1986) Hospital Ownership and the Practice of Medicine: Evidence from the Physician's Perspective. This volume.

Noie, Nancie E., Stephen M. Shortell, and Michael A. Morrisey (1983) A Survey of Hospital Medical Staffs—Part 1. *Hospitals* 57(December 1):80-84.

Palmer, R. Heather, and Margaret C. Reilly (1979) Individual and Institutional Variables Which May Serve as Indicators of Quality of Medical Care. *Medical Care* 17(July):693-717.

Perrow, Charles (1963) Goals and Power Structures: A Historical Case Study. Pp. 112-145 in Eliot Freidson (ed.), *The Hospital in Modern Society*. New York: Free Press.

Rosoff, Arnold (1984) The "Corporate Practice of Medicine" Doctrine: Has Its Time Passed? Supplement to *Health Law Digest* 12(December).

Scott, W. Richard (1982) Managing Professional Work: Three Models of Control for Health Organizations. *Health Services Research* 17(Fall):213-240.

Shortell, Stephen M. (1973) Patterns of Referral Among Internists in Private Practice: A Social Exchange Model. *Journal of Health and Social Behavior* 14(December):335-348.

Shortell, Stephen M. (1983) Physician Involvement in Hospital Decision Making. Pp. 73-101 in Bradford H. Gray, ed. *The New Health Care for Profit*. Washington, D.C.: National Academy Press.

Shortell, Stephen M. (1985) The Medical Staff of the Future: Replanting the Garden, *Frontiers of Health Services Management* 1(February):3-48.

Shortell, Stephen M., and James P. LoGerfo (1981) Hospital Medical Staff Organization and Quality of Care: Results for Myocardial Infarction and Appendectomy. *Medical Care* 19(October):1041-1056.

Smith, Harvey L. (1955) Two Lines of Authority Are One Too Many: The Hospital's Dilemma. *Modern Hospital* 84(March):59-64.

Starr, Paul (1983) *The Social Transformation of American Medicine*. New York: Basic Books.

Tatge, Mark, and Cynthia Wallace (1985) Hospital Chains Entering Insurance Business to Attract Patients, Fill Beds. *Modern Healthcare* 15(March 1):56, 58.

Vladeck, Bruce (1976) Why Nonprofits Go Broke. *The Public Interest* 42(Winter):86-101.

Waldholz, Michael (1985) More Firms Are Telling Patients Which Doctors They Should Use. *Wall Street Journal* (March 18):37.

# *10* Summary and Conclusions

This inquiry has focused on questions about for-profit health care organizations, particularly investor-owned multihospital systems, and about the fiduciary role of physicians in a health care system increasingly characterized by commercial and entrepreneurial activities. In examining the many topics covered in this report—the sources and uses of capital funds for health facilities, access to care, the costs and quality of care, involvement in medical research and education, and the relationships of physicians to organizations to which they refer patients or in which they treat patients—the committee found that only limited quantitative evidence was available on many important points. However, the committee was charged to use its broad experience and diversity to make its best considered judgments about the meaning and importance of the available evidence for the future. Thus, in addition to summarizing the major findings from the previous chapters, this chapter also presents the committee's view of the major implications of these findings and offers some recommendations, acknowledging that its conclusions and recommendations reflect not only the empirical evidence but also the committee's considered judgments about the meaning of this evidence.

As befits the controversy regarding for-profit health care, this study has examined not only factual matters about organizational behavior but also the value conflicts raised by changes taking place in the organization of health care in America. These value conflicts color people's interpretations of data and persist after all empirical studies have been reviewed.

Thus, some observers believe that the rise of for-profit health care threatens the values and ideals that should guide the activities of health professionals and health care organizations and that, if realized, distinguish professional work from commerce. Concern has also been expressed that the growth of for-profit health care may exacerbate current problems in the health care system. Problems frequently mentioned include inadequate availability of services for people who lack the means to pay, duplicative high-cost technologies and facilities for health care delivery, deficiencies in the availability of good primary care and services for patients with chronic disease, and highly variable rates of elective surgery. It is feared that something essential will be lost if a service ethos—expressed in terms such as caring, community responsiveness, fiduciary responsibility—is abandoned or replaced with a principle based on economic goals. Many who express these concerns also are opposed to the perpetuation of a multi-tiered health care system based on the ability to pay. They believe that scarce health resources should be allocated not by whether their provision will generate profits but by their effectiveness in improving the health of individuals and populations.

On the other hand, advocates of markets and competition—rather than governmental planning and cost controls—as a way of distributing services see the problem not in the behavior of profit-seeking organizations but in the failure of public policy. We fail, they say, to provide the financial means that would allow people who need care to obtain it, as well as to structure payment incentives to reward cost-effectiveness. These advocates believe that a more economically based ethic that emphasizes competition, businesslike efficiency, and responsiveness to demand has become possible with the increasing ability of patients to afford care (a result of third-party payment, including Medicare and Medicaid) and to participate in decisions about their care and with the greater ability of payers to monitor the services they purchase. Furthermore, they tend to be skeptical about the past realization of selfless ideals by practitioners and institutions.

This study took place in a swiftly changing environment. Available evidence about costs, quality, and access to care in for-profit and not-for-profit hospitals comes from a period that was dominated by Medicare's cost-based reimbursement and that saw little price competition among providers for the business of other payers. Now, Medicare's prospective payment system for hospitals is reversing the incentives presented by cost-based reimbursement. The consequences of this singularly important change are not yet well understood. In other developments, various forms of price competition (discounting, expansion of HMOs and preferred-provider arrangements, contracting in state Medicaid programs) are rapidly emerging, and the growing supply of physicians is having perceptible effects. Because some of the committee's findings about hospitals pertain to institutional differences in response to economic incentives, they must

now be regarded as a point of reference, a freeze-frame in a film of rapid action. The comparative performance of for-profit and not-for-profit hospitals could well change in the future.[1]

Major organizational changes in health care in recent years include (1) the development of a significant for-profit component among almost all types of providers; (2) the emergence and rapid growth of investor-owned for-profit organizations, whose owners are mostly not involved in the operation of the organization (in contrast to traditional "proprietary" organizations); (3) the proliferation and growth of multi-institutional arrangements among both for-profit and not-for-profit health care organizations; (4) the emergence of several types of for-profit/not-for-profit hybrid organizations; (5) the increasing numbers of vertically integrated organizations[2] and the growth of organizations (including, but not limited to HMOs) that are involved in both the financing and provision of care; and (6) a new wave of physician entrepreneurship.[3]

Available data do not always distinguish investor-owned from other for-profit or proprietary organizations. However, investor ownership can now be found in all types of health care organizations—acute care hospitals, psychiatric hospitals, HMOs, nursing homes (which have long been predominantly for-profit), home health agencies, substance abuse facilities, and proliferating types of ambulatory care, diagnostic, and rehabilitation facilities. Although the goal of this study has been to gain an understanding of the implications of for-profit health care organizations in general, most comparative information about the behavior of for-profit and not-for-profit health care organizations pertains to hospitals, where the for-profit presence is relatively small, notwithstanding the dynamism and rapid growth of the investor-owned companies.

Investor ownership of general hospitals constitutes only 13 percent of hospitals and 9 percent of beds. However, because investor ownership is concentrated in certain states and regions (in the South, Southwest, and West), it constitutes one-third to one-half of the hospitals in a few states. Approximately 60 percent of the 540 general hospitals owned by the six largest investor-owned hospital companies in 1984 had been acquired from other for-profit owners. The others were divided almost equally between hospitals that had previously been public or not-for-profit facilities and hospitals that were constructed by the investor-owned companies. To date, the growth of investor ownership of hospitals has had little effect on the ownership mix of for-profit/not-for-profit/public hospitals. Yet, much consolidation of the investor-owned hospital sector has occurred (a pattern that has taken place to some degree among for-profit nursing homes as well), and the larger hospital companies are expanding rapidly into other sectors of the health care economy, as are the larger not-for-profit multihospital systems.

## THE FOR-PROFIT/NOT-FOR-PROFIT DISTINCTION

Although many differences between for-profit and not-for-profit institutions can be identified (see Table 1.1 in Chapter 1), most positive and negative expectations about the supposed tendencies of for-profit or not-for-profit health care organizations stem from some key legal differences.[4] Not-for-profit organizations are generally exempted from federal, state, and local taxes and are chartered for limited purposes—charitable, scientific, educational, benevolent, or religious. Their income and assets must be used for these purposes. The people who operate the organizations have no claim on such income and assets; they do, however, receive compensation for their services. Not-for-profit organizations are typically responsible to a voluntary, unpaid board of trustees.

For-profit organizations are owned by and accountable to investors, who ultimately receive the profits either in the form of divi-

dends or increased equity. The property rights that accompany equity ownership give the for-profit organization more incentive than the not-for-profit organization to act on relatively narrow economic grounds. A for-profit organization has options that have not been available to not-for-profit organizations to allocate profits either to its investors or to entirely different types of businesses.

It is true that in recent years many not-for-profit health care organizations have undergone corporate reorganizations and have created for-profit entities that operate under their control (or in joint ventures). Although these developments have blurred the distinction between for-profit and not-for-profit organizations to some extent and have given not-for-profits more flexibility than was historically the case, the after-tax surpluses from the for-profit activities of not-for-profit organizations are nevertheless ultimately returned to the not-for-profit organization.

Different types of ownership have access to different sources of capital. Some public institutions receive governmental appropriations; not-for-profit organizations have access to tax-exempt bond financing as well as to philanthropic contributions (which today constitute only a small fraction of capital financing); for-profit organizations have access to equity capital from investors.[5] Each of these sources of financial capital is tied to certain expectations. Governmental appropriations are for well-defined purposes, as are large philanthropic contributions in most cases. Various requirements designed to ensure continued creditworthiness and the continued value of pledged assets are attached to debt financing. Investor equity financing of health care companies has generally entailed the strong expectation of growth in earnings.

Investor-owned companies have powerful motives for expansion. The price of their stock—and, therefore, their continued access to equity capital, as well as the value of the assets of their stockholders—depends heavily on growth in earnings,[6] particularly for companies that represent themselves to investors as growth companies. In a field such as acute hospital care, in which the market is maturing, achieving increased earnings may require increasing the market share or moving into new markets. Growth can often be achieved more easily through acquisitions than through internal operations. Hence, some observers believe that the growth imperative of the investor-owned sector could change the overall for-profit/not-for-profit/public composition of health care even more in the future than it has in the past.

Implications of the formal differences in type of ownership can be overdrawn. As governmental and philanthropic grants have declined (totaling less than 8 percent of the funds for capital construction in 1981), debt and retained earnings have become the source of almost all capital needs for all ownership types of hospitals. Thus, not-for-profit organizations share with for-profit organizations the need to generate operating surpluses for building reserves that can be used as working capital and for future renovation, equipment purchases, and new services. Although investor-owned hospitals' "profit margins" on patient care services have surpassed the margins of not-for-profit hospitals, when all hospital revenues (including nonpatient care income such as gifts and investment income) are added, and the accrued taxes of investor-owned hospitals are subtracted therefrom, the margins of surplus of not-for-profit and for-profit hospitals are very similar on a national basis.[7] However, more not-for-profit than investor-owned hospitals operate at a loss.

The same features (organizational size, diversity, and ample revenue margins) that attract investors of equity are also attractive to the investors who lend money to not-for-profit and for-profit organizations. Changes in methods of payment for services and in sources of capital have made economic performance a more dominant factor in most health care organizations. Both for-profit and not-for-profit hospitals are increasingly organizing into multi-institutional arrangements, becoming more market oriented and more concerned with controlling expenses. Yet fundamental differences in ownership, accountability, and tax status remain.

## FINDINGS ABOUT FOR-PROFIT ENTERPRISE IN HEALTH CARE

The differences between for-profit and not-for-profit organizations in their values, tax status, and sources of capital have prompted both theory and assumptions about their behavior regarding hospital costs, pricing, quality, service to patients who are unable to pay, involvement in research and education, access to capital, and relationships with medical staffs. As summarized below, the committee's examination of the evidence shows that many of these assumptions are false and that others are only partly true.[8] Furthermore, findings about for-profit and not-for-profit hospitals may or may not typify performance in other types of health care organizations at this point, something that is largely unknown at this point.

### Health Care Costs

The committee studied the cost implications of for-profit health care by examining studies that compared for-profit and not-for-profit health care organizations. Almost all available data pertain to hospitals.

*The committee found that the rise in investor ownership of hospitals has increased health care costs to payers under both the original cost-based reimbursement approach used by Medicare and some other third-party payers and the charge-based reimbursement methods still used by a large number of third-party payers.*

#### Price

Both the amounts charged by investor-owned hospitals to charge-paying patients and the amounts they collect for the care of cost-paying patients (e.g., Medicare before DRGs and many Blue Cross plans) have been higher than comparable figures for not-for-profit hospitals. Studies show that collections per case from cost-based payers are from 8 to 15 percent higher in investor-owned chain hospitals than in not-for-profit hospitals, and that prices paid by charge-based payers are 17 to 24 percent higher. On a per-day basis, charges range up to 29 percent higher in investor-owned hospitals.

## Expenses

Studies of expenses incurred in the hospital care of cost-paying patients (Medicare) show that per-day expenses are 3 to 10 percent higher in investor-owned hospitals than in not-for-profit hospitals. (See Table 4.1 in Chapter 4.) On a per-admission basis, expense differences are smaller because of shorter average lengths of stay in investor-owned hospitals. Studies generally show higher per-case expenses in investor-owned hospitals, but the differences are not always statistically significant.

## Acquisitions and Costs

The acquisition activities of health care companies have resulted in increased costs to payers, because of the capital costs involved and because of aggressive pricing by the acquiring organizations. The extent to which acquisitions by investor-owned companies have prevented deterioration or closure of institutions that meet important local needs or have contributed to the nation's oversupply of hospital beds is unknown, as is the answer to a similar question about the new hospitals they and others have constructed. With national occupancy rates among all hospitals at 65 percent, the problem of excess capacity transcends the for-profit sector, but occupancy rates at for-profit hospitals are particularly low (approximately 10 percent lower than not-for-profit hospi-

tals). Among both for-profit and not-for-profit providers, it seems likely that more efforts will have to be exerted to find productive uses for unused space (e.g., extended care, ambulatory services).

## Nonhospital Settings

Data from nonhospital settings add complexity to the relationship between costs and type of ownership in health care. Nursing homes, for which approximately 50 percent of payments is prospectively determined, show expenses per patient day to be higher in not-for-profit than in for-profit homes and show little difference in pricing.

The growth in various types of ambulatory care, home care services, and diagnostic centers has brought about some impressive reductions in unit costs, when comparisons are made with in-hospital care and services to which full hospital overhead expenses are allocated. However, in the absence of studies comparing costs in for-profit and not-for-profit centers, these savings cannot be attributed to the for-profit mode. Furthermore, although the unit costs of services that are provided appropriately on an ambulatory basis are likely to be lower than the same services performed on an inpatient basis, the effect on total costs may not be the same. Because new facilities add to the total capital stock of health care organizations, because hospitals cannot always eliminate their fixed costs (which are then spread over fewer cases), and because total utilization rates have not been carefully studied, the existence and magnitude of total cost savings through ambulatory services are uncertain.

## Discussion

In sum, although standard economic theory predicts greater efficiency[9] in for-profit than in not-for-profit organizations, *the expected ability of investor-owned for-profit organizations to produce the same services at lower cost than their not-for-profit coun-*

*terparts has not been demonstrated.* Large organizations theoretically benefit from economies of scale and reduced transaction costs, but such savings may be offset by central-office costs, higher capital costs resulting from a growth orientation, and the payment of taxes and dividends.

Medicare's new prospective payment system and the growth of price competition change the incentives. Will investor-owned institutions then provide services more efficiently? If so, how, and with what impact on patients? These questions cannot now be answered. However, in nursing homes where payment by Medicaid has typically been by fixed, prospectively determined rates, for-profit homes have lower average expenses on such budget categories as food, housekeeping, and other patient care services, and higher expenses for capital costs and rent than do not-for-profit homes. Although direct analogy to hospitals ignores many important differences in the two types of institutions (including the shortage of nursing home beds, which restricts choice and, hence, minimizes punishment by market factors), the nursing home experience is a reminder that the responses of for-profit and not-for-profit hospitals to prospective payment should be closely monitored. The efficiencies that some expect of investor ownership may yet emerge, but it is also possible that a tightening on the revenue side will lead to undesirable cuts in services to patients, particularly in institutions that have a heavy burden of uncompensated care or that are under pressure to increase earnings and also must pay taxes.

### Access to Care

The major concerns about for-profits and access to care are the extent to which they serve patients who are unable to pay, the extent to which they offer services that are needed in the community but that are not profitable, and their impact on institutions that provide substantial amounts of uncom-

pensated care[10] and unprofitable services such as medical education and community services.

These concerns should be considered in light of the possibility that the investor-owned health care companies' construction and acquisition activities have made services more convenient and readily available to the people that they serve. Also, they have tended to locate in areas of relatively rapid population growth and in areas that do not have high bed-to-population ratios (Watt et al., 1986), and at least some of the hospitals they have acquired were not in sound financial condition (Pattison, 1986; Brown and Klosterman, 1986). Such facts suggest that they have enhanced access. On the other hand, their occupancy rates of around 50 percent indicate the presence of unneeded beds, and only 9 of the 365 hospitals on the Health Care Financing Administration's list of "sole community hospitals" are for-profit, which suggests that relatively few patients served by for-profit hospitals are without some alternative sources of hospital care.[11]

The provision of uncompensated care by health care providers is vital in a nation where 35 million people are uninsured and not eligible for public programs and millions more are underinsured and unprepared for the expenses of a major illness. Nationally, uncompensated care (charity care plus bad debt) provided by hospitals amounts to less than 5 percent of their revenues, a figure that at best meets only some of the needs of the people who are unable to pay for care. All studies show that public facilities provide a disproportionately large amount of uncompensated care. This may be bearable if they receive sufficient governmental subsidies, but the financial position of many of these institutions on which so many people depend is weakening.

*The committee found that most sources of evidence show that for-profit hospitals proportionately provide less uncompensated care than do not-for-profit hospitals, although there are substantial variations in the mag-*

*nitude of this difference. In several states where for-profit hospitals are numerous, the uncompensated care difference between for-profit and not-for-profit hospitals is substantially larger than is shown in national data.*

National data are available from American Hospital Association (AHA) surveys and from a compulsory survey of all hospitals that was conducted in 1981 by the Office for Civil Rights (OCR) in the Department of Health and Human Services. The OCR data show that a lower percentage of patients in for-profit than in not-for-profit hospitals were uninsured (6.0 percent versus 7.9 percent). (No such difference was found on service to uninsured emergency room patients.) Uninsured patients are a reasonable, if imperfect, proxy for "patients who are unable to pay," and the OCR data provide the only national figures available on the numbers of such patients served by hospitals of different types of ownership.

The AHA annual survey of hospitals provides data on the most widely used measure of uncompensated care—the percentage of revenues that are accounted for by the sum of bad debt and charity care. The 1983 AHA data show the same pattern as the OCR data, with not-for-profit hospitals reporting more uncompensated care than for-profit hospitals (4.2 percent versus 3.1 percent). This difference was smaller in 1982 (Table 5.5), when the level of uncompensated care among all types of hospitals was somewhat smaller.

Although differences of the magnitude shown in the OCR data and the 1983 AHA data are hardly negligible, they could be accounted for by factors (such as differences in size, rural-urban location, or region) that are not controlled in available analyses of the data; that is, the differences could result from factors other than a greater willingness of for-profits to turn uninsured patients away untreated, a matter about which systematic comparative data are not available.[12] However, it should also be noted that bad debts go directly to the bottom line of a not-for-

profit organization, whereas in a for-profit organization that has made a profit, the impact of bad debt is cushioned by the fact that it reduces income taxes.

The committee examined data from five states in which there are substantial numbers of for-profit hospitals (Table 5.6). In California, there was little difference between for-profit and not-for-profit hospitals in the amount of uncompensated care provided, but in Florida, Texas, Tennessee, and Virginia, not-for-profit hospitals provided substantially more uncompensated care (in some instances twice as much) than did for-profit hospitals. The differences are important, because in these states there are both large numbers of uninsured patients and large numbers of investor-owned hospitals (30-40 percent of hospitals). The committee's majority believes that the comparatively low levels of uncompensated care in for-profit hospitals in such states is strong evidence that the presence of these hospitals contributes to the problem of access to care for people who lack the means to pay.[13]

An institution's unwillingness to serve patients who may not pay can affect not only the patients but also other institutions that do not adopt the same policies. Efforts are being made at many types of institutions to reduce the amount of uncompensated care. Nevertheless, the provision of disproportionately small amounts of uncompensated care by some hospitals can threaten the financial well-being of nearby hospitals that serve larger numbers of people who are unable to pay. It seems likely that this is happening in states where there are many for-profit hospitals that provide comparatively small amounts of uncompensated care, but no systematic studies are available on whether certain institutions are diminishing the ability of other institutions to support indigent care or how often this might be attributable to for-profit rather than not-for-profit hospitals.[14] Some data show the for-profit/not-for-profit discrepancy in uncompensated care to be smaller outside of metropolitan areas, which may suggest that for-profit hospitals are more willing to provide uncompensated care when patients have fewer alternative sources of care.

Concerns about access also have been raised regarding the various types of ambulatory care centers that offer services that have traditionally been provided by hospitals. Although these centers, many of which are physician owned, often attempt to facilitate access in some sense of the term (i.e., though convenient locations and hours), many follow policies—such as requiring payment at the time service is rendered and accepting patients only on referral—that allow the organization to provide services almost exclusively to paying patients. To the extent that these paying patients are attracted away from hospitals that subsidize uncompensated care with revenues from paying patients, the ability of such hospitals to provide uncompensated care is diminished.

Further complicating the question of for-profits and access to care is the nursing home example, where Medicaid patients, who are generally less lucrative than private-pay patients and who are therefore often discriminated against in admissions, are served in proportionately larger numbers by for-profit homes than by not-for-profit homes. The committee was unable to obtain data that might document whether there are ownership differences in the care of other patients who have difficulty securing access to nursing homes—most notably "heavy care" patients who are sometimes discriminated against when reimbursement is fixed, and patients who have exhausted their funds but are not eligible for Medicaid.

Finally, the committee found that the question of whether for-profit hospitals are less likely to offer unprofitable services could not be answered empirically. AHA survey data do show that many services are not offered in as many for-profit hospitals as in not-for-profit hospitals of similar size. However, no systematic data are available on which services are profitable (on their own or because of other services whose use they stimulate) and which are not.

## Quality of Care

*The limited indicators of hospital quality that are now available—primarily hospital accreditation, board certification of staff physicians, and amount of nursing personnel—show no overall pattern of either inferior or superior quality in investor-owned chain hospitals when compared with not-for-profit hospitals.* On most quality-related measures, differences between investor-owned and not-for-profit institutions are small, and the direction of the differences varies.

On the most general measure available—accreditation by the Joint Commission on Accreditation of Hospitals—investor-owned hospitals (of which more than 90 percent are accredited) fare slightly better than not-for-profit hospitals. Regarding their medical staffs, investor-owned hospitals accept a slightly higher proportion of physician-applicants and have a slightly higher proportion of physicians who are not board certified, although in neither case were differences among different types of multihospital systems statistically significant.[15] AHA data on nursing personnel per 100 patients show virtually no difference between investor-owned and not-for-profit hospitals. Hospital board chairmen in investor-owned chains report more concern with some issues that are related to quality than do chairmen of not-for-profit hospital boards, but the relationship of such survey data to reality can be questioned. An American Medical Association survey conducted at the committee's request showed physician evaluations—including physicians with privileges at investor-owned hospitals—to be slightly less favorable toward for-profit than not-for-profit hospitals, and almost one-fourth of the physicians with privileges in for-profit hospitals said they believed the quality of care was better in the not-for-profit sector (Musacchio et al., 1986). The only available data on outcomes and investor ownership of hospitals was from a study conducted for the committee, which examined mortality rates among Medicare patients who had undergone elective surgery between 1974 and 1981 (Gaumer, 1986). No consistent patterns associated with type of hospital ownership were found.

Although the committee does not regard the data just reviewed as sufficient for a definitive determination of whether there are differences in quality of care, it concludes that there is no strong pattern of evidence to suggest that the quality of care in investor-owned hospitals is markedly better or worse than in not-for-profit hospitals.

The growth of the investor-owned hospital chains may have resulted in improved overall quality of hospital care, because the individual hospitals most commonly acquired were independent proprietary hospitals where accreditation rates tend to be notably low. Two small studies in California and Florida also suggest that hospitals acquired by investor-owned chains were financially weak and may have been poorly managed, conditions that could well have quality implications. More than 10 percent of the hospitals acquired by the four major hospital chains were subsequently replaced with new facilities, and an unknown number of additional hospitals were substantially renovated.

Nevertheless, the committee believes that the question of quality care will and should assume greater importance. Cost-based and charge-based reimbursement methods have provided hospitals with little incentive to take economizing steps that could lead to reductions in quality. With fundamental changes now taking place in methods of payment, standards of quality may change in all types of hospitals. Problems could develop in the form of too early discharge of patients, excessive reductions in maintenance schedules and replacement cycles of equipment, excessive reductions in staffing, or undue decreases in service intensity.

The committee recognizes that comparisons between nursing homes and hospitals have many limitations, but its concerns about quality were reinforced by the history of quality problems among nursing homes, which largely are paid prospectively set rates and which have long been mostly for-profit. A further concern about quality arises with the growth of freestanding ambulatory care centers, where quality assurance procedures are less well established than in hospitals.

*The committee concludes that the organizational, economic, and competitive changes taking place in health care make imperative the increased monitoring (by regulators and purchasers of care) of health care outcomes in all settings, including hospitals and freestanding centers and for-profit and not-for-profit institutions. Additional research is needed to develop and validate more sensitive measures of patient outcome and other indices of quality to illuminate the relationship between such measures and type of ownership.* (Chapter 6.)

## Education and Research

The past lack of involvement of investor-owned health care companies in health professional education and unsponsored research is documented in Chapter 8. The companies have been accused not only of unfairly benefiting from other institutions' commitment to education and research, but also of attracting away well-insured patients to an extent that makes it more difficult for teaching hospitals to generate patient revenues to subsidize education and research. Defenders of investor-owned facilities have pointed out that the hospitals these companies acquired were relatively small and had no history as teaching hospitals; further they have criticized cross-subsidization as a method of financing education and research.

During the course of this study, circumstances were changed by several visible examples of investor-owned companies becoming involved in medical education and research. These examples are too varied and experience is too limited to sustain firm conclusions. The committee does not foresee the acquisition of large numbers of teaching hospitals by investor-owned companies. Nevertheless, *the increased involvement of investor-owned companies in teaching hospitals suggests more willingness on their part to contribute to health professional education and biomedical research. It also raises many questions—about faculty control, institutional priorities, and different values— that deserve scrutiny as experience accumulates.*

## CONCLUSIONS ABOUT INVESTOR OWNERSHIP OF HEALTH CARE FACILITIES

*The committee concludes that available evidence on differences between for-profit and not-for-profit health care organizations is not sufficient to justify a recommendation that investor ownership of health care organizations be either opposed or supported by public policy. Substantive goals regarding cost, quality, access, education, and research are more appropriate than a goal of creating fair competition between for-profit and not-for-profit health care organizations.*

How the advantages and disadvantages of the for-profit mode are perceived depends to some degree on one's values and views about the past and future of the health care system.[16] However, the for-profit mode cannot now be seen as a possible solution to such important public policy issues as control of health care costs, ensuring access to care, or maintaining quality of care.

Studies comparing for-profit and not-for-profit hospitals show clear disadvantages of investor ownership regarding cost to payers and smaller disadvantages regarding expenses and service to patients who are un-

able to pay. Some count the past lack of involvement in medical education and research as a disadvantage of the investor-owned sector, although their becoming involved has also raised concern. No clear differences in quality have been demonstrated. The cost and quality of care, access to care, and the support of health professional education and academic health centers are all major public policy issues that must be addressed on their own terms, rather than primarily as an issue of for-profit health care. The need for increased monitoring of the performance of health care institutions and the urgent need for public policy actions to address the problem of uninsured patients are discussed in more detail later in this chapter.

The presence of a for-profit sector has some advantages that are not revealed in studies comparing its performance with that of not-for-profit institutions. First, the for-profit sector's access to equity capital (and the resulting enhanced access to debt capital) can help meet the health care sector's capital requirements and reduce the need for government to raise capital through taxes, which the federal government is unlikely to do in the forseeable future. However, over time, investor equity is an expensive source of capital, as discussed in Chapter 3. Furthermore, although investor equity is a capital source that is not available to the not-for-profit sector, viable alternative sources of capital now exist for much of the not-for-profit sector in health care.

Second, although there is little direct evidence, it is likely that the acquisition and construction activities of investor-owned companies have preserved or enhanced the availability of services for people who use the institutions. These acquisitions may also have improved the quality of care in acquired institutions.

A third, less-tangible impact of the for-profit sector pertains to competition, innovation, and change in the health care system. The influence of the for-profit sector can be exaggerated and probably cannot be quantified. However, the committee believes that the emergence of for-profit health care companies, along with other factors such as new payment methods, has in some instances provided alternative approaches and has stimulated new forms of service delivery, greater attention to the desires of patients as consumers of services, multi-institutional arrangements and the search for economies of scale, innovations for raising capital, and the development of more comprehensive health care organizations. Although some of these developments are not unique to for-profit organizations, the for-profit sector nevertheless has increased the pluralism of an already pluralistic, decentralized health care system. Great diffuseness of responsibility for the health care of populations is characteristic of such a system, but this country's political system has never found attractive the idea of a publicly dominated, centralized, hierarchical health care system, even though the need for a more cohesive and comprehensive set of public policies is continually debated.

## ISSUES, CONCLUSIONS, AND RECOMMENDATIONS

The presence of for-profit organizations in an increasingly competitive health care system is linked to a number of issues, including (1) the increasing importance of attention to economic incentives, (2) the social responsibilities of health care organizations, (3) the function and viability of not-for-profit organizations, (4) the growing problem of patients who are unable to pay, (5) questions of capital policy, (6) the future of the physician's fiduciary role, and (7) the need for careful monitoring of future developments.

### The Increasing Importance of Economic Incentives

Although systematic data are lacking, some observers believe that investor-owned health care organizations tend to follow economic incentives more quickly and closely than do not-for-profit organizations. Others believe that all types of health care providers are becoming more attuned to economic incentives. Whatever the case, in the committee's view it is becoming increasingly important to understand the operation of economic incentives in health care and to put in place incentives for providers to fulfill appropriate goals for quality and access, as well as cost. This is not to suggest that for-profit hospitals completely follow economic incentives. Even if they sought to do so, there are practical limits and considerations of public relations and social conscience. In addition, because of recent changes in reimbursement methods, all hospitals must be more mindful of economic incentives.

Those who argue that health care institutions should be highly responsive to economic incentives must consider whether it is possible to perfect the incentives sufficiently to avoid unfortunate results, such as providing unnecessary but lucrative services or not offering unprofitable services that are needed in the community. Those who argue that health care institutions should be selectively indifferent to economic incentives must consider how to encourage cost-effectiveness and the right selectivity (e.g., to concentrate surpluses on indigent care rather than on duplicating expensive technologies to "keep up with" neighboring hospitals). They must also face the question of whether the tradition of using revenues earned from patient care to subsidize indigent care and educational activities has virtue other than being the only practical way that institutions can engage in such activities in the absence of more explicit funding. Even if cross-subsidization is a virtue, it is in conflict with increasing efforts by governmental and other payers to reduce their expenditures for the care that they purchase. If it is at best a poor substitute for explicit financing, then the pursuit of such financing should be the goal. Increasingly, institutions are faced with the need to choose between economic realities and traditional concepts of mission and service.

Circumstances have developed whereby economic incentives make it difficult or impossible for institutions to subsidize uncompensated care from other patient care revenues, but in which the government has not made provision to deal with the problem. Without explicit public policy attention, an increasing number of people in need of care will suffer.

## The Social Responsibilities of Health Care Organizations

The social acceptability of a more competitive and pluralistic health care system that includes both for-profit and not-for-profit organizations depends on the degree of social responsibility with which institutions operate. The committee believes that all health care institutions have a basic moral obligation to respond to human need. This is consistent with the traditional values and purpose of not-for-profit and public hospitals. Even if they have not always responded adequately, the rules that pertain to the tax-exempt status of not-for-profit institutions and the accountability of public institutions provide, at the least, mechanisms for influencing their social responsibility. In the absence of such mechanisms, concerns have been raised about how for-profit health care organizations define their social responsibilities and to whom they are accountable in this regard.

The committee believes that if for-profit organizations are an impediment to the practical efforts of other institutions or of local or state governments to deal with unsolved problems in the provision of health services, as has been alleged by some, they will increasingly be seen by the public as part of the problem. As is discussed later in this chapter, the committee recognizes that the solution to the problem of uninsured and underinsured patients is essentially societal,

not institutional. The reasons for this—the failure of charity to keep pace with extraordinary increases in health care costs and the growing unwillingness of third-party payers to pay rates that permit institutions to subsidize indigent care—have little to do with the growth of for-profit health care. Nevertheless, any institution (of whatever ownership) that responds to the problem of the uninsured patient by refusing to provide care to people who are financial risks or by resisting arrangements to spread the burden of uncompensated care must expect to be seen as problematic. The for-profit sector would be well advised to resist the temptation to let tax obligations exclusively define social or moral obligations,[17] particularly in view of the fact that tax-supported programs now fail to assure the availability of funds to meet the needs of uninsured and underinsured patients. Although institutions must be mindful of their own economic realities, the committee concludes that no sector should absolve itself of the responsibility to help meet the needs of people who are unable to pay for health care.

This raises the question of what, if anything, should be expected from tax-exempt institutions that is not expected of a tax-paying institution. Because all health care institutions derive most of their income from charges for services, what should institutions do in exchange for the benefits of tax exemptions and eligibility to receive charitable contributions? Although there are many circumstances under which health care institutions should be expected to perform services for which they will not be paid, no standards exist to judge which institutions have done "enough" economically unrewarding activity (Brock and Buchanan, 1986). The committee believes that, just as the for-profit sector pays taxes, a reasonable relationship should be expected from not-for-profit institutions between (1) the amounts of charitable contributions that an institution receives plus the amount of taxes that it does not have to pay by virtue of its tax-exempt status (an amount that would vary according to the amount of the institution's surplus) and (2) the amount of uncompensated service that it provides in the form of charity care, unprofitable standby capacity, unsponsored research, and institutionally subsidized educational activities.

## The Future of Not-for-profit Institutions

The more that not-for-profit organizations are unable or unwilling to engage in activities that do not contribute directly or indirectly to their economic bottom line, and the more that for-profit organizations see their social obligations as limited to paying their taxes, the more the benefits of diversity could turn into liabilities from the standpoint of meeting some very important, but inadequately funded health care needs. This would be particularly true if no institution in a locale is both willing and able to assume the role of provider of last resort.

Not-for-profit and public institutions have long been essential in caring for the uninsured poor, in education and research, and in offering a wide variety of health care services, not all of which are profitable. They have embodied important values of giving, volunteering, self-help, and community involvement. Since their economic well-being has never been fully dependent on the generation of profits from operations, they have provided a degree of stability in the provision of needed services, rather than entering and leaving markets depending on profit opportunities. The not-for-profit bottom line is measured not only in the inevitable economic terms but also in terms of service to patients and communities. Performance in this regard is monitored, although sometimes more in theory than in fact, by governmental agencies, funding sources, and voluntary boards, whereas stockholders monitor the for-profit sector's bottom line of profitability. So long as the not-for-profit and public sectors act in accord with their

traditional values of charity, community involvement, and finding ways of meeting needs regardless of incentives, preservation of their vitality should be a major public policy concern.[18]

*Public concern is warranted about the continued vitality and even the survival of important not-for-profit and public health care institutions—particularly those that are sole community providers, those that provide large amounts of uncompensated care, and those that are valuable centers of education, research, and tertiary care.* Two issues are key to the future for-profit/not-for-profit composition of health care institutions: financing indigent care and meeting capital needs.

## The Indigent Care Problem

Unlike other developed nations that have some type of universal health insurance, the United States has never provided for the availability of care to all in need. Numerous commissions and researchers have pointed out this gap in public policy. The committee believes that the private sector's ability to deal with the consequences of this failure in public policy is limited and diminishing. It is essential that public debate focus on the financing of certain activities that are of public benefit, but that institutions on their own will find increasingly difficult to support. More than 35 million people have no private or public third-party payment coverage, millions more are seriously underinsured, and insurance coverage for long-term care needs is very limited. Except in the few states that have made some provision for the problem of the uninsured patient, public policy in the United States has never adequately dealt with the entire problem of assuring the availability of care to all who are unable to pay. In most states, the care of such patients depends on hospitals' and physicians' knowingly providing services that will not be paid for.

The fragility of the current arrangements

for indigent care must be appreciated. Approximately one-third of such care is provided by local or state government-owned hospitals, which typically receive direct public subsidies and are often chronically underfunded. However, about two-thirds of such care is provided by private (i.e., not tax-supported) hospitals. Not-for-profit hospitals, which own most of the beds and provide most of the indigent care, on average obtain about 5 percent of their revenues from sources other than patient care. (For-profit hospitals obtain less than 2 percent of their revenues from other sources.) The ability of institutions to subsidize indigent care from other patient care revenues is now seriously threatened. As governmental and other third-party payers change payment methods and amounts to minimize their health care costs, surplus patient care revenues will decline and disappear. More and more reports will be heard of indigent patients who are unable to obtain care and of institutions that are financially threatened because of their commitment to the care of uninsured patients, until there is governmental action.

*The committee concludes that public policy cannot rely indefinitely on the ability and willingness of health care institutions to generate the funds needed to provide care for those who are unable to pay. Ensuring adequate health care is a societal obligation, and government should make provision for its financing when private coverage is lacking.*

Various options merit consideration. A list of possible approaches to this problem appears at the end of Chapter 5 (note 21), but several possibilities can be noted here.

*Provisions should be made at the local, state, and federal levels to ensure that government-owned hospitals acquired either by investor-owned or not-for-profit chains continue their historical community service mission, particularly if the acquired hospital is the only source of uncompensated care or if a change in mission would jeopardize another hospital that provides a dispropor-*

*tionate share of uncompensated care.[19]* A similar recommendation might be made for not-for-profit hospitals that have had an important historical mission of providing indigent care and community service. Trustees of not-for-profit institutions should seek safeguards for that mission if sale or lease of a facility is contemplated.

In addition, *government should take steps to spread or ease the burden on institutions that provide a disproportionate amount of uncompensated care and to correct payment inequities resulting from hospitals' locations or the severity of the cases that they treat.* Such steps might include an expanded Medicaid program, adjustments to Medicare payments to take into account indigent care, or the creation of pools for indigent care at the state level. Institutions that have maintained a commitment to the poor have urged the Department of Health and Human Services to make adjustments in Medicare's DRG payment formulas to help institutions that carry an unusually large burden of uncompensated care. Legislative proposals to make such adjustments are mired in a debate about the appropriateness of using Medicare funds to subsidize the care of non-Medicare patients. Although this is a serious concern, it is less urgent than the growing problem of care for indigent patients and of the economic well-being of institutions that attempt to serve them.

Most of these approaches have little or nothing to do with the distinction between for-profit and not-for-profit health care institutions. However, there is one issue on which for-profit institutions' tax-paying status is directly relevant.

The not-for-profits pay no taxes on their surplus margins; investor-owned hospital companies have an effective tax rate of approximately 42 per cent, although in recent years they have been able to defer a substantial amount (almost half in 1983) of this tax obligation under provisions of current tax laws (Chapter 3).

Most of the taxes paid by investor-owned

health care companies—like all other tax-payers—are eventually spent for purposes other than health care.[20] However, unlike most other individual and corporate taxpayers, investor-owned hospital companies receive half of their revenues from tax-supported government programs. Thus, the corporate taxes paid by the investor-owned companies represent a complex and very indirect transfer of revenues from the Medicare and Medicaid programs to the Defense Department, interest on the national debt, and other governmental activities. *Ways should be explored whereby the taxes paid by investor-owned health care companies (whose revenues are so substantially derived from tax revenues) could be devoted to unmet health care needs—particularly the medical needs of indigent patients*, although there should be no illusions that the amount is adequate to meet such needs.

Other tax-related approaches also merit consideration. One option would be new dedicated taxes at the state or federal level to be used for paying health insurance premiums for people who are currently uninsured and not covered by public programs. A second approach is state programs, such as in Florida, that create a pool of money to pay for uncompensated care by taxing all hospitals a percentage of their net patient revenues. A third approach would be to give health care companies the option of providing service to indigent patients at marginal cost as a direct credit against taxes.

Conversely, as was suggested earlier, more consideration should be given to ensuring that hospitals, HMOs, home health agencies, and other not-for-profit institutions that receive charitable contributions and that benefit from a tax exemption provide public goods in the form of uncompensated care, unprofitable standby capacity, unsponsored research, or institutionally subsidized educational activities.

In the meanwhile, *it is essential that there be monitoring of and publicity about (1) the extent to which institutions that provide un-compensated care find themselves in financial distress and (2) the extent to which people are unable to get needed medical care.* Although the need for public policy action is already very apparent, it is important that there be ongoing public information about the dimensions of these problems.

### Financial Capital

Policy decisions regarding health care capital may affect the for-profit/not-for-profit balance of hospitals, because the need for financial capital is usually the force that pushes trustees of not-for-profit institutions to consider closure, sale to an investor-owned company, or joining a not-for-profit chain or alliance. (Discouragement or lack of commitment of hospital boards in the face of increasingly difficult economic circumstances also is clearly a factor in some instances. Declining occupancy rates and reduced revenues are leading some boards to question the value of keeping open all institutions in an area.) As the analysis in Chapter 3 shows, in the absence of governmental grant programs for financial capital, capital growth for all health care institutions depends on their financial condition and the prospect of future earnings. Institutions must generate sufficient earnings to cover not only current expenses but also to provide for future financial capital requirements.

The advantage that for-profit organizations have in this regard is clear: greater focus on economic goals and access to a unique and flexible source of capital, investor equity. But the not-for-profit sector also has certain advantages. Although only a small number of institutions obtain significant philanthropic support for their capital requirements, not-for-profit institutions' access to capital has been facilitated by the growth of multi-institutional arrangements, debt insurance mechanisms, and, most importantly, the availability of tax-exempt debt instruments.

In its examination of capital issues in health

care, the committee reached three general conclusions:

1. *The committee concludes that Medicare payments to health institutions must continue to include funds for capital.* This is important not only to the continuing vitality and standards of quality in health care but it could also affect the for-profit/not-for-profit composition of health institutions. Medicare is the largest single purchaser of care in a hospital industry that is highly dependent on reasonable retained earnings. Failure to incorporate a reasonable factor for capital costs would harm all hospitals, but particularly those whose location or mission results in their bearing unusually high costs for indigent care or for health professionals' education. In the absence of adequate funding, such institutions may find themselves unable to compete for paying patients, doctors, and capital and may be forced to abandon important aspects of their service, teaching, or research missions.

2. *The committee concludes that it is reasonable for capital costs to be built into the prospectively set prices of the Medicare program.* If this is done, there is no reason for differential treatment of institutions (for example, regarding return-on-equity payments) according to their for-profit/not-for-profit status. However, it is essential that provisions be made for institutions that are in exceptional situations—for example, tertiary care facilities with high costs for technology and specialized personnel and public facilities that are overaged and underequipped.

3. *The committee concludes that it is imperative that policymakers recognize the importance of tax-exempt bonds as the key source of capital for the not-for-profit health care sector.* It would be unwise to do away with such an important mechanism without much more study of the possible impact on the vitality of the not-for-profit sector and on health care costs. However, it would also be appropriate to review the requirements of eligibility for tax-exempt debt to make sure that institutions that obtain approval for tax-exempt bonds appropriately serve a public purpose regarding uncompensated care, unprofitable services, and education and research.

## The Future of the Physician's Fiduciary Role

### Physicians and Entrepreneurism

The committee examined entrepreneurial activity by physicians from the traditional ethical premise that the physician's first responsibility is to the patient. This primary role is becoming ever more complicated as a result of technological change, mounting economic pressures, and the widening range of organizations in which patient care takes place. Maintaining and transmitting the values on which the fiduciary aspects of the physician's role are based is a future task for professional organizations, medical education, and public policy.

Certain physician involvements in entrepreneurial activities can compromise the physician's fiduciary responsibilities to patients and the medical professions' moral authority. These involvements include (1) physicians who make substantial capital investment in office technology and equipment, which they then may overutilize to recoup their investment, (2) physicians who own interests in organizations to which they make referrals, or receive other economic benefits for making referrals, (c) bonus incentive arrangements for sharing an institution's earnings with physicians whose patient care decisions have influenced those earnings.

The committee reached conclusions on three such types of involvement.

1. *The committee concludes that purchasers of health care should favor physician compensation systems that break or attenuate the link between physicians' pa-*

tient care decisions and the money they make on investments in equipment or personnel in their own medical practices.

2. *The committee concludes that law and professional ethics should regard as unethical and unacceptable physicians having economic interests in health care facilities to which they make referrals or receiving payments for making referrals.* In the absence of prohibitions on such arrangements, it is essential that disclosure standards be developed so that patients, referring physicians, and third-party payers are aware of the conflict of interest.

3. *The committee concludes that bonus incentive plans, under which institutions offer physicians a share in surplus revenues generated by an organization in which they practice, are usually inconsistent with the physician's obligation of primary fidelity to the patient's interests.* Such plans present less difficulty when patients are a party to an agreement (as in a subscriber-owned HMO) or when they have been informed of an agreement in advance of their need for services (as when signing up with an HMO). The effects on patient care of the many varieties of physician-incentive arrangements designed to control costs are not well understood. Where they are implemented, their use should be closely studied and monitored.

### Physician Influence in Medical Institutions

In Chapter 9, the committee examined changes taking place in the control of health care organizations, particularly regarding physician influence. In the governance and management of medical institutions, power and influence conventionally are shared among physicians and other patient care personnel, administration or management, and governing boards. Although some goals are shared, the successful operation of an institution frequently requires some balancing of conflicting interests. Some past prob-

lems in the operation of institutions have been attributed to physicians' excessive power and influence. Now, however, the growth of centrally managed multi-institutional systems is removing certain types of decision making from the local level, and in independent institutions, boards and management are being forced to take a much stronger role in the face of more difficult competitive and economic conditions. An excessive emphasis on financial and managerial concerns could negatively affect patient care. The committee's concern is that there be a reasonable balance of power in institutions, not that physicians (or administrators/managers) should be in a position of complete control.

The committee examined two primary methods by which physicians can exercise influence: through their power to choose which institution to use with their patients (using the option of exiting the institution, if dissatisfied with it) or by having a significant voice in the decision-making bodies within the institution. Both of these options can be used on behalf of patients, although they have often been used for other purposes.

Regarding exit and voice mechanisms, staff physicians in investor-owned hospitals are now particularly likely to have multiple hospital privileges (thereby facilitating changes in admitting patterns), and these hospitals have particularly high levels of physician representation on their governing boards, although these boards typically have less authority than do the boards of independent institutions.

Future developments are difficult to foresee and the need for monitoring change is apparent, but the committee believes that physicians will increasingly be tied to particular institutions. If so, the option of taking their patients elsewhere will decline as a source of influence and the importance of physicians having a voice will increase. But a greater voice seems incompatible with the trends toward multi-institutional arrangements and ever-larger-scale organizations. Physician voice may take new forms, such as through physician corporations working jointly with hospitals, physician advisory councils to corporate system management, board membership by physicians, physician involvement in management, and key full-time clinical appointments. It is important that physicians and other patient care staff continue to play an effective role in ensuring that patient care concerns are not subordinated to economic concerns.

*The committee urges professional associations in the health occupations to develop their own criteria for defining appropriate modes of ensuring effective participation of practitioners in monitoring and sustaining the quality of care in both traditional and new forms of health care delivery and of discouraging excessive restriction of their voice in such issues.*

### The Need for Monitoring

Most questions about the comparative behavior of for-profit and not-for-profit institutions can now be answered only provisionally, because the behavior of institutions is affected by economic, competitive, and regulatory factors in their environment. In an era when these factors are changing rapidly, the behavior of different types of institutions also is likely to change.

Medicare's change from cost-based reimbursement to its prospective payment system (PPS) fundamentally changed incentives in ways that are affecting virtually all aspects of the American health care system. During the course of this study, most hospitals in this country began the transition to a system that put them at much greater financial risk, although operating margins have initially improved (American Hospital Association, 1985). However, no data were available to the committee about ownership differences in the way hospitals are responding to the

problems and opportunities presented by the new payment system, which will ultimately affect more than 40 percent of their revenues. Furthermore, little information is as yet available with which to assess the move among hospital companies and not-for-profit hospital chains to become involved in the financing of care by starting, acquiring, or joint venturing with an insurance company, in addition to providing health services. This and other trends toward vertical integration present some new incentives and challenge our ability to understand and measure implications for cost, quality, and access to services.

In several chapters of this report, attention has been called to the need for monitoring key aspects of the performance of health care organizations: indices of quality of care, cost of care, service to patients who are unable to pay, the auspices and values of health professional education, and the fiduciary role of the physician.

At the local level, a recast health planning program that is able to provide information to consumers, buyers, and policymakers could be valuable in monitoring performance by health care providers and in publishing reports that identify gaps, redundancies, and other problems. These activities should be concerned as much with quality as with cost and access. Professional review organizations (PROs) could provide much valuable public information. The Joint Commission on Accreditation of Hospitals also could be involved. There may also be a role for a new type of organization or agency to monitor and report on the performance of health care institutions.

At the national level, it would be useful for the National Center for Health Statistics to include in its annual report to the Congress, *Health, United States*, comparative information on the performance of all types of health care institutions on such measures as amount of uncompensated care, costs per adjusted admission, occupancy rates, bed turnover rates, profit margins, and quality indicators. Both theory and the evidence reviewed in this report suggest the importance of analyzing information about the performance of health care organizations in a way that illuminates the effects of type of ownership (for-profit, not-for-profit, public), membership in a multi-institutional system, and involvement in both the financing and provision of services.

As a result of acquisitions, mergers, and networking arrangements, health care organizations of considerable size and diversity have come into being. This is true not only among the investor-owned hospital companies but also among for-profit and not-for-profit HMOs and the affiliation organizations of not-for-profit hospitals. Several organizations now operate hundreds of facilities and generate billions of dollars in revenues. The element of scale or size has not yet been examined carefully, but it could prove to be as important as the distinction between for-profit and not-for-profit organizations or between independent institutions and those that are part of multi-institutional systems. Indeed, some observers believe that relatively few large organizations—with origins variously in today's investor-owned corporations, the organizations of affiliated not-for-profit hospitals, in HMOs, in insurance companies, and perhaps in major teaching hospitals or clinics— will come to dominate the American health care system in the same way that a few large national organizations dominate many areas of the U.S. economy.

However, although some organizations have clearly adopted aggressive growth strategies, the horizons of growth do not appear limitless. Future growth and consolidation are likely to be curbed by foreseeable limitations in Medicare payments for capital costs; by fear and likelihood that increasingly large organizations will attract more regulation; by a dearth in the number of territories where institutions are ripe for acquisition and where there are large numbers of well-insured, middle class people;

and by constraints on economies of scale in what remain essentially local marketplaces.

Studies that compare the behavior of institutions that are under different types of ownership and control provide hints of what a health care system dominated by ever larger and more comprehensive organizations would be like. However, some important questions about the increasing scale of health care organizations are probably not answerable by aggregating data from health care institutions. For example, how and in what ways will health care organizations of increasing size and diversity influence health care policy and public financing both nationally and at the state or local levels? Will they become an effective voice on behalf of those who need medical care? Will stories of corruption within the health care industry become more commonplace as larger and larger economic interests are involved? Will large organizations use their economic power and diversity to cut prices at selected institutions long enough to drive out local competition? What would happen if such companies, even if economically healthy, were to be sold to conglomerates or to foreign corporations for which American health care is, perhaps, only a minor line of business?

Other questions concern the impact of large-scale organizations on the policy environment. Might the growth of massive health enterprises increase the vulnerability of the political process to the sophisticated use of financial and lobbying pressures? Might the growing presence of multibillion dollar health care providers lead government to view health care as just another marketplace service of perhaps no particular public policy importance? If a direct relationship becomes evident between the amount of increase in federal health care expenditures and the amount of profit in the nation's health care companies, will there be movement toward a public utility model in which the amount of profit is negotiated between government and the providers of service?

## CONCLUSION

A health care system that is excessively responsive to short-term economic incentives would be unacceptable in terms of important social values, but a system that disregards economic constraints would quickly seal its own doom. The drive for a surplus of revenues over expenses is an essential goal of for-profit and not-for-profit providers, but it should not replace the broad goals regarding access to care, cost-effectiveness, quality of care, protection of the consumer, and the processes of education and research. As the investor-owned sector matures and the competitiveness of the environment increases, all institutions must be evaluated and monitored with respect to these broad goals, as well as with respect to the economic performance that is now followed so closely by investors. The issue of ownership will become more critical if these goals are jeopardized. The committee feels that our current path toward an increasingly competitive environment, with more investor-ownership, more for-profit activities by not-for-profit institutions, and larger multi-institutional networks, raises enough issues to warrant careful monitoring. Concurrently, more adequate public policy attention needs to be given to some key topics discussed in this report—the needs of uninsured patients, the maintenance of quality of care, and the fiduciary role of physicians—whose importance is heightened by the changing economic and market forces that affect the ways Americans receive health care.

## NOTES

[1] For this and other reasons, the committee also sought clues from the nursing home industry, in which the incentives generated by prospectively determined rates have long characterized state Medicaid program payments. More than 75 percent of nursing homes are for-profit operations and about half of their patients are paid through Medicaid. The committee hoped to compare proprietary and investor-owned nursing homes with not-for-profit homes concerning cost, quality, and patient access. Although available data have been included in this report, they are generally very inadequate on the major comparisons.

[2] Some diversification in hospitals goes beyond vertical integration, involving separate lines of business, usually through subsidiary organizations such as travel agencies, computer services, supplies, laundries, rental properties, and so forth. Such activities among not-for-profit organizations have led to concern about unfair competition with organizations that do not enjoy the not-for-profit organization's tax benefits. (See U.S. Small Business Administration, 1983.)

[3] Professional practices are themselves the scene of several trends—the decline of solo practice, the growth of practices under trade names, franchised practices (particularly in dentistry and optometry). For more on entrepreneurial trends in the health professions, see Trauner et al. (1982).

[4] Controversy about for-profit health care substantially concerns the relative advantages and disadvantages of two types of private corporations—for-profit and not-for-profit—not about government-owned versus privately owned health care organizations. See Horty and Mulholland (1983) for a more complete analysis of the legal differences between for-profit and not-for-profit health care organizations.

[5] In reality these distinctions in sources of capital are not so neat. Thus, government-owned institutions rely heavily on debt as a source of capital. Not-for-profit institutions that have entered into one of several types of for-profit/not-for-profit hybrid arrangements may have access to equity capital for certain purposes, and, under limited circumstances, for-profit institutions have been able to use tax-exempt debt financing.

[6] A vivid illustration of the importance of earnings growth is seen in the reaction of one Wall Street analyst to the merger of Hospital Corporation of America and American Hospital Supply Company that was proposed (and later derailed) early in 1985:

> We do not believe HCA will be able to maintain its pre-merger third-year growth rate expectation of 15-20 percent without subsequent acquisitions. From what we assess to be acquirable in the health care arena, further mergers would either be dilutive or a further drag on earnings growth. Then why is HCA taking such risks? We are still unsure, but unless, or until, the new proposed combined entity can justify higher growth expectations, we think its long-term expansion rate (assuming that merger is consummated) will hover over 12 percent. Thus, *we are removing Hospital Corporation from the Recommended List* (Shaw, 1985, emphasis in original).

[7] The American Hospital Association (1985) reports that the average U.S. hospital in 1983 had a net patient

margin of 1 percent and a total net margin of 5.1 percent. The Federation of American Hospitals (1983) reported the average after-tax margin among investor-owned acute care general hospitals to be 4.2 percent. Nonpatient revenues accounted for 5.2 percent of total net revenues of not-for-profit hospitals in 1983, but only 1.6 percent of the total net revenues of for-profit hospitals. (Data provided by telephone by the Center for Hospital Statistics at the American Hospital Association.)

[8] It should also be remembered when reviewing categorical comparisons of institutions that there are wide variations within categories. Although the data generally have not been analyzed and reported to show these variations, many of the differences between groups of hospitals of different types of ownership may be smaller than differences among hospitals of a given type of ownership.

[9] Few available data allow a true comparison of efficiency, because of the difficulty of establishing that different health care organizations are producing the same "product." For example, without more information than is generally available on the severity of illness for which patients are being treated in different institutions, doubt remains whether identical services are involved when expenses are being compared. However, there is no evidence that investor-owned hospitals treat more severe cases than comparable not-for-profit hospitals (i.e., nonteaching facilities). The Medicare case-mix index in investor-owned hospitals barely differs from the average for all hospitals.

[10] Although "charity" comprises a greater proportion of uncompensated care at not-for-profit hospitals than at for-profit hospitals, the committee concluded that the numbers that distinguish between bad debt and charity care are not reliable. Thus, the committee followed the common convention of using the measure "uncompensated care," which expresses the sum of bad debt and charity care as a percentage of gross patient revenues. However, this measure is a seriously flawed indicator either of charitable activities by institutions or of the extent to which the needs of those who are unable to pay are being met. It includes dollars of gross patient revenues that are written off either as charity care or as bad debt. Although these two concepts are quite different, they are not used consistently by different hospitals' accountants, in part because the only institutions that have any reason to account separately for charity care are not-for-profit and public hospitals that have an undischarged Hill-Burton "free care" obligation and hospitals that are located in states in which Blue Cross pays a portion of charity care. Uncompensated care that might be written off as charity care at one institution may be written off as bad debt at another.

[11] The Health Care Financing Administration uses a stringent definition of sole community provider (e.g.,

no other hospital within 50 miles), designed in part to minimize the number of such institutions. In a large number of communities, people may view their own hospital as the only one that is reasonably convenient and available. It should also be noted that the investor-owned hospital companies' activities likely include the management of some sole community hospitals.

[12] Hospitals may carry a relatively small uncompensated care burden because of location (which affects not only the demographic characteristics of the surrounding population but also the generosity of the state Medicaid program), the type of emergency services they offer, whether they offer services that may attract uninsured patients (e.g., obstetric services), the reputation and historical mission of the hospital and competing hospitals, and so forth. Thus, there are many circumstances that determine whether an institution that seeks to minimize bad debt and charity care actually has to refuse to provide services to certain patients.

[13] However, some members of the committee believe that before such a conclusion is drawn, more direct evidence is needed regarding the extent to which the ability to obtain care by people who are unable to pay was affected by the coming of investor-owned hospitals. The only two available studies of uncompensated care before and after acquisition by an investor-owned firm were both conducted for the committee. Their results are inconsistent and therefore inconclusive. Brown and Klosterman (1986) found in Florida that hospital acquisition by investor-owned companies was not followed by a decrease in the number of uncompensated care patients, although the percentage of such patients decreased because of an increase in total admissions. Pattison (1986) found in California that hospital acquisitions by investor-owned companies were followed by substantial decreases in uncompensated care, although it is not clear how much of this decrease resulted from changes in collection procedures rather than in admitting criteria. In the two states almost all of the hospitals acquired by investor-owned chains had previously been under for-profit ownership.

[14] Indeed, in one of the cities visited (in the committee's case studies) a public hospital closed its emergency room so as to shift some of its uncompensated care burden to two nearby not-for-profit hospitals.

[15] The physicians on the staff of for-profit hospitals are much more likely than those on the staff of not-for-profit hospitals to be in general or family practice (22 percent versus 13 percent) and much less likely to be in internal medicine (9 percent versus 18.5 percent) (Musacchio et al., 1986). (The distribution of specialists in public hospitals was similar to the distribution in for-profit hospitals.) However, without data about restrictions on privileges or about what physicians with different specialties actually do in different types of hospitals, the committee felt unable to interpret these differences in quality terms.

[16]Actions that may be seen as beneficial by one party—for example, a local government that does not want to make the expenditures necessary to replace an aging facility—may turn up as a third-party payer's increased costs or as an uninsured patient's reduced access to care. Furthermore, advocates and critics see the drive for income differently. For example, facility construction or acquisitions that kept open facilities that would otherwise have closed may have enhanced access to care for many patients and facilitated the practices of many physicians. Critics argue that the low average occupancy rates in these companies' hospitals show that investor ownership has helped to overcapitalize the nation's acute health care system. The higher expenses and charges that resulted from their investments increased costs to third-party payers, including Medicare. However, proponents contend that unrealistically low pre-acquisition price structures and inadequate provision for future capital needs had created problems that could best be met at many institutions through an infusion of outside capital, which had to be paid for.

[17]Statements to this effect appear from time to time. One of the most fully articulated ones comes from a Humana certificate-of-need application for West Hernando Medical Center in Florida:

> Public policy in the United States has determined that providing hospital care to indigent patients is a government responsibility. In order to meet this responsibility, various levels of government collect taxes and make funds available to certain hospitals for this purpose. As a taxpayer, Humana contributes to the provision of this care through payment of property taxes, sales taxes, income taxes, franchise taxes, and other taxes. As a result of public policy and their status as taxpayers, Humana hospitals do not have the responsibility to provide hospital care for the indigent except in emergencies or in those situations where reimbursement for indigent patients is provided.

[18]The health of the not-for-profit sector may also have spill-over effects that benefit the for-profit sector. Indeed, some leaders of investor-owned companies believe that they can survive and prosper so long as the reimbursement and regulatory environment permits the survival of not-for-profit institutions. For example, Richard Ragsdale, senior executive vice president of Republic Health Corp., was recently quoted in *Forbes* as arguing that being in the same business as not-for-profit institutions provides "a political umbrella. . . . If the government gets to the point of hurting us, it will also be pushing some not-for-profits out of business. That's not politically feasible" (Teitelman, 1985).

[19]The concern about potential changes in historical missions or in behavior following acquisitions by investor-owned chains has arisen in several states. The only two studies of changes associated with acquisitions were done for this committee (Brown and Klosterman, 1986; Pattison, 1986). Although both studies are small and include few examples of acquisitions of not-for-profit and public hospitals, both studies show post-acquisition changes (e.g., reductions in uncompensated care) that could signal a change in hospitals' historical missions.

[20]Income taxes (which are paid by for-profit but not by not-for-profit medical institutions) purchase health care that is provided by the Defense Department, Veteran's Administration, and Public Health Service, in addition to 75 percent of Part B of Medicare (approximately $25 billion—the other 25 percent comes from premiums paid by beneficiaries), and the federal share of the Medicaid program (approximately $23 billion). (At the federal level, Part A of the Medicare program is paid for by payroll taxes—a tax that does not distinguish between for-profit and not-for-profit institutions.) Only about 12 percent of the total federal budget of more than $925 billion (1985) goes for health care (Office of Management and Budget, 1984).

## REFERENCES

American Hospital Association (1985) *Economic Trends* 1(Spring).

Brock, Dan W., and Allen Buchanan (1986) Ethical Issues in For-Profit Health Care. This volume.

Brown, Kathryn J., and Richard E. Klosterman (1986) Hospital Acquisitions and Their Effects: Florida, 1979-1982. This volume.

Federation of American Hospitals (1983) *Statistical Profile of the Investor-Owned Hospital Industry, 1983*. Washington, D.C.: Federation of American Hospitals.

Gaumer, Gary (1986) Medicare Patient Outcomes and Hospital Organizational Mission. This volume.

Horty, John F., and Daniel M. Mulholland (1983) Legal Differences Between Investor-Owned and Non-Profit Health Care Institutions. Pp. 17-34 in Bradford H. Gray (ed.), *The New Health Care for Profit*. Washington, D.C.: National Academy Press.

Musacchio, Robert A., Stephen Zuckerman, Lynn E. Jensen, and Larry Freshnock (1986) Hospital Ownership and the Practice of Medicine: Evidence from the Physician's Perspective. This volume.

Office of Management and Budget (1984) *Budget of the U.S. Government, FY 1985*. Washington, D.C.: U.S. Government Printing Office.

Pattison, Robert V. (1986) Response to Financial Incentives Among Investor-Owned and Not-for-Profit Hospitals: An Analysis Based on California Data, 1978-1982. This volume.

Shaw, Seth H. (1985) Hospital Corporation of America (an "Equity Research Company Comment" from Shearson Lehman Brothers). May 2.

Teitelman, Robert (1985) Selective Surgery. *Forbes* (April 22):75-76.

Trauner, Joan B., Harold S. Luft, and Joy O. Robinson (1982) *Entrepreneurial Trends in Health Care Delivery: The Development of Retail Dentistry and Freestanding Ambulatory Services*. Washington, D.C.: Federal Trade Commission.

U.S. Small Business Administration (1983) *Unfair Competition by Nonprofit Organizations with Small Business: An Issue for the 1980s*. Washington, D.C.: U.S. Small Business Administration.

Watt, J. Michael, Steven C. Renn, James S. Hahn, Robert A. Derzon, and Carl J. Schramm (1986) The Effects of Ownership and Multihospital System Membership on Hospital Functional Strategies and Economic Performance. This volume.

SUPPLEMENTARY STATEMENT ON

# For-Profit Enterprise in Health Care

Alexander M. Capron, Eliot Freidson, Arnold S. Relman, Steven A. Schroeder, Katharine Bauer Sommers, Rosemary Stevens, and Daniel Wikler

The work of the committee and its staff and consultants has been thorough and thoughtful. Although we concur with most of the report, we add this statement to stress certain findings and implications that are important for public policy and need more emphasis.

In our opinion, the major finding of this report is that the investor-owned hospital chains have so far demonstrated no advantages for the public interest over their not-for-profit competitors. The report shows that on average the for-profit hospitals have been slightly less efficient, have charged payers more, and have rendered less uncompensated care to uninsured patients than not-for-profit hospitals. Their most notable capability has been their greater access to capital, which in some places may have allowed them to build or renovate needed facilities. However, the current underutilization of hospital beds, most evident among the investor-owned hospitals, suggests that easy access to capital has also encouraged overexpansion of inpatient facilities and may not always be a virtue.

Second, data are lacking on many significant points. The data do not allow an adequate comparison of the quality or kinds of services provided at for-profit and not-for-profit hospitals. Moreover, the committee did not measure the effect of for-profit hospitals' practices on not-for-profit institutions. Since the committee focused on national data, the special problems in states where the for-profits are concentrated and have a large share of the beds were not analyzed. We were therefore unable to lay to rest fears expressed by some observers that, particularly in those states, the for-profits are skimming the profitable patients and dumping the unprofitable ones, thus threatening the solvency of hospitals that adhere to a policy of not turning away medically indigent patients.

Finally, we are concerned about what would happen if for-profit institutions assumed a dominant role in our health care system as a whole. Nationally, less than 15 percent of private acute care hospitals (the main focus of the committee report) are for-profit, but a majority of nursing homes and private psychiatric hospitals are for-profit; and investor-owned businesses are expanding into other parts of the system. A substantial increase in the for-profit sector's share of the health system could

1. Put further pressure on hospitals, voluntary organizations, and other facilities that provide needed but less profitable services;
2. Create powerful centers of influence to affect public policy; and
3. Increase the drift of the health care system toward commercialism and away from medicine's service orientation.

These concerns reinforce the implication of the committee's report that we would have little to gain, and possibly much to lose, if for-profit corporations came to dominate our health care system.

# Part II
## PAPERS ON
# For-Profit Enterprise in Health Care

*For-Profit Enterprise in Health Care.* 1986.
National Academy Press, Washington, D.C.

# An Exchange on For-Profit Health Care

Arnold S. Relman and Uwe Reinhardt

August 23, 1984

Professor Uwe E. Reinhardt
Woodrow Wilson School of Public
  and International Affairs
Princeton University
Princeton, NJ 08544

Dear Uwe:

I have just read your entertaining piece in the July 23 issue of *Medical Economics*, debunking the "cost-crisis" in health care, and I wanted to make a brief comment.

In general, I agree with your argument—which has the usual Reinhardt style and panache—that as a nation, we *could* spend much more on health care if we wanted to (particularly in the public sector). But it seems to me that you ignore the crisis caused by the maldistribution of the burden of the cost. We have a crisis in the private sector because employers can't continue adding the rising costs of their employees' health insurance to the price of their products without becoming non-competitive in world markets. And we have a crisis in the public sector because the government, having made a commitment to provide care for the poor and the elderly, is no longer willing to pay the bills, and local taxpayers are unwilling to pick up the slack. So, I don't think you help the public understanding of our dilemma by asserting that there is no "crisis." The problem is that we want to have our cake and eat it too. We want more and better health care, but we don't have a system of paying for it that distributes the cost equitably or assures equal access for all citizens. That is what I would call a real "crisis."

Turning to another aspect of your article: I was puzzled by your comment about the economic behavior of "health-care providers." You say that the public shouldn't be concerned about the "remuneration ranging from good to excellent" now being earned by people and institutions in the health-care "industry." "Somehow they expect health-care providers to behave differently from the purveyors of other goods and services."

Why shouldn't the public expect health-care providers to be different from other "purveyors"? Do you really see no difference between physicians and hospitals on the one hand, and "purveyors of other goods and services" on the other? Do you regard the health care system as just another industry, and physicians as just another group of businessmen? Where does the professional commitment to service fit into your view of medical care? Do hospitals have no responsibility to serve the community, or do you reserve that obligation *only* for the public tax-supported hospitals?

It seems to me that this issue goes to the heart of the matter we have been discussing in the IOM [Institute of Medicine] committee. As a physician, I believe the medical profession's first responsibility is to serve as a trusted agent and adviser for patients. Physicians should be adequately compensated for their time and effort, but not as businessmen. Unfortunately, too many physicians nowadays are succumbing to the lure of easy profits, and are becoming entrepreneurs. The investor-owned hospital corporations obviously are businesses and tend to think of health care as a business. It is also true that many voluntary hospitals are becoming more businesslike in their orientation towards sales, marketing, cost control and so forth. But does this mean that the health-care system *really is* fundamentally the same as any other business, or that we should encourage it to become so?

As an economist, you may not see any distinction between the practice of medicine and a business, but that point of view would be strongly contested by many people outside of economics, including the great majority of health professionals. It would also be contested by almost anyone who has had a major personal encounter with medical care. Sick or frightened patients do not regard their physicians as they would "purveyors of other goods and services," nor do they think of the hospital where they go for treatment as simply another department store.

In any event, this is an issue that needs to be discussed in more depth at our committee meetings, and certainly deserves thoughtful consideration in our final report.

With kindest regards.

Sincerely yours,

Arnold S. Relman, M.D.

September 6, 1984

Arnold S. Relman, M.D.
Editor
*New England Journal of Medicine*
10 Shattuck Street
Boston, MA 02115

Dear Bud:

Many thanks for your letter of August 23rd concerning my recent piece in *Medical Economics*. For starters, let me mention that the piece was actually written by one of their editors, after an interview that, in turn, was based upon my paper entitled, "What Percentage of its GNP Should a Nation Spend on Health Care?".

Be that as it may, the thrust of the article is certainly mine, and I am willing to defend it. You register two criticisms against the piece: (a) that I mislead the public by arguing that cost is not the essence of our health care crisis, and (b) that I do not expect physicians' behavior to be different from that of "purveyors of other goods and services." Let me respond to both criticisms in turn, with emphasis on the second, because it bears on the matter before our IOM committee.

It is my sense that you misread the intent of my remarks on costs. Because you are an astute reader, other readers may have misread it as well. Thus, I plead mea culpa for inadequate communication.

Let me draw your attention to a sentence in the piece that really constitutes the heart of the argument:

All I'm saying is that we're dodging the real issue when we pretend that God has spoken from on high and told us: "Sorry: folks, you can't spend any more on health care or you'll be running around naked!" The real issue—and it's tough enough—is how much we *want* to spend on health care, and how to apportion the cost [to individual members of society.] [Unfortunately, the editors eliminated the section in brackets from the draft I had approved.]

I do not believe, as you apparently do, that premiums for employee health insurance have rendered American business noncompetitive. In Europe and (I believe) in Japan, the bulk of health care is typically payroll financed. Collectively, German and French business firms bear a larger share of the nation's total health bill than do American firms. There are more compelling reasons why American business firms find it hard to compete abroad.

Nor do I believe that our public sector could not absorb additional expenditures on health care. Let me not dwell on the $400 hammers we have no difficulty buying from our defense contractors. In 1983, we spent $22 billion on farm support programs—expenditures designed to pay farmers not to grow food or to grow surplus food the government must store in its warehouses. A nation that can do this year after year has no case arguing that it cannot afford additional public health care expenditures.

In sum, I stand by the argument that references to the percent of GNP [gross national product] we spend on health care, to the plight of business or of David Stockman, or to physicians' average income are smoke screens to hide the true dimension of the crisis before us: an apparent unwillingness of society's well-to-do to pay for the economic and medical maintenance of the poor. It is not an externally imposed economic or cost crisis; it is a moral crisis. That is what I meant by the statement that "the real issue is how to apportion the cost of our health care to individual members of society." And, as you mention, you agree.

Let me now come to the more important part of your letter. In it you argue that the American public should expect health care providers to be different from the "purveyors of other goods and services," and you wonder why I think otherwise. Furthermore, you argue that this question goes to the heart of the matter before our IOM committee.

In view of the central role you have played on the committee, I think that it is only fair to take your question head-on. Unfortunately, I shall not be able to attend the next two meetings. Permit me, therefore, to respond to your question with a commentary that goes much beyond the customary length of a letter. My ultimate objective will be to extract from you: (a) a positive definition of the kind of health care system you would find acceptable on ethical grounds, and (b) a statement explaining precisely in what sense American physicians differ from other "purveyors of goods and services"—purveyors you do not seem to hold in high regard. I shall proceed with a series of pointed questions.

Do I understand you to imply that you would like to see the U.S. health care system converted to something akin to the Swedish system? In Sweden, comprehensive health care is the responsibility of the county governments. Most Swedish doctors are salaried employees of the counties, that is, they are truly not-for-profit providers of health care. Only 5 percent of Swedish physicians are private, for-profit practitioners on the U.S. model. Are you not ultimately asking that such a system be introduced in the United States as well? Of course, in such a system physicians and others working in it would have to be paid the "good to excellent" wages earned by other "purveyors" in the economy, because the health sector must compete with other industries for the available pool of manpower. The time is long past when as vast and technically complex a sector as the health care sector could be run by missionaries and candy-stripers. It is a real industry now, whether we like it or not, and it must pay wages competitive with other industries.

Actually, I have never heard you make that plea for the Swedish system before our com-

mittee, nor have I seen you make it in print. Let me therefore assume, in what follows, that you do not advocate the Swedish model outright, but merely wish us to revert to the U.S. status quo circa 1970, that is, to the world as it was before the for-profit institutions appeared on the scene. It was a world in which physicians had the right to organize their practice as private entrepreneurs on a for-profit or for-income or for-honorarium or for-whatever-you-want-to-call-it basis, and in which they were supported by non-profit institutions that were financed by someone else, but freely available to physicians as their workshops. If this is the world to which you would have us return, then I must confront you with yet another set of questions, some of which may not be altogether tactful. These questions will center strictly on physicians and not on other parts of the health care industry. I would like to explore with you what role model your own profession has been to other purveyors of health care.

Let me, then, turn your question around and ask: What, in the history of the American medical profession, aside from that profession's own rhetoric, should lead a thoughtful person to expect from physicians a conduct significantly distinct from the conduct of other purveyors of goods and services? I do not deny that there have been grand and noble physicians among the lot, just as there have been grand and noble financiers, lawyers, and even economists. Rather, I am referring here to central tendencies, to the mainstream of American medicine as it has revealed itself through the ages to a paying public. What, then, in the conduct of mainstream American medicine should have led a thoughtful person to expect from physicians a conduct distinct from other ordinary mortals who sell their goods and services for a price? And what in the history of mainstream American medicine would you have serve as a role model for the emerging for-profit institutions delivering health services?

Surely you will agree that it has been one of American medicine's more hallowed tenets that piece-rate compensation is the sine qua non of high quality medical care. Think about this tenet. We have here a profession that openly professes that its members are unlikely to do their best unless they are rewarded in cold cash for every little ministration rendered their patients. If an economist made that assertion, one might write it off as one more of that profession's kooky beliefs. But physicians are saying it!

Ordinary mortals, not blessed by professional courtesy, experience the application of this piece-rate principle whenever they pass the physician's cashier on the way out: one is asked to pay, on the spot, with cash or valid check. Indeed, it is not uncommon that one makes a down payment or even a complete prepayment for obstetrical care or surgery— "cash on the barrelhead," as lesser mortals would put it. Why would patients who undergo this routine not think of the physician as a regular business person? If you do not like the imagery, perhaps you object to fee-for-service compensation. Again, if you object to fee-for-service medicine, why have you not made this clear to our IOM committee?

You will recall that, for many decades, our nation has been plagued by a maldistribution of physicians. Careful empirical research has established scientifically what was known to any cab driver all along: physicians, like everyone else, like to locate in pleasant areas where there is money to be had. Thus, our favorite areas have been said to be vastly overdoctored, while other areas, notably the inner cities, have been sorely underserved. As a nation we have been able to solve this problem only through the importation of thousands of FMGs [foreign medical graduates]. (Let us thank them one and all!) Because I do not think ill of ordinary mortals, and because I think of physicians as ordinary mortals, I would not look down upon physicians for their locational preferences. They have simply behaved like certain Ivy League professors who lavish their pedagogic skills on the offspring of America's well-to-do instead of teaching students who really need them. But how does someone imputing a more lofty social role to physicians reconcile the physicians' locational choices with the lofty ideal? Do you really believe that physicians are more civic in their behavior than the rest of us? Do you think they could come even close to members of the voluntary fire brigade? Let me put the question to you even more bluntly: Do you sincerely believe that

our for-profit hospitals will leave in their wake as much neglect of uninsured, sick Americans as American physicians have, collectively, in the past and are likely to leave in the future?

You ask me whether hospitals have no responsibility to serve the community, and whether I reserve that obligation *only* for the public tax-supported hospitals. This question involves principles of law and principles of ethics, and I am neither a lawyer nor an ethicist— just a little country economist from rural New Jersey. But perhaps I can make some headway by seeking guidance in your own profession's code of ethics. After all, the human capital of physicians (their training) has traditionally been largely tax-financed. Let us examine, then, what obligation for community service physicians believe they have shouldered in return for a largely tax-financed education. From that ethos we might derive some clues on the social obligation of a hospital that is wholly investor-financed and not tax-financed. Specifically, if physicians believe they owe no community service for their public subsidies, can we legitimately saddle investor-owned hospitals with such an obligation?

According to a recent article in *Medical Economics* (Jack E. Horsley, J.D., "Who Can Sue You for not Rendering Care?" August 20, 1984), the AMA [American Medical Association] Principles of Medical Ethics include the following tenet: Physicians are free to choose whom they will serve. Further on in the piece the author opines that "an AMA legal analysis states that 'a physician is not required to accept as patients all who apply to him for treatment. He may *arbitrarily* refuse to accept any person as patient, *even though no other physician is available.*'" (Italics added.) Finally, the author advises the reader, "You have a perfect right to refuse patients who are not insured or on welfare." As we all know, many American physicians have acted on these ethical precepts. They have refused to accept Medicaid patients because they considered the cash yield for treating such patients inadequate. They have "skimmed the cream," so to speak.

You and some of your colleagues seem troubled now by the thought that for-profit hospitals may "skim the cream" and refuse to treat uninsured, poor patients. You have made much of this point in our committee meetings. Here comes yet another question for you: Given that the medical profession, in its own code of ethics, actually has laid the moral and legal foundation for such refusals, have you at any time prior to the emergence of for-profit hospitals ever railed against your own profession's code of ethics?* If so, I would love to see that literature. If not, why have you not?

You may have noted in our committee's public hearing last fall that the representative of the AMA steadfastly refused to be goaded into saying something negative about for-profit hospitals, particularly on this issue. That was very decent of him, and very appropriate, too, because people in glass houses should not throw stones, as the old saw goes.

My own thoughts on the matter, for what they are worth, are these. Society should not expect private physicians or private hospitals (for-profit or not) to absorb the cost of whatever social pathos washes onto their shores. We as a society have a moral duty to compensate the providers of health care for treating the poor. If providers do give some charity care, our thanks to them. Ultimately, however, it is the responsibility of the citizenry at large to pay for the economic and medical maintenance of their less fortunate peers.

It follows that I do not consider it sensible to nit-pick over how much charity care for-profit hospitals do or do not give. Our committee has wasted too much time on that irrelevant question. In any event, to the extent that they refuse to render such care, they can point to the medical code of ethics as a moral justification for their policy, and they can buttress their case by pointing to the neglect your profession has traditionally visited upon low-

___

*Incidentally, I am not saying that the medical profession departs from the celebrated Hippocratic Oath our medical graduates swear. As I read that oath, I see no reference in it to charity care. It is merely required that physicians do the utmost, without corruption, for patients whose house they do (choose to) enter. There is the added promise that "you will be loyal to the profession and just and generous to its members," and there is the wish that "prosperity and good repute be ever yours." I saw nothing explicit about charity care in the version I reviewed. Maybe there is a longer one that does make reference to it. If so, I stand to be enlightened.

income Americans. Examine, if you will, the data presented in the graph's overleaf. Would you interpret the sudden upswing in the physician care received by America's poor since the mid 1960s as: (a) a massive attack of unrequited noblesse oblige seizing members of your profession shortly after 1964, or (b) a sudden decrease in the health status of America's hitherto unusually robust and healthy poor, or (c) the emergence of federal *financing* of physician care for America's poor, many of whom were sick all along?

My money is on (c). If I am correct, the graphs are not exactly monuments to the beneficence of American medicine, are they? And, if I am correct, other "purveyors" probably would have traced out similar graphs under similar circumstances, would you not agree? Real estate developers are one example that comes to mind; they have done much for the poor since federal funds began to pay them for it. If we pay the for-profit hospitals for treating the uninsured poor, they will treat them, too, as many American physicians (though not all) did in response to the onset of federal financing.*

And what of the profits the investor-owned hospitals will reap in the process? You will recall that you and I have had quite a few exchanges on the level of these profits. As you probably know, economists decompose a physician's income into at least three parts: (a) a rate of remuneration for hours of work, (b) a rate of return to the investment in fixed facilities (the practice), and (c) a rate of return to the investment the physician has made in his or her own training. Research has shown the latter rate to be certainly on par with the rate-of-return to shareholders' equity earned in industry, the hospital industry included.

Recently I read that over 70 percent of all cataract extractions in this country are covered by Medicare. If you look up the prevailing charges for that operation and relate these to the time it takes to perform a cataract extraction, you will arrive at a quite handsome hourly

___

*I do not deny that even prior to Medicaid, some American physicians did treat some of our poor on a charity basis. It is also true that our for-profit hospitals now do treat some uninsured poor on a charity basis.

rate of physician remuneration for that kind of work. Properly viewed, it implies quite a handsome rate of return to the investments made by ophthalmologists in their training. My legendary inbred tact stops me from dwelling on the rates of return our nephrologists have been able to extract from taxpayers via the Medicare program. But let me raise the following question: If it is all right for physicians to earn a handsome rate of return on their investments, what is so evil about paying a handsome rate of return also to the non-M.D.s who have let their savings be used for the brick and mortar of health care facilities against nothing more than the piece of hope-and-prayer paper lawyers refer to as a "common stock certificate?" Do you think that, in its final report, our committee can fairly get into the issue of the rates of return earned by the shareholders of investor-owned hospitals without exploring also the rates of return physicians earn on their investments? Might you not agree that we had best drop that entire issue as well?

So far, I have argued that, as individuals, American physicians have traditionally conducted themselves in a style that casts them into the role of a regular purveyor of a service. I do not judge it to be a style ordinary mortals need behold with awe. It is tempting to buttress the case further with reference to the activities of *organized* American medicine. I shall refrain from reciting that history, however, because Clark Havighurst of Duke University has already done so quite effectively before our committee. Suffice it to say that one would be hard put to distinguish organized American medicine from the trade association of any other group of purveyors of goods and services. Would you not agree with that as well?

In this connection, you may also wish to read Paul Feldstein's chapter "The Political Economy of Health Care" in his book *Health Economics.** In that chapter he demonstrates rather persuasively that the political activities of organized medicine are best explained with a simple model of economic self-interest. Feldstein asks, inter alia, why a profession that professes to be deeply concerned over the

quality of health care has been opposed so long to strict, effective periodic relicensing on the model of, say, periodic relicensing of airline pilots, all the while invoking the issue of quality in the defense of restrictive licensure laws that exclude would-be competitors from the primary health care market. Economists are neither shocked nor surprised by such a posture nor, however, does it persuade them that physicians stand much apart from the rest of mankind.

You might argue that all I have said about American physicians is perfectly true, but beside the point you wish to make: that such things just should not be true. But then I must repeat my earlier question, to wit: do you not really ask for a health system something like the Swedish one? I raise the issue again because nothing short of such a revolution will rid our health system of the conflicts of interest you seem to deplore. At a minimum, you should want our system to be converted totally to nonprofit HMOs that pay physicians a salary and do not—I repeat, *do not*—distribute to physicians any year-end bonuses based on the HMO's economic performance. Is that your plea?

You suggest that, when people are sick, they are often frightened and can, thus, be easily exploited by a for-profit provider. Is that true only when the provider is a for-profit institution, but not true when the provider is a fee-for-service (i.e., for-profit) practitioner? Do you really believe that the executives of a for-profit hospital naturally lack the decency and integrity self-employed physicians naturally have? Let me ask you this question in yet another way. It is well known that the hourly remuneration physicians earn for inpatient physician services exceeds that for ambulatory physician care. Would you not agree that, given the entrepreneurial practice setup American physicians have always preferred, and given the pressure on physician incomes likely to come from a physician surplus, this disparity in hourly remuneration may lead to needless testing, hospitalization, and length of stay, even if all hospitals in our country were not-for-profit?

I put to you the proposition that this question goes to the heart of our debate. Whatever the ownership of the hospitals in which Amer-

*New York: John Wiley and Sons, 1979.

ican physicians work, the ethical standards by which our health care sector operates will ultimately be driven by the ethical standards of our physicians. To make the case you have sought to make to our committee—unconvincingly, in my view—you must present us at least with a testable theory according to which the ethical standards of essentially unsupervised, self-employed, fee-for-service physicians affiliated with nonprofit hospitals can withstand even the severest economic pressure (mortgage, kids in college, alimony, lovers with expensive tastes, and so on) in the face of ample opportunity to be venal, while the ethical standards of physicians affiliated with for-profit hospitals, or employed at a salary by the latter, will wilt at the mere suggestion by some corporate officer to set aside medical ethics for the sake of corporate profits that do not even accrue, dollar for allegedly corrupt dollar, to the allegedly corrupt M.D.? Make that case convincingly, and you will walk away with our committee.

Until you do make that case convincingly, I shall continue to subscribe to the theory that, whatever erosion in medical ethics we shall observe in the future will be the product of excess capacity all around. When a nation decides to finance the operation of, say, only 90 percent of the human and material health care capacity it has put into place, there will be a scramble for the health-care dollar among health care providers. In that scramble, medical ethics may be bent. I hold to the proposition that it matters little if those who scramble for health care dollars define what they grab as "honoraria," "income," or "profits." These are semantic differences of little practical import for, when faced with economic extinction, nonprofit enterprises are unlikely to fight nicely nor, I suspect, will unsupervised, self-employed, fee-for-service physicians.

Let me assure you that all of us on the committee appreciate and, indeed, share your concern over the quality of American health care. Unfortunately, you seem to be shooting at the wrong target. The AMIs, HCAs, and NMEs*

---

*The acronyms refer to American Medical International, Hospital Corporation of America (HCA), and National Medical Enterprises (NME).

of the world strike me as nothing other than the logical end product of a trend originally nutured by none other than this country's medical profession. To be sure, it is a development which, from the profession's perspective, went out of control. But your profession nourished it along; physicians served as the role models. For better or for worse, we must now expect the for-profit corporations in health care to follow in your profession's tracks.

Throughout this century, American medicine has prided itself on its rugged individualism. If one looked for die-hard champions of free enterprise and libertarian thought, one could always find them among our physicians. As Clark Havighurst remarked before our committee, American medicine fought valiantly to defend its right to entrepreneurship in health care, and it fought just as valiantly to deny almost everyone else that right. It was a seductive strategy, but, alas, a dangerous one. Somewhere along the way the profession's erstwhile, tight control over the distribution of entrepreneurial rights in health care slipped out of its hands. My guess is that the tension between the profession's claim for an exalted social position and its earthy fight for an exclusive entrepreneurial franchise ultimately strained the credulity and patience even of medicine's friends. And, thus, the individual American physician finds him- or herself today reduced somewhat in stature, though not in wealth, almost a mere peer among an ever-increasing number of profit-oriented purveyors of health care, each competing vigorously for the health care dollar.

If you deplore this outcome, you should have started writing eons ago. By now, as Paul Ellwood has put it, the targets you ought to want to hit are already much beyond our reach. We are left with the search for incentives that make our for-profit or for-income or for-honorarium providers of health care do good by doing well. It probably can be done, although I cannot guarantee it. We shall see.

David Rogers once told me that I seem to be one of the few social scientists who does not hate physicians. He is right. I really do not hate physicians, nor do I begrudge them their income. I like them and respect them just about as much as I do other Americans (business people included) most of whom are very decent folk. This has not always been so. During my student days at Yale I did develop a certain disdain for physicians, but I write that off as a lack of maturity. You see, until those days I had thought of physicians as people somehow apart and above the rest of us. Naively, I had accepted the imagery physicians like to project of themselves. It was the dissonance between this imagery and the empirical record all around me that pained me enough to lash out in anger at your profession. Now I have mellowed. Years of both casual and careful empiricism have persuaded me that physicians really are not very different from other "purveyors." If one accepts them on that level, they come across as truly fine purveyors—expensive, to be sure—but truly fine, nevertheless. By and large, I like what they sell, and I like them, too.

Write me off as an economist or, alternatively, call me a realist. But it so happens that I am more comfortable dealing with a well-trained, competitive, self-professed professional entrepreneur who drives a Lincoln than I am with a well-trained, competitive, self-professed saint who insists on driving a Cadillac. *Chacun a son gout*, I suppose.

Until we meet again, with my best wishes,

Sincerely,

Uwe E. Reinhardt

September 25, 1984

To: Professor Uwe E. Reinhardt

Dear Uwe:

Thanks for taking the time to give such a detailed and thoughtful response to my letter.

For someone who declares that he really likes and respects physicians, you certainly have managed to roast the medical profession to a crisp. I shudder to contemplate the fate of a debating adversary you *didn't* like!

The questions I was trying to raise with you concern broad issues of public policy and social philosophy. Does the concept of a profession, as applied to physicians and other health care professionals, have any meaning in our society and, if so, does that meaning imply ethical obligations for health professionals that do not apply with equal force to businessmen? Are there differences between health care and other services that would justify different public expectations for the behavior of health care institutions and business firms?

My purpose in writing to you was simply to solicit your views on these questions, because I consider them to be at the very heart of the problem our IOM committee is wrestling with. Some members of the committee apparently believe that there basically is no difference between health care and other goods and services, or between physicians (as they are, or *ought* to be) and businessmen. It, therefore, would be logical for them to conclude that the investor-owned health industry is a pseudo-problem. Others, starting from the opposite assumption, think that it is self-evident there *is* a problem which needs looking into. Oddly enough, our committee has so far devoted virtually no attention to this matter, despite its crucial importance for our deliberations. That is why I was hoping you would respond directly to my questions and help generate some interest among our colleagues in giving further consideration to the issue.

Unfortunately, you have avoided a direct answer by inveighing against the moral hypocrisy of the medical profession. You seem to be saying that since there are so many profit-oriented entrepreneurial physicians out there, and since "the ethical standards by which our health care sector operates will ultimately be driven by the ethical standards of our physicians," how can I, as a physician, even raise questions about the ethics and social value of selling health care in a commercial market?

Suppose I were not a physician and were asking the same questions about investor-owned health care. Would your response be the same? Would you say that physicians will have to discipline themselves more effectively, or change their economic *modus operandi* before we can even look into the for-profit industry?

You have also dodged my questions by asking a lot of your own. There isn't time for me to deal here with all the questions you have raised about my personal views, even if they were germane to our committee agenda—which they are not. Perhaps we can continue the dialogue on another occasion. However, some of my opinions are already on record. I enclose a copy of an article I wrote in *Health Affairs* ("The Future of Medical Practice") in case you haven't seen it. It summarizes many of my views about the fee-for-service system and entrepreneurial health care, and it outlines some of the reforms I think physicians can and should institute. I haven't yet written about my concept of the "ideal" health care system because I am not at all sure I know what that is. I do, however, have pretty definite and well-known views about the ethical obligations of physicians, whatever the economic environment.

I happen to believe that your description of physicians as "almost a mere peer among an ever-increasing number of profit-oriented purveyors of health care" is exaggerated. It has some truth, but it overlooks the basic element in our health care system, which is the relation between doctor and patient. That relation is based on trust by the patient and a commitment by the doctor to serve the patient's interest first. The fact that most doctors are also interested in being well paid for their services, whether by salary or on a fee-for-service basis, doesn't change the primacy of their ethical commitment to the patient. This commitment is unfortunately being more and more eroded by new economic forces, but it is still there, and it is one of the several reasons why health care is different from other economic goods and services. Other reasons include the virtually total dependence of the consumer on the advice of the physician, and the often intimate and immediate relation of health care to the quality and quantity of life. You will probably attribute such views to the hubris of doctors, but I believe they are correct. Do you challenge these statements? If so, I hope you will tell the committee why.

In my view, these ethical considerations ought to be part of our committee's agenda. They boil down to the question of whether there is something special about health care which makes distribution of health services in a commercial marketplace problematic and inappropriate. A second issue (or set of issues) for our committee is whether there is in fact any empirical evidence of differences between not-for-profit and investor-owned health care in terms of process, product or broader social consequences. In my opinion, it would be as

serious an omission to avoid discussion of the first issue as it would be to assume, without objective examination of all the available evidence, that we know the answers to the second.

With kindest regards.

Sincerely yours,

Arnold S. Relman, M.D.


October 16, 1984

To: Arnold S. Relman, M.D.

Dear Bud:

Many thanks for your letter of September 25 concerning the issues before the IOM Committee on For-Profit Health Care. Your letter, and especially your paper on "The Future of Medical Practice" enclosed with that letter, finally put to us concisely the central question that appears to have troubled you all along. I take it to be the following question:

What revisions in the medical profession's code of ethics need to be made to minimize the conflicts of interest inherent in the transformation of health care from a labor-intensive to a more capital-intensive activity?

This question is rather distinct from (although not totally unrelated to) the question we seem to have pursued during the past year, namely:

Relative to health care delivered by not-for-profit institutions, what effect does the for-profit motive have on (a) the quality of care, (b) the cost of care, and (c) access by the poor to the care rendered by investor-owned institutions?

The second question is obviously interesting in its own right and thus worth pursuing. But it is at best tangential to the first question which you now declare to lie at the heart of our inquiry.

You seem to argue now that the primary focus of our inquiry should have been the *physician* and not the *hospital*. If that is so, then you surely bear a good part of the blame for our straying from the course. After all, you have rather consistently oriented the committee toward the for-profit hospital as the quintessential threat to the quality and fairness of American health care. In your comments and letters to the committee, you have drawn our attention to the relative markups for-profit and nonprofit hospitals charge on ancillary services, to the relative ratios of total charges to total costs, to relative profit rates, and to relative rates of charity care. None of these issues is really central to the issue you raise in your paper on "The Future of Medical Practice." In that paper the focus is squarely on the physician. It is not clear to me whether the committee will be able to shift so late in the game to zero in on the focus you now propose.

In your paper you speak of the "commercialization" of health care, just as Eli Ginzberg in his well-known paper speaks of the "monetarization" of health care. These phenomena are, of course, American adaptations to an underlying change in the technology of health care: the increasing reliance of modern medicine on sophisticated and expensive capital equipment. One need not be a confirmed Marxian economic determinist to believe that this underlying technological change lies at the heart of the changes you and Eli deplore.

The shift from labor-intensive to more capital-intensive medicine confronts society with two distinct questions:

1. Who should finance, own, and control the equipment and structures used in modern health care?
2. Should physicians ever be among the owners?

Some societies—for example, Canada and most European nations—appear to have decided that the capital used in health care should be financed and owned primarily by the public sector. In these societies, health-care capital is rarely owned by private investors, and not even by physicians. West Germany furnishes the only major exception to this pattern. (Although hospital care in that country is given almost exclusively by salaried physicians, some physicians do own small hospitals. Furthermore, the physicians in ambulatory care fill their private offices with all sorts of laboratory and therapeutic equipment. Many of them earn money simply by blowing hot air on patients' heads or by performing similarly weird capital-intensive procedures. More and more, West German physicians have become capitalists.)

In the United States, we have increasingly looked to private capital markets as sources of financing health-care capital, and physicians rank prominently among the investors. We have answered both of the two questions raised above with a definite yes. Presumably, we believe that patients are competent enough to cope with whatever economic conflicts of interest physicians as capitalists face under this arrangement.

In your paper you take issue with premises underlying the emerging pattern of capitalist medical practice in this country. As I interpret your policy recommendation on pages 17-18, you argue that physicians should not enter joint ventures with other entities in the ownership of health-care capital and, presumably, that they should not own expensive medical equipment as sole proprietors either. In making that recommendation you tacitly accept, do you not, that the physician's professional ethics are apt to be malleable—that a physician who must worry about the break-even volume of an X-ray machine, laboratory, or treadmill exerciser is unlikely to be impervious to such economic pressures in composing treatments for patients. I am persuaded by that argument, particularly because I view physicians as regular-issue human beings. Perhaps other members of the committee will be persuaded as well. You should press the argument at the next meeting, if only to test the waters.

But suppose the committee agreed on the recommendation that, wherever it is technically feasible, physicians should minimize the conflict of interest they already face under fee-for-service compensation by avoiding direct or indirect ownership of health-care capital. Would it necessarily follow from this recommendation that health-care capital should then also not be owned by other private laypersons? If you are prepared to make that argument, you should develop your case carefully. At this time I am still of the view that investor-owned hospitals, for example, are quite compatible with the strict code of medical ethics you espouse. As long as physicians can keep their noses clean of economic conflicts of interest in their role as the patients' agents, they should be able to act as their patients' powerful ombudsmen in dealing with investor-owned institutions.* That was the central thrust of the argument in my earlier letter of September 6. Do you have a problem with that line of reasoning? If so, voice it loudly and explicitly. It is my sense that our committee will arrive at some such proposition in its final report.

It is my sense that at least some of the for-profit hospitals might go along with the strict code of ethics you would impose on physicians. In a paper he prepared for last year's Duke University Private Sector Conference on Health Care, for example, HCA chairman Don MacNaughton argued explicitly against joint cooperative economic arrangements between hospitals and physicians. Don seemed worried that, in the long run, such joint ventures might impair the image of the hospital industry. I think he is right. It may not be good for the patient's fiscal and physical health to have both the physician's and the hospital's economic incentives aligned in the same direction, namely, against the patient. Of course, if one throws this argument against joint ventures between fee-for-service physicians and hospitals, one should be prepared also to lob it with equal force against HMOs [health maintenance organizations]. One unfortunate feature of an HMO is that, by "meshing" the physician's and the HMO's incentives in one direction, the physician may lose independence in his/her role as the patient's ombudsman. That is precisely why the champions of the poor tend to be so alarmed whenever it is proposed to force the poor into HMOs. Profit-sharing or bonus-giving HMOs are joint ventures.

You mention in your letter that you have not yet developed your own conception of an ideal health care system—one that minimizes the economic conflict of interest faced by physicians. It is time that you work on the articulation of such a system, lest your commentary be written off as destructive criticism. Perhaps you might begin by listing all of the arrangements to which you object. By a process of elimination you might then arrive at the set of acceptable arrangements. That set may in-

clude only "salaried medical practice." It might also include, however, the relatively more harmless fee-for-service system used in Canada in conjunction with essentially publicly owned or controlled hospitals. (Physicians in Canada own little capital.) If you wish the committee to be responsive to your thinking, you cannot go on forever without offering more *constructive* criticism of our present system.

Let me now come to some of the other questions in your recent letter. Although you have chosen not to answer any of the pointed questions I put to you in my previous letter—which is a pity—I shall nevertheless try to answer yours. I am that nice of a guy.

You ask me again whether I truly see no differences between physicians and other purveyors of goods and services. Honestly, I don't. Physicians are not the only purveyors whose work I am not technically competent to judge. The craftsmen who repair our cars and homes perform a similar agency role. Although we read of corrupt repairmen, just as we read about doctors who run Medicaid mills or push pills for profit, I have always been struck by the integrity of most of the craftsmen and businessmen in whose ethics I must necessarily trust. Physicians really should not be offended when one likens them to such "purveyors."

You and Dr. Donald M. Nutter, in a recent piece in your journal, contrast the presumably venal "business ethic" with your profession's presumably more lofty code of ethics. If you ever sat in on the board meetings of large corporations, you would be surprised to learn how often business people forego easy profits for the sake of ethical standards. And you would be surprised to learn what they could get away with, if they were as venal as is implied in your use of the term "business ethic." I honestly believe that a corporation has as much concern over the decency with which it treats its customers as physicians have over their patients. In short, I stand by the conception of physicians I expressed in my letter of September 6. They are as decent as other human beings, and just as frail under severe economic pressure.

Frankly, I remain a little puzzled by your own views on medical ethics. Sometimes you seem to suggest that physicians are endowed with a strong commitment to ethical conduct.

*I realize that a physician may have to please the hospital to enjoy privileges there. But that applies with equal force to nonprofit hospitals as well.

If that is true, why do you worry so? At other times you lament the erosion of medical ethics in the face of capitalist medicine. If medical ethics erode so easily, what then does set physicians apart from "other purveyors?"

You ask me in your letter whether we (the IOM) shall have to wait for the medical profession to clean up its act before we can even look into the for-profit hospital industry. The answer is: No, we don't have to wait, and we did not wait. After all, our committee *is* looking into the behavior of for-profit hospitals without even looking at the behavior of physicians. Unfortunately, no major policy recommendations are likely to emerge from such a study. Besides, our inquiry into this facet misses the central question you raise, for reasons indicated above.

Finally, you ask me whether there is something special about health care which makes it problematic to distribute it through the marketplace. The answer to that question depends on two issues. First, what distributional ethics do we wish to impose on health care? And, second, quite aside from the distributional ethics, do the consumers of health care possess sufficient consumer sovereignty to fend for themselves in the market for health care?

The first of these questions involves social values. Most societies treat health care not as a consumer good, but as a community service that is to be distributed on an egalitarian basis, on the basis of medical need. While that lofty goal may not always be attained, it is at least espoused. It is my sense that Americans have now decided to treat health care as essentially a private consumer good of which the poor might be guaranteed a basic package, but which is otherwise to be distributed more and more on the basis of ability to pay. What I personally think about this ethic is uninteresting. In thinking about policy recommendations for the United States, I must take the prevailing ethic as a state of nature. For better or for worse, it now points to two-class medicine.

The second question is a purely empirical one. The champions of free markets in health care obviously are persuaded that individual patients can muster adequate countervailing power even against systems in which the physician's and the hospital's economic incentives are fully aligned against the patient. Paul Ell-

wood seems to be in this school of thought. Frankly, I harbor some doubts on this point. I am not aware of any conclusive empirical research on the ability of patients with different health status and from different socioeconomic and demographic groups to muster effective countervailing power in the health care market. In this area we seem to proceed on preconceived notions, as any debate on the subject in our committee is apt to reveal. We certainly should discuss the issue, if only to bare our preconceptions.

Until we meet again, Bud, keep on trucking. I salute you for having the courage to propose for your brethren a strict code of ethics on the ownership of health care capital. Unfortunately, you propose this code just at a time when your brethren have come increasingly to look upon the ownership of capital as a substitute source of income, in the face of declining patient-physician ratios. You propose to kill the goose expected to lay your brethren's future golden eggs. It takes guts to go to their fiscal jugular in this fashion. As to the success of your campaign, I can only send you that old Navajo salute: Mazeltov!

With my best regards,

Cordially,

Uwe E. Reinhardt

December 3, 1984

To: Professor Uwe E. Reinhardt

Dear Uwe:

I am afraid you misunderstood the point I was trying to make in my last (September 25th) letter. I never said, nor even implied, that the committee should abandon its analysis of investor-owned health care institutions in favor of a new focus on the ethics of the medical profession. All I proposed was that we include in our report some discussion of the underlying ethical and social questions (as they apply to both health care institutions and physicians). I believe that public policy choices depend at least as much on these underlying questions as on the empirical and historical questions to which we have devoted most of our attention so far.

Clearly, it is of the utmost importance for us to marshall and evaluate all the available evidence on the characteristics and behavior of for-profit hospitals and other investor-owned health care facilities. It is essential that we try to determine whether the type of ownership of health care services makes any difference to their cost, efficiency, quality, availability, and responsiveness to community need. We also should consider how the growing presence of for-profit facilities has affected, and will affect, the viability of public and voluntary facilities in the same community. These questions have been high on our committee's agenda, as they should be, but I believe that our report should also recognize that there are other important considerations that the public and the government ought to be thinking about as they consider future policy on health care.

Is there something special about health care that makes it socially undesirable for facilities to be owned by private investors, or for physicians to be entrepreneurial businessmen? What will be the social consequences of the growing commercialization of our health care system? If we are to do a thorough job of evaluating the for-profit phenomenon, I believe we should discuss these kinds of questions along with the other topics we have been considering. I recognize that there may be no clearly right or wrong answers to such questions, and that we are not likely to get a committee consensus. Nevertheless, it would be a useful exercise to at least lay out the issues. Our report will be widely read and quoted, and it seems to me that we would do a public service by at least pointing out the questions that need to be addressed and the arguments pro and con. I suspect that many committee members, whatever their opinions about for-profit health care, would agree with me on this point, and I hope you will too. We still have several months in which to prepare the first draft of our report, and I see no reason why it shouldn't be possible to include some of this kind of analysis and still meet our deadline.

I now want to comment on some of the views you express in the remainder of your letter:

1. You say that in the United States (as op-posed to Canada and most European nations), we have decided that "private capital markets" and physicians should "own and control the equipment and structures used in modern health care." I can't agree. Certainly, it is true that much private capital has recently been invested in health care, and the trend is growing. That is what our report is all about. I see no evidence, however, that a political decision has been made to rely on this method of financing health care—or that the implications of such a decision have even been explored or publicly discussed. As I see it, our report is one of the first steps in the process of examining and debating public policy on this subject. The growth of the investor-owned health care industry, and the extent of any future involvement of the medical profession in this industry, will depend on decisions yet to be made. Our report could influence those decisions.

2. Yes, you interpret me correctly. I do advocate that physicians should neither enter joint business ventures with health care facilities (for-profit *or* not-for-profit) nor hold any equity interest in health care businesses. You raise the interesting question of physician ownership of expensive medical equipment. Exactly where the line should be drawn between permissible, relatively inexpensive items of office equipment and impermissible, more expensive equipment in the office or elsewhere, is a difficult question that I cannot answer, but I recognize the problem. You may be interested to know that the Judicial Committee of the AMA is currently studying conflicts of interest in physician ownership of health care capital and will shortly offer some guidelines.

3. You say that you believe physicians should avoid direct or indirect ownership of health-care capital, but you do not believe this stricture needs to be extended to other private investors. You think that investor-owned hospitals are compatible with the strict code of medical ethics I espouse because "as long as physicians can keep their noses clean of economic conflicts of interest in their role as the patients' agents, they should be able to act as their patients' powerful ombudsman in dealing with institutions."

I agree that physicians must avoid conflicts of interest if they are to represent their patients and protect them against exploitation by investor-owned health care businesses, and have urged this policy on many occasions. I am not convinced, however, that such a policy will be sufficient. Much depends upon how much authority and independence the medical profession will have in a system that may be increasingly dominated by for-profit corporations and by business managers who focus primarily on the bottom line. For example, how effectively will doctors be able to represent their patients' interests when the doctors are employed by for-profit institutions, or when a for-profit hospital chain is the only game in town?

Be that as it may, I find your position on this issue to be puzzling. You say that physicians need to be ombudsmen for their patients, and yet you also insist that there are "no differences between physicians and other purveyors of goods and services." How could that be? Are salesmen and other commercial purveyors also supposed to be ombudsmen for their customers?

4. In defending your claim of no difference between doctors and businessmen, you say that "physicians are not the only purveyors whose work I am not technically competent to judge. The craftsmen who repair our cars and homes perform a similar agency role." And a little later, you say that businessmen and corporations deal with their customers just as ethically as physicians do with their patients.

I think you avoid the main issue here. Of course there are many services which, like medical care, consumers are technically incompetent to judge. And, of course, physicians are not inherently more virtuous or honest than business people, or maybe even than corporations. But I would maintain that there is something unique about the doctor-patient relation which clearly distinguishes it from the relation between a car mechanic, a home repairman, or any other commercial purveyor and his customer.

It is not that there aren't experts other than doctors on whom clients or customers have to depend for technical advice. It is simply that a sick patient is dependent upon his doctor in a peculiarly critical and intimate way that isn't matched by any commercial rela-

tionship. Up to now, at least, society has recognized this special relation by surrounding it with a network of legal and ethical constraints on the behavior of physicians which make it very clear that physicians are *not* to be regarded simply as purveyors of expert services in a commercial market. The ethical obligations of a car mechanic or any other purveyor are to be honest in his business dealings, and to offer a good product or service, if the customer *wants* it enough to pay the price.

An ethical physician's obligations to his patient go far beyond that. The sick patient must rely on the physician to ensure that he gets the services he *needs*, and to make choices for him, upon which the quality and quantity of his life may depend. Financial considerations are secondary. There are some superficial resemblances, but no one who has ever been really sick would take your analogy between a car mechanic and a physician very seriously. Some authors, in attempting to understand how medical services differ from those ordinarily provided in a commercial market, draw the distinction between *needs* and *wants*. This strikes me as a useful and illuminating insight. Markets are driven by customers' *wants*; the medical care system is supposed to consider health *needs*.

Maybe in the future, society will want to change this special relationship between doctor and patient by "deregulation" of the practice of medicine, as Milton Friedman and other free market zealots suggest. I doubt that very much, however, because most people understand how dangerous to health that radical step would be.

5. You suggest "Americans have now decided to treat health care as essentially a private consumer good of which the poor might be guaranteed a basic package, but which is otherwise to be distributed more and more on the basis of ability to pay." I can't agree. As with your earlier opinion about the role of private capital markets and physician entrepreneurial ownership of health care facilities (page 2), I believe the issue hasn't been discussed or analyzed sufficiently to say what the American people really do believe. It is certainly true that we have been drifting towards a marketplace mechanism for distribution of health

care, but the public hasn't given its approval of that trend, and many people haven't even thought about it.

There are strong egalitarian feelings about health care in this country. I doubt that a two-tier system, such as would inevitably develop with market-determined distribution of health care, would be politically acceptable. In any event, I believe the issue is still open. One of our responsibilities in this study is to discuss the probable effects of an expanding for-profit sector on the distribution of care, so that intelligent policy decisions can be made. Voluntarism and cross-subsidization in our not-for-profit institutions formerly accounted for a large share of free care. If we replace these institutions with investor-ownership we will either require much larger tax subsidies for the poor, or we will have to deny the poor access to services. Given the choice, the public may decide that new policies favoring the preservation of the voluntary system may be preferable to either of these outcomes. It is also conceivable that within 5 or 10 years, perhaps in a new political climate, a tax-supported national health insurance system might be seen as a viable option again.

6. Finally, I want to respond to your comments where you urge me to offer my own version of the "ideal" health care system, lest my objections to the marketplace approach be written off as simply destructive criticism. In the first place, I don't see that the committee's report needs to be concerned with my personal views—or with anyone else's, for that matter. We are supposed to be analyzing the implications of investor-owned health care, not expressing any particular view of the "ideal" system. If there are cogent reasons to be concerned about the for-profit approach, as I believe there are, I don't see why those criticisms should be set aside simply because they are not coupled with a blueprint for the solution to all our health care problems.

In criticizing the for-profit system, I fully recognize the limitations of the system it seems to be replacing. And in decrying entrepreneurialism in investor-owned hospitals, I also decry similar behavior by voluntary hospitals and among physicians. I am frank to admit, however, that I am not sure what the best alternative would be. I do believe that we will need considerable reform in the present fee-for-service practice of medicine, and that we will also need more, not less, public regulation and subsidization of health care. But I still don't have a clear idea of what the "ideal" system for the United States would look like. All I am sure about at the moment is that a commercial marketplace isn't the answer.

I apologize for the length of this missive, but your last letter was so interesting that I couldn't resist trying to set my own thoughts straight on the many provocative points you raised. I think that I have now said all that I should. If you choose to reply—as I hope you will—I promise I will not attempt another rebuttal. You can have the last word. I have learned a lot from this exchange and have enjoyed it enormously. Thanks for staying with it.

I will be looking forward to seeing you at one of our next committee meetings.

With best regards.

Sincerely yours,

Arnold S. Relman, M.D.

*For-Profit Enterprise in Health Care.* 1986.
National Academy Press, Washington, D.C.

# Ethical Issues in For-Profit Health Care

Dan W. Brock and Allen Buchanan

The American health care system is undergoing a rapid socioeconomic revolution. Within a general environment of heightening competition, the number of investor-owned for-profit hospitals has more than doubled in the past 10 years, while the number of independent proprietary for-profit hospitals has declined by half.[1] Investor-owned for-profit corporations are controlled ultimately by stockholders who appropriate surplus revenues either in the form of stock dividends or increased stock values. Independent proprietary institutions are for-profit entities owned by an individual, a partnership, or a corporation, but which are not controlled by stockholders. Nonprofit corporations are tax-exempt and are controlled ultimately by boards of trustees who are prohibited by law from appropriating surplus revenues after expenses (including salaries) are paid. Although the increase in investor-owned hospitals has been most dramatic and publicized, a rise in investor-owned health care facilities of other types, from dialysis clinics to outpatient surgery and "urgent care" centers has also occurred.

The above definitions treat "for-profit" rather narrowly as a legal status term referring to investor-owned and independent proprietary institutions. However, much of the current concern over "for-profit health care" has a wider, though much less clear focus. It is often said, for instance, that health care in America is being transformed from a profession into a business like any other because of the growing dominance of those types of motivation, decision-making techniques, and organizational structures that are characteristic of large-scale commercial enterprises.

A recent book published by the Institute of Medicine bears the title *The New Health Care for Profit*, with the subtitle *Doctors and Hospitals in a Competitive Environment*. The difference in scope between the title and subtitle is but one example of a widespread tendency of discussions of "for-profit health care" to run together concerns about the effects of increasing competition in health care, which affects both "for-profit" and "nonprofit" institutions in the legal sense, and special concerns about the growth of those health care institutions which have the distinctive "for-profit" legal status.

This essay will focus primarily on the ethical implications of the growth of for-profit health care institutions in the legal sense. However, although the ethical problems we shall explore have been brought to public attention by the rapid rise of for-profit institutions (in the legal sense), it would be a mistake to assume that they are all peculiar to institutions that have this legal form.

In what follows, "for-profit" will be used only to denote a distinctive legal status and not as a vague reference to "commercial" motivation or decision making and organizational structure, or as a synonym for the equally nebulous concept of "competitive health care." We shall explore, however, some moral concerns about the rise of for-profit institutions in the legal sense that focus on the profit motivation, decision-making forms, and organizational structures common to those institutions.

Serious moral criticisms of for-profit health care have been voiced, both within and outside of the medical profession. Before they can be evaluated, these criticisms must be more

Dr. Brock is professor and chairman of the Philosophy Department of Brown University. Dr. Buchanan is a professor with the Department of Philosophy at the University of Arizona as well as the Division of Social Perspectives in Medicine in the university's College of Medicine.

carefully articulated than has usually been done. In each case, after clarifying the nature of the criticism, we shall try to answer two questions: (1) Is the criticism valid as a criticism of for-profit health care? (2) If the criticism is valid, is its validity restricted to for-profit health care?

The most serious ethical criticisms of for-profit health care can be grouped under six headings. For-profit health care institutions are said to (1) exacerbate the problem of access to health care, (2) constitute unfair competition against nonprofit institutions, (3) treat health care as a commodity rather than a right, (4) include incentives and organizational controls that adversely affect the physician-patient relationship, creating conflicts of interest that can diminish the quality of care and erode the patient's trust in his physician and the public's trust in the medical profession, (5) undermine medical education, and (6) constitute a "medical-industrial complex" that threatens to use its great economic power to exert undue influence on public policy concerning health care. Each of these criticisms will be examined in turn.

## FOR-PROFITS EXACERBATE THE PROBLEM OF ACCESS TO HEALTH CARE

Twenty-two to twenty-five million Americans have no health care coverage, either through private insurance or through government programs including Medicare, Medicaid, and the Veterans Administration. Another 20 million have coverage that is inadequate by any reasonable standards.[2] The charge that for-profits are exacerbating this already serious problem takes at least two forms. First, it is said that for-profits contribute directly to the problem by not providing care for nonpaying patients. This is an empirical question to which the accompanying Institute of Medicine (IOM) report devotes a chapter. The data are not fully consistent on whether for-profit hospitals provide less or as much uncompensated care as do nonprofit hospitals; data from several states show that they provide less, but national data show minimal differences between for-profits and nonprofits, both of which do much less than publicly owned hospitals. In any event, our concern here is to analyze the arguments

that have been advanced regarding the issue of uncompensated care.

Second, it is also alleged that for-profits worsen the problem of access to care in an indirect way because the competition they provide makes it more difficult for nonprofits to continue their long-standing practices of "cross-subsidization." Cross-subsidization is of two distinct types: nonprofits have traditionally financed some indigent care by inflating the prices they charge for paying patients, and they have subsidized more costly types of services by revenues from those that are less costly relative to the revenues they generate.

It is sometimes assumed that, in general, for-profits are more efficient in the sense of producing the same services at lower costs and that these production efficiencies will be reflected in lower prices. At present, however, there is insufficient empirical evidence to show that for-profits on the whole are providing significant price competition by offering the same services at lower prices, though this may change in the future. In fact, what little data there are at present indicate that costs, especially of ancillary services, tend to be higher, not lower, in the for-profits.[3]

However, the argument that for-profits are making it more difficult for nonprofits to continue the practice of cross-subsidization does not depend upon the assumption that for-profits are successful price competitors in that sense. Instead it is argued that for-profits "skim the cream" in two distinct ways. First, they capture the most attractive segment of the patient population, as noted earlier, by locating in more affluent areas, leaving nonprofits with a correspondingly smaller proportion of paying patients from which to subsidize care for nonpaying patients. Second, by concentrating on those services that generate higher revenues relative to the costs of supplying them, for-profits can achieve greater revenue surpluses, which provide opportunities either for lower prices or for investment in higher quality or more attractive facilities, both of which may worsen the competitive position of nonprofits, making it more difficult for them to cross-subsidize.

Critics of for-profits predict that access to care will suffer in two ways: fewer nonpaying patients will be able to get care and some paying patients, i.e., some who are covered by public or private insurance, will be unable to find providers who will treat them for certain "unprofitable" conditions.

Although these predictions have a certain a priori plausibility, they should be tempered by several important considerations. First, as already indicated, there is at present a dearth of supporting data concerning differences in the behavior of for-profits and nonprofits, and this is hardly surprising since the expansion of the for-profit sector has been so recent and rapid. However, preliminary data do support two hypotheses which tend to weaken the force of the criticism that for-profits are exeracerbating the problem of access to care by making it more difficult for nonprofits to continue cross-subsidization. One is that at present there seems to be no significant difference in the proportion of nonpaying care rendered by for-profits and nonprofits.[4] The other is that at present the proportion of nonpaying care rendered by nonprofits is on average only about 3 percent of their total patient care expenditures.[5] Here again, however, it may be important to separate from the overall data for nonprofits, the public hospitals in which the proportion of nonpaying care is both higher than in the for-profits and substantially in excess of 3 percent of overall total patient care expenditures.[6] If the public hospitals experience a decrease in their paying patients, their ability to carry out their mission of serving the indigent could be seriously jeopardized.

A third reason for viewing predictions about the effects of for-profits on access to care with caution is that there are other variables at work that may be having a much more serious impact. In particular, the advent of a prospective reimbursement system for Medicare hospital services and other efforts for cost-containment by state and federal regulatory bodies and businesses, as well as the general increase in competition throughout the health care sector, are making it more difficult for any institution to cross-subsidize.

In addition, as defenders of for-profits have been quick to point out, in some cases for-profits have actually improved access to care not only by locating facilities in previously underserved areas thus making it more convenient for patients to use them, but also by making certain services more affordable to more people by removing them from the more expensive hospital setting. The growth of outpatient surgical facilities in suburban areas, for example, has improved access to care in both respects. Indeed, there is some reason to believe that by making decisions on the basis of the preferences of their boards of trustees (which may be shaped more by their own particular preferences or considerations of prestige than by demands of sound medical practice or response to accurate perceptions of consumer demand), nonprofits have in some cases duplicated each other's services and passed up opportunities for improving access by failing to expand into underserved areas.

This latter point drives home the complexity of the access issue and the need for careful distinctions. For-profits may improve access to care in the sense of better meeting some previously unmet demand for services by paying patients, while at the same time exacerbating the problem of access to care for nonpaying patients. However, there is clearly a sense in which the latter effect on access is of greater moral concern. We assumed that the members of a society as affluent as ours have a collective moral obligation to ensure that everyone has access to some "decent minimum" or "adequate level" of care, even if they are not able to pay for it themselves. Surely providing basic care for those who lack any coverage whatsoever then should take priority over efforts to make access to care more convenient for those who already enjoy coverage and over efforts to reduce further the financial burdens of those who already have coverage, by providing services for which they are already insured in less costly nonhospital settings.

So far we have examined the statement that "cream skimming" by for-profits exacerbates the problem of access to care. Ultimately this is largely an empirical question about which current data are inconclusive. There is another way in which the "cream skimming" charge can be understood. Sometimes it is suggested that for-profits are acting irresponsibly or are not fulfilling their social obligations by failing to provide their "fair share" of indigent care and unprofitable care, as well as making it more difficult for nonprofits to bear their fair share through cross-subsidization. To this allegation of unfairness, defenders of for-profits have a ready reply: "No one is *entitled* to the cream; so for-profits do no wrong when they skim it. Further, for-profits discharge *their* social obligations by paying taxes. Finally, since the surplus revenues that nonprofits use to subsidize nonpaying or unprofitable care are themselves the result of overcharging—charging higher prices than would have existed in a genuinely competitive market—then it is all the more implausible to say that they are entitled to them."

While this reply is not a debate-stopper, it should give the critic of for-profits pause since it draws attention to the unstated—and controversial—premises underlying the contention that cream-skimming by for-profits is unfair because it constitutes a failure to bear a fair share of the costs of nonpaying or unprofitable patients. The most obvious of these is the assumption that, in general, nonprofits are (or have been) bearing their fair share.

To determine whether for-profits or nonprofits are discharging their obligations we must distinguish between two different types of obligations—general and special. For-profit corporations, like individual citizens, can argue that they are discharging their *general* obligation to subsidize health care for the poor by paying taxes. To see this, assume that the fairness of the overall tax system is not in question, and in particular its taxation of corporate profits. For-profits can then reasonably claim that they are doing their fair share to support *overall* government expenditures by paying taxes. If the government is subsidizing health care for the poor as part of overall government expenditures, then for-profits would appear to be doing their fair share towards supporting subsidized health care for the poor. If the government is providing inadequate subsidization of health care for the poor, then the fair share funded by the for-profits' taxes will in turn be inadequate, but proportionately no more so than every other taxpayer's share is inadequate, and *not unfair* relative to the subsidization by other taxpayers. The responsibility for this inadequacy, in any case, would be the government's or society's, not the for-profit health care corporation's.

A for-profit hospital chain cannot say that if it is paying, for example, $30 million in taxes, it is providing $30 million towards funding health care for the poor. Its taxes, whether at the federal, state, or local level, should be understood as a contribution to the overall array of tax-supported programs at those levels. But it can claim to be subsidizing health care for the poor with the portion of its taxes proportionate to the portion of overall government expenditures devoted to subsidizing health care for the poor.

On the other hand, those who raise the issue of fairness have apparently assumed that health care institutions have *special* obligations to help care for indigents. Even if this assumption is accepted, however, it is not obvious that in general nonprofits have been discharging the alleged special obligation successfully for the reasons already indicated. First, even if cross-subsidization is widespread among nonprofits, the proportion of nonpaying and nonprofitable care that is actually provided by many nonprofits appears not to be large. Second, some of the revenues from "overcharging" paying patients apparently are not channeled into care for nonpaying patients or patients with unprofitable conditions.

It was noted earlier that while many *publicly owned* nonprofit hospitals provide a substantial proportion of care for nonpaying patients, nonpublicly owned nonprofits ("voluntaries") as a group do not provide significantly more uncompensated care than for-profits. One rationale for granting tax-exempt status is that this benefit is bestowed in exchange for the public service of providing care for the indigent. If it turns out that many nonprofit health care institutions are in fact not providing this public service at a level commensurate with the benefit they receive from being tax-exempt, then this justification for granting them tax-exempt status is undermined.

It is also crucial to question the assumption that for-profit health care institutions have special obligations to help subsidize care for the needy over and above their general obligation as taxpayers. As the for-profits are quick to point out, supermarkets are not expected to provide free food to the hungry poor, real estate developers are not expected to let the poor live rent-free in their housing, and so forth. Yet food and housing, like health care,

are basic necessities for even a minimal sub-sistence existence. If there are basic human rights or welfare rights to some adequate level of health care, it is reasonable to think there are such rights to food and shelter as well as health care.

Whose obligation is it then to secure some basic health care for those unable to secure it for themselves? Assuming that private markets and charity leave some without access to what-ever amount of health care that justice re-quires be available to all, there are several reasons to believe that the obligation ulti-mately rests with the federal government. First, the obligation to secure a just or fair overall distribution of benefits and burdens across so-ciety is usually understood to be a general so-cietal obligation. Second, the federal government is the institution society com-monly employs to meet society-wide distrib-utive requirements. The federal government has two sorts of powers generally lacking in other institutions, including state and local governments, that are necessary to meet this obligation fairly. With its taxing power, it has the revenue-raising capacities to finance what would be a massively expensive program on any reasonable account for an adequate level of health care to be guaranteed to all. This taxing power also allows the burden of financ-ing health care for the poor to be spread fairly across all members of society and not to de-pend on the vagaries of how wealthy or poor a state or local area happens to be. With its nationwide scope, it also has the power to co-ordinate programs guaranteeing access to health care for the poor across local and state bound-aries. This is necessary both for reducing inef-ficiencies that allow substantial numbers of the poor to fall between the cracks of the patch-work of local and state programs, and for en-suring that there are not great differences in the minimum of health care guaranteed to all in different locales within our country.

If we are one society, a *United* States, then the level of health care required by justice for all citizens should not vary greatly in different locales because of political and economic con-tingencies of a particular locale. It is worth noting that food stamp programs and housing subsidies, also aimed at basic necessities, sim-ilarly are largely a federal, not state or local,

responsibility. These are reasons for the fed-eral government having the obligation to guar-antee access to health care for those unable to secure it for themselves. It might do this by directly providing the care itself, or by pro-viding vouchers to be used by the poor in the health care marketplace. *How* access should be guaranteed and secured—and in particular, to what extent market mechanisms ought to be utilized—is a separate question.

Granted that the obligation to provide ac-cess to health care for the poor rests ultimately with the federal government, is there any rea-son to hold that for-profit health care institu-tions such as hospitals have any special obligations to provide such care? The usual reason offered is that health care institutions, whether nonprofit or for-profit, are heavily subsidized directly or indirectly by public ex-penditures for medical education and research and by Medicare and Medicaid reimburse-ment which have created the enormous pre-dictable demand for health care services that has enabled health care institutions to flourish and expand so dramatically since the advent of these programs in 1965. However, we be-lieve it is less clear than is commonly supposed that these subsidies redound to the benefit of the for-profit institution in such a way as to ground a special institutional obligation to sub-sidize health care for the poor.

The legal obligation of nonprofit hospitals to provide free care to the poor is principally derived from their receipt of Hill-Burton fed-eral funds for hospital construction. However, the for-profit hospital chains secure capital for construction costs in private capital markets and do not rely on special federal subsidies. Even when they purchase hospitals that have in the past received Hill-Burton monies, they presumably now pay full market value for the hospitals. If there is a subsidy that has not been worked off in free care, that redounds to the nonprofit seller, not the for-profit purchaser. What of other subsidies?

There is heavy governmental subsidy of medical education; it is widely agreed that physicians do not pay the full costs of their medical education. Perhaps then they have a reciprocal duty later to pay back that subsidy, though it would need to be shown why the form that duty should take is to provide free care to the poor as opposed, for example, to reimbursing the government directly. However that may be—it is physicians and not the for-profit hospitals who are the beneficiaries of medical education subsidies. Physicians are the owners of these publicly subsidized capital investments in their skills and training, and are able to sell their subsidized skills at their full market value. Physicians, and not the owners of for-profit health care institutions in which they practice or are employed, are the beneficiaries of education subsidies and so are the ones who have any obligation there may be to return those subsidies by in turn subsidizing free care for the poor.

Another important area of public subsidy in the health care field is medical research. Much medical research has many of the features of a public good, providing good reason for it to be publicly supported and funded. (Where these reasons do not apply, as for example in drug research, the research is largely privately funded by the drug companies.) Medical research makes possible new forms of medical technology, knowledge, and treatment. Because it is publicly funded, and once developed is generally freely available for use by the medical profession, for-profit health care institutions are able to make use of the benefits of that research in their delivery of health care without sharing in its cost.

But who ultimately are the principal beneficiaries of this public subsidy of research? Not, we believe, the for-profits, but rather the patients who are the consumers of the new or improved treatments generated by medical research. It may or may not be true that for-profits will not bear the research costs of these treatments as part of their delivery costs. But if, as is increasingly the case, the for-profits operate in a competitive environment concerning health care costs or charges, they will be forced to pass on these subsidies to consumers or patients. (And if they operate in a largely noncompetitive environment, there will be a strong case for some form of regulation of their rates.) The price that patients pay for health care treatments whose research costs were subsidized by the government will not include those research costs and so will not reflect true costs. It is then consumers of health care, not the for-profits, who principally ben-

efit from research subsidies, and any obligation arising from this subsidy presumably lies on them.

Finally, consider the large public subsidy represented by Medicare and Medicaid. These programs created a vast expansion in the market for health care which many for-profits serve and from which they benefit. This is new health care business which heretofore did not exist and on which they make a profit. Perhaps this benefit grounds a special obligation of for-profit institutions to provide subsidized care for the poor. The most obvious difficulty with such a view is that the subsidized health care consumers, not the deliverers of the health care, are by far the principal beneficiaries of Medicare and Medicaid. Any profit that the for-profits receive from serving Medicare and Medicaid patients is only a small proportion of the overall cost of their care.

It must be granted, nevertheless, that the for-profits do earn profits from these subsidized patients. But it is difficult to see how this fact by itself is sufficient to ground a special obligation of the for-profits to subsidize free care for the poor. In the first place, for-profits can again respond that they pay taxes on these profits, like other profit-making enterprises. Moreover, they can point out that in no other cases of government-generated business of for-profit enterprises is it held that merely earning a profit from such business grounds a special obligation similar to that claimed for for-profit health care enterprises. Virtually no one holds that defense contractors, supermarkets who sell to food stamp recipients, highway builders, and so forth have any analogous special obligation based on the fact that their business is created by government funds. Nor is it ever made clear why this fact should itself ground any special obligation of for-profits in health care to provide access to health care for the poor. Thus, we conclude that none of the current forms of public subsidy of health care will establish any significant *special* obligation of for-profits to provide free care, and so the claim cannot be sustained that for-profits do not do their fair share in providing access to health care for the poor. We emphasize that we believe there *is* an obligation to guarantee some adequate level of health care for all, but the obligation is society's and ultimately the federal government's and not a special obligation of for-profit health care institutions.

Even if there are insufficient grounds for the assumption that for-profit health care institutions, or health care institutions as such, have special obligations to provide a "fair share" of uncompensated care, it can be argued that a nation or a community, operating through a democratic process, can impose such a special obligation on the institutions in question as a condition of their being allowed to operate. According to this line of thinking, a community may, through its elected representatives, require that any hospital doing business in that community provide some specified amount of indigent care, either directly or by contributing to an indigent care fund through a special tax on health care institutions (so far as they are not legally exempt from taxes) or through a licensing fee.

Whether or not such an arrangement would be constitutional or compatible with statutory law in various jurisdictions is not our concern here. One basic ethical issue is whether the imposition of such special obligations would unduly infringe on the individual's occupational and economic freedoms. Although no attempt to examine this question will be made here, this much can be said: a community's authority to impose a special obligation to contribute a portion of revenues (as opposed to an obligation to contribute services) for indigent care seems no more (or less) ethically problematic than its authority to levy taxes in general.

A second basic ethical issue is then whether such taxes, or requirements to provide uncompensated care as conditions of doing business for health care institutions, fairly distribute the costs of providing care to the indigent. That will depend on the details of the particular tax or requirement to provide uncompensated care, but since any are likely to be ultimately a tax on the sick, it is doubtful that such provisions will be fairer than financing care for the indigent through general tax revenues.

There is, moreover, an additional difficulty with any claim that by skimming the cream for-profits fail to fulfill an existing special obligation to bear a fair share of the burden of providing at least some minimum level of care for all who need it but cannot afford it. This is the assumption that in the current U.S. health care system any determinate sense can be given to the notion of a "fair share" of the burden of ensuring access to care (in the absence of specific legislation such as the Hill-Burton Act). Unless a rather specific content can be supplied for the notion of a fair share, the nature and extent of an institution's alleged special obligation will be correspondingly indeterminate. In particular, it will be difficult if not impossible to determine whether for-profits have met such a special obligation. But it will also be problematic to assert what some defenders of nonprofits imply, namely that nonprofits have in the past done their fair share through cross-subsidization.

The current U.S. health care system is a patchwork—or, less charitably, a crazy quilt—of private insurance and public program entitlements. There is no generally accepted standard for a "decent minimum" or "adequate level" of care to be ensured for all, no system-wide plan for coordinating local, state, and federal programs, charity, and private insurance so as to achieve it, and no overall plan for distributing the costs of providing care for those who are unable to afford it from their own resources. Absent all of this, no determinate sense can be given to the notion of an institution's special obligation to provide a "fair share" of the burden of ensuring an "adequate level" or "decent minimum" of care for everyone.

Furthermore, even if it were possible at present to determine, if only in some rough and ready way, what an institution's "fair share" is, this would still not be enough. Whether an institution has an *obligation*—a duty whose fulfillment society can require—will depend upon whether it can do so without unreasonable risks to its own financial well-being. But in a competitive environment, determining whether one institution is contributing its "fair share" will be unreasonably risky for it will depend upon whether other institutions are doing *their* "fair share."

The establishment of a coordinated system-wide scheme in which institutions share the costs of providing some minimum level of care for all is a "public good" in the economist's sense. Even if every governing board of every institution agrees that it is desirable or even imperative to ensure some level of care for all, so long as contribution to this good is strictly voluntary, each potential institutional contributor may attempt to take a free ride on the contribution of others with the result that the good will not be achieved.

It is important to understand that failure to produce the public good of a fair system for distributing the costs of care by voluntary efforts does *not* depend upon the assumption that potential contributors are crass egoists. Even if the potential contributor has no intention of taking a free ride on the contributions of others, he may nonetheless be unwilling to contribute his fair share unless he has *assurance* that others will do their fair share. For unless he has this assurance, to expect him to contribute his fair share is to expect him to bear an unreasonable risk—a cost which might put him at a serious competitive disadvantage. In the absence of an *enforced* scheme for fairly distributing the costs of care for the needy, the current vogue for containing costs by increasing competition in health care will only exacerbate this free-rider and assurance problem. And unless an institution can shoulder its fair share without unreasonable risk to itself, it cannot be said that it has an *obligation* that it has failed to fulfill. Granted that this is so, what is needed is an effective mechanism for enforcing a coordinated scheme for distributing the costs of providing some minimal level of care for all without imposing unreasonable competitive disadvantages on particular institutions.

It is important not to overstate this point. Although the notion of unreasonable risk is not sharply defined, it is almost certainly true that many for-profit (and nonprofit) institutions could be spending more than they currently are for nonpaying or unprofitable patients without compromising their financial viability. So it is incorrect to conclude simply from this that in the current state of affairs institutions have no special obligations whatsoever. The point, rather, is that debates over which institutions are or are not fulfilling their obligations are of limited value and that the energy they consume could be more productively used to develop a system in which institutional obligations could be more concretely specified and in which

society would be morally justified in holding those who control the institutions, whether government or private, accountable for the fulfillment of those obligations.

Moreover, there is at least one obligation which *now* can be justifiably imputed to for-profit (and nonprofit) health care institutions and that is the obligation to cooperate in developing a system in which determinate obligations (whether general or special) can be fairly assigned and enforced. It is much less plausible to argue that the initial efforts needed *to develop* a coordinated, enforced system would undermine an institution's competitive position, even if it is true that in the absence of such a system an institution's acting on a strictly voluntary basis to help fund indigent care would subject it to unreasonable risks.

Assuming that as members of this society we all share a collective obligation to ensure an "adequate level" or "decent minimum" of health care for the needy, those who control health care institutions, as individuals, have the same obligations the rest of us have. However, because of their special knowledge of the health care system and the disproportionate influence they can wield in health policy debates and decisions, health care professionals may indeed have an additional *special* obligation beyond the general obligations of ordinary citizens to help ensure that a just system of access to health care is established.

It can still be argued that whether or not they fail to fulfill their obligations, for-profits have at least contributed to the decline of cross-subsidization and that the cross-subsidization system has made some contribution toward coping with the problem of access to care. Whether this provides a good reason for social policy designed to restrain or modify the behavior of for-profits will depend upon the answer to two further questions: (1) Are cross-subsidization arrangements the best way of coping with the access problem, and, just as important, (2) is it now feasible in an increasingly competitive environment to preserve cross-subsidization even if we wish to do so?

Objections to cross-subsidization are not hard to find. On the one hand, cross-subsidization can be viewed as an inefficient, uncoordinated welfare system hidden from public view and unaccountable to the public or to its representatives in government. Further, it can be argued that widespread cross-subsidization is incompatible with effective efforts to curb costs. Surely an effective solution to both the access and cost containment problems requires a more integrated, comprehensive, and publicly accountable approach. Consequently, the demise of cross-subsidization should be welcomed, not lamented.

This last conclusion, however, is simplistic. It assumes that an explicit public policy designed to improve access for those not covered by private or public insurance is presently or in the foreseeable future politically feasible. Perhaps the strongest argument for cross-subsidization is the claim that it does—though admittedly in a haphazard and inefficient way—what is not likely to be done through more explicit social policies.

It might be tempting to protest that even if this is so, cross-subsidization ought to be rejected as an unauthorized welfare system since it did not come about through the democratic political process as a conscious social policy. However, if providing some minimum of care for the needy is a matter of right or enforceable societal obligation and not a matter of discretion, then the lack of a democratic pedigree may not be fatal, since rights and obligations place limitations on the scope of the democratic process.

Controversy over the ethical status of cross-subsidization may soon become moot if a point is reached where it is no longer feasible to shore up or rebuild an environment in which cross-subsidization is economically viable for health care institutions. So even if cross-subsidization has been the best feasible way of coping with the problem of access it does not follow that it will continue to be a viable option. Perhaps too much energy has already been wasted in policy debates defending or attacking cross-subsidization when the real issue is: How can we now best achieve the purpose that cross-subsidization was supposed to serve?

## FOR-PROFITS ARE UNFAIR COMPETITION FOR NONPROFITS

This criticism of for-profits can be interpreted in either of two different ways. The first understands it as a charge we have already examined in detail, that for-profits skim the cream and gain a competitive advantage over nonprofits by failing to discharge their institutional obligations to bear their fair share of the costs of providing care for indigents and those with unprofitable diseases. But the metaphor of cream-skimming suggests another possible aspect of the charge of unfair competition that it is worth saying a little more about. This is that besides not taking a fair share of the "bad" (unprofitable) patients, the for-profits also take more than their share of the "good" (profitable) patients.

As we noted above, if no one is *entitled* to the profitable patients, it is unclear why seeking to get as many as possible of them is unfair. Nor is it clear that the nonprofits do not also seek as many as possible of the profitable patients. If the for-profits get a disproportionate share of the profitable patients, which may be true at some places but not others, why would that be? Since paying patients have a choice about where and from whom they receive care, their choice of for-profits must in significant part reflect their view that for-profits offer a more attractive product: for example, more convenient location, more modern and higher quality facilities, additional amenities, cost-saving efficiencies, and so forth. It is difficult to see why getting a disproportionate share of the profitable patients simply because one offered a better product is unfair. Of course, when for-profits get more of the profitable patients because of factors such as tie-in arrangements with physicians, this may constitute unfair competition, but nonprofits may engage in such anticompetitive practices as well.

According to the second interpretation of the unfair competition charge, nonprofit health care institutions make a distinctive and valuable social contribution—one that is so important that they ought to be protected from the threat of extinction through competition with for-profits. Three main arguments can be given in favor of perpetuating the nonprofit legal status for health care institutions and, hence, for social policies that are designed to protect them from destructive competition from for-profits. First, nonprofit health care institutions are properly described as charitable institutions. As such they help nurture and perpetuate the virtue of charity among members of our otherwise highly self-interested society, and this virtue is of great value. The nonprofit legal form stimulates charity by exempting charitable institutions from taxes. Because it also ensures that those who administer charitable funds do not appropriate revenue surpluses, the nonprofit legal form encourages charity by providing potential donors with the assurance that they will not be taken advantage of and that their donations will be used for the purposes for which they were given. This assurance is especially vital in the case of donations for health care because donors usually lack the knowledge and expertise to determine whether the providers they support are using their resources properly.

Second, nonprofit health care institutions both function as and are perceived to be an important community resource, serving the entire community, rather than a commercial enterprise ultimately serving its shareholders and restricted to "paying customers." Like the virtue of charity, the sense of community is an important though fragile value in modern American society, and institutions that contribute significantly to it should not be lightly discarded.

Third, nonprofit health care institutions nurture a professional ethos that is more likely to keep the patient's interest at center stage than do for-profit institutions, in which the commercial spirit is given freer rein. Hence nonprofits are valuable because they protect quality of care. The quality-of-care argument will be examined in detail later.

The first argument above assumes that most nonprofit health care institutions are properly described as charitable institutions in the sense that a substantial portion of their financial resources comes from donations. At present, however, most nonprofit hospitals are not charitable institutions in this sense; they are "commercial" rather than "donative" institutions insofar as the major portion of their resources comes from selling services rather than from donations.[7] The more closely nonprofit health care institutions approximate the purely "commercial" nondonative type, which is becoming the dominant form among nonprofit hospitals, the weaker the value of charity appears as a justification for perpetuating the nonprofit legal status. Nevertheless, even if only a small portion of most nonprofits' revenues comes from charitable donations and is in turn used for unpaid care, nonprofits may still be properly regarded as "charitable" *if* they do in fact serve as the provider of last resort for those who are unable to pay for their care and who are not covered by any insurance or government program to fund their care. Even if such care represents only a small portion of a hospital's overall revenues, it may still be perceived as an important charitable activity and thereby reinforce altruistic and charitable motivations.

It should be clear that the charity and community arguments are not unrelated. It is partly because nonprofits stand ready to provide unpaid health care to the poor (if they do) that they are seen to be a community resource available to the entire community. They can serve to symbolize a shared community commitment that no member of the community should be denied access to an adequate level of health care. This commitment is especially important in the mission of public hospitals. Moreover, control of nonprofits will commonly rest with a board of trustees composed of members of the local community, rather than with a board of directors of a large national or multinational chain. This effect of nonprofits on the sense of community as shared by members of the community is somewhat intangible and difficult to measure. It is also certainly true that nonprofit hospitals are not the only institutions supporting this sense of community, or even the only means of supporting it within health care, and that for-profit hospitals can often contribute to it as well. Nevertheless, we believe the nonprofits are in general more likely than the for-profits to promote this significant value of community.

## FOR-PROFITS TREAT HEALTH CARE AS A COMMODITY TO BE BOUGHT AND SOLD IN THE MARKETPLACE RATHER THAN AS A RIGHT OF EVERY CITIZEN

This next collection of ethical concerns about the growth of for-profit health care is steeped in stirring rhetoric. We are told that "health care is not a commodity," that "health care ought not be left to the market," that "access to health care ought not depend on ability to pay," and that "everyone ought to have access to a single level of health care." And it is often said that the ethical acceptability of for-profit health care delivery systems depends on whether health care is properly viewed as a right or as a commodity.[8] In this section we attempt to sort out just what the implications of claims like these are for for-profit health care.

The slogan that health care is not a commodity is best understood as a normative, rather than a purely descriptive claim. As a descriptive claim, it is quite false: if a commodity is defined as something which has a market price or relative exchange value, then health care is a commodity since various treatments, tests, and services are assigned a market price in our society. (Until recently, of course, codes of professional ethics for physicians, backed up by the coercive power of legislation, have made it difficult for most consumers to learn the market price of most forms of health care; but this is a fact about the profession's success in restricting consumer information about health care, not a fact about the nature of health care.)

As a normative claim, the slogan that health care is not, that is, should not be treated as, a commodity implicitly depends on two sorts of assumptions: (1) empirical assumptions about what health care will be distributed to which persons if production and distribution of health care are carried out by for-profit institutions in a marketplace and (2) moral assumptions about what is a just distribution of health care, and what moral right, if any, there is to health care. With regard to the moral assumptions, we believe it is crucial to distinguish the claim that justice requires some level of access to health care for all from the claim that it requires equal access for all persons. We shall argue here that only the view that justice requires *equality* in access to health care, not merely that it implies a right to health care, is incompatible with for-profit provision of health care in a free marketplace.

If the goal is only to ensure that everyone is guaranteed access to some minimally adequate level of health care, why not leave its distribution to the market and so to for-profit institutions? The difficulties with doing so are well known and need not be rehearsed in de-

tail here. Generally, a market system for the distribution of health care, like a market distribution of all other goods and services, will be influenced by the initial natural endowments and wealth that people bring to the market, rather than simply by their need for health care. The market distribution of health care, as with other goods, will only be just if the distribution of initial assets, including income and wealth, is just.

However, there are specific characteristics of health care, and of health care markets, which further ensure that a market distribution of health care will fail to satisfy the demands of any theory of justice requiring that some minimally adequate level of access to health care be guaranteed to all. Health care needs are highly unpredictable for any particular individual, vary greatly between different individuals (unlike other basic needs for food or shelter), and in the context of modern health care are very expensive relative to most other goods and services. As a result, it is difficult if not impossible for any but the very richest to budget their health care expenditures.

The market solution to this situation, of course, is the development of a market in insurance, a device for *risk-sharing* that enables individuals to protect themselves from substantial unforeseen financial losses and to secure very expensive professional help in coping with disease or disability when it occurs. However, competition in the market for health care insurance will lead to differentiation of risk pools. Different insurance packages, with different premiums, will be developed for different groups of individuals with similar risks of sickness and disability with the result that those individuals who have the greatest risk of ill health—that is, those who need insurance the most—will find it prohibitively costly. Regulatory measures requiring community rating of insurance risks and unlimited access to insurance pools can be used to counter risk-pool differentiation, although a market proponent will view these as inefficient interferences in the operation of health care markets.

With either different risk pools or community rating, however, health care insurance will remain extremely expensive, and beyond the financial reach of substantial numbers of the poor in this country. This would be true even if access to health insurance were less closely tied to employment than it is in the United States today. Thus, even with health insurance the market will make access to even some minimally adequate level of health care depend upon ability to pay, an ability that many millions of Americans today lack (and would lack even under a system of perfectly competitive markets for the distribution of income).

On virtually any general theory of distributive justice, and in particular any theory of justice in health care other than a rather austere libertarian view, no one in a country as wealthy as ours ought to have to go without access to at least a minimally adequate level of health care. There is a general moral obligation of society to ensure that level of access for all, and we have argued that the obligation falls ultimately on the federal government. While general theories of rights are not well developed, nevertheless, we believe this obligation supports the claim that there is a moral right of all Americans to that level of health care. Market distribution systems employing for-profit health care delivery systems will fail to meet this obligation, or to secure the correlative right, and so will distribute health care in an unjust way.

To this extent, then, the rhetoric with which we began this section is correct: the distribution of health care ought not be left to the market and ought not depend on ability to pay. But this fact provides no reason for preferring for-profit health care to nonprofit health care, or for attempting to protect nonprofits or to stem the growth of for-profits. As noted earlier, until quite recently nonprofit institutions have dominated the health care system, but they did not solve the problem of access to care. The greatest extension of access to care to those who previously had virtually no access came from Medicare and Medicaid, not from the private insurance market working within a largely nonprofit system. Whether or not a predominantly nonprofit system, a predominantly for-profit system, or a more evenly mixed system will remedy the ethical deficiencies of a purely market distribution of health care will depend upon the specific arrangements for modifying the market distribution by subsidizing care for the worse off.

In a system in which virtually all health care institutions were of the for-profit form, the distributional inequities of the market might be avoided by the use of health insurance vouchers for the poor, financed by taxes, including taxes of health care institutions. Of course, if some health care markets are sufficiently noncompetitive so that supply problems still remain, for example in poor rural or inner-city ghetto areas, then supplementary, nonmarket direct provision programs such as the National Health Service Corps may be needed. The fundamental point, however, is that unjust gaps in access left by a market system of health care distribution require redistributive measures (probably by the government), whether the overall health care system is predominantly nonprofit or for-profit, and that redistributive means are available for either a nonprofit or for-profit system. So here, as with the charge that for-profits exacerbate the access problem, analysis of a criticism which at first appears to be directed only at for-profit health care leads us back to more fundamental issues of distributive justice—issues that would perhaps be just as urgent if for-profit health care had never appeared on the scene.

If acknowledgment of a right to health care is compatible with either a nonprofit or for-profit delivery system, both of which require redistributive measures to fund access for the poor, why is it so often thought that for-profits and markets are incompatible with that right? A principal explanation, we believe, is the confusion of a right of all persons to an *adequate* level of health care (the right we have appealed to above) with a right of all persons to the *same* level of health care. A right to an adequate level requires some minimal floor of health care access below which no one should be allowed to fall. That level does not, on the other hand, constitute a ceiling above which no one is permitted to rise, and so is compatible with individuals using their resources to purchase in the market more or better health care or health care insurance than the adequate level guarantees.

Without trying to specify what an "adequate level" would be, it also seems clear that it would be less than all medically beneficial care. A right to an adequate level of health care, then, is only minimally egalitarian in requiring an equal minimal level of access for all while

236 FOR-PROFIT ENTERPRISE IN HEALTH CARE

permitting departures from equality in an upward direction from that minimum. A right of all persons to the same level of health care, on the other hand, is strongly egalitarian in not permitting departures from equality in either a downward or upward direction from the level specified by the right. If that level is something less than all medically beneficial health care, as we believe it inevitably would have to be, such a right would have the effect of prohibiting anyone from using his or her resources to purchase more or better health care than is guaranteed to all.

This strong egalitarian position regarding health care distribution is incompatible with the unconstrained purchase and sale of health care in a market, *whether the seller is a for-profit or nonprofit institution.* Limited market price competition among providers offering only a single level of care to all would be possible, and so equality in health care does not foreclose all use of market competition, though it is likely that such competition would spread to quality and quantity of care, thereby undermining the single level of care for all. However, if markets for different amounts or quality of health care are allowed to exist alongside whatever system ensures the equal level to all, then any differences between persons in either income and wealth and/or preferences for health care as opposed to other goods and services will produce inequalities in the overall distribution of health care.

As several commentators have noted, the necessary prohibition of markets for health care to enforce this equality in health care, understood as requiring both a floor and ceiling, would have the effect of permitting persons to use their resources to purchase nonessential luxury goods like Mercedes Benz cars and Caribbean vacations while prohibiting their use for the basic and essential good of health care.[9] Without pursuing the matter further here, we believe this would require a stronger commitment to equality than is either plausible or widely accepted in American society, while at the same time conflicting with the freedom of individuals to decide for themselves how they will use their justly acquired resources.

There is another version of the concern that health care is a right whereas for-profits treat it as a commodity to be bought and sold in the marketplace. The important distinction here is between health care *needs* and market-expressed *wants* or preferences for health care. For-profits, it is argued, will respond to consumer wants for health care even if they are for frivolous amenities such as champagne breakfasts for obstetric patients and however unrelated they may be to the patient's true health care needs. The right to health care, on the other hand, is to some level of health care adequate to meet the patient's objectively determined, basic health care needs. There are two versions of this concern with a health care system that responds to wants rather than needs that should be distinguished.

The first rejects the identification of patients' well-being or just claims to health care with the satisfaction of even their *fully informed* preferences or wants. This view depends implicitly on some objective account of human well-being that does not ultimately reduce to the satisfaction of fully informed wants, or on an account of individuals' just claims to health care that depends on some objective features or ranking of health care (for example, its effects on a person's range of opportunity as in Norman Daniels'[10] theory of justice in health care). To evaluate this version of the concern would require us to evaluate the underlying objective theories of human well-being or the nonpreference-based theories of justice in health care. Most of these theories are not sufficiently well developed to permit their evaluation, and that task is in any case beyond the scope of this paper.

The second version of the concern about a health care system that responds to wants rather than needs is the more common one. It is that the actual expressed wants for health care of real patients in real conditions often deviate sharply from both their objective health care needs and what their fully informed preferences for health care would be.

As we have noted above and will discuss further, health care consumers are commonly in a poor position to evaluate for themselves their own need for health care. They lack information about the nature of their medical condition and of what alternative treatments might positively affect it in what ways. Moreover, in circumstances of serious illness, patients are often anxious, fearful, confused, and dependent in ways that further impair their capacities to assess for themselves their health care needs in an informed and rational fashion. Thus, their actual health care wants will often be both ill-informed and unusually vulnerable to influence and manipulation by health care professionals. It is these fundamental features of the setting in which decisions are made to utilize health care that support the importance both of the physician's commitment to act in the patient's best interests and of the patient's trust that the physician will do so.

One concern about the growth of for-profits is that they may contribute to strengthening physicians' motivations to act in their own economic interests and thereby weaken their commitment to their patients' well-being; we pursue this possible adverse impact on the physician/patient relationship later in this paper. The other potential effect of health care coming increasingly to be viewed as a commodity to be aggressively marketed is that physicians will cater to ill-informed patient wants at the expense of their true health needs or take advantage of patients' vulnerable positions to manipulate their wants. In either case, the result will be the delivery of health care that fails best to meet patients' true health needs. We believe this is a reasonable worry that warrants careful future monitoring, although the data do not yet exist to show to what extent, if any, the phenomenon has begun to occur.

However, not all increased responsiveness to consumer wants constitutes a shift from serving patients' health needs to serving their mere wants. Increased responsiveness to consumer wants makes a genuine contribution to patient well-being to the extent that which treatment, if any, best promotes a patient's well-being depends at least in part on the particular aims and values of that patient. If for-profits promote this form of responsiveness to patients they are to be commended, not condemned.

## FOR-PROFITS DAMAGE THE PHYSICIAN/PATIENT RELATIONSHIP, ERODE TRUST, CREATE NEW CONFLICTS OF INTEREST, AND DIMINISH QUALITY OF CARE

It is undeniable that for-profit health care involves potential conflicts between the interests of providers (physicians, managers, administrators, and stockholders) and those of patients. In the most general terms, the conflict is simply this: an institution with a strong if not an overriding commitment to maximizing profit may sometimes find that the best way to do this is not to act in its patients' best interests.

This fundamental potential conflict of interest is said to be of special concern in health care, not only because health care interests are so important, but also because the "consumer" of health care, unlike the consumer of most other goods and services provided by profit-seeking firms, is in an especially vulnerable position for two reasons. First, he will often lack the special knowledge and expertise needed for judging whether a particular health service is necessary or would be beneficial, whether it is being rendered in an appropriate way, and even in some cases whether it has been successful. Second, because illness or injury can result in anxiety and loss of self-confidence, the patient may find it difficult to engage in the sort of self-protective bargaining behavior expressed in the admonition "caveat emptor."

Whether this conflict of interest will damage the physician/patient relationship will depend on the extent that it also exists outside for-profit settings. And it is quite clear that this fundamental potential for conflict of interest is not peculiar to for-profit health care. A health care institution may exhibit a strong commitment to maximizing profit, and this commitment may result in practices that are not in patients' best interests, even if the institution is of nonprofit form. When we ask whether an institution's or an individual's pursuit of profits is prejudicial to the patient's interests, the appropriate sense of the phrase "pursuit of profits" is quite broad, not the narrower legal sense in which nonprofit institutions do not by definition pursue profits. After all, the issue is whether the opportunities for attaining *benefits* for themselves provide incentives that influence behavior on the part of providers that is not in patients' best interest. Whatever form these incentives take and whatever kinds of benefits are pursued, they may all run counter to the patient's interests.

In any form of medical practice operating under a fee-for-service system, under any system of prepayment (as in health maintenance organizations [HMOs]), and under any system of capitation, where physicians are paid a salary determined by the number of patients they treat (as in independent practice associations [IPAs]), a basic conflict of interest will exist, regardless of whether the organization is for-profit or nonprofit. In a fee-for-service system, the conflict is obvious: physicians have an incentive to overutilize services because their financial return will thereby be increased. The incentive for overutilization of services can conflict with the patient's interest in three distinct ways: it can lead physicians to (1) provide services whose *medical costs* to the patient outweigh their *medical benefits* (as in the case of surgery or X-rays that actually do more medical harm than good), (2) impose financial costs on the patient that exceed the medical benefits provided (greater out-of-pocket expenses for the patient), and (3) contribute to higher health care costs (including higher insurance premiums) for everyone.

In prepayment or capitation systems, providers are subject to conflicts of interest because of incentives to underutilize care. In HMOs, providers have an incentive to limit care because the overall financial well-being of the organization requires it and because salary increases and year-end bonuses as well as new personnel, new equipment, and new services are all financed by these savings. In IPAs and other organizations that operate on a capitation system, conflicts of interest due to the incentive for underutilization are equally clear: spending less time and using fewer scarce resources enable physicians to handle a larger number of patients, and this results in a larger salary. Whether, or to what extent, these incentives actually result in reduced quality of care is an extremely difficult question. But what is clear is that they create conflicts of interest, in both for-profit and nonprofit settings.

Some analysts have recognized that the preceding sorts of conflicts of interest are unavoidable because they result from two features that will be found in any form of health care institution or organization: (1) the patient's special vulnerability and (2) the need to provide some form of incentive for providers that is related in some fashion to the amount and kind of services they provide. They have then gone on to argue that what makes conflicts of interest especially serious in for-profits is that for-profits provide physicians with opportunities for *secondary income*. This secondary income may come either from charges for services, which they themselves do not provide but which they recommend or which are provided by others under their supervision, or from being a shareholder in the for-profit health care corporation.

Secondary income, however, and the conflict of interest it involves, is also neither a new phenomenon in health care nor peculiar to for-profits. Several forms of "fee splitting" are practiced by physicians working in nonprofit settings. One of the most common is an arrangement whereby a physician receives a percentage of the fee charged for X-rays, laboratory tests, other diagnostic procedures, physical therapy, or drug or alcohol counseling that he recommends but which are performed by people he employs or supervises. In some cases, licensing and certification laws and reimbursement eligibility requirements for Medicare, Medicaid, and private insurance require nonphysician health care professionals to be supervised by a physician, thus creating a dependence which makes it possible for physicians to reap this secondary income. Physicians may also charge fees for interpreting diagnostic tests, such as electrocardiograms, that they recommend and which are performed by others even if they do not split the fee for the procedure itself.

It may still be the case that the opportunities for secondary income and other conflicts of interest tend to be *greater* in most for-profit institutions than in most nonprofit institutions. At present, however, neither the extent of these differences, nor, more importantly, the extent to which they are taken advantage of in ways that reduce quality of care, increase costs, or otherwise compromise patients' interests is documented. It may also be the case that even though serious conflicts of interest, from secondary income and other sources, already exist in nonprofit health care, the continued growth of for-profits, both in their own activities and the influence they have on the behavior of nonprofits, will result in a significant worsening of the problem. Our current lack of data, however, makes it premature to predict that this will happen or when it will happen.

There is another form of the charge that for-profit health care creates new conflicts of interest or exacerbates old ones. Some fear that even if the physician's behavior toward patients is not distorted by incentives for secondary income or by equity ownership, physicians in for-profits will be subject to greater control by management and that this control will make it more difficult for physicians to serve the patient's interests rather than the corporation's. There can be little doubt that American physicians are increasingly subject to control by others, especially by managers and administrators, many of whom are not physicians.

There are two major factors that have led to this loss of "professional dominance" which are quite independent of the growth of for-profits.[11] One is the institutionalization of medicine which itself arose from a variety of factors, including the proliferation of technologies and specializations which call for large-scale social cooperation and cannot be rendered efficiently, if they can be rendered at all, by independent practitioners. The other is the increased pressure for cost containment in a more competitive environment, which has led to a greater reliance on professional management techniques within health care institutions and more extensive regulatory controls by government. At most, the growth of for-profits may be accelerating the loss of professional dominance.

It should not simply be assumed, however, that diminished physician control will result in an overall lowering of the quality of care or a worsening of the problem of conflict of interests. Whether it will depends upon the answer to three difficult questions. To what extent will management or shareholders of for-profits exercise their control over physicians in the pursuit of profit and at the expense of patient interests or will their pursuit of profit be restrained by ethical considerations? To what extent will management and stockholders act on the belief that, in the long run, profits will be maximized by serving patients' interests? To what extent have physicians, in the physician-dominated system that has existed up until recently, actually acted in the best interests of their patients? The answers to the first two questions await data not yet available.

The third question is especially difficult to answer because of an ambiguity in the notion of the "patient's best interests." In a fee-for-service, third-party payment system in which physicians exercise a great deal of control in ordering treatments and procedures, a physician who makes decisions according to what is in the individual patient's best medical interests will tend to order any treatment or test whose expected net medical benefit is greater than zero, no matter how small the net benefit may be. Under such a system, the traditional ethical principles of the medical profession, which require the physician to do what is best for the patient (or to minimize harm to him), and the principle of self-interest speak with one voice, at least so long as the patient's interests are restricted to his medical interests. Indeed, even if the physician considers the patient's overall interests—financial as well as medical—so long as a third party is picking up the major portion of the bill, the physician may still conclude that acting in the patient's best interest requires doing anything that can be expected to yield a nonzero net medical benefit. Yet, as has often been noted, the cumulative result of large numbers of such decisions, each of which may be in the best interest of the particular patient, is that health care is overutilized and a cost crisis results.

"Overutilization" here does not mean the use of medically unnecessary care, i.e., care having no net medical benefit or which is positively harmful; instead what is meant is what one author has called "noncostworthy care"— care which yields less benefit than some alternative use to which the same resources could be put, either for other health care services or for nonhealth care goods.[12] Overutilization of health care in this sense, not just overutilization as nonbeneficial care, is clearly contrary to everyone's interest. If continued professional dominance means perpetuation of this problem of overutilization, then even if a continued loss of professional dominance will lead to medical decisions that are not, considered in isolation, in the individual patient's best interest, it may result in the elimination of one important conflict of interest and collective irrationality in the current system.

This does not rule out the possibility, of course, that greater control by nonphysicians will also lead to overutilization. If this occurs, then one system which works against everyone's best interest will merely have been replaced by another that does the same thing.

We have seen that in the fee-for-service, third-party payment system in nonprofit as well as for-profit settings the cumulative result of many physicians acting on the desire to do what is best for the individual patient can result in overutilization that is contrary to all patients' best interest. Some critics of for-profits suggest that we must either pay the price of this overutilization or cope with it by methods that do not undermine physicians' commitments to doing what is best for their individual patients. They then conclude that even if it could be shown that the growth of for-profits would restrain overutilization by introducing greater price competition into health care, the price would be too high to pay because the physician's all-important commitment to do his best for each patient would eventually be eroded by the increasing "commercialization" of health care that is being accelerated if not caused by the growth of for-profits.

The force of this objection to for-profits depends, of course, not only upon the correctness of the prediction that the growth of for-profits will in fact contribute to a weakening of the physician's commitment to do the best he can for each patient; it also depends upon the assumption that under the current system that commitment has been a dominant force in physician behavior. This last point may be cast in a slightly different way. How concerned we should be about the tendency for the behavior of physicians to become more like that of businessmen depends upon how great the difference in behavior of the two groups is and has been. If one assumes that as a group physicians have been significantly more altruistic

than businessmen and if one also assumes that altruism is the only effective safeguard against exploitation of the patient's special vulnerability, then one will oppose any development, including the growth of for-profit health care, which can be expected to make physicians more like businessmen.

Those who make the first assumption tend to overlook two points which call it into question. First, our society does in fact expect, and in some cases enforces by the power of the law, significant restrictions on the pursuit of profit by "mere businessmen." In fact, it can be argued that the moral obligations of businessmen to their customers are not significantly less demanding than those of physicians toward their patients *when equally important interests are at stake*. Robert Veatch has observed that if a physician becomes aware that another physician is acting on misinformation or performing a procedure incorrectly, then the first physician is under an obligation to bring this to the attention of the second and perhaps to help him remedy the defect.[13]

Veatch then goes on to say that a businessman who learns that a competitor is acting on misinformation or using sloppy production techniques is under no obligation to point this out to the competitor. Veatch's contrast between the moral obligations of physicians and businessmen, however, is overdrawn if not outright mistaken. It is not clear that a physician has a moral obligation to inform another physician that he is misinformed or even that his technique is deficient unless significant patient interests are at stake. It may be true, however, that important interests are more frequently potentially at stake in health care than in ordinary business transactions.

Yet surely a businessman has a moral obligation to inform a competitor that he is unwittingly endangering people's lives even if in giving his competitor this information he prevents his competitor from ruining himself and, thereby, foregoes a chance to eliminate the competition. Moreover, if a businessman lies to or defrauds a customer, we conclude not only that he has done something illegal but that he has acted immorally. And even if he breaks no law, we may nonetheless condemn him morally as a cheat and a scoundrel. All of this is simply to emphasize a simple point that critics of the "commercialization" of health care sometimes overlook, namely, that we customarily do apply not only legal but also moral standards to the behavior of businessmen. One would not want a physician who was motivated exclusively by financial reward, but then one wouldn't want an electrician who was either. Nevertheless, even if there is a tendency to overstate the contrast between ethical and legal constraints on business transactions and the physician/patient relationship, we typically do expect a somewhat higher standard of conduct from physicians.

Many outside the medical profession and some within it greet the claim that physicians as a class are especially altruistic with some skepticism. This attitude is not groundless. One of the difficulties of determining the strength of altruistic motivation among physicians is that until very recently, the fee-for-service, third-party payment system has produced a situation in which altruism and self-interest converge: doing what is best for the patient (pursuing all treatment that promises nonzero benefits) was often doing what was financially best for the physician. Nevertheless, critics of the thesis that physicians are especially altruistic can marshall a good deal of evidence to support their view, such as the profession's historical opposition to HMOs and to Medicare and Medicaid, each of which promised significant extensions of access to health care,[14] its failure to overcome the chronic geographical maldistribution of physicians in this country, and its support of strict entry controls to the profession through medical licensure together with relatively weak oversight of the continuing competence of those already licensed. We can make no attempt to evaluate such evidence here, but the self-interest of the profession seems a better prima facie explanation of it than does an altruistic concern for the health of the ill. It is important to emphasize that explanations of these phenomena need not assume that self-interest here is exclusively or even primarily *financial* self-interest. The profession's resistance to Medicare, for example, was probably more an attempt to preserve physician *autonomy*.

In assessing these questions of conflict of interest, we think it is helpful to distinguish the behavior of physicians acting as an organized profession addressing matters of health policy from the behavior of individual physicians toward individual patients. As we have noted above, much behavior of medicine as an organized profession (as reflected for example in the political role the American Medical Association (AMA) has played in seeking to maintain physician dominance in the health care profession) to protect and enhance physician incomes, and so forth, has served the self-interest of physicians. Controversial is the extent to which the self-interested function of the motivation for supporting such practices as medical licensure is manifest or latent, explicit or implicit. In considering the conduct of professional trade associations such as the AMA, we believe that forwarding the economic and other interests of the members of the profession is often the explicit and conscious intent of the representatives of the profession. To the extent that the profession has been successful in forwarding its members' interests, we would expect to find an institutional, organizational, and legal structure shaping the practice of medicine that serves the economic and other interests of members of the profession. Moreover, it would be hard to look back over the evolution in this century of the position and structure of the medical profession without concluding that the profession has had considerable success in promoting its interests.

It would be completely implausible to attribute a high level of altruism to the medical profession if that was interpreted to mean a high level of economic self-sacrifice in favor of the public's health needs. The exceptionally high levels of physician incomes would belie that. Nor is it plausible to claim that the organized profession has led efforts to address some of the most serious moral deficiencies in our health care system, such as the continued lack of access to health care of large numbers of the poor.

As we noted above, the history of the profession's opposition to national health insurance and to Medicare and Medicaid belies any such role of altruism or moral leadership. Nor finally have many members of the profession acting as individuals been remarkably self-sacrificing or acted as moral leaders in addressing these problems. Occasionally physicians have, of course, located in undesirable geographical areas to meet pressing health care needs or have provided substantial unpaid care to the poor, but such behavior has not been sufficiently widespread to have a major impact on these problems.

Despite the extent that the profession has forwarded its members' interests and that individual members have not been self-sacrificing in addressing the most serious deficiencies in the health care system, we believe it would be a serious mistake to conclude that the patient-centered ethic that has defined the traditional physician/patient relationship is mere sham and rhetoric, a thin guise overlaying the physician's self-interest.

An alternative, and we believe more plausible, perspective is that in part just because the medical profession has been exceptionally successful in promoting and protecting an institutional and organizational setting that well serves physicians' economic and other interests, individual physicians have thereby been freed to follow the traditional patient-centered ethic in their relations with their individual patients. Put oversimply, a physician whose overall practice structure assures him a high income need not weigh economic benefits to himself when considering treatment recommendations for his individual patients. As we have argued above, conflicts of interest between physicians and patients have long existed and are hardly a heretofore unknown consequence of for-profit health care institutions. As one commentator has argued, much of medicine can be viewed as a conflict for the physician between self-interest and altruism, requiring a balancing of these sometimes conflicting motivations.[15]

What we are suggesting is that the self-interested organized professional behavior and institutional structure of medicine may have helped protect the possibility of altruistic behavior on the part of the physician when guiding treatment with his individual patients. (This hypothesis, of course, requires careful qualification. In some cases the self-interested behavior of organized medicine has clearly had a negative impact on patient interests. For example, licensure and other forms of self-regulation by the profession have often failed to protect patients from chemically dependent or otherwise incompetent physicians and have

exacerbated the problem of access by inhibiting the development of less expensive forms of care utilizing nonphysician providers such as midwives and nurse practitioners.)

One virtue of this more complex perspective is that it allows us to accommodate the elements of truth that exist in each of two otherwise seemingly incompatible perspectives, each of which taken only by itself appears extreme and incomplete. One perspective views the physician simply as an economically self-interested businessman in his dealings with patients. Those who support this perspective can point to the various ways in which the actions of the medical profession and the institutional and financing structure in which medicine is practiced serve the interests of physicians, as we have done above, but they often end up denying any significant reality to the physician's commitment to promoting his patients' best interests. On the other hand, many defenders of physicians viewed as devoted professionals committed to the well-being of their patients seem also to feel it necessary to deny the extent to which medical practices and institutional structures serve physicians' interests.

Either perspective is by itself stubbornly one-sided in its view of physicians simply as self-interested economic accumulators or as devoted altruists. We favor a view which recognizes that these two perspectives are *not* incompatible and accepts the elements of truth in each of them.

One advantage of this more balanced perspective is that it permits the recognition of the reality and importance of the traditional patient-centered ethic, without denying the conflicts of interest between physician and patient that we have discussed above or the important historical role played by economic interests of physicians. A perspective that encompasses a balance between self-interested and altruistic motivations on the part of physicians can help articulate the concern of many observers that the rise of for-profit medicine while *not* representing an entirely new phenomenon nevertheless *does* pose a danger to the traditional physician/patient relationship by shifting the traditional *balance* between self-interested and altruistic motivations because it tends to bring motivations of economic self-interest more directly and substantially into the physician's relations with individual patients.

What, more specifically, is the worry about the erosion of the physician/patient relationship by the rise of for-profit health care institutions? We think that worry can be most pointedly brought out by initially overstating the possible effect. The traditional account of the patient-centered ethic makes the physician the agent of the patient, whose "highest commitment is the patient."[16] The physician is to seek to determine together with the patient that course of treatment which will best promote the patient's well-being, setting aside effects on others, including effects on the physician, the patient's family, or society.

This commitment to the patient's well-being responds to the various respects discussed above in which patients are in a very poor position to determine for themselves what health care, if any, they need. Because the patient is unusually dependent on the physician, it is especially important to the success of their partnership in the service of the patient's well-being that the patient believe that the physician will be guided in his recommendations solely by the patient's best interests. Patients have compelling reasons to want the physician/patient relationship to be one in which this trust is warranted, quite apart from the putative therapeutic benefits of such trust.

Suppose the rise of for-profit health care so eroded this traditional relationship, and in its place substituted a commercial relationship, that patients came to view their physicians as they commonly now view used car salesmen. We emphasize that such a radical shift in view is not to be expected. We use this "worst-case" example of a caveat emptor commercial relationship only because it focuses most pointedly the worry about the effect on the physician/patient relationship of the commercialization of health care. Many factors will inhibit such a shift from actually taking place in patients' views of their physicians, including traditional codes of ethics in medicine, requirements of informed consent, fiduciary obligations of physicians, as well as powerful traditions of professionalism in medicine. Recognizing that the stereotype of the used car salesman substantially overstates what there is any reason to

expect in medicine, nevertheless what would a shift in this direction do to the physician/patient relationship?

Most obviously and perhaps also most importantly, it would undermine the trust that many patients are prepared to place in their physicians' commitment to seek their (the patients') best interests. In general, there is no such trust of a used car salesman, but rather his claims and advice are commonly greeted with a cool skepticism. He is viewed as pursuing his own economic interests, with no commitment to the customer's welfare. It is the rare (and probably in the end sorry) consumer who places himself in the hands of the car salesman. Anything like the fiduciary relationship in which a patient trusts the physician's commitment first to the patient's interest is quite absent with the used car salesman.

This is not to say that some additional consumer skepticism of physician recommendations and increased attempts by patients to become knowledgeable health care consumers would not be a good thing—they would. It is rather to say that many of the various inequalities in the physician/patient relationship are sufficiently deep and difficult to eradicate that some substantial trust of the physician's commitment to the patient is likely to remain necessary and valuable. The commercial model of arms-length, caveat emptor bargaining is not promising for the physician/patient relation.

While there has been deception of patients by physicians, it seems to have markedly decreased in recent decades, and in the past this deception in medicine was justified as for the patient's own good (even if in fact it often was not). However, one does not expect the truth, the whole truth, and nothing but the truth from a used car salesman, nor that shadings of the truth are done for the customer's own good. We expect some concealment and distortion of information in order to make the sale, although this is not to say that some outright deception in commerce may not be fraudulent and immoral. It is also commonly believed that businessmen are in business to sell as much of their product as possible, however much the consumer may not "need" the expensive car being pushed by the salesman, whereas physicians are expected not to encourage needless consumption. Businessmen respond to consumer wants, not needs, and will do their best to manufacture such wants where they do not already exist.

A shift towards commercialization of health care could be expected to result in increasing emphasis on marketing strategies to secure an increasing segment of the market. Moreover, we expect no unprofitable products or service from a car salesman in response to consumer need. We have argued that the moral obligation to ensure access to health care for the poor is ultimately the government's, not an individual physician's or hospital's by way of cross-subsidization. Nevertheless, in the face of unmet need, physicians and health care institutions often do, and are often expected to, respond to that need by furnishing the needed care. Other norms important to the practice of medicine have a weakened or nonexistent place in most commercial transactions, such as the requirement of confidentiality concerning information about the patient.

One must be careful not to overstate the contrast between medicine and commerce— we have already seen it is certainly not the case that commerce takes place in the absence of any ethical constraints (or legal constraints, reflecting ethical norms) or that the medical profession is never moved by self-interest. However, we believe there is a genuine and important difference in the ethos of the two enterprises that plays out in important differences in the physician/patient and businessman/consumer transaction. Oversimplifying, it is commonly believed that in business transactions individuals pursuing their own interests, though admittedly within some ethical and legal constraints, will best promote the overall social good. It is this view of the motivation of self-interest as ethically acceptable that quite reasonably worries many as medicine becomes increasingly commercialized. Since physicians are, of course, human like the rest of us and naturally concerned with their own interests, it is reasonable to view their primary commitment to the patient's well-being as inevitably fragile and always in danger of being undermined. In that light, it is unnecessary to view for-profit institutions as introducing a qualitatively new dimension of commercialization and new set of conflicts of interest into health care. As we have argued,

such a view is indefensible. Nor need it be expected that physicians' concern with their patient's well-being will just disappear as soon as they go on the payroll of a for-profit hospital or, more likely, establish other types of contractual relations with it. That view too would be indefensible, indeed downright silly.

The realistic worry, concerning which the data are not yet in, is rather that over time the increased importance of investor-owned for-profit institutions may permit considerations of economic self-interest increasingly to invade the heretofore somewhat protected sphere of the physician/patient relationship, and thereby weaken the patient-centered ethic on which that relationship has traditionally depended. The difference would only be one of degree, but no less important for that. As we have noted above, there are other independent factors putting similar pressures on that relationship such as the expected oversupply of physicians. It would be a mistake to think that these possible adverse effects on the physician/patient relationship are uniquely due to the rise of for-profits. However, that is not a reason to be unconcerned with these effects of for-profits, but only a reason not to focus one's concerns solely on for-profits.

We emphasize that the traditional patient-centered ethic need not be incompatible with greater attention to costs in health care utilization decisions and practices. Utilization of health care should reflect the financial costs as well as benefits of care, but that will not be appropriately achieved by, nor need it inevitably lead to, physicians making utilization decisions solely according to their own economic self-interest. Whatever the right mix of incentives for reasonably limiting health care utilization and costs, simply making physicians fully subject to incentives of economic self-interest by breaking down the patient-centered ethic seems not the path to that mix. A physician weighing the true financial costs of care against its medical benefits *to the patient* is entirely different from one who simply weighs the economic consequences *to himself* of the patient utilizing care.

The most obvious worry, then, is that the increasing prominence of for-profits may contribute to a shift in physicians' patient-oriented behavior, which may in turn affect the patient trust important to a well-functioning physician/patient relationship. The test of that hypothesis would then be the extent to which physician behavior is actually different within for-profit settings. But it is important to realize that patient trust may be eroded, and so the physician/patient relationship adversely affected, even in the absence of any actual shift toward more self-interested behavior by physicians. Even if outward behavior does not change, a change in the motivations of the behavior, and in turn of perceptions by others of those motivations, may be important. If physicians are increasingly perceived by patients as motivated by self-interest rather than by a commitment to serving their patient, then even in the absence of a change in physicians' behavior, it is reasonable to expect an erosion in patient *trust* that physicians will act for their patients' best interests. Part of what is important to patients in health care is the reassurance that the professional *cares* about them and their plight. (This is one respect in which other health care professionals, for example nurses, are often more important than physicians in patient care.) A change in a physician's motivations, or even in the patient's perceptions of those motivations, may be enough to affect the patient's belief about whether the physician "really cares" about him. This point should give pause to those who propose to test the effects of for-profits on the physician/patient relationship and on patient trust by looking only at changes in physician behavior.

## FOR-PROFITS UNDERMINE MEDICAL EDUCATION

The charge that for-profits undermine medical education parallels the claim examined previously that for-profits exacerbate the problem of access to care. Medical education, like care for indigents, is in part funded through cross-subsidization, and for-profits are believed to be contributing to the demise of cross-subsidization. It is thought that not only will for-profits themselves refrain from providing medical education because to do so would not be profitable for them, but also that they will make it increasingly difficult for nonprofit institutions such as university hospitals to carry

on medical education and still remain competitive.

Much of what was said regarding cross-subsidization of indigent care applies here as well. Even if the growth of for-profits is contributing to the crisis in funding for medical education it is difficult to estimate the magnitude of its contribution, and it is clear that other factors are at work as well. Faced with growing pressures for cost containment, nonprofit institutions would presumably have strong incentives to reduce all "unprofitable" activities, including medical education, even in the absence of competition from for-profits. And here, as in the case of cross-subsidization for indigent care, whether one laments these developments or welcomes them will depend upon one's views on the efficiency and ethical acceptability of a system which in effect disguised the true costs of medical education and upon whether one thinks that the political process is likely to produce a workable alternative system for funding medical education through explicit public policy choices.

Furthermore, before a convincing answer can be given to the question of what obligations institutions or individuals have to help support medical education, several basic ethical issues must be resolved which the cross-subsidization system has effectively kept out of the public view. Perhaps most importantly, to what extent should medical education be subsidized by public resources?

To the extent that physicians benefit from the skills which they sell at their full market value there is a presumptive case for making them bear the costs of their own training. However, there are several countervailing considerations which may overcome this presumption. First, it can be argued that if medical education is publicly subsidized we will all benefit from a higher level of skills than would be possible under a system in which individuals had to bear the full costs of their training. Second, public subsidization makes it possible for persons from lower socioeconomic groups to become physicians and this is desirable, not only because it promotes equality of opportunity, but also because there is some reason to believe that physicians from the same socioeconomic background as their patients may be better able to communicate with those patients and to serve them effectively.

Third, it may also be that a strong system of medical education, like medical research, has some of the features of a public good. Medical education does not simply build economic assets for physicians. At both the graduate and post-graduate levels it also sets, transmits, and improves standards and methods of sound medical practice. Because the average patient is in a poor position to evaluate for him- or herself the quality of care provided by a particular physician, all patients benefit from a high-quality system of medical education that provides some assurance of the high quality of training and skills of the physicians produced by that system. If public subsidization of medical education facilitates training geared more toward the quality of patient care and less toward the economic value to physicians of the skills produced, that may be of benefit to patients, that is, the public.

While it would be unjustified to maintain that the growth of for-profits is a major source of the reported crisis in funding for medical education, it can perhaps be said that for-profits are one element in a complex array of changes which will test the strength of the public commitment to medical education and challenge the moral assumptions on which that commitment is based.

## FOR-PROFITS AND THE POLITICAL POWER OF THE MEDICAL-INDUSTRIAL COMPLEX

The widespread view that the medical profession's dominance in the U.S. health care system is waning has already been noted. One important aspect of the weakening of professional dominance is said to be the decreasing effectiveness of organized medicine's lobbying efforts in recent years. Whether or not one greets this development with enthusiasm or regret will depend, of course, upon the extent to which one believes that these efforts to influence public policy have promoted or impeded the public interest. However, both the supporters and the critics of professional dominance have voiced a concern that it may be replaced by the dominance of a few extremely wealthy—and politically powerful—giant health

care corporations forming a medical-industrial complex.[17] The fear is that a handful of the largest corporations might "capture" the regulators, molding public policy to their own needs through lobbying, campaign contributions, and use of the media to sway the electorate.

The real concern here should be the political effects of highly concentrated *corporate* power in health care—not simply the power of *for-profit* health care corporations. While it is true that the hospital "industry" is becoming increasingly concentrated, it is important to point out that some of the largest hospital chains are owned or operated by large nonprofit corporations. Further, there is nothing to prevent large nonprofit corporations from using their wealth and power to influence public policy and little reason to believe that they will in general be less willing to do so than large for-profit corporations. At present, however, it is difficult to predict how concentrated the health care sector will become or to what extent the disparate interest groups within and across health care institutions can be welded together under corporate leadership to function as a unified influence on public policy.

The issue, then, is whether it may become necessary in the future to utilize regulation or some other form of societal control to neutralize or minimize the political effects of the economic power wielded by large health care corporations, whether nonprofit or for-profit. Some possible, even if not politically likely, controls include limitations on campaign contributions and on political advertisements in the media, special laws designed to disqualify legislators or regulators with conflicts of interest, or limitations on the maximum size of corporations.

It has often been remarked that it is a hallmark of a profession to be self-regulating. In the case of the medical profession, the idea that the physician/patient relationship is fiduciary along with the belief that medicine is a service for healing and comfort rather than simply one commercial enterprise among others have buttressed the profession's claim that it can be trusted to regulate itself.

Until recently it was widely assumed not only that the medical profession should regulate itself, but that it should also be chiefly responsible for regulating health care in general. This position rested on three main premises: (1) physicians and only physicians have the technical training and knowledge needed for informed control of their own professional activities, (2) physicians' professional activities are largely autonomous from other activities in health care, (3) the activities of other health care professionals are almost exclusively dependent upon physicians' decision making. The recognition that some of the most perplexing decisions concerning the use of medical treatments require complex moral, social, and legal judgments has undermined the first premise. (Decisions to forgo life-sustaining treatments for terminally ill or comatose patients are only the most obvious cases where medical judgment is not sufficient for guiding the physicians' own professional activities. These decisions require moral judgments because they rest on assumptions about the nature of individuals' rights and the quality and value of life.) The second and third premises also become dubious once it is seen that physicians' professional activities are increasingly dependent, not only upon decisions of other types of health care professionals (such as biomedical engineers and laboratory and radiology technicians) who sometimes possess specialized knowledge which physicians lack, but also upon a complex web of institutional functions, including planning, investment, and allocation of resources.

Some of the same reasons that make it implausible to leave regulation of health care to physicians make it equally implausible to entrust it to corporations or groups of corporations. In particular, the vast commitment of public resources to health care grounds a legitimate public concern that the resources be used efficiently and fairly, and the growing list of ethical dilemmas concerning the uses of medical technology is no more amenable to the administrative expertise of the corporate manager than to the professional judgment of the physician. There is, however, one reason why the public is perhaps even less likely to tolerate self-regulation by health care corporations than by the medical profession. If health care is perceived to be controlled by corporations—whether for-profit or nonprofit—that are in many respects indistinguishable from other commercial enterprises, then the presumption in favor of self-regulation, which flourished under professional dominance, will erode. For if the key decision makers in health care are perceived to be businessmen rather than fiduciaries committed to healing and comfort, an important barrier to societal regulation of all forms of health care will have fallen. Whether new forms of regulation will be needed to constrain the political influence of large health care corporations can only be determined after careful study not only of the impact that these organizations have on public policy, but also of the expected effectiveness of proposed regulations.

## CONCLUSION

Any summary conclusion of our examination of the ethical issues in for-profit health care will inevitably oversimplify. The one continuing theme running through our analysis of the moral objections commonly voiced against for-profits is that those objections need to be both framed and evaluated more carefully than they usually are. In many instances these objections also rest on empirical claims for which the data are not yet available.

We have been generally critical of the argument that for-profits fail to do their fair share in providing health care to poor or unprofitable patients. That argument assumes that for-profits have special obligations to care for these patients, that a determinate content can now be given to that obligation, and that the obligation can be discharged without unreasonable sacrifice on the part of the for-profit. These assumptions are problematic. It is a mistake to focus on how for-profits exacerbate or ameliorate access. The debate could more profitably concentrate on the need for a coordinated societal response to the serious injustices in access to health care that now exist.

We have also been skeptical of the claim that for-profits represent unfair competition for nonprofits, though for-profits may have possible adverse effects on charitable motivations and a sense of community. We have again been critical of a common objection to for-profits, that they wrongly treat health care as a commodity rather than a right. It is only the view that all persons should have one *sin-*

*gle* level of health care, not the recognition of a right to an adequate level of health care, that is incompatible with market provision of health care by for-profit institutions.

The arguments in each of the first three sections of the paper ultimately raise deeper issues of great importance about the just distribution of health care that go beyond the for-profit/nonprofit debate. We have argued that potential adverse effects on medical education, like those on access, may indeed be worrisome, but the data on them are at this point very limited and they probably arise more from other forces such as cost containment efforts than from for-profits. Similarly, although the possibility that a small number of large health care corporations may come to wield disproportionate influence on public policy is a serious matter for concern and vigilance, it would be a mistake to assume that the potential for political abuse of economic power exists only with for-profit corporations, rather than with large institutions generally.

We believe that perhaps the most serious ethical concern with the growth of for-profits is their potential adverse effects on the physician/patient relationship and on the quality of care. Here too, potential conflicts of interest between patient and provider are not new. Indeed, they are fundamental to the physician/patient relationship in either for-profit or nonprofit settings. Moreover, other powerful forces besides the growth of for-profits, in particular cost containment efforts and increased competition, are impinging on the physician/patient relationship. But the importance of the patient's trust in his physician, and the fragile balance between the physician's commitment to serve the patient and his natural concern with his own interests, give reason for serious continuing attention to this potential effect of for-profits.

## NOTES

[1] While the number of investor-owned, as opposed to independent for-profit hospitals has risen, hospital ownership, classified by broad categories—federal, state, and local government, nonprofit and for-profit—has changed little in the past decade. Gray, B. H. (1984) Overview: origins and trends. Keynote address, Annual Health Conference, The New Entrepeneurialism in Health Care, held by the Committee on Medicine in Society of the New York Academy of Medicine, *Bulletin of The New York Academy of Medicine*, second series, Vol. 61, No. 1, pp. 7-22.

[2] *Securing Access to Health Care* (1983) Report of the President's Commission for the Study of Ethical Problems in Medicine and Biomedical and Behavioral Research (Washington, D.C.: U.S. Government Printing Office) Vol. 1, pp. 92-101.

[3] This statement is based on a preliminary draft of the report of the Institute of Medicine Committee on For-Profit Health Care. Additional data may be included in the final report.

[4] Ibid.

[5] Ibid.

Brown, Kathryn J., and Richard E. Klosterman. Hospital acquisitions and their effects: Florida, 1979-1982. This volume.

[7] Hansmann, Henry D. (1980) The role of nonprofit enterprise. *Yale Law Journal* 89(5):835-901.

[8] Robert M. Veatch seems to take this position in Ethical dilemmas of for-profit enterprise in health care, *The New Health Care For Profit*, B. H. Gray, ed. (Washington, D.C.: National Academy Press, 1983), p. 143. Cf. also Outka, Gene, Social justice and equal access to health care in *Ethics and Health Policy*, R. Veatch and R. Branson, eds. Cambridge: Ballinger Publishing Co.

[9] See, for example, Guttman, Amy (1983) For and against equal access to health care, and Brock, Dan W. Distribution of health care and individual liberty, both in *Securing Access to Health Care, Volume Two: Appendices. Sociocultural and Philosophical Studies*, Report of the President's Commission for the Study of Ethical Problems in Medicine and Biomedical and Behavioral Research (Washington, D.C.: U.S. Government Printing Office).

[10] Daniels, Norman (1985) *Just Health Care* (New York: Cambridge University Press).

[11] Starr, P. (1982) *The Social Transformation of American Medicine* (New York: Basic Books).

[12] Menzel, P. (1983) *Medical Costs, Moral Choices* (New Haven: Yale University Press) p. 17.

[13] Veatch, R. (1983) Ethical dilemmas of for-profit enterprise in health care, B. H. Gray, ed., *The New Health Care for Profit* (Washington, D.C.: National Academy Press) pp. 145-146.

[14]Starr, P. (1982) *The Social Transformation of American Medicine* (New York: Basic Books).

[15]Jonson, A. (1983) Watching the doctor, Sounding Board, *New England Journal of Medicine*, 308(25): 1531-1535.

[16]*American College of Physicians Ethics Manual* (1984) p. 7.

[17]The term "medical-industrial complex" is borrowed from an article by Relman, A. (1980) The new medical-industrial complex, *The New England Journal of Medicine*, 303(17):963-970. Relman expresses a number of the concerns about for-profits analyzed in the present essay, including the fear that large for-profit corporations may exert undue influence on public policy.

For-Profit Enterprise in Health Care. 1986.
National Academy Press, Washington, D.C.

# Trends in the Growth of the Major Investor-Owned Hospital Companies

Elizabeth W. Hoy and Bradford H. Gray

Some of the most basic facts about the growth of the investor-owned hospital companies have never been documented, although they have often been topics of conjecture and speculation. To what extent have these companies grown through the construction versus the acquisition of facilities? Does the previous ownership of acquired hospitals suggest that the investor-owned sector is replacing the public or not-for-profit sectors? To what extent have these companies closed hospitals? How similar are the major companies in such growth patterns?

To provide at least a partial answer to such questions, we have examined the growth of six of the largest investor-owned hospital chains, which owned 58 percent of the 890 such hospitals as of September 30, 1984 (as shown in the 1985 directory of the Federation of American Hospitals [FAH]). These companies are the Hospital Corporation of America (HCA) which owns 200 hospitals; American Medical International (AMI) with 115 hospitals; Humana, Inc., with 87 hospitals; National Medical Enterprises (NME) with 47 hospitals; Charter Medical Corporation (Charter) with 41 hospitals; and Republic Health Care Corporation (Republic), with 24 hospitals. Although several of these companies own psychiatric hospitals, the analysis presented in this paper is confined to 540 domestic hospitals that the American Hospital Association (AHA) classifies as "short-term, general, and other special hospitals." Included are all such hospitals that were constructed, bought, leased, sold, merged, or closed between the inception of each company and the time of their 1984 filings with the Securities and Exchange Commission (SEC).[1]

Our primary sources of information about these hospitals were the companies' annual reports and filings with the SEC, especially their 10-K reports.[2] These reports, which must be filed annually by all publicly traded companies, are comprehensive statements that describe principal products and markets, the location and character of principal properties, a summary of the events of the previous fiscal year, and financial statements. Other sources of information were the AHA annual *Guide to the Health Care Field* and the FAH annual *Directory of Investor-Owned Hospitals*. The few questions about hospitals' histories that could not be answered from these published sources were taken to the companies themselves, which provided answers and in several cases checked our other data.

## SOURCES OF GROWTH

As Table 1 shows, acquisitions through purchases (68 percent of growth) and leases (12 percent of growth) have far outdistanced construction (20 percent) as a source of the growth of the six companies. Companies varied widely in sources of growth with HCA, Humana, and Charter having originally constructed more than 25 percent of their hospitals, while none of Republic's and only 4 percent of AMI's hospitals were built by those companies. These differences are undoubtedly partly a matter of strategy, although Republic's relative youth may also be a factor. Most of the companies studied did not construct hospitals in their first few years of operation.

The data on new hospital construction do not fully measure the construction activities of these companies. Table 2 shows three types of such activities—new construction, replacement of existing facilities, and addition of beds to existing facilities.

Part of the increase in these six companies' bed capacity came from capital improvements to facilities they had previously constructed or

**TABLE 1**  Sources of Growth of Short-Term General and Other Special Hospitals by Six Selected Corporations, All Hospitals Acquired Through 1984

| Activity | All Six | HCA[a] | Humana | AMI | NME | Republic | Charter |
|---|---|---|---|---|---|---|---|
| Total hospitals acquired | 540 | 202 | 124 | 114 | 50 | 31 | 19 |
| Constructed (%) | 20 | 27 | 26 | 4 | 12 | 0 | 26 |
| Purchased (%) | 68 | 62 | 56 | 88 | 80 | 76 | 58 |
| Leased (%) | 12 | 11 | 18 | 8 | 8 | 24 | 16 |

[a] HCA data are through 1983.

acquired. Renovations and expansions occurred in 23 percent of facilities owned by these companies. The beds added through these activities account for 7 percent of the total number of beds owned by the six companies. The six companies completely replaced 11 percent of their facilities with newly constructed buildings. Beds added in the process account for 2 percent of current bed capacity (7,983 beds).

The magnitude of expansion/replacement activities varied widely among the six companies. At the high end, 11 percent of the bed capacity of the HCA derives from capital expenditures at facilities already owned; 50 percent of their hospitals were affected. At the other end, 3 percent of AMI's beds derive from capital expenditures at facilities they owned, and 21 percent of hospitals were affected. Republic Health Corporation did not expand or replace any hospitals during the period examined. (See Table 1.)

### Growth Trends Over Time

Table 3 displays growth trends data for the six companies. Clearly, construction accounted for a much larger share of these companies' growth during the 1970s than either before or after. However, the percentage decline in share of growth via construction (from 27 percent between 1975 and 1979 to 11 percent between 1980 and 1984) resulted primarily from a surge in acquisition activity, not to a substantial slowing of construction.

Through 1969, only 49 hospitals were owned by these six companies. Beginning around 1970, the three companies that are the largest today began a period of rapid expansion. Between 1970 and 1972, HCA added 27 hospitals, 13 of which were constructed. Humana added 36 hospitals, 4 of which were constructed. AMI added 31 hospitals; one of these was constructed and 21 were acquired in a merger with Chanco in 1972, more than doubling the size of the company. Charter and NME exhibited much slower growth in short-term general hospitals during this period. This probably reflects the greater diversification of these two companies while they were entering the general hospital market.

During the mid-1970s, HCA and Humana both began constructing more of their new hospitals. Twenty-seven of the 50 hospitals added to HCA between 1973 and 1979 were constructed by the company. All but two of the 23 hospitals added by Humana between 1973 and 1977 were constructed. AMI did not grow during this period, having previously made the acquisition of the Chanco hospitals that had more than doubled the company.

In the late 1970s and early 1980s, growth through the acquisition of other investor-owned chains by the larger ones became particularly notable. HCA acquired three smaller chains (i.e., General Care Corporation, General Health Services, Inc., and Hospital Affiliates International, Inc. [HAI]) in 1980 and 1981. These 48 hospitals represented 60 percent of their growth in those 2 years. Humana acquired 39 hospitals through its merger with American Medicorp in 1978, almost doubling their capacity. AMI continued its strategy of growth primarily through the acquisition of chains, by acquiring Hyatt (eight hospitals) and Brookwood Health Services (11 hospitals) in 1981 and 1982, respectively, and in 1984, AMI acquired Lifemark's 27 hospitals through a corporate merger.

**TABLE 2** Growth of Selected For-profit Multi-institutional Systems from Construction of New Facilities and Expansion of Existing Facilities, Through 1984

| Activity | All | | HCA[a] | | Humana | | AMI | | NME | | Republic | | Charter | |
|---|---|---|---|---|---|---|---|---|---|---|---|---|---|---|
| | Hospitals | Beds | Hospitals | Beds | Hospitals | Beds | Hospitals | Beds | Hospitals | Beds | Hospitals | Beds | Hospitals | Beds |
| New facilities constructed | 104 | 15,893 | 55 | 7,571 | 33 | 5,803 | 5 | 853 | 6 | 973 | 0 | 0 | 5 | 693 |
| Replacement facilities | 58 | 7,983 | 31 | 4,243 | 19 | 2,611 | 6 | 797 | 2 | 332 | 0 | 0 | 0 | 0 |
| Beds added to existing facilities | | 5,359 | | 2,676 | | 1,385 | | 492 | | 685 | | 0 | | 121 |
| Change totals[b] | 102[c] | 22,618 | 54[c] | 10,809 | 32[c] | 7,900 | 5 | 1,312 | 6 | 1,783 | 0 | 0 | 5 | 814 |

[a]HCA data are through 1983.

[b]This row shows the net change in numbers of hospitals and beds as a result of construction, replacement, and additions. Change totals are affected by replacement facilities having different numbers of beds from the facility that was replaced.

[c]The change total for hospitals is smaller than the number of new facilities because of two instances in which two old facilities were replaced with one new one.

TABLE 3   Growth in Four Time Periods of Short-Term
General and Other Special Hospitals by Six
Investor-Owned Corporations[a]

| Activity | Total All Years | Before 1969 | 1970-1974 | 1975-1979 | 1980-1984[b] |
|---|---|---|---|---|---|
| Total hospitals acquired | 540 | 49 | 131 | 111 | 249 |
| Constructed (%) | 20 | 4 | 35 | 27 | 11 |
| Purchased (%) | 68 | 90 | 58 | 56 | 75 |
| Leased (%) | 12 | 6 | 7 | 17 | 14 |

[a]HCA, Humana, AMI, NME, Republic, and Charter.
[b]HCA data are through 1983.

Republic was founded in 1981 by four former executives of HAI and has grown to the fifth largest investor owner of general hospitals by purchasing two-thirds of its hospitals from other investor-owned chains. They purchased 16 hospitals from HCA in 1983, 8 of which were former HAI hospitals. Then in 1984, they acquired Health Resources (three hospitals), two hospitals from Humana, and one general hospital (along with several psychiatric or substance abuse hospitals) with their acquisition of Horizon Health—the owner of Raleigh Hills substance abuse hospitals.

## TYPES OF HOSPITALS ACQUIRED

### Previous Ownership

Table 4 shows that these six companies have grown primarily through the acquisition of other hospital chains (45 percent of all hospitals acquired) and independent proprietary hospitals (33 percent of all hospitals acquired). (This figure has been adjusted to compensate for the 22 hospitals that changed hands in transactions among the six companies.) Twelve percent of the acquired hospitals were previously under private not-for-profit ownership (mostly voluntary rather than religious), and 10 percent were previously owned by state and local governments.

Previous ownership also shows definite trends when examined over time (Table 5). Initially, most hospitals acquired were small independent proprietary hospitals. Not-for-profit and governmental hospitals did not assume a significant portion of acquisitions until the most recent period examined—1980-1984.

It is often difficult to determine the original ownership of hospitals that were acquired by these six companies from other proprietary chains. The most complete data we have come from the set of hospitals acquired by HCA through General Care Corporation, General Health Services, Inc., and HAI. These hospitals were almost exclusively either independent proprietary hospitals before they were acquired by any chain or they were constructed by a chain. This pattern appears to hold for the other companies studied, although we were unable to assemble complete data.

Once acquired by a hospital chain, a hospital can go through a series of changes of ownership as a result of the merger and acquisition activity among hospital chains. Perhaps the most vivid example are two California hospitals, Community Hospital of Sacramento and Laurel Grove Hospital, that went through the following changes. Both were physician-owned proprietary hospitals until their acquisition by Beverly Enterprises in the early 1970s. They were sold by Beverly to AID, Inc., a subsidiary of the Insurance Company of North America (INA) in the mid-1970s. After INA acquired HAI, the AID hospitals were moved into the HAI division, which was sold to HCA in 1981. In 1983 the two hospitals were among eight that HCA sold to Republic, their present owner.

TABLE 4  Previous Ownership of Hospitals Acquired (Purchased and Leased), Through 1984

| Ownership at Acquisition | HCA[a] | | Humana | | AMI | | NME | | Republic | | Charter | | Total | |
|---|---|---|---|---|---|---|---|---|---|---|---|---|---|---|
| | No. | % | No. | % | No. | % | No. | % | No. | % | No. | % | No. | % |
| Investor-owned chain | 51 | 35 | 43 | 48 | 68 | 62 | 10 | 23 | 22 | 71 | 0 | 0 | 194 | 45 |
| Investor-owned independent | 51 | 35 | 34 | 38 | 27 | 25 | 18 | 41 | 4 | 13 | 12 | 86 | 146 | 33 |
| Voluntary not-for-profit | 15 | 10 | 6 | 7 | 5 | 4 | 10 | 23 | 4 | 13 | 1 | 7 | 41 | 9 |
| Religious not-for-profit | 7 | 5 | 2 | 2 | 0 | 0 | 2 | 4 | 0 | 0 | 1 | 7 | 12 | 3 |
| State and local government | 23 | 15 | 5 | 5 | 10 | 9 | 4 | 9 | 1 | 3 | 0 | 0 | 43 | 10 |
| Total | 147 | 100 | 90 | 100 | 110 | 100 | 44 | 100 | 31 | 100 | 14 | 100 | 436 | 100 |

[a]HCA data are through 1983.

TABLE 5 Trends in Previous Ownership of Short-Term General and Other Special Hospitals Acquired by Six Investor-Owned Companies[a]

| Ownership at Acquisition | Total | Before 1969 | 1970- 1974 | 1975- 1979 | 1980- 1984[b] |
|---|---|---|---|---|---|
| Investor-owned chain | 194 | 0 | 24 | 51 | 119 |
| Investor-owned independent | 146 | 45 | 48 | 16 | 37 |
| Voluntary not-for-profit | 41 | 1 | 7 | 5 | 28 |
| Religious not-for-profit | 12 | 0 | 2 | 3 | 7 |
| State and local government | 43 | 1 | 5 | 7 | 30 |
| Total | 436 | 47 | 86 | 82 | 221 |

[a]HCA, Humana, AMI, NME, Republic, and Charter.
[b]HCA data are through 1983.

## Size of New Hospitals

Data on the size of hospitals constructed, purchased, and leased are displayed in Table 6. For the six companies, the average size of the hospitals constructed (153 beds) was slightly larger than the size of hospitals purchased (though not smaller than leased hospitals). For all three modes of acquisition, the size peaked in the period 1975-1979.

## Geographic Patterns

In 1969, the six investor-owned chains owned hospitals in only 10 states with 75 percent of them concentrated in California, Texas, Alabama, and Tennessee. By 1984, they owned hospitals in 35 states, with 74 percent of their hospitals in seven states (the four listed and Florida, Louisiana, and Georgia). Clearly the areas of greatest growth and concentration have remained in the South and Southwest. Since 1969, there has been a gradual spread into the Midwest and the Rocky Mountain area, but the six chains acquired no hospitals in several New England and Mid-Atlantic states.

## The Relationship Between Contract Management and Acquisition

HCA was the only company that provided enough information in their 10-K reports to track the relationship between management contracts and subsequent purchase of hospitals. Since becoming a public corporation through 1983, HCA managed a total of 220 hospitals in 39 states. Of these, 33 contracts were terminated, presumably at the end of the

TABLE 6 Average Number of Beds per Acquired Hospitals, Six Investor-Owned Companies,[a] Through 1984

| Hospital Type | Total | Before 1969 | 1970- 1974 | 1975- 1979 | 1980- 1984[b] |
|---|---|---|---|---|---|
| All acquired hospitals | 142 | 128 | 118 | 171 | 144 |
| Constructed hospitals | 153 | 44 | 152 | 180 | 131 |
| Purchased hospitals | 136 | 134 | 102 | 153 | 145 |
| Leased hospitals | 156 | 84 | 77 | 212 | 152 |

[a]HCA, Humana, AMI, NME, Republic, and Charter.
[b]HCA data are through 1983.

contract life. Seventeen managed hospitals were acquired by HCA during the course of the contract, and one was acquired after the contract had terminated. These represent 8 percent of HCA's total acquisitions. Seven of the 18 hospitals acquired were replaced by company-built hospitals during the term of the contract and were recorded as constructed hospitals in our data. At the end of our data collection period, HCA managed 169 hospitals in 38 states. Contract management is clearly a separate line of business rather than a vehicle for acquisition.

### DIVESTITURES

An oft-stated concern about the for-profit ownership of hospitals by for-profit entities is that such owners might be too willing to close a hospital that was not satisfying profitability goals. Although some studies (Sloan et al., 1986; Mullner et al., 1982) have shown that for-profit hospitals are disproportionately represented among hospitals that close, little data on closure activity of *investor-owned* for-profit hospitals have heretofore been available. For this reason, we also compiled data on divestitures by the six largest investor-owned hospital companies.

For the six companies combined, there were a total of 87 divestitures during the period studied—75 sales and 12 closures (Table 7). This is a total of 16 percent of all hospitals acquired during this period. The percentage of hospitals divested varies by company, with Humana having the highest percentage of total divestitures (31 percent of the hospitals they

bought or constructed) and NME having a low 6 percent. Republic has not divested any hospitals, but this may be a factor of the relatively young age of the company. For the first years of these companies' existence, there were very few divestitures (Table 8).

Only 2 percent of all the hospitals acquired by the six companies during the period studied were subsequently closed. In several of these cases, the closure was associated with, and compensated by, the addition of new beds at another area hospital owned by the same company; one was converted to a psychiatric hospital. None of the hospitals that were closed appeared to be the only hospital in a community. AMI exhibited the highest absolute number of closures (six). NME and Republic did not close a hospital.

Table 9 shows the number of years between the time of acquisition and the time of divestiture for the 87 hospitals that were closed or sold by these three companies through 1984. Divestitures appear to fall into several patterns. Sometimes companies acquire chains and then divest themselves relatively quickly of hospitals that do not fit well with the company. Of the hospitals divested through sale or closure, 45 percent took place within 3 years of the year of acquisition. Another cluster of hospital divestitures appears around 5 to 6 years after acquisition. One can speculate that these were hospitals that did not meet the acquiring companies' expectations regarding profitability. A third group of hospitals have been divested after 10 years or more of ownership. One can speculate that these are hospitals that have outlived their investment potential (i.e.,

**TABLE 7** Divestitures of Short-Term General and Other Special Hospitals by Six Companies, Through 1984

| Activity | Total | HCA[a] | Humana | AMI | NME | Republic | Charter |
|---|---|---|---|---|---|---|---|
| Total hospitals divested | 87 | 26 | 39 | 14 | 3 | 0 | 5 |
| Number sold | 75 | 23 | 38 | 8 | 3 | 0 | 3 |
| Number closed | 10 | 3 | 1 | 6 | 0 | 0 | 2 |
| Percent divested as percentage of total hospitals acquired[b] | 16 | 13 | 31 | 12 | 6 | 0 | 26 |

[a] HCA data are through 1983.

[b] As shown in Table 1.

**TABLE 8**  Divestitures as a Percentage of All Hospitals
Acquired by the Six Companies,[a] in Four Time Periods

| Activity | Total | Before 1969 | 1970-1974 | 1975-1979 | 1980-1984[b] |
|---|---|---|---|---|---|
| Total hospitals divested | 87 | 0 | 4 | 27 | 56 |
| Total hospitals acquired | 540 | 49 | 131 | 111 | 249 |
| Divestitures as percentage of acquisitions | 16 | 0 | 4 | 24 | 22 |

[a]HCA, Humana, AMI, NME, Republic, and Charter.
[b]HCA data are through 1983.

they are reaching the end of their depreciable life) and that their cash-flow value to the company may have declined.

## CONCLUSIONS

Several major findings from this compilation of information about the acquisition and divestiture activities of the six largest investor-owned hospital companies through 1984 are worthy of note and commentary:

● Most growth has been through acquisition of existing facilities; only 20 percent (104 hospitals) of all hospitals owned or leased by the companies during this period were originally constructed by the companies.

● Approximately 13 percent of the hospitals purchased or leased by the companies were subsequently replaced. Replacement and renovation activities added almost as many beds to the system as did the construction of new facilities.

● Almost half of the hospitals acquired by these six companies were acquired in 1980 or later, with acquisitions of and mergers with other companies playing an important role. However, projections of future growth based on trends shown in this paper would be unwarranted in light of changing economic circumstances brought about by Medicare and private third-party payers.

● As has been widely assumed, most hospitals acquired were previously under for-profit ownership. However, 22 percent of purchased hospitals were acquired from a not-for-profit or governmental owner. Such sources increased in prominence during the last period studied (1980-1984). However, as noted above, growth trends of the late 1970s and early 1980s may not continue.

● The size of hospitals purchased (and leased) and constructed peaked in the period 1975-1979 before declining in the 1980-1984 period.

● Although significant geographic dispersal took place during the period studied, a high

**TABLE 9**  Length of Time Between Acquisition and Divestiture for 87 Hospitals Sold or Closed by Six Investor-Owned Hospital Companies,[a] 1970-1984

| Length of Time | Total | HCA[b] | Humana | AMI | NME | Republic | Charter |
|---|---|---|---|---|---|---|---|
| 1-3 years[c] | 39 | 21 | 10 | 5 | 1 | 0 | 2 |
| 4-8 years | 33 | 3 | 22 | 4 | 1 | 0 | 3 |
| 9 or more years | 15 | 2 | 7 | 5 | 1 | 0 | 0 |

[a]HCA, Humana, AMI, NME, Republic, and Charter.
[b]HCA data are through 1983.
[c]Based on year of acquisition and sale, not on exact dates.

degree of geographic concentration still characterizes these six companies, with almost 75 percent of their hospitals being located in seven states.

• Acquisition by an investor-owned company can lead to subsequent changes in ownership. Sixteen percent of the hospitals built or purchased by these six companies had undergone a subsequent change in ownership. At the extreme, two examples were presented of hospitals that had changed hands five times after their initial purchase from local physician owners.

• Closure of a hospital after acquisition by one of these companies has been rare. Only 12 of the 540 hospitals owned by these companies during the period were closed, and several of these closures were the result of the replacement of two old facilities by one new one.

• There are substantial variations in the growth and divestiture patterns of different companies. Whether this is due to broad strategies or to ideosyncratic circumstances and events has not been determined.

### NOTES

[1]An exception was the HCA for which the most recent data used was from its 1983 filings with the SEC. Hospitals that these companies operated under management contracts were not included in the figures on acquisitions and divestitures.

[2]Beginning with the first year that each company filed with the SEC and owned one or more hospitals, the following information was compiled (and usually obtained) about each hospital owned by each company:

• The name and location of the hospital
• Year acquired
• How acquired (i.e., constructed, purchased, or leased)
• Type of previous ownership
• Whether the hospital was previously managed by the company (if available)
• Initial licensed bed capacity upon acquisition
• Any additions to bed capacity and the year they occurred
• If the hospital was replaced, when, and the number of beds in the replacement facility
• Current licensed bed capacity (1984 data)
• Any additions to ancillary capacity, and the year they occurred
• If the hospital was divested, how and when

Growth derives from construction, purchase, and lease. Constructed hospitals were recorded in the year they began operating rather than the year construction began. Hospitals constructed for other owners and then leased by the corporation under a capitalized lease arrangement were counted as constructed hospitals. Hospitals acquired after construction had begun and completed while owned by the corporation were counted as constructed rather than acquired hospitals. Hospitals that were constructed by others under agreements with the corporation and then acquired upon completion were categorized as either purchased or leased.

The 10-K reports must list properties that are leased, but need not differentiate between capitalized and noncapitalized leases. Both capitalized and noncapitalized leases are included in our data under the category "leased." However, the majority of leases by investor-owned chains are capitalized leases; for example, 18 of the 22 leases recorded by Humana are capitalized leases. A capitalized lease, also known as a financing lease, is a leasing agreement that is followed by the option to purchase at a nominal price and is treated on the financial statements as both the borrowing of funds and the acquisition of an asset by the lessee (in this case, the investor-owned chain). Both the liability and the asset are recognized on the balance sheet. Expenses consist of both the interest on the debt and the amortization of the asset. The lessor treats the lease as the sale of the asset in return for a series of future cash receipts. An operating lease, or noncapitalized lease, grants the lessee no rights to the asset and the rental payments are accounted for as expenses of the period, not a liability. The lessor retains rights to the property and shows the rental payments as revenues.

Purchased hospitals include those acquired through poolings of interest. When an investor-owned chain acquires a hospital (or hospital chain) through a pooling of interest, it exchanges previously unissued capital stock for the stock of the hospital and accepts responsibility to discharge the liabilities of the acquired firm. In accounting terminology, a pooling of interest combines the two firms by adding together the *book value* of the assets and equities of the two firms. When a hospital is purchased, the transaction is accounted for by adding the acquired company's assets, valued at the *price paid* for them, to the acquiring company's assets. Because the assets are put on the books at current, rather than original cost, the depreciation expense (and its associated cash flow) is higher and the reported net income is generally lower under this method than under the pooling-of-interest method. Acquisitions are required to be accounted for as purchases unless all of the criteria for a pooling are met.

For our purposes, poolings and purchases are both included in the terminology "purchased." Since the difference between a capitalized lease and a purchase is only one of the timing of the expenditure, leases and purchases have been combined under the term "acquisition" in some tables.

## REFERENCES

Mullner, Ross M., Calvin S. Byre, Paul Levy, and Joseph D. Kubal (1982) Closure among U.S. community hospitals, 1976-1980. A descriptive and a predictive model. *Medical Care* 20(July):699-709.

Sloan, Frank A., Joseph Valvona, and Ross Mullner (1986) Identifying the issues: A statistical profile. In Frank A. Sloan, James F. Blumstein, and James M. Perrin, eds., *Uncompensated Hospital Care: Rights and Responsibilities*. Baltimore, Md.: The Johns Hopkins University Press.

*For-Profit Enterprise in Health Care.* 1986.
National Academy Press, Washington, D.C.

# The Effects of Ownership and Multihospital System Membership on Hospital Functional Strategies and Economic Performance

J. Michael Watt, Steven C. Renn, James S. Hahn, Robert A. Derzon, and Carl J. Schramm

## INTRODUCTION

The hospital industry is undergoing major structural change. Shifts in Medicare and Medicaid reimbursement policies, increasing private concern about health care costs, technological change, and the growth of organized delivery systems such as health maintenance organizations (HMOs) and preferred provider organizations (PPOs) have radically altered the environment facing hospitals. Hospitals have responded in two primary ways: (1) by diversifying away from inpatient acute care services to find new revenues from services such as ambulatory care, home care, and skilled nursing care (vertical integration); and (2) by joining existing multihospital systems or forming new ones (horizontal integration) or starting non-health-care businesses such as construction (diversification).

Both of these strategies aim to improve the potential service benefits and economics of hospital operations, the first primarily by raising service volumes by assuring continuity in referrals, and the second primarily by achieving administrative economies of scale and better access to capital. These trends have resulted in the large numbers of corporate reorganizations of hospitals and the steady growth in

*Mr. Watt is a principal, Lewin and Associates, Inc., San Francisco, California. Mr. Renn is a research associate, The Johns Hopkins Center for Hospital Finance and Management, and the Department of Health Policy and Management, The Johns Hopkins University, Baltimore, Maryland. Mr. Hahn is a research assistant, Lewin and Associates, Inc. Mr. Derzon is vice president, Lewin and Associates, Inc. Dr. Schramm is director, The Johns Hopkins Center for Hospital Finance and Management, and associate professor, the Department of Health Policy and Management, The Johns Hopkins University, Baltimore, Maryland.

numbers of hospitals in multihospital systems that have been seen over recent years.

This paper focuses on the second of these phenomena—the behavior of multihospital systems—and examines differences in the location, strategies, and economic performance of five classes of community hospitals: investor-owned multihospital system (IOMS) members, not-for-profit multihospital system (NFPMS) members, and investor-owned (IO) freestanding, NFP freestanding, and government hospitals. This study attempts to separate differences associated with system membership from those associated with ownership form and to develop answers to the following questions:

● Are there differences in demographics, reimbursement systems, and regulatory structures between areas where multihospital system members are located and those in which freestanding hospitals are located? Are there differences between the areas where IO and NFP hospitals locate?

● Do multihospital systems produce economies in patient care or employ different financial strategies compared with freestanding hospitals? Are there differences in the advantages multihospital system membership gives IO or NFP hospitals?

● Are the inter-hospital differences that may be attributed to ownership—IO versus NFP—greater than the differences that may be due to organizational form—chain-affiliated versus freestanding?

● What does the historical record say about the potential of each type of hospital for success in a world in which purchasers of care are increasingly price-conscious?

Issues of comparative quality of care and access, while also important, were beyond the scope of our analysis of economic performance.

## METHODS

We analyzed a sample of hospitals that is national in scope and includes about 10 percent of all U.S. community hospitals, ranging from urban academic health centers to small rural facilities.

### The Sample

The sample was chosen by a stratified random sampling technique from the universe of 4,491 Medicare-certified, nonfederal, and nonstate general acute care hospitals with lengths of stay between 3 and 13 days in 1980. Using the *Guide to Multihospital Systems* of the American Health Association (AHA) and the *Directory* of the Federation of American Hospitals (FAH), each of the hospitals was classified based on ownership and system affiliation. We selected from this universe a sample of hospitals totaling 800 in aggregate. We originally hypothesized that there would be little difference (other than greater direct receipt of public funds) between voluntary hospitals and those organized as county and hospital district entities. However, in the models presented here, to control for differences such as sunshine laws, limitations on outside contracting, and restrictions on governing board composition that may remain even after adjusting for public subsidies, we included a category for government hospitals.

The original sample of 800 was reduced to 561 due to cost reports missing important schedules or covering periods of less than 9 or more than 15 months. The number of sample hospitals in each of the five strata are as follows: IOMS members—122; NFPMS—114; IO freestanding hospitals—148; NFP freestanding hospitals (voluntary or religious-sponsored)—93; and government (county or hospital district) hospitals—84.

We tested each of the samples against the eligible universe from which it was drawn, using two-tailed t-tests of the difference between means. We found the samples to represent their classes well in hospital size, occupancy, length of stay, and the ratio of outpatient to total gross revenue, as shown in Table 1, with two exceptions. First, the freestanding IO hospitals in our sample are slightly smaller and

the sampled chain IOs slightly larger than their classes overall. We do not believe these differences have important consequences for the results that follow because we explicitly control for number of beds in each equation. Second, the inpatient proportion of total revenue differs between the sampled freestanding NFPs and their class. However, a variable to control for this factor is also included in the equations.

There is little evidence of "response bias"—differences between the chosen random sample and the final usable sample. The sample has a good distribution of hospitals from the major multihospital systems. However, several large public system teaching hospitals in New York and California could not be included in the sample due to our inability to disaggregate some key financial data for the individual hospitals. Kaiser hospitals were excluded for similar reasons.

### Data

Several measures of hospital costs and revenues, utilization, and balance sheet strength were taken from audited Medicare cost reports. Data on the number of births, surgical admissions, urban/rural location of the hospital, and contract management and membership status in NFP systems in 1980 were taken from the AHA's *Annual Survey*. Demographic and physician supply information from the county where each hospital is located was taken from the U.S. Bureau of Health Professions' *Area Resource File*. Figures for the percentage of admissions covered by each type of third-party payer were constructed from the U.S. Office for Civil Rights' *1980 Survey of Hospitals*.[1] Finally, the Health Care Financing Administration (HCFA) supplied wage and case-mix indices and lists of hospitals that were sole community providers. This data base was checked for consistency among sources and within each hospital record.

### Techniques

Financial data were standardized to a common, 12-month fiscal period ending December 31, 1980, using trend factors based on monthly expense data from the AHA's *Panel Survey*. Expense and statistical data from hos-

**TABLE 1**   Sample Compared to Universe, 1980

| | Beds per Hospital | | Occupancy Rate | | Average Length of Stay | | Ratio of Inpatient Gross Revenue to Total Gross Revenue | |
|---|---|---|---|---|---|---|---|---|
| | N | Mean | N | Mean | N | Mean | N | Mean |
| Chain-affiliated investor-owned | | | | | | | | |
| Sample | 122 | 167.48 | 122 | 0.62 | 122 | 6.17 | 122 | 0.91 |
| Universe | 310 | 146.19* | 307 | 0.63 | 307 | 6.37 | 306 | 0.90 |
| Chain-affiliated not-for-profit | | | | | | | | |
| Sample | 114 | 220.77 | 114 | 0.69 | 114 | 6.58 | 114 | 0.88 |
| Universe | 436 | 223.32 | 416 | 0.70 | 418 | 6.80 | 413 | 0.87 |
| Freestanding investor-owned | | | | | | | | |
| Sample | 148 | 94.01 | 148 | 0.63 | 148 | 6.80 | 142 | 0.91 |
| Universe | 213 | 111.63* | 213 | 0.64 | 213 | 6.57 | 209 | 0.91 |
| Freestanding not-for-profit | | | | | | | | |
| Sample | 93 | 220.73 | 93 | 0.70 | 93 | 6.94 | 93 | 0.88 |
| Universe | 2,397 | 221.01 | 2,306 | 0.72 | 2,306 | 7.24 | 2,287 | 0.87*** |
| Government | | | | | | | | |
| Sample | 84 | 103.56 | 84 | 0.60 | 84 | 5.96 | 82 | 0.87 |
| Universe | 1,264 | 108.41 | 1,244 | 0.61 | 1,247 | 6.16 | 1,221 | 0.87 |

NOTE: Levels of statistical significance are denoted by asterisks as follow: *probability <.10; **probability <.05; ***probability <.01 that observed difference is due to chance.

SOURCE: Sample: Lewin and Associates and The Johns Hopkins University; Universe: American Hospital Association *Annual Survey of Hospitals.*

pitals with reporting periods of other than 366 days were adjusted by the ratio of the days in the period to 366. Edits were used to check the consistency of the measures calculated, and all outliers were verified.

We then analyzed this data set through ordinary least squares multiple regression on the models discussed below. Multiple regression was chosen to overcome two limits of the matched-pairs methodology we have applied in other studies. First, regression permits larger sample sizes, because there is no need to match hospitals explicitly in the respective samples under study. This allows the study to be national in scope, rather than limited only to states in which the hospital classes under study are located, and increases one's confidence that the measures calculated represent average relationships nationwide. Second, because the regression technique is not limited in its application to two equal-sized samples, differences among IO and NFP system hospitals and

IO and NFP freestanding hospitals can be examined explicitly at the same time.

### Dependent Variables

The 28 dependent variables included measures of case mix, operating revenues and costs, capital structure, markups and profitability, and activity and productivity. With few exceptions, these measures were taken from the Medicare cost reports directly or calculated from them, as we felt this was the most reliable and consistent source. Table 2 shows the dependent variables, their sources, and their mean values for each of the hospital classes.

*Severity and mix of cases* are indicators of patient selection strategies by the hospitals. These operate through decisions on siting, service offerings, and recruitment of different types of physicians to the medical staff. We measured severity and mix of cases by the Medicare case-mix index, inpatient surgeries per

**TABLE 2** Descriptive Statistics: Dependent Variables

| Variable | Source: Definition | N | Mean | Standard Deviation |
|---|---|---|---|---|
| **Case mix** | | | | |
| Case-mix index (1980) | HCFA, *Federal Register* | 561 | 0.9894 | 0.0822 |
| Inpatient surgeries per 100 admissions | AHA *Survey* | 560 | 37.3481 | 17.3455 |
| Births per 100 admissions | AHA *Survey* | 560 | 6.6276 | 6.6465 |
| Outpatient revenue to total gross revenue (ratio) | Medicare Cost Report (MCR) | 559 | 0.1092 | 0.0659 |
| **Revenues and costs** | | | | |
| Total patient care revenue per adjusted admission ($) | MCR, adjusted for case mix, wage rate, and outpatient differences | 490 | 1,888.6383 | 607.3580 |
| Net patient care revenue per adjusted admission ($) | MCR, as above | 495 | 1,589.7865 | 455.5115 |
| Total operating expenses per adjusted admission ($) | MCR, as above | 543 | 1,598.0947 | 467.9824 |
| Total patient care expenses per adjusted admission ($) | MCR, as above | 510 | 1,440.0125 | 399.4624 |
| General and administrative costs per adjusted admission ($) | MCR, as above | 510 | 696.3724 | 230.4583 |
| Home office costs per adjusted admission ($) | MCR, as above | 495 | 19.0471 | 40.1001 |
| **Capital structure** | | | | |
| Debt-to-asset ratio | MCR: total liabilities/total assets | 548 | 0.5315 | 0.3193 |
| Current ratio | MCR: current assets/current liabilities | 540 | 2.7231 | 2.2946 |
| Capital cost percent A (excluding ROE, percent of operating costs) | MCR: depreciation, interest, and capital leases/total operating costs | 550 | 7.1173 | 4.2766 |
| Capital cost percent B (including ROE, percent of operating costs) | MCR: depreciation, interest, capital leases and Medicare ROE/total operating costs | 550 | 7.8796 | 4.5876 |
| Accounting average age of plant | MCR: accumulated depreciation plant/depreciation expense | 442 | 4.9781 | 5.7084 |
| Total fixed assets per bed ($) | MCR: fixed assets/beds | 497 | 35,690.5042 | 25,489.4713 |
| **Markups and profitability** | | | | |
| Gross patient care markup ratio | MCR: gross patient revenues/operating expenses | 536 | 1.1935 | 0.1654 |
| Revenue deduction ratio | MCR: (gross patient revenues − net patient revenues)/gross patient revenues | 538 | 0.1455 | 0.0823 |
| Nonoperating revenue to total gross revenue | MCR: nonoperating revenue/(operating revenue + nonoperating revenue) | 531 | 0.0301 | 0.0324 |
| Total markup ratio | MCR: (gross patient revenue + net nonpatient revenue)/total operating expense | 537 | 1.2299 | 0.1595 |
| Return on total assets | MCR: total net income/total assets | 529 | 0.0573 | 0.1067 |
| Return on equity or fund balance | MCR: total net income/equity or fund balance | 517 | 0.1861 | 0.3550 |

TABLE 2   *Continued*

| Variable | Source: Definition | N | Mean | Standard Deviation |
|---|---|---|---|---|
| Activity and productivity ratios | | | | |
| Total asset turnover ratio | MCR: gross revenue/assets | 537 | 1.5215 | 0.9312 |
| Current asset turnover ratio | MCR: gross revenue/current assets | 533 | 4.2029 | 1.9565 |
| Case flow | MCR: admissions/beds | 561 | 37.2416 | 11.0268 |
| FTEs per adjusted daily census | MCR, supplemented by AHA: full-time equivalent personnel/adjusted average daily census | 518 | 2.3923 | 0.8455 |
| Occupancy rate | MCR: inpatient days/total days available | 561 | 64.7465 | 17.0570 |
| Medical education | | | | |
| Interns and residents: total expense per bed ($) | MCR: interns and residents expense/beds | 561 | 278.1697 | 1,097.9548 |

100 admissions, births per 100 admissions, and outpatient proportion of total gross revenue (a proxy for outpatient volumes).

*Operating revenues and costs per case* were examined as indicators of differences in hospital pricing strategies, productive efficiency, and the costs imposed by the home offices of system members. Our measures for operating revenues and costs were total patient care revenue (gross charges), net patient care revenue, total operating expense, total patient care expense, general and administrative costs, and home office costs, all per admission and adjusted for outpatient volume, case mix, reporting period length and end, and wage rate differences. We also measured total intern and resident costs per bed.

Financial ratios addressing the *capital structure* of hospitals yield insight into the financial strategies followed by hospitals in the different classes as well as their differential access to capital. These were measured by total fixed assets per bed, debt-to-asset and current ratios, capital costs as a percentage of operating costs, and accounting age of plant (defined as accumulated depreciation divided by depreciation expense).

*Markups and profitability measures* reflect other aspects of managerial strategy as well as the relative success of the hospitals' policies. The patient care markup ratio (gross patient revenues divided by patient care expenses), revenue deduction ratio (gross patient revenues minus net patient revenues, divided by gross patient revenues), ratio of nonoperating revenue to total net revenue, total markup ratio (total gross revenue divided by total operating cost), return on total assets, and return on equity (ROE) were used as measures of markups and profitability.

Finally, measures of *activity and productivity* were included as dependent variables to show differences that might exist in the efficiency of use of assets across the hospital classes. These measures were total asset turnover, current asset turnover, case flow (admissions per bed), and full-time equivalent staff (FTEs) per adjusted average census.

We controlled for case mix and wage differences from the outset using the methods employed by HCFA to standardize hospital data for these factors under the Prospective Payment System (PPS). Additionally, dependent variables measuring revenues and costs were adjusted for outpatient volume using the technique of the AHA. Finally, as described above, all financial data were standardized to a 12-month reporting period ending December 31, 1980. Thus, all revenue and cost-dependent variables were standardized for case-mix differences, wage rate differences, and differences in outpatient volume before they entered the regressions.

## Independent Variables and Hypotheses

The independent variables of primary interest were those representing ownership and system membership, specified as a construct of four dummy variables, with NFPF being the omitted reference group; and length of affiliation and contract management, which were specified as a construct of three dummy variables. Other independent variables consisted of five types that may also affect hospital economic performance:

1. *Competition and regulation* were measured by two proxies—sole community provider status under Medicare (a measure of lack of competition) and percentage of admissions under state rate-setting programs.

2. *Case mix and patient selection* was measured by the Medicare case-mix index, surgeries per 100 admissions, births per 100 admissions, and percent charge-based payers. We expected both higher case-mix indices and percentages of surgical admissions to be associated with higher revenues and costs per case.

3. *Input costs and regional practice differences* were examined through three measures, the HCFA area wage index, a dummy equal to 1 if the hospital was in a Standard Metropolitan Statistical Area (SMSA), and a second dummy equal to 1 if the hospital was in Census Region nine—the West Coast. This last variable was specified following preliminary regressions that found only this region to show different hospital performance on many of our measures. Higher wage indices and urban location were expected to be associated with higher revenues and costs.

4. *Productive capacity and utilization* were measured by the hospital's number of beds, ratio of outpatient to total gross revenue, occupancy rate, and, in some models, length of stay. Higher numbers of beds and lower occupancy rates were expected to be associated with higher costs per stay. We entered the linear form of the bed variable because preliminary regressions showed it fit as well as quadratic and other formulations.

5. Finally, *medical education commitment* was measured by the medical resident and intern expense per bed from the Medicare cost

report, and was expected to be associated with higher costs.

The sources and means of the independent variables are shown in Table 3.

We developed initial hypotheses about the effects of the independent variables on the dependent variables and tested them through the regressions. From our previous studies,[2] we hypothesized that IO system hospitals would tend to be located in the sunbelt states characterized by faster population growth, higher proportions of charge-based reimbursement, and less regulation. They would show case mixes about equal in total (Medicare case-mix index) and surgical proportions, and lower in obstetrical and outpatient proportions than NFP freestanding ones.

We hypothesized that IOMS revenues and administrative and home office costs per case would be higher than either freestanding or system NFPs, but their total operating and patient care expenses per case would be equivalent to the NFPs. We believed they would show lower asset values per bed, higher debt-to-asset ratios, higher capital costs as a percentage of operating costs and younger plants (by accounting-based measures) than NFPs, and that these strategies would result in higher markups and profitability. Finally, we expected IO system hospitals to show faster asset turnover on revenue-based measures, and greater productivity measured by full-time equivalent staff per occupied bed.

Our hypotheses regarding NFP system hospitals were that they would exhibit similarities to both NFP freestanding hospitals (which most of them once were) and IO system hospitals (due to similar opportunities to achieve system-derived economies and access to capital). Therefore, for many relationships, our hypotheses were indeterminate. However, we expected their case mixes to be somewhat higher overall and relatively richer in obstetrical and outpatient services than IO system hospitals. Like the IO systems, we expected that their home office costs would increase administrative and general costs relative to NFP freestanding facilities. Because one of the reasons for forming a multihospital system is the ability to pool resources to improve access to capital, we expected to see relatively higher

**TABLE 3**  Descriptive Statistics: Independent Variables

| Variable | Source | N | Mean | Standard Deviation |
|---|---|---|---|---|
| **Ownership and affiliation** | | | | |
| Investor-owned chain (D) | ⎫ | 561 | 0.2175 | 0.4129 |
| Not-for-profit chain (D) | | 561 | 0.2032 | 0.4027 |
| Investor-owned | American Hospital Association | | | |
| freestanding (D) | (AHA) *Guide*, Federation of | 561 | 0.2638 | 0.4411 |
| Government (D) | American Hospitals (FAH) | 561 | 0.1497 | 0.3571 |
| Not-for-profit | *Directory*, and Medicare | | | |
| freestanding (D) | Cost Reports (MCRs) | 561 | 0.1658 | 0.3722 |
| (omitted reference group) | ⎭ | | | |
| **Contract management and length of affiliation** | | | | |
| Contract managed in 1980 (D) | ⎫ | 561 | 0.0963 | 0.2952 |
| Chain affiliated in 1977 and 1980 (D) | AHA Special Run | 561 | 0.2175 | 0.4129 |
| Contract managed in 1977 and 1980 (D) | ⎭ | 561 | 0.0250 | 0.1561 |
| **Competition and regulation** | | | | |
| Sole community provider (D) | Health Care Financing Administration (HCFA) | 561 | 0.0303 | 0.1716 |
| Percent of admissions covered by rate setting | Office for Civil Rights (OCR) survey and state rate-setting agencies | 559 | 5.8147 | 21.0005 |
| **Case mix and patient selection** | | | | |
| Case-mix index | HCFA, *Federal Register* | 561 | 0.9894 | 0.0822 |
| Inpatient surgeries per 100 admissions | AHA *Annual Survey* | 560 | 37.3481 | 17.3455 |
| Births per 100 admissions | AHA *Annual Survey* | 560 | 6.6276 | 6.6465 |
| Percent of admissions covered by charge-based payers | OCR survey and Blue Cross Association | 539 | 41.3264 | 18.0965 |
| **Input cost and regional practice differences** | | | | |
| Wage index | HCFA, *Federal Register* | 561 | 0.9927 | 0.1595 |
| Located in Census Region 9 (D) | AHA | 561 | 0.1569 | 0.3640 |
| **Capacity and facility utilization** | | | | |
| Number of beds | MCR (available beds) | 561 | 158.1854 | 173.2655 |
| Occupancy rate (percent) | MCR | 561 | 64.7465 | 17.0570 |
| Outpatient revenue to total gross revenue (ratio) | MCR (includes outpatient ancillary and ER) | 559 | 0.1092 | 0.0659 |
| Average length of stay | MCR | 561 | 6.5147 | 1.6238 |
| **Medical education** | | | | |
| Interns and residents: total expense per bed ($) | MCR | 561 | 278.1697 | 1,097.9548 |

NOTE: D = dummy variable: value equals 1 if hospital has attribute, 0 otherwise.

debt-to-asset ratios and newer physical plants among system NFPs than freestanding NFPs.

Based on an earlier Lewin and Associates study,[3] we expected many similarities between IO freestanding hospitals and IO system members. However, we expected higher proportions of surgical admissions and a lower overall case-mix index at freestanding IOs than freestanding or system NFPs, lower overhead costs due to the absence of home office costs, and lower fixed assets per bed and debt-to-asset ratios than system IOs.

We hypothesized that in many ways government hospitals would resemble freestanding NFPs. However, they would have higher outpatient volumes, older plants, lower ratios of capital to operating costs, and higher FTEs per occupied bed than NFPs (due to the public service employer role of some of these facilities). After adjusting to control for public subsidies, we expected little difference in the markups or proportion of nonoperating to total revenue between government and NFP hospitals.

Several studies have shown that it often takes several years for the advantages of multihospital system membership to be realized. Therefore, we expected that hospitals affiliated with systems for more than 3 years would show better results than hospitals with shorter histories. We hypothesized similar relationships for contract-managed hospitals. Hospitals managed for less than 3 years would show poorer financial performance (because correcting such situations is a primary reason for becoming managed), but performance would be better in hospitals managed for a longer time.

### Regression Models

The regression models were developed by including, for each dependent variable, the independent variables which we hypothesized would have an effect. To ease discussion of the results and to provide a more complete explanation of the effects and relationships between variables, we included the same set of independent variables in almost all the equations.

Two sets of regression equations were calculated. First, freestanding NFP hospitals were used as the reference group against which other classes of hospitals were compared. These re-

sults are presented in the tables of regression results (Tables 5-9), which show the freestanding NFPs as the omitted reference group. Then the model was recalculated with the chain-affiliated NFP hospitals as the omitted reference group in order to explicitly measure the magnitude and statistical significance of the differences between NFP and IO system hospitals. This result is shown near the bottom of the tables as "IOMS compared to NFPMS." The changed reference group does not affect the coefficients or significance level values of any of the independent variables except the ownership construct, due to the mathematical relationships involved.

Standard tests eliminated variables sufficiently collinear to bias the results. However, our research has four limitations. First, in some cases the data we were able to obtain may not represent completely the effects we were trying to capture. For example, our payer-mix data are based on *anticipated* source of payment, not actual payer source.

Second, several factors that affect a hospital's performance are inadequately represented due to poor data with which to construct measures. An example is that our measure of the competitive environment is whether the hospital was a Medicare-designated sole community provider—a negative measure that does not distinguish between cases in which a hospital may be ringed by five larger ones and cases in which the sample hospital is the dominant one in a three-hospital town.[4]

Third, other factors that may be important to strategies and performance, such as the way in which strategies are formulated and communicated, the nature of the incentives placed on management, and management skill, could not be included in the current study. Finally, our model is cross-sectional and, thus, limits the inferences that can be made about causality rather than association.

### RESULTS

Our results include findings on six groups of issues: siting and service area characteristics, case mix, operating revenues and expenses, markups and profitability, capital structure, and productivity in the use of assets.

## Siting and Service Area Characteristics

Hospitals of the five classes considered in this study differ in their geographic distribution as a result of historical and economic factors. Table 4 shows the distribution of hospitals across U.S. Census regions.

IO chain facilities are concentrated in the South Atlantic region, including Florida (region 3), the East South Central region, including Tennessee (region 5), the West South Central region, including Texas (region 7), and the Pacific region, including California (region 9)—essentially the "sunbelt," characterized by faster population growth than other areas of the country. NFP systems are also somewhat concentrated, but in different regions: the East North Central region (Midwest—region 4), West North Central region (the Plains states—region 6), and the Mountain states (region 8). They overlap the IO systems in the Pacific and West South Central regions. Freestanding IO hospitals are highly concentrated in the West South Central and Pacific regions, but also remain on the Eastern Seaboard. NFP freestanding hospitals are well distributed across census regions. The government hospitals in our sample tend to be the county and district-sponsored facilities prominent in the South. Since the geographic regions differ in demographics, income, and health care industry regulation, as well as other factors, the broad differences in the locations of hospitals of the five classes influence our findings on five types of siting characteristics.

### Urban, Suburban, and Rural

Overall, about 60 percent of the hospitals in our sample were located in counties or aggregates of counties defined as SMSAs, compared with about 51 percent of U.S. hospitals overall. A higher proportion (74 percent) of IOMS hospitals, and a significantly lower proportion of government hospitals (27 percent), were urban.[5] Differences were sharper when subregions of SMSAs were examined. About 30 percent of the hospitals in the sample overall were located in suburban areas (non-central cities) of the SMSAs. However, about 40 percent of the chain IOs and 42 percent of freestanding IOs were located outside central city

city areas—significantly higher than the percentages of the freestanding NFP hospitals that were located in suburban areas. NFPMS and government hospitals were about as likely as freestanding NFPs to be located in suburban metropolitan areas, but less likely than IO chains to be in the suburbs.

### Wage Index and Sole Community Provider Status

As a consequence of their differing patterns of urban-rural location, the wage indices developed by HCFA were slightly higher for the investor-owned hospitals (both those in multihospital systems and freestanding ones) and lower for the government hospitals in our sample than for the NFPs.

No IO hospitals in our sample had been given Medicare sole community provider status, a designation indicating that a hospital lacks local competition from other hospitals. Hospitals must apply for this designation, and the benefit of doing so in 1980 was to exempt the hospital from Section 223 controls on routine costs under Medicare. Therefore, fewer sole community providers among the IOs could indicate either fewer rural hospitals among the IOs (supported by our findings above) or fewer hospitals needing relief from the cost limits. Of the 17 sole community providers in our sample, 6 were government hospitals, 3 were freestanding NFPs, and 8 were members of NFP systems.

### Area Demographics

On average, about 14 percent of the population in the counties in which the sample hospitals were located were below the poverty level in 1980. The figure was highest for government hospitals (about 16 percent). IO hospitals, both freestanding and chain-affiliated, also had slightly higher rates of poverty in their home counties than did the average freestanding or multihospital system NFP hospital in our sample, but when the broad census regions of the hospitals were controlled for (e.g., New England and Pacific), none of these differences was significant. The hospitals' home counties showed essentially no difference in the percentage of their populations over 65

**TABLE 4** Geographic Distribution of Hospitals in the Sample Compared to All U.S. Community Hospitals, 1980

Ownership Status and Chain Affiliation

| Census Region: States Included | Not-for-profit Freestanding | Investor-Owned Chain-Affiliated | Not-for-profit Chain-Affiliated | Investor-Owned Freestanding | Government | Total All Sample | Total U.S. |
|---|---|---|---|---|---|---|---|
| 1: Conn., Maine, Mass., N.H., R.I., Vt. | 0.08 | 0.00 | 0.00 | 0.02 | 0.00 | 0.02 | 0.06 |
| 2: N.J., N.Y., Pa. | 0.14 | 0.01 | 0.02 | 0.12 | 0.00[a] | 0.06 | 0.12 |
| 3: Del., D.C., Fla., Ga., Md., N.C., S.C., Va., W. Va. | 0.16 | 0.25 | 0.06 | 0.15 | 0.19 | 0.16 | 0.15 |
| 4: Ill., Ind., Mich., Ohio, Wis. | 0.18 | 0.01 | 0.22 | 0.03 | 0.12 | 0.10 | 0.16 |
| 5: Ala., Ky., Miss., Tenn. | 0.09 | 0.20 | 0.06 | 0.09 | 0.15 | 0.12 | 0.08 |
| 6: Iowa, Kans., Minn., Mo., Nebr., N. Dak., S. Dak. | 0.10 | 0.03 | 0.19 | 0.06 | 0.21 | 0.11 | 0.13 |
| 7: Ark., La., Okla., Tex. | 0.12 | 0.20 | 0.17 | 0.32 | 0.20 | 0.21 | 0.12 |
| 8: Ariz., Colo., Idaho, Mont., Nev., N. Mex., Utah, Wyo. | 0.03 | 0.07 | 0.18 | 0.01 | 0.02 | 0.06 | 0.07 |
| 9: Alaska, Calif., Hawaii, Oreg., Wash. | 0.10 | 0.23 | 0.11 | 0.21 | 0.10 | 0.16 | 0.12 |
| Total[b] | 1.00 | 1.00 | 1.01 | 1.01 | 0.99 | 1.00 | 1.01 |

[a]Although a few New York Health and Hospitals Corporation hospitals were selected in the random sampling, they are not in our final sample since we were unable to obtain hospital-specific balance sheet data. Similarly, our final sample does not include any Kaiser or Los Angeles County hospitals.
[b]Totals differ from 1.00 due to rounding.

SOURCE: Lewin and Associates and The Johns Hopkins University; American Hospital Association *Annual Survey of Hospitals*, 1980 (U.S. total).

years of age. While the home counties of the IO hospitals showed higher percentages of nonwhite population (about 20 percent versus 16 percent in the sample overall), these differences were primarily related to the differences in the census regions in which the hospitals were located.

### Area Health Care Capacity and Utilization

The home counties of NFP chain hospitals showed higher ratios of beds per 1,000 persons than the sample as a whole (about 5.3 compared with 4.8 overall). The counties in which the government hospitals in our sample were located showed lower rates of hospitalization as measured by admissions per 1,000 persons (156 versus 175 overall) and surgical operations per 1,000 persons (65 versus 80 overall) compared to freestanding NFPs.

These differences are measured after controlling for regional differences in capacity and use, which other studies have found to be large and significant. When these regional differences in practice were not controlled for, the sampled NFP chain hospitals, located primarily in the Midwest and Rocky Mountain states, show higher rates of admission per 1,000 persons than the other classes of hospitals in the sample.

### Third-Party Coverage and Rate Setting

We found essentially no difference in the percentage of admissions covered by Medicare and Medicaid across the hospitals. However, the shares of the insurance market held by Blue Cross and the bases for Blue Cross payment differ across geographic regions and show in lower proportions of Blue Cross admissions at the IO and government hospitals than at the NFPs of both classes. IO chain hospitals had a significantly higher proportion (35 percent versus 31 percent overall) of their admissions covered by insurance. Coupled with the fact that Blue Cross more often paid charges in their service areas, this led the IO system sample to have higher proportions of charge-based payers (48 percent versus 41 percent overall) than any other group. Virtually none of the IO

chain hospitals and few freestanding IOs were located in rate-setting states in 1980.

### Discussion

We believe these findings, taken together, suggest several important differences in the siting strategies of IO and NFP hospitals. First, IO hospitals in 1980 preferred to locate in areas with rising populations—the sunbelt and the suburban areas, rather than the Midwest, central cities, and rural areas which were losing population. As a consequence of this difference, IO hospitals had higher wage indices than the average NFP hospital in our sample or the government hospitals, which were primarily rural. Also, the lower proportion of rural hospitals among the IOMS systems in 1980 suggests they may have favored areas in which they could be the second provider in town, where they could differentiate the services they offered from those of the existing provider and become the hospital of choice for scheduled medical-surgical patients.[6]

Second, at least at the county level, the service areas of the IO hospitals do not show evidence of attempts to "cream-skim." IO hospitals did not avoid counties with relatively higher rates of poverty, proportions of nonwhite population, or high proportions of elderly. Below the county level, however, we have no data, except for whether the hospital is located in the suburban area or the central city of an SMSA. Their more frequent location in suburban areas may afford the IO hospitals immediate service areas relatively richer in charge-paying patients.

A third difference concerns per capita hospital capacity. Even after controlling for regional differences, NFPMS members are located in areas of higher hospital capacity (measured in beds per 1,000), which is one measure of the extent of hospital competition in an area. IOMS multihospital system members, on the other hand, have not located in areas of high bed-to-population ratios. NFP system hospitals may believe that they will be the survivors in competition in overbedded areas, or may have joined the systems to improve their chances.

Fourth, the lower use of health services in the home counties of the government hospitals may indicate access barriers in rural areas primarily served by government hospitals. However, we cannot conclude from our sample that the presence of NFP chain or IO chain hospitals either drives up use rates or is associated with higher rates of hospital use.

Finally, in 1980, IO hospitals of both classes avoided rate-setting states and ones in which Blue Cross penetration was high or its discount deep.

### Case Mix

Table 5 presents the results of our models of four indicators of case-mix differences: the Medicare case-mix index, inpatient surgeries per 100 admissions, births per 100 admissions, and outpatient revenue to total gross revenue.

IOMS hospitals, when compared to NFPMS facilities, had slightly lower Medicare case-mix indices (0.999 versus 1.017), fewer births per 100 admissions (4.79 versus 7.36), and lower proportions of outpatient to total revenue (0.099 compared to 0.119). We did not find any significant difference between the two groups on the measure of inpatient surgeries per 100 admissions.

NFPMS members were not significantly different from freestanding NFP hospitals on any of the measures, but showed slightly higher case-mix indices and outpatient proportions, and lower surgeries and births per 100 admissions than freestanding NFPs.

IO freestanding hospitals had the lowest case-mix indices (0.982) of any of the groups in our sample. Both they and government hospitals had significantly lower numbers of surgeries per 100 admissions than did freestanding NFPs. Freestanding IOs also had lower numbers of births per 100 admissions than did freestanding NFPs—about half of the freestanding NFP value.

Whether a hospital was contract managed, how long it was contract managed, and how long a hospital had been part of a system had little effect on any of the measures of case mix.

Independent variables from each of the other categories had important effects on hospital case mix. Hospitals in regulated rate-setting states (i.e., Maryland, Massachusetts, New Jersey, New York, Connecticut, and Washington) had slightly lower case-mix indices

(hospitals having 100 percent admissions under rate setting would have had indices averaging about 4 percentage points less than the sample overall); more surgeries per 100 admissions, and higher proportions of outpatient to total revenue.

The variables showing interrelationships among the case-mix measures suggest that higher case-mix indices are associated with higher values for births or surgeries per 100 admissions; higher proportions of births are associated with lower proportions of surgeries and vice versa, and higher proportions of charge-based payers are associated with higher proportions of surgical and obstetrical admissions, but lower proportions of outpatient to total revenue.

Three proxies for differences in input prices and regional medical practices also were associated with differences in the case-mix measures. The wage index, a direct measure of unit labor cost levels and a proxy for urban location, was related to greater numbers of surgeries per 100 admissions. The more direct measure of urban location—location in an SMSA—showed that urban hospitals had higher case-mix indices than rural ones, whether due to more co-morbidities in urban areas, better medical record reporting, or other factors. Hospitals located in the Pacific region also had higher case-mix indices and higher outpatient proportions of total revenue, suggesting that in the Pacific region less acutely ill patients who in other areas may be admitted (reducing the overall case-mix index) were instead treated as outpatients.

Variables measuring hospital capacity and utilization have statistically significant but practically negligible effects on the case-mix measures over reasonable ranges of differences in the independent variables.

### Discussion

In our view, three of these findings on case mix are most important. First, the differences among the case-mix indices of these classes of hospitals are small, even though they are statistically significant. Second, within each ownership type, the hospitals affiliated with multihospital systems have indices slightly higher than those of the freestanding hospitals.

**TABLE 5**   Regression Results: Case Mix Measures

| Variable | Case Mix Index | Inpatient Surgeries per 100 Admissions | Births per 100 Admissions | Outpatient Revenue to Total Gross Revenue |
|---|---|---|---|---|
| Dependent variable mean (whole sample) | 0.990 | 37.341 | 6.632 | 0.109 |
| Not-for-profit freestanding (reference group) dependent mean | 1.010 | 41.052 | 8.027 | 0.115 |
| Ownership and affiliation | | | | |
| Investor-owned chain | −0.011 | −1.449 | −3.237*** | −0.016* |
| Not-for-profit chain | 0.007 | −2.007 | −0.666 | 0.004 |
| Investor-owned freestanding | −0.028*** | −4.865** | −3.707*** | −0.011 |
| Government | −0.002 | −6.913*** | 0.096 | 0.011 |
| Contract management and length of affiliation | | | | |
| Contract managed in 1980 | 0.003 | 1.486 | 0.680 | 0.010 |
| Chain affiliated in 1977 and 1980 | 0.011 | −0.264 | −0.521 | −0.004 |
| Contract managed in 1977 and 1980 | −0.013 | −3.401 | −1.244 | 0.002 |
| Competition and regulation | | | | |
| Sole community provider | −0.014 | −3.834 | 1.513 | 0.020 |
| Percent of admissions covered by rate setting | $-3.836E-4$*** | 0.052* | 0.013 | $2.148E-4$* |
| Case mix and patient selection | | | | |
| Case-mix index | — | 68.970*** | 12.133*** | 0.137*** |
| Inpatient surgeries per 100 admissions | 0.001*** | — | −0.060*** | $-4.278E-4$** |
| Births per 100 admissions | 0.001 | −0.341*** | — | $4.854E-4$ |
| Percent of admissions covered by charge-based payers | $-1.729E-4$ | 0.215*** | 0.072*** | −0.001*** |
| Input cost and regional practice differences | | | | |
| Wage index | — | 25.306*** | 1.666 | 0.021 |
| Located in an SMSA | 0.020*** | — | — | — |
| Located in Census Region 9 | 0.055*** | −1.585 | −0.385 | 0.032*** |
| Capacity and facility utilization | | | | |
| Number of beds | $6.126E-5$*** | 0.009** | 0.006*** | $-4.260E-6$ |
| Occupancy rate (percent) | 0.001*** | 0.064 | 0.001 | $-7.431E-5$ |
| Outpatient revenue to total gross revenue (ratio) | 0.090* | −21.804** | 4.417 | — |
| Average length of stay | — | — | −1.639*** | −0.013*** |

**TABLE 5** *Continued*

| Variable | Case Mix Index | Inpatient Surgeries per 100 Admissions | Births per 100 Admissions | Outpatient Revenue to Total Gross Revenue |
|---|---|---|---|---|
| Medical education Interns and residents: total expense per bed | 9.423E − 6*** | − 0.001 | 0.001*** | 3.273E − 6 |
| Intercept | 0.845*** | − 62.497*** | 3.007 | 0.079** |
| N | 535 | 535 | 535 | 535 |
| Adjusted R² | 0.4335 | 0.3656 | 0.3391 | 0.2413 |
| IOMS compared to NFPMS | − 0.018* | 0.558 | − 2.571*** | − 0.020** |

NOTE: Levels of statistical significance are denoted by asterisks as follow: * probability <.10; ** probability <.05; ***probability <.01 that observed difference is due to chance.

Although these differences were measured before "diagnosis-related group (DRG) maximization," they suggest that hospitals in multihospital systems may have had tougher cases or better medical records systems in these years. Clearly, medical records is an area where economies of scale could allow systems to attract better staff and purchase software to improve the positions of their hospitals. Finally, our results confirm others' findings that IO hospitals of both classes have been considerably less active than NFPs in obstetrics, a service traditionally considered unprofitable.

### Operating Revenues and Expenses

Table 6 presents the results of regression models explaining differences in per-case revenue and expense measures. All these dependent variables were adjusted to control for case mix, wage index, and outpatient volume differences.

Chain-affiliated IO hospitals had total patient care revenues per adjusted admission $378 (21 percent) higher than NFP system hospitals, net patient care revenues per adjusted admission $185 (12 percent) higher, and home office costs per adjusted admission $57 (377 percent) higher. IO and NFP system facilities were much more similar on measures of operating, patient care, and administrative costs per case; these differences were not statistically significant.

NFP system hospitals showed no statistically significant differences from freestanding NFPs in revenues or expenses, except of course in their home office costs. Freestanding IO hospitals also showed no statistically significant differences from freestanding NFPs on any revenue or cost measure. Unlike the system IOs, however, the patient care costs per case of the freestanding IO hospitals appeared lower than those of the freestanding NFPs. Finally, government hospitals had lower revenues and costs per case than freestanding NFPs, especially lower administrative costs.

Hospitals contract managed for less than 3 years, whether by IO or NFP managers, in 1980 had home office costs per adjusted admission $18 higher than hospitals that were not contract managed, but hospitals that had been managed for 3 years or more showed only slightly higher home office costs than those not managed ($17.72 − $15.46 = $2.26). Similarly, hospitals affiliated with systems for longer periods had lower home office costs than those recently joining systems.

The presence of a mandatory state rate-setting program was associated with lower net patient care revenue per adjusted admission ($205 lower, if all admissions were covered under the program) of hospitals operating under it, as well as lower total operating expenses ($154 lower). Sole community provider status was significantly associated only with higher home office costs.

**TABLE 6** Regression Results: Case-Mix-Adjusted Revenues and Operating Costs per Adjusted Admission

| Variable | Total Patient Care Revenue | Net Patient Care Revenue | Total Operating Expenses | Total Patient Care Expenses |
|---|---|---|---|---|
| Dependent variable mean (whole sample) | $1,882.64 | $1,586.15 | $1,593.32 | $1,436.19 |
| Not-for-profit freestanding (reference group) dependent mean | 1,926.19 | 1,611.63 | 1,630.14 | 1,515.91 |
| Ownership and affiliation | | | | |
| Investor-owned chain | 289.98*** | 137.94** | 82.74 | −8.84 |
| Not-for-profit chain | −87.85 | −46.60 | 4.02 | −35.27 |
| Investor-owned freestanding | 104.44 | 22.37 | 44.47 | −73.86 |
| Government | −65.98 | −80.09 | −66.93 | −87.56 |
| Contract management and length of affiliation | | | | |
| Contract managed in 1980 | 42.86 | 39.68 | 89.94 | 54.76 |
| Chain affiliated in 1977 and 1980 | −58.48 | −47.17 | −73.13 | −59.35 |
| Contract managed in 1977 and 1980 | 196.84 | 164.57 | 115.49 | 135.35 |
| Competition and regulation | | | | |
| Sole community provider | 119.79 | 56.64 | 31.26 | 25.11 |
| Percent of admissions covered by rate setting | −1.51 | −2.05** | −1.54* | −1.15 |
| Case mix and patient selection | | | | |
| Case-mix index | — | — | — | — |
| Inpatient surgeries per 100 admissions | 6.09*** | 3.55*** | 3.71*** | 2.91*** |
| Births per 100 admissions | −21.56*** | −19.65*** | −18.34*** | −16.14*** |
| Percent of admissions covered by charge-based payers | −5.46*** | −1.18 | −2.43** | −2.55*** |
| Input cost and regional practice differences | | | | |
| Wage index | — | — | — | — |
| Located in an SMSA | 140.72** | 132.33*** | 128.39*** | 113.57*** |
| Located in Census Region 9 | 245.66*** | 185.28*** | 210.49*** | 81.55* |
| Capacity and facility utilization | | | | |
| Number of beds | 0.91*** | 0.63*** | 0.62*** | 0.49*** |
| Occupancy rate (percent) | 3.70** | 0.57 | −2.13* | −2.37** |
| Outpatient revenue to total gross revenue (ratio) | — | — | — | — |
| Average length of stay | — | — | — | — |
| Medical education | | | | |
| Interns and residents: total expense per bed | 0.08*** | 0.09*** | 0.10*** | 0.09*** |
| Intercept | 1,442.16*** | 1,364.78*** | 1,568.09*** | 1,561.87*** |
| N | 469 | 473 | 520 | 487 |
| Adjusted R² | 0.4146 | 0.3814 | 0.3402 | 0.3155 |
| IOMS compared to NFPMS | 377.83*** | 184.55*** | 78.72 | 26.43 |

**TABLE 6**   *Continued*

| Variable | General and Administrative Costs | Home Office Costs | Interns and Residents: Total Expense per Bed |
|---|---|---|---|
| Dependent variable mean (whole sample) | $694.48 | $19.10 | $   276.87 |
| Not-for-profit freestanding (reference group) dependent mean | 738.45 | 0.68 | 547.56 |
| Ownership and affiliation | | | |
| Investor-owned chain | 8.34 | 71.38*** | −65.32 |
| Not-for-profit chain | −34.74 | 14.43*** | 336.89** |
| Investor-owned freestanding | −23.78 | −0.78 | 8.69 |
| Government | −77.04** | −1.83 | 86.53 |
| Contract management and length of affiliation | | | |
| Contract managed in 1980 | 24.14 | 17.72*** | −134.31 |
| Chain affiliated in 1977 and 1980 | −30.82 | −8.75** | −154.22 |
| Contract managed in 1977 and 1980 | 109.69* | −15.46 | 131.08 |
| Competition and regulation | | | |
| Sole community provider | 1.94 | 14.10* | −60.33 |
| Percent of admissions covered by rate setting | 0.09 | 0.05 | 3.53* |
| Case mix and patient selection | | | |
| Case-mix index | — | — | 1,807.76*** |
| Inpatient surgeries per 100 admissions | 1.18* | −0.18* | −2.78 |
| Births per 100 admissions | −8.24*** | −0.37 | 19.47*** |
| Percent of admissions covered by charge-based payers | −1.68*** | 0.12 | −6.88** |
| Input cost and regional practice differences | | | |
| Wage index | — | — | 920.11*** |
| Located in an SMSA | 50.68** | 2.34 | — |
| Located in Census Region 9 | −14.38 | −7.60* | −397.32*** |
| Capacity and facility utilization | | | |
| Number of beds | 0.26*** | 0.01 | 2.22*** |
| Occupancy rate (percent) | −3.13*** | −0.14 | 1.38 |
| Outpatient revenue to total gross revenue (ratio) | — | — | 859.81 |
| Average length of stay | — | — | 39.38 |
| Medical education | | | |
| Interns and residents: total expense per bed | 0.06*** | 8.41E−4 | — |
| Intercept | 916.65*** | 12.07 | −2,935.69 |
| N | 487 | 472 | 535 |
| Adjusted $R^2$ | 0.2864 | 0.4684 | 0.3168 |
| IOMS compared to NFPMS | 43.08 | 56.95*** | −402.20*** |

NOTE: Levels of statistical significance are denoted by asterisks as follow: *probability <.10; **probability <.05; ***probability <.01 that observed difference is due to chance.

As expected, case-mix differences were associated with important differences in most measures of hospital revenues and costs. The results confirm the hypothesis that surgery is a profitable service for hospitals and obstetrics an unprofitable one. Each additional inpatient surgery per 100 admissions raised the hospitals' gross patient revenues by about $6 per case, net revenues by almost $4 per case, and total patient care expenses by less than $3 per case. On the other hand, each additional birth per 100 admissions *reduced* average gross patient care revenue per case by about $22, net patient care revenues by about $20, but expenses by only $16.

Higher percentages of charge-based payers also were associated with lower revenues and costs per case. The reason is not entirely clear, but may be related to fewer co-morbidities and shorter lengths of stay among the younger patients most often covered by charge-based insurance (an explanation of the cost difference) and a decreased need to "cost shift" in order to earn a target net revenue figure (a possible explanation for the relationship between higher charge-based percentages and lower gross revenues). This second hypothesis is supported by the fact that gross revenues declined more than five times faster than net revenues for each percentage increase in charge-based payers.

Urban hospitals and those located in the Pacific region also had higher revenues and costs than rural hospitals and ones located elsewhere in the country, perhaps due to regional practice differences. The only exceptions to these patterns were (1) in home office costs, where we found no difference between urban and rural hospitals, and (2) in general and administrative and home office costs, where hospitals in the Pacific region showed somewhat lower costs.

Hospitals' capacity and utilization of staffed beds, and their financial commitment to graduate medical education affected their charges and costs to a much lesser degree than many of the other factors in the equations. Each additional bed above the mean of the sample added less than $1 to the hospitals' revenues and costs per case, but more to revenues than to costs. Each additional percentage point of occupancy increased the hospital's total pa-

tient care revenue per case by about $4, but *reduced* total operating expenses per case by about $2, total patient care expenses per case by about $2.50, and the general and administrative component of total operating costs per case by a little over $3. Finally, in 1980, before the Medicare revenue enhancements for medical education, each additional dollar of expense for residents and interns per bed added only about 9 cents to the total patient care expense per admission and about 8 cents to total patient care revenues per admission.

The financial commitment to graduate medical education varied across the classes of hospitals. In the raw data, NFP chain-affiliated hospitals averaged about $733 in expenses for interns and residents per bed per year. NFP freestanding hospitals averaged $543; government hospitals $199; but IO freestanding hospitals only $34 and chain-affiliated IOs less than $3. Controlling for a wide range of factors other than hospital class, the regression model predicts that the average differences among the classes would be much less. The highest predicted value is that for members of NFPMS— intern and resident expenses per bed per year of about $884; government hospitals were the second highest ($634), followed by NFP and IO freestanding hospitals ($548 and $556, respectively). IO chain hospitals in 1980 were predicted to have the lowest financial commitment to medical education in our sample ($482).

### Discussion

In 1980, hospitals in IO systems charged significantly more per case, even after adjusting for case mix differences, relative input costs, and other factors, than did freestanding or system-affiliated NFP hospitals. Freestanding IOs appear to have charged somewhat more per case as well. Even after discounts, allowances, and reserves for bad debt, the net patient revenues of IO system hospitals—one measure of their costs to their communities—were higher than those of NFP hospitals.

However, we found no significant differences in patient care expenses or total operating expenses per case across the classes of hospitals. Indeed, the ownership and affiliation dummy variables as a group did not together explain a significant part of the variance in hospital costs per case.

These findings reinforce the hypothesis that, during the era of cost-based reimbursement, IO hospitals earned higher profits by charging more rather than by being more efficient. While this strategy appears to have been followed by both classes of IO hospitals, it was stronger among those in multihospital systems.

Home office costs per case were considerably higher in IO systems than NFP systems. This may indicate that the IO systems were more centrally organized than NFPs and provided more services centrally. It also, however, may reflect the more active building and acquisition efforts undertaken by the IOs to support their faster rates of growth.

### Markups and Profitability

Table 7 presents the results for the markup and profitability dependent variables. Gross patient care markup, defined as total patient charges divided by total operating costs, is a conservative measure of the profit margins hospitals built into their charges. The revenue deduction ratio measures contractual allowances, free care, discounts, and bad debts as a proportion of gross patient revenues. The third measure shows the proportion of the hospitals' total gross revenues derived from nonoperating sources. The total markup ratio, total revenue divided by total expense, measures the overall profitability of the hospital. Return on total assets (total net income divided by assets) and return on equity (net income divided by owner's equity—not to be mistaken for the add-on capital payment that Medicare pays to IO hospitals) are measures that relate profitability to the investment required to generate it.

Chain-affiliated IO hospitals took higher markups than NFP multihospital system members, both in total (12.8 percentage points higher) and on their patient care services (14.2 percentage points higher), but had higher deductions from gross revenues due to their higher charges, and lower ratios of nonoperating revenue to total revenue. These pricing strategies allowed IO system hospitals to generate better profitability as measured by return on assets (5.5 percentage points higher) and return on

equity (34 percentage points higher) than NFP system hospitals in 1980.

NFP system members, somewhat surprisingly, had significantly lower markups on both their patient care services and in total than freestanding NFPs, and therefore had lower operating surpluses than the freestanding NFPs. Freestanding and system NFPs were virtually identical, however, on the proportions of their revenues derived from nonoperating sources, and higher on this measure than either class of IO hospital. Nonoperating revenue was a larger portion of the total gross revenues of government hospitals than of freestanding NFPs, but these classes of hospitals differed little on markups and profitability.

Freestanding IO hospitals achieved a better return on equity (ROE) than freestanding NFPs on only slightly higher markup ratios and while earning less nonoperating revenue as a percentage of total revenue. Thus, their higher ROE was due largely to the higher proportion of debt financing among the IO hospitals than the NFPs. That IO hospitals of both classes had lower proportions of nonoperating revenue to total revenue than the NFP or government hospitals probably reflects the fact that IO hospitals are rarely the beneficiaries of either private philanthropy or tax revenues, important sources of nonoperating revenues for some NFP and government hospitals, respectively.

The length of affiliation with chains or under contract management had no significant relationships with hospital markups and profitability.

We found no evidence that sole community providers take advantage of their status to charge higher markups or generate "monopoly" profits. We found no statistically significant relationships between the presence of a state rate-setting program and levels of markups or deductions from gross revenues. However, hospitals in rate-setting states had slightly lower returns on assets than hospitals elsewhere.

We found no relationship between either the overall case-mix index of a hospital or its proportion of surgical cases and its markups or profitability. However, hospitals with higher proportions of maternity cases had lower profitability. Hospitals with higher percentages of charge-based payers showed lower revenue

TABLE 7 Regression Results: Markups and Profitability

| Variable | Gross Patient Care Markup Ratio | Revenue Deduction Ratio | Nonoperating Revenue to Total Gross Revenue | Total Markup Ratio | Return on Total Assets | Return on Equity or Fund Balance |
|---|---|---|---|---|---|---|
| Dependent variable mean (whole sample) | 1.193 | 0.144 | 0.031 | 1.230 | 0.059 | 0.188 |
| Not-for-profit freestanding (reference group) dependent mean | 1.190 | 0.152 | 0.035 | 1.233 | 0.039 | 0.075 |
| Ownership and affiliation | | | | | | |
| Investor-owned chain | 0.105*** | 0.039*** | −0.020*** | 0.089*** | 0.045*** | 0.315*** |
| Not-for-profit chain | −0.037* | −0.011 | −0.001 | −0.040* | −0.010 | −0.028 |
| Investor-owned freestanding | 0.029 | 0.009 | −0.012*** | 0.019 | 0.018 | 0.144*** |
| Government | 0.011 | 0.008 | 0.012** | 0.024 | 0.021 | 0.026 |
| Contract management and length of affiliation | | | | | | |
| Contract managed in 1980 | −0.015 | 0.010 | −0.001 | −0.018 | −0.008 | 0.012 |
| Chain affiliated in 1977 and 1980 | 0.007 | 0.003 | 0.004 | 0.010 | −0.003 | 0.016 |
| Contract managed in 1977 and 1980 | 0.020 | 0.012 | −0.011 | 0.003 | −0.040 | −0.067 |
| Competition and regulation | | | | | | |
| Sole community provider | 0.030 | 0.024 | 0.011 | 0.037 | 0.009 | −0.006 |
| Percent of admissions covered by rate setting | $-3.513E-4$ | $5.929E-5$ | $1.109E-4$ | $-2.128E-4$ | $-4.180E-4*$ | −0.001 |
| Case mix and patient selection | | | | | | |
| Case-mix index | −0.073 | −0.076 | −0.033 | −0.075 | 0.053 | 0.058 |

| | | | | | | |
|---|---|---|---|---|---|---|
| Inpatient surgeries per 100 admissions | 5.562E−4 | 2.041E−4 | −6.584E−5 | 0.001 | −1.902E−4 | −2.544E−4 |
| Births per 100 admissions | −8.323E−4 | 0.001** | −6.447E−5 | −3.682E−4 | −0.003*** | −0.005* |
| Percent of admissions covered by charge-based payers | −0.001*** | −0.001*** | 2.226E−5 | −0.001*** | 0.001* | 0.002** |
| Input cost and regional practice differences | | | | | | |
| Wage index | 0.137** | 0.098*** | −0.012 | 0.117** | 0.043 | 0.126 |
| Located in Census Region 9 | 0.039 | 0.011 | −0.008* | 0.024 | 0.026 | −0.011 |
| Capacity and facility utilization | | | | | | |
| Number of beds | 7.664E−5 | 4.594E−5* | 1.924E−5* | 1.089E−4** | 4.300E−5 | 1.259E−4 |
| Occupancy rate (percent) | 0.004*** | 0.001*** | −3.988E−4*** | 0.004*** | 0.002*** | 0.004*** |
| Outpatient revenue to total gross revenue (ratio) | −0.228** | −0.184*** | 0.053** | −0.168 | −0.038 | 0.261 |
| Average length of stay | −0.002 | 0.003 | −2.454E−4 | −0.003 | −0.012*** | −0.010 |
| Medical education | | | | | | |
| Interns and residents: total expense per bed | −1.708E−5** | −9.155E−6** | 1.034E−6 | −1.760E−5* | −4.218E−6 | −1.234E−5 |
| Intercept | 0.903*** | 0.047 | 0.102*** | 0.996*** | −0.104 | −0.344 |
| N | 512 | 514 | 507 | 513 | 506 | 497 |
| Adjusted $R^2$ | 0.2872 | 0.2502 | 0.1832 | 0.2396 | 0.1546 | 0.1826 |
| IOMS compared to NFPMS | 0.142*** | 0.050*** | −0.018*** | 0.128*** | 0.055*** | 0.343*** |

NOTE: Levels of statistical significance are denoted by asterisks as follow: *probability $<.10$; **probability $<.05$; ***probability $<.01$ that observed difference is due to chance.

deductions, and required lower markup ratios (measured as *gross* revenues to costs) to achieve higher profitability.

Hospitals in areas with higher wage indices took higher total markups of revenues over costs. Pacific Coast hospitals earned less of their total revenue from nonoperating sources than hospitals in the remainder of the county.

Capacity and utilization variables were statistically significant, but explained only small proportions of the differences in markups and profitability across the classes of hospitals. Increased occupancy allowed hospitals to earn higher markups on patient services and in total, and was therefore associated with increased revenue deductions and higher return on assets and return on equity. Increased outpatient proportions of total revenue were associated with lower patient service markups and deductions, but with higher proportions of the hospital's revenue coming from nonoperating sources. Longer average lengths of stay were associated with lower return on assets (1.2 percent decrease for each additional day).

Finally, higher medical education costs per bed were associated with slightly lower patient and total markups in the hospitals.

## Discussion

These results support our earlier findings on revenues and costs: the IO hospitals in multihospital chains took higher markups and earned higher returns than did NFP hospitals of either type. Freestanding IO facilities were somewhat more moderate in their pricing practices, but both classes of IO hospitals earned higher returns on equity than the NFP hospitals. NFP system hospitals took relatively lower markups than freestanding NFPs, and earned only modest returns.

All hospitals, regardless of ownership, must earn operating surpluses in order to remain attractive to lenders of debt capital and to be able to replace their plant and equipment. All five classes of hospitals in our sample, on average, were able to do so in 1980. However, the higher surpluses of the IO hospitals, coupled with their ability to issue stock, give them a flexibility in developing capital that is not matched by the ability of the NFP hospitals

to attract and accept donations or government grants.

### Capital Structure

Table 8 shows the results of equations examining capital structure variables. Chain-affiliated IOs had higher debt-to-asset ratios than NFP system members (about 0.66 versus 0.46); higher capital costs as a percentage of total operating costs, whether excluding or including Medicare's return-on-equity payment; younger plants, as measured by the ratio of accumulated depreciation to depreciation expense (2.22 versus 6.50 years); and lower fixed-asset values per bed ($6,533 less). While we found no statistically significant differences between the NFP hospitals in our sample in systems and those that were freestanding, the NFP system sample showed slightly lower debt-to-asset ratios, current ratios, and capital costs as percentages of total operating costs; older plants; and lower fixed-asset values per bed than freestanding NFPs.

Freestanding IOs had higher debt-to-asset ratios (0.15 higher), younger plants (1.95 years younger), and considerably lower fixed-asset values per bed ($22,386 less) than freestanding NFPs. On the fixed-asset value measure, the freestanding IO figure is about half the NFP freestanding one. Government hospitals had lower debt-to-asset ratios (0.13 lower), lower capital costs as a percentage of operating costs, and lower fixed-asset values per bed ($9,559 less) than freestanding NFPs.

Hospitals contract-managed for less than 3 years had higher debt-to-asset ratios (0.19 higher) than freestanding NFPs that were not contract-managed. Our results also showed contract-managed hospitals as having less depreciated plants (about 2 years lower in accounting age of plant than freestanding NFPs). Variables measuring the length of affiliation with a chain or under contract management had no significant effects on capital structure.

Our variables reflecting competition and regulation in the hospitals' environments yielded only two strong relationships. First, sole community providers appear to not have capital structures significantly different from those of the average hospital in our sample. Second, hospitals operating under rate-setting

TABLE 8 Regression Results: Capital Structure

| Variable | Debt-to-Asset Ratio | Current Ratio | Capital Cost Percent A[a] | Capital Cost Percent B[b] | Accounting Average Age of Plant | Total Fixed Assets per Bed |
|---|---|---|---|---|---|---|
| Dependent variable mean (whole sample) | 0.527 | 2.724 | 7.146 | 7.907 | 4.963 | $ 35,481.12 |
| Not-for-profit freestanding (reference group) dependent mean | 0.477 | 2.587 | 7.146 | 7.146 | 5.497 | 46,768.00 |
| Ownership and affiliation | | | | | | |
| Investor-owned chain | 0.187*** | −0.115 | 0.371 | 2.418*** | −3.276*** | −8,489.38** |
| Not-for-profit chain | −0.020 | −0.034 | −0.853 | −0.767 | 1.005 | −1,956.81 |
| Investor-owned freestanding | 0.154*** | −0.156 | −0.095 | 1.228* | −1.953*** | −22,385.80*** |
| Government | −0.126*** | 0.472 | −1.323** | −1.441** | 1.169 | −9,559.21*** |
| Contract management and length of affiliation | | | | | | |
| Contract managed in 1980 | 0.193*** | −0.467 | 0.964 | 0.619 | −1.608* | −1,646.94 |
| Chain affiliated in 1977 and 1980 | 0.040 | −0.419 | −0.386 | −0.689 | 0.276 | 1,738.47 |
| Contract managed in 1977 and 1980 | −0.080 | −0.119 | −0.122 | 0.072 | 2.667 | −1,037.91 |
| Competition and regulation | | | | | | |
| Sole community provider | −0.075 | −0.274 | −0.428 | −0.483 | 0.194 | 4,936.26 |
| Percent of admissions covered by rate setting | 0.001** | −0.011** | −0.006 | −0.007 | −0.004 | −8.96 |
| Case mix and patient selection | | | | | | |
| Case-mix index | −0.317 | −1.205 | 5.009 | 7.259** | −1.559 | 67,267.87*** |
| Inpatient surgeries per 100 admissions | 0.002** | −0.013* | 0.030** | 0.028** | 0.008 | 43.78 |
| Births per 100 admissions | 3.936E−4 | −0.020 | −0.065* | −0.071** | 0.044 | −4.52 |
| Percent of admissions covered by charge-based payers | 7.036E−5 | 8.988E−5 | 0.022* | 0.020 | −0.006 | 130.39** |

282

**TABLE 8** *Continued*

| Variable | Debt-to-Asset Ratio | Current Ratio | Capital Cost Percent A[a] | Capital Cost Percent B[b] | Accounting Average Age of Plant | Total Fixed Assets per Bed |
|---|---|---|---|---|---|---|
| Input cost and regional practice differences | | | | | | |
| Wage index | 0.318*** | -1.969** | -0.786 | -2.521 | -0.886 | 131.37 |
| Located in Census Region 9 | -0.018 | 0.400 | -0.683 | -0.449 | -1.115 | -446.16 |
| Capacity and facility utilization | | | | | | |
| Number of beds | 6.991E-5 | 3.442E-4 | 0.002 | 0.002 | -0.002 | 11.26 |
| Occupancy rate (percent) | -0.001 | 0.003 | -0.050*** | -0.055*** | -0.067*** | 248.90*** |
| Outpatient revenue to total gross revenue (ratio) | -0.082 | 1.056 | -8.656*** | -9.054*** | 3.827 | -420.06 |
| Average length of stay | 0.012 | -0.135 | -0.158 | -0.185 | 0.454* | -412.44 |
| Medical education | | | | | | |
| Interns and residents: total expense per bed | -1.290E-5 | 1.057E-5 | -2.983E-4 | -2.715E-4 | -7.043E-5 | 0.87 |
| Intercept | 0.319 | 7.138*** | 6.821** | 7.105** | 9.285** | -45,231.77*** |
| N | 523 | 516 | 525 | 525 | 420 | 477 |
| Adjusted $R^2$ | 0.2231 | 0.0584 | 0.1139 | 0.2034 | 0.1201 | 0.3136 |
| IOMS compared to NFPMS | 0.208*** | -0.082 | 1.225** | 3.185*** | -4.281*** | -6,532.57** |

NOTE: Levels of statistical significance are denoted by asterisks as follow: *probability $<.10$; **probability $<.05$; ***probability $<.01$ that observed difference is due to chance.

[a]Capital-related cost as a percentage of total operating cost.
[b]Capital-related cost plus Medicare return on equity payments as a percentage of total operating cost.

programs had higher debt-to-asset ratios and lower current ratios than those in less regulated states. The higher debt-to-asset ratio may indicate both that hospitals in these states required more borrowing and that these states assisted hospitals to borrow by issuing "comfort orders" explaining that debt service was an allowable expense under the rate-setting program.

Few other independent variables were strongly associated with differences in capital structure. Higher case-mix indices were associated with slightly higher capital cost as a percentage of operating costs and higher fixed assets per bed, confirming the need for sophisticated and costly equipment to render more intensive care. Higher numbers of surgical procedures per 100 admissions were related to higher debt-to-asset ratios, lower current ratios, and higher capital cost as a percentage of operating costs. However, we found no significant relationship between higher surgeries and higher fixed assets per bed. Higher percentages of births among a hospital's case load were associated with lower capital cost as a percentage of operating costs, but had no strong effects on any of the other measures of capital structure. Higher wage indices, often indicating urban areas, were linked to higher debt-to-asset and lower current ratios.

Capacity and facility utilization had statistically significant but small effects on capital structure ratios. Higher occupancy rates resulted in lower capital cost as a percentage of total operating costs, showing the effect of spreading the fixed capital costs over greater volumes. Higher occupancy also was present in younger physical plants and in hospitals with higher fixed assets per bed. This may indicate that new physical plants tend to be built in areas of need where the capacity will be utilized by growing populations. An alternative hypothesis, that patients are attracted to new buildings, is less in accord with our experience. Higher proportions of total revenue from outpatient services, including ancillaries, were associated with lower capital cost as a percentage of operating costs. Finally, hospitals with longer stays apparently also had somewhat older physical plants.

## Discussion

Despite their better access to capital, IO multihospital systems appear to be more judicious in its use, as shown by their lower fixed-asset values per bed. The significantly lower fixed-asset figures for freestanding IO hospitals are consistent with their lower case-mix indices and smaller size, and indicate hospitals which probably provide fewer sophisticated services.

Consistent with national studies, IO hospitals of both classes had higher capital costs as a percentage of their total operating costs than other hospitals. This is due to their higher leverage, and also, in part, due to the younger age of their physical plants on accounting-based measures. However, since "accounting age" is affected by sales of hospitals (revaluation of the assets, which Medicare until recently allowed, "reset the accounting clock"), it is not clear whether other hospitals in fact will require replacement or major capital projects earlier than IO hospitals. Clearly, in the short run, IO hospitals would be less advantaged by a payment system that would include capital as a fixed-percentage add-on to the DRG rates. IO hospitals might be disadvantaged over the long term as well, unless their higher capital costs in fact show the financing of more "future costs," rather than being accounting artifacts of more recent purchase of plant assets of the same physical age as those of the NFPs.

## Activity and Productivity

Table 9 presents the estimated coefficients for the activity and productivity regressions. The total asset turnover ratio measures the revenue dollars a hospital generates for each dollar invested in fixed assets, and the current asset turnover ratio measures revenue per dollar of current assets. Case flow is measured as admissions per bed, and is, thus, directly related to occupancy and inversely related to length of stay.

Chain-affiliated IO hospitals showed better use of assets on those measures based on dollars—total and current asset turnover ratios—than NFP system hospitals (ratios 0.39 and 2.32 higher), due to their higher charges and lower asset values. However, they showed

TABLE 9 Regression Results: Activity and Productivity Ratios

| Variable | Total Asset Turnover Ratio | Current Asset Turnover Ratio | Case Flow | Occupancy Rate | FTEs per Adjusted Daily Census |
|---|---|---|---|---|---|
| Dependent variable mean (whole sample) | 1.504 | 4.200 | 37.293 | 64.650 | 2.372 |
| Not-for-profit freestanding (reference group) dependent mean | 1.043 | 3.469 | 37.949 | 69.841 | 2.588 |
| Ownership and affiliation | | | | | |
| Investor-owned chain | 0.578*** | 2.286*** | −2.485 | −5.104** | −0.222** |
| Not-for-profit chain | 0.194* | −0.037 | −0.059 | −1.363 | 0.062 |
| Investor-owned freestanding | 1.106*** | 0.637*** | −1.666 | −1.621 | −0.036 |
| Government | 0.101 | −0.230 | −2.348 | −2.959 | 0.069 |
| Contract management and length of affiliation | | | | | |
| Contract managed in 1980 | 0.246* | 0.052 | −3.017* | −5.038** | −0.058 |
| Chain affiliated in 1977 and 1980 | −0.046 | 0.651*** | 2.443* | 3.484* | −0.026 |
| Contract managed in 1977 and 1980 | 0.226 | 0.361 | −0.354 | 2.099 | 0.013 |
| Competition and regulation | | | | | |
| Sole community provider | −0.097 | −0.089 | 0.570 | −4.299 | −0.054 |
| Percent of admissions covered by rate setting | 0.001 | 0.004 | 0.062*** | 0.110*** | −0.002 |
| Case mix and patient selection | | | | | |
| Case-mix index | −1.334** | −0.717 | 6.622 | 42.064*** | 0.869* |
| Inpatient surgeries per 100 admissions | 0.001 | −0.002 | 0.075** | 0.078* | 0.002 |

|  | (1) | (2) | (3) | (4) | (5) |
|---|---|---|---|---|---|
| Births per 100 admissions | 0.002 | 0.012 | 0.362*** | 0.008 | 0.017*** |
| Percent of admissions covered by charge-based payers | −0.003 | 0.009* | 0.120*** | 0.025 | 0.001 |
| Input cost and regional practice differences |  |  |  |  |  |
| Wage index | 1.299*** | 1.981*** | −5.073 | −2.941 | 0.255 |
| Located in Census Region 9 | 0.032 | −0.840*** | −2.589* | −10.937*** | 0.372*** |
| Capacity and facility utilization |  |  |  |  |  |
| Number of beds | −0.001** | 1.894E−4 | −0.014*** | 0.009** | −6.159E−5 |
| Occupancy rate (percent) | 0.002 | 0.004 | — | — | 0.025*** |
| Outpatient revenue to total gross revenue (ratio) | −0.322 | −1.342 | 12.241 | −4.720 | 1.649*** |
| Average length of stay | −0.019 | 0.007 | — | 2.139*** | −0.029 |
| Medical education |  |  |  |  |  |
| Interns and residents: total expense per bed | 1.691E−5 | −4.899E−5 | 1.207E−4 | 3.337E−4 | 1.455E−4*** |
| Intercept | 1.248** | 1.715 | 27.571*** | 0.061 | −0.606 |
| N | 513 | 509 | 535 | 535 | 495 |
| Adjusted R² | 0.3350 | 0.3185 | 0.1533 | 0.2995 | 0.4540 |
| IOMS compared to NFPMS | 0.383*** | 2.323*** | −2.426* | −3.740* | −0.284*** |

NOTE: Levels of statistical significance are denoted by asterisks as follow: *probability $<.10$; **probability $<.05$; ***probability $<.01$ that observed difference is due to chance.

weaker performance on case flow (2.4 fewer admissions per staffed bed per year), a productivity measure based on use of beds in service, due to their significantly lower occupancy. However, despite their lower occupancy, IO chain hospitals employed 0.28 fewer FTEs per adjusted average daily census than NFP system hospitals. NFP system members showed slightly better total asset turnover numbers than freestanding NFPs, but showed no other significant differences from NFPs on these measures of activity and productivity. Government hospitals were also similar to freestanding NFPs on these measures. Unlike the chain-affiliated IOs, however, freestanding IO hospitals did not use fewer FTEs per average daily census than NFP hospitals.

Hospitals chain-affiliated for 3 or more years showed higher turnover of current assets (ratio 0.65 higher), better case flows (2.4 more admissions per bed per year), and higher occupancy than hospitals that had joined multihospital systems more recently, but showed no better productivity in the use of personnel. Hospitals newly contract managed had fewer admissions per bed and lower occupancy than other hospitals in the sample.

Case flow was faster and occupancy higher in hospitals in rate-setting states (several states encouraged more admissions per bed through low-occupancy penalties in their reimbursement systems), but activity and productivity apparently were little affected otherwise by our competition and regulation variables.

Hospitals with higher case-mix indices apparently had somewhat lower total asset turnover, primarily due to their higher asset values. They also showed higher occupancy, graduate medical education (GME) costs, and ratios of personnel to daily census than did hospitals with less intense caseloads. Higher numbers of surgeries and births per 100 admissions were associated with better case flow and somewhat higher FTEs per adjusted average daily census. Higher proportions of charge-based payers also were associated with better case flow, perhaps through shorter stays.

Higher area wage indices, perhaps due to their relation to urban areas, were associated with slightly higher asset turnover ratios and higher GME costs, but not with better personnel productivity. Pacific Coast hospitals showed lower current asset turnover, occupancy, and GME costs, but better personnel productivity than hospitals elsewhere.

Larger hospitals had lower current asset turnover, higher occupancy, and slower case flow (0.009 fewer admissions per bed per year for each additional bed) than the smaller hospitals in our sample, but were not different in personnel productivity. They also had higher GME costs. Occupancy, oddly, appears to be directly related to the number of FTEs per adjusted average daily census (0.025 *increase* per each 1 percent increase in occupancy). More expected results are that the proportion of a hospital's revenue from outpatient services also increases FTEs per adjusted daily census (0.086 additional FTE for each additional percent of outpatient revenue), as does GME. Longer lengths of stay are also associated with higher occupancy.

### Discussion

IO hospitals of both classes, due to their higher markups and lower asset values per bed, generate more revenue per dollar of total or current assets than do NFP hospitals. They also operate with fewer staff per occupied bed. While IO hospitals did not translate their higher productivity into lower costs per case in 1980, they achieved better productivity despite operating at much lower occupancy rates than NFP hospitals. Thus, IO hospitals, particularly those in systems, stand to benefit more than NFP hospitals from improvements in facility utilization, which will allow them to spread their higher administrative costs and lower their overall costs per case. While their higher charges would disadvantage them in contracting with organizations like PPOs and HMOs which can shift blocks of patients, their cost functions might encourage the IO system facilities to offer the deeper discounts necessary to secure greater patient volumes.

### CONCLUSIONS

This study of a national sample of community hospitals has shown a number of differences in economic performance across hospitals of different ownership and affiliation classes from which differences in strategies may be inferred. On 24 of our 28 measures of case mix, revenues and operating costs, markups and profitability, capital structure, and activity and productivity, statistical tests showed that hospital ownership and system affiliation were significant factors in explaining the differences across hospitals. However, on most measures except revenues per case, home office costs, and debt-to-asset ratios, other factors such as hospital capacity were also important explanatory factors.

## Ownership and Chain Affiliation

The clear pattern that emerges from this study is that in 1980 there were much greater similarities among hospitals of the same ownership type (IO or NFP) than among hospitals of the same organizational type (multihospital system or freestanding). IO hospitals, whether freestanding or members of systems, were similar on the majority of measures in the study. The NFP members of multihospital systems in our study differed from freestanding NFPs only on the measures of home office costs, markup ratios, and asset turnover. Clearly, in 1980 the strategies and performance of IO and NFP multihospital system hospitals had not converged as some observers believe they have today.

## Functional Strategies

The study suggests several conclusions about the functional strategies of IO and NFP hospitals. First, *patient selection* by the IO hospitals appears largely a function of siting and service-offering decisions. In 1980, as in 1984, less than 30 IO system hospitals, and none in our sample, were Medicare sole community providers, indicating that their service areas lacked competition. IO hospitals are primarily (74 percent) suburban or urban, and located in areas of relatively more rapid population growth and moderate bed-to-population ratios than characterize the home counties of NFP hospitals. They appear to have preferred to be the second hospital in town, which allows them to differentiate their service offerings from those of other providers. This type of service decision was shown in 1980 in their less frequent offering of obstetrical services, ones which ap-

pear to be unprofitable among the hospitals in our sample. IO multihospital systems in 1980 also preferred to locate in areas where Blue Cross paid charges; this resulted in higher percentages of their patients being covered by charge-based insurance than the patients of the other classes of hospitals in our sample.

NFP multihospital systems, on the other hand, appear to have hospitals more evenly distributed across locations ranging from central cities to rural communities. Although several NFP system hospitals in our sample are sole community providers, on average, the NFP multihospital system facilities are located in areas with more competition, as indicated by bed-to-population ratios, than any other class of hospital.

Second, in 1980 *pricing* was the key to the IO hospitals' higher profitability. Services in IO systems in 1980 cost the public more than in other classes of hospitals, even when adjusted for differences in case mix, wage rates, and outpatient volumes, and controlling for a wide range of other factors affecting costs. The NFP system members in our sample, on the other hand, earned somewhat lower returns than other classes of hospitals by marking up their patient care services less in relation to their costs.

Third, the *financial strategies* of IO hospitals of both types enabled them to earn higher returns for their investors and gave the IO hospitals an advantage in access to capital. These strategies combined higher patient service prices with financing a higher proportion of their assets through debt than the NFPs.

Finally, the *costs of medical education* in 1980 were virtually all borne by NFP hospitals. The direct expenses associated with training interns and residents were dramatically higher in hospitals in NFP multihospital systems than in IO ones. While not quantified in this study, it is intuitive that the indirect costs of teaching were also higher in NFP multihospital systems.

## Multihospital System Economies

This study does not show evidence of net economies achieved through multihospital system operation in either the IO or the NFP sector. The total patient care costs and total operating expenses per adjusted admission of the multihospital system hospitals were not significantly different from those of freestanding NFPs. This may be due in part to the incentives of the Medicare reimbursement system in place in 1980, under which hospitals were paid on the basis of costs rather than revenues. However, it is also important to note that these operating cost and patient care cost results were obtained by system hospitals despite their home office costs, a category of costs not borne by freestanding facilities. The total general and administrative costs per admission (including home office costs) of the IO chains were only slightly higher than those of freestanding NFPs, and those of multihospital system NFPs were lower than those of freestanding hospitals. This suggests that the home office operations of both types of systems, in the main, substituted for costs borne by hospitals locally and may, in fact, have resulted in some offsetting direct cost savings as well.

### Potential for Future Success

The environment that hospitals of all classes face in 1984 is considerably different from the world of 1980. HMOs, PPOs, employers, and insurers have begun to "shop" for hospital services. Medicare has set prospective prices, and other public payers have experimented with contracting with selected hospitals. New types of providers such as surgicenters have also emerged that chip away at the edges of hospitals' traditional markets. This snapshot of the behavior and performance of hospitals under cost reimbursement, while not conclusive, may allow some inferences about the potential successes of the classes of hospitals in a more price-competitive environment.

First, the considerably higher prices per case among the IO system facilities, wider geographic dispersion (rather than regional concentration), and their less frequent offering of outpatient and obstetric services may put them at a disadvantage to NFP hospitals in winning contracts to provide services for organized local groups of patients. However, this expectation could be tempered by three factors. First, through multiunit operation, systems can subsidize lower prices and profits in areas where competition is keen, with profits from hospi-

tals in less challenging environments. This strategy is open to all systems, but not to freestanding hospitals. Second, the greater capital available in systems makes them more able to offer their own insurance products. Finally, the IO chains' cost and profit performance has been achieved in hospitals with generally low occupancy. Winning or offering contracts to improve occupancy might result in greater economies of scale in the IO hospitals, allowing them to achieve their historical profit margins despite the necessarily lower net prices of services. IO hospitals might use these factors to erode the NFP hospitals' initially greater attractiveness to payers, but they will need to run faster and farther than the NFPs to do so.

Second, faced with potentially shrinking margins, IO systems may redeploy capital to develop other sources of revenues. Humana, for example, was initially a nursing home company, but left that business to concentrate on hospitals. In recent years, it has sold more hospitals than it has acquired, and concentrated on freestanding centers and insurance products. If changing market economics force hospitals to become price-takers and allow insurers to be price-setters, IO systems may increasingly redefine themselves as insurers to capture the higher margins possible from other levels of the health care industry. NFP hospitals, whether freestanding or in systems, may be slower to change their historical missions.

Third, their higher capital costs as a percentage of operating costs would disadvantage IO hospitals in the short run if a method were enacted to pay for capital as a fixed percentage increment to operating costs. This disadvantage would persist in the long run as well to the extent that the IO hospitals' higher current capital costs are an artifact of the revaluation of older assets on purchase, rather than related to physically newer buildings.

Fourth, the current magnitude of the indirect teaching cost adjustment under Medicare gives teaching hospitals an edge over nonteaching ones that may become even more important as the payment formula becomes based more on national averages. Along with their desire to integrate more vertically, this may be part of the reason that IO chain hospitals have sought to acquire several major teaching hospitals recently. However, the future of this adjustment factor is in doubt. Current proposals suggest halving the indirect allowance factor and freezing allowable salary and benefit costs per intern and resident at some historical level. The advantage of more favorable reimbursement to teaching hospitals may be quickly eroded.

Finally, for multihospital systems of both classes, the challenge of the new environment will be to use their greater capital resources effectively and achieve the scale economies that theory suggests should be possible through system operation. Neither the IO nor the NFP multihospital systems demonstrated solid evidence of such economies in 1980. Basic issues such as how to motivate physicians and staff, reduce the costs of service, increase patient volumes in maturing markets, anticipate the behavior of third-party payers, and develop new revenue sources will be a large part of the new equation. The question of relative future success thus depends significantly on the managerial creativity and leadership each sector of the industry brings to solving problems. On these factors of production, no sector of the industry has a monopoly.

## ACKNOWLEDGMENTS

The authors gratefully acknowledge the technical assistance of George D. Pillari.

This research was supported in part by Associated Hospital Systems. The views expressed are solely those of the authors.

## NOTES

[1] Using a matrix for each state, these data were used to construct the "percent charge-based" and "percent of admissions subject to rate-setting" variables described below.

[2] Watt, J. M., R. A. Derzon, S. C. Renn, and C. J. Schramm, J. S. Hahn, and G. D. Pillari (1986) The comparative economic performance of investor-owned and not-for-profit hospitals, *New England Journal of Medicine* 314:89-96; Lewin and Associates (1981) Studies in the Comparative Performance of Investor-Owned and Not-for-Profit Hospitals, Vol. 1: Industry Analysis (Washington, D.C.: Lewin and Associates); and Lewin, L., R. Derzon, and R. Margulies (1981) Investor-owneds and nonprofits differ in economic performance, *Hospitals* 55:52-58.

[3] Lewin and Associates (1976) *Investor-Owned Hospitals: An Examination of Performance* (Chicago: Health Services Foundation).

[4] This measure is also more restrictive than those based solely on distance between hospitals, e.g., no other hospitals in a 15-mile radius. Using the Medicare designation, none of the IO hospitals in our sample are sole community providers. However, using other definitions, HCA, among other systems, may have a large number of sole community provider hospitals.

[5] In this chapter, "significant" indicates $p < .05$. Here, significant differences are measured against not-for-profit freestanding hospitals, which constitute the majority of the hospitals in the universe from which our samples were drawn.

[6] This inference is supported by our earlier case study research. See Lewin and Associates, Inc. (1981) *Studies in the Comparative Performance of Investor-Owned and Not-For-Profit Hospitals. Volume III: Two Case Studies of Competition Between Hospitals* (Washington, D.C.: Lewin and Associates).

*For-Profit Enterprise in Health Care.* 1986.
National Academy Press, Washington, D.C.

# Response to Financial Incentives Among Investor-Owned and Not-for-Profit Hospitals: An Analysis Based on California Data, 1978-1982

Robert V. Pattison

This report presents findings from an investigation conducted for the Institute of Medicine's project on the implications of for-profit organization in health care. The investigation focuses on the dynamic aspects of financial performance by the nonprofit (public and private) and investor-owned (independent and "chain") sectors of the hospital industry in California over a 4-year period, from 1977-1978 to 1981-1982. Data have been examined for 240 acute care, fee-for-service (non-HMO) hospitals in the 76 to 250 bed-size range.

The research is an extension and refinement of a study by Pattison and Katz, "Investor-Owned and Not-for-Profit Hospitals: A Comparison Based on California Data" published on August 11, 1983 in *The New England Journal of Medicine*. In that study, utilizing California Health Facilities Commission (CHFC) data for 1978-1980 (CHFC Cycle 5), the authors analyzed differences in financial performance by ownership class among small to midsize urban hospitals.

Among the principal findings of that study are the following:

• There was no evidence that investor-owned (IO) hospitals were more cost effective than nonprofit or public hospitals of comparable size and service complexity. This was true for either independent or multi-institutional affiliated (chain) IO hospitals, and was true whether costs (operating expenses) were measured on either a per-day or per-admission basis.
• The profitability and the growth of IO chain sectors were attributed to an aggressive use of pricing and marketing strategies.
• There was no evidence that ownership per se was influential in the payer mix of pa-

tients served (Medicare, Medicaid, and private pay). Hospital size, location, and type appeared to be the principal factors.

Those findings raised questions for further investigation. In particular, issues were raised regarding financial performance over time—the ways in which the IO and not-for-profit sectors of the industry had responded to financial incentives. It is the purpose of this study to examine these issues.

## SUMMARY OF PRINCIPAL FINDINGS

The principal findings of the current study are:

1. Corroborating our earlier study, no evidence was found to support a hypothesis that IO hospitals are more cost effective than their private not-for-profit or public counterparts. Operating costs per discharge were higher and the rate of increase in operating costs over the 4-year period was at least as high for IO as for not-for-profit facilities.
2. Higher operating expenses in IO hospitals were attributable to overhead expenses. Administrative and fiscal costs were higher as a percent of operating expenses for the IO than for the not-for-profit sector.
3. For all sectors, capital costs increased at a rate in excess of other operating expenses over the period. This was much more pronounced in the IO independent sector than in the others.
4. All of the sectors apparently became more aggressive in their use of pricing strategies, shifting inpatient revenues toward ancillary and away from daily (room and board) services. Not surprisingly, this phenomenon was more pronounced in the IO sector, followed by the voluntary sector, and finally by public hospitals.
5. For nearly all financially important daily

Dr. Pattison is Executive Vice President of the Health Services Research Foundation.

and ancillary services, charges per service unit (prices) were highest in the IO sector and lowest in the public sector.

6. Over the 4-year period, operating margins improved for the IO chains, but remained constant or deteriorated for the other sectors.

7. The mix of patients (Medicare, Medi-Cal, and other) stayed relatively constant within each sector over the period. There was little difference between the voluntary and IO sectors. Public hospitals cared for a significantly greater share of Medi-Cal patients and a lesser share of Medicare. Other (private-pay) patients also comprised relatively less of the volume for public hospitals.

8. Public hospitals provided a disproportionately large share of services to Medi-Cal beneficiaries, both inpatient and outpatient. The stringency of Medi-Cal reimbursement during this period adversely affected their ability to maintain break-even or profitable operations.

9. During the time period studied, the principal acquisition targets for the IO chains in California were independent IO hospitals.

10. As compared to nonacquired facilities, the IO independent hospitals acquired were typically older, more depreciated, unprofitable facilities with higher than average uncollectable charges. Following acquisition, profitability improved, bad debts were reduced, and the accounting value of assets, debt, equity, and capital expenses increased dramatically.

11. The major source of capital for the acquisition of hospitals by the IO chains was not ownership (or equity) capital, but new long-term debt.

## DATA BASE AND METHODS

Our analysis is based on CHFC annual disclosure data. Three CHFC reporting cycles were analyzed: Cycle 3 (fiscal years ending between June 30, 1977 and June 29, 1978), Cycle 5 (1979-1980), and Cycle 7 (1981-1982). The 4 years examined in this study were those preceding the implementation of revolutionary changes in hospital reimbursement in California. During the time period covered by the study, reimbursement for both Medicare and Medi-Cal inpatient services was based on ret-

rospectively determined costs, and most private payers paid billed charges.

We examined data for short-term, acute care, fee-for-service (non-Kaiser) hospitals of between 76 and 250 beds. This selection method eliminated teaching hospitals; large, complex facilities; small and rural hospitals; and specialty hospitals or those with a long-term-care emphasis. Four subsectors of the sample were analyzed: voluntary not-for-profit (including religious and secular), public (including city/county and district), IO independent, and IO chain hospitals.

As Table 1 illustrates, the method provided a relatively homogeneous sample in terms of bed size, occupancy, and length of stay. Furthermore, the sample included most of the California hospitals owned by the large, investor-owned national management companies (referred to in this report as IO chains).

## RESULTS

### General Observations

Table 1 reflects major structural changes in the California hospital industry. While the total number of hospitals and beds in the sample remained almost constant over the 4-year period (a net decline of 11 hospitals and 1,210 beds, or 5 and 3 percent, respectively), this was not true within individual ownership categories. The greatest growth, either in absolute or percentage terms, was in the IO chain sector, which experienced a net increase of seven hospitals and 1,066 beds. The greatest decrease was in the IO independent sector, which experienced a decrease of 14 hospitals and 1,795 beds. This suggests that the growth of the IO chain sector was due principally to acquisitions of IO independent hospitals, rather than either voluntaries or publics. A detailed analysis of the data revealed this to be true. We identified nine hospitals acquired by the major national management companies at some time during the 4-year period studied. All nine were acquired from independent IO hospitals or from a small, regional multi-institutional system. (A discussion of these hospitals as a separate group follows in a later section of this paper.)

Beds per hospital changed very little for any

**TABLE 1**   General Characteristics of Hospitals in the Study

| Cycle/Variable | All[a] | Voluntary | Public | Investor-Owned Independent | Investor-Owned Chain |
|---|---|---|---|---|---|
| **Cycle 3 (1977–1978)** | | | | | |
| Number of hospitals | 242 | 105 | 33 | 59 | 45 |
| Beds | 35,372 | 16,016 | 5,221 | 7,789 | 6,346 |
| Inpatient days (1,000s) | 7,804 | 3,803 | 1,230 | 1,439 | 1,333 |
| Discharges (1,000s) | 1,276 | 610 | 193 | 241 | 231 |
| Beds/hospital | 146 | 153 | 158 | 132 | 141 |
| Occupancy (%) | 60 | 65 | 65 | 51 | 58 |
| Length of stay (days) | 6.1 | 6.2 | 6.4 | 6.0 | 5.8 |
| **Cycle 5 (1979–1980)** | | | | | |
| Number of hospitals | 236 | 107 | 32 | 46 | 51 |
| Beds | 34,763 | 16,783 | 4,913 | 5,951 | 7,116 |
| Inpatient days (1,000s) | 7,616 | 3,937 | 1,191 | 1,045 | 1,442 |
| Discharges (1,000s) | 1,230 | 624 | 187 | 177 | 242 |
| Beds/hospital | 147 | 157 | 154 | 129 | 140 |
| Occupancy (%) | 60 | 64 | 66 | 48 | 56 |
| Length of stay (days) | 6.2 | 6.3 | 6.4 | 5.9 | 6.0 |
| **Cycle 7 (1981–1982)** | | | | | |
| Number of hospitals | 231 | 100 | 34 | 45 | 52 |
| Beds | 34,162 | 15,283 | 5,473 | 5,994 | 7,412 |
| Inpatient days (1,000s) | 8,113 | 4,016 | 1,491 | 1,064 | 1,547 |
| Discharges (1,000s) | 1,388 | 677 | 246 | 185 | 280 |
| Beds/hospital | 148 | 153 | 161 | 133 | 143 |
| Occupancy (%) | 65 | 72 | 75 | 49 | 57 |
| Length of stay (days) | 5.8 | 5.9 | 6.1 | 5.7 | 5.5 |

Column group header: Ownership Category (spanning All, Voluntary, Public, Investor-Owned Independent, Investor-Owned Chain)

[a]Includes general acute care, non-Kaiser (HMO) hospitals between 76 and 250 beds.

of the sectors during the time period studied. For the most recent year (1981-1982), it ranged from a low of 133 in the IO independent hospitals to a high of 161 in the public hospitals.

Occupancy rates improved considerably for both the voluntaries and publics over the period, increasing respectively from 65 to 72 percent and from 65 to 75 percent. This increase came mostly between the fifth and sixth cycles. For the IO sector, this figure worsened slightly.

Lengths of stay declined for all sectors. The figure was lowest for the IO chains (5.5 days) and highest for the publics (6.1 days). Overall hospital case-mix intensity and acuity measures were not available, so it is not possible to say whether the increased lengths of stay in the voluntaries and publics were attributable to a more severe case load.

## Profitability and Growth

The two most widely used measures of profitability are operating margin (profits expressed as a percent of revenues) and return on equity (profits expressed as a percent of owners' investment). By either of these two measures, the IO chain sector was the most profitable and the public sector the least.

Table 2 reveals that operating margins, defined here as net operating revenues divided by total operating revenues, were highest for the IO chains, followed in order by the voluntaries, IO independents, and publics. Public hospitals consistently operated at a loss, and this loss worsened over the period, from 11 percent in 1977-1978 to 14 percent in 1981-1982. These operating losses were recovered principally by public subsidies. Interestingly, margins remained constant or deteriorated for

**TABLE 2** Profitability, Assets, and Growth

| Year/Variable | Ownership Category | | | | |
|---|---|---|---|---|---|
| | All | Voluntary | Public | Investor-Owned Independent | Investor-Owned Chain |
| 1977–1978 | | | | | |
| Operating margin | .02 | .03 | −.11 | .02 | .08 |
| Return on equity | .08 | .08 | .05[a] | .08 | .12 |
| Accounting age of facility (yrs) | 6.0 | 6.2 | 7.8 | 4.6 | 4.7 |
| Invested capital (assets) per bed | 61,278 | 68,597 | 57,249 | 34,109 | 79,467 |
| Net plant, property, and equipment per bed | 32,163 | 38,878 | 29,559 | 13,691 | 40,028 |
| 1979–1980 | | | | | |
| Operating margin | .02 | .03 | −.09 | .03 | .06 |
| Return on equity | .10 | .10 | .06 | .25 | .16 |
| Accounting age of facility (yrs) | 6.0 | 6.4 | 7.3 | 5.0 | 4.2 |
| Invested capital (assets) per bed | 75,740 | 86,829 | 74,388 | 40,852 | 79,694 |
| Net plant, property, and equipment per bed | 40,231 | 49,006 | 39,210 | 15,916 | 40,572 |
| 1981–1982 | | | | | |
| Operating margin | .01 | .03 | −.14 | .01 | .10 |
| Return on equity | .13 | .13 | .05 | .10 | .27 |
| Accounting age of facility (yrs) | 5.9 | 6.3 | 7.8 | 4.2 | 4.0 |
| Invested capital (assets) per bed | 96,108 | 112,771 | 90,208 | 59,382 | 95,392 |
| Net plant, property, and equipment per bed | 49,491 | 57,802 | 47,991 | 24,857 | 53,383 |
| Percent growth (4-year period from FYE 6/30/77–6/29/78 to FYE 6/30/81–6/29/82) | | | | | |
| Number of beds | −3 | −5 | 5 | −23 | 17 |
| Total invested capital (assets) | 51 | 57 | 65 | 34 | 40 |
| Invested capital per bed | 57 | 64 | 58 | 74 | 20 |
| Net plant property and equipment per bed | 53 | 48 | 62 | 81 | 33 |

[a]Return on equity is not a useful measure for public hospitals because many fail to report equity.

all but the IO chains, in which they increased from 8 to 10 percent. The margins for the chains in 1981-1982 were 10 times the average for the cohort of hospitals studied.

Further attesting to the profitability of the national IO chain hospitals is the figure on return on equity. This increased dramatically for these hospitals, from 12 percent to 27 percent. Return on equity improved for all sectors except for the publics. (The reader is cautioned, however, that this measure has little validity for public hospitals, which frequently do not report equity capital on their balance sheets.)

In the previous study, based only on 1979-1980 data, net income (after tax profit) per discharge was highest for the voluntaries, followed in order by the IO chains, publics, and

IO independents. Analysis of the three time periods reveals a different pattern for 1977-1978 and 1981-1982, with the IO chains highest, followed respectively by the voluntaries, publics, and IO independents. This figure showed little change for the publics over the 4-year period, rising by only $3 or 9 percent. However, for the IO chains, the growth was substantial, rising by $100 over the period or a percentage increase of 149 percent.

The accounting age of facility figures demonstrates that investment in depreciable assets was taking place relatively more rapidly in the investor-owned sector than in the not-for-profit. The age of these facilities' assets fell a little over 4.5 years to just slightly over 4 years. During the same time, the age of not-for-profits increased slightly or remained the same. Accounting age is computed by dividing accumulated depreciation by annual depreciation. It is an imprecise measure, and does not distinguish between investment in new construction and equipment or acquisition of an existing facility by a new owner. Thus, the purchase of relatively older IO independent hospitals by the IO chains would have the effect of reducing the accounting age of each of the two sectors, as these more depreciated facilities were acquired and depreciation schedules reestablished subsequent to the change in ownership.

The growth in total assets was highest in the publics, followed by the voluntaries, IO chains, and IO independents. However, an examination of growth in assets *per bed* yields quite different results. IO independents become the highest (74 percent) and IO chains the lowest (20 percent). This phenomenon, closely related to that discussed in the preceding paragraph, occurs because the IO chains were acquiring relatively older and more depreciated IO independent hospitals. Thus, as those older hospitals' beds and assets were removed from the books of the IO independent sector and added to those of the IO chain sector (at a value reflecting the acquisition price), the growth rate in assets *per bed* increased for the former and decreased for the latter.

Whereas in 1977-1978 the IO chain hospitals had the greatest investment in assets per bed, by 1981-1982, investment was highest for the voluntaries. This was due to the high rate of growth in the voluntary sector. It is also interesting to compare the publics with the IO chains. In 1977-1978, public hospitals' assets per bed were only 72 percent of the IO chains. Because of the rate of investment in the public sector, this figure had risen to 95 percent by 1981-1982. Thus, the public and voluntary hospitals in this group, even though somewhat older, became as heavily "capitalized" as the IO chain hospitals, and significantly more so than the IO independents.

## Pricing Strategies

The growth of the IO chains has been attributed to the aggressive and successful use of pricing and marketing strategies rather than to economies of scale or centralization, which would have been reflected in lower cost per day or per discharge. This study confirms this finding and further demonstrates that (1) over the time period studied, all ownership sectors adopted a more aggressive pricing structure, and (2) the IO chains were the leaders in adoption of these strategies.

Gross patient revenues (patient charges) were highest for the IO chains, followed by IO independents, voluntaries, and publics (Table 3). For 1977-1978, IO chain charges were 114 percent of the group mean, and by 1981-1982, this had risen to 117 percent. In contrast, public hospitals' average charges were 86 percent of the group mean in 1977-1978, but had fallen to 82 percent by 1981-1982.

As revealed in Table 4, the increase in the ratio of inpatient ancillary to daily service charges indicates that all sectors adopted a pricing strategy in which ancillary services became relatively more important as a revenue source when compared to daily (room and board) services. Two factors can explain this:

1. The decrease in length of stay for all sectors, which may indicate either a more intense case mix or more intense treatment modalities, and/or
2. A more aggressive pricing strategy in which an increasing proportion of revenues are generated from the services with relatively less price-elastic demand (inpatient ancillary services).

**TABLE 3** Charges, Deductions, Expenses, and Profits per Adjusted Discharge[a]

| Year/Variable | Ownership Category | | | | |
| | All | Voluntary | Public | Investor-Owned Independent | Investor-Owned Chain |
| --- | --- | --- | --- | --- | --- |
| 1977–1978 | | | | | |
| Gross patient charges | 1,777 | 1,708 | 1,536 | 1,908 | 2,022 |
| Deductions | 231 | 200 | 198 | 248 | 328 |
| Net patient revenue | 1,545 | 1,508 | 1,337 | 1,660 | 1,694 |
| Operating expense | 1,543 | 1,492 | 1,512 | 1,643 | 1,576 |
| Net income (profit) after tax | 47 | 55 | 39 | 14 | 68 |
| 1979–1980 | | | | | |
| Gross patient charges | 2,366 | 2,255 | 2,045 | 2,527 | 2,783 |
| Deductions | 390 | 314 | 357 | 394 | 608 |
| Net patient revenue | 1,977 | 1,940 | 1,688 | 2,133 | 2,175 |
| Operating expense | 1,969 | 1,914 | 1,895 | 2,099 | 2,046 |
| Net income (profit) after tax | 70 | 82 | 53 | 51 | 65 |
| 1981–1982 | | | | | |
| Gross patient charges | 3,012 | 2,894 | 2,462 | 3,399 | 3,527 |
| Deductions | 571 | 495 | 486 | 625 | 797 |
| Net patient revenue | 2,441 | 2,399 | 1,976 | 2,775 | 2,730 |
| Operating expense | 2,439 | 2,370 | 2,304 | 2,771 | 2,458 |
| Net income (profit) after tax | 99 | 112 | 42 | 25 | 168 |
| Percent increase (4-year period from FYE 6/30/77–6/29/78 to FYE 6/30/81–6/29/82) | | | | | |
| Gross patient charges | 70 | 69 | 60 | 78 | 74 |
| Deductions | 147 | 147 | 145 | 152 | 143 |
| Net patient revenue | 58 | 59 | 48 | 67 | 61 |
| Operating expense | 58 | 59 | 52 | 69 | 56 |
| Net income (profit) after tax | 110 | 106 | 9 | 75 | 149 |

[a]Adjusted discharges are the total discharges times the ratio of total patient revenue (inpatient and outpatient) to inpatient revenue.

Despite the shift across all sectors, however, the intersectoral differences were still extreme, with the most aggressive use of this strategy employed by the IO chains, and the least aggressive by the publics. It is tempting to speculate that the profitability and financial solvency of public hospitals could have been improved by a more vigorous adoption of these pricing strategies. However, it is unlikely that the public hospitals could successfully have employed these strategies given their relatively small proportion of patients covered by insurance plans that paid billed charges.

The relative importance of outpatient charges was virtually unchanged over time for each of the four ownership categories. As a percent of inpatient charges, outpatient charges were twice as high for the publics as for IO hospitals, with voluntaries close to the IO sector and significantly below the publics. Public hospitals care for relatively more Medi-Cal patients (see Table 5). This accounts for much of the observed difference since Medi-Cal patients consume relatively more outpatient services than the population at large.

Tables 6 and 7 demonstrate the differences in pricing strategies on a service-specific basis. The importance of individual ancillary services to the hospitals' revenues is illustrated by the example of pharmacy, which comprised 9 percent of patient charges in 1981-1982, or almost half the revenues generated by medical/surgical daily services. Pharmacy ranged in importance from a low of 6 percent in the public

**TABLE 4**   Charge Structure: Ratios of Daily Service, Inpatient Ancillary, and Outpatient Charges

| Year/Ratio | Ownership Category | | | | |
|---|---|---|---|---|---|
| | All | Voluntary | Public | Investor-Owned Independent | Investor-Owned Chain |
| 1977–1978 | | | | | |
| Inpatient ancillary/ | | | | | |
| daily services charges | 1.18 | 1.07 | 0.92 | 1.44 | 1.42 |
| Outpatient/inpatient charges | 0.19 | 0.19 | 0.33 | 0.14 | 0.15 |
| 1979–1980 | | | | | |
| Inpatient ancillary/ | | | | | |
| daily services charges | 1.27 | 1.25 | 0.103 | 1.56 | 1.56 |
| Outpatient/inpatient charges | 0.19 | 0.19 | 0.33 | 0.14 | 0.15 |
| 1981–1982 | | | | | |
| Inpatient ancillary/ | | | | | |
| daily services charges | 1.43 | 1.33 | 1.08 | 1.70 | 1.81 |
| Outpatient/inpatient charges | 0.19 | 0.19 | 0.33 | 0.14 | 0.13 |

hospitals to a figure approximately double that, 12 to 13 percent in the IO sector.

Charges per unit of service for nearly all services were uniformly higher in the IO sector than in either the voluntary or public hospitals. Again, comparisons of individual services between the IO and public hospitals reveal extreme differences.

**Operating Expenses**

Table 3 confirms that operating expenses per adjusted discharge in 1981-1982 were highest for the IO independents, followed respectively by the IO chains, voluntaries, and publics. For all four sectors, this figure rose by 58 percent over the 4-year period. This is the equivalent of an average annual compounded rate of about 12 percent. The rate of increase was highest for IO independents (69 percent) and lowest for publics (52 percent). Gross patient charges increased by 70 percent, equivalent to an average annual increase of 14 percent. The range was from a low of 60 percent (publics) to a high of 74 percent (IO chains). These increases in charges, however, did not translate directly into increases in patient revenues, as deductions from revenue (which include Medicare and Medi-Cal contractual allowances as well as charity care, bad debts,

and other contractual allowances) increased by 147 percent. Because of these deductions, the growth in net patient revenues (amounts actually received for the provision of care) almost exactly matched the growth in operating expenses in the voluntaries and IO independents. For the publics, revenues grew 4 percent slower than expenses, and for the IO chains the situation was reversed, with revenues growing 5 percent faster than expenses.

In Table 8, we examined data for the major expense categories of research, education, general service (costs associated with laundry, dietary, housekeeping, etc.), fiscal services (accounting), administrative services (administration, taxes), and daily and ancillary services (e.g., costs associated with nursing services and ancillary departments). For the IO sector, fiscal and administrative costs (which include, in the case of the IO chains, allocated home office costs) totaled between 28 and 30 percent of operating expenses. For the not-for-profit sector, these costs were 22 to 24 percent.

The IO chains, in support of their claims of increased efficiencies (as reflected, for example, in lower ratios of employees (full-time equivalents or FTEs) per discharge, incurred expenses for general services and daily and ancillary services equal to $1,745 per adjusted discharge in 1981-1982. These costs amounted

**TABLE 5**   Deductions from Revenue as a Percent of Total Patient Charges

| Year/Variable | Ownership Category | | | | |
| | All | Voluntary | Public | Investor-Owned Independent | Investor-Owned Chain |
|---|---|---|---|---|---|
| **1977–1978** | | | | | |
| Medicare contractual allowance | 7 | 6 | 4 | 7 | 9 |
| Medi-Cal contractual allowance | 3 | 3 | 5 | 3 | 3 |
| Charity | 0 | 0 | 0 | 0 | 0 |
| Bad debt | 2 | 2 | 2 | 2 | 2 |
| Other | 1 | 1 | 2 | 1 | 2 |
| Total deductions | 13 | 12 | 13 | 13 | 16 |
| **1979–1980** | | | | | |
| Medicare contractual allowance | 9 | 8 | 5 | 9 | 13 |
| Medi-Cal contractual allowance | 4 | 3 | 5 | 3 | 4 |
| Charity | 0 | 0 | 1 | 0 | 0 |
| Bad debt | 2 | 2 | 3 | 3 | 2 |
| Other | 1 | 1 | 3 | 1 | 3 |
| Total deductions | 16 | 14 | 17 | 16 | 22 |
| **1981–1982** | | | | | |
| Medicare contractual allowance | 10 | 10 | 6 | 10 | 14 |
| Medi-Cal contractual allowance | 5 | 4 | 6 | 4 | 5 |
| Charity | 0 | 0 | 1 | 0 | 0 |
| Bad debt | 3 | 2 | 6 | 3 | 2 |
| Other | 1 | 1 | 1 | 1 | 2 |
| Total deductions | 19 | 17 | 20 | 18 | 23 |

to $1,801 for the voluntaries. Thus, the IO chains experienced savings of $56 per adjusted discharge in these two categories.

These savings may represent efficiencies at the hospital level. However, fiscal and administrative costs were $119 less in the voluntaries than in the IO chains. The net effect was a savings of $63 per discharge in the voluntaries. The same analysis holds for a comparison that includes the publics and IO independents.

**Patient Selection**

Tables 5 and 9 reveal intersectoral differences in the relative importance of Medicare, Medi-Cal, and private-pay patients. Part A of Table 8, which provides information on the percentage of charges by payer category, is the

best indication of the volume of services consumed by each category. It reveals that public hospitals cared for a disproportionately high share of Medi-Cal patients and a disproportionately low share of Medicare. This was true for all years. There was relatively little difference between the other sectors.

Medicare contractual allowances are a reflection of (1) the percent of patient care provided to Medicare beneficiaries and (2) the spread between charges and allowable costs (as determined by the Medicare fiscal intermediary). For each of the three cycles studied, these allowances were highest for the IO chains, followed by IO independents, voluntaries, and publics.

As a percent of total charges, Medi-Cal contractual allowances were highest for the pub-

**TABLE 6**   Important Daily and Ancillary Charges as a Percentage of Total Patient Charges, 1981–1982

| Year/Variable | Ownership Category | | | | |
| | All | Voluntary | Public | Investor-Owned Independent | Investor-Owned Chain |
|---|---|---|---|---|---|
| Daily services | | | | | |
| Medical/surgical acute | 22 | 24 | 20 | 20 | 19 |
| Psychiatric acute | 1 | 1 | 4 | 1 | 1 |
| Obstetrics acute | 2 | 1 | 2 | 1 | 1 |
| Medical/surgical intensive care | 4 | 4 | 3 | 4 | 4 |
| Coronary intensive care | 2 | 2 | 2 | 1 | 1 |
| Total daily services[a] | 35 | 37 | 36 | 32 | 31 |
| Ancillary services | | | | | |
| Clinical labs | 8 | 7 | 7 | 11 | 9 |
| Pharmacy | 9 | 7 | 6 | 13 | 12 |
| Diagnostic radiology | 5 | 4 | 5 | 6 | 4 |
| Surgery | 6 | 6 | 4 | 6 | 6 |
| Central service and supply | 6 | 5 | 3 | 7 | 9 |
| Emergency | 3 | 3 | 4 | 3 | 3 |
| Inhalation therapy | 4 | 3 | 3 | 5 | 4 |
| Total ancillary services[a] | 65 | 63 | 64 | 68 | 69 |

[a]Individual service figures do not equal total figure because minor services are not included in the table.

lics, followed respectively by the IO chains, then the voluntaries and IO independents. The reason for this difference was the relatively greater percent of Medi-Cal patients served in public hospitals as well as the greater per-cent of revenues derived from outpatient services. (Medi-Cal paid for outpatient services according to a fee schedule, which was lower than accounting costs for most hospitals and significantly lower than billed charges.)

**TABLE 7**   Patient Charges per Unit of Service[a] for Important Daily and Ancillary Services, 1981–1982

| Year/Variable | Ownership Category | | | | |
| | All | Voluntary | Public | Investor-Owned Independent | Investor-Owned Chain |
|---|---|---|---|---|---|
| Daily services | | | | | |
| Medical/surgical acute | 191 | 192 | 180 | 187 | 200 |
| Medical/surgical intensive care | 464 | 463 | 419 | 479 | 486 |
| Ancillary services | | | | | |
| Clinical labs | 0.98 | 0.92 | 0.71 | 1.24 | 1.19 |
| Pharmacy | 49.34 | 40.20 | 22.18 | 84.11 | 85.14 |
| Diagnostic radiology | 7.28 | 6.90 | 7.43 | 8.92 | 6.79 |
| Surgery | 4.65 | 4.43 | 3.53 | 6.07 | 5.22 |
| Central service and supply | 32.26 | 24.95 | 16.21 | 44.00 | 58.85 |
| Emergency | 46.80 | 44.41 | 41.96 | 57.49 | 52.65 |
| Inhalation therapy | 16.46 | 17.78 | 12.79 | 16.10 | 16.98 |

[a]Units of service are defined by the California Health Facilities Commission.

**TABLE 8** Operating Expense Structure as a Percentage of Total Operating Expenses

| Year/Expense Category | All | Voluntary | Public | Investor-Owned Independent | Investor-Owned Chain |
|---|---|---|---|---|---|
| 1977–1978 | | | | | |
| Research | 0 | 0 | 0 | 0 | 0 |
| Education | 0 | 0 | 2 | 0 | 0 |
| General service | 14 | 15 | 15 | 13 | 13 |
| Fiscal service | 7 | 7 | 8 | 6 | 7 |
| Administrative | 20 | 18 | 16 | 25 | 22 |
| Daily and ancillary service | 59 | 60 | 59 | 56 | 58 |
| 1979–1980 | | | | | |
| Research | 0 | 0 | 0 | 0 | 0 |
| Education | 0 | 0 | 2 | 0 | 0 |
| General service | 14 | 15 | 15 | 13 | 13 |
| Fiscal service | 7 | 7 | 8 | 6 | 7 |
| Administrative | 19 | 17 | 15 | 23 | 22 |
| Daily and ancillary service | 60 | 61 | 60 | 59 | 58 |
| 1981–1982 | | | | | |
| Research | 0 | 0 | 0 | 0 | 0 |
| Education | 1 | 0 | 2 | 0 | 0 |
| General service | 13 | 14 | 14 | 12 | 12 |
| Fiscal service | 5 | 4 | 5 | 4 | 6 |
| Administrative | 21 | 20 | 17 | 26 | 22 |
| Daily and ancillary service | 61 | 62 | 61 | 58 | 59 |

Finally, the previous study noted the absence of charity care provided by this cohort of hospitals. Table 10 confirms that finding. However, broadening the definition of uncompensated care to include bad debts as well as charity reveals the public hospitals to be significantly more involved in this effort, with allowances equal to 7 percent of total charges in 1981-1982, compared to 3 percent in the nearest sector. This figure rose from 2 percent in 1977-1978, when publics were identical to the other sectors, and was accounted for entirely by an increase in the bad debt component. The data do not reveal whether this was due to the recession environment during 1981-1982 or to less aggressive management of accounts receivable, but it is clear that bad debts became a significant problem for the public hospitals over the period.

## Hospitals That Changed Ownership During the Period

Our previously published study based on a single year's data (1979-1980) left unanswered two critical questions: What were the financial characteristics of hospitals acquired by the IO chains during the preprospective payment system environment? What financial changes did these hospitals undergo in the years immediately following acquisition?

We were able to identify definitively nine hospitals which, during our study period, went from IO independent (freestanding) to IO chain status through acquisition. While a sample of nine is an insufficient number upon which to base sweeping conclusions, the comparison of these hospitals with their other IO counterparts, presented in Table 10, is instructive. The table presents comparative figures for 1977-1978 and 1981-1982 for IO hospitals that remained independent throughout the period, IO independent hospitals acquired by a national chain at some time during the period,

**TABLE 9**  Patient Mix and Contractual Allowances

| Year/Variable | Ownership Category | | | | |
| | All | Voluntary | Public | Investor-Owned Independent | Investor-Owned Chain |
|---|---|---|---|---|---|
| *Part A: Percent of Gross Patient Charges by Payer Class* | | | | | |
| 1977–1978 | | | | | |
| Medicare | 37 | 40 | 29 | 35 | 38 |
| Medi-Cal | 16 | 13 | 27 | 16 | 14 |
| Other | 47 | 47 | 44 | 50 | 48 |
| 1981–1982 | | | | | |
| Medicare | 41 | 44 | 31 | 41 | 43 |
| Medi-Cal | 16 | 14 | 29 | 13 | 13 |
| Other | 43 | 42 | 40 | 46 | 44 |
| *Part B: Contractual Allowances as Percent of Charges to Each Payer* | | | | | |
| 1977–1978 | | | | | |
| Medicare | 18 | 16 | 13 | 19 | 25 |
| Medi-Cal | 21 | 211 | 19 | 20 | 25 |
| Other | 7 | 5 | 9 | 7 | 7 |
| All payers | 13 | 12 | 13 | 13 | 16 |
| 1981–1982 | | | | | |
| Medicare | 25 | 23 | 18 | 24 | 32 |
| Medi-Cal | 28 | 29 | 20 | 27 | 40 |
| Other | 10 | 7 | 21 | 9 | 8 |
| All payers | 19 | 17 | 20 | 17 | 23 |
| *Part C: Percent of Net Patient Revenues by Payer Class* | | | | | |
| 1977–1978 | | | | | |
| Medicare | 35 | 38 | 29 | 32 | 34 |
| Medi-Cal | 14 | 12 | 25 | 14 | 13 |
| Other | 51 | 51 | 45 | 53 | 53 |
| 1981–1982 | | | | | |
| Medicare | 38 | 41 | 32 | 37 | 38 |
| Medi-Cal | 14 | 12 | 28 | 12 | 10 |
| Other | 48 | 47 | 40 | 51 | 52 |

and IO hospitals owned by a chain throughout the 4-year period.

The table reveals that

• Pre-acquisition, the purchased hospitals were somewhat older, under-capitalized facilities as compared to either the nonacquired IO independents or previously acquired IO chain hospitals.

• They were unprofitable, incurring after-tax losses of $1.38 per day. This is compared to daily profits of $3.00 for the independents and $11.72 for the chains.

• Their losses were attributable at least in part to three factors: (1) low occupancy rates (48 percent), (2) high daily expenses ($286 versus $274 for each of the other groups), and (3) a relatively high level of uncollectable accounts (2.7 percent of billed charges).

• Investment per bed was the lowest of the three subsectors and, correspondingly, these hospitals were carrying little debt. Of course, given their unprofitability, low occupancy, and relatively high cost, they would not have been attractive prospects for lenders.

**TABLE 10** Comparison of Financial Indicators, Investor-Owned Hospitals, 1977–1978 and 1981–1982

| Variable | 1977–1978 | | | 1981–1982 | | |
|---|---|---|---|---|---|---|
| | Independent | Acquired | Chain | Independent | Acquired | Chain |
| Number of hospitals | 50 | 9 | 45 | 45 | 9 | 43 |
| Occupancy (%) | 51 | 48 | 58 | 49 | 50 | 59 |
| After-tax profits per day | 3.00 | −1.38 | 11.72 | 4.39 | 23.70 | 32.00 |
| Bad debts (% of charges) | 2.4 | 2.7 | 1.6 | 3.2 | 0.2 | 2.6 |
| Inpatient charges per day ($) | 317 | 334 | 351 | 591 | 631 | 639 |
| Total expenses per day ($) | 274 | 286 | 274 | 482 | 467 | 441 |
| Capital costs per day ($) | 12 | 11 | 23 | 34 | 55 | 39 |
| Assets per bed ($) | 34,401 | 32,565 | 79,467 | 59,382 | 98,832 | 94,687 |
| Debt per bed ($) | 10,991 | 7,767 | 34,832 | 23,845 | 57,678 | 38,684 |
| Accounting age (yrs) | 4.6 | 4.8 | 4.7 | 4.2 | 2.7 | 4.3 |

• About 2.5 years following acquisition, on average, a dramatic turnaround became evident. This group's average daily profits not only recovered, but rose to $23.70. This compares to $4.39 for those hospitals remaining independent throughout the period.

• This increase in profitability was not attributable to filling empty beds; occupancy rates remained almost the same, rising only to 50 percent.

• A significant factor in their turnaround was the extraordinary drop in bad debts to only 0.2 percent of total charges. Unfortunately, data do not reveal whether this decrease was due exclusively to more aggressive management of accounts receivable, or whether policies were instituted to deny all but emergency services to unsponsored patients (those without private insurance or government program coverage).

• The companies appear to have instituted operating cost efficiencies. Daily expenses for this group, which were $12 more than the non-acquired hospitals in 1977-1978, became $15 less than the still-independent hospitals in 1981-1982.

• The accounting value of assets per bed increased from $32,565 in 1977-1978 to $98,832 4 years later. A significant share of this increase was the revaluation of assets to fair market value (typically acquisition cost) upon change of ownership. Another part was due to new construction and equipment added after acquisition. A detailed analysis of each hospital's books would be necessary to reveal the importance of each.

• These new asset values were financed principally by additional debt. In 1977-1978, the debt-to-asset ratio (obtained by dividing debt per bed by assets per bed) was 0.24 for this group compared with 0.32 and 0.44 for the independent and chain groups, respectively. By 1981-1982 this ratio had risen to 0.58 for this group compared with 0.40 and 0.41 for the independent and chain groups, respectively.

• Partly as a consequence of this new debt, capital costs rose from 4 percent of total expenses to 12 percent. This figure includes depreciation expenses on the newly revalued facility as well as interest costs on the debt.

These observations are consistent with intuitive and anecdotal evidence regarding purchases of independent IO hospitals by the chains during the late 1970s and early 1980s. The policy implications are less clear, especially as the hospital industry enters a new financial environment in which the targets for acquisition appear increasingly to be more complex, larger teaching facilities.

**CONCLUDING STATEMENT**

The results of this study confirm most of the findings of our previous study (and others, e.g., those of Lewin and Associates and the Florida Cost Containment Board). In addition, these results, by demonstrating the more vigorous response of the IO sector to the previous cost-based incentives reimbursement system, help to shed light on what we may expect in the new reimbursement environment being implemented in California and in may other parts of the United States.

If the IO sector, as demonstrated in our analysis, is quickest to respond to these new incentives, we may expect its growth to continue or even to accelerate. Until now, targets for acquisition in California have been confined primarily to smaller, independent, IO hospitals. However, we may expect to see acquisitions occur among larger, complex, teaching facilities as these institutions find themselves in financial difficulty. These facilities have traditionally borne much of the burden of provision of "unprofitable" services and care of unsponsored patients. Whether these services will continue to be provided and these patients to be served at historical levels is unclear.

## ACKNOWLEDGMENTS

This analysis was supported by a grant from the James Irvine Foundation, San Francisco, California. The author wishes to acknowledge with gratitude the assistance of Piruz Alemi.

*For-Profit Enterprise in Health Care.* 1986.
National Academy Press, Washington, D.C.

# Hospital Acquisitions and Their Effects: Florida, 1979-1982

Kathryn J. Brown and Richard E. Klosterman

The rapid emergence of investor-owned hospital corporations as a major influence in the provision of hospital care has been greeted with both alarm and accolades (Relman, 1980; Larson, 1983). While much of this discussion has been based on opinion or personal philosophy, empirical evidence is becoming available on the similarities and differences between investor-owned and not-for-profit hospitals, and between system and nonsystem hospitals (Lewin et al., 1981; Sloan and Vraciu, 1983; and Pattison and Katz, 1983). However, to date, no studies have been published on the effects of changes in ownership of hospitals. This study examines hospital acquisitions in Florida in the years 1979-1982.

New hospital construction has received substantial attention in the past due to the relentless debate over the effectiveness of state certificate-of-need legislation (Kushman and Nuckton, 1977). Hospital closures have recently been the subject of a series of important articles (Mullner et al., 1983). However, the characteristics of hospital acquisitions have received only limited attention to date (Florida Hospital Cost Containment Board, 1983). This paper will contribute to an understanding of these issues by examining two major questions: (1) Prior to an ownership change, are there significant differences between hospitals that change ownership and other hospitals? (2) After a change in ownership, are there significant differences in the behavior of hospitals that experience an ownership change and other

hospitals? Since 60 percent of the hospitals that underwent a change in ownership in Florida between 1979 and 1983 were acquired by investor-owned firms, these acquisitions receive detailed consideration.

## RESEARCH DESIGN

These questions are examined using data from Florida for 1979 to 1982. Florida is an appropriate study location due to the large number of hospitals in the state (216 acute care general hospitals in 1982), the high proportion of investor-owned hospitals (approximately 35 percent), and the large number of recent changes of hospital ownership (53 acute care general hospitals between 1978 and 1983). In addition, a unique data source is available through the Florida Hospital Cost Containment Board (HCCB), a state hospital rate review agency that has collected uniform hospital data annually since 1979; data through 1982 were available at the time of this analysis. Most of the analyses reported herein are for the 27 hospitals that changed ownership between 1979 and 1982 and for which HCCB data were available for all 4 years.

Data on several dimensions of hospital characteristics are available for examining differences—both before and after a change in ownership—between hospitals that had a change in ownership and control hospitals that did not. These include information on revenues, profitability, sources of payment for patients treated, the efficiency of operations, resources available for patient care, and the hospital's regional characteristics. The 24 variables used to measure these dimensions are summarized in Table 1.

Two major analyses were conducted. The first used a cross-sectional design to compare the characteristics of hospitals that experi-

Ms. Brown is the former director of research for the Florida Hospital Cost Containment Board and is now assistant executive director of the Edwin Shaw Hospital, Akron, Ohio. Dr. Klosterman is associate professor in the Department of Urban Studies, University of Akron.

**TABLE 1**   Variables Used in the Analysis

Profitability

    Operating margin—pre-tax net operating revenue less expenses, as a percentage of pre-tax net operating revenue.

    Total margin—after-tax net operating and nonoperating revenues less expenses as a percentage of net operating revenue.

Types of Patients Treated

    Percent Medicare patients—Medicare acute care patient days as a percentage of total acute care patient days.

    Percent Medicaid patients—Medicaid acute care patient days as a percentage of total acute care patient days.

    Percent charity and bad debt patients—deductions from revenue due to bad debt and charity patients as a percent of total patient care revenues.

Efficiency of Operations

    Operating expense per adjusted admission—a ratio of total operating expense and total adjusted admissions.

    Percent occupancy—hospital utilization based on acute licensed beds and acute patient days.

    Average length of stay (ALOS)—a ratio of total acute patient days and total acute admissions.

    Salary expense per adjusted admission—a ratio of total personnel expense and adjusted admissions.

    Salary per full-time equivalent employee—the average employee's salary.

    Man-hours per adjusted patient day—the number of employee hours per average adjusted patient day.

Revenues

    Gross revenue per adjusted admission—total patient charges for an average admission.

    Net revenue per adjusted admission—the average amount of revenue the hospital receives for an average admission.

    Ancillary revenue per adjusted admission—average patient charges for services not covered in the room charge.

Available Resources

    Number of licensed beds—a direct measure of hospital size.

    Service index score—a weighted index based on the presence or absence of 27 services and with a maximum score of 81.3. (See Appendix A for additional details.)

    Physician-mix score—an unweighted index based on the presence or absence of 24 physician specialties and with a maximum score of 24. (See Appendix B for additional details.)

    Percent patient care salary expense—the proportion of personnel resources devoted to direct patient care.

    Number of residents—the number of residents in hospitals with approved residency programs.

Regional characteristics

    Per capita income—a ratio of total county income to total county population in 1980.

    Percent over 65—a ratio of total county population over 65 to total county population in 1980.

    Number of hospitals in county—the number of acute care general hospitals in the county.

    Number of physicians in county—a ratio of active physicians in the county to the total county population divided by 1,000.

    Geographic price level index—county level index score developed by the Florida Hospital Cost Containment Board and based on the Florida Price Level Index and data reported to the board.

enced a change of ownership with hospitals that did not. The second used a longitudinal design to compare the behavior of hospitals after a change in ownership with the behavior of hospitals that did not change ownership.

    The cross-sectional analysis compared the characteristics of the hospitals that experienced an ownership change between 1979 and 1982 to the characteristics of hospitals that did not. The analysis was performed on data for 1979 at two levels of aggregation. The first analysis compared 27 hospitals that changed ownership in 1979, 1980, and 1981 to 168 hospitals that did not. (The remaining acute care hospitals were excluded because of incomplete reporting.) The second analysis focused on hospitals purchased by the most actively acquiring sector of the industry—investor-owned chains. Hospitals acquired by investor-owned chains were partitioned into those that changed hands when one corporation acquired another corporation (and the hospitals that it owned) and those that were acquired individually. The analysis examines how both types of acquired hospitals differed from other hospitals, and whether the nature of the acquisition (i.e., corporate takeover or individual purchase) affected the results. Additional analysis compared the hospitals already owned by investor-owned chains to the hospitals they acquired during that period.

The longitudinal analysis compared rates of change in the institutional variables in Table 1 for the acquired and comparison hospitals between the pre-acquisition period, 1979, and the post-acquisition period, 1982. The regional characteristics were omitted from this analysis because they did not change significantly during this period. The longitudinal analysis was conducted for the total populations of hospitals that did and did not undergo an ownership change and for each of the subcategories of hospitals acquired by investor-owned chains.

The cross-sectional and longitudinal analyses used the student's *t* statistic to test for significant differences between the mean values for hospitals that changed ownership and comparison hospitals that did not. The total population of 27 cases of hospital ownership changes is rather small for statistical testing. Partitioning by ownership category further reduces the sample sizes. As a result, variables that are found to be statistically significant in this study are particularly important.

## DESCRIPTION OF HOSPITALS THAT CHANGED OWNERSHIP

Fifty-three acute care general hospitals changed ownership in Florida during the period between 1978 and 1983 (see Table 2). Seventy-nine percent of these were due to for-profit organizations acquiring for-profit hospitals. Thus, while a reconfiguration of the hos-

TABLE 2  Hospital Acquisitions in Florida, 1978–1983

| Year | Number of Acute Care General Hospitals |
|------|----------------------------------------|
| 1978 | 6 |
| 1979 | 7 |
| 1980 | 10 |
| 1981 | 13 |
| 1982 | 14 |
| 1983 | 3 |
| Total | 53 |

pital industry was supposedly occurring, most change was occurring in one sector of the industry. The number of ownership changes increased each year between 1978 and 1982 and sharply decreased in 1983. It is likely that the introduction of prospective Medicare reimbursement and the accompanying uncertainty affected the number of acquisitions in that year.

As Table 3 demonstrates, the hospitals that underwent an ownership change were quite diverse. They ranged in size from 27 to 771 licensed beds; in service index scores from 12 to 62; in Medicare caseloads from 18 to 74 percent; in Medicaid caseloads from 0 to 48 percent, and in total margins from −54 percent to 9 percent.

Most ownership changes took place in sections of the state that are characterized by seasonal populations or tourists. Southeast Florida, which includes Miami, had 37 percent of the ownership changes. Northwest Florida, which is less densely populated and has fewer seasonal residents, lower income levels, and fewer elderly, had the smallest percentage, 11 percent.

Table 3 also demonstrates that most of the hospitals that underwent an ownership change were investor-owned both before (74 percent) and after (81 percent) the change. Investor-owned chains were the most active acquiring organizations, making almost 56 percent of the acquisitions. A single firm (Hospital Corporation of America) accounted for 73 percent of the purchases by investor-owned chains. Investor-owned chains also owned more than half (8 of 15) of the hospitals acquired by other chains; 40 percent of the hospitals acquired by chains were previously independent investor-

**TABLE 3**   1979 Characteristics of Acquired Hospitals

| Characteristic | Mean | Range |
|---|---|---|
| Number of licensed beds | 192.3 | 27.0–771 |
| Service index (see Table 1) | 27.7 | 11.9–62.5 |
| Physician mix (see Table 1) | 15.9 | 3.0–24 |
| Number of residents | 15.1 | 0.0–368 |
| Percent Medicare patients | 44.9 | 17.9–74.1 |
| Percent Medicaid patients | 7.6 | 0.0–48.2 |
| Average length of stay (days) | 7.1 | 4.0–9.2 |
| Percent occupancy | 62.5 | 19.6–92.4 |
| Operating margin (percent) | 1.85 | − 73.3–14.9 |
| Total margin (percent) | 0.76 | − 54.7–9.1 |
| Acquired hospitals with management contracts: | 25% | |

| Locations | Number | Percent |
|---|---|---|
| Northwest Florida | 3 | 11.1 |
| Southeast Florida (6 in Miami) | 10 | 37.0 |
| West Coast of Florida | 7 | 25.9 |
| Central and Northeast Florida | 7 | 25.9 |
| Total | 27 | 100.0 |

| Changes in Organizational Form | Number | Percent |
|---|---|---|
| Government to— | | |
| Not-for-profit | 4 | 14.8 |
| Not-for-profit to— | | |
| Not-for-profit | 1 | 3.7 |
| Independent investor-owned | 1 | 3.7 |
| Chain investor-owned | 1 | 3.7 |
| Independent investor-owned to— | | |
| Independent investor-owned | 6 | 22.2 |
| Chain investor-owned | 6 | 22.2 |
| Chain investor-owned to— | | |
| Chain investor-owned | 8 | 29.6 |
| Total | 27 | 100.0 |

owned hospitals. Only one not-for-profit hospital was acquired by an investor-owned chain.

Table 4 provides additional background on the hospitals that changed ownership by comparing them with other hospitals according to their pre-change (1979) type of ownership. The three not-for-profit hospitals that underwent a change of ownership were dramatically smaller and less complex than other not-for-profit hospitals and other hospitals that changed ownership.

Government-owned hospitals whose ownership did not change were notable in their low percentage of Medicare patients and high Medicaid caseloads, and this pattern was particularly true for the four government hospitals that subsequently changed ownership. All four

government hospitals that changed ownership became not-for-profit hospitals. In addition, these four hospitals were, on average, larger and more complex than other government hospitals as well as other hospitals that changed ownership. They included the two largest hospitals in the study as well as two of the smallest. All four of these hospitals were located in counties with low per capita income levels.

Investor-owned chain hospitals that underwent a subsequent change of ownership had much higher Medicaid caseloads and lower Medicare case loads than did investor-owned hospitals whose ownership did not change.

The independent investor-owned hospitals that did not change ownership had notably low occupancy levels in 1979, although this had changed by 1982. They also were located in areas of unusually high per capita income levels and high elderly concentrations. The independent investor-owned hospitals that changed ownership (almost 50 percent of all independent investor-owned hospitals) were operating at more typical occupancy levels and in areas of more modest income levels and average elderly concentrations.

Thus, there were several differences among hospitals in the pre-acquisition period. Not-for-profit hospitals that subsequently changed ownership were small and unsophisticated. The acquired government hospitals that underwent an ownership change were on average larger, more complex, and had smaller Medicare caseloads than other government hospitals and other hospitals that had an ownership change. Investor-owned hospitals, both chain and independent, that subsequently changed ownership had higher Medicaid and lower Medicare levels than other investor-owned hospitals, although their levels were about average for hospitals that underwent a change in ownership. These differences are examined further in the following section.

## ANALYSIS OF PRE-ACQUISITION CHARACTERISTICS

Are hospitals that change ownership different from those that do not? It seems unlikely that organizations motivated by profit maximization, status enhancement, medical staff satisfaction, community interest, or any of the other objectives that have been attributed to hospitals (e.g., White, 1979) would randomly select facilities for acquisition or that random facilities would be available for acquisition. Possible acquisition objectives range from public service efforts such as saving a distressed hospital, to protecting market position by preventing new competition from entering the area, to gaining access to growing markets, to bed banking (the purchase of a hospital to enable the parent facility to trade some portion of those beds for a certificate of need) (Gersh, 1982). Possible objectives for corporate reorganization include enhancement of reimbursement, reductions in government regulation, and improved compensation for top executives (Tillet et al., 1982).

For investor-owned companies, a most compelling rationale is undoubtedly the search for increased levels of profitability, consistent with overall goals for the parent firm. This suggests that the attractive acquisition candidate would have either good profitability or the potential for increases in profitability and that steps would be taken after the acquisition of a hospital to improve profit levels. Possible avenues available for increasing the profitability of an acquired institution include changing the patient mix by source of payment, improving the efficiency of operations (including increased volume), increasing price levels, and realigning the resources available for patient care. The profitability of the acquired hospitals and the potential for improving these profits through each of the avenues is considered in the following section.

### Profitability

The data in Table 5 indicate that the total population of hospitals that underwent an ownership change had unusually low profit levels in the pre-acquisition period. Both operating margin and total margin were below those for other hospitals. For total margin the difference is statistically significant at the .10 percent level.

Table 5 also reveals that hospitals acquired by investor-owned chains had lower total margins but higher operating margins than the total population of hospitals that did not change ownership. This reflects the fact that operating margin is a pre-tax measure that includes revenues eventually paid as taxes by for-profit institutions. In comparison to investor-owned hospitals whose ownership did not change, these operating margins are low (see Table 5). Thus, the hospitals acquired by investor-owned chains conform to the general finding of low pre-acquisition margins, especially in comparison to existing investor-owned hospitals, despite the fact that the levels of these margins were higher than for other hospitals that underwent an ownership change.

### Types of Patients Treated

The makeup of a hospital's patient population by source of payment can have a direct

TABLE 4  Characteristics of Hospitals That Subsequently Changed Ownership and Hospitals Whose Ownership Was Unchanged, by 1979 Type of Ownership (means)

| Year | Not-for-profit | | Government | | Investor-Owned Chain | | Independent Investor-Owned | |
|---|---|---|---|---|---|---|---|---|
| | Unchanged (N = 71) | Changed (N = 3) | Unchanged (N = 54) | Changed (N = 4) | Unchanged (N = 30) | Changed (N = 8) | Unchanged (N = 13) | Changed (N = 12) |
| **1979** | | | | | | | | |
| Licensed beds | 302.96 | 73.67** | 216.35 | 330.25 | 199.17 | 166.38 | 193.38 | 190.58 |
| Service index | 37.24 | 15.15** | 28.06 | 41.60 | 30.75 | 24.58** | 27.33 | 27.18 |
| Physician mix | 19.17 | 6.50* | 11.50 | 15.25 | 18.13 | 17.90 | 17.08 | 16.42 |
| Percent Medicare | 50.97 | 60.66 | 41.51 | 29.60 | 56.19 | 47.53* | 60.69 | 50.83 |
| Percent Medicaid | 3.57 | 9.00 | 7.58 | 8.02 | 2.05 | 7.13** | 4.09 | 6.85 |
| Average length of stay (days) | 7.44 | 7.41 | 7.23 | 6.30 | 6.89 | 7.16 | 7.23 | 7.52 |
| Percent occupancy | 66.39 | 63.81 | 65.64 | 68.42 | 61.67 | 57.02 | 46.35 | 62.24** |
| Per capita income ($) | 11,373.00 | 9,886.00 | 11,332.00 | 8,275.00*** | 11,461.00 | 11,696.00 | 12,433.00 | 11,680.00 |
| Percent over 65 | 16.96 | 20.72 | 17.74 | 16.09 | 20.00 | 16.62 | 20.66 | 17.79 |
| **1982** | | | | | | | | |
| Licensed beds | 311.25 | 73.67** | 219.78 | 331.75 | 213.00 | 165.38 | 193.23 | 207.92 |
| Service index | 37.84 | 17.00** | 29.68 | 43.08 | 30.89 | 23.28** | 29.91 | 27.22 |

309

| | | | | | | | |
|---|---|---|---|---|---|---|---|
| Physician mix | 19.87 | 8.00** | 12.70 | 15.75 | 18.73 | 18.75 | 18.85 | 19.33 |
| Percent Medicare | 53.22 | 60.76 | 43.84 | 32.26 | 59.96 | 53.92 | 61.64 | 54.55 |
| Percent Medicaid | 3.43 | 5.59 | 8.88 | 9.14 | 1.77 | 5.84** | 3.79 | 7.82 |
| Average length of stay (days) | 7.43 | 7.33 | 7.38 | 6.13 | 7.17 | 7.76 | 7.43 | 7.73 |
| Percent occupancy | 71.55 | 65.05 | 70.89 | 67.66 | 69.57 | 57.50** | 60.49 | 65.03 |
| Percentage change (1979–1982) | | | | | | | | |
| Licensed beds | 2.74 | 0.00 | 1.59 | 0.45 | 6.94 | -0.61 | -0.08 | 9.10 |
| Service index | 1.60 | 12.21 | 5.76 | 3.55 | 0.46 | -5.29 | 9.43 | 0.16 |
| Physician mix | 3.67 | 23.08** | 10.47 | 3.28 | 3.31 | 4.90 | 10.36 | 17.77 |
| Percent Medicare | 4.41 | 0.16 | 5.59 | 8.95 | 6.71 | 13.43 | 1.57 | 7.32*** |
| Percent Medicaid | -3.92 | -37.96 | 17.16 | 13.95 | -13.57 | -18.08 | -7.33 | 14.15 |
| Average length of stay (days) | -0.13 | -1.18 | 2.11 | -2.71 | 3.92 | 8.39 | 2.77 | 2.83 |
| Percent occupancy | 7.78 | 1.94 | 8.01 | -1.11 | 12.82 | 0.85 | 30.51 | 4.48*** |

*** .10 level of significance.
** .05 level of significance.
* .01 level of significance.

TABLE 5  1979 Characteristics of Hospitals That Underwent a Subsequent Ownership Change and Hospitals That Did Not Change Ownership (means)

| Variable | All Hospitals with Unchanged Ownership (N = 168) | Investor-Owned Hospitals with Unchanged Ownership (N = 30) | All Hospitals Whose Ownership Changed (N = 27) | Hospitals Acquired by Investor-Owned Chains | |
|---|---|---|---|---|---|
| | | | | Corporate Takeovers (N = 8) | Individually Acquired (N = 7) |
| Profitability (percent) | | | | | |
| Operating margin | 2.89 | 11.98 | 1.85 | 4.07 | 5.48 |
| Total margin | 4.32 | 5.88 | 0.76*** | 2.34 | 3.22 |
| Types of patients treated | | | | | |
| Percent Medicare | 49.49 | 56.19 | 44.90 | 47.53[a] | 56.97 |
| Percent Medicaid | 4.52 | 2.05 | 7.60*** | 7.13[a] | 2.49 |
| Percent charity and bad debt | 7.32 | 3.46 | 8.90 | 5.08[a] | 5.41[a] |
| Efficiency of operations | | | | | |
| Operating expense/ adjusted admission | 1,559.20 | 1,519.14 | 1,615.20 | 1,708.90 | 1,741.60 |
| Percent occupancy | 63.74 | 61.67 | 62.50 | 57.02 | 65.60 |
| Average length of stay (days) | 7.29 | 6.89 | 7.08 | 7.16 | 7.63 |
| Average number of admissions | 7,780.00 | 6,501.00 | 5,924.00 | 4,837.00 | 6,518.00 |
| Salary expense/ adjusted admission ($) | 725.17 | 614.90 | 699.56 | 696.59 | 710.66 |
| Salary expense/full- time equivalent ($) | 11,094.00 | 11,338.00 | 11,334.00 | 13,165.00[a]* | 10,849.00 |

311

| | | | | | |
|---|---|---|---|---|---|
| Man-hours/adjusted patient day | 18.78 | 16.40 | 18.22 | 15.46* | 17.87 |
| Revenues ($) | | | | | |
| Gross revenue/adjusted admission | 1,993.00 | 2,206.44 | 2,057.50 | 2,298.30 | 2,155.50 |
| Net revenue/adjusted admission | 1,605.80 | 1,725.94 | 1,645.70 | 1,781.46 | 1,842.80 |
| Ancillary revenue/adjusted admission | 1,169.10 | 1,421.21 | 1,271.30 | 1,411.90 | 1,323.30 |
| Available resources | | | | | |
| Licensed beds | 243.45 | 199.17 | 192.30 | 166.40 | 210.90 |
| Service index | 32.60 | 30.75 | 27.70 | 24.58 | 27.56 |
| Physician mix | 16.30 | 18.13 | 15.90 | 17.90 | 17.70 |
| Percent patient care salary expense | 65.40 | 68.68 | 64.50 | 65.60 | 64.90 |
| Regional characteristics (county) | | | | | |
| Per capita income ($) | 11,490.00 | 11,461.00 | 11,521.00 | 11,696.00 | 11,835.00 |
| Percent over 65 | 18.02 | 20.00 | 17.29 | 16.62 | 20.64 |
| Number of hospitals | 10.74 | 10.40 | 11.52 | 15.50* | 9.57 |
| Number of physicians | 2.07 | 1.83 | 2.35 | 2.24 | 2.12 |
| Geographic index | 98.46 | 98.86 | 100.03 | 102.23 | 100.54 |

NOTE: Significance computed for difference in means between hospitals with no ownership change and each other category: ***.10 level of significance; *.01 level of significance.

[a]Significant difference in means between investor-owned hospitals with unchanged ownership and the two categories of acquisitions by investor-owned chains.

impact on overall profitability. From a reimbursement standpoint, patients can be ranked with respect to the portion of their charges that will actually be paid. Insured charge-paying patients are most likely to reimburse the hospital fully, followed in order by Medicare and Medicaid patients who pay allowable costs rather than full charges. Bad debt and charity cases are least desirable because their charges must be written off (although in some cases public funds may help offset the losses). As a result, hospitals with a sizable charity and bad debt burden are likely to have low profit levels or even losses and comparatively high charges because paying patients must subsidize patients receiving uncompensated care.

In 1979, hospitals in Florida wrote off 7.4 percent of assessed charges to charity care and bad debts. For government hospitals, which have played a major role historically in providing this kind of care, the figure was 14.2 percent. A hospital that can modify its patient mix to increase the proportion of Medicare and fully insured patients can improve its profit levels without changing its charges or costs. Improved collections of bad debts can also reduce the percentage of cases attributed to that category and improve profits, if collection costs do not exceed revenues.

The results in Table 5 suggest that the hospitals that subsequently changed ownership had the potential for changes in patient mix since their Medicaid caseloads and their charity and bad debt level were higher than those of other hospitals. In addition, the Medicare caseload for the hospitals whose ownership subsequently changed was comparatively low.

Hospitals that investor-owned chains subsequently acquired deviated from this pattern with bad debt and charity write-offs that were low compared to the total population of hospitals whose ownership did not change. However, bad debt and charity figures were nevertheless higher than for the investor-owned hospitals whose ownership remained unchanged (see Table 5). Hospitals acquired individually by the investor-owned chains also had extremely low Medicaid caseloads (although above average for investor-owned hospitals) and comparatively high Medicare case loads (average for investor-owned hospitals). Thus, from a reimbursement standpoint the

patient mix of hospitals acquired individually by investor-owned chains was particularly desirable.

**Efficiency of Operations**

Profit levels can be enhanced by reducing expenses, for example, through reductions in staffing levels, or by increasing volume without commensurate increases in expenses. The data in Table 5 suggest that some potential for efficiency improvements existed among hospitals that subsequently underwent a change of ownership. Operating expenses per adjusted admission were slightly higher for such hospitals, even after adjustments were made for differences in hospital input prices and despite the fact that hospitals whose ownership changed had a slightly lower case-mix score than other hospitals (as measured by the Health Care Financing Administration's case-mix score based on 1980 data). Some sources of these higher expenses can be identified. Occupancy levels were slightly lower. And because staffing levels and salary expense per adjusted admission were lower, the hospitals whose ownership changed must have had higher nonsalary expenses. The hospitals subsequently acquired by investor-owned chains had the highest levels of operating expense per admission of all hospitals that changed ownership. Expenses other than salaries were the primary source of this differential.

**Revenues**

The data in Table 5 reveal that hospitals whose ownership subsequently changed had higher average revenues and collected more per adjusted admission than did other hospitals in 1979. Their ancillary revenues were also higher. Since markups are typically higher on ancillary services than on room services, this indicates that charges for the hospitals that were subsequently acquired were already relatively high for the more profitable portion of the patient bill.

The hospitals subsequently acquired by investor-owned chains mirrored the general pattern, although their revenues were higher than average for hospitals that underwent a subsequent ownership change. Again, hospitals subsequently acquired individually by investor-owned chains had the most desirable revenue profile with the highest average net revenue per admission.

## Available Resources

Also important to hospital growth and long-term profitability is the range of resources available for patient care—particularly the medical staff profile. Physicians are the gate-keepers for any hospital, determining that a hospital admission is necessary and advising patients on where they should be admitted. Without a minimal number of physicians and a core of medical specialties, it may be difficult to compete for patients. On the other hand, certain physician specialties tend to admit complex cases that are costly to treat. Depending upon the reimbursement sources for these patients, overall profitability may be affected.

The range of services that a facility offers is also important. Certain resources are essential to attract or keep particular physician specialties and their patients, even though they may increase costs. Hospitals must deal with these frequently conflicting considerations in light of their own definition of the hospital's mission. Management strategies focused on profit maximization could expand into new clinical areas that have potential for reasonable levels of returns, or attempt to perform better with the existing mix of services, or eliminate unprofitable services.

The results in Table 5 suggest that the hospitals that had a subsequent change of ownership were only marginally smaller and less complex than other hospitals in 1979. Their physician-mix score was slightly lower. The hospitals subsequently acquired by investor-owned chains followed the general pattern for available resources with the exception of physician mix, where their physician-mix scores were slightly higher than the average for all hospitals, but slightly below average for investor-owned hospitals whose ownership did not change (see Table 5).

## Regional Characteristics

The potential for improvements in profits can also be affected by a hospital's location.

Locations in affluent areas or in areas with large elderly populations may have greater potential for volume growth and revenue enhancement than do locations in low-income areas where there are larger numbers of uninsured people. Locations with relatively large numbers of physicians and few competing hospitals also have greater potential for developing the desired medical staff profile. Finally, hospitals located in regions with lower input prices should be able to operate at lower cost, other things being equal.

The data in Table 5 reveal that per capita income levels and the number of physicians in the county were higher in 1979 for the hospitals that underwent a subsequent ownership change, but elderly populations were more prominent in the area of hospitals whose ownership remained unchanged. In addition, the hospitals that subsequently changed ownership were generally located in areas with comparatively high input prices (actually above the state average) and an above-average number of facilities. Hospitals subsequently acquired by investor-owned chains through corporate takeovers mirrored the regional pattern for hospitals that underwent an ownership change. Hospitals acquired individually were different in several important ways. Most dramatic was the high elderly concentration in the counties where these facilities were located. These concentrations undoubtedly accounted for the high Medicare caseloads noted above and are consistent with typical locations of other investor-owned hospitals in Florida. Also noteworthy is the smaller average number of acute care general hospitals in the counties where these facilities were located. Thus, the individually acquired facilities again had a particularly desirable profile.

## Overall Characteristics of Hospitals That Subsequently Changed Ownership

In conclusion, the hospitals that subsequently underwent an ownership change differed from other hospitals in several important ways. They had significantly lower total profit margins, which were not due to lower charges (their charges were actually slightly higher) but to slightly higher operating costs, fewer admissions, and the more frequent necessity

TABLE 6  Mean Percentage Changes in Hospitals That Underwent an Ownership Change and Hospitals That Did Not Change Ownership, 1979–1982

| Variable | All Hospitals with Unchanged Ownership (N = 168) | Investor-Owned Hospitals with Unchanged Ownership (N = 30) | All Hospitals Whose Ownership Changed (N = 27) | Hospitals Acquired by Investor-Owned Chains | |
|---|---|---|---|---|---|
| | | | | Corporate Takeovers (N = 8) | Individually Acquired (N = 7) |
| Profitability (percent) | | | | | |
| Operating margin | 38.79 | 30.88 | 205.50 | 37.64 | 62.74 |
| Total margin | 24.47 | 41.94 | 446.57*** | 23.27 | 66.53 |
| Types of patients treated | | | | | |
| Percent Medicare | 5.16 | 6.71 | 9.65*** | 13.43[a]** | 4.55 |
| Percent Medicaid | 4.88 | −13.57 | 0.29 | 18.09 | 84.33[a] |
| Percent charity and bad debt | 5.36 | 1.51 | −19.90* | −34.60** | −14.18 |
| Efficiency of operations | | | | | |
| Operating expense/ adjusted admission | 58.15 | 54.28 | 66.68 | 82.04[a]*** | 60.25 |
| Percent occupancy | 9.43 | 12.82 | 2.54*** | 0.85** | 5.92 |
| Average length of stay | 1.25 | 3.92 | 2.69 | 8.40*** | 3.28 |

|  | | | | | |
|---|---|---|---|---|---|
| Average number of admissions | 11.22 | 16.11 | 3.75 | −7.52[a]* | 13.99 |
| Salary/adjusted admission | 58.71 | 56.33 | 58.96 | 63.31 | 56.70 |
| Salary/full-time equivalent | 45.84 | 39.97 | 41.77 | 29.24** | 51.08 |
| Man-hours/adjusted patient day | 8.02 | 7.11 | 9.34 | 15.86 | 3.34 |
| Revenues | | | | | |
|   Gross revenue/ adjusted admission | 67.48 | 68.69 | 76.38 | 82.91 | 67.12 |
|   Net revenue/ adjusted admission | 60.01 | 61.05 | 73.01*** | 84.99[a]*** | 66.28 |
|   Ancillary revenue/ adjusted admission | 76.09 | 108.45 | 189.93*** | 101.35** | 78.60[a] |
| Available resources | | | | | |
|   Service index | 5.08 | 0.46 | 0.18 | −5.29 | 6.69 |
|   Physician mix | 9.31 | 3.31 | 16.49 | 4.90 | 18.75 |
|   Percent patient care salary expense | −0.52 | −2.76 | 0.16 | −3.51 | 1.23 |

NOTE: Significance computed for difference in means between hospitals with no ownership change and each other category: ***.10 level of significance; **.05 level of significance; *.01 level of significance.

[a]Significant difference in means between investor-owned hospitals with unchanged ownership and the two categories of acquisitions by investor-owned chains.

of paying taxes out of profits. Although slightly smaller and less complex than other hospitals, the hospitals that subsequently changed ownership had higher costs and a less desirable patient mix with more Medicaid patients and more bad debt and charity. While only the low total margin and high Medicaid caseload measures were statistically significant, the findings suggest both why these hospitals might have been candidates for being sold and what types of management strategies might have been expected to increase their profitability after acquisition.

Hospitals subsequently acquired by investor-owned chains (and particularly those acquired individually) had a more desirable profile in the pre-acquisition period (e.g., higher margins and better patient mix for reimbursement purposes) than the acquired hospital that underwent a subsequent ownership change. As a result, the magnitude of post-acquisition change in these facilities may well be less dramatic than might otherwise occur because their starting point was relatively favorable.

## ANALYSIS OF POST-ACQUISITION BEHAVIOR

Hospital behavior in the post-acquisition period was examined by comparing rates of change for the acquired and other hospitals (i.e., those whose ownership was unchanged) between 1979 and 1982 for most of the measures noted in Table 1. The five regional variables were not examined because they did not change significantly in the 3-year period. Again comparisons were made between the total population of hospitals that had an ownership change and the total population of hospitals acquired by investor-owned chains, whose ownership did not change.

The analysis of the pre-acquisition characteristics revealed that the hospitals that had an ownership change had consistently lower profit levels than the other hospitals, which may explain why they were available for acquisition. Several possible approaches for increasing the profitability of acquired hospitals were proposed including: changing the patient mix, improving the efficiency of operations, increasing revenues, and realigning available resources. The actual changes experienced in

the post-acquisition period are discussed in the following section.

### Profitability

The data in Table 6 reveal that the profit margins for the hospitals that underwent an ownership change increased dramatically faster between 1979 and 1982 than they did for the hospitals whose ownership did not change. Operating margins for the hospitals whose ownership changed increased at a rate of over 200 percent in the 3-year period, compared to approximately 38 percent for other hospitals. During this period average total margin for the hospitals whose ownership changed increased by over 400 percent compared to less than 25 percent for other hospitals. Even so, these increases brought the average total margin of hospitals whose ownership changed to 4.16 percent in 1982, a level still below the 5.38 percent total margin for hospitals whose ownership had not changed.

The hospitals acquired by investor-owned chains experienced less dramatic increases in margins than did other hospitals that changed ownership, partially because of their comparatively high margins in the pre-acquisition period. Hospitals acquired through corporate takeovers had rates of increase that were actually less than in hospitals with unchanged ownership; as a result, total margins in 1982 for these facilities were lower than those for either the average hospital that had changed ownership or the average hospital whose ownership had not changed. Hospitals acquired individually by investor-owned clinics achieved more substantial rates of increase in margin and as a result in 1982 exceeded the operating margin and equaled the total margin of the average hospital that had not changed ownership. Even with those substantial rates of increase, their average margins were less than those of the average investor-owned hospital whose ownership had not changed.

### Types of Patients Treated

Significant post-acquisition changes took place in patient mix, with the percentage of revenues written off to charity and bad debt diminishing on average almost 20 percent in hospitals that underwent an ownership change while they increased by more than 5 percent for other hospitals. This difference is significant at the .01 percent level. It should be noted that the absolute dollar amount written off by hospitals that underwent an ownership change increased in this period, but at a slower rate than the increase in average charge per admission. These figures suggest that the average number of bad debt or charity cases that could have been treated actually decreased even though the dollar amount written off increased.

Medicare caseloads for hospitals that underwent an ownership change increased at a rate nearly twice that for other hospitals and almost equalized levels between the two categories of hospitals. This difference was also statistically significant. Medicaid caseloads increased less than three-tenths of 1 percent for the hospitals that changed ownership and by almost 5 percent for other ones. These increases still did not eliminate the dramatic difference in Medicaid caseloads that existed in 1979 between hospitals that changed ownership and those that did not. In sum it appears that the hospitals that changed ownership changed their patient mix in the post-acquisition period to reduce their dependence on less reliable revenue sources and to increase the proportion of patients with more reliable reimbursement.

The hospitals acquired by investor-owned chains mirrored the general pattern of reductions in the percentage of revenue written off to bad debt and charity care, despite the fact that these facilities had comparatively low bad debt and charity writeoffs in the pre-acquisition period. Consistent with the general pattern, Medicare caseloads increased both absolutely and as a percent of all cases for both types of hospitals acquired by investor-owned chains, although the individually acquired facilities, which already had unusually high Medicare caseloads, experienced smaller increases. Medicaid caseloads actually decreased (both as a proportion and in absolute numbers) for the hospitals acquired under corporate takeovers. The dramatic increase in Medicaid caseload for the hospitals acquired individually reflects both the low levels in the pre-acquisition period and a sizable increase for one of these seven facilities. With the ex-

ception of this one hospital, the hospitals acquired by investor-owned chains continued to improve their patient profile from a reimbursement standpoint. The hospitals acquired individually had a less dramatic change, probably because of their comparatively desirable patient profiles in the pre-acquisition period.

### Efficiency of Operations

While efficiency improvements and resulting cost reductions are frequently cited expectations for hospital acquisition, expenses increased faster for the hospitals that underwent an ownership change than for other hospitals. Occupancy levels and the number of admissions also increased at much slower rates than for the hospitals whose ownership was unchanged (significantly slower for occupancy levels). Personnel costs increased at approximately the same rate for both groups of hospitals, indicating that the nonsalary components of expense were the primary cause of the different rates of increase in overall operating expense.

Although the data do not make it possible to determine exactly which components of the nonsalary expenses caused these changes, the findings of an earlier study on acquired hospitals in Florida (Florida HCCB, 1983) identified several potential sources. That study (based on some of the hospitals included in this study) attributed above-average increases in operating expense by acquired hospitals to high interest expense associated with high levels of debt financing, high depreciation expense associated with the rapid increase in asset value upon acquisition, and in at least one case, high rental expenses paid to related parties. The finding here that nonsalary expenses contributed at above-average levels to expense increases is consistent with these earlier findings.

The hospitals acquired by investor-owned chains exhibited faster rates of increase in expenses than did all hospitals whose ownership was unchanged and than did investor-owned hospitals whose ownership did not change (see Table 6). These increases were in addition to their comparatively high expense levels in the pre-acquisition period. Expense increases for hospitals acquired during corporate takeovers were statistically significant. As in the general case, nonsalary expenses contributed disproportionately to these increases in expense levels.

### Revenue

All measures of revenue showed faster rates of increase for the hospitals that changed ownership than they did for other hospitals. The net revenue figure reflects not only increases in charges, but also the modifications in patient mix by reimbursement category pointed out above. The dramatic increase in ancillary revenue suggests that increases in the number of ancillary services provided and/or in the charges for ancillary services contributed significantly to the increase in revenues.

The hospitals acquired by investor-owned chains exhibited increases in revenues which, with one exception, exceeded the average changes for hospitals that had an ownership change. Gross revenue per adjusted admission increased somewhat slower for individually acquired hospitals than for hospitals whose ownership did not change. The rate of increase on net revenue was significantly higher for the hospitals acquired under corporate takeovers than for hospitals that did not change ownership. It appears that despite comparatively high revenue levels in the pre-acquisition period, the hospitals acquired by investor-owned chains (and particularly those acquired under corporate takeovers) experienced unusually high revenue increases after acquisition.

### Available Resources

Virtually no changes were observed in the average service mix of hospitals that underwent an ownership change. Increases in their physician-mix index exceeded the rate for other hospitals. This suggests that the acquired hospitals attempted to attract new patients by adding new physician specialties. This finding is consistent with the modifications in patient mix that occurred during the period.

The hospitals acquired by investor-owned chains under corporate takeovers experienced modest rates of increase in the physician-mix index and decreased their service index score in the post-acquisition period. Those acquired individually increased both their service index and physician-mix scores at rates faster than those for other hospitals.

### Overall Changes in the Post-Acquisition Period

The findings reveal that the profitability of hospitals whose ownership changed dramatically increased in the post-acquisition period. This was accomplished by modifying their patient mix, increasing revenues (especially ancillary revenues), and attempting to enter new patient markets. Improved efficiency was not a contributing factor as operating expenses for these hospitals actually increased faster than they did for hospitals whose ownership was unchanged.

The post-acquisition behavior of the hospitals acquired by investor-owned chains was also substantially different from the behavior of hospitals whose ownership was unchanged. The pre-acquisition characteristics of these hospitals may explain many of these differences. Hospitals acquired through corporate takeovers followed the general pattern for all hospitals whose ownership changed, but at faster rates. The major exception was that profit margins, which were comparatively high in 1979, increased at comparatively modest rates in the post-acquisition period. Hospitals acquired individually by investor-owned chains had comparatively high margins and a fairly desirable patient profile in the pre-acquisition period, so post-acquisition increases were smaller than increases for other hospitals whose ownership changed, though these increases still generally exceeded those for the hospitals whose ownership was unchanged.

### DISCUSSION

The observed differences between hospitals that experienced an ownership change and other hospitals in Florida raise several interesting policy issues. Primary among these is the issue of profitability itself. The study reveals that the hospitals that changed ownership had significantly lower profit margins than other hospitals prior to the ownership change. The 1979 average total margin for hospitals that subsequently changed ownership was 0.76 percent, a very low figure compared to margins for the average hospital in the state or for other industries. The often-cited capital crisis of the 1980s and the resulting fierce competition for capital will require an ongoing accumulation of profits if hospitals are to engage successfully in the major capital expenditures which eventually face all institutions. From this standpoint the acquisition process may be extremely beneficial in substantially improving margins for hospitals that have been unable or unwilling to generate necessary and healthy margins.

The study reveals that overall increases in profit levels for hospitals that changed ownership in the 3-year period were dramatic; operating margins increased by an average of more than 200 percent and average total margins increased by over 400 percent. As a result, average profit margins for the 27 institutions reached a level of 4.16 percent in 1982. However, the range in these margins (from 15.9 percent to −44.5 percent) suggests that these hospitals did not benefit uniformly from the change in ownership.

The profitability experience of the hospitals acquired by investor-owned chains was less dramatic but also exhibited much variability. In the 3-year period between 1979 and 1982, 5 of the 15 hospitals acquired by investor-owned chains had reached margins that were average for that comparatively profitable sector, and 2 others had margins that exceeded the average for hospitals that had not changed ownership. However, 2 of the 15 hospitals acquired by investor-owned chains had negative margins in 1982. Thus, these findings do not provide strong support for the argument that acquisition by investor-owned hospitals will lead to excessive profiteering. On the other hand, the fact that some facilities achieved substantial after-tax margins (the high was 10.8 percent) when pre-acquisition levels were low or negative suggests that the concern cannot be totally dismissed.

Perhaps of more concern than profitability are the social effects of the management strategies that the acquiring firms used to increase profit margins. Intentionally or not, the hospitals whose ownership changed previously served as a major source of Medicaid, bad debt, and charity care. While these categories of patients may not be desirable from a reimburse-

ment standpoint, as the most needy segment of society they clearly require access to the hospital system. However, the hospitals whose ownership changed collectively reduced bad debt and charity and held Medicaid increases to a minimum.

For the hospitals acquired by investor-owned chains the findings are similar, showing reductions in Medicaid and bad debt and charity burdens in facilities that generally were already low on these measures. Some of the reduction in bad debt may have resulted from improved collection techniques rather than through reductions in access to care; however, the fact that in the same period the hospitals whose ownership did not change had an increase in bad debt and charity raises the possibility that some of the reduction may have been accomplished by channeling these patients to other facilities.

Also troubling is the finding that hospital acquisition is a cost-inducing process. Undoubtedly some of the increased expenditures were necessary and would have occurred in any case. However, some earlier evidence is available to suggest that a significant portion of these cost increases was a result of the financing strategies and operating arrangements employed by the acquiring firms. Such cost increases do not lead to significant improvements in operating efficiencies or service levels.

For the hospitals acquired by investor-owned chains, these same concerns apply perhaps more strongly since it is for this sector of the industry that the benefit of operating efficiency is so often claimed. The rapid increases in operating expenses on top of unusually high levels in the pre-acquisition period call that claim into question.

A direct consequence of the escalation in expenses due to hospital acquisition was a sizable increase in patient charges. A major source of the improved profitability for the hospitals that underwent an ownership change was the increased price of an admission. In cases where facilities were operating at a loss, this may have been an essential management step. However, in cases where revenues were already high, the necessity for further increases can be questioned.

This last concern is particularly appropriate

for hospitals acquired by investor-owned chains. Post-acquisition revenues for these facilities increased faster than expenses; as a result, margins increased. The result of acquisition by investor-owned chains included, among other things, dramatic increases in charges that were already comparatively high.

It should be noted that revenue increases for hospitals acquired individually by investor-owned chains were less dramatic than those for hospitals acquired under corporate takeover. It is perhaps not surprising that these facilities, which had been individually selected for acquisition, could achieve increased margins with less dramatic increases in charges and could modify operations with less dramatic increases in expenses. It is not clear if this pattern can be maintained as fewer "desirable" acquisition candidates remain.

The fact that facilities acquired under corporate takeovers had such dramatic increases in expenses and revenues is also understandable. Decisions regarding these acquisitions were made on the basis of larger considerations than the characteristics of a few hospitals in Florida. The number of facilities involved in these takeovers nationally would make it difficult to modify operations quickly and efficiently. Likewise the amount of debt necessitated by these takeovers could have a direct effect on interest and depreciation expenses. Regardless of the reasons, the consequences were dramatic. This study's findings suggest a serious concern with the impact of corporate takeovers on system costs and resulting patient charges.

The introduction of prospective reimbursement under Medicare will undoubtedly affect future decisions concerning hospital acquisitions and the behavior of those facilities after acquisitions. The incentives under the new system for reducing costs and service utilization and for promoting the provision of care in profitable diagnostic categories will probably change significantly the behavior of indi-

vidual hospitals and corporate chains. This study suggests that the effects of hospital acquisition deserve thorough study in the years ahead. If existing patterns of increased charges and expenses and reduced provision of care to indigents continue under that system as well, the hospital acquisition process may help contribute to a reconfigured hospital system that is less responsive to society's needs.

### REFERENCES

Gersh, David L. (1982) Hospital acquisitions demand caution. *Modern Healthcare* 12:94-96.

Florida Hospital Cost Containment Board (HCCB) (1983) Impact of Acquisition on Hospital Finances. Unpublished manuscript.

Kushman, John Everett, and Carole Frank Nuckton (1977) Further evidence on the relative performance of proprietary and nonprofit hospitals. *Medical Care* (March):189-204.

Larson, John G. (1983) Factors in the success of the investor-owned hospitals: Implications for the not-for-profits. *Hospital and Health Services Administration* (March/April):43-49.

Lewin, Lawrence S., Robert A. Derzon, and Rhea Margulies (1981) Investor-owned and nonprofits differ in economic performance. *Hospitals* 55:52-58.

Mullner, Ross, Calvin S. Byre, and Joseph D. Kubal (1983) Hospital closure in the United States, 1976-1980: A descriptive overview. *Health Services Research* 18(3):437-450.

Pattison, Robert V., and Hallie M. Katz (1983) Investor-owned and not-for-profit hospitals: A comparison based on California data. *New England Journal of Medicine* 309(6):347-353.

Relman, Arnold S. (1980) The new medical-industrial complex. *New England Journal of Medicine* 303(17):963-970.

Sloan, Frank A., and Robert A. Vraciu (1983) Investor-owned and not-for-profit hospitals: Addressing some issues. *Health Affairs* 2:25-37.

Tillet, J. William, R. Bruce Linklater, and Randy A. Sucher (1982) Survey reveals trends in corporate reorganizations. *Hospital Financial Management* (September):38-45.

White, William D. (1979) Regulating competition in a nonprofit industry: The problem of for profit hospitals. *Inquiry* 16:50-61.

# APPENDIX A

## VARIABLES INDEX SCORE

| Service | Weight | Service | Weight |
|---|---|---|---|
| 1. Substance Abuse Unit | 2.2 | 14. Recovery Services | 2.6 |
| 2. Medical/Surgical Intensive Care | 4.7 | 15. Blood Bank | 3.4 |
| 3. Coronary Care | 4.7 | 16. Cardiac Catheterization Laboratory | 4.0 |
| 4. Combined Intensive Med/Surgical Coronary Care | 5.0 | 17. CT Scanner | 4.0 |
| | | 18. X-Ray or Cobalt Therapy | 3.7 |
| 5. Neonatal Intensive Care | 4.4 | 19. Respiratory Therapy | 2.3 |
| 6. Burn Intensive Care | 5.0 | 20. Physical Therapy | 2.0 |
| 7. Emergency Services with 24-hour In-House Physicians Only | 3.4 | 21. Occupational Therapy | 2.0 |
| | | 22. Speech-Language Pathology | 1.8 |
| 8. Emergency Services with 24-hour On-Call Physicians Only | 2.3 | 23. Renal Dialysis Inpatient or Outpatient | 3.7 |
| 9. Ambulatory Surgery Services | 2.7 | 24. Organ Bank | 2.7 |
| 10. Ambulance Services | 2.3 | 25. Social Work Services | 2.0 |
| 11. Labor and Delivery Services | 3.0 | 26. Pharmacy—Full-Time Registered Pharmacist | 3.0 |
| 12. Neurological Surgery | 4.2 | | |
| 13. Open-Heart Surgery | 5.0 | 27. Psychiatric Acute Care | 2.5 |

# APPENDIX B

## SPECIALTIES INCLUDED IN PHYSICIAN-MIX SCORE

1. Allergy and Immunology
2. Anesthesiology
3. Cardiovascular Diseases
4. Colon and Rectal Surgery
5. Emergency Medicine
6. Endocrinology
7. Family/General Practice
8. Gynecology (Surgical)
9. General Surgery
10. Internal Medicine
11. Neurosurgery
12. Obstetrics and Gynecology
13. Oncology-Hematology
14. Ophthamology
15. Orthopedic Surgery
16. Otorhinolaryngology
17. Pathology
18. Pediatrics
19. Plastic Surgery
20. Psychology
21. Pulmonary Diseases
22. Radiology
23. Thoracic/Cardiovascular Surgery
24. Urological Surgery
25. Other Clinical Specialties

*For-Profit Enterprise in Health Care.* 1986.
National Academy Press, Washington, D.C.

# Hospital Ownership and Comparative Hospital Costs

Craig G. Coelen

## INTRODUCTION

Proprietary hospitals have become increasingly common in the United States in the past decade, and this trend has provoked a debate about the relative cost of patient care in proprietary versus nonprofit hospitals. Of particular concern have been the implications of the growth of proprietary chains, through construction and acquisition. Advocates of proprietary ownership point to the advantages of economies of scale and the profit-related incentive for efficiency. Detractors raise concerns about high costs of capital, high charge/cost ratios, and limitations on access for charity cases and Medicaid beneficiaries.

Previous empirical studies of comparative costs among different types of hospitals do not provide uniform conclusions. Ermann and Gabel (1986) review a dozen studies and conclude that "the consensus . . . is that [proprietary and nonprofit chains] increase the cost of care [relative to independent hospitals]. The conclusion holds whether costs are measured as hospital expenses, revenues, or charges, on a per admission or per diem basis." Because half of the studies indicate that proprietary hospitals and/or proprietary chains are less expensive or, at worst, no more expensive than nonprofit hospitals, it is our view that there is no consensus in the existing evidence.

The 12 studies reviewed by Ermann and Gabel differ widely with respect to measures of cost, research samples, analytic techniques, and controls for possible differences in case mix. Most studies compare costs among hospitals in only one or a few states and warn readers about the danger of generalizing their results to other areas. In most cases, the sample sizes are so small that multivariate statistical techniques cannot be used to account for the influence of cost determinants other than ownership. Because case mix is not accounted for explicitly in any of the studies, the reader is left with conclusions of the form: "Unless the patients admitted to proprietary hospitals are sicker (less sick) than those admitted to nonprofit hospitals, proprietary hospitals are more expensive (less expensive) than similar nonprofit institutions."

Reexamining the relationship between hospital ownership and the cost of hospital care, we hope to improve upon earlier research in several ways. First, we use data for a generalizable sample of community hospitals in the 48 contiguous states and the District of Columbia. Second, by presenting the dispersion of cost per patient among hospitals within each group and then comparing the distributions across groups, we are able to assess the relative homogeneity of different groups. Third, by explicitly adjusting for cross-sectional differences in case mix in our analysis, we are able to limit the degree to which we must qualify our conclusions about comparative costs.

We confine our discussion of interhospital differences to the following set of indicators of hospital performance:

- Level and annual rate of change of expense per discharge
- Average length of stay
- Level and annual rate of change of number of discharges
- Total, routine, and ancillary charges per discharge and
- Margins on patient revenue and total revenue.

Although we do not provide detailed statistical results, we have examined other indica-

---

Dr. Coelen is with Abt Associates, Inc., Cambridge, Massachusetts.

tors during our analysis and will refer to the findings as relevant.

## DATA

Data are drawn from information compiled for a large evaluation of hospital prospective reimbursement programs for the Health Care Financing Administration (HCFA). The principal facts about our data are the following:

- Measures of hospital expense, utilization, and margins are drawn from hospitals' Medicare cost reports, although information from American Hospital Association (AHA) annual surveys has been used extensively to test for errors in coding and keypunching.
- Measures of total, routine, and ancillary charges per discharge are drawn from a 20 percent sample of Medicare patients with selected medical problems.[1] Comparing total charges per patient from this source with hospital-wide average charges per patient from cost reports, we find that Medicare-only charges accurately reflect differences in gross patient service revenue across groups of hospitals.
- Hospital expense has been divided by a uniquely derived measure of adjusted discharges. The adjustment for outpatient services and inpatient days in skilled nursing facility (SNF) units is accomplished by regressing the annual rate of change of expense on annual rates of change of acute care discharges, length of stay, SNF days per acute care discharge, outpatient visits per acute care discharges, and a variety of variables measuring the characteristics of hospital catchment areas. Regression coefficients from this short-term cost function are then used to convert SNF days and outpatient visits to equivalent values of acute care discharges.

## RESEARCH SAMPLE

Unlike the samples used in most other studies of comparative hospital costs, our sample is representative of the 48 contiguous states and the District of Columbia. The sample was selected as follows:

- A 25 percent simple random sample of community hospitals was selected. Specialty hospitals, those run by federal or state agencies, and those with median values of average length of stay from 1969 to 1981 in excess of 15 days were excluded.
- All remaining eligible hospitals in the 15 states with prospective reimbursement programs of interest to HCFA were added to the proportional sample. The states were Arizona, Colorado, Connecticut, Indiana, Kentucky, Maryland, Massachusetts, Minnesota, Nebraska, New Jersey, New York, Pennsylvania, Rhode Island, Washington, and Wisconsin.
- For this study, hospitals run by local government agencies and hospitals with membership in the Council of Teaching Hospitals were excluded.
- For analyses of hospital expense, utilization rates, and charges, data are available for each year from 1975 to 1981. The analyses of hospital margins are based on data from 1975 to 1979.

Table 1 displays sample size by type of hospital and year. Because the sample over-represents states with prospective reimbursement programs (primarily in the northeast), all major analyses have been redone for a strictly proportional sample. Because findings about comparative cost across types of hospitals did not change when the proportional sample was used, only results for the complete sample are reported here.

## ANALYTIC METHODS

The method used to estimate costs, charges, utilization rates, and margins among groups of hospitals is multiple regression analysis. This technique computes intergroup differences that are adjusted for geographic location, catchment area characteristics, presence/absence of regulatory programs (prospective reimbursement, certificate-of-need programs, and binding professional standards review organization review [PSRO]), bed size, and case mix. Once the influence of these other potential determinants of hospital behavior has been taken into account, residual differences among groups of hospitals can be reliably attributed to differences in management.

Table A.1 in the appendix provides a list of all dependent and explanatory variables included in multiple regression models and pre-

**TABLE 1**    Sample Size by Type of Hospital and Year[a]

| Year | Proprietary Hospitals | | Nonprofit Hospitals | | All Four Types |
|------|-------|-------------|-------|-------------|-------|
|      | Chain | Independent | Chain | Independent |       |
| 1975 | 92  | 188 | 419 | 1,083 | 1,782 |
| 1976 | 96  | 170 | 419 | 1,073 | 1,758 |
| 1977 | 100 | 157 | 424 | 1,065 | 1,746 |
| 1978 | 100 | 141 | 424 | 1,046 | 1,711 |
| 1979 | 104 | 132 | 423 | 1,020 | 1,679 |
| 1980 | 108 | 128 | 424 | 1,004 | 1,664 |
| 1981 | 108 | 129 | 418 | 982   | 1,637 |

[a]The sample excludes hospitals that opened after 1977; sample size by 1981 is lower by about 60 hospitals than would otherwise be the case. The sample size decreases over time as the result of hospital closures.

sents means and standard deviations for the set of observations used in analyses. The explanatory variables are

• Six dummy variables for the year to which data apply; these constitute a more flexible specification of secular influences than a simple linear time trend (dummy variable for 1975 is omitted).
• Three dummy variables for type of ownership; since a dummy variable for independent (nonchain) nonprofit hospitals is omitted, all three coefficients for ownership variables measure differences with respect to this omitted, and most common, category of hospital.
• The logarithm of the hospital's Medicare case-mix index for 1982, propagated to all other years, as a rough measure of differences in case type across hospitals (but not across years).
• Four dummy variables representing urban, nonurban, and regional location of hospitals;
• Three dummy variables indicating presence/absence of regulatory programs for each hospital year—prospective reimbursement, binding PSRO utilization review, and certificate of need; and
• Sixteen continuous variables to control for relevant characteristics of the catchment areas (counties) served by each hospital—socioeconomic characteristics of the population, economic conditions, insurance coverage, and availability of physicians and nursing home beds.

For selected measures of hospital perfor-

mance we present comparative histograms to indicate differences in distributions across the four groups of hospitals. Although multiple regression analyses provide estimates of differences in adjusted means and indicate the statistical significance of those differences, they do not provide an adequate indication of dispersion within a group and relative dispersion across groups. The comparative histograms complement the results of regression analyses by indicating the degree to which statistically significant differences in means are typical of most hospitals or are the result of large differences between a minority of hospitals in each group (so called outliers).

## RESULTS

Table 2 presents estimated differences across the four groups of hospitals for 10 indicators of performance. These estimates, derived from multiple regression analyses reported in the appendix, are adjusted for differences in location, catchment area characteristics, presence/absence of regulatory programs directed at hospitals, bed size and case mix. Figure 1, comparing the dispersion of case mix among hospitals across the four groups, illustrates the degree to which these potential determinants of hospital behavior vary across the four groups. Proprietary chain hospitals, for example, are concentrated primarily in southern and western states, whereas other types of hospitals are more equally distributed geographically. Independent proprietary hospitals tend to have

TABLE 2   Estimated Differences in Cost, Utilization, Charges, and Margins Among Hospitals: Summary of Results from Regression Analyses

| Performance Measure[a] | Difference Relative to Independent Nonprofit Hospitals | | |
|---|---|---|---|
| | Proprietary Chains | Proprietary Independents | Nonprofit Chains |
| Total expense per adjusted discharge (% difference) | 5.8[b] | − 4.2[b] | 1.9[b] |
| Annual rate of change of expense per case (percentage point difference in rate of growth) | −0.4 | − 1.2[b] | −0.2 |
| Average length of stay (% difference) | 0.2 | 2.2[b] | 1.3[b] |
| Number of discharges (% difference) | − 7.7[b] | − 2.3 | 2.2[b] |
| Annual rate of change of number of discharges (percentage point difference in rate of growth) | 1.0[b] | 0.3 | 0.5[b] |
| Medicare charges/case (% difference) | 19.0[b] | 11.2[b] | 3.5[b] |
| Medicare routine charges/case (% difference) | −1.2 | 7.4[b] | 2.2[b] |
| Ancillary charges per case (% difference) | 33.9[b] | 14.5[b] | 5.1[b] |
| Margin on patient revenue (percentage point difference) | 5.5[b] | 3.3[b] | −0.6[b] |
| Margin on total revenue (percentage point difference) | 1.8[b] | 1.1[b] | −0.6[b] |

[a]Estimates in each of the 10 rows of the table are derived from Appendix tables A.2 through A.11. All measures except Medicare charges per case apply to the entire hospital and all patients.

[b]Probability that measured differences are due to chance is less than 5 percent.

fewer beds than other types of hospitals and a higher frequency of low-intensity case mix. Only those differences in performance indicators across groups that are not associated with differences, location, case mix, and other factors are reflected in our measures of differences due to ownership.

### Experience per Discharge

Total hospital expense per adjusted discharge varies by as much as 10 percent among the average hospitals in each of the four groups, or by as much as $250 per case in 1981 dollars.[2]

Independent hospitals are less expensive than chain-operated hospitals, and among independent institutions, proprietary hospitals are 4 percent less expensive than nonprofit hospitals. Nonprofit chains are 2 percent more expensive, on average, than independent nonprofit institutions. Proprietary chains are the most expensive of all four groups—6 percent more costly than nonprofit independents and 10 percent more expensive than proprietary independents. Our results clearly dispute the presumed advantages of chain-operated hospitals in general, and proprietary chains in

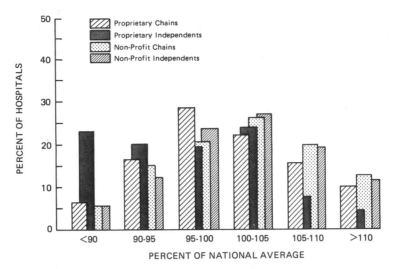

**FIGURE 1**    Comparative dispersion of Medicare case-mix index (year 1980).

particular, from economies of scale and profit-related incentives for minimization of cost.[3]

In addition to providing care at the most economical cost, independent proprietary hospitals have been more effective than other hospitals in slowing the annual rate of increase of costs. There are no statistically significant differences in annual rates of increase of expense per case among average hospitals in the other three of the four groups. Among independent proprietary hospitals, average annual increases were 1.2 percentage points lower than was the case among other hospitals. Over a 7-year period (1975 through 1981, the span of our data), this lower annual rate of growth produces a cumulative compound savings of 8 percent, large enough by itself to account for the 4 percent average difference in the level of cost between proprietary independents and nonprofit independents.

Figure 2 presents the comparative dispersion of expense per case among the four groups of hospitals. The comparative histograms are not adjusted for differences in location, case mix, and other factors among groups of hospitals. Relative to similar comparisons to be presented later, the distributions of expense per case among hospitals in each group are quite similar. The relatively high cost per case of proprietary chains is not readily apparent

from the histograms and appears only as a result of multivariate adjustment for differences in case mix and bed size.[4] The moderate cost advantage of independent proprietary hospitals appears to result from a relatively high frequency of very low-cost hospitals within this group (22 percent with cost per case 30 percent or more below the national average).[5]

### Utilization Rates

After differences in case mix and other factors have been taken into account, relatively small, if any, differences in average length of stay exist across the four groups of hospitals. Independent proprietary and chain-operated nonprofit hospitals have longer adjusted average stays than other hospitals, but the differences represent only one to three additional days of stay for every 20 patients. Proprietary chains treat slightly fewer patients, on average, and independent nonprofit hospitals slightly more patients, on average, than other hospitals. Occupancy rates are lowest for the average proprietary chain and slightly above average for the average nonprofit chain.[6]

The average chain-operated hospital appears to be growing slightly faster than the average independent institution. Annual discharges grew by a half a percentage point faster

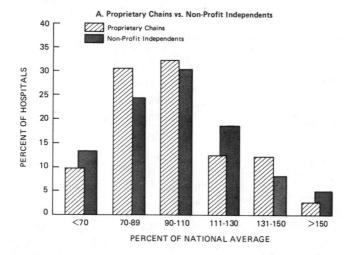

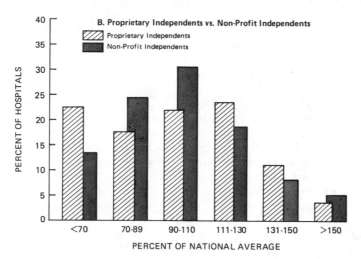

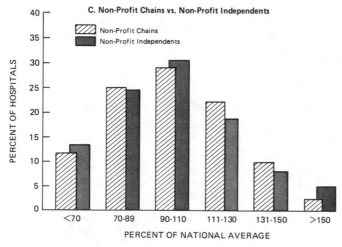

**FIGURE 2**   Dispersion of hospital expense per discharge among hospitals (years 1975 through 1981).

per year for the average nonprofit chain and by a full percentage point faster per year for the average proprietary chain than for independent nonprofit institutions. Compounded over the 7-year span of our data, these differentials in annual growth account for about 300 to 400 extra patients, respectively, for nonprofit and proprietary chains.

### Charges per Discharge

Earlier studies by Lewin et al. (1981) and by Pattison and Katz (1983) indicated that, at least for hospitals in California, Florida, and Texas, hospital charges per discharge are much higher for the average proprietary hospital than for the average nonprofit hospital. The difference, according to these studies, is due to very large differentials for ancillary charges; routine charges per case differ by very moderate amounts for average hospitals in each group.[7]

Our results, shown in Table 2, confirm the findings of those earlier studies. Total charges per case, from our data, are substantially higher among proprietary hospitals (19 and 11 percent, respectively, for chain-operated and independent facilities) and slightly higher among chain-operated nonprofit hospitals (3.5 percent) than among independent nonprofit hospitals. Routine charges per case are about the same, on average, across three of the four groups, but are moderately above average for independent proprietary hospitals. For ancillary charges per case, however, differences are quite large: compared to nonprofit independents, proprietary chains bill 34 percent more per patient for ancillary services on average; proprietary independents bill 15 percent more; and nonprofit chains bill 5 percent more.

Figure 3 compares the dispersion of expense and ancillary charges per case among hospitals in each of the four groups. For both types of proprietary hospitals, a very distinctive pattern is obvious—a very high frequency (30 percent of hospitals) of very high ancillary charges per case despite a very low frequency (2 to 3 percent of hospitals) of very high expense per case. In contrast, the dispersions of expense and ancillary charges among nonprofit hospitals are quite similar. Lacking data on units of ancillary services and charge/cost ratios by type of service, we cannot evaluate the

finding of Pattison and Katz, for California hospitals, that high ancillary charges per case among proprietary hospitals are due to a combination of high utilization and high markups.

### Margins on Revenue

Using 1978 data for hospitals in California, Florida, and Texas, Lewin et al. (1981) found that proprietary hospitals achieved margins on patient revenue about 9 percentage points on average above those of nonprofit hospitals (+6.5 percent versus −2.7 percent) and after-tax margins on total revenue about 2.5 percentage points above those of nonprofit hospitals (3.7 percent versus 1.3 percent). Using 1980 data for hospitals only in Florida, Sloan and Vraciu (1983) found that proprietary hospitals achieved slightly lower after-tax margins on total revenue than those of nonprofit hospitals (5.4 percent versus 5.6 percent).

Sloan and Vraciu argue that after-tax margins on total revenue provide a more equitable basis for comparison of the "profitability" of proprietary and nonprofit hospitals than do pretax margins on patient revenue. The former measure reflects the gain to nonprofits from contributions and the burden to proprietary hospitals of federal and state taxes on profits.

Our results, based on a nationally representative sample of hospitals for the years from 1975 to 1979 and shown in Table 2, indicate that differences in margins across groups of hospitals are not as large as those reported by Lewin et al. or as small as reported by Sloan and Vraciu. Margins on patient revenue are 3 to 5 percentage points higher among proprietary hospitals than among nonprofit hospitals, and margins on total revenue are 1 to 2 percentage points higher for proprietary hospitals.[8] All intergroup differences are statistically significant.

Figure 4 presents the comparative dispersions of margins on patient revenue among hospitals in each of the four groups. Between 20 and 23 percent of proprietary hospitals have operating losses of more than 3 percent, compared to 31 to 35 percent of nonprofit hospitals.

At the other end of the spectrum, 34 percent of proprietary chains have operating profits of more than 8 percent, compared to 12 percent of independent proprietary hospitals and 3 percent of nonprofit hospitals. Differentials in relative frequency of operating profits of more than 8 percent do not change very much when one examines margins on total revenue (not shown in Figure 4): 33 percent of proprietary chains versus 14 percent of proprietary independents and 8 to 9 percent of nonprofits. Data on comparative distributions are valuable because they indicate that, despite modest differences among averages for the four groups, two to four times as high a proportion of proprietary hospitals achieve margins on total revenue of more than 8 percent than do nonprofit hospitals.

## DISCUSSION

Our statistical results indicate that the truth lies somewhere in between the two polar positions taken in the debate about the advantages and disadvantages of proprietary ownership of hospitals. On the one hand, our results tend to disprove the claim that proprietary chains can operate more cost effectively than the traditional independent nonprofit hospital as a result of economies of scale. Although independent proprietary hospitals operate at a 4 percent cost advantage relative to independent nonprofit institutions, proprietary chains operate, on average, at a 6 percent cost disadvantage.

On the other hand, proprietary hospitals achieve smaller differential profit rates than some previous studies indicate. If one accepts the argument of Sloan and Vraciu that performance should be compared in terms of after-tax margins on total income, proprietary hospitals achieve a very small 1 to 2 points differential in net income as a percentage of revenue.

Other aspects of our comparisons indicate areas in which proprietary hospitals have taken some additional advantage of the reimbursement system for hospital care. Despite our measures being adjusted for differences in case mix and other factors, proprietary hospitals operate with very high ancillary charges per patient. Higher-than-average ancillary charges are most common among chain-operated proprietary hospitals.

Even though they operate with higher cost and higher markup of revenue over cost than other hospitals, proprietary chains managed to achieve a higher growth of admissions during the years from 1974 to 1981. This latter point illustrates the insensitivity of the market for hospital care to differences in cost and reimbursement rates during the late 1970s and early 1980s.

Until recently, the reimbursement system for hospital care has not encouraged efficient behavior. Cost-based reimbursement for Medicare, Medicaid, and in many locations, Blue Cross imposed a penalty for cost economy. The mix of cost-based reimbursement for the large payers and charge-based reimbursement for others, however, tended to encourage the type of differential pricing reflected in above-average ancillary charges among proprietary hospitals. The advent of Medicare's Prospective Payment System and various competitive strategies (preferred provider organizations and competitive contracting) can be expected to provide stronger incentives for cost economy.

Looking at data for the later years of the 1980s, one should not be surprised to see, in the type of comparisons we have provided here, proprietary hospitals using different strategies, achieving lower than average costs, and deriving larger differentials on margins than they have obtained to date.

## NOTES

[1]Patients admitted for elective surgery and urgent care (e.g., acute myocardial infarction or congestive heart failure) are those included. See Gaumer (1986) for a description of the selection of types of patients.

[2]Presuming a 12 percent annual inflation rate between 1981 and 1985 and no change in relative costs, one would find an average difference of $400 per case today.

[3]When admissions, length of stay, SNF unit days, and outpatient visits are added to multiple regression models, to approximate a cost function specification, the estimated differences in cost per case among groups of hospitals remain virtually unchanged. Therefore, the hypothesis that chain-operated hospitals benefit from improved economic and technical efficiency is rejected by our results.

[4]Expense per case among proprietary chains is only 2 to 3 percent higher than among nonprofit indepen-

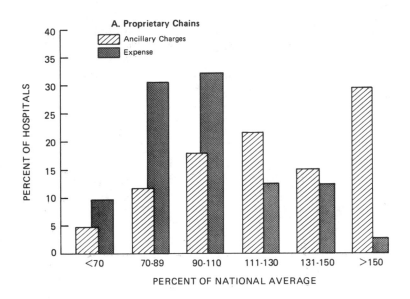

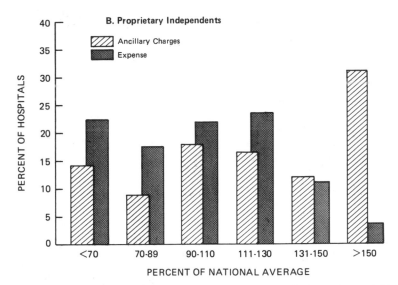

**FIGURE 3**  Comparative dispersion of expense and ancillary charges per discharge (years 1975 through 1981).

dents when no adjustment is made for bed size or case mix. Adjustment for regional location and catchment area characteristics is not sufficient to change the magnitude or statistical insignificance of differences computed from completely unadjusted data. The 6 percent differential reported in Table 2 results, therefore, primarily from adjustment for case mix and bed size.

[5]The cost advantage of proprietary independents relative to independent nonprofits actually declines as the result of adjustment for bed size and case mix, from 10 percent to the 4 percent differential shown in Table 2.

[6]Because number of beds appears as an explanatory variable in the equations for length of stay and number of discharges, the sum of differences shown in Table 2 for length of stay and discharges can be interpreted as the average difference in occupancy rates across groups of hospitals.

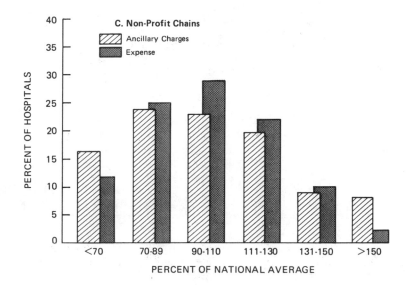

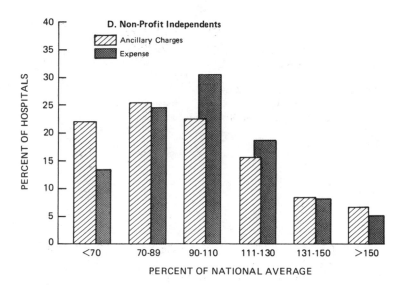

**FIGURE 3** *Continued*

[7]Pattison and Katz, using data not available from Medicare cost reports, attribute differences with respect to ancillary charges per case to a combination of high markups over cost on ancillary services by proprietary hospitals and to high utilization of ancillary services by patients served in those institutions.

[8]Our data do not permit taxes on profits to be broken out as a separate element of nonoperating expense. In fact, it is likely that some proprietary hospitals did not include profit tax in their computation of net income on total revenue (see Lewin et al. [1981:58] on this point). Hence, our measure of margin on total revenue may overstate after-tax margins for proprietary hospitals.

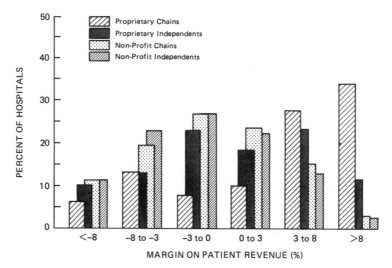

**FIGURE 4**   Comparative dispersion of margins on patient revenue (years 1975 through 1979).

## REFERENCES

Ermann, Dan, and Jon Gabel (1986) Investor-owned multihospital systems: A synthesis of research findings. This volume.

Gaumer, Gary (1986) Medicare patient outcomes and hospital organizational mission. This volume.

Lewin, Lawrence S., Robert A. Derzon, and Rhea

Margulies (1981) Investor-owned and nonprofits differ in economic performance. *Hospitals* July 1:52-58

Pattison, Robert V., and Hallie M. Katz (1983) Investor-owned and not-for-profit hospitals. *New England Journal of Medicine* 309:347-353.

Sloan, Frank A., and Robert A. Vraciu (1983) Investor-owned and not-for-profit hospitals: Addressing some issues. *Health Affairs* (Spring):25-37.

APPENDIX

# Multiple Regression Results

TABLE A.1
MEANS AND STANDARD DEVIATIONS
FOR VARIABLES USED IN REGRESSION ANALYSES

| VARIABLE | LABEL | MEAN | STANDARD DEVIATION |
|---|---|---|---|
| LN_TEPC | LOG(TOTAL EXPENSE PER DISCHARGE) | 7.14393129 | 0.42968610 |
| DLN_TEPC | 1ST DIFF.: LOG(TOTAL EXP. PER CASE) | 0.13072625 | 0.08192271 |
| LN_LOS | LOG(AVERAGE LENGTH OF STAY) | 1.90646589 | 0.26065975 |
| LN_ADM | LOG(NUMBER OF DISCHARGES) | 8.40192812 | 0.93039566 |
| DLN_ADM | 1ST DIFF.: LOG(ACUTE CARE ADMISSIONS) | 0.00532770 | 0.08949911 |
| LN_TCPC | LOG(TOTAL CHARGES PER DISCHARGE) | 7.68403061 | 0.48315669 |
| LN_RCPC | LOG(ROUTINE CHARGES PER DISCHARGE) | 6.83670713 | 0.46305114 |
| LN_ACPC | LOG(ANCILLARY CHARGES PER DISCHARGE) | 7.01767578 | 0.52595390 |
| MARGIN_O | MARGIN ON PATIENT REVENUE (PERCENT) | -1.48074353 | 6.63296577 |
| MARGIN_T | MARGIN ON TOTAL REVENUE (PERCENT) | 2.06467098 | 5.35894781 |
| D76 | 1976 YEAR DUMMY | 0.85121483 | 0.35589144 |
| D77 | 1977 YEAR DUMMY | 0.70443350 | 0.45631604 |
| D78 | 1978 YEAR DUMMY | 0.55865409 | 0.49656851 |
| D79 | 1979 YEAR DUMMY | 0.41579694 | 0.49287943 |
| D80 | 1980 YEAR DUMMY | 0.27561159 | 0.44684059 |
| D81 | 1981 YEAR DUMMY | 0.13667863 | 0.34352211 |
| DPRF_CHN | DUMMY: PROPRIETARY CHAINS | 0.05911330 | 0.23584648 |
| DPRF_IND | DUMMY: PROPRIETARY INDEPENDENTS | 0.08725056 | 0.28221366 |
| DVOL_CHN | DUMMY: NON-PROFIT CHAINS | 0.24638891 | 0.43092566 |
| LN_CMIX | LOG.--MEDICARE CASEMIX INDEX FOR 1982 | 0.00604356 | 0.13425821 |
| LN_BEDS | LOG.--MEAN # BEDS STAFFED DURING YEAR | 4.84067526 | 0.85166201 |
| DSMSA | COUNTY LOCATED IN AN SMSA | 0.60674626 | 0.48849274 |
| N_EAST | NORTHEASTERN STATES | 0.50613676 | 0.49998321 |
| SOUTH | SOUTHERN STATES | 0.20163647 | 0.40123889 |
| N_CNTR | NORTH CENTRAL STATES | 0.11972948 | 0.32465849 |
| DPR | PROSPECTIVE REIMBURSEMENT DUMMY | 0.58336812 | 0.49302135 |
| DPSRO | HOSPITAL COVERED BY REVIEW IN YEAR | 0.49762044 | 0.50001521 |
| CON | CONDATE LE YEAR | 0.87082498 | 0.33540755 |
| LN_AFDC | LOG.--PCT. OF POPULATION IN AFDC | 1.26309585 | 0.67194638 |
| LN_BIRTH | LOG.--BIRTHS PER CAPITA | 7.34143570 | 0.18688081 |
| LN_EDUC | LOG.--AVE. YRS. OF EDUCATION | 2.47241290 | 0.05911934 |
| LN_WHT | LOG.--WHITES AS PCT. OF POPULATION | 4.47801812 | 0.15247607 |
| LN_POP | LOG.--POPULATION IN COUNTY | 12.00383042 | 1.69636084 |
| DLN_POP | 1ST DIFF.: LOG(COUNTY POPULATION) | 0.00857844 | 0.01671109 |
| LN_DNSTY | LOG.--POPULATION PER SQ. MILE | 5.44910080 | 1.99278780 |
| LN_INC | LOG.--INCOME PER CAPITA | 8.73022157 | 0.28555216 |
| LN_CPI | LOG.--PCT. CHG. IN CPI | 4.68715883 | 0.02094053 |
| LN_URT | LOG.--UNEMPLOYMENT RATE | 1.91542408 | 0.31632421 |
| LN_INS | LOG.--PCT. OF POPULATION WITH PRIV. INS. | 4.44337987 | 0.14238733 |
| LN_HMO | LOG.--PCT. OF POPULATION IN HMOS | -7.88693213 | 7.37437366 |
| LN_T18 | LOG.--PCT. OF POPULATION IN MEDICARE | 2.41400512 | 0.28734909 |
| LN_MDS | LOG.--PHYSICIANS PER CAPITA | 4.68524887 | 0.89041483 |
| LN_SPMD | LOG.--SPECIALISTS AS PCT. OF MDS | 3.69663029 | 3.17626883 |
| LN_NHB | LOG.--NURSING HOME BEDS PER CAPITA | 6.21639847 | 2.34280319 |

334

TABLE A.2

MULTIPLE REGRESSION RESULTS
TOTAL EXPENSE PER ADJUSTED DISCHARGE

DEP VARIABLE: LN_TEPC  LOG.--TOTAL EXPENSES PER CASE

| SOURCE | DF | SUM OF SQUARES | MEAN SQUARE | F VALUE | PROB>F |
|---|---|---|---|---|---|
| MODEL | 34 | 5836001 | 171647 | 716.163 | 0.0001 |
| ERROR | 7797 | 1868753 | 239.676 | | |
| C TOTAL | 7831 | 7704754 | | | |

| | | | |
|---|---|---|---|
| ROOT MSE | 15.481469 | R-SQUARE | 0.7575 |
| DEP MEAN | 7.260595 | ADJ R-SQ | 0.7564 |
| C.V. | 213.2259 | | |

| VARIABLE | DF | PARAMETER ESTIMATE | STANDARD ERROR | T FOR H0: PARAMETER=0 | PROB > |T| | TOLERANCE | VARIABLE LABEL |
|---|---|---|---|---|---|---|---|
| INTERCEP | 1 | 4.393025 | 0.923434 | 4.757 | 0.0001 | | INTERCEPT |
| D76 | 1 | 0.132845 | 0.009848823 | 13.488 | 0.0001 | 0.387085 | 1976 YEAR DUMMY |
| D77 | 1 | 0.103884 | 0.008204595 | 12.662 | 0.0001 | 0.320077 | 1977 YEAR DUMMY |
| D78 | 1 | 0.104984 | 0.008064107 | 13.019 | 0.0001 | 0.271013 | 1978 YEAR DUMMY |
| D79 | 1 | 0.082742 | 0.009714368 | 8.518 | 0.0001 | 0.186417 | 1979 YEAR DUMMY |
| D80 | 1 | 0.106547 | 0.008166134 | 13.047 | 0.0001 | 0.323852 | 1980 YEAR DUMMY |

| Variable | | Coefficient | Std. Error | t | p | | Description |
|---|---|---|---|---|---|---|---|
| D81 | 1 | 0.13699 | 0.008310737 | 16.476 | 0.0001 | 0.555127 | 1981 YEAR DUMMY |
| DPRF_CHN | 1 | 0.057602 | 0.011286 | 5.104 | 0.0001 | 0.872411 | DUMMY: FOR-PROFIT & PART OF CHAIN |
| DPRF_IND | 1 | -0.041836 | 0.012147 | -3.444 | 0.0006 | 0.876692 | DUMMY: FOR-PROFIT & INDEPENDENT |
| DVOL_CHN | 1 | 0.018850 | 0.005015712 | 3.758 | 0.0002 | 0.843602 | DUMMY: NONPROFIT & PART OF CHAIN |
| LN_CMIX | 1 | 0.770431 | 0.037656 | 20.459 | 0.0001 | 0.669558 | LOG.--MEDICARE CASEMIX INDEX FOR 1982 |
| LN_BEDS | 1 | 0.061898 | 0.004637734 | 13.347 | 0.0001 | 0.512707 | LOG.--MEAN # BEDS STAFFED DURING YEAR |
| DSMSA | 1 | 0.023291 | 0.007500733 | 3.105 | 0.0019 | 0.448490 | COUNTY LOCATED IN AN SMSA |
| N_EAST | 1 | 0.051707 | 0.009668328 | 5.348 | 0.0001 | 0.189970 | NORTHEASTERN STATES |
| SOUTH | 1 | -0.164672 | 0.009885235 | -16.658 | 0.0001 | 0.280488 | SOUTHERN STATES |
| N_CNTR | 1 | -0.00374886 | 0.012272 | -0.305 | 0.7600 | 0.410036 | NORTH CENTRAL STATES |
| DPR | 1 | -0.034298 | 0.005397139 | -6.355 | 0.0001 | 0.632507 | PROSPECTIVE REIMBURSEMENT DUMMY |
| DPSRO | 1 | 0.015192 | 0.00552669 | 2.749 | 0.0060 | 0.564384 | HOSPITAL COVERED BY REVIEW IN YEAR |
| CON | 1 | 0.073528 | 0.007101301 | 10.354 | 0.0001 | 0.742583 | CONDATE LE YEAR |
| LN_AFDC | 1 | 0.006144351 | 0.005752722 | 1.068 | 0.2855 | 0.351143 | LOG.--PCT. OF POPULATION IN AFDC |
| LN_BIRTH | 1 | -0.024595 | 0.018235 | -1.349 | 0.1775 | 0.437401 | LOG.--BIRTHS PER CAPITA |
| LN_EDUC | 1 | 0.198236 | 0.068333 | 2.901 | 0.0037 | 0.618738 | LOG.--AVE. YRS. OF EDUCATION |
| LN_WHT | 1 | 0.028499 | 0.022721 | 1.254 | 0.2098 | 0.403691 | LOG.--WHITES AS PCT. OF POPULATION |
| LN_POP | 1 | 0.055844 | 0.003452849 | 16.173 | 0.0001 | 0.197776 | LOG.--POPULATION IN COUNTY |
| DLN_POP | 1 | 0.405723 | 0.186855 | 2.171 | 0.0299 | 0.522262 | 1ST DIFF.: LOG(COUNTY POPULATION) |
| LN_DNSTY | 1 | 0.030034 | 0.003319183 | 9.049 | 0.0001 | 0.145665 | LOG.--POPULATION PER SQ. MILE |
| LN_INC | 1 | 0.051273 | 0.189899 | 2.577 | 0.0100 | 0.163257 | LOG.--INCOME PER CAPITA |
| LN_CPI | 1 | 0.107525 | 0.180540 | 0.596 | 0.5515 | 0.279727 | LOG.--PCT. CHG. IN CPI |
| LN_URT | 1 | 0.016823 | 0.010060 | 1.672 | 0.0945 | 0.487328 | LOG.--UNEMPLOYMENT RATE |
| LN_INS | 1 | -0.135774 | 0.027171 | -4.997 | 0.0001 | 0.289386 | LOG.--PCT. OF POPULATION WITH PRIV. INS. |
| LN_HMO | 1 | 0.0002119212 | 0.0003926013 | 0.540 | 0.5894 | 0.496484 | LOG.--PCT. OF POPULATION IN HMOS |
| LN_T18 | 1 | 0.107875 | 0.011365 | 9.492 | 0.0001 | 0.548277 | LOG.--PCT. OF POPULATION IN MEDICARE |
| LN_MDS | 1 | 0.032021 | 0.006038877 | 5.303 | 0.0001 | 0.417430 | LOG.--PHYSICIANS PER CAPITA |
| LN_SPMD | 1 | 0.001517538 | 0.001937766 | 0.783 | 0.4336 | 0.831510 | LOG.--SPECIALISTS AS PCT. OF MDS |
| LN_NHB | 1 | -0.00826069 | 0.001823569 | -4.530 | 0.0001 | 0.876711 | LOG.--NURSING HOME BEDS PER CAPITA |

TABLE A.3

MULTIPLE REGRESSION RESULTS
ANNUAL PERCENTAGE CHANGE OF EXPENSE PER CASE

DEP VARIABLE: DLN_TEPC 1ST DIFF.: LOG(TOTAL EXP. PER CASE)

| SOURCE | DF | SUM OF SQUARES | MEAN SQUARE | F VALUE | PROB>F |
|---|---|---|---|---|---|
| MODEL | 34 | 25528.170 | 750.829 | 24.553 | 0.0001 |
| ERROR | 7797 | 238428 | 30.579517 | | |
| C TOTAL | 7831 | 263957 | | | |

| | | |
|---|---|---|
| ROOT MSE | 5.529875 | R-SQUARE | 0.0967 |
| DEP MEAN | 0.128058 | ADJ R-SQ | 0.0928 |
| C.V. | 4318.247 | | |

| VARIABLE | DF | PARAMETER ESTIMATE | STANDARD ERROR | T FOR H0: PARAMETER=0 | PROB > |T| | TOLERANCE | VARIABLE LABEL |
|---|---|---|---|---|---|---|---|
| INTERCEP | 1 | 0.034443 | 0.329844 | 0.104 | 0.9168 | | INTERCEPT |
| D76 | 1 | -0.028792 | 0.003517932 | -8.184 | 0.0001 | 0.387085 | 1976 YEAR DUMMY |
| D77 | 1 | -0.0099651 | 0.002930625 | -3.400 | 0.0007 | 0.320077 | 1977 YEAR DUMMY |
| D78 | 1 | -0.00777311 | 0.002880444 | -2.699 | 0.0070 | 0.271013 | 1978 YEAR DUMMY |
| D79 | 1 | 0.0002059189 | 0.003469906 | 0.059 | 0.9527 | 0.186417 | 1979 YEAR DUMMY |
| D80 | 1 | 0.014400 | 0.002916887 | 4.937 | 0.0001 | 0.323852 | 1980 YEAR DUMMY |

| Variable | Coef. | | Std. Err. | t | | | Description |
|---|---|---|---|---|---|---|---|
| D81 | 0.034373 | 1 | 0.002968538 | 11.579 | 0.0001 | 0.555127 | 1981 YEAR DUMMY |
| DPRF_CHN | -0.00375053 | 1 | 0.004031124 | -0.930 | 0.3522 | 0.872411 | DUMMY:  FOR-PROFIT & PART OF CHAIN |
| DPRF_IND | -0.012007 | 1 | 0.004339001 | -2.767 | 0.0057 | 0.876692 | DUMMY:  FOR-PROFIT & INDEPENDENT |
| DVOL_CHN | -0.00177251 | 1 | 0.001791578 | -0.989 | 0.3225 | 0.843602 | DUMMY:  NONPROFIT & PART OF CHAIN |
| LN_CMIX | 0.009174012 | 1 | 0.013451 | 0.682 | 0.4952 | 0.669558 | LOG.--MEDICARE CASEMIX INDEX FOR 1982 |
| LN_BEDS | 0.002468797 | 1 | 0.001656567 | 1.490 | 0.1362 | 0.512707 | LOG.--MEAN # BEDS STAFFED DURING YEAR |
| DSMSA | 0.007008708 | 1 | 0.002679211 | 2.616 | 0.0089 | 0.448490 | COUNTY LOCATED IN AN SMSA |
| N_EAST | -0.00842524 | 1 | 0.003453461 | -2.440 | 0.0147 | 0.189970 | NORTHEASTERN STATES |
| SOUTH | -0.000709545 | 1 | 0.003530938 | -0.201 | 0.8407 | 0.280488 | SOUTHERN STATES |
| N_CNTR | -0.00245869 | 1 | 0.004383624 | -0.561 | 0.5749 | 0.410036 | NORTH CENTRAL STATES |
| DPR | -0.00923704 | 1 | 0.001927821 | -4.791 | 0.0001 | 0.632507 | PROSPECTIVE REIMBURSEMENT DUMMY |
| DPSRO | 0.004833304 | 1 | 0.001974096 | 2.448 | 0.0144 | 0.564384 | HOSPITAL COVERED BY REVIEW IN YEAR |
| CON | -0.010598 | 1 | 0.002536536 | -4.178 | 0.0001 | 0.742583 | CONDATE LE YEAR |
| LN_AFDC | 0.004811479 | 1 | 0.002054833 | 2.342 | 0.0192 | 0.351143 | LOG.--PCT. OF POPULATION IN AFDC |
| LN_BIRTH | 0.020927 | 1 | 0.006513506 | 3.213 | 0.0013 | 0.437401 | LOG.--BIRTHS PER CAPITA |
| LN_EDUC | 0.026260 | 1 | 0.024408 | 1.076 | 0.2820 | 0.618738 | LOG.--AVE. YRS. OF EDUCATION |
| LN_WHT | 0.030971 | 1 | 0.008115935 | 3.816 | 0.0001 | 0.403691 | LOG.--WHITES AS PCT. OF POPULATION |
| LN_POP | 0.003423178 | 1 | 0.001233334 | 2.776 | 0.0055 | 0.197776 | LOG.--POPULATION IN COUNTY |
| DLN_POP | -0.121309 | 1 | 0.066743 | -1.818 | 0.0692 | 0.522262 | 1ST DIFF.: LOG(COUNTY POPULATION) |
| LN_DNSTY | -0.00433477 | 1 | 0.001185589 | -3.656 | 0.0003 | 0.145665 | LOG.--POPULATION PER SQ. MILE |
| LN_INC | 0.000807826 | 1 | 0.007107656 | 0.114 | 0.9095 | 0.163257 | LOG.--INCOME PER CAPITA |
| LN_CPI | -0.037851 | 1 | 0.064488 | -0.587 | 0.5573 | 0.279727 | LOG.--PCT. CHG. IN CPI |
| LN_URT | -0.00374804 | 1 | 0.003593432 | -1.043 | 0.2970 | 0.487328 | LOG.--UNEMPLOYMENT RATE |
| LN_INS | -0.015971 | 1 | 0.009705316 | -1.646 | 0.0999 | 0.289386 | LOG.--PCT. OF POPULATION WITH PRIV. INS. |
| LN_HMO | -0.000131082 | 1 | 0.0001402345 | -0.935 | 0.3500 | 0.496484 | LOG.--PCT. OF POPULATION IN HMOS |
| LN_T18 | 0.002612362 | 1 | 0.004059379 | 0.644 | 0.5199 | 0.548277 | LOG.--PCT. OF POPULATION IN MEDICARE |
| LN_MDS | -0.00325915 | 1 | 0.002157046 | -1.511 | 0.1308 | 0.417430 | LOG.--PHYSICIANS PER CAPITA |
| LN_SPMD | -0.000228716 | 1 | 0.0006911569 | -0.330 | 0.7411 | 0.831510 | LOG.--SPECIALISTS AS PCT. OF MDS |
| LN_NHB | 0.0001985006 | 1 | 0.0006513664 | 0.305 | 0.7606 | 0.876711 | LOG.--NURSING HOME BEDS PER CAPITA |

TABLE A.4

MULTIPLE REGRESSION RESULTS
AVERAGE LENGTH OF STAY

DEP VARIABLE: LN_LOS    LOG.--LENGTH OF STAY, ACUTE CARE SERV.

| SOURCE | DF | SUM OF SQUARES | MEAN SQUARE | F VALUE | PROB>F |
|--------|-----|-----------------|-------------|---------|--------|
| MODEL | 34 | 1263436 | 37159.897 | 256.908 | 0.0001 |
| ERROR | 7797 | 1127782 | 144.643 | | |
| C TOTAL | 7831 | 2391218 | | | |

| | | | |
|---|---|---|---|
| ROOT MSE | 12.026764 | R-SQUARE | 0.5284 |
| DEP MEAN | 1.969712 | ADJ R-SQ | 0.5263 |
| C.V. | 610.5849 | | |

| VARIABLE | DF | PARAMETER ESTIMATE | STANDARD ERROR | T FOR H0: PARAMETER=0 | PROB > |T| | TOLERANCE | VARIABLE LABEL |
|----------|-----|--------------------|----------------|-----------------------|-----------|-----------|----------------|
| INTERCEP | 1 | 3.246190 | 0.717369 | 4.525 | 0.0001 | | INTERCEPT |
| D76 | 1 | 0.004148848 | 0.007651049 | 0.542 | 0.5877 | 0.387085 | 1976 YEAR DUMMY |
| D77 | 1 | 0.006127407 | 0.006373731 | 0.961 | 0.3364 | 0.320077 | 1977 YEAR DUMMY |
| D78 | 1 | 0.005635207 | 0.006264593 | 0.900 | 0.3684 | 0.271013 | 1978 YEAR DUMMY |
| D79 | 1 | 0.006564022 | 0.007546597 | 0.870 | 0.3844 | 0.186417 | 1979 YEAR DUMMY |
| D80 | 1 | 0.007161095 | 0.006343853 | 1.129 | 0.2590 | 0.323852 | 1980 YEAR DUMMY |

| Variable | | Coefficient | Std. Error | t | | | Description |
|---|---|---|---|---|---|---|---|
| D81 | 1 | -0.010548 | 0.006456188 | -1.634 | 0.1023 | 0.555127 | 1981 YEAR DUMMY |
| DPRF_CHN | 1 | -0.00214612 | 0.008767175 | -0.245 | 0.8066 | 0.872411 | DUMMY: FOR-PROFIT & PART OF CHAIN |
| DPRF_IND | 1 | 0.022387 | 0.009436768 | 2.372 | 0.0177 | 0.876692 | DUMMY: FOR-PROFIT & INDEPENDENT |
| DVOL_CHN | 1 | 0.012522 | 0.003896451 | 3.214 | 0.0013 | 0.843602 | DUMMY: NONPROFIT & PART OF CHAIN |
| LN_CMIX | 1 | 0.084036 | 0.029253 | 2.873 | 0.0041 | 0.669558 | LOG.--MEDICARE CASEMIX INDEX FOR 1982 |
| LN_BEDS | 1 | 0.089170 | 0.003602819 | 24.750 | 0.0001 | 0.512707 | LOG.--MEAN # BEDS STAFFED DURING YEAR |
| DSMSA | 1 | 0.025166 | 0.005826937 | 4.319 | 0.0001 | 0.448490 | COUNTY LOCATED IN AN SMSA |
| N_EAST | 1 | 0.218024 | 0.007510831 | 29.028 | 0.0001 | 0.189970 | NORTHEASTERN STATES |
| SOUTH | 1 | 0.113815 | 0.007679335 | 14.821 | 0.0001 | 0.280488 | SOUTHERN STATES |
| N_CNTR | 1 | 0.164688 | 0.009533817 | 17.274 | 0.0001 | 0.410036 | NORTH CENTRAL STATES |
| DPR | 1 | 0.015222 | 0.004192762 | 3.630 | 0.0003 | 0.632507 | PROSPECTIVE REIMBURSEMENT DUMMY |
| DPSRO | 1 | -0.00400155 | 0.004293404 | -0.932 | 0.3514 | 0.564384 | HOSPITAL COVERED BY REVIEW IN YEAR |
| CON | 1 | 0.024330 | 0.005516638 | 4.410 | 0.0001 | 0.742583 | CONDATE LE YEAR |
| LN_AFDC | 1 | -0.00236081 | 0.004468997 | -0.528 | 0.5973 | 0.351143 | LOG.--PCT. OF POPULATION IN AFDC |
| LN_BIRTH | 1 | -0.114696 | 0.014166 | -8.097 | 0.0001 | 0.437401 | LOG.--BIRTHS PER CAPITA |
| LN_EDUC | 1 | 0.117009 | 0.053084 | 2.204 | 0.0275 | 0.618738 | LOG.--AVE. YRS. OF EDUCATION |
| LN_WHT | 1 | -0.081508 | 0.017651 | -4.618 | 0.0001 | 0.403691 | LOG.--WHITES AS PCT. OF POPULATION |
| LN_POP | 1 | 0.021402 | 0.002682342 | 7.979 | 0.0001 | 0.197776 | LOG.--POPULATION IN COUNTY |
| DLN_POP | 1 | -0.322318 | 0.145158 | -2.220 | 0.0264 | 0.522262 | 1ST DIFF.: LOG(COUNTY POPULATION) |
| LN_DNSTY | 1 | 0.021545 | 0.002578504 | 8.356 | 0.0001 | 0.145665 | LOG.--POPULATION PER SQ. MILE |
| LN_INC | 1 | -0.128904 | 0.015458 | -8.339 | 0.0001 | 0.163257 | LOG.--INCOME PER CAPITA |
| LN_CPI | 1 | -0.157779 | 0.140252 | -1.125 | 0.2606 | 0.279727 | LOG.--PCT. CHG. IN CPI |
| LN_URT | 1 | -0.00756201 | 0.007815251 | -0.968 | 0.3333 | 0.487328 | LOG.--UNEMPLOYMENT RATE |
| LN_INS | 1 | 0.026646 | 0.021108 | 1.262 | 0.2069 | 0.289386 | LOG.--PCT. OF POPULATION WITH PRIV. INS. |
| LN_HMO | 1 | -0.000006992 | 0.0003049919 | -0.023 | 0.9817 | 0.496484 | LOG.--PCT. OF POPULATION IN HMOS |
| LN_T18 | 1 | 0.151732 | 0.008828625 | 17.186 | 0.0001 | 0.548277 | LOG.--PCT. OF POPULATION IN MEDICARE |
| LN_MDS | 1 | -0.00845856 | 0.004691296 | -1.803 | 0.0714 | 0.417430 | LOG.--PHYSICIANS PER CAPITA |
| LN_SPMD | 1 | -0.00122258 | 0.001505352 | -0.812 | 0.4167 | 0.831510 | LOG.--SPECIALISTS AS PCT. OF MDS |
| LN_NHB | 1 | -0.0040011 | 0.001416638 | -2.824 | 0.0047 | 0.876711 | LOG.--NURSING HOME BEDS PER CAPITA |

## TABLE A.5

### MULTIPLE REGRESSION RESULTS
### NUMBER OF DISCHARGES

DEP VARIABLE: LN_ADM  LOG.--ADMISSIONS, ACUTE CARE SERV.

| SOURCE | DF | SUM OF SQUARES | MEAN SQUARE | F VALUE | PROB>F |
|---|---|---|---|---|---|
| MODEL | 34 | 20815659 | 612225 | 2148.514 | 0.0001 |
| ERROR | 7797 | 2221778 | 284.953 | | |
| C TOTAL | 7831 | 23037437 | | | |

| | | |
|---|---|---|
| ROOT MSE | 16.880547 | R-SQUARE | 0.9036 |
| DEP MEAN | 9.118228 | ADJ R-SQ | 0.9031 |
| C.V. | 185.1297 | | |

| VARIABLE | DF | PARAMETER ESTIMATE | STANDARD ERROR | T FOR H0: PARAMETER=0 | PROB > [T[ | TOLERANCE | VARIABLE LABEL |
|---|---|---|---|---|---|---|---|
| INTERCEP | 1 | 4.224544 | 1.006886 | 4.196 | 0.0001 | | INTERCEPT |
| D76 | 1 | -0.00926329 | 0.010739 | -0.863 | 0.3884 | 0.387085 | 1976 YEAR DUMMY |
| D77 | 1 | 0.0000650438 | 0.00894605 | 0.007 | 0.9942 | 0.320077 | 1977 YEAR DUMMY |
| D78 | 1 | 0.006897025 | 0.00879287 | 0.784 | 0.4328 | 0.271013 | 1978 YEAR DUMMY |
| D79 | 1 | 0.016345 | 0.010592 | 1.543 | 0.1229 | 0.186417 | 1979 YEAR DUMMY |
| D80 | 1 | 0.009727569 | 0.00890411 | 1.092 | 0.2747 | 0.323852 | 1980 YEAR DUMMY |

| Variable | | Estimate | Std Error | t | p | | Description |
|---|---|---|---|---|---|---|---|
| D81 | 1 | 0.016675 | 0.009061788 | 1.840 | 0.0658 | 0.555127 | 1981 YEAR DUMMY |
| DPRF_CHN | 1 | -0.077176 | 0.012305 | -6.272 | 0.0001 | 0.872411 | DUMMY: FOR-PROFIT & PART OF CHAIN |
| DPRF_IND | 1 | -0.023006 | 0.013245 | -1.737 | 0.0824 | 0.876692 | DUMMY: FOR-PROFIT & INDEPENDENT |
| DVOL_CHN | 1 | 0.021700 | 0.005468988 | 3.968 | 0.0001 | 0.843602 | DUMMY: NONPROFIT & PART OF CHAIN |
| LN_CMIX | 1 | 0.407648 | 0.041060 | 9.928 | 0.0001 | 0.669558 | LOG.--MEDICARE CASEMIX INDEX FOR 1982 |
| LN_BEDS | 1 | 0.946845 | 0.005056852 | 187.240 | 0.0001 | 0.512707 | LOG.--MEAN # BEDS STAFFED DURING YEAR |
| DSMSA | 1 | -0.00828159 | 0.008178583 | -1.013 | 0.3113 | 0.448490 | COUNTY LOCATED IN AN SMSA |
| N_EAST | 1 | -0.121991 | 0.010542 | -11.572 | 0.0001 | 0.189970 | NORTHEASTERN STATES |
| SOUTH | 1 | -0.00456492 | 0.010779 | -0.424 | 0.6719 | 0.280488 | SOUTHERN STATES |
| N_CNTR | 1 | -0.173809 | 0.013381 | -12.989 | 0.0001 | 0.410036 | NORTH CENTRAL STATES |
| DPR | 1 | 0.001595226 | 0.005884884 | 0.271 | 0.7863 | 0.632507 | PROSPECTIVE REIMBURSEMENT DUMMY |
| DPSRO | 1 | -0.00338508 | 0.006026144 | -0.562 | 0.5743 | 0.564384 | HOSPITAL COVERED BY REVIEW IN YEAR |
| CON | 1 | 0.009670051 | 0.007743053 | 1.249 | 0.2118 | 0.742583 | CONDATE LE YEAR |
| LN_AFDC | 1 | 0.008869099 | 0.006272602 | 1.414 | 0.1574 | 0.351143 | LOG.--PCT. OF POPULATION IN AFDC |
| LN_BIRTH | 1 | 0.040275 | 0.019883 | 2.026 | 0.0428 | 0.437401 | LOG.--BIRTHS PER CAPITA |
| LN_EDUC | 1 | -0.322237 | 0.074508 | -4.325 | 0.0001 | 0.618738 | LOG.--AVE. YRS. OF EDUCATION |
| LN_WHT | 1 | 0.087507 | 0.024775 | 3.532 | 0.0004 | 0.403691 | LOG.--WHITES AS PCT. OF POPULATION |
| LN_POP | 1 | -0.009595 | 0.003764887 | -2.549 | 0.0108 | 0.197776 | LOG.--POPULATION IN COUNTY |
| DLN_POP | 1 | 2.074609 | 0.203742 | 10.183 | 0.0001 | 0.522262 | 1ST DIFF.: LOG(COUNTY POPULATION) |
| LN_DNSTY | 1 | -0.00328882 | 0.003619141 | -0.909 | 0.3635 | 0.145665 | LOG.--POPULATION PER SQ. MILE |
| LN_INC | 1 | 0.072053 | 0.021697 | 3.321 | 0.0009 | 0.163257 | LOG.--INCOME PER CAPITA |
| LN_CPI | 1 | -0.156081 | 0.196856 | -0.793 | 0.4279 | 0.279727 | LOG.--PCT. CHG. IN CPI |
| LN_URT | 1 | 0.034705 | 0.010969 | 3.164 | 0.0016 | 0.487328 | LOG.--UNEMPLOYMENT RATE |
| LN_INS | 1 | 0.080173 | 0.029627 | 2.706 | 0.0068 | 0.289386 | LOG.--PCT. OF POPULATION WITH PRIV. INS. |
| LN_HMO | 1 | -0.000831067 | 0.000428081 | -1.941 | 0.0522 | 0.496484 | LOG.--PCT. OF POPULATION IN HMOS |
| LN_T18 | 1 | -0.205539 | 0.012392 | -16.587 | 0.0001 | 0.548277 | LOG.--PCT. OF POPULATION IN MEDICARE |
| LN_MDS | 1 | 0.020138 | 0.006584617 | 3.058 | 0.0022 | 0.417430 | LOG.--PHYSICIANS PER CAPITA |
| LN_SPMD | 1 | 0.008157806 | 0.002112885 | 3.861 | 0.0001 | 0.831510 | LOG.--SPECIALISTS AS PCT. OF MDS |
| LN_NHB | 1 | 0.002273354 | 0.001988367 | 1.143 | 0.2529 | 0.876711 | LOG.--NURSING HOME BEDS PER CAPITA |

TABLE A.6

MULTIPLE REGRESSION RESULTS
ANNUAL PERCENTAGE CHANGE, NUMBER OF DISCHARGES

DEP VARIABLE: DLN_ADM   1ST DIFF.:  LOG(ACUTE CARE ADMISSIONS)

| SOURCE | DF | SUM OF SQUARES | MEAN SQUARE | F VALUE | PROB>F |
|---|---|---|---|---|---|
| MODEL | 34 | 11977.091 | 352.267 | 12.447 | 0.0001 |
| ERROR | 7797 | 220663 | 28.300973 | | |
| C TOTAL | 7831 | 232640 | | | |

| | | | |
|---|---|---|---|
| ROOT MSE | 5.319866 | R-SQUARE | 0.0515 |
| DEP MEAN | 0.013878 | ADJ R-SQ | 0.0473 |
| C.V. | 38334.07 | | |

| VARIABLE | DF | PARAMETER ESTIMATE | STANDARD ERROR | T FOR H0: PARAMETER=0 | PROB > $|T|$ | TOLERANCE | VARIABLE LABEL |
|---|---|---|---|---|---|---|---|
| INTERCEP | 1 | -0.448405 | 0.317318 | -1.413 | 0.1577 | | INTERCEPT |
| D76 | 1 | 0.009300978 | 0.003384331 | 2.748 | 0.0060 | 0.387085 | 1976 YEAR DUMMY |
| D77 | 1 | -0.00556802 | 0.002819328 | -1.975 | 0.0483 | 0.320077 | 1977 YEAR DUMMY |
| D78 | 1 | -0.00451021 | 0.002771053 | -1.628 | 0.1036 | 0.271013 | 1978 YEAR DUMMY |
| D79 | 1 | 0.009935739 | 0.003338128 | 2.976 | 0.0029 | 0.186417 | 1979 YEAR DUMMY |
| D80 | 1 | 0.012042 | 0.002806112 | 4.291 | 0.0001 | 0.323852 | 1980 YEAR DUMMY |

| Variable | | Coefficient | Std. Error | t | | | Description |
|---|---|---|---|---|---|---|---|
| D81 | 1 | -0.017574 | 0.002855802 | -6.154 | 0.0001 | 0.555127 | 1981 YEAR DUMMY |
| DPRF_CHN | 1 | 0.009724243 | 0.003878034 | 2.508 | 0.0122 | 0.872411 | DUMMY:  FOR-PROFIT & PART OF CHAIN |
| DPRF_IND | 1 | 0.002599906 | 0.004174218 | 0.623 | 0.5334 | 0.876692 | DUMMY:  FOR-PROFIT & INDEPENDENT |
| DVOL_CHN | 1 | 0.004530165 | 0.001723539 | 2.628 | 0.0086 | 0.843602 | DUMMY:  NONPROFIT & PART OF CHAIN |
| LN_CMIX | 1 | 0.063312 | 0.012940 | 4.893 | 0.0001 | 0.669558 | LOG.--MEDICARE CASEMIX INDEX FOR 1982 |
| LN_BEDS | 1 | -0.00242179 | 0.001593655 | -1.520 | 0.1286 | 0.512707 | LOG.--MEAN # BEDS STAFFED DURING YEAR |
| DSMSA | 1 | 0.0003123146 | 0.002577462 | 0.121 | 0.9036 | 0.448490 | COUNTY LOCATED IN AN SMSA |
| N_EAST | 1 | -.0000028414 | 0.003322308 | -0.001 | 0.9993 | 0.189970 | NORTHEASTERN STATES |
| SOUTH | 1 | 0.004721915 | 0.003396843 | 1.390 | 0.1645 | 0.280488 | SOUTHERN STATES |
| N_CNTR | 1 | -0.010316 | 0.004217147 | -2.446 | 0.0145 | 0.410036 | NORTH CENTRAL STATES |
| DPR | 1 | -0.000937787 | 0.001854608 | -0.506 | 0.6131 | 0.632507 | PROSPECTIVE REIMBURSEMENT DUMMY |
| DPSRO | 1 | -0.00245383 | 0.001899125 | -1.292 | 0.1964 | 0.564384 | HOSPITAL COVERED BY REVIEW IN YEAR |
| CON | 1 | 0.001013911 | 0.002440206 | 0.416 | 0.6778 | 0.742583 | CONDATE LE YEAR |
| LN_AFDC | 1 | -0.00642747 | 0.001976796 | -3.251 | 0.0012 | 0.351143 | LOG.--PCT. OF POPULATION IN AFDC |
| LN_BIRTH | 1 | -0.00157353 | 0.006266142 | -0.251 | 0.8017 | 0.437401 | LOG.--BIRTHS PER CAPITA |
| LN_EDUC | 1 | -0.059105 | 0.023481 | -2.517 | 0.0119 | 0.618738 | LOG.--AVE. YRS. OF EDUCATION |
| LN_WHT | 1 | -0.011733 | 0.007807715 | -1.503 | 0.1329 | 0.403691 | LOG.--WHITES AS PCT. OF POPULATION |
| LN_POP | 1 | 0.000112924 | 0.001186495 | 0.095 | 0.9242 | 0.197776 | LOG.--POPULATION IN COUNTY |
| DLN_POP | 1 | 0.576221 | 0.064209 | 8.974 | 0.0001 | 0.522262 | 1ST DIFF.: LOG(COUNTY POPULATION) |
| LN_DNSTY | 1 | 0.001186008 | 0.001140564 | 1.654 | 0.0983 | 0.145665 | LOG.--POPULATION PER SQ. MILE |
| LN_INC | 1 | -0.00969697 | 0.006837727 | -1.418 | 0.1562 | 0.163257 | LOG.--INCOME PER CAPITA |
| LN_CPI | 1 | 0.145629 | 0.062039 | 2.347 | 0.0189 | 0.279727 | LOG.--PCT. CHG. IN CPI |
| LN_URT | 1 | -0.00576304 | 0.003456964 | -1.667 | 0.0955 | 0.487328 | LOG.--UNEMPLOYMENT RATE |
| LN_INS | 1 | 0.009898124 | 0.009336735 | 1.060 | 0.2891 | 0.289386 | LOG.--PCT. OF POPULATION WITH PRIV. INS. |
| LN_HMO | 1 | -0.000358159 | 0.0001349088 | -2.655 | 0.0080 | 0.496484 | LOG.--PCT. OF POPULATION IN HMOS |
| LN_T18 | 1 | 0.005667027 | 0.003905215 | 1.451 | 0.1468 | 0.548277 | LOG.--PCT. OF POPULATION IN MEDICARE |
| LN_MDS | 1 | 0.004359629 | 0.002075127 | 2.101 | 0.0357 | 0.417430 | LOG.--PHYSICIANS PER CAPITA |
| LN_SPMD | 1 | 0.0009435266 | 0.0006658707 | 1.417 | 0.1565 | 0.831510 | LOG.--SPECIALISTS AS PCT. OF MDS |
| LN_NHB | 1 | -0.000718311 | 0.0006266293 | -1.146 | 0.2517 | 0.876711 | LOG.--NURSING HOME BEDS PER CAPITA |

TABLE A.7

MULTIPLE REGRESSION RESULTS
TOTAL CHARGES PER DISCHARGE
MEDICARE CASES ONLY

DEP VARIABLE: LN_TCPC  LOG.--TOTAL CHG. PER CASE

| SOURCE | DF | SUM OF SQUARES | MEAN SQUARE | F VALUE | PROB>F |
|---|---|---|---|---|---|
| MODEL | 34 | 38725.016 | 1138.971 | 465.841 | 0.0001 |
| ERROR | 7797 | 19063.477 | 2.444976 | | |
| C TOTAL | 7831 | 57788.494 | | | |

| | | | |
|---|---|---|---|
| ROOT MSE | 1.563642 | R-SQUARE | 0.6701 |
| DEP MEAN | 7.855673 | ADJ R-SQ | 0.6687 |
| C.V. | 19.90462 | | |

| VARIABLE | DF | PARAMETER ESTIMATE | STANDARD ERROR | T FOR H0: PARAMETER=0 | PROB > [T[ | TOLERANCE | VARIABLE LABEL |
|---|---|---|---|---|---|---|---|
| INTERCEP | 1 | 8.363637 | 1.046306 | 7.993 | 0.0001 | | INTERCEPT |
| D76 | 1 | 0.140049 | 0.012014 | 11.657 | 0.0001 | 0.433229 | 1976 YEAR DUMMY |
| D77 | 1 | 0.093655 | 0.009895572 | 9.464 | 0.0001 | 0.331408 | 1977 YEAR DUMMY |
| D78 | 1 | 0.102059 | 0.009579821 | 10.654 | 0.0001 | 0.272278 | 1978 YEAR DUMMY |
| D79 | 1 | 0.048172 | 0.011222 | 4.293 | 0.0001 | 0.185906 | 1979 YEAR DUMMY |
| D80 | 1 | 0.091895 | 0.009091264 | 10.108 | 0.0001 | 0.324729 | 1980 YEAR DUMMY |

| Variable | | Estimate | Std Error | t | Prob | | Description |
|---|---|---|---|---|---|---|---|
| D81 | 1 | 0.083569 | 0.008826978 | 9.467 | 0.0001 | 0.556436 | 1981 YEAR DUMMY |
| DPRF_CHN | 1 | -0.012016 | 0.013489 | -0.891 | 0.3731 | 0.875137 | DUMMY: FOR-PROFIT & PART OF CHAIN |
| DPRF_IND | 1 | 0.073644 | 0.013640 | 5.399 | 0.0001 | 0.867440 | DUMMY: FOR-PROFIT & INDEPENDENT |
| DVOL_CHN | 1 | 0.021537 | 0.005825263 | 3.697 | 0.0002 | 0.842597 | DUMMY: NONPROFIT & PART OF CHAIN |
| LN_CMIX | 1 | -0.202206 | 0.045292 | -4.465 | 0.0001 | 0.656178 | LOG.--MEDICARE CASEMIX INDEX FOR 1982 |
| LN_BEDS | 1 | 0.088747 | 0.005294646 | 16.762 | 0.0001 | 0.507425 | LOG.--MEAN # BEDS STAFFED DURING YEAR |
| DSMSA | 1 | -0.00793606 | 0.008411336 | -0.943 | 0.3455 | 0.441024 | COUNTY LOCATED IN AN SMSA |
| N_EAST | 1 | 0.169946 | 0.011389 | 14.922 | 0.0001 | 0.181212 | NORTHEASTERN STATES |
| SOUTH | 1 | -0.123984 | 0.011702 | -10.595 | 0.0001 | 0.283832 | SOUTHERN STATES |
| N_CNTR | 1 | 0.055036 | 0.013973 | 3.939 | 0.0001 | 0.386067 | NORTH CENTRAL STATES |
| DPR | 1 | -0.045650 | 0.006229532 | -7.328 | 0.0001 | 0.637124 | PROSPECTIVE REIMBURSEMENT DUMMY |
| DPSRO | 1 | 0.005811865 | 0.006377287 | 0.911 | 0.3621 | 0.564774 | HOSPITAL COVERED BY REVIEW IN YEAR |
| CON | 1 | 0.120057 | 0.008541008 | 14.056 | 0.0001 | 0.747119 | CONDATE LE YEAR |
| LN_AFDC | 1 | 0.025878 | 0.006441597 | 4.017 | 0.0001 | 0.356915 | LOG.--PCT. OF POPULATION IN AFDC |
| LN_BIRTH | 1 | -0.165071 | 0.020910 | -7.894 | 0.0001 | 0.430972 | LOG.--BIRTHS PER CAPITA |
| LN_EDUC | 1 | 0.189386 | 0.082260 | 2.302 | 0.0213 | 0.669431 | LOG.--AVE. YRS. OF EDUCATION |
| LN_WHT | 1 | -0.032696 | 0.026169 | -1.249 | 0.2115 | 0.393700 | LOG.--WHITES AS PCT. OF POPULATION |
| LN_POP | 1 | 0.013617 | 0.004011534 | 3.394 | 0.0007 | 0.187060 | LOG.--POPULATION IN COUNTY |
| DLN_POP | 1 | -0.188202 | 0.207550 | -0.907 | 0.3645 | 0.537288 | 1ST DIFF.: LOG(COUNTY POPULATION) |
| LN_DNSTY | 1 | 0.078307 | 0.003770412 | 20.769 | 0.0001 | 0.138262 | LOG.--POPULATION PER SQ. MILE |
| LN_INC | 1 | 0.064631 | 0.022130 | 2.920 | 0.0035 | 0.174631 | LOG.--INCOME PER CAPITA |
| LN_CPI | 1 | -0.494147 | 0.202795 | -2.437 | 0.0148 | 0.290559 | LOG.--PCT. CHG. IN CPI |
| LN_URT | 1 | 0.084570 | 0.011328 | 7.466 | 0.0001 | 0.506358 | LOG.--UNEMPLOYMENT RATE |
| LN_INS | 1 | 0.193828 | 0.031397 | 6.173 | 0.0001 | 0.278159 | LOG.--PCT. OF POPULATION WITH PRIV. INS. |
| LN_HMO | 1 | 0.00293551 | 0.0004586592 | 6.400 | 0.0001 | 0.471609 | LOG.--PCT. OF POPULATION IN HMOS |
| LN_T18 | 1 | 0.070396 | 0.012362 | 5.695 | 0.0001 | 0.583389 | LOG.--PCT. OF POPULATION IN MEDICARE |
| LN_MDS | 1 | -0.00978927 | 0.006409674 | -1.527 | 0.1267 | 0.447968 | LOG.--PHYSICIANS PER CAPITA |
| LN_SPMD | 1 | -0.000979527 | 0.002058877 | -0.476 | 0.6343 | 0.813822 | LOG.--SPECIALISTS AS PCT. OF MDS |
| LN_NHB | 1 | -0.00831239 | 0.002431358 | -3.419 | 0.0006 | 0.881812 | LOG.--NURSING HOME BEDS PER CAPITA |

346

TABLE A.8

MULTIPLE REGRESSION RESULTS
ROUTINE CHARGES PER DISCHARGE

MEDICARE CASES ONLY

DEP VARIABLE: LN_RCPC  LOG.--ROUTINE CHG. PER CASE

| SOURCE | DF | SUM OF SQUARES | MEAN SQUARE | F VALUE | PROB>F |
|---|---|---|---|---|---|
| MODEL | 34 | 45849.926 | 1348.527 | 571.878 | 0.0001 |
| ERROR | 7797 | 18385.849 | 2.358067 | | |
| C TOTAL | 7831 | 64235.774 | | | |

| | | | |
|---|---|---|---|
| ROOT MSE | 1.535600 | R-SQUARE | 0.7138 |
| DEP MEAN | 6.996510 | ADJ R-SQ | 0.7125 |
| C.V. | 21.94808 | | |

| VARIABLE | DF | PARAMETER ESTIMATE | STANDARD ERROR | T FOR H0: PARAMETER=0 | PROB > |T| | TOLERANCE | VARIABLE LABEL |
|---|---|---|---|---|---|---|---|
| INTERCEP | 1 | 6.957624 | 1.027541 | 6.771 | 0.0001 | | INTERCEPT |
| D76 | 1 | 0.110604 | 0.011799 | 9.374 | 0.0001 | 0.433229 | 1976 YEAR DUMMY |
| D77 | 1 | 0.068897 | 0.009718107 | 7.090 | 0.0001 | 0.331408 | 1977 YEAR DUMMY |
| D78 | 1 | 0.083706 | 0.009408019 | 8.897 | 0.0001 | 0.272278 | 1978 YEAR DUMMY |
| D79 | 1 | 0.063724 | 0.011020 | 5.782 | 0.0001 | 0.185906 | 1979 YEAR DUMMY |
| D80 | 1 | 0.063941 | 0.008928224 | 7.162 | 0.0001 | 0.324729 | 1980 YEAR DUMMY |

| Variable | | Estimate | Std Error | t | Prob | | Description |
|---|---|---|---|---|---|---|---|
| D81 | 1 | 0.111033 | 0.00898817 | 12.353 | 0.0001 | 0.556436 | 1981 YEAR DUMMY |
| DPRF_CHN | 1 | 0.189920 | 0.013735 | 13.827 | 0.0001 | 0.875137 | DUMMY: FOR-PROFIT & PART OF CHAIN |
| DPRF_IND | 1 | 0.111510 | 0.013889 | 8.029 | 0.0001 | 0.867440 | DUMMY: FOR-PROFIT & INDEPENDENT |
| DVOL_CHN | 1 | 0.034742 | 0.00593164 | 5.857 | 0.0001 | 0.842597 | DUMMY: NONPROFIT & PART OF CHAIN |
| LN_CMIX | 1 | 0.202544 | 0.046119 | 4.392 | 0.0001 | 0.656178 | LOG.--MEDICARE CASEMIX INDEX FOR 1982 |
| LN_BEDS | 1 | 0.086280 | 0.005391333 | 16.003 | 0.0001 | 0.507425 | LOG.--MEAN # BEDS STAFFED DURING YEAR |
| DSMSA | 1 | 0.009648761 | 0.008564938 | 1.127 | 0.2600 | 0.441024 | COUNTY LOCATED IN AN SMSA |
| N_EAST | 1 | 0.135781 | 0.011597 | 11.709 | 0.0001 | 0.181212 | NORTHEASTERN STATES |
| SOUTH | 1 | -0.055866 | 0.011916 | -4.688 | 0.0001 | 0.283832 | SOUTHERN STATES |
| N_CNTR | 1 | 0.079737 | 0.014228 | 5.604 | 0.0001 | 0.386067 | NORTH CENTRAL STATES |
| DPR | 1 | -0.080206 | 0.006343291 | -12.644 | 0.0001 | 0.637124 | PROSPECTIVE REIMBURSEMENT DUMMY |
| DPSRO | 1 | 0.009724973 | 0.006493744 | 1.498 | 0.1343 | 0.564774 | HOSPITAL COVERED BY REVIEW IN YEAR |
| CON | 1 | 0.087348 | 0.008696978 | 10.043 | 0.0001 | 0.747119 | CONDATE LE YEAR |
| LN_AFDC | 1 | 0.006026765 | 0.006559229 | 0.919 | 0.3582 | 0.356915 | LOG.--PCT. OF POPULATION IN AFDC |
| LN_BIRTH | 1 | -0.054304 | 0.021292 | -2.550 | 0.0108 | 0.430972 | LOG.--BIRTHS PER CAPITA |
| LN_EDUC | 1 | 0.293549 | 0.083762 | 3.505 | 0.0005 | 0.669431 | LOG.--AVE. YRS. OF EDUCATION |
| LN_WHT | 1 | -0.064263 | 0.026646 | -2.412 | 0.0159 | 0.393700 | LOG.--WHITES AS PCT. OF POPULATION |
| LN_POP | 1 | 0.048105 | 0.00408479 | 11.777 | 0.0001 | 0.187060 | LOG.--POPULATION IN COUNTY |
| DLN_POP | 1 | 0.420700 | 0.211340 | 1.991 | 0.0466 | 0.537288 | 1ST DIFF.: LOG(COUNTY POPULATION) |
| LN_DNSTY | 1 | 0.043506 | 0.003839265 | 11.332 | 0.0001 | 0.138262 | LOG.--POPULATION PER SQ. MILE |
| LN_INC | 1 | 0.040573 | 0.022535 | 1.800 | 0.0718 | 0.174631 | LOG.--INCOME PER CAPITA |
| LN_CPI | 1 | -0.578392 | 0.206498 | -2.801 | 0.0051 | 0.290559 | LOG.--PCT. CHG. IN CPI |
| LN_URT | 1 | 0.071550 | 0.011534 | 6.203 | 0.0001 | 0.506358 | LOG.--UNEMPLOYMENT RATE |
| LN_INS | 1 | -0.100088 | 0.031970 | -3.131 | 0.0018 | 0.278159 | LOG.--PCT. OF POPULATION WITH PRIV. INS. |
| LN_HMO | 1 | 0.002626424 | 0.0004670349 | 5.624 | 0.0001 | 0.471609 | LOG.--PCT. OF POPULATION IN HMOS |
| LN_T18 | 1 | 0.096060 | 0.012587 | 7.631 | 0.0001 | 0.583389 | LOG.--PCT. OF POPULATION IN MEDICARE |
| LN_MDS | 1 | 0.022850 | 0.006526723 | 3.501 | 0.0005 | 0.447968 | LOG.--PHYSICIANS PER CAPITA |
| LN_SPMD | 1 | 0.001792208 | 0.002096475 | 0.855 | 0.3927 | 0.813822 | LOG.--SPECIALISTS AS PCT. OF MDS |
| LN_NHB | 1 | -0.00875042 | 0.002475758 | -3.534 | 0.0004 | 0.881812 | LOG.--NURSING HOME BEDS PER CAPITA |

## TABLE A.9

MULTIPLE REGRESSION RESULTS
ACUTE CARE LENGTH OF STAY

### MEDICARE CASES ONLY

DEP VARIABLE: LN_ACPC LOG.--ANCILL. CHG. PER CASE

| SOURCE | DF | SUM OF SQUARES | MEAN SQUARE | F VALUE | PROB>F |
|---|---|---|---|---|---|
| MODEL | 34 | 28654.265 | 842.772 | 182.534 | 0.0001 |
| ERROR | 7797 | 35999.236 | 4.617062 | | |
| C TOTAL | 7831 | 64653.500 | | | |

| | | | |
|---|---|---|---|
| ROOT MSE | 2.148735 | R-SQUARE | 0.4432 |
| DEP MEAN | 7.159953 | ADJ R-SQ | 0.4408 |
| C.V. | 30.01047 | | |

| VARIABLE | DF | PARAMETER ESTIMATE | STANDARD ERROR | T FOR H0: PARAMETER=0 | PROB > $|T|$ | TOLERANCE | VARIABLE LABEL |
|---|---|---|---|---|---|---|---|
| INTERCEP | 1 | 8.708266 | 1.437819 | 6.057 | 0.0001 | | INTERCEPT |
| D76 | 1 | 0.148836 | 0.016510 | 9.015 | 0.0001 | 0.433229 | 1976 YEAR DUMMY |
| D77 | 1 | -0.072042 | 0.013598 | -5.298 | 0.0001 | 0.331408 | 1977 YEAR DUMMY |
| D78 | 1 | 0.040785 | 0.013164 | 3.098 | 0.0020 | 0.272278 | 1978 YEAR DUMMY |
| D79 | 1 | 0.049232 | 0.015421 | 3.193 | 0.0014 | 0.185906 | 1979 YEAR DUMMY |
| D80 | 1 | 0.119355 | 0.012493 | 9.554 | 0.0001 | 0.324729 | 1980 YEAR DUMMY |

| Variable | DF | Parameter Estimate | Standard Error | T | Prob | | Description |
|---|---|---|---|---|---|---|---|
| D81 | 1 | 0.120052 | 0.012351 | 9.720 | 0.0001 | 0.556436 | 1981 YEAR DUMMY |
| DPRF_CHN | 1 | 0.339065 | 0.018875 | 17.964 | 0.0001 | 0.875137 | DUMMY: FOR-PROFIT & PART OF CHAIN |
| DPRF_IND | 1 | 0.145416 | 0.019086 | 7.619 | 0.0001 | 0.867440 | DUMMY: FOR-PROFIT & INDEPENDENT |
| DVOL_CHN | 1 | 0.051425 | 0.00815178 | 6.309 | 0.0001 | 0.842597 | DUMMY: NONPROFIT & PART OF CHAIN |
| LN_CMIX | 1 | 0.343951 | 0.063376 | 5.427 | 0.0001 | 0.656178 | LOG.--MEDICARE CASEMIX INDEX FOR 1982 |
| LN_BEDS | 1 | 0.075435 | 0.007408696 | 10.182 | 0.0001 | 0.507425 | LOG.--MEAN # BEDS STAFFED DURING YEAR |
| DSMSA | 1 | 0.013222 | 0.011770 | 1.123 | 0.2613 | 0.441024 | COUNTY LOCATED IN AN SMSA |
| N_EAST | 1 | 0.153168 | 0.015936 | 9.611 | 0.0001 | 0.181212 | NORTHEASTERN STATES |
| SOUTH | 1 | 0.026951 | 0.016375 | 1.646 | 0.0998 | 0.283832 | SOUTHERN STATES |
| N_CNTR | 1 | 0.138477 | 0.019552 | 7.082 | 0.0001 | 0.386067 | NORTH CENTRAL STATES |
| DPR | 1 | -0.097591 | 0.008716863 | -11.196 | 0.0001 | 0.637124 | PROSPECTIVE REIMBURSEMENT DUMMY |
| DPSRO | 1 | 0.017976 | 0.008923614 | 2.014 | 0.0440 | 0.564774 | HOSPITAL COVERED BY REVIEW IN YEAR |
| CON | 1 | 0.055252 | 0.011951 | 4.623 | 0.0001 | 0.747119 | CONDATE LE YEAR |
| LN_AFDC | 1 | -0.017567 | 0.009013602 | -1.949 | 0.0513 | 0.356915 | LOG.--PCT. OF POPULATION IN AFDC |
| LN_BIRTH | 1 | 0.068399 | 0.029259 | 2.338 | 0.0194 | 0.430972 | LOG.--BIRTHS PER CAPITA |
| LN_EDUC | 1 | 0.204573 | 0.115105 | 1.777 | 0.0756 | 0.669431 | LOG.--AVE. YRS. OF EDUCATION |
| LN_WHT | 1 | -0.119634 | 0.036617 | -3.267 | 0.0011 | 0.393700 | LOG.--WHITES AS PCT. OF POPULATION |
| LN_POP | 1 | 0.069881 | 0.005613261 | 12.449 | 0.0001 | 0.187060 | LOG.--POPULATION IN COUNTY |
| DLN_POP | 1 | 1.210646 | 0.290420 | 4.169 | 0.0001 | 0.537288 | 1ST DIFF.: LOG(COUNTY POPULATION) |
| LN_DNSTY | 1 | 0.019595 | 0.005275865 | 3.714 | 0.0002 | 0.138262 | LOG.--POPULATION PER SQ. MILE |
| LN_INC | 1 | 0.014447 | 0.030967 | 0.467 | 0.6409 | 0.174631 | LOG.--INCOME PER CAPITA |
| LN_CPI | 1 | -0.641883 | 0.283767 | -2.262 | 0.0237 | 0.290559 | LOG.--PCT. CHG. IN CPI |
| LN_URT | 1 | 0.074424 | 0.015850 | 4.695 | 0.0001 | 0.506358 | LOG.--UNEMPLOYMENT RATE |
| LN_INS | 1 | -0.331980 | 0.043933 | -7.556 | 0.0001 | 0.278159 | LOG.--PCT. OF POPULATION WITH PRIV. INS. |
| LN_HMO | 1 | 0.002787071 | 0.0006417929 | 4.343 | 0.0001 | 0.471609 | LOG.--PCT. OF POPULATION IN HMOS |
| LN_T18 | 1 | 0.129041 | 0.017297 | 7.460 | 0.0001 | 0.583389 | LOG.--PCT. OF POPULATION IN MEDICARE |
| LN_MDS | 1 | 0.048934 | 0.008968932 | 5.456 | 0.0001 | 0.447968 | LOG.--PHYSICIANS PER CAPITA |
| LN_SPMD | 1 | 0.0000495919 | 0.002880947 | 0.017 | 0.9863 | 0.813822 | LOG.--SPECIALISTS AS PCT. OF MDS |
| LN_NHB | 1 | -0.012147 | 0.003402152 | -3.570 | 0.0004 | 0.881812 | LOG.--NURSING HOME BEDS PER CAPITA |

350

TABLE A.10

MULTIPLE REGRESSION RESULTS
MARGIN OF PATIENT REVENUE

DEP VARIABLE: MARGIN_O MARGIN ON PATIENT REVENUE (PERCENT)

| SOURCE | DF | SUM OF SQUARES | MEAN SQUARE | F VALUE | PROB>F |
|---|---|---|---|---|---|
| MODEL | 32 | 27763.188 | 867.600 | 22.668 | 0.0001 |
| ERROR | 4603 | 176174 | 38.273746 | | |
| C TOTAL | 4635 | 203937 | | | |

| | | |
|---|---|---|
| ROOT MSE | 6.186578 | R-SQUARE | 0.1361 |
| DEP MEAN | -1.478065 | ADJ R-SQ | 0.1301 |
| C.V. | -418.559 | | |

| VARIABLE | DF | PARAMETER ESTIMATE | STANDARD ERROR | T FOR H0: PARAMETER=0 | PROB > [T[ | TOLERANCE | VARIABLE LABEL |
|---|---|---|---|---|---|---|---|
| INTERCEP | 1 | -387.995 | 64.875403 | -5.981 | 0.0001 | | INTERCEPT |
| D76 | 1 | 1.993789 | 0.523172 | 3.811 | 0.0001 | 0.150477 | 1976 YEAR DUMMY |
| D77 | 1 | -0.516365 | 0.399928 | -1.291 | 0.1967 | 0.214443 | 1977 YEAR DUMMY |
| D78 | 1 | -1.668933 | 0.359277 | -4.645 | 0.0001 | 0.256320 | 1978 YEAR DUMMY |
| D79 | 1 | -2.214585 | 0.519726 | -4.261 | 0.0001 | 0.168150 | 1979 YEAR DUMMY |

| | | | | | | | |
|---|---|---|---|---|---|---|---|
| DPRF_CHN | 1 | 5.485966 | 0.502451 | 10.918 | 0.0001 | 0.849150 | DUMMY: FOR-PROFIT & PART OF CHAIN |
| DPRF_IND | 1 | 3.279229 | 0.397531 | 8.249 | 0.0001 | 0.783585 | DUMMY: FOR-PROFIT & INDEPENDENT |
| DVOL_CHN | 1 | -0.625017 | 0.226175 | -2.763 | 0.0057 | 0.859741 | DUMMY: NONPROFIT & PART OF CHAIN |
| LN_CMIX | 1 | 6.256465 | 1.524685 | 4.103 | 0.0001 | 0.590501 | LOG.--MEDICARE CASEMIX INDEX FOR 1982 |
| LN_BEDS | 1 | 0.918827 | 0.166672 | 5.513 | 0.0001 | 0.414360 | LOG.--MEAN # BEDS STAFFED DURING YEAR |
| DSMSA | 1 | 0.802412 | 0.312433 | 2.568 | 0.0103 | 0.345518 | COUNTY LOCATED IN AN SMSA |
| N_EAST | 1 | -0.953267 | 0.434781 | -2.193 | 0.0284 | 0.175965 | NORTHEASTERN STATES |
| SOUTH | 1 | -0.215167 | 0.473936 | -0.454 | 0.6499 | 0.253426 | SOUTHERN STATES |
| N_CNTR | 1 | -0.516066 | 0.543200 | -0.950 | 0.3421 | 0.251546 | NORTH CENTRAL STATES |
| DPR | 1 | -0.988989 | 0.231263 | -4.276 | 0.0001 | 0.659459 | PROSPECTIVE REIMBURSEMENT DUMMY |
| DPSRO | 1 | -0.046269 | 0.253157 | -0.183 | 0.8550 | 0.529735 | HOSPITAL COVERED BY REVIEW IN YEAR |
| CON | 1 | -1.045155 | 0.268991 | -3.885 | 0.0001 | 0.763421 | CONDATE LE YEAR |
| LN_AFDC | 1 | 0.466656 | 0.222420 | 2.098 | 0.0360 | 0.382105 | LOG.--PCT. OF POPULATION IN AFDC |
| LN_BIRTH | 1 | 2.203341 | 0.698873 | 3.153 | 0.0016 | 0.520863 | LOG.--BIRTHS PER CAPITA |
| LN_EDUC | 1 | 7.813408 | 2.127667 | 3.672 | 0.0002 | 0.539638 | LOG.--AVE. YRS. OF EDUCATION |
| LN_WHT | 1 | 3.556875 | 0.901017 | 3.948 | 0.0001 | 0.478245 | LOG.--WHITES AS PCT. OF POPULATION |
| LN_POP | 1 | -0.144172 | 0.156466 | -0.921 | 0.3569 | 0.118169 | LOG.--POPULATION IN COUNTY |
| DLN_POP | 1 | 1.618374 | 6.817999 | 0.237 | 0.8124 | 0.612433 | 1ST DIFF.: LOG(COUNTY POPULATION) |
| LN_DNSTY | 1 | -0.108043 | 0.140777 | -0.767 | 0.4428 | 0.105419 | LOG.--POPULATION PER SQ. MILE |
| LN_INC | 1 | 1.978795 | 0.794063 | 2.492 | 0.0127 | 0.210015 | LOG.--INCOME PER CAPITA |
| LN_CPI | 1 | 69.610185 | 13.698792 | 5.081 | 0.0001 | 0.122151 | LOG.--PCT. CHG. IN CPI |
| LN_URT | 1 | -1.286775 | 0.472716 | -2.722 | 0.0065 | 0.332582 | LOG.--UNEMPLOYMENT RATE |
| LN_INS | 1 | -2.446158 | 1.242100 | -1.969 | 0.0490 | 0.298419 | LOG.--PCT. OF POPULATION WITH PRIV. INS. |
| LN_HMO | 1 | -0.055822 | 0.018864 | -2.959 | 0.0031 | 0.452025 | LOG.--PCT. OF POPULATION IN HMOS |
| LN_T18 | 1 | 0.285001 | 0.445960 | 0.639 | 0.5228 | 0.534037 | LOG.--PCT. OF POPULATION IN MEDICARE |
| LN_MDS | 1 | 0.129511 | 0.135449 | 0.956 | 0.3390 | 0.593499 | LOG.--PHYSICIANS PER CAPITA |
| LN_SPMD | 1 | 0.011404 | 0.031286 | 0.365 | 0.7155 | 0.679994 | LOG.--SPECIALISTS AS PCT. OF MDS |
| LN_NHB | 1 | 0.326727 | 0.045027 | 7.256 | 0.0001 | 0.867273 | LOG.--NURSING HOME BEDS PER CAPITA |

TABLE A.11
MULTIPLE REGRESSION RESULTS
MARGIN ON TOTAL REVENUE

DEP VARIABLE: MARGIN_T MARGIN ON TOTAL REVENUE (PERCENT)

| SOURCE | DF | SUM OF SQUARES | MEAN SQUARE | F VALUE | PROB>F |
|---|---|---|---|---|---|
| MODEL | 32 | 12061.650 | 376.927 | 14.332 | 0.0001 |
| ERROR | 4598 | 120930 | 26.300478 | | |
| C TOTAL | 4630 | 132991 | | | |

| | | |
|---|---|---|
| ROOT MSE | 5.128399 | R-SQUARE | 0.0907 |
| DEP MEAN | 2.065781 | ADJ R-SQ | 0.0844 |
| C.V. | 248.2548 | | |

| VARIABLE | DF | PARAMETER ESTIMATE | STANDARD ERROR | T FOR H0: PARAMETER=0 | PROB > [T[ | TOLERANCE | VARIABLE LABEL |
|---|---|---|---|---|---|---|---|
| INTERCEP | 1 | -178.381 | 53.794785 | -3.316 | 0.0009 | | INTERCEPT |
| D76 | 1 | 0.981569 | 0.434528 | 2.259 | 0.0239 | 0.150389 | 1976 YEAR DUMMY |
| D77 | 1 | -0.679133 | 0.331721 | -2.047 | 0.0407 | 0.214566 | 1977 YEAR DUMMY |
| D78 | 1 | -0.654919 | 0.298111 | -2.197 | 0.0281 | 0.256063 | 1978 YEAR DUMMY |
| D79 | 1 | -0.906524 | 0.431013 | -2.103 | 0.0355 | 0.167856 | 1979 YEAR DUMMY |
| DPRF_CHN | 1 | 1.776233 | 0.417417 | 4.255 | 0.0001 | 0.849878 | DUMMY: FOR-PROFIT & PART OF CHAIN |

| Variable | | Coef. | Std. Err. | t | p | | Description |
|---|---|---|---|---|---|---|---|
| DPRF_IND | 1 | 1.105497 | 0.330233 | 3.348 | 0.0008 | 0.784694 | DUMMY: FOR-PROFIT & INDEPENDENT |
| DVOL_CHN | 1 | -0.571699 | 0.187606 | -3.047 | 0.0023 | 0.860459 | DUMMY: NONPROFIT & PART OF CHAIN |
| LN_CMIX | 1 | 4.874901 | 1.260521 | 3.867 | 0.0001 | 0.592899 | LOG.--MEDICARE CASEMIX INDEX FOR 1982 |
| LN_BEDS | 1 | 1.011530 | 0.138292 | 7.314 | 0.0001 | 0.415192 | LOG.--MEAN # BEDS STAFFED DURING YEAR |
| DSMSA | 1 | 0.596168 | 0.258948 | 2.302 | 0.0214 | 0.346006 | COUNTY LOCATED IN AN SMSA |
| N_EAST | 1 | -0.613977 | 0.360821 | -1.702 | 0.0889 | 0.175753 | NORTHEASTERN STATES |
| SOUTH | 1 | 0.861544 | 0.393043 | 2.192 | 0.0284 | 0.252777 | SOUTHERN STATES |
| N_CNTR | 1 | 0.141658 | 0.451038 | 0.314 | 0.7535 | 0.252947 | NORTH CENTRAL STATES |
| DPR | 1 | -0.781976 | 0.191642 | -4.080 | 0.0001 | 0.660331 | PROSPECTIVE REIMBURSEMENT DUMMY |
| DPSRO | 1 | -0.074430 | 0.209743 | -0.355 | 0.7227 | 0.530952 | HOSPITAL COVERED BY REVIEW IN YEAR |
| CON | 1 | -0.736091 | 0.223292 | -3.297 | 0.0010 | 0.764283 | CONDATE LE YEAR |
| LN_AFDC | 1 | -0.023457 | 0.183879 | -0.128 | 0.8985 | 0.382906 | LOG.--PCT. OF POPULATION IN AFDC |
| LN_BIRTH | 1 | 1.686173 | 0.579500 | 2.910 | 0.0036 | 0.514639 | LOG.--BIRTHS PER CAPITA |
| LN_EDUC | 1 | 1.965805 | 1.751331 | 1.122 | 0.2617 | 0.531573 | LOG.--AVE. YRS. OF EDUCATION |
| LN_WHT | 1 | 0.781383 | 0.728959 | 1.072 | 0.2838 | 0.485525 | LOG.--WHITES AS PCT. OF POPULATION |
| LN_POP | 1 | -0.040520 | 0.129698 | -0.312 | 0.7547 | 0.118385 | LOG.--POPULATION IN COUNTY |
| DLN_POP | 1 | -1.047920 | 5.651739 | -0.185 | 0.8529 | 0.609206 | 1ST DIFF.: LOG(COUNTY POPULATION) |
| LN_DNSTY | 1 | -0.354456 | 0.116393 | -3.045 | 0.0023 | 0.106186 | LOG.--POPULATION PER SQ. MILE |
| LN_INC | 1 | 2.331559 | 0.657131 | 3.548 | 0.0004 | 0.208618 | LOG.--INCOME PER CAPITA |
| LN_CPI | 1 | 29.314931 | 11.362482 | 2.580 | 0.0099 | 0.121854 | LOG.--PCT. CHG. IN CPI |
| LN_URT | 1 | -0.632155 | 0.391344 | -1.615 | 0.1063 | 0.334028 | LOG.--UNEMPLOYMENT RATE |
| LN_INS | 1 | -0.235068 | 1.033998 | -0.227 | 0.8202 | 0.295072 | LOG.--PCT. OF POPULATION WITH PRIV. INS. |
| LN_HMO | 1 | -0.048677 | 0.015642 | -3.112 | 0.0019 | 0.452313 | LOG.--PCT. OF POPULATION IN HMOS |
| LN_T18 | 1 | 0.136456 | 0.370010 | 0.369 | 0.7123 | 0.530296 | LOG.--PCT. OF POPULATION IN MEDICARE |
| LN_MDS | 1 | 0.403946 | 0.112403 | 3.594 | 0.0003 | 0.591518 | LOG.--PHYSICIANS PER CAPITA |
| LN_SPMD | 1 | -0.027327 | 0.026129 | -1.046 | 0.2957 | 0.684237 | LOG.--SPECIALISTS AS PCT. OF MDS |
| LN_NHB | 1 | 0.093098 | 0.036178 | 2.573 | 0.0101 | 0.859080 | LOG.--NURSING HOME BEDS PER CAPITA |

For-Profit Enterprise in Health Care. 1986.
National Academy Press, Washington, D.C.

# Medicare Patient Outcomes and Hospital Organizational Mission

Gary Gaumer

The objective of this paper is to examine the relationship between indicators of quality of care and ownership status in a large sample of U.S. hospitals. Very little is known about the determinants of interhospital differences in patient outcomes and even less about the relationship between organizational mission and patient care. Work by Luft (1980), Scott et al. (1979), and Bunker et al. (1969) has established that significant disparities in hospital mortality rates exist which are, in part, associated with hospital organizational attributes such as size, nurse staffing, teaching mission, physician experience, and administrative span of control. No studies have yet examined the relationship between proprietary status and patient outcomes, nor has the influence of multihospital system affiliation on outcomes been studied.

This paper examines several types of measures which, taken together, may be indicative of differences in patient care practices and quality of care across groups of hospitals with differing organizational missions. The measures we analyze include

- Post-operative mortality for Medicare elective surgical admissions—measured over the stay and within 180 days of admission
- 90-day post-discharge readmission rates for Medicare elective surgery admissions
- Status regarding acccreditation by the Joint Commission on Accreditation of Hospitals (JCAH)
- Two measures of Medicare case mix.

## METHODS

The hospital sample used for our analyses includes two components:

1. A 25 percent simple random sample of all continental U.S. hospitals with a median length of stay of 15 days or less over the 1970-1978 period
2. All other similarly defined short-term hospitals in the 15 states with prospective payment programs.[1]

The surgical admissions we studied included inguinal hernia repair, hysterectomy, cholecystectomy, hemorrhoidectomy, open prostatectomy, transurethral resection of prostate, excision of bladder lesion, and mastectomy. Patient data were taken from the Health Care Financing Administration's (HCFA) MEDPAR file, containing clinical and billing data on Medicare inpatient stays for 20 percent of Medicare beneficiaries. Data were gathered for the 1974-1981 period on each sample hospital. Table 1 shows the resultant sample sizes. Table 2 shows characteristics of sample hospitals.

Constructing measures of readmission rates and post-discharge fatality rates required special processing of the HCFA files. A 90-day readmission indicator (0, 1) was created for each study patient by scanning the entire MEDPAR file across years to see if patients discharged from study hospitals were readmitted to *any* hospitals within 90 days of the date of discharge. For 180-day post-admission death rates, a similar process was used, except that HCFA's Medicare eligibility files were used to determine if beneficiary death occurred within 180 days of the admission.

Unpublished accreditation data were obtained from JCAH. Status codes were obtained that reflect full (2- or 3-year) accreditation and

---

Mr. Gaumer is Vice President of health care research with Abt Associates, Inc., Cambridge, Massachusetts.

**TABLE 1** Sample Sizes

| | Number of Hospitals | | | | Number of Elective Surgery Cases | | | |
|---|---|---|---|---|---|---|---|---|
| Year | Chain Proprietary | Independent Proprietary | Chain Nonproprietary | Independent Nonproprietary | Chain Proprietary | Independent Proprietary | Chain Nonproprietary | Independent Nonproprietary |
| 1974 | 94 | 173 | 417 | 1,245 | 965 | 1,296 | 8,032 | 21,265 |
| 1975 | 93 | 173 | 421 | 1,226 | 893 | 1,192 | 7,569 | 19,340 |
| 1976 | 94 | 160 | 419 | 1,233 | 1,057 | 1,502 | 8,812 | 22,046 |
| 1977 | 96 | 148 | 425 | 1,236 | 1,169 | 1,378 | 8,684 | 22,161 |
| 1978 | 96 | 135 | 426 | 1,248 | 1,088 | 1,131 | 7,966 | 20,589 |
| 1979 | 104 | 123 | 427 | 1,272 | 1,255 | 983 | 8,409 | 20,713 |
| 1980 | 108 | 121 | 440 | 1,300 | 1,368 | 1,229 | 8,014 | 24,138 |
| 1981 | 107 | 117 | 435 | 1,310 | 1,405 | 1,129 | 8,757 | 25,184 |
| *Composition of Elective Surgery Cases in 1981* | | | | | | | | |
| Hemorrhoidectomy | | | | | 50 | 36 | 266 | 715 |
| Cholecystectomy | | | | | 240 | 141 | 1,369 | 3,559 |
| Inguinal hernia | | | | | 262 | 242 | 1,643 | 5,143 |
| Open prostatectomy | | | | | 41 | 62 | 295 | 992 |
| Transurethral resection of prostate | | | | | 461 | 341 | 3,188 | 8,469 |
| Hysterectomy | | | | | 112 | 76 | 543 | 1,751 |
| Excision of bladder lesion | | | | | 147 | 151 | 822 | 2,762 |
| Mastectomy | | | | | 92 | 80 | 631 | 1,793 |

**TABLE 2**   Characteristics of Sample Hospitals,[a] 1981 Data

| Variable | Proprie-tary Chain | Proprie-tary Inde-pendent | Non-profit[b] Chain | Non-profit Inde-pendent |
|---|---|---|---|---|
| Number of hospitals in sample | 107 | 117 | 435 | 1,310 |
| Average number of beds staffed | 148 | 103 | 199 | 185 |
| Minimum | 40 | 11 | 15 | 8 |
| Maximum | 638 | 400 | 872 | 969 |
| Average Medicare case-mix index | 1.00 | 0.97 | 1.02 | 1.02 |
| Minimum | 0.79 | 0.71 | 0.72 | 0.56 |
| Maximum | 1.20 | 1.22 | 1.39 | 1.75 |
| Percent fully JCAH-accredited[c] | 0.79 | 0.50 | 0.74 | 0.55 |
| Percent covered by state prospective payment program | 0.17 | 0.44 | 0.57 | 0.64 |
| Percent located in SMSA[d] | 0.78 | 0.68 | 0.61 | 0.60 |
| *County Characteristics (unweighted mean)* | | | | |
| Percent population on AFDC[e] | 3.9 | 4.3 | 4.2 | 4.2 |
| Births per 100,000 population | 1,675 | 1,568 | 1,658 | 1,506 |
| Per capita income | 8,756 | 8,540 | 8,307 | 8,423 |
| Percent population with health insurance | 75.5 | 81.5 | 82.2 | 87.2 |
| Percent population on Medicare | 11.5 | 12.8 | 13.0 | 13.4 |
| Number of hospital beds per 100,000 population | 537 | 638 | 787 | 770 |
| M.D.s per 100,000 population | 161 | 153 | 144 | 145 |
| Percent M.D.s who are specialists | 0.81 | 0.75 | 0.71 | 0.75 |
| HMO penetration rate | 0.065 | 0.041 | 0.038 | 0.035 |
| Percent population white | 0.80 | 0.81 | 0.88 | 0.89 |
| Median years of education | 11.9 | 11.8 | 11.9 | 11.9 |
| Unemployment rate | 7.2 | 7.3 | 7.6 | 7.7 |

[a]Excludes government hospitals and members of the Council of Teaching Hospitals.

[b]American Hospital Association data for 1981-1982 were used to assign this ownership status indicating membership in a multihospital system.

[c]Joint Commission on Accreditation of Hospitals.

[d]Standard metropolitan statistical area.

[e]Aid to Families with Dependent Children.

**TABLE 3**  Unadjusted In-Hospital Mortality Rates by Hospital Type

| | Proprietary Chain | Proprietary Independent | Nonprofit[a] Chain | Nonprofit Independent |
|---|---|---|---|---|
| All eight elective procedures | | | | |
| 1975 | 0.010 | 0.013 | 0.012 | 0.013 |
| 1977 | 0.009 | 0.009 | 0.014 | 0.012 |
| 1979 | 0.010 | 0.007 | 0.011 | 0.011 |
| 1981 | 0.011 | 0.004 | 0.011 | 0.012 |
| 1981 by procedure | | | | |
| Hemorrhoidectomy | 0.000 | 0.000 | 0.000 | 0.004 |
| Cholecystectomy | 0.042 | 0.014 | 0.032 | 0.032 |
| Inguinal hernia | 0.004 | 0.004 | 0.006 | 0.004 |
| Open prostatectomy | 0.000 | 0.000 | 0.014 | 0.015 |
| Transurethral resection of prostate | 0.009 | 0.000 | 0.009 | 0.010 |
| Hysterectomy | 0.000 | 0.013 | 0.002 | 0.006 |
| Excision of bladder lesion | 0.000 | 0.000 | 0.010 | 0.012 |
| Mastectomy | 0.000 | 0.012 | 0.015 | 0.006 |

[a]American Hospital Association data for 1981-1982 were used to assign this ownership status indicating membership in a multihospital system.

only 1-year accreditation as a result of the survey. For analytic purposes, we used an indicator of whether the hospital was fully (2- or 3-year) accredited or not.[2]

Medicare case-mix data for 1981 were coded from the September 30, 1983 *Federal Register*.

Several measures of organizational mission were developed from AHA's annual survey designation of proprietary status. An indicator of affiliation with a proprietary hospital system was coded from 1974-1981 annual directories of the Federation of American Hospitals. AHA's 1982 annual survey data were used to deter-

**TABLE 4**  Unadjusted 180-Day Mortality Rates by Hospital Type

| | Proprietary Chain | Proprietary Independent | Nonprofit[a] Chain | Nonprofit Independent |
|---|---|---|---|---|
| All eight elective procedures | | | | |
| 1975 | 0.049 | 0.045 | 0.050 | 0.013 |
| 1977 | 0.063 | 0.057 | 0.058 | 0.012 |
| 1979 | 0.062 | 0.070 | 0.054 | 0.011 |
| 1981 | 0.055 | 0.041 | 0.056 | 0.054 |
| 1981 by procedure | | | | |
| Hemorrhoidectomy | 0.020 | 0.000 | 0.029 | 0.025 |
| Cholecystectomy | 0.059 | 0.067 | 0.083 | 0.076 |
| Inguinal hernia | 0.027 | 0.043 | 0.029 | 0.026 |
| Open prostatectomy | 0.051 | 0.032 | 0.055 | 0.040 |
| Transurethral resection of prostate | 0.077 | 0.041 | 0.063 | 0.064 |
| Hysterectomy | 0.000 | 0.026 | 0.019 | 0.019 |
| Excision of bladder lesion | 0.095 | 0.039 | 0.083 | 0.095 |
| Mastectomy | 0.033 | 0.037 | 0.047 | 0.037 |

[a]American Hospital Association data for 1981-1982 were used to assign this ownership status indicating membership in a multihospital system.

mine if the hospital was a member of a multihospital system. Using these data, for-profit affiliations were available for all hospital years, but nonprofit chain affiliation was only captured at one point in time.

## DESCRIPTIVE STATISTICS

Tables 3, 4, and 5 contain means on patient outcome measures.[3] The unadjusted outcome data often show large differences across types of ownership, and considerable instability over time—no doubt arising, in part, from the relatively small samples of patients for some procedure groups.

### Mortality During the Stay

For the aggregate of eight elective procedures, death rates averaged about 1.1 percent. No significant trends are apparent. Death rates generally appear lower in proprietary hospitals, particularly in the independent investor-owned hospitals. Post-operative death rates are often zero for procedures such as open prostatectomy and excision of bladder lesion. Mortality rates for the specific procedures show the instability in measures that arises from infrequent deaths and relatively small samples.

### Mortality Rates Within 180 Days of Admission

Six-month mortality rates average about 5 percent for all elective surgery, often somewhat lower in proprietary hospitals. No trends are apparent. Among the specific procedures, bladder lesions and gall bladder removals have highest death rates. Patterns of mortality by hospital organizational types are very inconsistent across the specific procedures.

### Readmission Rates Within 90 Days of Discharge

Readmission rates for the eight procedures are about 9 percent. There is a slight upward trend in these rates. Readmission rates show similar performance of nonprofit and proprietaries, although on balance, mean rates for proprietaries are slightly higher. Readmission rates are low for hernia repair, hysterectomy, and mastectomy, and highest for procedures relating to the bladder and prostate.

The descriptive data suggest that it may not be meaningful to statistically examine many of the specific procedures separately due to the combined consequences of rare outcomes and small samples of cases for particular ownership

**TABLE 5**  Unadjusted 90-Day Readmission Rates by Hospital Type

|  | Proprietary Chain | Proprietary Independent | Nonprofit[a] Chain | Nonprofit Independent |
|---|---|---|---|---|
| All eight elective procedures |  |  |  |  |
| 1975 | 0.067 | 0.083 | 0.084 | 0.081 |
| 1977 | 0.104 | 0.101 | 0.103 | 0.094 |
| 1979 | 0.088 | 0.093 | 0.084 | 0.083 |
| 1981 | 0.111 | 0.089 | 0.093 | 0.089 |
| 1981 by procedure |  |  |  |  |
| Hemorrhoidectomy | 0.140 | 0.056 | 0.079 | 0.073 |
| Cholecystectomy | 0.083 | 0.072 | 0.092 | 0.087 |
| Inguinal hernia | 0.077 | 0.075 | 0.058 | 0.052 |
| Open prostatectomy | 0.098 | 0.081 | 0.110 | 0.081 |
| Transurethral resection of prostate | 0.136 | 0.129 | 0.115 | 0.113 |
| Hysterectomy | 0.063 | 0.013 | 0.057 | 0.064 |
| Excision of bladder lesion | 0.190 | 0.099 | 0.114 | 0.139 |
| Mastectomy | 0.076 | 0.063 | 0.076 | 0.047 |

[a]American Hospital Association data for 1981-1982 were used to assign this ownership status indicating membership in a multihospital system.

categories. We examined standardized outcomes for the following types of procedures:

- All elective procedures taken together
- Cholecystectomy
- Hernia repair
- Transurethral resection of prostate.

Figures 1, 2, 3, and 4 show further detail on the unadjusted patient outcome rates for these four procedure categories. Data on length of stay are also included for reference purposes. All tables show means weighted by number of admissions in the particular surgical category. The tables show four bed-size categories.

### Size of Hospital

Patient outcomes for elective procedures seem to vary systematically with respect to hospital size. Larger hospitals have longer lengths of stay, higher in-hospital fatality rates, and lower readmission rates. Inguinal hernia repair is the only exception, where no pattern in readmission rates is apparent. The pattern is different for mortality rates within 180 days of admission; generally, the fatality rates are much lower for very small hospitals. Cholecystectomy is an exception, where no size pattern is seen.

### Medicare Case Mix

Hospitals were classified on the basis of the HCFA-published 1981 Medicare diagnosis-related group (DRG) case-mix index. As with size, patterns are evident in the raw data. Readmission patterns are quite uniform; hospitals with a more complex (costly) Medicare case mix have lower readmission rates and shorter lengths of stay for these elective procedures. Mortality rate patterns are not so uniform. Excepting cholestectomy, the in-hospital and 180-day mortality rates are generally higher in hospitals with higher case-mix values. No pattern is evident for cholecystectomy.

### Organization of Hospital

Looking first at differences between pro-

prietary and voluntary hospitals, the weighted means show that proprietary hospitals have comparable or lower mortality rates. In-hospital mortality rates are lower for all eight procedures taken together (.008 compared to .012) and for transurethral resection of the prostate (.004 compared to .010). Proprietary hospitals have lower 180-day mortality rates for all eight procedures together (.049 compared to .055) and for cholecystectomy (.061 versus .076). The only observed instance where proprietary hospitals have much higher mortality is hernia repair, where 180-day post-admission mortality is 3.7 percent compared to 2.7 percent for nonprofit hospitals. Readmission rates are generally much higher in proprietary hospitals, excepting cholecystectomy, where the reverse is true. Length-of-stay differences are nonexistent or quite small, though for the aggregate of eight procedures and prostate surgery the proprietary hospitals have slightly lower lengths of stay.

When subgroups of investor-owned hospitals are compared to their voluntary chain and nonchain counterparts, some patterns emerge. Independent proprietary hospitals have the lowest values on both mortality rate measures of all four groups of hospitals except for cholecystectomy; for this procedure, in-hospital fatality rates are equal to their voluntary counterparts and 180-day mortality is higher than in other types of hospitals. Readmission rates and length of stay for independent proprietaries are generally equal to or higher than for independent voluntary hospitals. The exception is hernia repair, where independent proprietary hospitals have the lowest readmission rate.

The pattern for proprietary chains is similar; for readmission rates, proprietary chains have higher rates than voluntary chains, except for hernia repair. But unlike the independent proprietaries, the investor-owned chain hospitals have *lower* lengths of stay than the voluntary chain hospitals. For chain hospitals there is no pattern whatsoever for mortality rates across procedure categories; for the aggregate of eight procedures, proprietary chains have mortality rates about equal to those observed in voluntary chain hospitals.

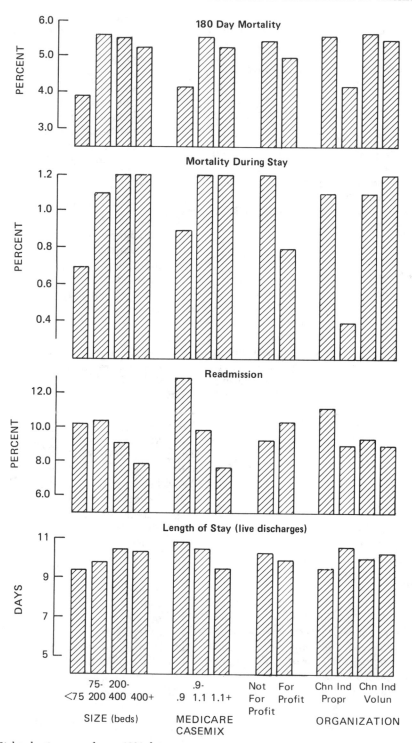

FIGURE 1   Eight elective procedures, 1981 data.

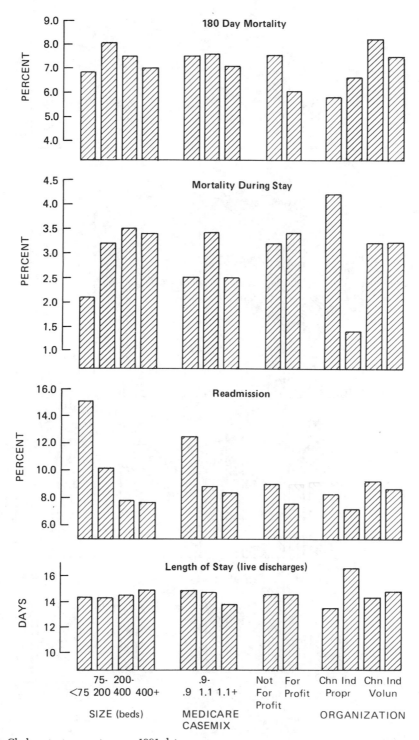

**FIGURE 2** Cholecystectomy outcomes, 1981 data.

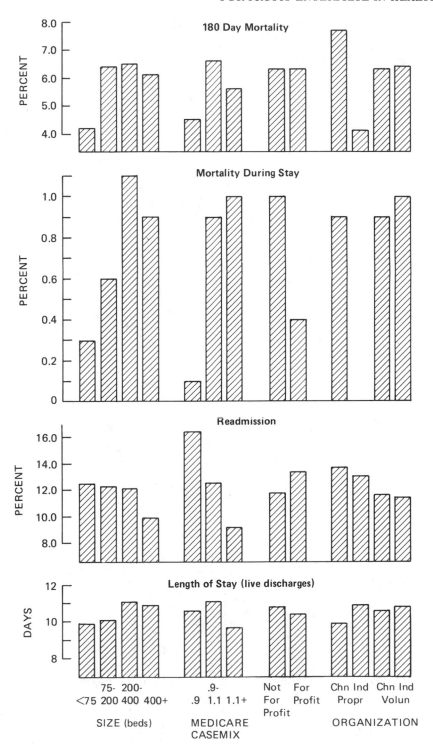

**FIGURE 3**  Inguinal hernia repair, 1981 data.

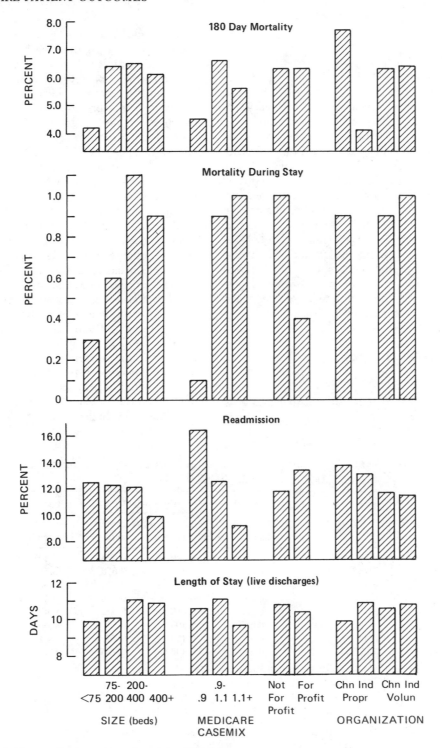

**FIGURE 4** Transurethral resection of prostate, 1981 data.

## Accreditation Trends

The trends in accreditation status have not been pronounced, although there are clear differences across groups of hospitals. Table 6 and Figure 5 show the unadjusted data on full JCAH accreditation rates (percent fully accredited). There is a clear demarcation between chain and nonchain hospitals, but little difference between proprietary and nonprofit independents. For the chain affiliates, about 65 to 75 percent of hospitals maintain full accreditation. For independents, full accreditation rates in 1981 were 50 to 55 percent, with the proprietaries up from 40 percent in the early 1970s.

Table 6 also shows the specific accreditation status of hospital years being studied. Lower accreditation rates for proprietary independents are apparently due to lower rates of participation in the JCAH program.

## STATISTICAL RESULTS

### Mortality During the Stay

Table 7 shows the results of statistical tests on the ratio of actual to expected death rates

at discharge.[4] The table shows various differences of interest (rows) for each of the aggregate and individual elective procedures (columns). If probability is less than 0.10 the coefficient is reported which, because of the log form, is interpreted as the difference between the indicated groups of hospitals expressed in percentage terms (e.g., mortality rates are x percent higher in the first-listed group of hospitals than in the other). If the coefficient was not significant ($p < .10$), only the direction of differences is reported. For example, the first cell in the table (.119) indicates that chain-affiliated hospitals have in-hospital mortality rates for all elective procedures combined that are 11.9 percent higher than for nonchain hospitals, *cet par*.

The dominant conclusion from these tests is that hospital ownership may not be a strong or consistent influence on postoperative mortality rates; significant results are not propagated across all procedures categories. The data are not without patterns, though they may fail to be fully persistent; proprietary status is frequently found to be associated with lower in-hospital mortality, and chain affiliation is often associated with higher mortality. There is no

**TABLE 6** Trends in Accreditation by the Joint Commission on Accreditation of Hospitals (JCAH)

| Year | Percent with 2-Year Accreditation[a] | | | |
| | Proprietary Chain | Proprietary Independent | Nonprofit[b] Chain | Nonprofit Independent |
| --- | --- | --- | --- | --- |
| 1974 | 0.660 | 0.399 | 0.724 | 0.605 |
| 1975 | 0.688 | 0.387 | 0.679 | 0.586 |
| 1976 | 0.649 | 0.400 | 0.623 | 0.505 |
| 1977 | 0.688 | 0.399 | 0.640 | 0.514 |
| 1978 | 0.729 | 0.415 | 0.662 | 0.492 |
| 1979 | 0.663 | 0.398 | 0.710 | 0.522 |
| 1980 | 0.676 | 0.496 | 0.730 | 0.547 |
| 1981 | 0.785 | 0.496 | 0.736 | 0.547 |
| *Accreditation Status: All Years Combined* | | | | |
| Percent full | 69 | 42 | 69 | 54 |
| Percent provisional | 10 | 10 | 14 | 12 |
| Percent other | 21 | 48 | 18 | 34 |

[a]The balance of hospitals either did not seek JCAH accreditation, had status of unaccredited, or were accredited for only 1 year.

[b]American Hospital Association data for 1981-1982 were used to assign this ownership status for nonprofits, indicating membership in a multihospital system.

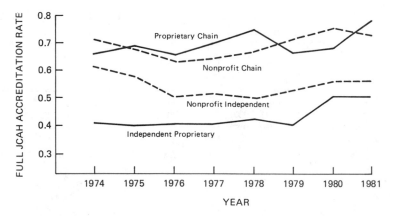

**FIGURE 5** Accreditation trends by hospital status.

significant evidence that proprietary chains are significantly different from other proprietary hospitals.

We are concerned that the pattern (higher mortality in chains; lower mortality in proprietaries) may be confounded with severity. Although mortality rates were standardized for the age/sex/co-morbid status and covariates provide control for aggregate case-mix and size differences, we still worry that the differences in mortality may be partially due to severity differences which are not captured in our standardization approach. In part, our concern stems from the pattern of case-mix results below—showing that proprietary hospitals may have a less complex case mix.

### 180-Day Post-Admission Mortality

The statistical results for tests on this measure generally tend to be the reverse of those found for in-hospital mortality, though usually less consistent. Compared to voluntary hospitals, chain hospitals are not consistently different from their independent counterparts, though they have significantly lower mortality rates for prostate surgery. Investor-owned hospitals have higher 180-day mortality rates, though these differences are statistically significant only in the hernia repair and prostate models. The effect of switching to proprietary status is measured directly as Test 3; here we find no significant differences to support the

pattern of higher 180-day mortality in investor-owned hospitals.

Results are also inconsistent on the differences between independent proprietary hospitals and their chain-affiliated counterparts. There is some indication that switching from independent to chain status is associated with lower 180-day mortality rates; this pattern is statistically significant for the aggregate of eight procedures, and the signs are consistent for the other procedure-specific tests.

### 90-Day Readmission Rates

The readmission tests in Table 7 show only one consistent pattern. Chain affiliates are often found to have higher readmission rates. There is also some evidence that proprietary chains have higher readmission rates than other proprietary hospitals.

### Accreditation Rates

Table 8 shows the statistical results for accreditation rates. The likelihood of full (2-year) accreditation with JCAH is consistently related to the organizational measures; no doubt this reflects, in part, mission and image differences which differentially affect the propensities of hospitals to seek JCAH accreditation. All the tested models show that chain-affiliated hospitals are more often ac-

TABLE 7   Statistical Results on Patient Outcomes: Percentage Differences in Adverse Outcome Rate[a] (*p* value in parentheses)

| Test Statistic | All Eight Electives | Cholecystectomy | Inguinal Hernia Repair | Transurethral Resection of Prostate |
|---|---|---|---|---|
| Inhospital mortality | | | | |
|   Chain vs. independent | .119 (.033) | .120 (.033) | .124 (.056) | — |
|   Proprietary vs. voluntary | −.401 (.000) | — | −.181 (.096) | + |
|   Switch from voluntary to proprietary | — | — | + | − |
|   Proprietary chain vs. proprietary independent | — | + | + | − |
|   Switch from proprietary independent to proprietary chain | + | + | + | − |
| 180-day mortality | | | | |
|   Chain vs. independent | — | + | + | −.181 (.002) |
|   Proprietary vs. voluntary | + | + | .172 (.001) | .171 (.000) |
|   Switch from voluntary to proprietary | + | + | — | − |
|   Proprietary chain vs. proprietary independent | — | + | + | .157 (.062) |
|   Switch from proprietary independent to proprietary chain | −.248 (.099) | — | — | − |
| 90-day readmission rate | | | | |
|   Chain vs. independent | + | + | .197 (.001) | + |
|   Proprietary vs. voluntary | − | − | + | − |
|   Switch from voluntary to proprietary | − | + | + | − |
|   Proprietary chain vs. proprietary independent | .204 (.057) | — | −.420 (.024) | − |
|   Switch from proprietary independent to proprietary chain | — | .873 (.035) | .764 (.063) | + |

[a]Dependent variable is natural log of ratio of actual to expected rate. Only coefficients with $p < .10$ are shown (*p* value in parentheses). Positive values indicate higher adverse outcome rates in the first-listed category of hospital.

credited than others. Results also indicate that, after standardization, proprietary chains have significantly higher accreditation rates than other investor-owned hospitals. Both models that test the effect of switching status show similar patterns, though differences are not statistically significant.

### Case Mix

Case-mix differences were examined by means of two measures made on *Medicare* admissions. One measure, available only for 1981, is the Medicare case-mix index based on ICD9 DRGs which was developed for the Tax Equity and Fiscal Responsibility Act (TEFRA). The other measure is the *expected* 180-day post-admission mortality rate for the aggregate of Medicare elective surgery cases.[5] The former measure is a form of resource use index; the latter is a measure of severity or prognosis.

Results are not fully consistent, though generally both measures show that proprietary hospitals have a simpler case mix than others, *cet par.*

**TABLE 8** Statistical Results for Accreditation and Case Mix

| | Percentage Difference* | | |
|---|---|---|---|
| | Full Accreditation Rate | Expected 180-Day Mortality for Elective Surgery | 1981 Medicare Case-Mix Index |
| Chain versus independent | .087 (.000) | + | + |
| Proprietary versus voluntary | −.114 (.000) | −.001 (.078) | −.019 (.001) |
| Switch from voluntary to proprietary | − | − | NA |
| Proprietary chain versus proprietary independent | .170 (.000) | − | + |
| Switch from proprietary independent to proprietary chain | + | + | NA |

*Coefficients are interpreted as the percentage difference between the indicated groups. Only coefficients with $p < .10$ are shown.

## SUMMARY AND DISCUSSION

### Findings on Investor-Owned Hospitals

The analysis of quality-of-care indicators provides no evidence for concluding that the profit motive, in the aggregate, has compromised patient care to the point of causing large and systematic differences in post-operative mortality or readmission. Results indicate that Medicare post-operative mortality rates are often lower in proprietary hospitals, after standardizing for patient age, sex, and co-morbidity; and controlling for interhospital differences in hospital size and other hospital and market characteristics. This pattern does not persist for mortality rates within 180 days of admission; proprietary hospitals have somewhat higher mortality rates although they are not sufficiently higher than the levels in voluntary hospitals to be considered statistically significant. The findings on readmission rates admit to no pattern whatsoever—again providing no support for the view that investor-owned hospitals have poorer patient outcomes. In sum, the patient outcome findings do not show any persisting pattern that would support a conclusion that proprietary hospitals are providing poorer quality of care.

Analysis of accreditation status with JCAH shows that proprietaries are consistently less likely to be fully (2-year) accredited. Whether this finding has a bearing on quality of care is, of course, problematic due to the nature of the JCAH survey and the fact that the accreditation program is voluntary. The data indicate that lower rates of participation in the JCAH program are largely responsible for the lower rates of full accreditation, implying that the statistical findings may have little or no bearing on the quality of the patient care process in investor-owned hospitals.

### Findings on Chain Influences for Investor-Owned Hospitals

There is very inconsistent evidence on the issue of how proprietary chains may be distinctive from independent proprietaries in terms of quality indicators. No significant differences or pattern of results is seen when mortality rates are compared directly. Switching from independent to chain affiliation is weakly associated with higher in-hospital mortality and lower 180-day mortality. Patterns in readmission differences are not seen. JCAH accreditation rates are also found to be more favorable in proprietary chains than in other

investor-owned hospitals. Finally, chain affiliation is associated with more complex case
mix.

These results are, without question, not a
conclusive test on the issue of quality of care.
Aside from the usual caveats about correla-
tional analysis and a nonrandomized design
and imperfect indicators of quality, we are concerned about several statistical issues. Deaths
(and even readmissions) are relatively rare
events for elective surgery. Given small sample sizes per hospital, we observe fairly extreme variability in our measures. While the
use of weighted least squares and the continuity correction factor will tend to minimize
this problem, we still observe quite "noisy"
data—tending to make it less likely to reject
the null hypothesis. That is, differences between groups need to be quite large before it
is likely that they are considered statistically
significant. While we use a liberal critical confidence limit ($p<0.10$), it still appears that intergroup differences in outcome rates smaller
than 10 to 12 percent or so are not detectable.

The sample size issue is most germane to
consideration of the use of the results stemming from the four-way design. This difficulty
is unfortunate because this approach essentially allows each hospital to be its own control,
which is a strong hedge against confounding
stemming from omitted determinants of outcomes that are unique to individual hospitals.
The number of hospitals that switch status is
quite small. Estimates of the effects of switching from proprietary independent to proprietary chain status are based on about 1.2 percent
of the sample of hospital years (N = 15,422
in total). Estimates of the effects of switching
to proprietary status (versus nonprofit) are based
on only about 3.7 percent of the sample, where
such switches occur. Consequently, the results of the four-way model tests are not likely
to be reliable.

The failure to detect persistent patterns may,
in part, derive from these statistical power
considerations. We can conclude, however, that
no apparent pattern of *large* ownership differences exist for serious patient outcomes following elective surgery.

## NOTES

[1] These states are Arizona, Colorado, Connecticut,
Indiana, Kentucky, Maryland, Massachusetts, Minnesota, Nebraska, New Jersey, New York, Pennsylvania (western), Rhode Island, Washington, and
Wisconsin.
[2] We followed Dowling et al. (1976) who reported
that separating 1-year from full accreditation status offers a more sensitive measure of accreditation status.
[3] Hospital year means have been weighed by number
of admissions in specific surgical categories.
[4] The ratio of actual to expected outcomes is used to
standardize outcomes for interhospital differences in
patient age, sex, and co-morbid status. Appendix A
describes the standardization approach as well as other
aspects of the statistical method.
Appendix B contains the full results of the statistical
models that are summarized in this section.
[5] These rates are developed on the basis of patient
age, sex, procedure, and existence (or not) of a second
diagnosis on admission.

## REFERENCES

Bunker, J., W. Forrest, F. Mosteller, and L. Vandam,
eds. (1969) *The National Halothane Study*, National
Institute of General Medical Sciences, Bethesda, Md.
Dowling, William et al. (1976) The Evaluation of
Blue Cross in Medicaid Prospective Reimbursement
Systems in Downstate New York. Final Report, DHEW
Contract HEW-OS-74-248.
Luft, H. (1980) The relationship between surgical
volume and mortality: An exploration of causal factors
and alternative models. *Medical Care*, 18(9), Septem-
ber.
Scott, W., B. Flood, and W. Ewy (1979) Organiza-
tional determinants of services, quality, and cost of care
in hospitals, *Milbank Memorial Fund Quarterly*, 57(2).

# APPENDIX A

# Statistical Methods

## CONTROLLING FOR SEVERITY

A principal analytic issue in evaluating interhospital differences is controlling for prognosis or expected outcome on admission. Our approach was to adjust or normalize the measured outcome rate for factors known to affect prognosis. The ratio of the *measured* outcome to the *expected* outcome provides a measure of severity-adjusted outcomes for a given hospital year.

These "expected" rates are the cell means on each outcome measure (fatality and readmission rates) for a 20 percent sample of Medicare admissions patients in all years (1974-1981) from a 25 percent random sample of short-term U.S. hospitals. The 96 cells were defined by procedure (eight categories), age (three categories 65-74, 75-84, over 84), sex (two categories), and presence of a second diagnosis (two categories). Two sets of norms (means) were used: 1974-1978 and 1979-1981. This was done to acknowledge the shift to ICD9-CM coding on Medicare files which began in 1979. After the patient file for each year was scored with appropriate means, both the actual and "expected" outcome rates were computed for each hospital year observation by summing across patients and dividing by the number of cases.

## SPECIFYING OWNERSHIP MEASURES

Three basic forms of ownership influence were examined in the study. The first two specify the ownership influence within the two-way or treatment-control design:

*Model 1*: Prop (= 1 if proprietary, 0 otherwise), and
Chain (= 1 if member of chain, 0 otherwise)
*Model 2*: Prop (= 1 if proprietary, 0 otherwise), and
Chain (= 1 if member of chain, 0 otherwise), and

Prochain (= 1 if proprietary chain, 0 otherwise)

The coefficients on the organization measures in the Model 1 specification tests for differences between chain and nonchain hospitals and between proprietary and nonproprietary hospitals. In Model 2, the coefficient on the Prochain variable tests whether proprietary chain hospitals are different from other proprietary hospitals. Both models test for differences in means between groups of hospitals (e.g., proprietary versus other), controlling for differences in means between groups on other covariates we include.

A third specification uses a different test: measuring the difference between groups in their pre/post change. This four-way (pre/post-treatment/control) design reduces the risk that unmeasured baseline differences between the groups of institutions are confounding the results. This design is intrinsically preferable to the treatment-control approach used in the first two models, but suffers here due to several factors: the small number of hospitals that actually change status (between profit and nonprofit and between chain and independent) over the study period; and the inability to gather *time series* data on nonprofit chain affiliation. Hence, the hypothesis test

$$H_0: (Q_{\text{post}} - Q_{\text{pre}})_{\text{PROPR}} -$$
$$(Q_{\text{post}} - Q_{\text{pre}})_{\text{NONPROP}} = 0$$

is highly leveraged on those few cases where ownership status changed. We do test this approach, acknowledging the problem, allowing the results to be considered by the reader as *part of* the overall pattern of findings. The specification is

*Model 3*: Prop (see other), and
DProchain (see other), and
DChain (= 1 if ever chain affiliated)[1]
Prop (= 1 in years when proprietary, 0 otherwise), and
DProp (= 1 if ever proprietary), and

FOR-PROFIT ENTERPRISE IN HEALTH CARE

Chain (= 1 for years when affiliated with a chain)[1]

In Model 4, the coefficient on Prop tests whether the change to proprietary status influenced outcomes. The coefficient on Prochain in Model 3 tests whether a change from an independent proprietary to a chain-affiliated proprietary influenced the outcomes.

### COVARIATES

The characteristics of hospitals in various ownership groups of interest are different. Of course, without random assignment this problem of noncomparability is always a problem, precluding simple hypothesis tests of differences in means. We use a multivariate (regression) approach to standardize groups for differences in many of these hospital characteristics. Table 2 presents descriptive data on the values of covariates across ownership groups. In addition to those measures shown in the table, the regression models include covariate as

• Whether binding review by a professional standards review organization (PSRO) was conducted in the hospital for the year
• Whether the hospital was subject to state certificate-of-need (CON) authority for each year
• Percentage increase in the CPI for the SMSA
• County population
• County population per square mile
• A set of year-specific, dummy (0,1) variables
• A set of region-specific dummy variables
• Number of staffed beds—following Luft (1980). This measure captures scale effects on outcomes.

### ESTIMATION

For the patient outcome analyses, a weighted regression (OLS) was used to estimate the basic models. This is done to remove heteroscedastic (systematic) variances in residuals across hospital year observations which, if uncorrected, make all parameter estimates inefficient (though unbiased). These patterns are likely in our model because our hospital year

outcome measures are based on samples of patients of widely varying sizes, and while the 20 percent sample is probably random, the variances of these estimates are likely to be systematically related to the number of cases in each hospital year on which the mean was computed.

### CONTINUITY CORRECTION FACTOR

Another estimation problem is that, for some measures, we can expect to observe a cluster of zeros for outpatient outcome variables. With small samples per hospital year, for example, it is plausible that no deaths or readmissions will be observed even though some cases were admitted. The number of zeros in the data approaches 50 percent for some types of elective surgery. Consequently, we observe a bimodal distribution on our measures. The approach for dealing with the clusters of cases at zero (and at high extreme values) is the use of a "continuity correction factor." This approach is a standard technique for smoothing the "ends" of a distribution on a binary variable (e.g., values approaching 0 and values approaching 1).[2]

### SIGNIFICANCE LEVELS

In all statistical analyses we report coefficients that are significant at the $p = .10$ level or better (two-tailed test). There are two reasons for reporting at a level of significance somewhat lower than the $p = .05$ that is customary in the literature. First, we are concerned that measurement errors in the MEDPAR file may elevate the standard errors in the model, causing significant differences to be overlooked if tolerance levels are too stringent. Second, we believe that the policy applications of this work require that we allow less than the usual chance of committing false negative (type II) errors (ignoring an adverse difference because a critical significance level is too stringent).

### NOTES

[1] AHA data for 1981-1982 were used to assign this ownership status for nonprofits indicating membership in a multihospital system.

[2]Following techniques suggested by Cox (1970) and Bishop et al. (1975), we can use an adjustment of the form:

$$R_i = \frac{A_i + 1/6}{N_i + 1/3}$$

where $A_i$ = the observed number of adverse outcomes for the hospital year; $N_i$ = the number of cases; and $R_i$ = the adjusted adverse outcome rate. The constants (1/6, 1/3), which define the value of this Taylor expansion on $n$ are suggested by Mosteller and Tukey (1977). The choice remains somewhat arbitrary, though larger fractions tend to have more dramatic "smoothing" effects.

## REFERENCES

Bishop Y., S. Fienberg, and P. Holland (1975) *Discrete Multivariate Analysis*. Cambridge, Mass.: MIT Press.

Cox, D. R. (1970) *Analysis of Binary Data*. London: Chapman and Hall.

Luft, H. (1980) The relationship between surgical volume and mortality. *Medical Care* 18, September.

Mosteller, F., and J. Tukey (1977) *Data Analysis and Regression*. Reading, Mass.: Addison Wesley.

# APPENDIX B

# Model Results

**TABLE B-1** Statistical Results on Post-Operative Mortality Rates: Percentage Difference in Mortality Rate During the Stay[a]

| Model | Surgical Category | | | |
| --- | --- | --- | --- | --- |
| | All Elective Surgery | Cholecystectomy | Inguinal Hernia Repair | Transurethral Resection of Prostate |
| Model 1 | | | | |
| Chain[b] | 0.119 (0.033) | 0.120 (0.033) | 0.124 (0.056) | — |
| Proprietary[c] | −0.401 (0.000) | — | −0.181 (0.096) | + |
| Model 2 | | | | |
| Chain | 0.129 (0.023) | 0.116 (0.031) | + | + |
| Proprietary | — | — | — | + |
| Prochain[d] | — | + | + | — |
| Model 3 | | | | |
| DChain[e] | — | — | — | + |
| Prochain | + | + | + | — |
| Proprietary | −0.274 (0.035) | — | — | — |
| Model 4 | | | | |
| DProprietary[f] | — | — | — | — |
| Proprietary | — | — | + | — |
| Chain | 0.129 (0.032) | 0.121 (0.032) | + | + |

[a]Dependent variable is natural log of ratio of actual to expected mortality rate at discharge. Only coefficients with $p < .10$ are shown ($p$ value in parentheses).

[b]Chain = 1 if chain affiliated in year.

[c]Proprietary = 1 if proprietary in year.

[d]Prochain = 1 if proprietary and chain.

[e]DChain = 1 for all years if ever chain affiliated.

[f]DProprietary = 1 for all years if ever proprietary.

**TABLE B-2**   Statistical Results on Readmission Rate: Percentage Difference in Readmission Rate[a]

| Model | Surgical Category | | | |
|---|---|---|---|---|
| | All Elective Surgery | Cholecystectomy | Inguinal Hernia Repair | Transurethral Resection of Prostate |
| Mastectomy | | | | |
| Model 1 | | | | |
| Chain[b] | + | + | 0.197 (0.001) | + |
| Proprietary[c] | − | − | + | − |
| Model 2 | | | | |
| Chain | + | + | 0.222 (0.000) | + |
| Proprietary | + | − | 0.268 (0.045) | + |
| Prochain[d] | 0.204 (0.057) | − | −0.420 (0.024) | − |
| Model 3 | | | | |
| DChain[e] | − | −1.167 (0.004) | −1.176 (0.004) | − |
| Prochain | − | 0.873 (0.035) | 0.764 (0.063) | + |
| Proprietary | + | + | 0.382 (0.000) | + |
| Model 4 | | | | |
| DProprietary[f] | + | + | + | + |
| Proprietary | − | + | + | − |
| Chain | + | + | + | + |

[a]Dependent variable is natural log of ratio of actual to expected rate. Only coefficients with $p < .10$ are shown ($p$ value in parentheses).
[b]Chain = 1 if chain affiliated in year.
[c]Proprietary = 1 if proprietary in year.
[d]Prochain = 1 if proprietary and chain.
[e]DChain = 1 for all years if ever chain affiliated.
[f]DProprietary = 1 for all years if ever proprietary.

**TABLE B-3** Statistical Results on 180-Day Mortality Rate: Percentage Difference in Mortality Rate[a]

| Model | Surgical Category | | | |
|---|---|---|---|---|
| | All Elective Surgery | Cholecystectomy | Inguinal Hernia Repair | Transurethral Resection of Prostate |
| Mastectomy | | | | |
| Model 1 | | | | |
| Chain[b] | − | + | + | − 0.081 (0.002) |
| Proprietary[c] | + | + | 0.172 (0.001) | 0.171 (0.000) |
| Model 2 | | | | |
| Chain | − | + | + | − 0.089 (0.001) |
| Proprietary | + | + | 0.141 (0.004) | + |
| Prochain[d] | − | + | + | 0.157 (0.062) |
| Model 3 | | | | |
| DChain[e] | + | + | 0.116 (0.021) | − 0.430 (0.033) |
| Prochain | − 0.248 (0.099) | − | − | − |
| Proprietary | + | + | 0.116 (0.021) | + |
| Model 4 | | | | |
| DProprietary[f] | + | + | 0.337 (0.035) | + |
| Proprietary | + | + | − | − |
| Chain | − | + | + | − 0.081 (0.002) |

[a]Dependent variable is natural log of ratio of acutal to expected rate. Only coefficients with $p < .10$ are shown ($p$ value in parentheses).

[b]Chain = 1 if chain affiliated in year.

[c]Proprietary = 1 if proprietary in year.

[d]Prochain = 1 if proprietary and chain.

[e]DChain = 1 for all years if ever chain affiliated.

[f]DProprietary = 1 for all years if ever proprietary.

**TABLE B-4**   Statistical Results on Case Mix and JCAH Measures[a]

|  | JCAH Status (1 = 2 Year, 0 Otherwise)[b] | Expected 180-Day Mortality Rate for All Elective Surgeries | 1981 Medicare Case-Mix Index |
|---|---|---|---|
| Model 1 |  |  |  |
| Chain | 0.087 (0.000) | + | + |
| Proprietary | −0.114 (0.000) | −0.001 (0.078) | −0.019 (0.001) |
| Model 2 |  |  |  |
| Chain | 0.066 (0.000) | + | + |
| Proprietary | −0.177 (0.000) | − | −0.024 (0.001) |
| Prochain | 0.170 (0.000) | − | + |
| Model 3 |  |  | NA |
| Proprietary | −0.182 (0.000) | − |  |
| DChain | 0.199 (0.000) | + |  |
| DProchain | + | − |  |
| Model 4 |  |  | NA |
| DProprietary | −0.085 (0.008) | − |  |
| Proprietary | − | − |  |
| Chain | 0.088 (0.000) | + |  |

[a]Coefficients indicate differences for the indicated group expressed in percentage terms: numbers in parentheses are $p$ values.

[b]Models of the Joint Commission on Accreditation of Hospitals (JCAH) used ordinary least-squares estimation.

*For-Profit Enterprise in Health Care.* 1986.
National Academy Press, Washington, D.C.

# Compliance of Multihospital Systems with Standards of the Joint Commission on Accreditation of Hospitals

Daniel R. Longo, Gary A. Chase, Lynn A. Ahlgren,
James S. Roberts, and Carol S. Weisman

## BACKGROUND

A major challenge to the hospital industry is to provide available and accessible high-quality, cost-effective health and medical services. Historically, the individual voluntary hospital has been the focus of the industry's efforts to meet community health care needs. This type of organization has been quite successful in the past in meeting the challenges in an environment of abundant resources, moderate regulation, and cost-based reimbursement.

Today's environment, however, is a very different one. Increasingly constrained resources, more regulation, advances in medical technology, greater diversity of delivery systems, growing public demand and awareness, increased burden of liability protection, and pressure of capital financing have all contributed to creating the current "less supportive" (Longest, 1980) and "hostile" (Dowling, 1983) environment in which the individual hospital is striving to remain viable.

Georgopoulos (1972) described the hospital as being an "adaptive system" in that each hospital is a dynamic, self-regulating system that is in constant interchange with its external environment. The adaptive strategy for many individual hospitals in today's environment is increasingly the formation of interdependent organizational linkages.

According to statistics from the American Hospital Association (AHA), multihospital systems, one of the major forms of hospital linkages, have grown from 10 percent of all hospitals in 1970 to approximately 33 percent of all hospitals today. This increase in interorganizational relationships represents a dramatic change in the structure of the hospital industry. Previous research indicates that the organizational structure of the multihospital system represents a healthy adaptation to environmental pressures (Longo, 1982; Longo and Chase, 1984). Most important, however, is to understand the potential impact of these changes on patient care.

There has been much discussion in the literature of the relative merits of the various types of organizational arrangements developing in health care in response to this new environment. The majority of these commentaries and investigations have focused on the ability of these structures to control the costs of health care; an undeniably important concern. However, in conjunction with the cost issue, it is essential to address the impact of these new structures on the quality of patient care.

The primarily anecdotal literature to date investigating differences in cost and quality between system and autonomous hospitals finds few, if any, differences (Ermann and Gabel, 1984). However, potential advantages of multihospital system arrangements to individual hospitals and their surrounding communities are frequently identified in the literature. The advantages of systems cited in the literature that are thought to directly affect the quality of patient care include the following:

- improved availability and access to care
- more comprehensive scope of services
- improved continuity of care

Dr. Longo is Director of Research at the Joint Commission on Accreditation of Hospitals (JCAH), Chicago, Illinois, and Visiting Scholar, Northwestern University, Evanston, Illinois. Ms. Ahlgren is associate director, JCAH. Dr. Roberts is Vice President for Accreditation, JCAH. Dr. Chase is a professor and Dr. Weisman an associate professor, The Johns Hopkins University, School of Hygiene and Public Health, Baltimore, Maryland.

• greater ability to attract and retain clinical and management manpower

• improved continuing education programs

• greater resources available for quality assurance activities

• greater ability to conduct comparative studies.

The assumption that quality of patient care would be a result of some of these multihospital system attributes has not yet been adequately substantiated by empirical studies. In fact, the question of whether there is any difference between the performance of multihospital systems and autonomous hospitals is identified by Brown (1979) and Kaluzny (1982) as a research issue that still needs to be addressed.

Contributing to the lack of empirical investigations addressing the quality of care in different organizational structures is the difficulty in operationalizing quality. However, empirical investigations have been done which evaluate the impact of specific organizational attributes on health outcomes.

The effects of board composition and structure on hospital efficiency, as measured by cost per patient day and case, and quality, as measured by post-surgical complications rate and medical-surgical death rate, were investigated by Kaufman et al. (1979). Shortell et al. (1976) also used surgical death rate and post-surgical complication rate as indications of quality patient care to evaluate the impact of management practices. Patient satisfaction was the quality index Fleming (1981) used to look at the effects of ownership and teaching status on good patient care.

While these investigations have explored the importance of a variety of organizational attributes to outcomes, studies which investigate differences between multihospital systems and autonomous hospitals have been conducted only to a limited degree.

Ruchlin et al. (1973) compared investor-owned system hospitals with not-for-profit independent (autonomous) hospitals on a number of variables. It is important to note that the differences identified between investor-owned and not-for-profit is confounded by organizational structure. That is, differences identified may be due to the fact that a facility is part of a system versus being an independent (autonomous) hospital rather than due to their type of ownership (investor-owned versus not-for-profit). With this limitation in mind, these two types of facilities were found to be similar with respect to medical staff composition, average length of stay by service, the majority of mortality/morbidity and utilization measures, educational programs, and accreditation status. However, significant differences were found in the gross death rates, admissions from emergency, and some patient treatments.

Not-for-profit independent hospitals had a significantly greater gross death rate than the investor-owned system facilities. The authors speculate that this may be because the not-for-profit independent facilities are admitting patients with more serious medical conditions. Supporting this possibility of case-mix differences are their findings that not-for-profit independent hospitals have a significantly greater tendency to admit patients who were first seen in their emergency rooms. Furthermore, investor-owned system facilities were reported to provide significantly less therapeutic and occupational therapy treatments per inpatient day than the not-for-profit, independent hospitals.

The investigation by Ruchlin et al. (1973) is one of the few extensive empirical studies in the literature that addresses the differences between system and autonomous hospitals. In addition to the confounding variable limitation, however, there are several other limitations of this study for drawing conclusions. The results are based on samples that have been matched on organizational characteristics, such as size, which would restrict the number of differences that may be found. The exclusion of not-for-profit system hospitals and autonomous investor-owned hospitals from this study affects the ability to generalize the study results. The study used 1970 data and, given the dynamic environment of health care delivery, similar results may not be found in the 1980s. In addition, no distinction was made between religious affiliation within the two comparison groups that were used. Indeed, there are a variety of organizational variables that may result in differences in a hospital's provision of quality patient care.

As one example, Sloan and Vraciu (1983)

showed that "ownership (investor-owned versus not-for-profit) is a poor predictor of a hospital's willingness to treat low-income patients, costs to the community, and profitability." However, they compared investor-owned system hospitals and all not-for-profit hospitals only. Therefore, they have the same limitation as Ruchlin et al. (1973) in that it is possible that differences found might be related to whether a facility is part of a system or not, independent of their ownership status. In addition, there may be differences found within the not-for-profit group such as Catholic systems compared to voluntary nonreligious systems.

Because of the variety of multihospital system types, the most accurate assessment of their impact on quality would need to differentiate between the different organizational structures found in systems. The most comprehensive evaluation of quality would include the evaluation of all varying types of structures in order to better determine what feature may be responsible for differences found. The present study investigates differences in quality of care between multihospital systems and autonomous hospitals and includes the evaluation of a variety of organizational characteristics that may be important in the appropriate assignment of factors contributing to differences found.

## RESEARCH QUESTIONS

Compliance with Joint Commission on Accreditation of Hospitals (JCAH) standards indicates that accredited facilities have mechanisms in place that help an organization to provide quality care. The W. K. Kellogg Foundation–funded project, "New Frontiers in Patient Care Assessment," has as one of its objectives to "explore the implications of the growth and development of multihospital systems for JCAH standards and develop appropriate changes in these standards." The assumption implicit in this objective is that because most JCAH standards were developed before the extensive growth of hospital systems, they may not adequately reflect proper system structure and function and, thus, result in an inappropriately high level of noncompliance.

As one attempt to meet this objective, the present study investigates differences between system and autonomous hospitals' compliance with JCAH standards. The broad research questions investigated are

• What differences, if any, exist between autonomous hospitals and hospitals that are members of a multihospital system with respect to compliance with JCAH standards?
• If differences are found, what hospital characteristics are associated with these differences?

## METHODS

The research data set constructed to assess issues of comparative performance between system and autonomous hospitals includes selected JCAH variables and AHA variables from the AHA *Annual Survey of Hospitals*. The latter data were used to measure specific organizational characteristics not included in the JCAH data set. The JCAH hospital survey records selected for inclusion in this data set were all hospitals surveyed between June 1, 1982, and May 31, 1983. The JCAH data set contains variables collected at the time of an accreditation survey. This combined data set has been chosen for analysis because it represents the most recent complete year of data during which the process of data collection was nearly uniform.

The total number of hospitals surveyed by the JCAH's Hospital Accreditation Program during this time period is 1,657. Of these 1,657 facilities, 1,202 were autonomous and 455 were system hospitals.

An initial comparison was made of accreditation outcome measures (accredited without contingency, accredited with contingency, and nonaccredited). Next, an analysis was conducted of specific standard areas (or standard Survey Report Form [SRF] items) which contributed to determining accreditation outcome.

To facilitate the analysis of compliance with these numerous survey items, a standards compliance severity scale was used (see Table 1). On this scale, degrees of compliance with standards for each variable are ranked in ascending order from 1 (full compliance) to 5

**TABLE 1**  Standards Compliance
Severity Scale

| Rank Order | Code |
|---|---|
| Compliant | 1 |
| Recommendation[a] | 2 |
| Recommendation of significance | 3 |
| Recommendation with special warning | 4 |
| Recommendation with contingency | 5 |

[a]This category excludes recommendations with contingencies, with special warnings, and of significance.

(sufficient degree of noncompliance to warrant a contingency), thus permitting ready identification of the severity of each recommendation. A contingency is defined as a recommendation of serious enough merit that failure to comply within a specific time period may cause nonaccreditation.

The first step of SRF item analysis was to determine the percentages of total hospitals receiving each score (1-5) on each item. As a result of this procedure, it was possible to obtain a ranking of items that have the greatest number of hospitals receiving recommendations (2-4) and a second ranking of items that have the greatest number of hospitals receiving contingencies—in other words, the standard areas with which hospitals have the most difficulty in compliance. This ranking was identified for system and autonomous hospitals separately so that differences in their 25 top problem areas could be investigated. These top problem SRF items for both recommendations and contingencies were then grouped into their standard chapters. SRF items are grouped into sections that relate directly to chapters in the *Accreditation Manual for Hospitals*.

In order to identify those items likely to discriminate between system and autonomous hospitals, the second step of the SRF item analysis was conducted. Thus, items were identified in which 10 percent or more of the hospitals surveyed were in less than full compliance. (Items with greater variance in the scores would be more likely to differentiate between types of hospitals.)

A ranking of sections by the number of items within each section that had 10 percent or more

of the hospitals surveyed receiving less than full compliance and/or missing values, divided by the total number of items in that section, was calculated similarly to the methods used in previous analyses of JCAH standards (Longo et al., 1983).

## SYSTEM/AUTONOMOUS DIFFERENCES

Cross-tabulations and chi-square tests of significant associations were calculated comparing system and autonomous hospitals for each item that passed the variance screen, that is, those items in which 10 percent or more of the hospitals had less than full compliance. The 1-5 severity scores were first collapsed into three categories: compliance (1), recommendations (2, 3, 4), and contingencies (5) in order to eliminate cells with too few entries to allow for valid statistical test results. A second set of cross-tabulations and chi-square tests were calculated for items in which the severity scores were collapsed into two categories: compliance (1) versus all other recommendations and contingencies (2-5). The two categories were used to further eliminate the problem of small cells.

Items were identified in which a significant association was found between the item score and the type of hospital (system or autonomous). By grouping the items into the SRF sections, rankings were obtained of the SRF sections by the percent of total possible items that were significant. This percentage was calculated by dividing the number of items significant at the $p < .05$ level by the total number of items in each section. For those items found to be significant, the specific hospital type having better compliance with JCAH standards was identified.

The methods discussed above provide a description of differences between system and autonomous hospitals. However, while these differences do reflect the status of facilities surveyed by the JCAH, they do not control for potential confounding variables. It is possible that the differences identified between system and autonomous hospitals may, in fact, be due to other characteristics associated with these organizational structures, rather than a direct result of the organizational structures themselves.

To investigate these associations, bivariate analyses were conducted comparing organizational variables from the AHA *Annual Survey of Hospitals* with hospital type (see Appendix). Because of the high percentage of investor-owned hospitals that are members of systems, accreditation outcomes were compared among four groups: system/investor-owned, system/not-for-profit, autonomous/investor-owned, and autonomous/not-for-profit.

Similar to the two-way comparisons between system and autonomous hospitals, the differences in compliance performance among these four groups may be influenced by confounding variables and, therefore, represent only a preliminary description of these differences. Controlling for possible confounding variables in multivariate analyses may affect the differences identified through these methods. As a result, regression analyses were conducted to determine which organizational variables were the best predictors of accreditation outcome.

## RESULTS

This section of the paper describes the results of the analytic process outlined above. The findings are divided into two sections: (1) compliance with JCAH standards and (2) accreditation decisions.

### Compliance with JCAH Standards

In a typical hospital, JCAH asks approximately 2,400 questions, each designed to judge compliance with specific JCAH standards. In developing data sets across a 2-year period, 2,045 questions remained. The difference re-

flects changes in the survey report form from 1982 to 1983. In the analysis of the 1,657 hospitals in this study, there were 942 questions for which more than 10 percent of these hospitals were not in full compliance. When one analyzes these questions for differences in compliance between system and autonomous hospitals, only 34 items show significant variation. These data are summarized in Table 2. These findings indicate that there are very few differences found between system and autonomous hospitals in meeting JCAH standards. However, when these few differences are found, in virtually all cases the system hospitals were found more in compliance with JCAH standards.

### Top 25 Contingency Items

The results show that for system hospitals, the percent that received contingencies for one or more of these items ranged from 8.6 percent to 26.8 percent. For autonomous hospitals, the percent that received contingencies for these items ranged from 11.5 percent to 29.6 percent.

The vast majority of the top 25 items resulting in contingencies, 23 out of 25 (92 percent), were the same for both system and autonomous hospitals, although not necessarily in the same rank order. The two SRF items resulting in the highest level of contingencies were the same for both types of hospitals:

1. Do the minutes of the monthly medical staff or department/major clinical service meetings document the recommendations, conclusions, and action instituted, resulting from the review of the care and treatment of patients served by the hospitals?

**TABLE 2**  Items with Variation Between Autonomous Hospitals and Hospitals in Multihospital Systems

| Data Set | Number | Percent |
|---|---|---|
| Total questions asked | 2,045 | 100.0 |
| Questions with possible variance | 942 | 46.0 (942/2,045) |
| Significant differences between system/autonomous | 34 | 3.6 (34/942) |
| System more compliant | 33 | 97.0 (33/34) |
| Autonomous more compliant | 1 | 3.0 (1/33) |

**TABLE 3** Comparisons of Accreditation Decisions by Hospital Type (percentage)

| Type of Hospital | Accredited Without Contingencies | Accredited with Contingencies | Not Accredited |
|---|---|---|---|
| System | 44.8 | 54.3 | 0.9 |
| Autonomous | 36.9 | 61.9 | 1.2 |

2. Is the ongoing review of antibiotic use documented?

For the first item, 26.7 percent of the system hospitals received contingencies; 29.6 percent of the autonomous hospitals received contingencies. For the documentation of antibiotic review, 24.2 percent of system hospitals received contingencies; 24.4 percent of the autonomous hospitals received contingencies.

The next two items resulting in contingencies in the top 25 were also the same for both system and autonomous hospitals, although not in the same order:

1. Has there been action taken on the findings of the antibiotic use reviews made?
2. Is a regular (quarterly) review and evaluation of the quality, safety, and appropriateness of care performed and documented for each special care unit?

Actions taken on antibiotic review findings ranked third for system hospitals, and 21.3 percent received contingencies. This item was ranked fourth for autonomous hospitals, and 21.4 percent received contingencies.

Review and evaluation of special care units ranked fourth for system hospitals, and 16.9 percent received contingencies. This item was ranked third for autonomous hospitals, and 23.2 percent received contingencies. The results indicate that when hospitals experience difficulty in complying with JCAH standards, as measured by the receipt of a contingency, system and autonomous hospitals are very similar.

When the top 25 SRF items that result in contingencies were compared between system and autonomous hospitals, only 8 percent (2/25) of the items differed. The two items that were in the top 25 *contingencies for system hospitals* but not autonomous hospitals were—

1. Is there evidence of medical staff participation in medical record review relative to clinical pertinence?
2. Is there evidence of medical staff participation in medical record review relative to the record's completeness and adequacy as a medico-legal document?

The two items that were in the top 25 *contingencies for autonomous hospitals* but not system hospitals were—

1. Is there evidence that drug utilization and effectiveness in the hospital are reviewed?
2. Is a regular review and evaluation of the quality, safety, and appropriateness of care provided by the renal unit performed and documented?

**Accreditation Decisions**

When final accreditation decisions were compared, the majority of both system and autonomous hospitals were found to be accredited *with* contingencies (54 percent and 62 percent, respectively). However, system hospitals were found to be accredited *without* contingencies significantly more frequently than autonomous hospitals ($p = .013$), as shown in Table 3.

Looking at these data in more detail, we grouped hospitals into four categories and analyzed the accreditation outcomes for each, as shown in Table 4.

These results indicate that autonomous, not-for-profit hospitals tend, as far as contingencies are concerned, to have greater difficulty in complying with JCAH standards, whereas autonomous investor-owned tend to have a higher level of nonaccreditation. However, it is important to note that there was not a statistically significant association found between hospital type and accreditation outcome.

**Multivariate Analyses**

In the preceding analyses, all relevant factors (independent variables) were identified and explored as to their impact or contribution to accreditation outcome. In addition, step-

TABLE 4 Analysis of Accreditation Outcome

| Hospital Type | Accreditation Outcome | | |
| --- | --- | --- | --- |
| | Accredited Without Contingencies | Accredited with Contingencies | Not Accredited |
| System/investor-owned | 48.1 | 51.3 | 0.6 |
| System/not-for-profit | 43.2 | 55.8 | 1.0 |
| Autonomous/investor-owned | 46.4 | 51.8 | 1.8 |
| Autonomous/not-for-profit | 36.5 | 62.4 | 1.1 |

wise linear multiple regression was run to disentangle the confounding effects of the independent variables on the dependent variable. For example, when all variables are taken together, what variables best predict accreditation outcome? In addition, it is important to determine the strength of the relationship of the predictors; this is accomplished by a review of the "beta coefficients" that represent the correlation or strength of the association found through the use of the multiple regression. The independent variables that were entered into the regression based on the descriptive analyses are listed with their definitions in the Appendix.

Table 5 lists those variables that multivariate analysis indicate are the better predictors of accreditation. The variables are listed in descending order by the absolute value of the size of the "beta coefficient"; that is, the strength of the association measured after all variables are taken into consideration. The sign of the coefficient (positive or negative) indicates the direction of the relationship. Accreditation outcome is the dependent variable in the equation.

The results indicate that the best predictors of accreditation outcome are related to population size (as indicated by the SMSA [standard metropolitan statistical area] categories), region of the country (East Central, West Central, West South Central, and Mountain), community hospital status, multihospital system status, and bed size. However, the direction of the coefficient must be taken into account. Thus, hospitals are more likely to be accredited *without* contingencies that are located in areas with a population size of between 100,000 to 2,500,000 (indicated by the

positive coefficient of SMSA categories 4, 5, 3, and 2), a member of a multihospital system, *not* located in the West Central, East Central, West South Central, and Mountain regions (indicated by the negative coefficients), smaller bed size, and noncommunity hospitals. Notably, neither for-profit nor not-for-profit status is a good predictor of accreditation outcome. In fact, the $f$ value of the profit variable was not significant in any step of the multiple regression. Because profit status is somewhat correlated with the multihospital variable (0.392), profit status may directly influence accreditation outcome, but does not add any additional predictive value to the equation after the multihospital variable is included.

Also of note is that there are other variables that may predict accreditation outcome that

TABLE 5 Variables that Remain in Regression Equation

| Variable | Beta Coefficient |
| --- | --- |
| SMSA 4 (500,000–1,000,000)[a] | +0.09222 |
| SMSA 5 (1 million–2.5 million) | +0.09082 |
| West Central region | −0.08198 |
| East Central region | −0.07952 |
| West South Central region | −0.07403 |
| SMSA 3 (250,000–500,000) | +0.06435 |
| Mountain region | −0.06415 |
| SMSA 2 (100,000–250,000) | +0.05848 |
| Community hospital | −0.05808 |
| Multihospital system | +0.05617 |
| Large bed size | −0.05562 |

[a]Standard metropolitan statistical area (SMSA) category.

were not examined in this analysis. Furthermore, the SMSA and regional variables may be viewed as "dummy" variables that capture a wide variety of "environmental" characteristics such as hospital location, level of competition, numbers of patients, and the presence of resources that may possibly contribute to the ability of hospitals to comply with standards. For example, it may be possible that the negative coefficient for the East North Central region may actually measure the presence of older hospitals. However, the present analysis is unable to assess the specific characteristic of region or population size that influences the variables' ability to serve as a predictor of accreditation outcome. Future analyses should explore the impact of more specific characteristics upon accreditation outcome.

In summary, it is important to emphasize that the numerous characteristics' impact on a hospital's ability to comply with JCAH standards and that any of the results taken in isolation would not accurately represent the complicated profile of a hospital accredited without contingencies. Multivariate analyses assist in controlling for confounding variables, but may mask the possible direct influences of correlates of the variables that are included in the equation as the best predictors.

### LIMITATIONS

Limitations of this study include the exclusive use of available national data from the JCAH and AHA that measure structure and process. Therefore, outcome measures such as morbidity/mortality and patient satisfaction are not taken into account.

There are also limitations of the data set used, in particular the deletion of SRF items as the result of changes in JCAH standards during the study period. Thus, the impact of standards deleted or implemented during the study period cannot be determined.

In addition, it is not known whether systems acquire hospitals that were previously better or worse in complying with JCAH standards. Thus, additional research should use a longitudinal approach in investigating the impact of pre-acquisition accreditation history upon subsequent facility compliance as part of a system.

### SUMMARY AND CONCLUSIONS

Previous investigations have found that the organizational structure of a hospital may impact on performance. The present study examined differences in compliance with JCAH standards between the two predominant organizational structures—system and autonomous hospitals. A multistep approach was taken to investigate the two research questions outlined. These steps included descriptive statistics, including frequencies and percentages, the use of bivariate chi-square statistics, multiple comparison groups, and multiple regression.

The present study resulted in several findings concerning compliance and accreditation.

#### Compliance with Individual Standards

There was a remarkably similar level of compliance between system and autonomous hospitals. This is indicated by the following:

● Of the 2,045 items asked, there were only 46 percent (942) for which 10 percent or more of the hospitals showed important levels of noncompliance. Of the 942 items, only 3.6 percent (34) showed differences between system and autonomous hospitals and in 97 percent (33) of these, system hospitals showed significantly higher levels of compliance than autonomous hospitals.

● When the top 25 SRF items which resulted in contingencies were compared between system and autonomous hospitals, only 8 percent (2) of the items differed.

#### Accreditation Decisions

When final accreditation decisions were compared, the majority of both system and autonomous hospitals were found to be accredited *with* contingencies (54 percent and 62 percent, respectively). However, system hospitals were found to be accredited *without* contingencies significantly more frequently than autonomous hospitals (44.8 percent and 36.9 percent, respectively; $p = .013$).

The set of predictors of accreditation outcome are population size, region, community hospital status, multihospital system status, and bed size. Thus, hospitals accredited *without* contingencies are more likely to be located in areas where the population is between 100,000 and 2,500,000 people, located in a region other than the East Central, West Central, West South Central, and Mountain, not a community hospital, a member of a multihospital system, and of smaller bed size.

Finally, these findings do not support the suspicion that JCAH standards may possibly discriminate against hospitals that are part of multihospital systems.

## ACKNOWLEDGMENTS

Funded in part by a grant from the W. K. Kellogg Foundation, Battle Creek, Michigan. The authors wish to acknowledge the computer support of Teri Grey and Laura Merrigan and the secretarial support of Betty Johnson.

## REFERENCES

Brown, Montague (1979) Systems development: Trends, issues and implications. *Health Care Management Review* 4 Winter:1.

Dowling, William J. (1983) Multihospital systems face growth, constraints, unexploited options. *Hospital Progress* (April):48-53.

Ermann, Dan, and Jon Gabel (1984) Multihospital systems: Issues and empirical findings. *Health Affairs* 3(1):51-64

Fleming, G. V. (1981) Hospital structure and consumer satisfaction. *Health Services Research* 16(1):43-63.

Georgopoulos, Basil S. (1972) The hospital as an organization and problem solving system. In Georgopoulos, Basil S. (ed.), *Organizational Research on Health Institutions*. Ann Arbor: Institute for Social Research, University of Michigan.

Kaluzny, Arnold D. (1982) Present and future research on multihospital systems. *Health Services Research* 17(4):331-336.

Kaufman, Kenneth, Stephen Shortell, Selwyn Becker, and Duncan Neuhauser (1979) The effects of board composition and structure on hospital performance. *Hospital and Health Services Administration.* 24(1):37-62.

Longest, Jr., B. B. (1980) A conceptual framework for understanding the multihospital arrangement strategy. *Health Care Management Review* 4(Winter):17-23.

Longo, Daniel R. (1982) *A Case-Control Study of the Structural Determinants of Hospital Closure.* Baltimore: The Johns Hopkins University. Doctoral dissertation.

Longo, Daniel R., and Gary A. Chase (1984) Structural determinants of hospital closure. *Medical Care* (May):338-402.

Longo, Daniel R., Donald E. Widmann, and Peter Van Schoonhoven (1983) JCAH forum: Compliance with JCAH standards: National findings from 1982 surveys. *Quality Review Bulletin* 10(3):81-86.

Ruchlin, Hirsch S., Dennis D. Pointer, and Lloyd L. Cannedy (1973) A comparison of for-profit investor-owned chain and non-profit hospitals. *Inquiry* 10(December):13-23.

Becker, S. W., and D. Neuhauser (1976) The effects of management practices on hospital efficiency and quality of care. Pp. 90–107 in Shortell, S., and M. Brown (eds.), *Organizational Research in Hospitals*. Chicago: Blue Cross Association.

Sloan, Frank A., and Robert A. Vraciu (1983) Investor-owned and not-for-profit hospitals: Addressing some issues. *Health Affairs* 2(Spring):25-37.

## APPENDIX

## Variables Entered into the Regression

| *Variable* | *Definition* |
|---|---|
| Average length of stay | Average stay of inpatients during the reporting period. |
| Community hospital | All nonfederal short-term general and other special hospitals, excluding hospital units of institutions whose facilities and services are available to the public. This includes a variety of facilities including university hospitals (N = 5,900). |
| Multihospital system | An acute care facility owned or leased by a system, including acute care facilities operated by the Veterans Administration. |
| Investor ownership | A facility that is for-profit and operated by an individual, partnership, or corporation. |
| Region of the country | The nine U.S. Census regions. |
| Standard metropolitan statistical area | The seven categories designed by population size arranged in ascending order of population. |
| Occupancy | Ratio of average daily census to the average number of beds, that is, statistical beds, maintained during the reporting period. |
| Bed size | Number of beds set up and staffed for use in hospitals. |
| Number of registered nurses | The number of full-time registered nurses on the hospital payroll. |
| Percent Medicaid patients | The number of Medicaid patients divided by the total number of patients times 100. |
| Percent Medicare patients | The number of Medicare patients divided by the total number of patients times 100. |
| Control | The types of organization responsible for establishing policy concerning the overall operation of hospitals. The four major categories are government, nonfederal; nongovernment, not-for-profit; investor-owned (for-profit); and government, federal. |

For-Profit Enterprise in Health Care. 1986.
National Academy Press, Washington, D.C.

# Hospital Ownership and the Practice of Medicine: Evidence from the Physician's Perspective

Robert A. Musacchio, Stephen Zuckerman,
Lynn E. Jensen, and Larry Freshnock

The last two decades have witnessed significant changes in the structure of the hospital industry. While the total number of investor-owned hospitals has remained reasonably stable since the late 1960s, there has been significant growth in the number of investor-owned hospitals that are a part of multihospital systems. These hospitals have grown at an average annual rate of 10.3 percent between 1972 and 1983. Further, the concentration of the proprietary sector is quite high: the five largest chains control over 60 percent of all general acute care hospitals in the sector.

Concern over the implications of an emerging "medical-industrial complex" has raised a number of questions and sparked considerable debate (Relman, 1980, 1983). Issues pertaining to ethical provider behavior, quality of care, and the comparative economic performance of proprietary and not-for-profit hospitals have recently emerged (Lewin et al., 1981; Pattison and Katz, 1983; Sloan and Vraciu, 1983; and Sloan and Becker, 1985). Ermann and Gabel (1984) have recently published a comprehensive assessment of the issues and empirical findings on the subject of multihospital systems. Their review found, among other things, that there are no discernible differences between systems and independent hospitals in terms of access, service availability, and quality of care.

Thus far, all studies comparing the performance of systems versus independent hospitals and for-profit and not-for-profit hospitals

have focused on the hospital as the unit of analysis. Given the physicians' role as the central decision maker in the provision of health care services, additional insight can, however, be gained from analyzing physician involvement with for-profit hospitals from the physicians' perspective. Until recently the data necessary for such an analysis were unavailable. Data collected through the American Medical Association's (AMA's) Socioeconomic Monitoring System (SMS) and attitudinal research program allow us to examine these issues.

This paper describes the data sets used in the analysis, reviews differences in physician characteristics and practice patterns across hospital types, considers the variation in physicians' financial arrangements with hospitals, and examines physicians' attitudes toward for-profit hospitals. Finally, it summarizes our findings and suggests some areas for future research.

## DATA

Data are drawn from three sources: (1) the 1984 SMS Core Survey; (2) the 1984 AMA Physician Opinion Survey; and (3) the American Hospital Association's (AHA's) 1982 AHA Annual Survey of Hospitals. SMS is a quarterly telephone survey program that collects information from a random sample of nonfederal patient care physicians stratified by specialty and census division. Data collected include information on physician incomes, practice expenses, visits, hours worked, and fees, among other socioeconomic indicators. The core survey is conducted during the second quarter of each year and uses a sample approximately three times as large as those used in other quarters.

In 1984, 4,002 physicians were interviewed

Dr. Musacchio is Director, Department of Health Systems Analysis, Center for Health Policy Research; Dr. Zuckerman is Research Associate, Health Policy Center, The Urban Institute, Washington, D.C.; Dr. Jensen is Vice President, Health Services Policy Group; and Dr. Freshnock is Vice President, Lance V. Tarrance and Associates, Chicago, Illinois.

during the core survey. This survey included a supplemental series of questions on physicians' involvement with hospitals. These questions were developed in collaboration with staff of the Institute of Medicine for the purpose of analyzing differences among physicians in for-profit and not-for-profit facilities. Specific areas covered include the number of hospital privileges each physician has, the physician's financial arrangement with his/her primary hospital, the physician's evaluation of certain aspects of this hospital, and physician ownership interest in their primary hospital. This type of information is useful to determine the overall extent of physician involvement with for-profit enterprises and multihospital systems.

In addition, SMS also collected information on the physician's primary hospital so that hospital data from the 1982 AHA Annual Survey, the most recent one available at the time the research was conducted, could be merged with the SMS file. Merging data from both sources provided us with higher quality information on hospital ownership, organizational structure, utilization, and hospital capacity than would have been available from the physician. While we are aware that some hospitals may have been acquired by for-profit organizations between the time of the AHA survey and the SMS survey, we feel the procedures we followed gave us the best possible physician/hospital data set we could create. Details on the AHA Annual Survey of Hospitals may be found in Mullner et al. (1983).

For each SMS physician, the unit of analysis in our study, the hospital about which we are collecting information is the one at which the physician provides the most patient care services. Since the SMS sample is limited to nonfederal physicians, only two federal hospitals were picked up. As a result, the federal hospital classification has been excluded from our analysis. In addition, long-term hospitals have been excluded for reasons of homogeneity.

Findings from the 1984 Physician Opinion Survey are based on telephone interviews with 1,000 randomly selected physicians residing in the United States. The interviews were conducted during July 1984. The information presented here is part of a major attitudinal data base which is summarized in *Physician and*

*Public Attitudes on Health Care Issues*, available from the AMA upon request.

Table 1 compares AHA data to SMS data with regard to selected hospital characteristics. Several differences exist. Specifically, SMS appears to be picking up fewer nongovernment for-profit hospitals than the AHA survey. Despite the fact that almost 15 percent of all hospitals are categorized as for-profit, only 8.4 percent of the SMS physicians have their primary privileges at a hospital of this type. Furthermore, hospitals identified through SMS have higher annual admission rates and larger average bed sizes than the hospital population in general. We believe that these differences exist for two primary reasons. First, a large urban/rural difference exists between the two data sets. About 81 percent of the physicians in the SMS data set work primarily in hospitals in urban areas. In comparison, AHA data indicate that only 55 percent of the hospitals are located in these areas. Second, and probably more important, is that physicians' primary hospitals—the hospitals at which they provide the most patient care services—are not representative of hospitals in general. Due to the urban/rural differences and the characteristics of the physicians' primary hospital, the hospitals identified in this analysis do not mirror those in the AHA annual survey.

## PHYSICIAN CHARACTERISTICS AND PRACTICE PATTERNS

An analysis of physician involvement with for-profit hospitals should start by asking the question: Do physicians who have their primary privileges at for-profit hospitals differ from other physicians in any systematic way?

In addition, it will be useful to consider if physicians' practice patterns vary according to the type of hospital the physician works in. Given this focus, our analysis is limited to those physicians with admitting or medical staff privileges at some hospitals. Over 95 percent of physicians in the SMS sample had hospital privileges.

Table 2 shows the specialty distribution of physicians by hospital type. A chi-square test causes us to reject at the 99 percent confidence level the null hypothesis that physicians' specialty and hospital type are independent. Pri-

**TABLE 1** Comparison of Hospitals in American Health Association (AHA) Annual Survey to Those Represented by Physicians in SMS Sample

| Variable | Hospitals Represented in the AHA[a] Annual Survey | Hospitals Represented by Physicians in the SMS[b] Sample |
|---|---|---|
| Hospital type (%) | | |
|     Government nonfederal | 29.8 | 16.2 |
|     Nongovernment not-for-profit | 55.5 | 75.4 |
|     Nongovernment for-profit | 14.7 | 8.4 |
| Organizational structure (%) | | |
|     Multihospital system | 30.0 | 34.3 |
|     Independent hospital | 70.0 | 65.7 |
| Region (%) | | |
|     Northeast | 14.8 | 22.3 |
|     North Central | 28.7 | 23.0 |
|     South | 37.5 | 33.5 |
|     West | 18.9 | 21.2 |
| Location (%) | | |
|     Urban | 53.9 | 80.5 |
|     Rural | 46.1 | 19.5 |
| Hospital size | | |
|     Average bed size | 168.8 | 364.0 |
|     Admissions per year | 5,955 | 13,563 |

[a]American Hospital Association (AHA).

[b]Socioeconomic Monitoring System (SMS) of the American Medical Association (AMA).

SOURCE: 1982 AHA Annual Survey of Hospitals and 1984 AMA Socioeconomic Monitoring System Core Survey.

vate not-for-profit hospitals are staffed by a more specialized group of physicians than other hospitals. Nearly one out of every four physicians whose primary privileges are at a government or for-profit hospital is a general or family practitioner (GP/FP). On the other hand, only one out of eight physicians primarily affiliated with private not-for-profit hospitals is GP/FP. In addition, we find that physicians whose primary hospital is not-for-profit are twice as likely to be in some internal medicine subspecialty as physicians at for-profit hospitals; 18.5 percent as compared to 9.2 percent. To the extent that specialists treat different types of patients than GP/FPs, these specialty-mix differences may be indicative of variation in hospital case mix.

In addition to the growth in for-profit hospitals, the expansion of multihospital systems (MHS) represents a major change taking place in the hospital industry. Table 3 indicates that 34.3 percent of physicians have privileges at a hospital that is part of an MHS. There is a significant relationship between being part of an MHS and the ownership status of the physician's hospital. Only 17 percent of physicians primarily affiliated with government hospitals are in an MHS. The MHS structure is most prominent among for-profit hospitals. Seventy-five percent of the physicians with privileges at these hospitals claim MHS affiliation.

To explore further differences among physicians in for-profit hospitals and those in other facilities, data on selected physician characteristics are presented in Table 4. There are no statistically significant differences among physicians on the basis of experience (years since residency) across the hospital types shown. However, significant differences exist with regard to location of the medical school, em-

**TABLE 2**  Specialty Distribution of Physicians by Hospital Types (percentage)

| Specialty | Hospital Type | | |
| --- | --- | --- | --- |
| | Nonfederal Government | Private Not-for-profit | For-profit |
| General/family practice | 23.3 | 12.9 | 22.2 |
| Internal medicine | 12.7 | 18.5 | 9.2 |
| Surgery | 20.0 | 22.1 | 24.9 |
| Pediatrics | 7.2 | 8.4 | 5.5 |
| Obstetrics/gynecology | 7.6 | 7.8 | 8.5 |
| Radiology | 8.1 | 6.6 | 7.5 |
| Psychiatry | 4.1 | 6.6 | 5.5 |
| Anesthesiology | 4.6 | 5.8 | 6.5 |
| Pathology | 4.8 | 3.5 | 2.4 |
| Other specialties | 7.6 | 7.8 | 7.9 |

NOTE: Chi-square (18 d.f.) = 80.23, which is significant at the 99 percent level of confidence.

SOURCE: 1984 AMA Socioeconomic Monitoring System Core Survey.

ployment status, and type of practice. Foreign medical school graduates (FMGs) represent a greater proportion of physicians primarily affiliated with independent for-profit hospitals (31.5 percent) than they do at any other type of facility. For-profit hospitals that are part of an MHS do not have medical staffs that are as heavily dependent on FMGs. Only 20 percent of these physicians received their medical training abroad. This is quite comparable to physicians whose primary privileges are at independent not-for-profits (19.5 percent), independent government hospitals (18.7 percent), and MHS not-for-profits (17.7 percent).

The data also show that physicians who are full or part owners of their main practice—self-employed physicians—account for 88.2 percent of physicians primarily affiliated with MHS for-profit hospitals. This is a higher proportion than we found among physicians at any other types of hospitals. Other types of hospitals with above-average shares of self-employed physicians are MHS not-for-profits (81.3 percent) and independent for-profits (80.8 percent). Employee physicians, on the other hand, are most prevalent among government hospital staffs, making up 32.3 percent of the MHS group and 26.2 percent of the independent hospital group. These results suggest that for-profit hospitals have not attempted to influ-

**TABLE 3**  Distribution of Physicians Between Multihospital Systems and Independent Hospitals by Hospital Ownership Status

| Type | All Hospitals | Nonfederal Government | Private Not-for-profit | For-profit |
| --- | --- | --- | --- | --- |
| Multihospital system (%) | 34.3 | 17.0 | 33.5 | 75.1 |
| Independent hospital (%) | 65.7 | 83.0 | 66.5 | 24.9 |

NOTE: Chi-square (2 d.f.) = 292.3, which is significant at the 99 percent level of confidence.

SOURCE: 1984 AMA Socioeconomic Monitoring System Core Survey.

**TABLE 4**   Selected Physician Characteristics by Hospital Ownership Status (percentage of physicians)

| Variable | Multihospital System | | | Independent | | |
|---|---|---|---|---|---|---|
| | Nonfederal Government | Private Not-for profit | For-profit | Nonfederal Government | Private Not-for profit | For-profit |
| Years since residency | | | | | | |
| 0–5 years | 20.8 | 17.8 | 18.7 | 18.4 | 17.0 | 15.1 |
| 5–10 years | 22.9 | 19.1 | 19.6 | 19.2 | 20.7 | 13.7 |
| 10–20 years | 24.0 | 24.7 | 30.1 | 27.8 | 27.1 | 30.1 |
| 20–30 years | 17.7 | 20.7 | 20.1 | 20.9 | 18.3 | 19.2 |
| 30 or more years | 14.6 | 17.7 | 11.4 | 13.7 | 17.0 | 21.9 |
| Chi-square (20 d.f.) = 18.5 | | | | | | |
| Location of medical school | | | | | | |
| U.S. or Canada | 76.0 | 82.3 | 80.0 | 81.3 | 80.5 | 68.5 |
| Other foreign country | 24.0 | 17.7 | 20.0 | 18.7 | 19.5 | 31.5 |
| Chi-square (5 d.f.) = 9.9* | | | | | | |
| Board certification | | | | | | |
| No | 31.3 | 31.4 | 38.6 | 36.2 | 31.3 | 37.0 |
| Yes | 68.7 | 68.6 | 61.4 | 63.8 | 68.7 | 63.0 |
| Chi-square (5 d.f.) = 9.0 | | | | | | |
| Employment status in main medical practice | | | | | | |
| Employee | 32.3 | 18.7 | 11.8 | 26.2 | 22.1 | 19.2 |
| Self-employed | 67.7 | 81.3 | 88.2 | 73.8 | 77.9 | 80.8 |
| Chi-square (5 d.f.) = 29.7*** | | | | | | |
| Type of practice | | | | | | |
| Solo | 52.7 | 46.3 | 57.4 | 50.1 | 51.4 | 58.8 |
| Non-solo | 47.3 | 53.7 | 42.6 | 49.9 | 48.6 | 41.2 |
| Chi-square (5 d.f.) = 12.4** | | | | | | |

*Significant at the 90 percent level of confidence.
**Significant at the 95 percent level of confidence.
***Significant at the 99 percent level of confidence.

SOURCE: 1984 AMA Socioeconomic Monitoring System Core Survey.

ence physician practice patterns by placing the physician in an employee's role. Other financial mechanisms that could alter practice patterns are available to hospitals. Some of these will be discussed in the following section of this paper.

For-profit medical staffs also have a significantly higher proportion of solo practitioners than government or not-for-profit hospitals. The implications of this finding are not clear unless one can argue that practice patterns of group physicians are somehow more in tune with the objectives of not-for-profit hospitals than they are with other hospitals' objectives. We would

not be willing to make that argument here. If, however, the division of physicians between hospitals becomes increasingly a function of practice type, this area should be explored further. At present we do not see this as a major issue.

While we found that for-profit MHS medical staffs have the lowest extent of board-certified physicians, this result was not statistically significant. However, since some view board certification as an indicator of the quality of care delivered at a hospital, we explored this issue further (Table 5). We were particularly concerned that the significant specialty composition differences might be confounding our analysis of board certification, i.e., there might be significant differences in board certification for certain specialties but not for others. In examining board certification by specialty and hospital ownership status, we found statistically significant variations. In particular, we found that surgeons at for-profit MHS hospitals were the least likely group of surgeons to be certified. Since the extent of board certification clearly varies by specialty, general conclusions about the relationship between board certification and hospital type cannot be drawn.

Aspects of the relationships that exist between physicians and hospitals may also vary by hospital type. Data on hospital tenure, percent of time spent at the primary hospital, the total number of hospital privileges, and the percentage of physicians having solo admitting privileges are displayed in Table 6 as a means for studying these relationships. The data indicate that physicians with a primary for-profit affiliation have been working at this hospital for fewer years than physicians at both not-for-profit and government hospitals. We find this result particularly interesting in light of the similarity in physicians' years since residency across hospital types (see Table 4). The lower tenure suggests that the shift in physicians' hospital practices to the for-profit sector is a relatively recent phenomenon. This result

underscores—from the physicians' perspective—that the expansion of the for-profit hospital sector is fairly recent. If we analyze the data by system and nonsystem status we observe that the only real difference exists between the multifacility for-profit hospital and its independent counterpart. Physicians at a for-profit multifacility hospital have been affiliated with their hospital the fewest number of years (8.4).

Furthermore, physicians at for-profit hospitals have a greater number of hospital privileges than their not-for-profit counterparts. The greater number of privileges may be necessitated by the lower average bed size of for-profit hospitals. Although for-profit facilities have fewer beds on average, physicians at these for-profit facilities spend about the same number of hours at their primary facility as physicians at nonprofit hospitals. An alternative way to analyze physician hospital affiliations is to examine the percent of physicians with privileges at only one hospital. Overall, approximately 37 percent of the physicians surveyed indicate that they have solitary admitting privileges. Physicians primarily affiliated with an independent for-profit hospital are least likely to have privileges at only one hospital. At the other extreme, physicians at independent nonfederal government hospitals are the most likely to have single admitting privileges.

As noted, there has been considerable in-

TABLE 5   Percent of Physicians That Are Board Certified by Hospital Ownership Status and Selected Specialty Breakdowns

|  | Multihospital System | | | Independent | | |
|---|---|---|---|---|---|---|
|  | Nonfederal Government | Private Not-for-profit | For-profit | Nonfederal Government | Private Not-for-Profit | For-profit |
| All physicians | 68.7 | 68.6 | 61.4 | 63.8 | 68.7 | 63.0 |
| General/family specialty | [b] | 43.4 | 40.8 | 53.9 | 43.1 | [b] |
| Medical specialty | [b] | 67.3 | [b] | 65.0 | 70.3 | [b] |
| Surgical specialty | 76.5 | 79.3 | 66.7 | 73.8 | 76.4 | 85.0 |
| Other[a] | 75.9 | 70.1 | 67.2 | 63.2 | 70.0 | 73.9 |

NOTE: The variation in board certification by specialty and hospital status was found to be statistically significant using a chi-square test.

[a]Includes psychiatrists, radiologists, anesthesiologists, and pathologists.
[b]Insufficient number of observations to provide reliable estimates.

**TABLE 6** Dimensions of the Physician/Hospital Relationship by Type of Hospital

| | All Hospitals | Multihospital System | | | Independent | | |
|---|---|---|---|---|---|---|---|
| | | Nonfederal Government | Private Not-for-profit | For-profit | Nonfederal Government | Private Not-for-profit | For-profit |
| Number of years affiliated with primary hospital F test (5 d.f.) = 10.6** | 12.3 | 11.0 | 12.9 | 8.4 | 10.8 | 12.9 | 10.2 |
| Percent of hospital hours spent at primary hospital F test (5 d.f.) = 2.84* | 79.8 | 83.4 | 77.9 | 79.7 | 82.7 | 80.1 | 80.9 |
| Number of hospitals at which physician has hospital privileges F test (5 d.f.) = 19.5** | 2.1 | 1.9 | 2.4 | 2.7 | 1.8 | 2.0 | 2.6 |
| Percent of physicians having privileges at only one hospital F test (5 d.f.) = 19.5** | 36.7 | 38.5 | 26.4 | 27.3 | 48.3 | 40.5 | 20.5 |

*Significant variation at the 95 percent level of confidence.
**Significant variation at the 99 percent level of confidence.

SOURCE: 1984 AMA Socioeconomic Monitoring System Core Survey.

terest in the influence of hospital ownership on physician practice patterns. Table 7 shows that physicians' hours, visits, and hospital discharges vary according to the type of hospital at which they have their primary privileges. Physicians at independent nonfederal government hospitals work on average more total hours, have more patient visits, and discharge more patients from the hospital each week than physicians at the other types of hospitals. Physicians in multifacility for-profit hospitals see the fewest number of patients (22.7) on hospital rounds. This relatively low level of utilization in the hospital is somewhat offset by the fact that these physicians spend more time and see more patients in their offices. (Despite these differences in utilization, physicians' earnings do not vary significantly by hospital type.)

Another issue in the debate regarding hospital ownership and performance is whether payer mix in for-profit hospitals is different from the payer mix in other hospitals. Using the hospital as the unit of observation, Sloan and Vraciu (1983) found no significant differences in Medicare and Medicaid days as a percent of total acute patient days by ownership class.

To analyze this issue from the perspective of the physician, we examine whether variation exists in the number of inpatient visits that the physician makes with Medicare patients and the number of hospital discharges by hospital type. The data indicate that there is no significant variation in the weekly number of inpatient visits by hospital type. In addition, while there appears to be variation in the number of Medicare hospital discharges by hospital ownership status, it appears to be consistent with the pattern for total discharges. Taken together, these two results suggest that physicians in both for-profit and not-for-profit hospitals may be seeing their Medicare inpatients more frequently than physicians in government hospitals. As such, one might be led to conclude that concerns about the treatment of Medicare patients in for-profit hospitals may be unwarranted. The real distinction appears to be between hospitals in the public and private sectors.

TABLE 7  Selected Measures of Physician Utilization by Type of Hospital, 1984

| Measure | All Hospitals | Multihospital System | | | Independent | | | F Statistics |
|---|---|---|---|---|---|---|---|---|
| | | Nonfederal Government | Private Not-for-profit | For-profit | Nonfederal Government | Private Not-for-profit | For-profit | |
| Average hours worked per week | | | | | | | | |
| Total | 56.8 | 57.2 | 56.5 | 56.3 | 59.6 | 56.2 | 57.3 | 3.8* |
| Office | 27.1 | 28.0 | 26.8 | 30.1 | 28.2 | 26.4 | 29.8 | 4.1* |
| Hospital | 9.9 | 9.6 | 9.8 | 8.6 | 9.9 | 10.2 | 9.6 | 1.1 |
| Average visits per week | | | | | | | | |
| Total | 131.9 | 135.6 | 131.9 | 138.1 | 148.2 | 126.1 | 134.6 | 5.8* |
| Office | 76.0 | 68.1 | 77.4 | 88.6 | 82.8 | 72.0 | 80.5 | 4.6* |
| Hospital | 29.1 | 33.2 | 28.8 | 22.7 | 35.3 | 28.2 | 26.1 | 4.5* |
| Average Medicare visits per week | | | | | | | | |
| Total | 37.7 | 36.7 | 37.1 | 37.0 | 42.8 | 36.7 | 40.2 | 1.0 |
| Office | 20.4 | 15.4 | 20.3 | 22.6 | 20.9 | 20.0 | 25.4 | 1.1 |
| Hospital | 12.7 | 13.9 | 13.1 | 10.1 | 14.7 | 12.3 | 12.0 | 1.1 |
| Average hospital discharges per week | | | | | | | | |
| Total | 4.8 | 4.9 | 4.9 | 4.4 | 6.0 | 4.5 | 3.6 | 6.5* |
| Medicare | 1.9 | 2.4 | 1.9 | 1.5 | 2.5 | 1.7 | 1.7 | 3.2* |

*Significant variation at the 99 percent level of confidence; all F statistics are evaluated at 5 d.f.

SOURCE: 1984 AMA Socioeconomic Monitoring System Core Survey.

## FINANCIAL ARRANGEMENTS

One area which some analysts feel may be altered by the growth in the for-profit sector of the hospital industry is physicians' financial arrangements with hospitals. Shortell and Evashwick (1981) found that arrangements whereby physicians are compensated by the hospital are more common in for-profit rather than voluntary hospitals. Steinwald (1983), on the other hand, found that hospital ownership had little bearing on the compensation methods of the hospital-based physicians. Based on Steinwald's earlier research (Steinwald and Neuhauser, 1980), he had expected for-profits to "attract physicians by providing relatively lucrative and unencumbered working conditions." This hypothesis, however, was not supported by his data.

In this study, we examine three specific types of financial arrangements that physicians may have with hospitals. First, we consider the proportion of physicians who received some part of their 1983 income directly from their primary hospital. This may be viewed as the most basic category of physician/hospital contract. Second, we measure the extent of lease agreements that physicians have with hospitals. Under a lease agreement the physician or his practice compensates the hospital for the use of its facilities or services. Finally, we consider a phenomenon unique to the for-profit sector: the degree to which physicians have an ownership interest in their hospital.

Table 8 presents data on the first two arrangements to be considered. Column 3 shows that 23.5 percent of all physicians in our study either receive some type of direct payment for their hospital or had a lease agreement. This percentage varied significantly by hospital type. However, upon examination of direct payments and lease agreements separately we find that only the percent receiving direct payments showed significant variation. The probability of receiving a direct payment was highest for physicians at government hospitals (25.1 percent) and lowest for physicians at for-profit hospitals (11.4 percent). These results are supportive of Steinwald's hypothesis regarding "unencumbered working conditions" in for-profit hospitals. In particular, we find that physicians affiliated with hospitals that are a part

of for-profit chains are the least likely to receive payments from their hospital.

To control for differences in physician characteristics, we examine differences in financial arrangements using a linear probability model. Among the control variables we include physician specialty, location of medical school, board certification, employment status, sex, experience, type of practice, and hospital bed size. Holding these variables constant, we find (Table 9) that physicians in for-profit chains, not-for-profit chains, and independent not-for-profit hospitals are significantly less likely to receive direct payments than physicians in independent government hospitals (the omitted category). This supports the results of our univariate analysis. Lease agreements continue to remain unrelated to hospital ownership.

Data on the methods by which the hospital's direct payments are made are shown in Table 10. Despite the fact that variation by ownership status and organizational structure is not significant, the table provides useful information on compensation arrangements. The numbers shown do sum to over 100 percent across the rows since each physician may receive payments through a number of arrangements. Our results indicate that salary and fee-for-service compensation are the most common methods. Overall, 59.0 percent of those physicians receiving payments were paid some of it in the form of salary, while 37.7 percent received some fee-for-service payments. In this study, we define fee-for-service to include arrangements in which the physician receives a fixed percentage of a hospital's charges.

Even though there is a lack of statistical significance regarding compensation and organizational structure, it appears that government and not-for-profit hospitals are different from for-profits with regard to the methods of compensation. In particular, the physicians at for-profit chains seem least likely to be involved in a salaried relationship and most likely to receive payments on a fee-for-service basis or as a percent of net or gross department billings. These latter three methods can be viewed as incentive arrangements that are designed to align the financial interests of the physician with those of the hospital. Unfortunately, firm conclusions about the relationship between hospital type and methods of compensation

**TABLE 8**  Physicians' Financial Arrangements with Hospitals by Hospital Ownership Status and Organizational Structure (percentage of physicians)

|  | Direct Payments* | Lease Agreement** | Direct Payments or Lease*** |
|---|---|---|---|
| All physicians | 18.4 | 7.1 | 23.5 |
| Nonfederal government | 25.1 | 7.9 | 31.1 |
|   Multihospital system | 24.2 | 5.2 | 28.4 |
|   Independent hospital | 25.3 | 8.5 | 31.7 |
| Private not-for-profit | 17.8 | 7.1 | 22.6 |
|   Multihospital system | 16.5 | 6.0 | 21.1 |
|   Independent hospital | 18.4 | 7.6 | 23.3 |
| For-profit | 11.4 | 5.6 | 16.5 |
|   Multihospital system | 8.8 | 5.6 | 14.2 |
|   Independent hospital | 19.4 | 5.5 | 23.3 |

*3-way chi-square (2 d.f.) = 26.77; 6-way chi-square (5 d.f.) = 32.28, both significant at the 99 percent level of confidence.

**3-way chi-square (2 d.f.) = 1.55; 6-way chi-square (5 d.f.) = 4.99, neither significant.

***3-way chi-square (2 d.f.) = 27.39; 6-way chi-square (5 d.f.) = 31.91, both significant at the 99 percent level of confidence.

SOURCE: 1984 AMA Socioeconomic Monitoring System Core Survey.

cannot be drawn from this study due to the small number of physicians in our sample who have affiliations with for-profit hospitals and receive direct payments.

Data not shown in the tables indicate that few physicians with their primary privileges at for-profit hospitals have any ownership interest in the hospital. Fewer than one out of ten physicians on for-profit staffs indicated that they were full- or part-owners of their hospital. However, we do find that hospital ownership is significantly more prevalent among physicians whose privileges are at independent for-profit hospitals. Twenty-two percent of these physicians were hospital owners as compared to only 6 percent of physicians primarily affiliated with chain hospitals. In the case of chain hospitals, hospital ownership includes owning stock in the company that controls the hospital.

## PHYSICIAN ATTITUDES

In the preceding sections we examined the for-profit issue by analyzing a range of socio-economic variables. We found some substantive differences in the areas of medical school location, employment status, utilization, and financial arrangements. However, an equally important avenue for analysis is physicians' attitudes toward for-profit hospitals. If physicians, for whatever reason, were to oppose the for-profit concept, then continued growth in this sector could produce increased tension among medical staffs and hospital administrators. In considering these attitudinal results, it is important to remember that fewer than 10 percent of the physicians have their primary privileges at a for-profit hospital. Therefore, many of the opinions regarding for-profit hospitals are not likely to be based on firsthand experience.

Table 11 presents results from the 1984 AMA Physician Opinion Survey. The exact questions that were asked and the full range of potential responses are included in the table. According to question 1, only 52 percent of physicians believe that hospitals can be operated properly on a for-profit basis. This per-

**TABLE 9**  Determinants of Physicians' Financial Arrangements with Hospitals: A Multivariate Linear Probability Model (ordinary least squares estimate: N = 3,023)

| Independent Variables[a] | Dependent Variable | | |
|---|---|---|---|
| | Direct Payment | Lease Agreement | Direct Payment or Lease |
| *Physician Characteristics* | | | |
| Specialty | | | |
| Internal medicine | 0.14** | 0.00008 | 0.14** |
| | (6.56) | (0.01) | (5.46) |
| Surgery | −0.07** | 0.02 | −0.05* |
| | (3.73) | (1.12) | (2.04) |
| Pediatrics | −0.02 | −0.01 | −0.02 |
| | (0.66) | (0.70) | (0.69) |
| Obstetrics/gynecology | −0.05* | 0.0009 | −0.05 |
| | (1.99) | (0.05) | (1.53) |
| Radiology | 0.01 | −0.01 | 0.01 |
| | (0.39) | (0.57) | (0.34) |
| Psychiatry | 0.04 | −0.01 | 0.03 |
| | (1.43) | (0.35) | (0.84) |
| Anesthesiology | 0.01 | 0.01 | 0.02 |
| | (0.17) | (0.45) | (0.66) |
| Pathology | 0.49** | −0.0009 | 0.48** |
| | (12.14) | (0.03) | (10.32) |
| Other | 0.11** | 0.06** | 0.16** |
| | (4.07) | (2.71) | (5.11) |
| | | | |
| Years since residency | | | |
| 0–10 | 0.05 | 0.05 | 0.08 |
| | (0.76) | (0.91) | (0.98) |
| 10–20 | 0.03 | 0.02 | 0.04 |
| | (0.51) | (0.32) | (0.44) |
| 20–30 | 0.02 | 0.01 | 0.02 |
| | (0.33) | (0.11) | (0.24) |
| 30 or more | 0.001 | −0.01 | −0.01 |
| | (0.02) | (0.09) | (0.13) |
| | | | |
| Board certification | 0.0003 | −0.0007 | −0.004 |
| | (0.02) | (0.07) | (0.24) |
| | | | |
| Foreign medical school graduate | 0.01 | 0.004 | 0.001 |
| | (0.75) | (0.31) | (0.06) |
| Sex (male) | −0.04 | 0.03 | −0.02 |
| | (1.74) | (1.43) | (0.88) |
| Self-employed | 0.07** | −0.03* | 0.03 |
| | (3.66) | (2.22) | (1.55) |
| Solo practitioner | −0.003 | −0.02* | −0.02 |
| | (0.22) | (2.16) | (1.58) |
| | | | |
| *Hospital Characteristics* | | | |
| Bed size | −0.00002 | 0.00001 | −0.00002 |
| | (1.13) | (0.65) | (0.53) |

(*continued*)

**TABLE 9**  *Continued*

|                                          | Dependent Variable |                      |                                  |
|------------------------------------------|--------------------|----------------------|----------------------------------|
| Independent Variables[a]                 | Direct Payment     | Lease Agreement      | Direct Payment or Lease          |
| Ownership and structure                  |                    |                      |                                  |
| Government, multihospital system         | −0.03 (0.71)       | −0.01 (0.25)         | −0.04 (0.74)                     |
| Not-for-profit, independent hospital     | −0.06** (3.23)     | −0.01 (0.25)         | −0.07** (3.11)                   |
| Not-for-profit, multi- hospital system   | −0.05* (2.34)      | −0.02 (1.10)         | −0.06** (2.60)                   |
| For-profit, independent hospital         | −0.02 (0.46)       | 0.01 (0.20)          | −0.02 (0.49)                     |
| For-profit, multihospital system         | −0.10** (3.45)     | −0.02 (1.00)         | −0.10** (3.16)                   |
| Constant                                 | 0.08 (1.11)        | 0.08 (1.48)          | 0.17 (1.96)                      |
| R-square                                 | 0.11               | 0.02                 | 0.09                             |

[a]All variables are categorical variables that equal 1 if the physician has the indicated characteristics; 0 otherwise (t-statistics are shown in parentheses).
   *Significant at the 95 percent level of confidence.
   **Significant at the 99 percent level of confidence.

cent differs among physicians depending on their experience with the for-profit sector. Among physicians reporting some staff privileges at a for-profit hospital, 64 percent favor the for-profit concept. Only 47 percent of the remaining responded affirmatively to this question. More interesting, however, is the fact that 28 percent of the group with for-profit experience oppose the for-profit approach. Unfortunately, data from the Physician Opinion Survey could not be disaggregated in a way that allows us to contrast physicians practicing in MHS hospitals to those in independent hospitals.

Question 2 asks physicians to compare the quality of care in for-profit versus not-for-profit hospitals. The pattern of responses is similar to that for the preceding question. A slight majority of physicians believe quality is unaffected by the profit-nonprofit distinction. However, views toward quality differences are also affected by actual experience in for-profit hospitals. Twenty-four percent of physicians

who have some involvement in for-profit hospitals say quality of care is better in the not-for-profit sector. Part of the reason that physicians may view quality as being lower in the for-profit sector is that only 9 percent of them believe that for-profit hospitals afford them a greater degree of clinical discretion (question 3).

Changes in the health care sector are causing new ethical issues to emerge. A substantial majority of physicians believe that referring patients to facilities in which they have an ownership share is a conflict of interest. Physicians who have some experience in for-profit hospitals are less likely to indicate conflict of interest. However, even among this group, a majority of 59 percent agree with the conflict-of-interest position. This potential for conflict of interest may be the major reason why few physicians have ownership interests in hospitals.

As the for-profit hospital sector continues to grow, concerns intensify about graduate medical education and its evolving role in an environment increasingly affected by profit considerations. In question 5, physicians were polled concerning their views toward establishing residencies in profit-oriented hospitals. As indicated, a plurality of physicians believe that the quality of graduate medical education would be negatively affected by locating it in a for-profit hospital. Actual experience in for-profit hospitals makes no difference in the physicians' opinion on graduate medical education.

Physicians were then asked about their preference for practice in profit versus nonprofit hospitals. The most prevalent response among physicians interviewed is that no preference between for-profit and not-for-profit hospitals exists, but of those with a preference the not-for-profit hospital was the predominant choice. This seems to reflect the distribution of physicians across hospital types when viewed from the standpoint of their primary affiliation (Table 1).

In an effort to evaluate views on the quality of hospital care delivered, the SMS survey asked physicians to compare their primary hospital to other hospitals that they may be familiar with, along certain specific dimensions. These results are displayed in Table 12. We find that physicians primarily admitting to government MHS hospitals are least likely to view their facility as better than other facilities. In fact, almost half of these physicians see their hospitals as worse than other other hospitals with respect to technical resources and equipment offered.

Among physicians admitting to private-sector hospitals, opinions are mixed as to whether for-profits or not-for-profits are better. Few physicians at any of the private hospitals would rate their hospital as worse than other hospitals. In terms of nursing support, the for-profits get a higher rating than not-for-profits among physicians at independent hospitals, but a lower rating among the MHS group. We observe a similar mixed pattern in terms of physicians' evaluation of the level of patient satisfaction. In two areas, physician opinions on the for-profit/not-for-profit comparison are clearer, but are contradictory in their evaluation of hospitals. Physicians at for-profit hos-

**TABLE 10** Methods of Compensation by Hospital Ownership Status and Organizational Structure (percentage of physicians)

| Status/Structure | Salary | Fee for Service[a] | Share of Net Department Revenue | Share of Gross | Other |
|---|---|---|---|---|---|
| All physicians[b] | 59.0 | 37.7 | 8.0 | 12.1 | 24.6 |
| Nonfederal government | 60.4 | 35.5 | 8.8 | 12.6 | 24.8 |
| Multihospital system | 78.3 | 31.8 | 9.1 | 9.1 | 36.4 |
| Independent hospital | 56.5 | 36.2 | 8.7 | 13.3 | 22.6 |
| Private, not-for-profit | 59.5 | 37.5 | 7.2 | 11.5 | 24.0 |
| Multihospital system | 50.4 | 43.4 | 4.5 | 10.4 | 25.0 |
| Independent hospital | 63.5 | 35.0 | 8.3 | 12.1 | 23.6 |
| For-profit | 48.5 | 50.0 | 15.6 | 18.2 | 31.3 |
| Multihospital system | 36.8 | 57.9 | 11.1 | 26.3 | 27.8 |
| Independent hospital | 64.3 | 38.5 | 21.4 | 7.1 | 35.7 |

NOTE: In this table, none of the variation by hospital ownership status and organizational structure is statistically significant based on chi-square tests.

[a]Includes arrangements involving the physician receiving a percentage of hospital charges.
[b]Those receiving part of their 1983 income directly from hospital.

**TABLE 11**  Physician Attitudes on Issues Related to Hospital Ownership by Extent of Involvement with For-profit Hospitals (percentage)

| Question | Response | All Physicians | Involvement with For-profit Hospitals | |
|---|---|---|---|---|
| | | | Some | None |
| 1. As you may know, there has been a rapid growth of "for-profit" multihospital systems in recent years. Do you favor or oppose the view that hospitals can be operated properly as profit-making organizations? | Favor | 52 | 64 | 47 |
| | Oppose | 37 | 28 | 41 |
| | Unsure | 11 | 8 | 12 |
| 2. In general, do you believe that *not-for-profit* hospitals provide better, worse, or about the same quality of care as *for-profit* hospitals? | Better | 32 | 24 | 35 |
| | Worse | 5 | 8 | 4 |
| | Same | 50 | 59 | 46 |
| | Unsure | 13 | 9 | 14 |
| 3. In your opinion, do physicians have greater, less, or the same amount of clinical discretion at a for-profit hospital as they do at a not-for-profit hospital? | Greater | 9 | 11 | 8 |
| | Less | 28 | 27 | 28 |
| | Same | 37 | 50 | 32 |
| | Unsure | 27 | 12 | 32 |
| 4. Do you believe it is a conflict of interest for physicians to refer patients to a hospital or other health care facility in which they have an ownership interest? | Yes | 65 | 59 | 68 |
| | No | 28 | 35 | 26 |
| | Unsure | 7 | 7 | 6 |
| 5. Do you believe that graduate medical training in for-profit hospitals would be better, worse, or the same as that in not-for-profit hospitals? | Better | 5 | 7 | 4 |
| | Worse | 46 | 44 | 47 |
| | Same | 34 | 37 | 34 |
| | Unsure | 16 | 13 | 16 |
| 6. Assuming the medical staff privileges, compensation arrangements, and work conditions are the same, would you rather practice at a for-profit hospital, a not-for-profit hospital, or would you have no preference? | For-profit | 7 | 13 | 5 |
| | Not-for-profit | 42 | 31 | 48 |
| | No preference | 51 | 57 | 47 |

SOURCE: 1984 AMA Physician Opinion Survey.

pitals are more satisfied with the responsiveness of the hospital to their professional needs, but less satisfied with the available technical resources and equipment than their not-for-profit counterparts. On the basis of these results, no clear preferences are apparent among private-sector physicians.

**SUMMARY AND DISCUSSION**

The purpose of this paper has been to compare characteristics of physicians at for-profit hospitals to those of other physicians. In addition, we explored physician attitudes toward aspects of the growing for-profit hospital sector. At this point in time, physicians have limited experience with for-profit hospitals. Even so, the attitudinal data (Table 11) show that half of all physicians believe hospitals can be operated properly as profit-making organizations. However, data on specific areas of hospital operation (Table 12) produced mixed results with regard to preferences for particular hospital types. While we realize that our own data could suggest that physicians are not satisfied with for-profit hospitals, a more appropriate interpretation would be that physicians are clearly aware of and concerned about potential issues that could arise. A less tentative conclusion is unwarranted until more

TABLE 12   Physicians' Evaluation of Their Primary Hospital by Hospital Type (percentage)[a]

| Variable | Response | Multihospital System | | | Independent | | |
|---|---|---|---|---|---|---|---|
| | | Nonfederal Government | Private Not-for-profit | For-profit | Nonfederal Government | Private Not-for-profit | For-profit |
| Nursing support | Better | 29.0 | 59.7 | 48.2 | 50.0 | 56.3 | 63.1 |
| | Same | 59.2 | 38.3 | 46.7 | 42.4 | 40.2 | 33.9 |
| | Worse | 11.8 | 2.0 | 5.1 | 7.9 | 3.5 | 3.1 |
| Responsiveness of the hospital administration | Better | 29.7 | 47.3 | 60.2 | 43.5 | 46.8 | 60.9 |
| | Same | 45.1 | 42.6 | 32.8 | 14.7 | 41.9 | 31.3 |
| | Worse | 25.3 | 10.2 | 7.0 | 41.8 | 11.3 | 7.8 |
| Level of patient satisfaction | Better | 31.9 | 56.6 | 51.5 | 45.7 | 57.6 | 64.1 |
| | Same | 53.9 | 41.8 | 43.9 | 47.6 | 39.7 | 34.4 |
| | Worse | 14.3 | 1.7 | 4.6 | 6.7 | 2.8 | 1.6 |
| Technical resources and equipment | Better | 33.3 | 57.8 | 52.5 | 51.4 | 60.9 | 49.2 |
| | Same | 18.3 | 38.5 | 43.0 | 36.9 | 34.5 | 39.7 |
| | Worse | 48.4 | 3.8 | 4.5 | 11.8 | 4.6 | 11.1 |

[a]Physicians were asked to compare their primary hospital to other hospitals that they may be familiar with regarding the characteristics shown in this table.

SOURCE: 1984 Socioeconomic Monitoring System Core Survey.

physicians have firsthand contact with these facilities.

To summarize, examining the physician characteristic data, we identified a number of important differences between for-profit medical staffs and those at other hospitals. First, there are relatively more GP/FPs and relatively fewer internists on the staffs of for-profit hospitals. This may reflect differences in hospital case mix. Second, the typical physician on the staff of a for-profit MHS hospital is more likely to be self-employed than other physicians. Third, this same physician is least likely to receive any direct monetary compensation from his/her hospital. Taken together, these last two findings suggest that the financial link between the hospital and the physician may be weakest at for-profit MHS facilities, a result that may be counter to some views of the for-profit sector.

Finally, physicians primarily affiliated with for-profit hospitals discharge the fewest patients from the hospital in an average week. This, combined with their higher average rate of office visits, suggests that their practices may be somewhat less involved with the hospital than are those of other physicians. The lower level of hospital involvement is quite likely due to the specialty composition of these physicians and the case mix of their patients.

Our results show that, along several dimensions, medical staffs at for-profit hospitals differ from those at other facilities. It appears that the specialty composition differences may be the driving force behind our findings. The higher proportion of GP/FPs relative to internists at for-profit hospitals could result in less-hospital-oriented practices and the larger proportion of self-employed physicians that we observe. For-profit hospitals may be treating comparable types of patients with less specialized physicians. On the other hand, by virtue of their specialty differences, for-profit medical staffs may be admitting a different mix of cases to their hospitals. Our data do not allow us to choose between these competing hypotheses. The relationship between the observed specialty differences, case mix, and quality of care is an area that should receive further investigation.

This study was not designed to be an exhaustive analysis of the for-profit multihospital system issue. We feel a number of other fruitful areas for future research remain open with regard to the physician. One important area that might help us to better understand physician/hospital relations in general is: What factors cause a physician to seek privileges at a particular type of hospital? For example, do physicians affiliate with a for-profit hospital or multihospital system because it is the only one located near them, or are there specific aspects of the hospital environment that make for-profit hospitals more desirable to some physicians? Likewise, do for-profit hospitals grant hospital/physician privileges to different types of physicians? A second area of research that seems appropriate in light of our findings with regard to financial arrangements is: As for-profit hospitals grow, will new types of financial arrangements between physicians and hospitals develop? Physician/hospital joint ventures and physician ownership of stock in hospital management companies are two such developments that have the potential to alter practice patterns and, therefore, should be studied further. Finally, will Medicare's prospective pricing system, other regulatory devices, or competition change the need for a financial tie between hospitals and physicians.

Throughout most of this paper we have attempted to array the data so as to allow us to analyze differences among government, not-for-profit, and for-profit hospitals. On the basis of Table 7, we observe that physicians practicing primarily in government hospitals exhibit utilization patterns that are no more similar to the not-for-profit group than the for-profit group is to the not-for-profit group. In particular, physicians who practice at government hospitals have a higher rate of Medicare discharges. This higher rate may be indicative of a shift in the treatment of the aged towards the public sector. While these results are by no means conclusive, we feel that they suggest a need for further research on public/private differentials.

### ACKNOWLEDGMENTS

The views expressed in this paper are not necessarily those of the American Medical Association or the Urban Institute and its sponsors. The authors would like to thank Steven

D. Culler, Janet Willer, Bradford Gray, and two anonymous reviewers for their helpful comments and able assistance on this research project.

## REFERENCES

Ermann, D., and J. Gabel (1984) Multihospital systems: Issues and empirical findings. *Health Affairs* 3(1):50-64.

Lewin, L. S., A Derzon, and R. Margulies (1981) Investor-owned and nonprofits differ in economic performance. *Hospitals* 55:52-58.

Morrisey, M. (1984) The composition of hospital medical staffs. *Health Care Management Review* (Summer):11-20.

Mullner, Ross M., Calvin Byre, and Cleve L. Killingsworth (1983) An inventory of U.S. health care data bases. *Review of Public Data Use* 11(2):85-188.

Pattison, R. V., and H. M. Katz (1983) Investor-owned and not-for-profit hospitals: A comparison based on California data. *New England Journal of Medicine* 309:347-353.

Relman, A. S. (1980) The new medical-industrial complex. *New England Journal of Medicine* 303:963-970.

Relman, A. S. (1983) Investor-owned hospitals and health care costs. *New England Journal of Medicine* 309:370-372.

Rosett, R. M. (1974) Proprietary hospitals in the United States. Pp. 57-65 in *The Economics of Health and Medical Care*, M. Perlman, ed. New York: John Wiley and Sons.

Shortell, S. M., and C. Evashwick (1981) The structural configuration of U.S. hospital medical staffs. *Medical Care* 19:419-430.

Sloan, F., and E. Becker (1985) Hospital ownership and performance. *Economic Inquiry.* Vol 11.

Sloan, F., and R. Vraciu (1983) Investor-owned and not-for-profit hospitals: Addressing some issues. *Health Affairs* 2(1):25-37.

Steinwald, B. (1983) Compensation of hospital-based physicians. *Health Services Research* 18(1):17-43.

Steinwald, B., and D. Neuhauser (1980) The role of proprietary hospitals. *Law and Contemporary Problems* 35:817-838.

For-Profit Enterprise in Health Care. 1986.
National Academy Press, Washington, D.C.

# Physician Participation in the Administration and Governance of System and Freestanding Hospitals: A Comparison by Type of Ownership

Jeffrey A. Alexander, Michael A. Morrisey, and Stephen M. Shortell

## INTRODUCTION

This paper examines the type and extent of physician participation in the administration and governance of hospitals in multihospital systems. Particular emphasis is given to physician participation in investor-owned chain hospitals relative to freestanding hospitals and other system-affiliated institutions.

The advent of prospective pricing, coupled with the rise of multi-institutional arrangements in the hospital industry is thought to have major implications for the role of the physician in the hospital. The nature of many of these changes, however, is still open to empirical question. Brown (1979) and Reynolds and Studen (1978) suggest that hospital consolidation into systems may promote more formalized methods for securing physician input into hospital decision-making processes.[1,2] Others have argued, however, that physician power and influence in hospital policymaking and administration will be reduced in the context of multi-institutional arrangements and the "corporatization" of medicine.[3,4]

Physician involvement in hospital decision making represents a potentially important issue for several reasons. First, several national groups (i.e., American Hospital Association [AHA], Joint Commission on Accreditation of Hospitals [JCAH], American Medical Association [AMA]) perceive and endorse physician participation in hospital decision making as an important mechanism for conflict resolution among the administration, board members, and medical staff.[5] Second, such participation is seen to foster an institution-wide perspective among medical staff members, of particular importance under diagnosis-related group (DRG) reimbursement. Finally, studies by Neuhauser (1971), Shortell et al. (1976), Shortell and LoGerfo (1981), and Morlock et al. (1979) suggest that greater medical staff participation in governance is associated with higher quality hospital care.[6-9]

In light of the above, this study examines a series of structural variables related to physician involvement in hospital decision making. Two categories of involvement are considered: (1) physician participation in hospital governance, and (2) physician participation in hospital management.

The primary group under investigation are those hospitals owned or leased by investor-owned multihospital systems (IO hospitals). On a series of physician decision-making variables, these hospitals are compared to five other hospital groups: (1) freestanding hospitals or those not affiliated with a multihospital system; (2) hospitals owned or leased, by secular nonprofit multihospital systems; (3) hospitals owned, leased, or sponsored by religious multihospital systems; (4) hospitals owned or leased by public multihospital systems; and (5) hospitals contract-managed by all of the aforementioned system types.

## SAMPLE

The sample for this study was composed of 3,027 community hospitals located in the 48 contiguous states and the District of Columbia. The sample hospitals were chosen by random selection and represent 25 percent of all

Dr. Morrisey is in the Department of Health Care Organization and Policy and Dr. Alexander is in the Department of Health Services Administration, both at the University of Alabama at Birmingham. When this paper was written they were with the Hospital Research and Educational Trust, Chicago, Illinois. Dr. Shortell is with the J. L. Kellogg Graduate School of Management and Center for Health Services and Policy Research at Northwestern University, Evanston, Illinois.

community hospitals, augmented with additional, randomly selected hospitals in 22 states. These states were primarily those with mandatory or voluntary rate review programs.

Sample hospitals were sent a six-page survey questionnaire related to medical staff organization. Of the 3,027 sample hospitals, 2,065 responded to the survey, a response rate of 69.9 percent. These hospitals represented the final sample for this investigation.

It is important to note that the hospitals in this study are not representative of all community hospitals insofar as sample representation was greater for New England, Middle Atlantic, and West North Central regions than for the South East, East South Central, and West South Central regions. Sample hospitals were also more likely to be involved in teaching activities and less likely to be investor-owned than the population of community hospitals.[10]

## DATA

Data for this investigation were obtained from these sources: (1) the 1982 AHA Survey of Hospital Medical Staffs; (2) the 1982 AHA Annual Survey of Hospitals; and (3) the 1982 AHA Validation Survey of Multihospital Systems. The medical staff survey provided information on the type and extent of physician/medical participation in hospital decision making. The annual survey was used to obtain data on selected hospital characteristics (e.g., size, teaching involvement, and regional location). The validation survey indicated whether or not a hospital was part of a multihospital system, the ownership status of that system and the type of hospital affiliation with the system (i.e., owned, leased, sponsored, or contract-managed).

## MEASUREMENT

Physician participation in hospital governance was measured by four variables: (1) total number of physician members on the hospital governing board; (2) whether or not physician board members have voting privileges; (3) whether or not physicians serve on the board executive committee and; (4) whether or not the hospital chief executive officer (CEO) is a voting member of the hospital governing board.

The latter item, while not a direct indicator of physician involvement on the board, is indicative of participation and influence by the administrative component of the hospital, possibly complementing physician influence.

Physician involvement in hospital management activity was assessed by six variables: (1) whether or not any staff physicians hold salaried positions as part of the hospital's management team; (2) whether or not the chief of the hospital medical staff is compensated by the hospital; (3) whether or not the director of medical education is compensated by the hospital; (4) whether or not the hospital has a medical staff committee for long-range planning; (5) whether or not the hospital has a medical staff committee for cost containment/cost awareness; and (6) the total number of medical staff committees in the hospital.

Because many of the outcome measures described above may be influenced by factors other than multihospital system participation, several control variables were incorporated in the analysis. These included hospital size as measured by the total number of beds set up and staffed for use; regional location of hospital, indicated by whether the hospital is situated in the Northeast, South, North Central, or Western areas of the country; size of standard metropolitan statistical area (SMSA), measured by seven population categories ranging from 0 to over 2.5 million; teaching involvement, assessed by the number of house staff in the hospital; and system size as indicated by the number of owned, leased, sponsored, or managed hospitals in the system. Hospitals not affiliated with a system were assigned a value of 0 on this variable.

Descriptive statistics for the dependent, independent, and control variables are presented in Table 1.

## ANALYTIC APPROACH

Zero-order comparisons among investor-owned and other hospital categories were performed using chi-square tests of significance in the case of dichotomous variables, and difference-of-means t-tests in the case of continuous, dependent variables. IO hospitals were compared separately to each of the other five hospital categories.

Following zero-order comparisons, all de-

**TABLE 1** Descriptive Statistics for Hospital Sample (N = 2,067)

| Variables | Mean | Standard Deviation | Number in Sample[a] |
|---|---|---|---|
| *Independent Variables* | | | |
| Freestanding hospital | .71 | .45 | 1,469 |
| System characteristics | | | |
| System control | | | |
| Religious nonprofit | .12 | .32 | 247 |
| Secular nonprofit | .03 | .18 | 70 |
| Investor-owned | .06 | .24 | 126 |
| Public | .01 | .07 | 11 |
| Contract-managed | .07 | .25 | 144 |
| System size | 21.00 | 72.28 | |
| Hospital characteristics | | | |
| Number of beds | 190.76 | 179.53 | |
| Regional location | | | |
| Northeast | .23 | .42 | 468 |
| South | .26 | .44 | 542 |
| North Central | .32 | .47 | 660 |
| West | .19 | .39 | 397 |
| SMSA size[b] | | | |
| Non-SMSA | .45 | .50 | 929 |
| Under 100,000 | .02 | .12 | 32 |
| 100,000–250,000 | .09 | .28 | 178 |
| 250,000–500,000 | .09 | .29 | 187 |
| 500,000–1 million | .08 | .27 | 160 |
| 1 million–2.5 million | .14 | .35 | 297 |
| Over 2.5 million | .14 | .34 | 284 |
| House staff | 11.60 | 50.14 | |
| *Dependent Variables* | | | |
| Whether M.D.s receive salaries as administrators | .16 | .36 | 323 |
| Whether director of medical education paid | .19 | .39 | 392 |
| Whether chief of staff paid | .07 | .26 | 145 |
| Whether chief executive officer is voting member of governing board | .34 | .47 | 697 |
| Whether M.D.s on governing board of executive committee | .35 | .48 | 720 |
| Whether M.D. governing board members have voting rights | .70 | .46 | 1,437 |
| Whether hospital has committee for cost containment/awareness | .16 | .37 | 329 |
| Whether hospital has committee for medical staff long-range planning | .28 | .45 | 584 |

[a]For dichotomously scored variables only.
[b]Size of standard metropolitan statistical area (SMSA).

**TABLE 2** Comparison of Hospitals in For-profit Systems with Other Hospital Types: Number of Physicians on Governing Boards

| Hospitals in For-profit Systems | | Freestanding Hospitals | | Hospitals in Religious Systems | | Hospitals in Nonprofit Systems | | Hospitals in Public Systems | | Contract-Managed | |
|---|---|---|---|---|---|---|---|---|---|---|---|
| N | Mean (S.D.) | N | Mean (S.D.) | N | Mean (S.D.) | N | Mean (S.D.) | N | Mean (S.D.) | N | Mean (S.D.) |
| 125 | 3.83 (2.32) | 1,442 | 1.86*** (2.12) | 241 | 1.76*** (1.66) | 68 | 2.13*** (1.95) | 7 | 7.00** (14.22) | 142 | 1.42*** (1.77) |

***T significant at $p \leq .01$ when compared with hospitals in for-profit systems.
**T significant at $p \leq .05$ when compared with hospitals in for-profit systems.

pendent variables were subjected to multivariate analysis to assess the impact of hospital and environmental controls on the bivariate relationships. Two regressions were performed for each dependent variable. The first compared all system categories to freestanding hospitals. The second compared IO system hospitals to all other system categories and freestanding hospitals. In the case of dichotomous dependent variables, multiple logistic regression was performed. Ordinary least-squares regression was used for continuous dependent variables.

## RESULTS OF COMPARISONS

### Governance

Results of the zero-order comparisons between IO hospitals and other hospital groups are presented in Tables 2-11. Results of the multivariate analysis are contained in the appendix. In general, our findings suggest that

physician participation in hospital governance is greater in IO hospitals than in the five comparison groups. Table 2 indicates that with the exception of public system hospitals, IO hospitals have on average a greater number of physicians (X = 3.83) serving on their boards than the other system hospital groups or freestanding hospitals. These results are maintained even after the introduction of controls for system size, hospital size, region, SMSA size, and teaching involvement.

It is important to note that these board positions carry some influence insofar as 91 percent of the sample IO hospitals indicated that physician board members had voting privileges on the board (Table 3). Zero-order comparisons between IO hospitals and other groups also suggest that physician board members are more likely to have voting privileges in IO hospitals than in the other five hospital groups. With the introduction of the control variables, however, only differences between the IO and the secular nonprofit and public system hospitals are sustained.

**TABLE 3** Comparison of Hospitals in For-profit Systems with Other Hospital Types: Do Hospital Physician Governing Board Members Have Voting Privileges?

| Response | Hospitals in For-profit Systems | | Freestanding Hospitals | | Hospitals in Religious Systems | | Hospitals in Nonprofit Systems | | Hospitals in Public Systems | | Contract-Managed | |
|---|---|---|---|---|---|---|---|---|---|---|---|---|
| | N | Mean | N | Mean | N | Mean | N | Mean | N | Mean | N | Mean |
| Yes | 115 | 91.27 | 991 | 67.46 | 193 | 78.14 | 50 | 71.43 | 5 | 45.45 | 83 | 57.64 |
| No | 11 | 8.73 | 478 | 32.54*** | 54 | 21.86*** | 20 | 28.57*** | 6 | 54.55*** | 61 | 42.36*** |
| Total | 126 | 100.00 | 1,469 | 100.00 | 247 | 100.00 | 70 | 100.00 | 11 | 100.00 | 144 | 100.00 |

***Chi-square significant at $p \leq .01$ when compared with hospitals in for-profit systems.

**TABLE 4**    Comparison of Hospitals in For-profit Systems with Other Hospital Types: Are There Physicians on the Hospital Governing Board Executive Committee?

| Response | Hospitals in For-profit Systems | | Freestanding Hospitals | | Hospitals in Religious Systems | | Hospitals in Nonprofit Systems | | Hospitals in Public Systems | | Contract-Managed | |
|---|---|---|---|---|---|---|---|---|---|---|---|---|
| | N | % | N | % | N | % | N | % | N | % | N | % |
| Yes | 57 | 45.24 | 524 | 35.67 | 65 | 26.32 | 22 | 31.43 | 4 | 36.36 | 48 | 33.33 |
| No | 69 | 54.76 | 945 | 64.33** | 182 | 73.68*** | 48 | 68.57* | 7 | 68.64 | 96 | 66.67* |
| Total | 126 | 100.00 | 1,469 | 100.00 | 247 | 100.00 | 70 | 100.00 | 11 | 100.00 | 144 | 100.00 |

***Chi-square significant at $p \leq .01$ when compared with hospitals in for-profit systems.
**Chi-square significant at $p \leq .05$ when compared with hospitals in for-profit systems.
*Chi-square significant at $p \leq .10$ when compared with hospitals in for-profit systems.

Table 4 suggests that physicians are more likely to be members of the important board executive committee in IO hospitals relative to all other hospital groups except public system hospitals. However, only the difference between IO hospitals and religious system hospitals holds after the introduction of the control variables. Finally, Table 5 indicates strong involvement of IO hospital CEOs in hospital governance. Eighty percent of the sample IO hospital CEOs participated as voting members of their governing boards. This finding is particularly striking when compared to the low percentage of CEO board membership in freestanding hospitals (26 percent), secular nonprofit system hospitals (31 percent), and public system hospitals (9 percent). As the percentage differences would indicate, these IO hospital CEOs are significantly more likely to be members of their hospital governing board than the CEOs of the other five

hospital groups. The introduction of hospital and environmental controls does not alter these differences.

## Management

Comparisons related to physician involvement in hospital management suggest a pattern of results opposite that of physician participation in hospital governance. In general, physicians in IO hospitals appear to be less integrated into hospital managerial activities than physicians in other hospital categories.

Table 6, for example, indicates that physicians in IO hospitals are significantly less likely to hold salaried positions as part of the hospital's administrative team. Only 2 percent of the IO hospitals in the sample indicated that their physicians held such positions, by far the

**TABLE 5**    Comparison of Hospitals in For-profit Systems with Other Hospital Types: Is the Hospital CEO a Voting Member of the Governing Board?

| Response | Hospitals in For-profit Systems | | Freestanding Hospitals | | Hospitals in Religious Systems | | Hospitals in Nonprofit Systems | | Hospitals in Public Systems | | Contract-Managed | |
|---|---|---|---|---|---|---|---|---|---|---|---|---|
| | N | % | N | % | N | % | N | % | N | % | N | % |
| Yes | 101 | 80.16 | 385 | 26.21 | 162 | 65.59 | 22 | 31.43 | 1 | 9.09 | 26 | 18.06 |
| No | 25 | 19.84 | 1,084 | 73.79*** | 85 | 34.41*** | 48 | 68.57*** | 10 | 90.91*** | 118 | 81.94*** |
| Total | 126 | 100.00 | 1,469 | 100.00 | 247 | 100.00 | 70 | 100.00 | 11 | 100.00 | 144 | 100.00 |

***Chi-square significant at $p \leq .01$ when compared with hospitals in for-profit systems.

TABLE 6   Comparison of Hospitals in For-profit Systems with Other Hospital Types: Do Physicians Hold Salaried Positions as Part of Hospital's Administrative Team?

| Response | Hospitals in For-profit Systems | | Freestanding Hospitals | | Hospitals in Religious Systems | | Hospitals in Nonprofit Systems | | Hospitals in Public Systems | | Contract-Managed | |
|---|---|---|---|---|---|---|---|---|---|---|---|---|
| | N | % | N | % | N | % | N | % | N | % | N | % |
| Yes | 3 | 2.38 | 230 | 15.66 | 52 | 21.05 | 20 | 28.57 | 5 | 45.45 | 13 | 9.03 |
| No | 123 | 97.62 | 1,239 | 84.34*** | 195 | 78.95*** | 50 | 71.43*** | 6 | 54.55*** | 131 | 90.97** |
| Total | 126 | 100.00 | 1,469 | 100.00 | 247 | 100.00 | 70 | 100.00 | 11 | 100.00 | 144 | 100.00 |

***Chi-square significant at $p \leq .01$ when compared with hospitals in for-profit systems.
**Chi-square significant at $p \leq .05$ when compared with hospitals in for-profit systems.

lowest proportional representation among the six hospital groups. These findings remain unaltered, holding constant the five hospital and environmental control variables. Consistent with these findings, key medical staff officers in IO hospitals are also less likely to be compensated by the hospital (see Tables 7 and 8). Specifically, chiefs of staff and directors of medical education in IO hospitals are significantly less likely than those in all comparison groups, except contract-managed hospitals, to be paid by the hospital.

It should be noted, however, that when hospital and environmental variables are held constant, chiefs of staff in IO hospitals are less likely than those in secular nonprofit system hospitals to be compensated. Medical education directors in IO hospitals are less likely than their counterparts in freestanding hospitals and religious system hospitals to be compensated after introducing the control variables.

A second arena of administrative activity for physicians is reflected in the medical staff committee structure of the hospital. Table 9 suggests that with an average of 11, IO hospitals have fewer medical staff committees than all comparison groups except contract-managed hospitals. These differences, with the exception of hospitals in secular nonprofit systems, hold even after controlling for other hospital and environmental characteristics.

We also examined the presence or absence of two medical staff committees that have particular relevance for hospital administration: cost containment/awareness and long-range planning. IO hospitals appear to be significantly less likely to have medical staff committees on long-range planning (Table 10) relative to all other groups except public system and contract-managed hospitals. Few significant differences were obtained between IO hospitals and other hospital groups on the presence of a cost containment/awareness committee (Table 11). These differences are

TABLE 7   Comparison of Hospitals in For-profit Systems with Other Hospital Types: Is Hospital Chief of Staff Compensated?

| Response | Hospitals in For-profit Systems | | Freestanding Hospitals | | Hospitals in Religious Systems | | Hospitals in Nonprofit Systems | | Hospitals in Public Systems | | Contract-Managed | |
|---|---|---|---|---|---|---|---|---|---|---|---|---|
| | N | % | N | % | N | % | N | % | N | % | N | % |
| Yes | 2 | 1.59 | 103 | 7.01 | 20 | 8.10 | 13 | 18.57 | 2 | 18.18 | 5 | 3.47 |
| No | 124 | 98.41 | 1,366 | 92.99** | 227 | 91.90** | 57 | 81.43*** | 9 | 81.82** | 139 | 96.53 |
| Total | 126 | 100.00 | 1,469 | 100.00 | 247 | 100.00 | 70 | 100.00 | 11 | 100.00 | 144 | 100.00 |

***Chi-square significant at $p \leq .01$ when compared with hospitals in for-profit systems.
**Chi-square significant at $p \leq .05$ when compared with hospitals in for-profit systems.

**TABLE 8**   Comparison of Hospitals in For-profit Systems with Other Hospital Types: Is the Director of Medical Education Compensated?

| Response | Hospitals in For-profit Systems | | Freestanding Hospitals | | Hospitals in Religious Systems | | Hospitals in Nonprofit Systems | | Hospitals in Public Systems | | Contract-Managed | |
|---|---|---|---|---|---|---|---|---|---|---|---|---|
| | N | % | N | % | N | % | N | % | N | % | N | % |
| Yes | 9 | 7.14 | 286 | 19.47 | 67 | 27.13 | 16 | 22.86 | 5 | 45.45 | 9 | 6.25 |
| No | 117 | 92.86 | 1,183 | 80.53*** | 180 | 72.87*** | 54 | 77.14*** | 6 | 54.55*** | 135 | 93.75 |
| Total | 126 | 100.00 | 1,469 | 100.00 | 247 | 100.00 | 70 | 100.00 | 11 | 100.00 | 144 | 100.00 |

***Chi-square significant at $p \leq .01$ when compared with hospitals in for-profit systems.

eliminated with the introduction of the control variable set.

## Summary

In summary, IO hospitals, relative to free-standing hospitals, appear to have greater physician representation on hospital governing boards although these physicians are no more or less likely to have voting privileges or to serve on the board executive committee than physicians on freestanding hospital boards.

Relative to hospitals in other system categories, IO hospitals also have greater physician representation on hospital governing boards. Only hospitals in public systems have a higher mean number of physicians on the board. In addition, physician board members of IO hospitals are more likely to have voting privileges than those in secular nonprofit and public systems and are more likely to serve on the executive committee of the board relative to physicians in religious system hospitals.

It is important to note that CEOs of IO hospitals are more likely than those in freestanding hospitals to be voting members of the hospital board. This may suggest a more influential position of the IO hospital CEO on the board relative to physicians since no differences were obtained between IO hospitals and freestanding hospitals on physician voting privileges.

This same pattern holds when comparing IO hospitals with hospitals in other system groups. IO hospitals tend to be significantly more likely to have their CEOs serve as voting members of the board than hospitals in religious, secular, nonprofit, or public systems.

In terms of physician involvement in hospital administration, IO hospitals are less likely to have physicians as salaried administrators and to have fewer medical staff committees than freestanding hospitals. When controlling for other hospital and environmental attributes, however, no significant differences were obtained between IO and freestanding hos-

**TABLE 9**   Comparison of Hospitals in For-profit Systems with Other Hospital Types: Number of Medical Staff Committees

| Hospitals in For-profit Systems | | Freestanding Hospitals | | Hospitals in Religious Systems | | Hospitals in Nonprofit Systems | | Hospitals in Public Systems | | Contract-Managed | |
|---|---|---|---|---|---|---|---|---|---|---|---|
| N | Mean (S.D.) | N | Mean (S.D.) | N | Mean (S.D.) | N | Mean (S.D.) | N | Mean (S.D.) | N | Mean (S.D.) |
| 125 | 11.14 (6.26) | 1,442 | 13.55*** (9.36) | 241 | 15.97*** (8.70) | 68 | 14.06** (10.89) | 7 | 16.29* (6.58) | 142 | 9.68* (6.96) |

***T significant at $p \leq .01$ when compared with hospitals in for-profit systems.
**T significant at $p \leq .05$ when compared with hospitals in for-profit systems.
*T significant at $p \leq .10$ when compared with hospitals in for-profit systems.

**TABLE 10**  Comparison of Hospitals in For-profit Systems with Other Hospital Types: Does the Hospital Have a Committee for Medical Staff Long-Range Planning?

| Response | Hospitals in For-profit Systems | | Freestanding Hospitals | | Hospitals in Religious Systems | | Hospitals in Nonprofit Systems | | Hospitals in Public Systems | | Contract-Managed | |
|---|---|---|---|---|---|---|---|---|---|---|---|---|
| | N | % | N | % | N | % | N | % | N | % | N | % |
| Yes | 19 | 15.08 | 436 | 29.68 | 77 | 31.17 | 22 | 31.43 | 3 | 27.27 | 27 | 18.75 |
| No | 107 | 84.92 | 1,033 | 70.32*** | 170 | 68.83*** | 48 | 68.57*** | 8 | 72.73 | 117 | 81.25 |
| Total | 126 | 100.00 | 1,469 | 100.00 | 247 | 100.00 | 70 | 100.00 | 11 | 100.00 | 144 | 100.00 |

***Chi-square significant at $p \leq .01$ when compared with hospitals in for-profit systems.

pitals on compensation for key medical staff members or the existence of a medical staff committee on cost containment/awareness. However, IO hospitals are less likely than freestanding hospitals to have a medical staff committee on long-range planning.

In general, comparisons of IO hospitals with other system groups on variables related to administrative involvement varied by comparison groups. For example, IO hospitals were less likely to compensate their chief of medical staff only relative to secular nonprofit hospitals and less likely to compensate their director of medical education when compared to religious system hospitals. However, IO hospitals, relative to all other system types, were less likely to have physicians salaried as part of the hospital's administrative team.

## DISCUSSION AND IMPLICATIONS

The findings on physician involvement in hospital management and governance are of interest primarily in terms of their future implications. Increasingly, hospital trustees, managers, and medical staff members are going to have to make difficult trade-off decisions involving the volume and mix of services to offer to different kinds of potential consumers. These decisions will increasingly involve ethical considerations. Hospitals will be called upon to balance, in some way, health care as an economic good with the conception of health care as a social good. Physician and medical staff input into this process is critical and, therefore, the way in which hospitals solicit this input becomes important. The new environment requires a more integrated management structure involving closer relationships among trustees, hospital managers, and physicians in order to make decisions that balance economic and social considerations to the extent possible.

The present findings are of interest because they suggest that, to date, IO hospitals have solicited physician input in different ways from

**TABLE 11**  Comparison of Hospitals in For-profit Systems with Other Hospital Types: Does Hospital Have Committee for Cost Containment/Cost Awareness?

| Response | Hospitals in For-profit Systems | | Freestanding Hospitals | | Hospitals in Religious Systems | | Hospitals in Nonprofit Systems | | Hospitals in Public Systems | | Contract-Managed | |
|---|---|---|---|---|---|---|---|---|---|---|---|---|
| | N | % | N | % | N | % | N | % | N | % | N | % |
| Yes | 13 | 10.32 | 238 | 16.20 | 46 | 18.62 | 12 | 17.14 | 4 | 36.36 | 16 | 11.11 |
| No | 113 | 89.68 | 1,231 | 83.80 | 201 | 81.38* | 58 | 82.86 | 7 | 63.64* | 128 | 88.89 |
| Total | 126 | 100.00 | 1,469 | 100.00 | 247 | 100.00 | 70 | 100.00 | 11 | 100.00 | 144 | 100.00 |

*Chi-square significant at $p \leq .10$ when compared with hospitals in for-profit systems.

other kinds of hospitals, namely, greater involvement at the individual hospital board level than at the managerial level of the organization. In contrast, other hospitals have essentially done the reverse. No studies exist to suggest that one type of involvement is superior to another. It is likely that both types will be increasingly needed in the future. To the extent that this is true, one might expect to find the better performing IO hospitals moving to involve their physicians somewhat more in the managerial activities of the hospital, and the better performing voluntary hospitals moving toward greater involvement of their physicians in the governance and policymaking activities of the organization. This kind of "convergence" would be consistent with those who suggest that IO and nonprofit systems will become more similar in the future. It is clearly an issue for future research with the present findings serving as useful baseline data.

A final issue relevant to both investor-owned and voluntary systems is the *level of the system* at which physician involvement occurs. The findings discussed above have pertained to physician involvement at the individual hospital level. There are data that suggest that physicians are less involved at the divisional and corporate levels of systems.[4,11] To the extent that systems, whether investor-owned or voluntary, become larger and more centralized, physician involvement at these higher corporate levels would appear to be essential to addressing the larger socioeconomic trade-off issues that will exist. Several systems, both investor-owned and voluntary, are already moving toward greater physician involvement at higher levels, and future research should continue to document this trend and examine its impact on corporate decision making.

### ACKNOWLEDGMENT

This paper was funded in part by contract 0557-4176 from the Institute of Medicine, National Academy of Sciences. The opinions and conclusions expressed herein are solely those of the authors.

### NOTES

[1]Brown, M. (1979) Multihospital systems: Implications for physicians. *The Hospital Medical Staff* (August):2.

[2]Reynolds, J., and A. E. Stunden (1978) The organization of not-for-profit hospital systems. *Health Care Management Review* 3:23.

[3]Starr, P. (1982) *The Social Transformation of American Medicine.* New York: Basic Books.

[4]Morlock, L. L., J. A. Alexander, and H. Hunter (1985) Governing board—CEO—medical staff relations in multi-institutional arrangements. *Medical Care* 23:1193-1213.

[5]*The Hospital Medical Staff* (1978) AHA issues guidelines on physician involvement in hospital governance. 7:15.

[6]Neuhauser, D. (1971) The relationship between administrative activities and hospital performance. Research Series No. 28. Center for Health Administrative Studies, University of Chicago.

[7]Shortell, S. M., S. W. Becker, and D. Neuhauser (1976) The effects of management practices on hospital efficiency and quality of care. In *Organization Research in Hospitals*, S. M. Shortell and M. Brown, eds. Chicago: Blue Cross Association.

[8]Shortell, S. M., and J. P. LoGerfo (1981) Hospital medical staff organization and quality of care: Results for myocardial infarction and appendectomy. *Medical Care* 19:1041.

[9]Morlock, L. L., C. A. Nathanson, S. D. Horn, and D. N. Schumcher (1979) Organizational factors associated with quality of care in 17 general acute care hospitals. Paper presented at the annual meeting of the Association of University Programs in Health Administration, Toronto.

[10]Noie, N., S. Shortell, and M. Morrisey (1983) A survey of hospital medical staffs—Part 1 (1983) *Hospitals JAHA* 57(1).

[11]Alexander, J., and D. Cobbs (1984) MDs and multihospital systems. *The Hospital Medical Staff* 13(6):8-14.

# APPENDIX

**TABLE A-1**  Number of Physicians on the Governing Board

| | System Control Coefficients Relative to— | | | |
| | Freestanding Hospitals | | Investor-Owned Systems | |
| Variables | Coefficient | Standard Error | Coefficient | Standard Error |
|---|---|---|---|---|
| Freestanding hospital | | | −1.55 | .23*** |
| System characteristics | | | | |
| System control | | | | |
| Religious nonprofit | −.26 | .14* | −1.81 | .26*** |
| Secular nonprofit | −.06 | .25 | −1.49 | .33*** |
| Investor-owned | 1.55 | .23*** | | |
| Public | 4.23 | .80*** | 2.68 | .83*** |
| Contract-managed | −.29 | .21 | −1.85 | .25*** |
| System size (100s) | .22 | .08*** | .22 | .08*** |
| Hospital characteristics | | | | |
| Number of beds (100s) | .25 | .04*** | .25 | .04*** |
| Regional location | | | | |
| Northeast | .42 | .15*** | .42 | .15*** |
| South | −.27 | .14* | −.27 | .14* |
| North Central | −.49 | .13*** | −.49 | .13*** |
| SMSA size[a] | | | | |
| Under 100,000 | .40 | .37 | .40 | .37 |
| 100,000–250,000 | .46 | .17* | .46 | .17* |
| 250,000–500,000 | .89 | .17*** | .89 | .17*** |
| 500,000–1 million | .81 | .19*** | .81 | .19*** |
| 1 million–2.5 million | 1.00 | .15*** | 1.00 | .15*** |
| Over 2.5 million | 1.47 | .16*** | 1.47 | .16*** |
| House staff (100s) | −.54 | .11*** | −.54 | .11*** |
| Constant | 1.04 | .12*** | 2.59 | .25*** |
| Model Statistics | | | | |
| $R^2$ | .23 | | .23 | |
| N | 2,025 | | 2,025 | |

[a]Size of standard metropolitan statistical area (SMSA).
***Chi-square significant at $p \leq .01$.
**Chi-square significant at $p \leq .05$.
*Chi-square significant at $p \leq .10$.

**TABLE A-2**  Do Hospital Physician Governing Board Members
Have Voting Privileges?

| | System Control Coefficients Relative to— | | | |
| | Freestanding Hospitals | | Investor-Owned Systems | |
| Variables | Coefficient | Standard Error | Coefficient | Standard Error |
| --- | --- | --- | --- | --- |
| Freestanding hospital | | | −1.12 | .35*** |
| System characteristics | | | | |
| System control | | | | |
| Religious nonprofit | .44 | .18** | −.68 | .38* |
| Secular nonprofit | .30 | .29 | −.82 | .44* |
| Investor-owned | 1.12 | .35*** | | |
| Public | −1.47 | .75** | −2.59 | .82*** |
| Contract-managed | −.58 | .23** | −1.70 | .38*** |
| System size (100s) | .46 | .12*** | .46 | .12*** |
| Hospital characteristics | | | | |
| Number of beds (100s) | .30 | .05*** | .30 | .05*** |
| Regional location | | | | |
| Northeast | 1.31 | .19*** | 1.31 | .19*** |
| South | .18 | .16 | .18 | .16 |
| North Central | −.14 | .15 | −.14 | .15 |
| SMSA size[a] | | | | |
| Under 100,000 | .78 | .51 | .78 | .51 |
| 100,000–250,000 | .40 | .20** | .40 | .20** |
| 250,000–500,000 | .89 | .22*** | .89 | .22*** |
| 500,000–1 million | .28 | .23 | .28 | .23 |
| 1 million–2.5 million | .95 | .19*** | .95 | .19*** |
| Over 2.5 million | .39 | .20** | .39 | .20** |
| House staff (100s) | −.88 | .14*** | −.88 | .14*** |
| Constant | −.25 | .13* | .88 | .36** |
| Model statistics | | | | |
| Pseudo R | .35 | | .35 | |
| N | 2,067 | | 2,067 | |

[a]Size of standard metropolitan statistical area (SMSA).
***Chi-square significant at $p \leq .01$.
**Chi-square significant at $p \leq .05$.
*Chi-square significant at $p \leq .10$.

**TABLE A-3** Are There Physicians on the Governing Board Executive Committee?

| | System Control Coefficients Relative to— | | | |
| | Freestanding Hospitals | | Investor-Owned Systems | |
| Variables | Coefficient | Standard Error | Coefficient | Standard Error |
|---|---|---|---|---|
| Freestanding hospital | | | −.17 | .24 |
| System characteristics | | | | |
| System control | | | | |
| Religious nonprofit | −.57 | .16*** | −.74 | .28*** |
| Secular nonprofit | −.26 | .27 | −.43 | .35 |
| Investor-owned | .17 | .24 | | |
| Public | −.49 | .67 | −.66 | .71 |
| Contract-managed | −.03 | .23 | −.20 | .26 |
| System size (100s) | .12 | .09 | .12 | .09 |
| Hospital characteristics | | | | |
| Number of beds (100s) | .15 | .04*** | .15 | .04*** |
| Regional location | | | | |
| Northeast | .31 | .15** | .31 | .15** |
| South | −.03 | .15 | −.03 | .15 |
| North Central | −.31 | .15** | −.31 | .15** |
| SMSA size[a] | | | | |
| Under 100,000 | .03 | .40 | .03 | .40 |
| 100,000–250,000 | .55 | .18*** | .55 | .18*** |
| 250,000–500,000 | .59 | .17*** | .59 | .17*** |
| 500,000–1 million | .42 | .19** | .42 | .19** |
| 1 million–2.5 million | .59 | .16*** | .59 | .16*** |
| Over 2.5 million | .55 | .16*** | .55 | .16*** |
| House staff (100s) | −.29 | .12** | −.29 | .12** |
| Constant | −1.13 | .13*** | −.96 | .26*** |
| Model Statistics | | | | |
| Pseduo R | .19 | | .19 | |
| N | 2,067 | | 2,067 | |

[a]Size of standard metropolitan statistical area (SMSA).

***Chi-square significant at $p \leq .01$.

**Chi-square significant at $p \leq .05$.

**TABLE A-4**   Is the Hospital Chief Executive Officer a Voting Member of the Governing Board?

| | System Control Coefficients Relative to— | | | |
| | Freestanding Hospitals | | Investor-Owned Systems | |
| Variables | Coefficient | Standard Error | Coefficient | Standard Error |
|---|---|---|---|---|
| Freestanding hospital | | | −2.67 | .30*** |
| System characteristics | | | | |
| System control | | | | |
| Religious nonprofit | 1.82 | .16*** | −.86 | .32*** |
| Secular nonprofit | .32 | .29 | −2.35 | .39*** |
| Investor-owned | 2.67 | .30*** | | |
| Public | −2.24 | 1.11** | −4.92 | 1.14*** |
| Contract-managed | −.15 | .28 | −2.82 | .33*** |
| System size (100s) | .05 | .11 | .05 | .11 |
| Hospital characteristics | | | | |
| Number of beds (100s) | .23 | .04*** | .23 | .04*** |
| Regional location | | | | |
| Northeast | .36 | .17*** | .36 | .17*** |
| South | −.16 | .17 | −.16 | .17 |
| North Central | −.34 | .65** | −.34 | .16** |
| SMSA size[a] | | | | |
| Under 100,000 | 1.06 | .41*** | 1.06 | .41*** |
| 100,000–250,000 | .28 | .20 | .28 | .20 |
| 250,000–500,000 | .28 | .20 | .28 | .20 |
| 500,000–1 million | .45 | .21** | .45 | .21** |
| 1 million–2.5 million | .51 | .17*** | .51 | .17*** |
| Over 2.5 million | .59 | .18*** | .59 | .18*** |
| House staff (100s) | −.38 | .13*** | −.38 | .13*** |
| Constant | −1.89 | .15*** | .79 | .31** |
| Model Statistics | | | | |
| Pseudo R | .42 | | .42 | |
| N | 2,067 | | 2,067 | |

[a]Size of standard metropolitan statistical area (SMSA).
***Chi-square significant at $p \leq .01$.
**Chi-square significant at $p \leq .05$.

**TABLE A-5** Do Any Physicians Hold Salaried Positions as Part of Hospital's Administrative Team?

| | System Control Coefficients Relative to— | | | |
| | Freestanding Hospitals | | Investor-Owned Systems | |
| Variables | Coefficient | Standard Error | Coefficient | Standard Error |
|---|---|---|---|---|
| Freestanding hospital | | | 1.40 | .64* |
| System characteristics | | | | |
| System control | | | | |
| Religious nonprofit | .39 | .19** | 1.79 | .65*** |
| Secular nonprofit | .88 | .31*** | 2.28 | .69*** |
| Investor-owned | −1.40 | .64** | | |
| Public | .27 | .76 | 1.67 | .98* |
| Contract-managed | .11 | .38 | 1.51 | .67*** |
| System size (100s) | −.14 | .18 | −.14 | .18 |
| Hospital characteristics | | | | |
| Number of beds (100s) | .19 | .04*** | .19 | .04*** |
| Regional location | | | | |
| Northeast | .87 | .21*** | .87 | .21*** |
| South | −.32 | .23 | −.32 | .23 |
| North Central | −.06 | .21 | −.06 | .21 |
| SMSA size[a] | | | | |
| Under 100,000 | 1.19 | .47** | 1.19 | .47** |
| 100,000–250,000 | .65 | .27** | .65 | .27** |
| 250,000–500,000 | 1.12 | .24*** | 1.12 | .24*** |
| 500,000–1 million | 1.12 | .25*** | 1.12 | .25*** |
| 1 million–2.5 million | .91 | .23*** | .91 | .23*** |
| Over 2.5 million | 1.11 | .23*** | 1.11 | .23*** |
| House staff (100s) | .19 | .13 | .19 | .13 |
| Constant | −3.07 | .21*** | −4.47 | .66*** |
| Model Statistics | | | | |
| Pseudo R | .38 | | .38 | |
| N | 2,067 | | 2,067 | |

[a]Size of standard metropolitan statistical area (SMSA).
***Chi-square significant at $p \le .01$.
**Chi-square significant at $p \le .05$.
*Chi-square significant at $p \le .10$.

**TABLE A-6**   Is the Hospital Chief of Staff Compensated?

| | System Control Coefficients Relative to— | | | |
| | Freestanding Hospitals | | Investor-Owned Systems | |
| Variables | Coefficient | Standard Error | Coefficient | Standard Error |
|---|---|---|---|---|
| Freestanding hospital | | | .82 | .79 |
| System characteristics | | | | |
| System control | | | | |
|   Religious nonprofit | .17 | .27 | .99 | .81 |
|   Secular nonprofit | 1.11 | .37*** | 1.94 | .84** |
|   Investor-owned | −.82 | .79 | | |
|   Public | −.86 | .97 | −.03 | 1.24 |
| Contract-managed | .29 | .53 | 1.12 | .87 |
| System size (100s) | −.51 | .37 | −.51 | .37 |
| Hospital characteristics | | | | |
| Number of beds (100s) | .16 | .05*** | .16 | .05*** |
| Regional location | | | | |
|   Northeast | .50 | .28* | .50 | .28* |
|   South | −.10 | .31 | −.10 | .31 |
|   North Central | −.20 | .30 | −.20 | .30 |
| SMSA size[a] | | | | |
|   Under 100,000 | −6.15 | 24.96 | −6.15 | 24.96 |
|   100,000–250,000 | .32 | .54 | .32 | .54 |
|   250,000–500,000 | 1.34 | .40*** | 1.34 | .40*** |
|   500,000–1 million | 1.99 | .37*** | 1.99 | .37*** |
|   1 million–2.5 million | 1.91 | .34*** | 1.91 | .34*** |
|   Over 2.5 million | 1.67 | .36*** | 1.67 | .36*** |
| House staff (100s) | .23 | .14* | .23 | .14* |
| Constant | −4.32 | .35*** | −5.14 | .84*** |
| Model Statistics | | | | |
| Pseudo R | .39 | | .39 | |
| N | 2,067 | | 2,067 | |

[a]Size of standard metropolitan statistical area (SMSA).
***Chi-square significant at $p \leq .01$.
**Chi-square significant at $p \leq .05$.
*Chi-square significant at $p \leq .10$.

**TABLE A-7**  Is the Director of Medical Education Compensated?

| | System Control Coefficients Relative to— | | | |
| | Freestanding Hospitals | | Investor-Owned Systems | |
| Variables | Coefficient | Standard Error | Coefficient | Standard Error |
|---|---|---|---|---|
| Freestanding hospital | | | .71 | .45 |
| System characteristics | | | | |
| System control | | | | |
| Religious nonprofit | .06 | .19 | .78 | .46* |
| Secular nonprofit | −.18 | .37 | .54 | .55 |
| Investor-owned | −.71 | .45 | | |
| Public | −.44 | .80 | .28 | .91 |
| Contract-managed | −.50 | .45 | .21 | .54 |
| System size (100s) | −.17 | .20 | −.17 | .20 |
| Hospital characteristics | | | | |
| Number of beds (100s) | .51 | .05*** | .51 | .05*** |
| Regional location | | | | |
| Northeast | .03 | .20 | .03 | .20 |
| South | −1.01 | .23*** | −1.01 | .23*** |
| North Central | −.14 | .20 | −.14 | .20 |
| SMSA size[a] | | | | |
| Under 100,000 | 1.48 | .53*** | 1.48 | .53*** |
| 100,000–250,000 | 1.48 | .28*** | 1.48 | .28*** |
| 250,000–500,000 | 1.73 | .27*** | 1.73 | .27*** |
| 500,000–1 million | 2.02 | .28*** | 2.02 | .28*** |
| 1 million–2.5 million | 1.91 | .25*** | 1.91 | .25*** |
| Over 2.5 million | 2.13 | .26*** | 2.13 | .26*** |
| House staff (100s) | −.52 | .14*** | −.52 | .14*** |
| Constant | −3.68 | .24*** | −4.39 | .48*** |
| Model Statistics | | | | |
| Pseudo R | .51 | | .51 | |
| N | 2,067 | | 2,067 | |

[a]Size of standard metropolitan statistical area (SMSA).

***Chi-square significant at $p \leq .01$.

*Chi-square significant at $p \leq .10$.

**TABLE A-8**　Number of Medical Staff Committees

| | System Control Coefficients Relative to— | | | |
| | Freestanding Hospitals | | Investor-Owned Systems | |
| Variables | Coefficient | Standard Error | Coefficient | Standard Error |
|---|---|---|---|---|
| Freestanding hospital | | | 2.27 | .80*** |
| System characteristics | | | | |
| System control | | | | |
| Religious nonprofit | .55 | .49 | 2.82 | .88*** |
| Secular nonprofit | −1.02 | .86 | 1.25 | 1.12 |
| Investor-owned | −2.27 | .80*** | | |
| Public | −8.17 | 2.74*** | −5.92 | 2.84** |
| Contract-managed | −1.06 | .71 | 1.21 | .86 |
| System size (100s) | .11 | .28 | .11 | .28 |
| Hospital characteristics | | | | |
| Number of beds (100s) | 2.82 | .12*** | 2.82 | .12*** |
| Regional location | | | | |
| Northeast | 1.02 | .50** | 1.02 | .50** |
| South | −2.61 | .47*** | −2.61 | .47*** |
| North Central | −2.99 | .45*** | −2.99 | .45*** |
| SMSA size[a] | | | | |
| Under 100,000 | .88 | 1.25 | .88 | 1.25 |
| 100,000–250,000 | 3.79 | .59*** | 3.79 | .59*** |
| 250,000–500,000 | 1.55 | .67*** | 1.55 | .67*** |
| 500,000–1 million | 3.12 | .64*** | 3.12 | .64*** |
| 1 million–2.5 million | 4.23 | .51*** | 4.23 | .51*** |
| Over 2.5 million | 5.10 | .54*** | 5.10 | .54*** |
| House staff (100s) | −3.44 | .39*** | −3.44 | .39*** |
| Constant | 8.02 | .42*** | 5.75 | .84*** |
| Model statistics | | | | |
| $R^2$ | .45 | | .45 | |
| N | 2,025 | | 2,025 | |

[a]Size of standard metropolitan statistical area (SMSA).

***Chi-square significant at $p \leq .01$.

**Chi-square significant at $p \leq .05$.

**TABLE A-9** Does the Hospital Have a Committee for Cost Containment or Cost Awareness?

| | System Control Coefficients Relative to— | | | |
| | Freestanding Hospitals | | Investor-Owned Systems | |
| Variables | Coefficient | Standard Error | Coefficient | Standard Error |
|---|---|---|---|---|
| Freestanding hospital | | | .19 | .36 |
| System characteristics | | | | |
| System control | | | | |
| Religious nonprofit | .14 | .19 | .37 | .39 |
| Secular nonprofit | .05 | .34 | .24 | .47 |
| Investor-owned | −.19 | .36 | | |
| Public | .14 | .72 | .33 | .80 |
| Contract-managed | −.05 | .32 | .14 | .41 |
| System size (100s) | −.16 | .14 | −.16 | .14 |
| Hospital characteristics | | | | |
| Number of beds (100s) | .19 | .04*** | .19 | .04*** |
| Regional location | | | | |
| Northeast | .29 | .19 | .29 | .19 |
| South | −.02 | .19 | −.02 | .19 |
| North Central | −.44 | .19** | −.44 | .19** |
| SMSA size[a] | | | | |
| Under 100,000 | −.34 | .51 | −.34 | .51 |
| 100,000–250,000 | −.12 | .24 | −.12 | .24 |
| 250,000–500,000 | −.43 | .25* | −.43 | .25* |
| 500,000–1 million | −.16 | .25 | −.16 | .25 |
| 1 million–2.5 million | −.10 | .20 | −.10 | .20 |
| Over 2.5 million | −.16 | .21 | −.16 | .21 |
| House staff (100s) | .03 | .13 | .03 | .13 |
| Constant | −1.89 | .17*** | −2.07 | .38*** |
| Model statistics | | | | |
| Pseudo R | .14 | | .14 | |
| N | 2,067 | | 2,067 | |

[a]Size of standard metropolitan statistical area (SMSA).
***Chi-square significant at $p \leq .01$.
**Chi-square significant at $p \leq .05$.
*Chi-square significant at $p \leq .10$.

**TABLE A-10**   Does the Hospital Have a Committee for
Medical Staff Long-Range Planning?

| | System Control Coefficients Relative to— | | | |
| | Freestanding Hospitals | | Investor-Owned Systems | |
| Variables | Coefficient | Standard Error | Coefficient | Standard Error |
|---|---|---|---|---|
| Freestanding hospital | | | .93 | .32*** |
| System characteristics | | | | |
|   System control | | | | |
|     Religious nonprofit | −.04 | .16 | .90 | .34*** |
|     Secular nonprofit | .03 | .28 | .96 | .40** |
|     Investor-owned | −.93 | .32*** | | |
|     Public | −.65 | .73 | .29 | .79 |
|   Contract-managed | −.52 | .27* | .42 | .34 |
|   System size (100s) | .08 | .11 | .08 | .11 |
| Hospital characteristics | | | | |
|   Number of beds (100s) | .20 | .04*** | .20 | .04*** |
|   Regional location | | | | |
|     Northeast | .28 | .16* | .28 | .16* |
|     South | .01 | .16 | .01 | .16 |
|     North Central | −.06 | .15 | −.06 | .15 |
|   SMSA size[a] | | | | |
|     Under 100,000 | .15 | .40 | .15 | .40 |
|     100,000–250,000 | .14 | .19 | .14 | .19 |
|     250,000–500,000 | −.16 | .19 | −.16 | .19 |
|     500,000–1 million | .02 | .21 | .02 | .21 |
|     1 million–2.5 million | .10 | .17 | .10 | .17 |
|     Over 2.5 million | .22 | .17 | .22 | .17 |
|   House staff (100s) | −.34 | .13*** | −.34 | .13*** |
| Constant | −1.33 | .14*** | −2.26 | .33*** |
| Model statistics | | | | |
|   Pseudo R | .14 | | .14 | |
|   N | 2,067 | | 2,067 | |

[a]Size of standard metropolitan statistical area (SMSA).
***Chi-square significant at $p \leq .01$.
**Chi-square significant at $p \leq .05$.
*Chi-square significant at $p \leq .10$.

**TABLE A-11**   Descriptive Statistics for Hospital Sample Subset (N = 2,025)

| Variables | Mean | Standard Deviation | Number in Sample[a] |
|---|---|---|---|
| *Independent Variables* | | | |
| Freestanding hospital | .71 | .45 | 1,442 |
| System characteristics | | | |
| System control | | | |
|   Religious nonprofit | .12 | .32 | 241 |
|   Secular nonprofit | .03 | .18 | 68 |
|   Investor-owned | .06 | .24 | 125 |
|   Public | .003 | .06 | 7 |
| Contract-managed | .07 | .26 | 142 |
| System size (100s) | 21.31 | 72.97 | |
| Hospital characteristics | | | |
| Number of beds (100s) | 190.53 | 178.50 | |
| Regional location | | | |
|   Northeast | .23 | .42 | 460 |
|   South | .26 | .44 | 533 |
|   North Central | .32 | .47 | 647 |
|   West | .19 | .39 | 385 |
| SMSA size[b] | | | |
|   Non-SMSA | .45 | .50 | 906 |
|   Under 100,000 | .02 | .12 | 32 |
|   100,000–250,000 | .09 | .28 | 178 |
|   250,000–500,000 | .09 | .29 | 184 |
|   500,000–1 million | .08 | .27 | 155 |
|   1 million–2.5 million | .14 | .35 | 293 |
|   Over 2.5 million | .14 | .34 | 277 |
| House staff (100s) | 11.49 | 50.04 | |
| *Dependent Variables* | | | |
| Number of M.D.s on governing board | 1.96 | 2.27 | |
| Number of medical staff committees | 13.44 | 9.13 | |

[a]For dichotomously scored variables.
[b]Size of standard metropolitan statistical area (SMSA).

*For-Profit Enterprise in Health Care.* 1986.
National Academy Press, Washington, D.C.

# Medical Staff Size, Hospital Privileges, and Compensation Arrangements: A Comparison of System Hospitals

Michael A. Morrisey, Jeffrey A. Alexander, and
Stephen M. Shortell

## INTRODUCTION

Since 1975, multihospital systems have grown at a 3 to 4 percent annual rate (Ermann and Gabel, 1984). Many observers see fundamental changes in the practice of medicine as a result of this trend (Starr, 1982), particularly in regard to the investor-owned (IO) systems (Relman, 1980). Among the concerns are (1) potential conflict of interest between the profit motive and patient needs, (2) the ability of investor-owned system hospitals to deliver care in terms of the number and types of physicians that affiliate with such hospitals, (3) the degree to which IO system hospitals review privileges, and (4) the nature of the financial relationships between physicians and IO system hospitals.

The first issue is beyond the range of this paper. The remaining three are addressed in descriptive fashion by comparing IO system hospitals with freestanding hospitals and hospitals in other types of systems. The analysis uses available data from the American Hospital Association (AHA). The following section describes the three data sets used. This is followed by findings pertaining to the number and types of physicians, privilege criteria and review, and compensation arrangements. A concluding section discusses the implications

Dr. Morrisey is in the Department of Health Care Organization and Policy and Dr. Alexander is in the Department of Health Services Administration, both at the University of Alabama at Birmingham. When this paper was written they were with the Hospital Research and Educational Trust, Chicago, Illinois. Dr. Shortell is with the J. L. Kellogg Graduate School of Management and Center for Health Services and Policy Research at Northwestern University, Evanston, Illinois.

of the findings and makes suggestions for further study.

## DATA AND METHODS

Most of the medical staff data are drawn from the 1982 AHA Survey of Medical Staff Organization. This survey was mailed to 3,027 nonfederal, short-term, acute care hospitals in the 48 contiguous states and the District of Columbia. Because the survey was designed to test the effects of regulation, the sample hospitals were chosen by a 25 percent random design augmented with additional hospitals in 22 states. These states were primarily those with mandatory or voluntary rate-setting programs. The survey had an overall response rate of 69.9 percent. Due to the sampling design, the sample is not wholly representative of national data. The respondents are larger, more likely to be from the Northeast, Middle Atlantic, and West North Central regions, more likely to have a teaching program, and less likely to be IO hospitals (Shortell et al., 1985).

Data on the size, specialty composition, and physicians on the hospital payroll as well as all control variables were taken from the 1982 AHA Annual Survey of Hospitals. This universe survey had an overall response rate of 89.9 percent.

The data on hospital system participation are drawn from the 1982 AHA Validation Survey of Multihospital Systems. That survey collected information on the hospitals participating in the system, the date they joined, and the type of participation (i.e., owned, leased, sponsored, or contract-managed). To our knowledge, this is the most complete file of multihospital system hospitals in existence.

For purposes of this analysis, when two or more hospitals are owned, leased, or sponsored by another entity, they are categorized as being part of a system. System hospitals are then subdivided by ownership: religious, secular nonprofit, public (i.e., owned by a state or local government), and IO. Contract-managed hospitals are given a unique category as are freestanding hospitals. Federal hospitals have been excluded. This yields six mutually exclusive and exhaustive categories.

Two analyses are conducted for each variable of interest. First, simple comparisons across the six cells are presented. Statistical tests are performed comparing IO system hospitals with hospitals in each of the other cells. When the variables are continuous, t-tests of means are calculated; when the data are dichotomous, chi-squared tests are used.

Second, regression techniques are used to test for the same differences controlling for system, hospital, region, and urban location variables. Specifically, the equation controls for

• System size (the number of hospitals in the system);
• Staffed beds (the average number of beds set up and staffed over the course of the year);
• Teaching status (number of interns and residents on the hospital payroll);
• Northeast region (Connecticut, Maine, Massachusetts, New Hampshire, New Jersey, New York, Pennsylvania, Rhode Island, Vermont);
• South region (Alabama, Arkansas, District of Columbia, Delaware, Florida, Georgia, Kentucky, Louisiana, Maryland, Mississippi,

North Carolina, Oklahoma, South Carolina, Tennessee, Texas, Virginia, West Virginia);
• North Central region (Illinois, Indiana, Iowa, Kansas, Michigan, Montana, Missouri, Nebraska, North Dakota, Ohio, South Dakota, Wisconsin); and
• Standard metropolitan statistical area (SMSA) size (under 100,000, 100,000-250,000, 250,000-500,000, 500,000-1 million, 1 million-25 million, over 25 million).

For exploratory purposes these equations are estimated twice, once to allow comparisons of all system types to freestanding hospitals and once again to allow direct comparisons with IO system hospitals. Equations emphasizing continuous dependent variables are estimated using ordinary least squares regression techniques; dichotomous dependent variables are analyzed using logit regression.

Means and standard deviations of all variables are found in Appendix Tables A-1, A-2, A-3, and A-4. Because different sample sizes are available for different variables, four sets of summary statistics are reported.

### NUMBER AND TYPES OF PHYSICIANS

Table 1 presents data on the number of applications for medical staff membership received in 1981. The average IO system hospital received 16 applications. This is comparable to freestanding and voluntary system hospitals. However, publicly owned system hospitals received twice that number of applications;

**TABLE 1** Comparision of Investor-Owned System Hospitals with Other Types of Hospitals: How Many Physicians Applied for Active Staff Privileges During Calendar Year 1981?

| Investor-Owned Systems | | Freestanding | | Religious Systems | | Nonprofit Systems | | Public Systems | | Contract-Managed | |
|---|---|---|---|---|---|---|---|---|---|---|---|
| N | Mean (S.D.) | N | Mean (S.D.) | N | Mean (S.D.) | N | Mean (S.D.) | N | Mean (S.D.) | N | Mean (S.D.) |
| 117 | 16.11 (18.02) | 1,283 | 13.48 (20.71) | 223 | 19.22 (24.64) | 59 | 27.25 (51.62) | 6 | 33.50** (26.82) | 123 | 7.48*** (10.90) |

***T significant at $p \leq .01$ when compared to hospitals in investor-owned systems.
**T significant at $p \leq .05$ when compared to hospitals in investor-owned systems.

contract-managed hospitals only received 7.5 applications, on average.

These differences are related to differences in hospital size, location, and teaching status. When these factors are taken into account (Appendix Table A-5), it is only the secular nonprofit system hospitals that differ significantly from IO system hospitals. They receive on average 5.2 more applications annually than do IOs.

Table 2 shows that IO system hospitals accept a higher percentage of applicants (89.76 percent) than does any other hospital group. Appendix Table A-6 demonstrates that, controlling for other factors, this difference is even more pronounced. Nonprofit secular system hospitals approve 12 percent fewer applications, religious systems 8.9 percent fewer, and freestanding and contract-managed hospitals approve over 11 percent fewer applications than do IO system hospitals.

While IO system hospitals received and accepted more medical staff applications in 1981, these hospitals, nonetheless, had smaller medical staffs than did other system hospitals (Table 3A). However, the average of 91 physicians in IO system hospitals is comparable to freestanding hospitals and almost twice as large as contract-managed hospitals. This result is largely attributable to differences in hospital size across system control. Table 3B reports the number of physicians per 100 beds. When measured on this basis, IO system hospitals have over 61 physicians per 100 beds. This is larger than contract-managed, freestanding, and most system hospitals. Only voluntary sec-

ular system hospitals have more active and associate medical staff members per 100 hospital beds. As Appendix Table A-7 reports, however, while the relationship across hospital types continues to hold when other factors are introduced, it is only the public system, freestanding, and contract-managed hospitals that exhibit statistically significant differences from IO system hospitals.

The specialty composition of the staff was also examined, focusing on family practice, pediatrics, general internal medicine, other medical specialties, and general surgery. The simple comparisons are reported in Table 4. In general the IO system hospitals have as many or more physicians per 100 beds as hospitals in other categories. The principal exception is in pediatrics where voluntary secular system hospitals have more physicians. These findings hold when other factors are entered into the equations (Appendix Tables A-8, A-9, A-10, A-11, and A-12). Interestingly, the larger IO medical staffs appear to arise, in part, from larger numbers of internists and other medical specialists.

Table 5 reports the dependence of hospitals on the top five admitters to the hospital. All differences are statistically significant. Contract-managed hospitals derived over 63 percent of their admissions from five physicians or physician groups; public system hospitals only 12 percent. IO system hospitals fall in the lower end of the range with approximately 40 percent of their admissions provided through the top five admitters. When hospital size and other factors are controlled (Appendix Table

**TABLE 2**  Comparison of Investor-Owned System Hospitals with Other Types of Hospitals: What Percentage of the Physicians Who Applied for Active Staff Privileges During Calendar Year 1981 Were Accepted?

| Investor-Owned Systems | | Freestanding | | Religious Systems | | Nonprofit Systems | | Public Systems | | Contract-Managed | |
|---|---|---|---|---|---|---|---|---|---|---|---|
| N | Mean (S.D.) | N | Mean (S.D.) | N | Mean (S.D.) | N | Mean (S.D.) | N | Mean (S.D.) | N | Mean (S.D.) |
| 117 | 89.76 (23.39) | 1,283 | 81.39*** (34.99) | 223 | 86.75 (29.17) | 59 | 81.45 (35.57) | 6 | 72.93 (39.62) | 123 | 76.45*** (39.85) |

***T significant at $p \leq .01$ when compared to hospitals in investor-owned systems.

**TABLE 3A** Comparison of Investor-Owned System Hospitals with Other Types of Hospitals: How Many Practitioners (Total) Were on the Active or Associate Medical Staff as of September 30, 1982?

| Investor-Owned Systems | | Freestanding | | Religious Systems | | Nonprofit Systems | | Public Systems | | Contract-Managed | |
|---|---|---|---|---|---|---|---|---|---|---|---|
| N | Mean (S.D.) | N | Mean (S.D.) | N | Mean (S.D.) | N | Mean (S.D.) | N | Mean (S.D.) | N | Mean (S.D.) |
| 395 | 91.03 (93.89) | 3,453 | 90.32 (140.32) | 538 | 144.07*** (120.21) | 232 | 169.47*** (300.17) | 31 | 286.65** (449.59) | 355 | 46.73*** (78.41) |

***T significant at $p \leq .01$ when compared with hospitals in investor-owned systems.
**T significant at $p \leq .05$ when compared with hospitals in investor-owned systems.

A-13), IO system hospitals have a lower concentration of admissions than do voluntary secular system hospitals and contract-managed facilities.

Finally, Table 6 reports the percentage of the top five admitting physicians who are board certified. With the exception of contract-managed hospitals, which had a smaller percentage of board-certified heavy admitters, there was no statistically significant difference between hospitals in IO chains and other types of hospitals. This finding is born out by the multivariate analysis in Appendix Table A-14.

### PRIVILEGES CRITERIA AND REVIEW

Although IO sytem hospitals accept more applications (see Table 2), there is no statistically significant difference in the proportion of these hospitals that require at least some specialties to be board certified (Table 7). This

result holds when other factors are included in the regression as well (Appendix Table A-15).

Recently reported AHA data indicate that proprietary hospitals (not just IO system hospitals) have a somewhat higher number of board-certified staff members than do nonprofit hospitals (28.8 per 100 beds versus 24.6 per 100 beds) (American Medical Association, 1984). This finding is consistent with earlier AHA data. When earlier data are controlled for other factors, however, the difference loses statistical significance (Morrisey, 1984). Table 8 reports the proportion of active and associate medical staff members who were board certified in 1982. Sixty-one percent of the medical staff members of hospitals in IO chains were board certified. This percentage is not statistically different from hospitals in most other ownership control categories. Hospitals in religious systems had a higher proportion of board-

**TABLE 3B** Comparison of Investor-Owned System Hospitals with Other Types of Hospitals: How Many Practitioners (Total) Were on the Active or Associate Medical Staff per 100 Staffed Beds as of September 30, 1982?

| Investor-Owned Systems | | Freestanding | | Religious Systems | | Nonprofit Systems | | Public Systems | | Contract-Managed | |
|---|---|---|---|---|---|---|---|---|---|---|---|
| N | Mean (S.D.) | N | Mean (S.D.) | N | Mean (S.D.) | N | Mean (S.D.) | N | Mean (S.D.) | N | Mean (S.D.) |
| 395 | 61.39 (55.57) | 3,453 | 43.67*** (44.07) | 538 | 52.24*** (36.79) | 232 | 66.03 (73.14) | 31 | 61.61 (51.98) | 355 | 36.97*** (39.49) |

***T significant at $p \leq .01$ when compared to hospitals in investor-owned systems.

TABLE 4 Comparison of Investor-Owned System Hospitals with Other Types of Hospitals: How Many Practitioners Were on the Active or Associate Medical Staff per 100 Staffed Beds, by Specialty, as of September 30, 1982?

| Specialty | Investor-Owned Systems | | Freestanding | | Religious Systems | | Nonprofit Systems | | Public Systems | | Contract-Managed | |
|---|---|---|---|---|---|---|---|---|---|---|---|---|
| | N | Mean (S.D.) | N | Mean (S.D.) | N | Mean (S.D.) | N | Mean (S.D.) | N | Mean (S.D.) | N | Mean (S.D.) |
| General and family practice | 394 | 10.52 (7.09) | 3,415 | 8.73*** (8.33) | 531 | 8.45*** (6.48) | 228 | 10.05 (9.86) | 31 | 7.60** (8.40) | 336 | 9.79 (7.65) |
| Pediatrics | 394 | 2.72 (4.63) | 3,415 | 2.91 (7.69) | 531 | 2.98 (3.32) | 228 | 4.89*** (10.40) | 31 | 3.71 (5.09) | 336 | 1.95 (7.85) |
| Internal medicine | 394 | 7.74 (12.53) | 3,415 | 5.06*** (8.01) | 531 | 6.69 (6.78) | 228 | 7.56 (12.28) | 31 | 9.02 (12.11) | 336 | 3.91*** (7.30) |
| Other medical specialties | 394 | 7.29 (11.18) | 3,415 | 3.63*** (7.21) | 531 | 5.32*** (6.71) | 228 | 6.29 (11.53) | 31 | 7.53 (9.81) | 336 | 2.83*** (6.20) |
| General surgery | 394 | 5.30 (5.65) | 3,415 | 3.81*** (4.72) | 531 | 4.77 (4.21) | 228 | 4.99 (6.46) | 31 | 5.37 (6.38) | 336 | 3.40*** (3.61) |

***T significant at $p \leq .01$ when compared with hospitals in investor-owned systems.
**T significant at $p \leq .05$ when compared with hospitals in investor-owned systems.

**TABLE 5** Comparison of Investor-Owned System Hospitals with Other Types of Hospitals: What Percentage of Total Admissions During Calendar Year 1981 Were Admitted by the Five Highest Admitting Physicians?

| Investor-Owned Systems | | Freestanding | | Religious Systems | | Nonprofit Systems | | Public Systems | | Contract-Managed | |
|---|---|---|---|---|---|---|---|---|---|---|---|
| N | Mean (S.D.) | N | Mean (S.D.) | N | Mean (S.D.) | N | Mean (S.D.) | N | Mean (S.D.) | N | Mean (S.D.) |
| 117 | 40.54 (27.47) | 1,283 | 46.57** (33.54) | 223 | 32.65** (28.61) | 59 | 50.38* (35.54) | 6 | 12.38*** (2.22) | 123 | 63.56*** (31.81) |

  \*\*\*T significant at $p \leq .01$ when compared with hospitals in investor-owned systems.
   \*\*T significant at $p \leq .05$ when compared with hospitals in investor-owned systems.
    \*T significant at $p \leq .10$ when compared with hospitals in investor-owned systems.

**TABLE 6** Comparison of Investor-Owned System Hospitals with Other Types of Hospitals: What Percentage of Top Five Admitting Physicians Are Board Certified?

| Investor-Owned Systems | | Freestanding | | Religious Systems | | Nonprofit Systems | | Public Systems | | Contract-Managed | |
|---|---|---|---|---|---|---|---|---|---|---|---|
| N | Mean (S.D.) | N | Mean (S.D.) | N | Mean (S.D.) | N | Mean (S.D.) | N | Mean (S.D.) | N | Mean (S.D.) |
| 117 | 62.79 (35.34) | 1,236 | 60.98 (36.40) | 221 | 65.29 (33.44) | 57 | 60.61 (37.30) | 6 | 65.00 (28.11) | 121 | 52.66** (36.97) |

  \*\*T significant at $p \leq .05$ when compared with hospitals in investor-owned systems.

certified medical staff members, but this difference loses statistical significance in the multivariate analysis (Appendix Table A-16).

Further, IO system hospitals have longer probationary periods for new medical staff members than do either freestanding or contract-managed hospitals (Table 9). System hospitals, across the board, are similar in this respect. These differences disappear, however, when other factors are considered (Table A-17). The differences appear to be largely attributable to hospital and community size.

While no data are available from AHA surveys pertaining to utilization review and qual-

**TABLE 7** Comparison of Investor-Owned System Hospitals with Other Types of Hospitals: Is Board Certification Required for Any (or All) Specialties on Your Hospital's Active Staff?

| | Investor-Owned Systems | | Freestanding | | Religious Systems | | Nonprofit Systems | | Public Systems | | Contract-Managed | |
|---|---|---|---|---|---|---|---|---|---|---|---|---|
| | N | % | N | % | N | % | N | % | N | % | N | % |
| Yes | 35 | 29.91 | 396 | 30.87 | 54 | 24.22 | 20 | 33.90 | 2 | 33.33 | 29 | 23.58 |
| No | 82 | 70.09 | 887 | 69.13 | 169 | 75.78 | 39 | 66.10 | 4 | 66.67 | 94 | 76.42 |
| Total | 117 | 100.00 | 1,283 | 100.00 | 223 | 100.00 | 59 | 100.00 | 6 | 100.00 | 123 | 100.00 |

**TABLE 8**  Comparison of Investor-Owned System Hospitals with Other Types of Hospitals: What Proportion of Active and Associate Medical Staff in the Hospital Are Board Certified?

| Investor-Owned Systems | | Freestanding | | Religious Systems | | Nonprofit Systems | | Public Systems | | Contract-Managed | |
|---|---|---|---|---|---|---|---|---|---|---|---|
| N | Mean (S.D.) | N | Mean (S.D.) | N | Mean (S.D.) | N | Mean (S.D.) | N | Mean (S.D.) | N | Mean (S.D.) |
| 348 | 0.61 (0.22) | 3,062 | 0.61 (0.35) | 500 | 0.65*** (0.26) | 204 | 0.65 (0.41) | 30 | 0.58 (0.24) | 304 | 0.58 (0.25) |

***T significant at $p \leq .01$ when compared with hospitals in investor-owned systems.

ity assurance activities of different types of hospitals, some descriptive data are available from a recent AMA survey (1984). They report that a somewhat higher percentage of proprietary (not just IO system) hospitals formally review clinical decisions than do nonproprietary hospitals (83 percent versus 79.8 percent). A somewhat lower percentage of proprietary hospitals set guidelines to reduce length of stay (65.9 percent versus 71.8 percent); review length of stay after discharge (84.9 percent versus 90.1 percent); attempt to reduce the number of treatment procedures that physicians prescribe (26.7 percent versus 32.2 percent); and review the range of services that the hospital provides (6.7 percent versus 9.5 percent).

## COMPENSATION ARRANGEMENTS

Table 10, based on AHA annual survey data, compares the number of full-time and part-time physicians and dentists employed by the hospital in a clinical capacity. On average, public system hospitals employ over 80 physicians. Freestanding hospitals employ approximately seven physicians. All private voluntary system hospitals employ similar numbers. However, IO system hospitals employ less than one physician, on average. With the exception of the public system hospitals, none of these differences remain when one controls for hospital size, teaching commitment, and location (Appendix Table A-18). That is, except for public system hospitals, hospitals are quite similar in their employment of physicians.

Hospital-based physicians have historically had the greatest direct financial affiliation with hospitals. These affiliations involve employment, form of compensation, and billing arrangements. Tables 11 and 12 report the available data from the AHA Survey on Medical Staff Organization on the form of compen-

**TABLE 9**  Comparison of Investor-Owned System Hospitals with Other Types of Hospitals: What Is the Usual Number of Months for Provisional Appointment Before a Physician Is Awarded Full Privileges?

| Investor-Owned Systems | | Freestanding | | Religious Systems | | Nonprofit Systems | | Public Systems | | Contract-Managed | |
|---|---|---|---|---|---|---|---|---|---|---|---|
| N | Mean (S.D.) | N | Mean (S.D.) | N | Mean (S.D.) | N | Mean (S.D.) | N | Mean (S.D.) | N | Mean (S.D.) |
| 117 | 9.62 (4.54) | 1,283 | 8.80* (5.29) | 223 | 10.41 (4.98) | 59 | 9.44 (5.15) | 6 | 11.00 (2.45) | 123 | 7.85*** (4.25) |

***T significant at $p \leq .01$ when compared with hospitals in investor-owned systems.
  *T significant at $p \leq .10$ when compared with hospitals in investor-owned systems.

**TABLE 10** Comparison of Investor-Owned System Hospitals with Other Types of Hospitals: How Many Full-Time and Part-Time Physicians and Dentists Were on the Hospital Payroll as of September 30, 1982?

| Investor-Owned Systems | | Freestanding | | Religious Systems | | Nonprofit Systems | | Public Systems | | Contract-Managed | |
|---|---|---|---|---|---|---|---|---|---|---|---|
| N | Mean (S.D.) | N | Mean (S.D.) | N | Mean (S.D.) | N | Mean (S.D.) | N | Mean (S.D.) | N | Mean (S.D.) |
| 395 | 0.28 (1.58) | 3,453 | 6.91*** (30.67) | 538 | 5.87*** (14.91) | 232 | 7.77*** (22.94) | 31 | 80.48*** (150.90) | 355 | 1.03** (5.25) |

***T significant at $p \leq .01$ when compared with hospitals in investor-owned systems.

**T significant at $p \leq .05$ when compared with hospitals in investor-owned systems.

sation for anesthesiologists and radiologists. The results are similar—57 percent of public system hospitals compensate their physicians on a salary basis, and the remainder use an output-based arrangement such as a percentage of revenue, or the hospital or patient pays on a fee-for-service basis. Approximately 12 percent of freestanding and contract-managed hospitals use salary compensation. Secular nonprofit system hospitals are somewhat more likely and religious systems somewhat less likely to use salary arrangement than are freestanding hospitals. In marked contrast, IO system hospitals almost never use a salary form of compensation. These relationships are generally supported in the multivariate comparisons (Appendix Tables A-19 and A-20).

The form of compensation for pathologists is summarized in Table 13. Much larger proportions of hospitals of all types compensate these physicians with salary arrangements. It is still the case, however, that a smaller proportion of IO system hospitals use the salary form. The statistically significant differences with IO system hospitals are maintained only for religious and public system hospitals once other factors are considered (Appendix Table A-21).

Finally, Tables 14, 15, and 16 report the degree to which the hospital bills for physician services as one moves from anesthesiology to radiology to pathology. As with other measures of financial involvement with physicians, IO system hospitals are least likely to bill patients for physician services. In this regard they are most like religious system hospitals and least like freestanding hospitals and public system hospitals. These differences persist when other factors are controlled (Appendix Tables A-22, A-23, and A-24).

**TABLE 11** Comparison of Investor-Owned System Hospitals with Other Types of Hospitals: What Is the Primary Form of Compensation for Anesthesiologists?[a]

| | Investor-Owned Systems | | Freestanding | | Religious Systems | | Nonprofit Systems | | Public Systems | | Contract-Managed | |
|---|---|---|---|---|---|---|---|---|---|---|---|---|
| | N | % | N | % | N | % | N | % | N | % | N | % |
| Yes | 78 | 98.73 | 785 | 88.40*** | 143 | 94.70 | 33 | 82.50*** | 3 | 42.86*** | 61 | 88.41** |
| No | 1 | 1.27 | 103 | 11.60*** | 8 | 5.30 | 7 | 17.50*** | 4 | 57.14*** | 8 | 11.59** |
| Total | 79 | 100.00 | 888 | 100.00 | 151 | 100.00 | 40 | 100.00 | 7 | 100.00 | 69 | 100.00 |

[a]Yes = percent of revenue or fee-for-service; no = straight salary; "other" types not included.

***Chi-square significant at $p \leq .01$ when compared with hospitals in investor-owned systems.

**Chi-square significant at $p \leq .05$ when compared with hospitals in investor-owned systems.

TABLE 12   Comparison of Investor-Owned System Hospitals with Other Types of Hospitals: What Is the Primary Form of Compensation for Radiologists?[a]

| | Investor-Owned Systems | | Freestanding | | Religious Systems | | Nonprofit Systems | | Public Systems | | Contract-Managed | |
|---|---|---|---|---|---|---|---|---|---|---|---|---|
| | N | % | N | % | N | % | N | % | N | % | N | % |
| Yes | 77 | 97.47 | 782 | 88.06** | 146 | 96.69 | 34 | 85.00** | 3 | 42.86*** | 66 | 95.65 |
| No | 2 | 2.53 | 106 | 11.94** | 5 | 3.31 | 6 | 15.00** | 4 | 57.14*** | 3 | 4.35 |
| Total | 79 | 100.00 | 888 | 100.00 | 151 | 100.00 | 40 | 100.00 | 7 | 100.00 | 69 | 100.00 |

[a]Yes = percent of revenue or fee-for-service; no = straight salary; "other" types not included.
***Chi-square significant at $p \leq .01$ when compared with hospitals in investor-owned systems.
**Chi-square significant at $p \leq .05$ when compared with hospitals in investor-owned systems.

## DISCUSSION

After controlling for system size, hospital size, teaching activity, region of the country, and SMSA size, IO system hospitals tend to differ from other types of hospitals in the following ways:

1. They accept a somewhat higher percentage of medical staff applications than other types of hospitals.
2. They take essentially the same time to review physician performance before awarding full privileges as do other hospitals.
3. They have a larger number of physicians per bed.
4. They have a larger number of internists and other medical specialists than other hospitals, but fewer pediatricians than secular nonprofit hospitals.
5. They experience less concentration of ad-

missions than secular nonprofit hospital systems and contract-managed hospitals, but are similar to other hospitals.
6. They are less likely to have salaried arrangements with anesthesiologists, pathologists, or radiologists.
7. They are more likely to have hospital-based specialists directly bill for services.

On all other dimensions investigated, IOs are essentially similar to other types of hospitals, whether system owned or freestanding.

Because the study is descriptive and exploratory, no firm conclusions can be drawn. In reference to the original three issues (i.e., number and types of physicians, privilege criteria and review process, and compensation arrangements), the data do suggest the following observations and raise several questions for future investigation.

TABLE 13   Comparison of Investor-Owned System Hospitals with Other Types of Hospitals: What Is the Primary Form of Compensation for Pathologists?[a]

| | Investor-Owned Systems | | Freestanding | | Religious Systems | | Nonprofit Systems | | Public Systems | | Contract-Managed | |
|---|---|---|---|---|---|---|---|---|---|---|---|---|
| | N | % | N | % | N | % | N | % | N | % | N | % |
| Yes | 67 | 84.81 | 568 | 63.96*** | 99 | 65.56*** | 27 | 67.50* | 2 | 28.57*** | 58 | 84.06 |
| No | 12 | 15.19 | 320 | 36.04*** | 52 | 34.44*** | 13 | 32.50* | 5 | 71.43*** | 11 | 15.94 |
| Total | 79 | 100.00 | 888 | 100.00 | 151 | 100.00 | 40 | 100.00 | 7 | 100.00 | 69 | 100.00 |

[a]Yes = percent of revenue or fee-for-service; no = straight salary; "other" types not included.
***Chi-square significant at $p \leq .01$ when compared with hospitals in investor-owned systems.
*Chi-square significant at $p \leq .10$ when compared with hospitals in investor-owned systems.

**TABLE 14** Comparison of Investor-Owned System Hospitals with Other Types of Hospitals: Do Your Anesthesiologists Bill Patients Directly?

| | Investor-Owned Systems | | Freestanding | | Religious Systems | | Nonprofit Systems | | Public Systems | | Contract-Managed | |
|---|---|---|---|---|---|---|---|---|---|---|---|---|
| | N | % | N | % | N | % | N | % | N | % | N | % |
| Yes | 89 | 85.58 | 805 | 69.52*** | 170 | 84.16 | 37 | 68.52** | 5 | 50.00** | 54 | 54.55*** |
| No | 15 | 14.42 | 353 | 30.48*** | 32 | 15.84 | 17 | 31.48** | 5 | 50.00** | 45 | 45.45*** |
| Total | 104 | 100.00 | 1,158 | 100.00 | 202 | 100.00 | 54 | 100.00 | 10 | 100.00 | 99 | 100.00 |

***Chi-square significant at $p \leq .01$ when compared with hospitals in investor-owned systems.
**Chi-square significant at $p \leq .05$ when compared with hospitals in investor-owned systems.

## Medical Staff Size and Composition

The fact that IO system hospitals have a somewhat greater number of physicians per 100 beds and accept a higher percentage of applications to their staff suggests that they have at least as "adequate" a supply of medical staff resources as do other hospitals. If anything, IOs are expanding their medical staffs at a faster rate since the volume of applications to their staffs is comparable to other types of hospitals. It is not known whether the larger number of medical specialists per 100 beds is a matter of deliberate policy on the part of IO systems or more a reflection of the mix of physicians available in the communities in which IO system hospitals have located.

Among the questions for discussion and future exploration are the following:

• Do the larger staffs give IO system hospitals greater or lesser flexibility to expand or contract their service mix relative to other hospitals?

• Does the greater percentage of applications accepted suggest that IO system hospitals are "out-competing" other hospitals for the increasing supply of physicians? What are the implications for the type, volume, and quality of services that are offered to the community?

• Does the clinical behavior of physicians differ between those primarily affiliated with IO system hospitals versus those primarily affiliated with other types of hospitals? Diagnosis-specific, physician-specific data are needed to address these issues.

## Privilege Criteria and Review

This study indicates that at least as many IO system hospitals require board certification as a requirement of medical staff membership as do other hospitals. Combined with the other data indicating that IO system hospitals have a percentage of physicians who are board certified similar to that of nonproprietary hospitals, this suggests that IOs exhibit as much

**TABLE 15** Comparison of Investor-Owned System Hospitals with Other Types of Hospitals: Do Your Radiologists Bill Patients Directly?

| | Investor-Owned Systems | | Freestanding | | Religious Systems | | Nonprofit Systems | | Public Systems | | Contract-Managed | |
|---|---|---|---|---|---|---|---|---|---|---|---|---|
| | N | % | N | % | N | % | N | % | N | % | N | % |
| Yes | 87 | 83.65 | 630 | 54.40*** | 155 | 76.73 | 33 | 61.11*** | 5 | 50.00** | 58 | 58.59*** |
| No | 17 | 16.35 | 528 | 45.60*** | 47 | 23.27 | 21 | 38.89*** | 5 | 50.00** | 41 | 41.41*** |
| Total | 104 | 100.00 | 1,158 | 100.00 | 202 | 100.00 | 54 | 100.00 | 10 | 100.00 | 99 | 100.00 |

***Chi-square significant at $p \leq .01$ when compared with hospitals in investor-owned systems.
**Chi-square significant at $p \leq .05$ when compared with hospitals in investor-owned systems.

**TABLE 16**  Comparison of Investor-Owned System Hospitals with Other Types of Hospitals: Do Your Pathologists Bill Patients Directly?

| | Investor-Owned Systems | | Freestanding | | Religious Systems | | Nonprofit Systems | | Public Systems | | Contract-Managed | |
|---|---|---|---|---|---|---|---|---|---|---|---|---|
| | N | % | N | % | N | % | N | % | N | % | N | % |
| Yes | 56 | 53.85 | 200 | 17.27*** | 51 | 25.25*** | 15 | 27.78*** | 1 | 10.00** | 28 | 28.28*** |
| No | 48 | 46.15 | 958 | 82.73*** | 151 | 74.75*** | 39 | 72.22*** | 9 | 90.00** | 71 | 71.72*** |
| Total | 104 | 100.00 | 1,158 | 100.00 | 202 | 100.00 | 54 | 100.00 | 10 | 100.00 | 99 | 100.00 |

***Chi-square significant at $p \leq .01$ when compared with hospitals in investor-owned systems.

**Chi-square significant at $p \leq .05$ when compared with hospitals in investor-owned systems.

concern for attracting competent physicians as do other hospitals. This is further supported by the fact that IO system hospitals generally have as long a probationary period before granting full privileges as do other hospitals.

Among the questions for discussion and future examination are the following:

• Beyond meeting the basic structure and process accreditation standards of the Joint Commission on Accreditation of Hospitals, it would be useful to know what additional quality assurance mechanisms are used by different types of hospitals.

• Given competitive and cost-containment pressures, it would be useful to know the degree to which cost-effective physician performance will be used as a criterion for granting and renewing clinical privileges, and the extent to which this may differ across types of hospital ownership.

• Carefully designed outcome studies that control for differences in case mix and other relevant variables are also needed to identify the degree to which there may be differences in the quality of care provided by different types of hospitals.

### Compensation Arrangements

The fact that IO hospitals are less likely to have salaried relationships with their hospital-based specialists and more likely to have their physicians bill directly for their services suggests looser financial relationships between IO hospitals and these specialists. This may result from a philosophy of promoting physician au-

tonomy and, under cost-based reimbursement, may also have been viewed as financially advantageous.

Among the questions for discussion and future exploration are the following:

• The looser financial relationships may be the result of the regulatory environments in which IO system hospitals have located to date. It would be useful to know whether the new Medicare prospective payment system has changed these relationships.

• Does the new payment system, the increased number of physicians, and the apparent emergence of price competition suggest that new compensation arrangements are being developed between hospitals and physicians? If so, are arrangements likely to differ by hospital ownership. What implications do they have for the cost, volume, and quality of the service provided?

The relationships between hospitals and physicians are complex and rapidly changing as a result of changes in the environment. This exploratory study has documented some of the differences in relationships, but, in the end, has posed many more questions for future work.

### ACKNOWLEDGMENTS

This paper was funded, in part, by contract 0557-4176 from the Institute of Medicine, National Academy of Sciences, to the Hospital Research and Educational Trust. The opinions and conclusions expressed herein are solely those of the authors. The authors thank Robert

Anderson and Bonnie Lewis for excellent research assistance and advice.

## REFERENCES

American Medical Association (1984) *SMS Report* 3(4).

Ermann, D., and J. Gabel (1984) Multihospital systems: Issues and empirical findings. *Health Affairs* 3(1):50-64.

Morrisey, M. A. (1984) The composition of hospital medical staffs. *Health Care Management Review* 9(3):11-20.

Relman, A. S. (1980) The new medical-industrial complex. *The New England Journal of Medicine* 303:963-970.

Shortell, S. M., M. A. Morrisey, and D. A. Conrad (1985) Economic regulation and hospital behavior: The effects on medical staff organization and hospital-physician relationships. *Health Services Research* 20(5):597-628.

Starr, P. (1982) *The Social Transformation of American Medicine*. New York: Basic Books.

# APPENDIX

# Sample Characteristics and Multivariate Results

**TABLE A-1**  Descriptive Statistics for Hospitals in the Analysis of Practitioner and Medical Staff Size and Composition (N = 5,004)

| Variables | Mean | Standard Deviation | Sum |
|---|---|---|---|
| *Independent Variables* | | | |
| Freestanding hospital | 0.69 | 0.46 | 3,453 |
| System characteristics | | | |
| System control | | | |
| Religious nonprofit | 0.11 | 0.31 | 538 |
| Secular nonprofit | 0.05 | 0.21 | 232 |
| Investor-owned | 0.08 | 0.27 | 395 |
| Public | 0.01 | 0.08 | 31 |
| Contract-managed | 0.07 | 0.26 | 355 |
| System size | 24.09 | 77.20 | 120,553 |
| Hospital characteristics | | | |
| Number of beds | 181.80 | 177.40 | 909,724 |
| Regional location | | | |
| Northeast | 0.15 | 0.36 | 766 |
| South | 0.36 | 0.48 | 1,800 |
| North Central | 0.31 | 0.46 | 1,531 |
| West | 0.17 | 0.38 | 872 |
| SMSA size[a] | | | |
| Non-SMSA | 0.47 | 0.50 | 2,348 |
| Under 100,000 | 0.01 | 0.10 | 55 |
| 100,000-250,000 | 0.09 | 0.28 | 429 |
| 250,000-500,000 | 0.09 | 0.28 | 431 |
| 500,000-1 million | 0.09 | 0.28 | 426 |
| 1 million-2.5 million | 0.13 | 0.33 | 638 |
| Over 2.5 million | 0.14 | 0.34 | 677 |
| House staff | 10.53 | 45.54 | 52,709 |
| *Dependent Variables* | | | |
| Full-time and part-time *active* M.D.s and D.D.s on payroll | | | |
| Number | 6.35 | 29.58 | 31,779 |
| Number per 100 staffed beds | 2.22 | 7.99 | 11,123 |
| Total active and associate medical staff | | | |
| Number | 97.95 | 150.18 | 490,131 |
| Number per 100 staffed beds | 46.66 | 46.41 | 233,504 |
| By specialty group (N = 4,935)[b] | | | |
| General and family practice | 8.97 | 8.11 | 44,258 |
| Pediatrics | 2.93 | 7.31 | 14,482 |
| General internal medicine | 5.51 | 8.63 | 27,182 |
| Other medical specialty | 4.20 | 7.85 | 20,713 |
| General surgery | 4.07 | 4.82 | 20,074 |
| Proportion of active and associate medical staff that is board certified | 0.61 | 0.33 | 2,724 |

[a]Size of standard metropolitan statistical area (SMSA).

[b]Of the 5,004 community hospitals, 69 were missing one or more responses on number of medical staff by specialty.

*434*

**TABLE A-2**  Descriptive Statistics for Hospitals in the Analysis of Privilege Awarding and of Concentration of Admissions (N = 1,811)

| Variables | Mean | Standard Deviation | Sum |
|---|---|---|---|
| *Independent Variables* | | | |
| Freestanding hospital | 0.71 | 0.45 | 1,283 |
| System characteristics | | | |
| System control | | | |
| Religious nonprofit | 0.12 | 0.33 | 223 |
| Secular nonprofit | 0.03 | 0.18 | 59 |
| Investor-owned | 0.06 | 0.25 | 117 |
| Public | 0.00 | 0.06 | 6 |
| Contract-managed | 0.07 | 0.25 | 123 |
| System size | 21.15 | 72.36 | 38,295 |
| Hospital characteristics | | | |
| Number of beds | 192.87 | 171.98 | 349,295 |
| Regional location | | | |
| Northeast | 0.23 | 0.42 | 422 |
| South | 0.26 | 0.44 | 470 |
| North Central | 0.32 | 0.47 | 573 |
| West | 0.19 | 0.39 | 346 |
| SMSA size[a] | | | |
| Non-SMSA | 0.44 | 0.50 | 791 |
| Under 100,000 | 0.02 | 0.12 | 28 |
| 100,000-250,000 | 0.09 | 0.29 | 166 |
| 250,000-500,000 | 0.09 | 0.28 | 160 |
| 500,000-1 million | 0.08 | 0.28 | 150 |
| 1 million-2.5 million | 0.15 | 0.35 | 264 |
| Over 2.5 million | 0.14 | 0.35 | 252 |
| House staff | 9.79 | 42.35 | 17,728 |
| *Dependent Variables* | | | |
| Number who applied for *active* staff privileges | 14.47 | 22.54 | 26,198 |
| Percent who were accepted | 82.23 | 34.17 | 148,913 |
| *Usual* number of months of provisional appointment | 9.01 | 5.16 | 16,324 |
| Board certification is required | 0.30 | 0.46 | 536 |
| Percent of admissions by top five admitting physicians | 45.63 | 33.22 | 82,641 |
| Percent of top five admitting physicians who are board certified | 61.07 | 36.07 | 107,363 |

[a]Size of standard metropolitan statistical area (SMSA).

**TABLE A-3**  Descriptive Statistics for Hospitals in the Analysis of Physicians' Primary Form of Compensation (N = 1,234)

| Variables | Mean | Standard Deviation | Sum |
|---|---|---|---|
| *Independent Variables* | | | |
| Freestanding hospital | 0.72 | 0.45 | 888 |
| System characteristics | | | |
| System control | | | |
| Religious nonprofit | 0.12 | 0.33 | 151 |
| Secular nonprofit | 0.03 | 0.18 | 40 |
| Investor-owned | 0.06 | 0.24 | 79 |
| Public | 0.01 | 0.08 | 7 |
| Contract-managed | 0.06 | 0.23 | 69 |
| System size | 20.76 | 72.03 | 25,612 |
| Hospital characteristics | | | |
| Number of beds | 218.62 | 190.62 | 269,779 |
| Regional location | | | |
| Northeast | 0.26 | 0.44 | 316 |
| South | 0.26 | 0.44 | 320 |
| North Central | 0.29 | 0.46 | 364 |
| West | 0.19 | 0.39 | 234 |
| SMSA size[a] | | | |
| Non-SMSA | 0.36 | 0.48 | 440 |
| Under 100,000 | 0.02 | 0.13 | 22 |
| 100,000-250,000 | 0.10 | 0.30 | 127 |
| 250,000-500,000 | 0.10 | 0.30 | 123 |
| 500,000-1 million | 0.09 | 0.29 | 114 |
| 1 million-2.5 million | 0.17 | 0.37 | 204 |
| Over 2.5 million | 0.17 | 0.37 | 204 |
| House staff | 14.50 | 53.83 | 17,892 |
| *Dependent Variables* | | | |
| Anesthesiologists are paid a percent of revenues or a fee for service | 0.89 | 0.31 | 1,103 |
| Pathologists are paid a percent of revenues or a fee for service | 0.67 | 0.47 | 821 |
| Radiologists are paid a percent of revenues or a fee for service | 0.90 | 0.30 | 1,108 |

[a]Size of standard metropolitan statistical area (SMSA).

TABLE A-4 Descriptive Statistics for Hospitals in the Analysis of Physicians' Direct Patient Billing Decisions (N = 1,627)

| Variables | Mean | Standard Deviation | Sum |
|---|---|---|---|
| *Independent Variables* | | | |
| Freestanding hospital | 0.71 | 0.45 | 1,158 |
| System characteristics | | | |
| System control | | | |
| Religious nonprofit | 0.12 | 0.33 | 202 |
| Secular nonprofit | 0.03 | 0.18 | 54 |
| Investor-owned | 0.06 | 0.24 | 104 |
| Public | 0.01 | 0.08 | 10 |
| Contract-managed | 0.06 | 0.24 | 99 |
| System size | 20.21 | 70.53 | 32,884 |
| Hospital characteristics | | | |
| Number of beds | 212.37 | 183.63 | 345,533 |
| Regional location | | | |
| Northeast | 0.25 | 0.43 | 408 |
| South | 0.26 | 0.44 | 427 |
| North Central | 0.30 | 0.46 | 480 |
| West | 0.19 | 0.39 | 312 |
| SMSA size[a] | | | |
| Non-SMSA | 0.37 | 0.48 | 605 |
| Under 100,000 | 0.02 | 0.13 | 28 |
| 100,000-250,000 | 0.09 | 0.29 | 154 |
| 250,000-500,000 | 0.10 | 0.30 | 160 |
| 500,000-1 million | 0.09 | 0.29 | 154 |
| 1 million-2.5 million | 0.17 | 0.37 | 273 |
| Over 2.5 million | 0.16 | 0.36 | 253 |
| House staff | 13.55 | 53.36 | 22,053 |
| *Dependent Variables* | | | |
| Anesthesiologists bill patients directly | 0.71 | 0.45 | 1,160 |
| Pathologists bill patients directly | 0.22 | 0.41 | 351 |
| Radiologists bill patients directly | 0.59 | 0.49 | 968 |

[a]Size of standard metropolitan statistical area (SMSA).

**TABLE A-5**   How Many Physicians Applied for Active Staff Privileges at Your Hospital During Calendar Year 1981?

| | System Control Coefficients Relative to— | | | |
| | Freestanding Hospitals | | Investor-Owned Systems | |
| Variables | Coefficient | Standard Error | Coefficient | Standard Error |
|---|---|---|---|---|
| Freestanding hospitals | | | −3.43 | 2.16 |
| System characteristics | | | | |
|   System control | | | | |
|     Religious nonprofit | 2.52 | 1.33* | −0.90 | 2.40 |
|     Secular nonprofit | 8.61 | 2.40*** | 5.19 | 3.09* |
|     Investor-owned | 3.43 | 2.16 | | |
|     Public | −5.77 | 7.40 | −9.20 | 7.64 |
|   Contract-managed | 0.92 | 1.96 | −2.50 | 2.36 |
|   System size | −0.01 | 0.01 | −0.01 | 0.01 |
| Hospital characteristics | | | | |
|   Number of beds | 4.37 | 0.34*** | 4.37 | 0.34*** |
|   Regional location | | | | |
|     Northeast | −5.13 | 1.38*** | −5.13 | 1.38*** |
|     South | −2.79 | 1.31** | −2.79 | 1.31** |
|     North Central | −5.00 | 1.25*** | −5.00 | 1.25*** |
|   SMSA size[a] | | | | |
|     Under 100,000 | 1.66 | 3.46 | 1.66 | 3.46 |
|     100,000-250,000 | 1.57 | 1.58 | 1.57 | 1.58 |
|     250,000-500,000 | 5.54 | 1.60*** | 5.54 | 1.60*** |
|     500,000-1 million | 4.97 | 1.72*** | 4.97 | 1.72*** |
|     1 million-2.5 million | 12.12 | 1.39*** | 12.12 | 1.39*** |
|     Over 2.5 million | 15.38 | 1.47*** | 15.38 | 1.47*** |
|   House staff | 9.58 | 1.19*** | 9.58 | 1.19*** |
| Constant | 2.96 | 1.16** | 6.38 | 2.28*** |
| Model statistics | | | | |
|   $R^2$ | | 0.38 | | 0.38 |
|   N | | 1,811 | | 1,811 |

[a]Size of standard metropolitan statistical area (SMSA).

***T is significant at $p \leq .01$.

**T is significant at $p \leq .05$.

*T is significant at $p \leq .10$.

**TABLE A-6** What Percentage of the Physicians Who Applied for Active Staff Privileges During Calendar Year 1981 Were Accepted?

| | System Control Coefficients Relative to— | | | |
| | Freestanding Hospitals | | Investor-Owned Systems | |
| Variables | Coefficient | Standard Error | Coefficient | Standard Error |
|---|---|---|---|---|
| Freestanding hospitals | | | −11.84 | 4.05*** |
| System characteristics | | | | |
| System control | | | | |
| Religious nonprofit | 2.94 | 2.49 | −8.90 | 4.49** |
| Secular nonprofit | −0.19 | 4.50 | −12.03 | 5.78** |
| Investor-owned | 11.84 | 4.05*** | | |
| Public | −10.38 | 13.86 | −22.22 | 14.31 |
| Contract-managed | 0.26 | 3.67 | −11.58 | 4.43*** |
| System size | −0.02 | 0.01 | −0.02 | 0.01 |
| Hospital characteristics | | | | |
| Number of beds | 3.59 | 0.63*** | 3.59 | 0.63*** |
| Regional location | | | | |
| Northeast | 0.93 | 2.58 | 0.93 | 2.58 |
| South | −5.03 | 2.45** | −5.03 | 2.45** |
| North Central | −7.63 | 2.34*** | −7.63 | 2.34*** |
| SMSA size[a] | | | | |
| Under 100,000 | 12.46 | 6.48* | 12.46 | 6.48* |
| 100,000-250,000 | 9.63 | 2.95*** | 9.63 | 2.95*** |
| 250,000-500,000 | 5.46 | 3.01* | 5.46 | 3.01* |
| 500,000-1 million | 1.23 | 3.23 | 1.23 | 3.23 |
| 1 million-2.5 million | 3.97 | 2.60 | 3.97 | 2.60 |
| Over 2.5 million | −3.37 | 2.76 | −3.37 | 2.76 |
| House staff | −5.08 | 2.23** | −5.08 | 2.23** |
| Constant | 76.78 | 2.17*** | 88.62 | 4.28*** |
| Model statistics | | | | |
| $R^2$ | | 0.06 | | 0.06 |
| N | | 1,811 | | 1,811 |

[a]Size of standard metropolitan statistical area (SMSA).

***T is significant at $p \leq .01$.

**T is significant at $p \leq .05$.

*T is significant at $p \leq .10$.

**TABLE A-7**   How Many Practitioners (Total) Were on the Active or Associate Medical Staff per 100 Staffed Beds as of September 30, 1982?

| Variables | System Control Coefficients Relative to— | | | |
| --- | --- | --- | --- | --- |
| | Freestanding Hospitals | | Investor-Owned Systems | |
| | Coefficient | Standard Error | Coefficient | Standard Error |
| Freestanding hospitals | | | −8.54 | 2.72*** |
| System characteristics | | | | |
| System control | | | | |
| Religious nonprofit | 5.79 | 1.91*** | −2.75 | 3.14 |
| Secular nonprofit | 12.62 | 2.74*** | 4.08 | 3.65 |
| Investor-owned | 8.54 | 2.72*** | | |
| Public | −8.22 | 7.30 | −16.76 | 7.70*** |
| Contract-managed | −1.67 | 2.57 | 10.21 | 3.01*** |
| System size | 0.00 | 0.01 | 0.00 | 0.01 |
| Hospital characteristics | | | | |
| Number of beds | −3.62 | 0.45*** | −3.62 | 0.45*** |
| Regional location | | | | |
| Northeast | −10.96 | 2.04*** | −10.96 | 2.04*** |
| South | −18.58 | 1.68*** | −18.58 | 1.68*** |
| North Central | −22.77 | 1.71*** | −22.77 | 1.71*** |
| SMSA size[a] | | | | |
| Under 100,000 | 33.10 | 5.49*** | 33.10 | 5.49*** |
| 100,000-250,000 | 23.16 | 2.17*** | 23.16 | 2.17*** |
| 250,000-500,000 | 29.15 | 2.17*** | 29.15 | 2.17*** |
| 500,000-1 million | 36.02 | 2.23*** | 36.02 | 2.23*** |
| 1 million-2.5 million | 47.80 | 1.94*** | 47.80 | 1.94*** |
| Over 2.5 million | 49.13 | 1.96*** | 49.13 | 1.96*** |
| House staff | 14.55 | 1.57*** | 14.55 | 1.57*** |
| Constant | 44.59 | 1.58*** | 53.13 | 2.96*** |
| Model statistics | | | | |
| $R^2$ | | 0.26 | | 0.26 |
| N | | 5,004 | | 5,004 |

[a]Size of standard metropolitan statistical area (SMSA).

***T is significant at $p \leq .01$.

**TABLE A-8**  How Many General and Family Practice Medical Specialists Were on the Medical Staff per 100 Staff Beds as of September 30, 1982?

| Variables | System Control Coefficients Relative to— | | | |
| | Freestanding Hospitals | | Investor-Owned Systems | |
| | Coefficient | Standard Error | Coefficient | Standard Error |
| --- | --- | --- | --- | --- |
| Freestanding hospitals | | | −1.03 | 0.51** |
| System characteristics | | | | |
| System control | | | | |
| Religious nonprofit | 0.48 | 0.36 | −0.55 | 0.59 |
| Secular nonprofit | 0.67 | 0.52 | −0.35 | 0.69 |
| Investor-owned | 1.03 | 0.51** | | |
| Public | 1.09 | 1.36 | 0.05 | 1.44 |
| Contract-managed | 0.46 | 0.49 | −0.57 | 0.57 |
| System size | 0.00 | 0.00 | 0.00 | 0.00 |
| Hospital characteristics | | | | |
| Number of beds | −1.69 | 0.08*** | −1.69 | 0.08*** |
| Regional location | | | | |
| Northeast | −4.71 | 0.39*** | −4.71 | 0.39*** |
| South | −4.24 | 0.32*** | −4.24 | 0.32*** |
| North Central | −3.05 | 0.33*** | −3.05 | 0.33*** |
| SMSA size[a] | | | | |
| Under 100,000 | 0.96 | 1.06 | 0.96 | 1.06 |
| 100,000-250,000 | 2.06 | 0.41*** | 2.06 | 0.41*** |
| 250,000-500,000 | 2.82 | 0.41*** | 2.82 | 0.41*** |
| 500,000-1 million | 2.51 | 0.42*** | 2.51 | 0.42*** |
| 1 million-2.5 million | 2.88 | 0.36*** | 2.88 | 0.36*** |
| Over 2.5 million | 2.83 | 0.37*** | 2.83 | 0.37*** |
| House staff | 0.38 | 0.29 | 0.38 | 0.29 |
| Constant | 13.68 | 0.31*** | 14.71 | 0.56*** |
| Model statistics | | | | |
| $R^2$ | | 0.16 | | 0.16 |
| N | | 4,935 | | 4,935 |

[a]Size of standard metropolitan statistical area (SMSA).

***T is significant at $p \leq .01$.

**T is significant at $p \leq .05$.

**TABLE A-9**   How Many Pediatric Medical Specialists Were on the Medical Staff per 100 Staffed Beds as of September 30, 1982?

| | System Control Coefficients Relative to— | | | |
| | Freestanding Hospitals | | Investor-Owned Systems | |
| Variables | Coefficient | Standard Error | Coefficient | Standard Error |
| --- | --- | --- | --- | --- |
| Freestanding hospitals | | | 0.63 | 0.47 |
| System characteristics | | | | |
| System control | | | | |
| Religious nonprofit | −0.18 | 0.33 | 0.45 | 0.55 |
| Secular nonprofit | 1.11 | 0.48** | 1.74 | 0.64*** |
| Investor-owned | −0.63 | 0.47 | | |
| Public | −2.91 | 1.27** | −2.27 | 1.34* |
| Contract-managed | −0.08 | 0.46 | 0.55 | 0.53 |
| System size | 0.00 | 0.00 | 0.00 | 0.00 |
| Hospital characteristics | | | | |
| Number of beds | −0.18 | 0.08** | −0.18 | 0.08** |
| Regional location | | | | |
| Northeast | −0.68 | 0.36* | −0.68 | 0.36* |
| South | −1.00 | 0.30*** | −1.00 | 0.30*** |
| North Central | −1.87 | 0.31*** | −1.87 | 0.31*** |
| SMSA size[a] | | | | |
| Under 100,000 | 2.39 | 0.99** | 2.39 | 0.99** |
| 100,000-250,000 | 1.55 | 0.38*** | 1.55 | 0.38*** |
| 250,000-500,000 | 2.21 | 0.38*** | 2.21 | 0.38*** |
| 500,000-1 million | 3.54 | 0.39*** | 3.54 | 0.39*** |
| 1 million-2.5 million | 4.38 | 0.34*** | 4.38 | 0.34*** |
| Over 2.5 million | 3.85 | 0.34*** | 3.85 | 0.34*** |
| House staff | 2.53 | 0.27*** | 2.53 | 0.27*** |
| Constant | 2.37 | 0.28*** | 1.74 | 0.52*** |
| Model statistics | | | | |
| $R^2$ | | 0.11 | | 0.11 |
| N | | 4,935 | | 4,935 |

[a]Size of standard metropolitan statistical area (SMSA).
***T is significant at $p \leq .01$.
**T is significant at $p \leq .05$.
*T is significant at $p \leq .10$.

TABLE A-10 How Many General Internal Medical Specialists Were on the Medical Staff per 100 Staffed Beds as of September 30, 1982?

| Variables | System Control Coefficients Relative to— | | | |
|---|---|---|---|---|
| | Freestanding Hospitals | | Investor-Owned Systems | |
| | Coefficient | Standard Error | Coefficient | Standard Error |
| Freestanding hospitals | | | −2.04 | 0.53*** |
| System characteristics | | | | |
| System control | | | | |
| Religious nonprofit | 0.96 | 0.37*** | −1.07 | 0.61* |
| Secular nonprofit | 1.09 | 0.54** | −0.95 | 0.71 |
| Investor-owned | 2.04 | 0.53*** | | |
| Public | −1.12 | 1.42 | −3.16 | 1.50** |
| Contract-managed | 0.08 | 0.51 | −1.96 | 0.59*** |
| System size | 0.00 | 0.00 | 0.00 | 0.00 |
| Hospital characteristics | | | | |
| Number of beds | 0.13 | 0.09 | 0.13 | 0.09 |
| Regional location | | | | |
| Northeast | 0.02 | 0.40 | 0.02 | 0.40 |
| South | −2.81 | 0.33*** | −2.81 | 0.33*** |
| North Central | −3.46 | 0.34*** | −3.46 | 0.34*** |
| SMSA size[a] | | | | |
| Under 100,000 | 4.43 | 1.11*** | 4.43 | 1.11*** |
| 100,000-250,000 | 2.85 | 0.42*** | 2.85 | 0.42*** |
| 250,000-500,000 | 2.98 | 0.42*** | 2.98 | 0.42*** |
| 500,000-1 million | 4.10 | 0.43*** | 4.10 | 0.43*** |
| 1 million-2.5 million | 5.25 | 0.38*** | 5.25 | 0.38*** |
| Over 2.5 million | 6.68 | 0.38*** | 6.68 | 0.38*** |
| House staff | 2.20 | 0.30*** | 2.20 | 0.30*** |
| Constant | 4.31 | 0.32*** | 6.34 | 0.58*** |
| Model statistics | | | | |
| $R^2$ | | 0.20 | | 0.20 |
| N | | 4,935 | | 4,935 |

[a]Size of standard metropolitan statistical area (SMSA).

***T significant at $p \leq .01$.

**T significant at $p \leq .05$.

*T significant at $p \leq .10$.

**TABLE A-11**  How Many Other Medical Specialists Were on the Medical Staff per 100 Staffed Beds as of September 30, 1982?

| Variables | System Control Coefficients Relative to— | | | |
| | Freestanding Hospitals | | Investor-Owned Systems | |
| | Coefficient | Standard Error | Coefficient | Standard Error |
| --- | --- | --- | --- | --- |
| Freestanding hospitals | | | −2.46 | 0.48*** |
| System characteristics | | | | |
| System control | | | | |
| Religious nonprofit | 1.07 | 0.34*** | −1.39 | 0.56** |
| Secular nonprofit | 1.23 | 0.49** | −1.23 | 0.65* |
| Investor-owned | 2.46 | 0.48*** | | |
| Public | −0.55 | 1.29 | −3.01 | 1.36** |
| Contract-managed | 0.24 | 0.47 | −2.22 | 0.54*** |
| System size | 0.00 | 0.00 | 0.00 | 0.00 |
| Hospital characteristics | | | | |
| Number of beds | −0.14 | 0.08* | −0.14 | 0.08* |
| Regional location | | | | |
| Northeast | −1.63 | 0.37*** | −1.63 | 0.37*** |
| South | −1.80 | 0.31*** | −1.80 | 0.31*** |
| North Central | −2.72 | 0.31*** | −2.72 | 0.31*** |
| SMSA size[a] | | | | |
| Under 100,000 | 4.40 | 1.01*** | 4.40 | 1.01*** |
| 100,000-250,000 | 2.52 | 0.39*** | 2.52 | 0.39*** |
| 250,000-500,000 | 3.35 | 0.39*** | 3.35 | 0.39*** |
| 500,000-1 million | 4.31 | 0.39*** | 4.31 | 0.39*** |
| 1 million-2.5 million | 6.17 | 0.35*** | 6.17 | 0.35*** |
| Over 2.5 million | 7.31 | 0.35*** | 7.31 | 0.35*** |
| House staff | 1.84 | 0.28*** | 1.84 | 0.28*** |
| Constant | 2.92 | 0.29*** | 5.38 | 0.53*** |
| Model statistics | | | | |
| $R^2$ | 0.20 | | 0.20 | |
| N | 4,935 | | 4,935 | |

[a]Size of standard statistical metropolitan area (SMSA).

***T is significant at $p \leq .01$.

**T is significant at $p \leq .05$.

*T is significant at $p \leq .10$.

**TABLE A-12** How Many General Surgery Specialists Were on the Medical Staff per 100 Staffed Beds as of September 30, 1982?

| Variables | System Control Coefficients Relative to— | | | |
|---|---|---|---|---|
| | Freestanding Hospitals | | Investor-Owned Systems | |
| | Coefficient | Standard Error | Coefficient | Standard Error |
| Freestanding hospitals | | | −0.83 | 0.31*** |
| System characteristics | | | | |
| System control | | | | |
| Religious nonprofit | 0.91 | 0.22*** | 0.07 | 0.36 |
| Secular nonprofit | 0.54 | 0.31* | −0.30 | 0.42 |
| Investor-owned | 0.83 | 0.31*** | | |
| Public | −0.09 | 0.82 | −0.93 | 0.87 |
| Contract-managed | −0.07 | 0.30 | −0.90 | 0.34*** |
| System size | 0.00 | 0.00 | 0.00 | 0.00 |
| Hospital characteristics | | | | |
| Number of beds | −0.39 | 0.05*** | −0.39 | 0.05*** |
| Regional location | | | | |
| Northeast | −0.51 | 0.23** | −0.51 | 0.23** |
| South | −1.33 | 0.19*** | −1.33 | 0.19*** |
| North Central | −1.64 | 0.20*** | −1.64 | 0.20*** |
| SMSA size[a] | | | | |
| Under 100,000 | 1.60 | 0.64** | 1.60 | 0.64** |
| 100,000-250,000 | 1.62 | 0.25*** | 1.62 | 0.25*** |
| 250,000-500,000 | 2.10 | 0.25*** | 2.10 | 0.25*** |
| 500,000-1 million | 2.78 | 0.25*** | 2.78 | 0.25*** |
| 1 million-2.5 million | 3.49 | 0.22*** | 3.49 | 0.22*** |
| Over 2.5 million | 3.59 | 0.22*** | 3.59 | 0.22*** |
| House staff | 1.02 | 0.18*** | 1.02 | 0.18*** |
| Constant | 4.03 | 0.18*** | 4.87 | 0.34*** |
| Model statistics | | | | |
| $R^2$ | | 0.13 | | 0.13 |
| N | | 4,935 | | 4,935 |

[a]Size of standard statistical metropolitan area (SMSA).

***T is significant at $p \leq .01$.

**T is significant at $p \leq .05$.

*T is significant at $p \leq .10$.

**TABLE A-13**   What Percentage of Total Admissions During Calendar Year 1981 Were Admitted by the Five Highest Admitting Physicians?

| | System Control Coefficients Relative to— | | | |
| | Freestanding Hospitals | | Investor-Owned Systems | |
| Variables | Coefficient | Standard Error | Coefficient | Standard Error |
|---|---|---|---|---|
| Freestanding hospitals | | | 3.44 | 2.68 |
| System characteristics | | | | |
| System control | | | | |
| Religious nonprofit | −5.54 | 1.64*** | −2.10 | 2.96 |
| Secular nonprofit | 8.70 | 2.97*** | 12.13 | 3.82*** |
| Investor-owned | −3.44 | 2.68 | | |
| Public | −17.09 | 9.15* | −13.65 | 9.45 |
| Contract-managed | 7.96 | 2.43*** | 11.40 | 2.92*** |
| System size | −0.02 | 0.01** | −0.02 | 0.01** |
| Hospital characteristics | | | | |
| Number of beds | −10.72 | 0.41*** | −10.72 | 0.41*** |
| Regional location | | | | |
| Northeast | −2.58 | 1.70 | −2.58 | 1.70 |
| South | 8.00 | 1.62*** | 8.00 | 1.62*** |
| North Central | 10.51 | 1.55*** | 10.51 | 1.55*** |
| SMSA size[a] | | | | |
| Under 100,000 | −25.11 | 4.28*** | −25.11 | 4.28*** |
| 100,000-250,000 | −18.25 | 1.95*** | −18.25 | 1.95*** |
| 250,000-500,000 | −18.14 | 1.98*** | −18.14 | 1.98*** |
| 500,000-1 million | −17.72 | 2.13*** | 17.72 | 2.13*** |
| 1 million-2.5 million | −22.43 | 1.72*** | −22.43 | 1.72*** |
| Over 2.5 million | −21.57 | 1.82*** | −21.57 | 1.82*** |
| House staff | 13.44 | 1.48*** | 13.44 | 1.48*** |
| Constant | 72.20 | 1.43*** | 68.76 | 2.82*** |
| Model statistics | | | | |
| $R^2$ | | 0.57 | | 0.57 |
| N | | 1,811 | | 1,811 |

[a]Size of standard statistical metropolitan area (SMSA).

***T is significant at $p \leq .01$.

**T is significant at $p \leq .05$.

*T is signficant at $p \leq .10$.

**TABLE A-14**  Percentage of Top Five Admitting Physicians Who Are Board Certified

| Variables | System Control Coefficients Relative to— | | | |
|---|---|---|---|---|
| | Freestanding Hospitals | | Investor-Owned Systems | |
| | Coefficient | Standard Error | Coefficient | Standard Error |
| Freestanding hospitals | | | −2.61 | 4.27 |
| System characteristics | | | | |
| System control | | | | |
| Religious nonprofit | 0.70 | 2.63 | −1.91 | 4.73 |
| Secular nonprofit | −3.86 | 4.82 | −6.47 | 6.14 |
| Investor-owned | 2.61 | 4.27 | | |
| Public | −4.43 | 14.59 | −7.05 | 15.07 |
| Contract-managed | −5.68 | 3.91 | −8.30 | 4.67* |
| System size | 0.01 | 0.02 | 0.01 | 0.02 |
| Hospital characteristics | | | | |
| Number of beds | 4.94 | 0.67*** | 4.94 | 0.67*** |
| Regional location | | | | |
| Northeast | −2.75 | 2.76 | −2.75 | 2.76 |
| South | −7.87 | 2.60*** | −7.87 | 2.60*** |
| North Central | −6.30 | 2.49** | −6.30 | 2.49** |
| SMSA size[a] | | | | |
| Under 100,000 | 11.14 | 6.82 | 11.14 | 6.82 |
| 100,000-250,000 | 4.36 | 3.15 | 4.36 | 3.15 |
| 250,000-500,000 | −2.25 | 3.20 | −2.25 | 3.20 |
| 500,000-1 million | −1.53 | 3.43 | −1.53 | 3.43 |
| 1 million-2.5 million | 0.72 | 2.78 | 0.72 | 2.78 |
| Over 2.5 million | 0.02 | 2.95 | 0.02 | 2.95 |
| House staff | −0.03 | 2.41 | −0.03 | 2.41 |
| Constant | 56.06 | 2.30*** | 58.67 | 4.51*** |
| Model statistics | | | | |
| $R^2$ | | 0.067 | | 0.067 |
| N | | 1,758 | | 1,758 |

[a]Size of standard statistical metropolitan area (SMSA).
***T is significant at $p \leq .01$.
**T is significant at $p \leq .05$.
*T is significant at $p \leq .10$.

**TABLE A-15**   Is Board Certification Required for Any (or All) Specialties on Your Hospital Active Staff?

| | System Control Coefficients Relative to— | | | |
| | Freestanding Hospitals | | Investor-Owned Systems | |
| Variables | Coefficient | Standard Error | Coefficient | Standard Error |
|---|---|---|---|---|
| Freestanding hospitals | | | −0.08 | 0.28 |
| System characteristics | | | | |
| System control | | | | |
| Religious nonprofit | −0.33 | 0.18* | −0.41 | 0.31 |
| Secular nonprofit | 0.20 | 0.30 | 0.12 | 0.39 |
| Investor-owned | 0.08 | 0.28 | | |
| Public | −0.50 | 0.90 | −0.58 | 0.93 |
| Contract-managed | −0.06 | 0.26 | −0.13 | 0.31 |
| System size | −0.00 | 0.00 | −0.00 | 0.00 |
| Hospital characteristics | | | | |
| Number of beds | 0.10 | 0.04** | 0.10 | 0.04** |
| Regional locations | | | | |
| Northeast | 0.78 | 0.18*** | 0.78 | 0.18*** |
| South | 0.67 | 0.18*** | 0.67 | 0.18*** |
| North Central | 0.45 | 0.17*** | 0.45 | 0.17*** |
| SMSA size[a] | | | | |
| Under 100,000 | 0.53 | 0.40 | 0.53 | 0.40 |
| 100,000-250,000 | 0.09 | 0.20 | 0.09 | 0.20 |
| 250,000-500,000 | 0.18 | 0.20 | 0.18 | 0.20 |
| 500,000-1 million | 0.20 | 0.21 | 0.20 | 0.21 |
| 1 million-2.5 million | 0.37 | 0.17** | 0.37 | 0.17** |
| Over 2.5 million | 0.64 | 0.18*** | 0.64 | 0.18*** |
| House staff | 0.21 | 0.15 | 0.21 | 0.15 |
| Constant | −1.78 | 0.16*** | −1.70 | 0.30*** |
| Model statistics | | | | |
| Pseudo R | | 0.17 | | 0.17 |
| N | | 1,811 | | 1,811 |

[a]Size of standard statistical metropolitan area (SMSA).
***T is significant at $p \leq .01$.
**T is significant at $p \leq .05$.
*T is significant at $p \leq .10$.

**TABLE A-16** Proportion of Active and Associate Medical Staff Who Are Board Certified

| Variables | System Control Coefficients Relative to— | | | |
| | Freestanding Hospitals | | Investor-Owned Systems | |
| | Coefficient | Standard Error | Coefficient | Standard Error |
|---|---|---|---|---|
| Freestanding hospital | | | 0.02 | 0.02 |
| System characteristics | | | | |
| System control | | | | |
| Religious nonprofit | 0.02 | 0.02 | 0.04 | 0.03 |
| Secular nonprofit | 0.02 | 0.02 | 0.04 | 0.03 |
| Investor-owned | −0.02 | 0.02 | | |
| Public | −0.11 | 0.06* | −0.09 | 0.06 |
| Contract-managed | −0.02 | 0.02 | 0.00 | 0.03 |
| System size | 0.00 | 0.00 | 0.00 | 0.00 |
| Hospital characteristics | | | | |
| Number of beds | 0.02 | 0.00*** | 0.02 | 0.00*** |
| Regional location | | | | |
| Northeast | −0.03 | 0.02** | −0.03 | 0.02** |
| South | −0.05 | 0.01*** | 0.05 | 0.01*** |
| North Central | −0.08 | 0.01*** | −0.08 | 0.01*** |
| SMSA size[a] | | | | |
| Under 100,000 | 0.06 | 0.05 | 0.06 | 0.05 |
| 100,000-250,000 | 0.04 | 0.02** | 0.04 | 0.02** |
| 250,000-500,000 | 0.05 | 0.02*** | 0.05 | 0.02*** |
| 500,000-1 million | 0.07 | 0.02*** | 0.07 | 0.02*** |
| 1 million-2.5 million | 0.07 | 0.02*** | 0.07 | 0.02*** |
| Over 2.5 million | 0.06 | 0.02*** | 0.06 | 0.02*** |
| House staff | 0.01 | 0.01 | 0.01 | 0.01 |
| Constant | 0.59 | 0.01*** | 0.57 | 0.03*** |
| Model statistics | | | | |
| $R^2$ | | 0.043 | | 0.043 |
| N | | 4,448 | | 4,448 |

[a]Size of standard statistical metropolitan area (SMSA).

***T is significant at $p \leq .01$.

**T is significant at $p \leq .05$.

*T is significant at $p \leq .10$.

**TABLE A-17**   What Is the Usual Number of Months for Provisional Appointment Before a Physician Is Awarded Full Privileges?

| Variables | System Control Coefficients Relative to— | | | |
| | Freestanding Hospitals | | Investor-Owned Systems | |
| | Coefficient | Standard Error | Coefficient | Standard Error |
|---|---|---|---|---|
| Freestanding hospitals | | | −0.55 | 0.60 |
| System characteristics | | | | |
| System control | | | | |
| Religious nonprofit | 1.11 | 0.37*** | 0.56 | 0.67 |
| Secular nonprofit | 0.50 | 0.67 | 0.05 | 0.86 |
| Investor-owned | 0.55 | 0.60 | | |
| Public | 1.39 | 2.05 | 0.84 | 2.12 |
| Contract-managed | −0.43 | 0.54 | −0.98 | 0.66 |
| System size | 0.00 | 0.00 | 0.00 | 0.00 |
| Hospital characteristics | | | | |
| Number of beds | 0.56 | 0.09*** | 0.56 | 0.09*** |
| Regional location | | | | |
| Northeast | 0.48 | 0.38 | 0.48 | 0.38 |
| South | 0.00 | 0.36 | 0.00 | 0.36 |
| North Central | −0.18 | 0.35 | −0.18 | 0.35 |
| SMSA size[a] | | | | |
| Under 100,000 | 0.89 | 0.96 | 0.89 | 0.96 |
| 100,000-250,000 | 1.59 | 0.44*** | 1.59 | 0.44*** |
| 250,000-500,000 | 1.33 | 0.45*** | 1.33 | 0.45*** |
| 500,000-1 million | 1.83 | 0.48*** | 1.83 | 0.48*** |
| 1 million-2.5 million | 1.92 | 0.39*** | 1.92 | 0.39*** |
| Over 2.5 million | 1.56 | 0.41*** | 1.56 | 0.41*** |
| House staff | −1.25 | 0.33*** | −1.25 | 0.33*** |
| Constant | 6.88 | 0.32*** | 7.42 | 0.63*** |
| Model statistics | | | | |
| $R^2$ | | 0.10 | | 0.10 |
| N | | 1,811 | | 1,811 |

[a]Size of standard statistical metropolitan area (SMSA).
***T is significant at $p \leq .01$.

**TABLE A-18**  How Many Full-Time and Part-Time Physicians and Dentists Were on the Hospital Payroll as of September 30, 1982?

| | System Control Coefficients Relative to— | | | |
| | Freestanding Hospitals | | Investor-Owned Systems | |
| Variables | Coefficient | Standard Error | Coefficient | Standard Error |
|---|---|---|---|---|
| Freestanding hospitals | | | 1.53 | 1.67 |
| System characteristics | | | | |
| System control | | | | |
|   Religious nonprofit | −1.72 | 1.17 | −0.19 | 1.93 |
|   Secular nonprofit | −2.18 | 1.68 | −0.64 | 2.24 |
|   Investor-owned | −1.53 | 1.67 | | |
|   Public | 46.91 | 4.47*** | 48.44 | 4.72*** |
| Contract-managed | −0.48 | 1.57 | 1.05 | 1.85 |
| System size | 0.00 | 0.01 | 0.00 | 0.01 |
| Hospital characteristics | | | | |
| Number of beds | 2.41 | 0.28*** | 2.41 | 0.28*** |
| Regional location | | | | |
|   Northeast | 10.14 | 1.25*** | 10.14 | 1.25*** |
|   South | −1.28 | 1.03 | −1.28 | 1.03 |
|   North Central | 0.50 | 1.05 | 0.50 | 1.05 |
| SMSA size[a] | | | | |
|   Under 100,000 | −4.79 | 3.36 | −4.79 | 3.36 |
|   100,000-250,000 | −2.67 | 1.33** | −2.67 | 1.33** |
|   250,000-500,000 | −2.23 | 1.33* | −2.23 | 1.33* |
|   500,000-1 million | −4.97 | 1.36*** | −4.97 | 1.36*** |
|   1 million-2.5 million | 0.92 | 1.19 | 0.92 | 1.19 |
|   Over 2.5 million | 6.78 | 1.20*** | 6.78 | 1.20*** |
| House staff | 24.19 | 0.96*** | 24.19 | 0.96*** |
| Constant | −1.90 | 0.97* | −3.43 | 1.81* |
| Model statistics | | | | |
| $R^2$ | 0.32 | | 0.32 | |
| N | 5,004 | | 5,004 | |

[a]Size of standard statistical metropolitan area (SMSA).

***T is significant at $p \leq .01$.

**T is significant at $p \leq .05$.

*T is significant at $p \leq .10$.

**TABLE A-19**   The Primary Form of Compensation for Anesthesiologists Is a Percent of Revenue or Fee for Service

| | System Control Coefficients Relative to— | | | |
| | Freestanding Hospitals | | Investor-Owned Systems | |
| Variables | Coefficient | Standard Error | Coefficient | Standard Error |
|---|---|---|---|---|
| Freestanding hospitals | | | −1.49 | 1.07 |
| System characteristics | | | | |
| System control | | | | |
| Religious nonprofit | 0.53 | 0.39 | −0.95 | 1.12 |
| Secular nonprofit | −0.65 | 0.46 | −2.14 | 1.14* |
| Investor-owned | 1.49 | 1.07 | | |
| Public | −2.52 | 0.96*** | −4.01 | 1.41*** |
| Contract-managed | −0.52 | 0.50 | −2.00 | 1.09* |
| System size | 0.00 | 0.00 | 0.00 | 0.00 |
| Hospital characteristics | | | | |
| Number of beds | 0.09 | 0.08 | 0.09 | 0.08 |
| Regional location | | | | |
| Northeast | −1.20 | 0.32*** | −1.20 | 0.32*** |
| South | −0.12 | 0.36 | −0.12 | 0.36 |
| North Central | −0.14 | 0.34 | −0.14 | 0.34 |
| SMSA size[a] | | | | |
| Under 100,000 | 0.50 | 0.81 | 0.50 | 0.81 |
| 100,000-250,000 | 0.46 | 0.42 | 0.46 | 0.42 |
| 250,000-500,000 | 0.12 | 0.35 | 0.12 | 0.35 |
| 500,000-1 million | 1.11 | 0.47** | 1.11 | 0.47** |
| 1 million-2.5 million | 0.39 | 0.34 | 0.39 | 0.34 |
| Over 2.5 million | 0.18 | 0.32 | 0.18 | 0.32 |
| House staff | −0.93 | 0.20*** | −0.93 | 0.20*** |
| Constant | 2.36 | 0.34*** | 3.85 | 1.08*** |
| Model statistics | | | | |
| Pseudo R | | 0.28 | | 0.28 |
| N | | 1,234 | | 1,234 |

[a]Size of standard metropolitan statistical area (SMSA).
***Chi-square significant at $p \leq .01$.
**Chi-square significant at $p \leq .05$.
*Chi-square significant at $p \leq .10$.

TABLE A-20 The Primary Form of Compensation for Radiologists Is a Percent of Revenue or Fee for Service

| Variables | System Control Coefficients Relative to— | | | |
| | Freestanding Hospitals | | Investor-Owned Systems | |
| | Coefficient | Standard Error | Coefficient | Standard Error |
| --- | --- | --- | --- | --- |
| Freestanding hospitals | | | −0.62 | 0.87 |
| System characteristics | | | | |
| System control | | | | |
| Religious nonprofit | 1.23 | 0.49** | 0.60 | 0.98 |
| Secular nonprofit | −0.24 | 0.51 | −0.87 | 0.97 |
| Investor-owned | 0.62 | 0.88 | | |
| Public | −2.23 | 1.09** | −2.85 | 1.36** |
| Contract-managed | 0.28 | 0.74 | −0.35 | 0.96 |
| System size | 0.00 | 0.00 | 0.00 | 0.00 |
| Hospital characteristics | | | | |
| Number of beds | −0.03 | 0.07 | −0.03 | 0.07 |
| Regional location | | | | |
| Northeast | −1.44 | 0.34*** | −1.44 | 0.34*** |
| South | 0.14 | 0.41 | 0.14 | 0.41 |
| North Central | 0.01 | 0.39 | 0.01 | 0.39 |
| SMSA size[a] | | | | |
| Under 100,000 | −0.05 | 0.83 | −0.05 | 0.83 |
| 100,000-250,000 | 0.08 | 0.47 | 0.08 | 0.47 |
| 250,000-500,000 | −0.60 | 0.37 | −0.60 | 0.37 |
| 500,000-1 million | 0.81 | 0.52 | 0.81 | 0.52 |
| 1 million-2.5 million | −0.12 | 0.37 | −0.12 | 0.37 |
| Over 2.5 million | −0.95 | 0.32*** | −0.95 | 0.32*** |
| House staff | −0.70 | 0.20*** | −0.70 | 0.20*** |
| Constant | 3.14 | 0.36*** | 3.76 | 0.89*** |
| Model statistics | | | | |
| Pseudo R | | 0.41 | | 0.41 |
| N | | 1,234 | | 1,234 |

[a]Size of standard metropolitan statistical area (SMSA).
***Chi-square significant at $p \leq .01$.
**Chi-square significant at $p \leq .05$.

**TABLE A-21** The Primary Form of Compensation for Pathologists Is a Percent of Revenue or Fee for Service

| | System Control Coefficients Relative to— | | | |
| | Freestanding Hospitals | | Investor-Owned Systems | |
| Variables | Coefficient | Standard Error | Coefficient | Standard Error |
|---|---|---|---|---|
| Freestanding hospitals | | | −0.69 | 0.48 |
| System characteristics | | | | |
| System control | | | | |
| Religious nonprofit | −0.29 | 0.22 | −0.98 | 0.50* |
| Secular nonprofit | −0.11 | 0.40 | −0.80 | 0.60 |
| Investor-owned | 0.69 | 0.48 | | |
| Public | −1.57 | 1.00 | −2.26 | 1.09** |
| Contract-managed | 1.37 | 0.50*** | 0.68 | 0.51 |
| System size | −0.00 | 0.00** | −0.00 | 0.00** |
| Hospital characteristics | | | | |
| Number of beds | −0.09 | 0.05 | −0.09 | 0.05 |
| Regional location | | | | |
| Northeast | −2.58 | 0.23*** | −2.58 | 0.23*** |
| South | 0.10 | 0.24 | 0.10 | 0.24 |
| North Central | −0.28 | 0.23 | −0.28 | 0.23 |
| SMSA size[a] | | | | |
| Under 100,000 | −0.03 | 0.55 | −0.03 | 0.55 |
| 100,000-250,000 | 0.21 | 0.28 | 0.21 | 0.28 |
| 250,000-500,000 | −0.33 | 0.27 | −0.33 | 0.27 |
| 500,000-1 million | 0.03 | 0.29 | 0.03 | 0.29 |
| 1 million-2.5 million | −0.24 | 0.24 | −0.24 | 0.24 |
| Over 2.5 million | −0.28 | 0.24 | −0.28 | 0.24 |
| House staff | −0.57 | 0.21*** | −0.57 | 0.21*** |
| Constant | 1.91 | 0.22*** | 2.59 | 0.50*** |
| Model statistics | | | | |
| Pseudo R | | 0.48 | | 0.48 |
| N | | 1,234 | | 1,234 |

[a]Size of standard metropolitan statistical area (SMSA).
***Chi-square significant at $p \leq .01$.
**Chi-square significant at $p \leq .05$.
*Chi-square significant at $p \leq .10$.

**TABLE A-22**  Do Your Anesthesiologists Bill Patients Directly?

| | System Control Coefficients Relative to— | | | |
| | Freestanding Hospitals | | Investor-Owned Systems | |
| Variables | Coefficient | Standard Error | Coefficient | Standard Error |
|---|---|---|---|---|
| Freestanding hospitals | | | −0.78 | 0.35** |
| System characteristics | | | | |
| System control | | | | |
| Religious nonprofit | 0.44 | 0.22** | −0.33 | 0.40 |
| Secular nonprofit | −0.29 | 0.34 | −1.07 | 0.47** |
| Investor-owned | 0.78 | 0.35** | | |
| Public | −2.49 | 0.80*** | −3.26 | 0.86*** |
| Contract-managed | −0.40 | 0.28 | −1.17 | 0.37*** |
| System size | 0.00 | 0.00 | 0.00 | 0.00 |
| Hospital characteristics | | | | |
| Number of beds | 0.54 | 0.07*** | 0.54 | 0.07*** |
| Regional location | | | | |
| Northeast | −0.49 | 0.20** | −0.49 | 0.20** |
| South | −0.43 | 0.19** | −0.43 | 0.19** |
| North Central | −0.37 | 0.18** | −0.37 | 0.18** |
| SMSA size[a] | | | | |
| Under 100,000 | 1.36 | 0.64** | 1.36 | 0.64** |
| 100,000-250,000 | 0.63 | 0.23*** | 0.63 | 0.23*** |
| 250,000-500,000 | 0.95 | 0.23*** | 0.95 | 0.23*** |
| 500,000-1 million | 1.01 | 0.26*** | 1.01 | 0.26*** |
| 1 million-2.5 million | 1.09 | 0.21*** | 1.09 | 0.21*** |
| Over 2.5 million | 0.95 | 0.22*** | 0.95 | 0.22*** |
| House staff | −0.78 | 0.17*** | −0.78 | 0.17*** |
| Constant | −0.19 | 0.16 | −0.58 | 0.36 |
| Model statistics | | | | |
| Pseudo R | | 0.38 | | 0.38 |
| N | | 1,627 | | 1,627 |

[a]Size of standard metropolitan statistical area (SMSA).

***Chi-square significant at $p \leq .01$.

**Chi-square significant at $p \leq .05$.

*Chi-square significant at $p \leq .10$.

**TABLE A-23**   Do Your Radiologists Bill Patients Directly?

| | System Control Coefficients Relative to— | | | |
| | Freestanding Hospitals | | Investor-Owned Systems | |
| Variables | Coefficient | Standard Error | Coefficient | Standard Error |
|---|---|---|---|---|
| Freestanding hospitals | | | −1.26 | 0.33*** |
| System characteristics | | | | |
|   System control | | | | |
|     Religious nonprofit | 0.75 | 0.19*** | −0.51 | 0.37 |
|     Secular nonprofit | 0.31 | 0.31 | −0.95 | 0.43** |
|     Investor-owned | 1.26 | 0.33*** | | |
|     Public | −0.77 | 0.73 | −2.02 | 0.80** |
|   Contract-managed | 0.16 | 0.27 | −1.10 | 0.36*** |
|   System size | 0.00 | 0.00 | 0.00 | 0.00 |
| Hospital characteristics | | | | |
|   Number of beds | 0.29 | 0.05*** | 0.29 | 0.05*** |
|   Regional location | | | | |
|     Northeast | 0.01 | 0.17 | 0.01 | 0.17 |
|     South | 0.86 | 0.17*** | 0.86 | 0.17*** |
|     North Central | 0.44 | 0.16*** | 0.44 | 0.16*** |
|   SMSA size[a] | | | | |
|     Under 100,000 | 0.92 | 0.52* | 0.92 | 0.52* |
|     100,000-250,000 | 0.60 | 0.22*** | 0.60 | 0.22*** |
|     250,000-500,000 | 0.27 | 0.20 | 0.27 | 0.20 |
|     500,000-1 million | 0.52 | 0.22** | 0.52 | 0.22** |
|     1 million-2.5 million | 0.46 | 0.18*** | 0.46 | 0.18*** |
|     Over 2.5 million | −0.35 | 0.18* | −0.35 | 0.18* |
|   House staff | −0.33 | 0.00** | −0.33 | 0.00** |
| Constant | −0.85 | 0.15*** | 0.41 | 0.34 |
| Model statistics | | | | |
|   Pseudo R | 0.29 | | 0.29 | |
|   N | 1,627 | | 1,627 | |

[a]Size of standard metropolitan statistical area (SMSA).

***Chi-square significant at $p \leq .01$.

**Chi-square significant at $p \leq .05$.

*Chi-square significant at $p \leq .10$.

**TABLE A-24**  Do Your Pathologists Bill Patients Directly?

| Variables | System Control Coefficients Relative to— | | | |
| | Freestanding Hospitals | | Investor-Owned Systems | |
| | Coefficient | Standard Error | Coefficient | Standard Error |
|---|---|---|---|---|
| Freestanding hospitals | | | −1.43 | 0.29*** |
| System characteristics | | | | |
| System control | | | | |
|   Religious nonprofit | 0.35 | 0.19* | −1.08 | 0.32*** |
|   Secular nonprofit | 0.44 | 0.33 | −0.99 | 0.42** |
|   Investor-owned | 1.43 | 0.29*** | | |
|   Public | −2.10 | 1.21* | −3.52 | 1.24*** |
| Contract-managed | 0.87 | 0.28*** | −0.56 | 0.32* |
| System size | −0.00 | 0.00* | −0.00 | 0.00* |
| Hospital characteristics | | | | |
| Number of beds | −0.00 | 0.05 | −0.00 | 0.05 |
| Regional location | | | | |
|   Northeast | −1.51 | 0.28*** | −1.51 | 0.28*** |
|   South | 0.95 | 0.18*** | 0.95 | 0.18*** |
|   North Central | −0.03 | 0.19 | −0.03 | 0.19 |
| SMSA size[a] | | | | |
|   Under 100,000 | 1.09 | 0.45** | 1.09 | 0.45** |
|   100,000-250,000 | 0.78 | 0.23*** | 0.78 | 0.23*** |
|   250,000-500,000 | 0.09 | 0.25 | 0.09 | 0.25 |
|   500,000-1 million | 0.12 | 0.27 | 0.12 | 0.27 |
|   1 million-2.5 million | 0.42 | 0.21** | 0.42 | 0.21** |
|   Over 2.5 million | 0.43 | 0.23* | 0.43 | 0.23* |
| House staff | 0.42 | 0.14*** | 0.42 | 0.14*** |
| Constant | −1.88 | 0.18*** | −0.46 | 0.30 |
| Model statistics | | | | |
| Pseudo R | 0.34 | | 0.34 | |
| N | 1,627 | | 1,627 | |

[a]Size of standard metropolitan statistical area (SMSA).
***Chi-square significant at $p \leq .01$.
**Chi-square significant at $p \leq .05$.
*Chi-square significant at $p \leq .10$.

For-Profit Enterprise in Health Care. 1986.
National Academy Press, Washington, D.C.

# Hospitals and Their Communities: A Report on Three Case Studies

Jessica Townsend

The Institute of Medicine's (IOM's) Committee on the Implications of For-Profit Enterprise in Health Care reviewed and commissioned studies that use numerical data and statistical analysis to enhance understanding of the impact of for-profit providers on numerous aspects of the nation's health care system and those who use it. These studies quantify similarities and differences among health care providers of different ownership types. But observations derived from aggregated data cannot show how organizations interact at the community level. Nor can such data show how differences among providers affect other providers and residents of communities, or the dynamics of interactions among the diverse elements that comprise local health care systems.

To help fill some of these gaps, the IOM committee conducted three case studies in 1984, using site visits by committee members and staff. These studies were designed to illuminate several topics of interest to the committee. Two questions were of primary interest: in communities, what differences and similarities can be observed among health care organizations of different ownership types? What are the effects of the introduction of for-profit providers on a community's other health care providers and on those who seek care? Other topics that flow from these two questions relate to changes in the financial status of provider organizations, changes in the cost and quality of care and in access to care, changes in the competitive environment in the communities, and changes in relationships among physicians and institutions.

---

Ms. Townsend is a professional associate with the Institute of Medicine.

## METHODOLOGY

Three communities were selected as study sites. Selection was based on the following criteria:

1. Each community should include at least one investor-owned chain hospital and one not-for-profit hospital that was a member of a multihospital system. This criterion was to help ensure that similarities and differences between not-for-profit and investor-owned hospitals were likely to be related to ownership, rather than membership or nonmembership in a multi-institutional organization. It also was intended to enable investigation of similarities and differences in the relationship between not-for-profit and investor-owned hospitals and the systems that own them.

2. The investor-owned hospitals in different communities should each belong to a different corporation. This criterion was included to allow observation of differences among investor-owned corporations in the extent and type of control exercised over hospitals and in other characteristics that may differ according to corporate policy.

3. Each community should include no more than four hospitals so that a site-visit team would have sufficient time to visit all hospitals and other important facilities.

4. The communities should be in states in which investor-owned hospitals have substantial representation, and each site selected should be in a different state. These criteria were intended to ensure that the study sites were in states with characteristics (such as demographic or regulatory characteristics) typically selected by investor-owned corporations for the location of hospitals, and also that some differences among states would be reflected in the studies.

Communities that fulfilled these criteria were selected from the 1983 American Hospital Association *Guide to the Health Care Field*. Permission to visit the hospitals was requested from the hospital administrators and from headquarters of the multihospital systems. In one case permission to visit a hospital was refused by an investor-owned company (on the grounds that the hospital was not typical), and an alternative city was chosen that fulfilled the criteria and that included a hospital owned by the same company. Interviews were requested with people holding key administrative and medical positions in the hospitals—chief administrator; administrators in charge of finance, marketing, and planning; chairman and members of the governing board; medical director; chief of staff; physicians who admit significant numbers of patients to the hospital; and physicians who work under contract with the hospital. In addition, contact was made with owners and operators of the major nonhospital health facilities, such as ambulatory surgery centers and urgent care centers. All agreed to participate in the study, and all helped arrange the meetings we requested between members of our site visit teams and the people (or types of people) with whom we wished to meet.

In several cases, visits were also arranged to the home offices of the multihospital systems. Interviews were conducted with people holding positions such as chief executive officer, and directors of finance, planning, and marketing.

The site visit teams were composed of one physician and one nonphysician member of the IOM committee, and two staff members. Before the site visits, background information was obtained about demographic and economic aspects of the community and about the history and current status of the major health care providers. During the course of a 2- or 3-day visit to each of the three communities, all of the hospitals and most other significant health care organizations were visited. Interviews were generally conducted by teams of site visitors and were generally recorded. Interviews were based on lists of topics—some of which were explored in all three communities and some of which were specific to a particular community or a particular hospital.

Through preparation of these topic lists in advance and through periodic consultations during the course of a visit, efforts were made to cover the same topics in different communities and hospitals, as well as to learn about significant factors that were specific to a particular community or institution. Conclusions drawn from the case studies are based on numerous respondents confirming each other's views.

## THE COMMUNITIES

The names of all places and hospitals have been changed to preserve the anonymity of the communities, organizations, and the people interviewed, who gave most generously of their time.

### Valleyville

Valleyville, a city of 50,000 people, is the major trade and commerce center of a large semirural area. At the time of our visit, the effects of a 3-year economic recession were evident. Unemployment was higher than national and state averages. The city of Valleyville is located in Hill County, whose mainly white and growing population is, by most measures, poorer than the national average. The supply of physicians in Valleyville has grown with the population and is close to the national physician-to-population ratio.

There are three hospitals in Valleyville. The largest is the 200-bed Miracle Hospital. Since the 1940s this hospital has been owned by a Catholic multihospital system that owns several other hospitals in the state. The hospital has been rebuilt and enlarged to meet the health care needs of Valleyville's growing population, and provides high-technology services such as computed tomographic (CT) scanning, ambulatory surgery, and 24-hour emergency room coverage. Miracle Hospital is Valleyville's designated trauma center, and is the only hospital in the city that provides obstetrical and specialized cancer services.

The second largest hospital is Valley Hospital. This 150-bed hospital was built by a physician in the 1940s, subsequently sold to a group of doctors, who in turn sold the hospital to the current owner—a major investor-owned multihospital system. Valley Hospital, like Miracle, has grown over the years and provides a wide range of high-technology services. Valley Hospital has the only cardiac catheterization laboratory and rehabilitation unit in Valleyville.

At the time of our visit, Miracle and Valley hospitals were competing to attract physicians through the provision of a working environment that physicians would prefer, and by capturing specific segments of the market through the provision of specialized services. Physicians generally had admitting privileges at both hospitals which were about a 10-minute drive from each other. They frequently allowed patients to choose their place of hospitalization. The hospitals therefore also competed on patient amenities.

The third hospital is Hill County, which at its peak operated 150 beds, of which 100 were closed as Miracle and Valley hospitals expanded. This county-owned hospital has a history of financial problems dating back to the late 1970s. The board of county supervisors had at one time considered closing the hospital, and had offered to lease or sell the hospital. However, no acceptable offer was received. In 1983 a management contract with an investor-owned hospital company was signed under which the hospital was to be operated on an annually declining county subsidy, dropping to zero in the fifth year.

### Coast Town

Coast Town, a city of approximately 60,000 people, is the medical center for the surrounding three counties as well as the adjacent areas of two contiguous states. The city enjoys a stable economic base and weathered the recent recession well. Unemployment remained below the national level. However, the per capita personal income of the town and surrounding Sunshine County is substantially below state and national averages. Coast Town has a large (one-third of the population) black community. It has four hospitals.

The oldest hospital in Coast Town dates from 1915. It is 300-bed St. Mary's Hospital, owned by a Catholic multi-institutional system that owns hospitals in several states. St. Mary's Hospital is preeminent in pediatric care in Coast Town, operating a level II neonatal care unit

and a specialized children's hospital on the grounds. St. Mary's Hospital operates primary care centers that function as feeders to the hospital, and a freestanding ambulatory surgery center on the hospital campus.

A public hospital, Sunshine County Hospital was built in the 1940s. At the time of the site visit, this 150-bed hospital was in the first year of operation under a management contract with an investor-owned management company. Under the contract, the management team must set up data systems to put in order financial accounting procedures that had been in disarray. More importantly, because the county had decided to reduce and eventually eliminate county subsidies for the facility, the management company was in effect required to reduce uncompensated care and to seek to attract private-pay patients that had been drawn to Coast Town's private hospitals by their more attractive facilities and reputedly superior quality of care. The most controversial change made by the contract managers (with the county's agreement) to put the hospital on a more healthy financial base was closure of the emergency room.

Memorial Hospital is a large (500-bed) independent hospital that opened in the early 1950s, and built its census in part by drawing patients from Sunshine County Hospital. This church-affiliated hospital is becoming the nucleus of a small multi-institutional system through the purchase or contract-management of several hospitals in nearby small communities.

The most recent hospital to be built was investor-owned Coast Hospital located in a suburb of Coast Town. This 400-bed hospital opened in the 1970s with immediate access to a substantial patient base because of an agreement it made with a large multispecialty group practice (Health Clinic). This group practice, which included approximately half of the community's physicians, agreed with a major investor-owned hospital company to jointly buy land on which the company would build a hospital. Health Clinic physicians had been dissatisfied with the voice they were given in the administration of St. Mary's and Memorial hospitals, and with what they perceived as a cavalier attitude toward their group's needs at these two hospitals. They were, therefore, ready to work with a corporation that promised to be more responsive and would establish a hospital in which Health Clinic physicians would be a major power. The Health Clinic today numbers roughly 100 physicians, one-third of all Coast Town physicians, and provides almost all admissions to Coast Hospital.

The construction of Coast Hospital, and the loss of the Health Clinic's substantial volume of patients caused immediate severe census and revenue losses at St. Mary's and Memorial hospitals. Administrators at both hospitals devised strategies that had restored the health of their institutions by the time of our site visit, 8 years later. However, at the time of our visit to Coast Town, St. Mary's and Memorial hospitals were feeling the effects of the closing of the emergency room at Sunshine County Hospital. Increasing numbers of indigent patients, who formerly gained access to hospital care through the emergency room at the county hospital, were seeking care at nearby St. Mary's and Memorial.

## Center City

Center City is a town of over 100,000 people that is experiencing a sharp economic downturn after substantial economic and population growth in the 1950s and 1960s. The city is within an industrialized standard metropolitan statistical area (SMSA) that includes a relatively large (30 percent) black population and a high unemployment rate that is thrusting many people into medical indigency as union health benefits expire.

The major providers of health care in Center City consist of three private acute care hospitals, a psychiatric hospital, a dialysis center, three urgent care centers, a surgery center, and two diagnostic-imaging centers expected to be operational within a year. Absent from the array of health care providers is a public hospital. Many indigent patients travel out of the county for care at a public hospital.

The largest hospital in Center City is St. Ricardo, a 450-bed member of a Catholic multihospital system that operates in several states. This 90-year-old hospital was rebuilt and expanded as demand for a larger, more modern facility occurred. St. Ricardo is the leading

hospital in Center City in terms of size and level of care, operating the most active emergency room, cardiac catheterization laboratory, and open heart program in the city.

In the 1940s a protestant denomination felt they should also have a hospital and established Church Hospital which, like St. Ricardo, grew in response to growing demand for care to its present size of 350 beds. The hospital is one of several in the state that is owned by the church, but the hospitals are operated without centralized control. Like St. Ricardo, Church provides sophisticated services such as CT scanning and cardiac surgery, but fewer such procedures are performed. Church recently closed its maternity unit which had been losing money because of low utilization and few paying patients.

Center City's newest and smallest hospital is an investor-owned company's 250-bed Walnut Hospital. In the 1970s Center City was experiencing a shortage of hospital beds. Simultaneously a substantial number of physicians were becoming distressed at their inability to have an impact on decisions at St. Ricardo and Church hospitals. Furthermore, new physicians recruited by St. Ricardo Hospital appeared to be given favorable treatment, causing many physicians to fear that their influence would further diminish. In response, 60 physicians formed a partnership to buy land, and then sought an investor-owned corporation to finance, construct, lease, and operate a hospital. The physician investors bear no risks nor do they share in the profit of the hospital. What they sought to gain was a hospital in which the administration would be responsive to their desires. The hospital has become a place to which physicians admit paying patients needing uncomplicated care. Elective surgery is emphasized. Trauma, obstetrics, complex cardiology, and neurosurgery patients are admitted to the other hospitals.

Unlike the situation in Coast Town, the construction of the investor-owned Walnut Hospital did not cause immediate disruption at the existing hospitals, which had been operating with extremely high occupancy levels. Physicians in the group of investors in Walnut Hospital continued to admit patients to St. Ricardo and Church hospitals.

## THE CONTEXT

Site visits made in the summer of 1984 occurred at a time of change and disruption for many community hospitals. Nationally, occupancy rates were falling, and employers and others who pay for services or insurance were becoming increasingly aware of their bargaining power in the medical marketplace. Health care providers were responding to the new cost-consciousness of payers by developing new and less expensive types of care. Medicare's prospective payment system was being phased in. Many of the people interviewed in the course of the case studies commented on the impact of these changes. They contrasted the current focus on containing hospital expenses with earlier times. They described a time when competition between hospitals meant striving to provide more lavishly equipped facilities and a broader array of services. Sustaining occupancy rates was formerly of less concern than at the time of our site visits, when competition between hospitals was likely to mean working hard to keep physicians happy and revenues flowing. Future-minded hospital administrators were also starting to perceive that price competition could become a reality. Cost control—through physician cooperation as well as effective management—had already become reality with the start of prospective payment.

But, although these and other factors were changing the environment in which hospitals operate, one development caused several of the hospitals to make rapid and dramatic changes. That development was the advent of competition from providers of health care in freestanding centers such as surgery, urgent care, and diagnostic-imaging centers. In one community all the hospitals had reacted rapidly. They had reduced emergency room charges, and, more dramatically, they were developing freestanding centers themselves, often as a joint venture with physicians. In another community the hospital administrators, hearing that physicians were seeking financing to establish freestanding centers, attempted to engage in joint ventures. To the dismay of the administrators, other financiers had already concluded deals. Although in this latter case the hospitals reacted too slowly, the perception of administrators was that the cen-

ters were real threats that demanded immediate action.

Indeed, the ability to respond rapidly and flexibly to changes in their environment was one of the most striking features of many of the hospitals studied. This was particularly apparent in some not-for-profit hospitals that had to recoup their market positions after the construction of an investor-owned hospital. It was also notable in hospitals that altered, delayed, or cancelled expansion plans in response to diminished or changed demand. And it was notable in the response of hospitals to prospective payment—the acquisition of new data systems, the dissemination of cost data and other information to physicians, and the initiation of more stringent cost control.

Differences in the economic, political, and social environment of the communities appeared to affect the actions and reactions of members of the health care community to events or changes in their communities. For example, physicians' political stances appeared to affect their influence. Physicians in one community frequently spoke of their belief in traditional, solo practice and their dislike of the newer prepaid plans or preferred provider organizations, which some described as socialized medicine. These physicians, who valued their independence, showed little interest in uniting with other physicians to create power blocks to promote their interests in hospitals. In another example, the economic stability and growing population of a community enabled not-for-profit hospitals to rebuild their census after an investor-owned hospital opened its doors.

In sum, the hospitals, physicians, and other health care providers observed in the case studies exist in local and national environments. Each interacts with the other. The local environment was often a determinant of how people and institutions responded to changes in the larger national environment. And changes at the national level often produced responses in the local environment.

## COMPETITION

How the introduction of an investor-owned hospital affected the competitive climate of the communities involved and how the existing health care providers responded were to a great extent determined by the circumstances behind the advent of investor ownership. But it should be remembered that the impact of the newly built investor-owned hospitals involves more than the impact of investor ownership per se. The construction of a new hospital, regardless of ownership, is likely to affect existing providers. However, in these instances it was investor-owned companies that built (or bought) a hospital.

The impact of the advent of investor-owned hospitals on the competitive environment in the community was different in each case. These differences illustrate the importance of the circumstances surrounding the introduction of investor ownership to a community in determining how the competitive situation will be affected.

In Valleyville the purchase of an existing hospital by an investor-owned corporation was followed by improvements in plant and equipment. The newly upgraded hospital then became more serious competition to the existing not-for-profit hospital, although not a threat to its survival. The not-for-profit hospital remained financially healthy, carved out some specialty niches in which it dominated the market, and retained a reputation for superior quality in many of the hospitals' departments. The not-for-profit hospital also had lower charges than the investor-owned hospital—a factor that appeared to be becoming increasingly important as it became known and as physicians in Valleyville became more protective of patients' purses. Another event that some in Valleyville viewed as potentially changing the competitive balances among the hospitals was the recent management contract between the public hospital and an investor-owned corporation. If the new managers succeed in attracting more paying patients to the public hospital, the private hospitals will be the losers.

In Center City and Coast Town, the investor-owned hospitals were constructed with the support of groups of discontented physicians. In both cases administrators of existing hospitals were considered to be unresponsive to physician's needs and had balked at giving physicians the degree of control that they sought. In Center City, where demand was sufficiently high for new capacity to be absorbed and where physicians continued to admit to all hospitals, the introduction of an investor-owned hospital caused little disruption. Only when a recession later reduced demand for hospital care did the relative strengths and weaknesses of each hospital become apparent. Of the two not-for-profit hospitals the one with the stronger administration, greater financial resources, strength in specific services, and better relationship with medical staff appeared to be in sound economic condition at the time of our visit. The weaker not-for-profit appeared to be in marginal economic condition and was badly in need of more paying patients. Possibly its financial position would today be a little less precarious had the third hospital not been built.

By contrast in Coast Town, the construction of a new investor-owned hospital, which was connected with the large multispecialty physician group practice, immediately and radically changed the competitive situation among hospitals. The census at the two not-for-profit hospitals immediately dropped 30 to 50 percent, forcing prompt action to alleviate the situation. While these two hospitals took different approaches to restoring their financial health, the outcome was the creation of a fiercely competitive situation. The hospitals brought new physicians to the community (but not in such numbers or specialties as to upset their important admitters), provided office space, helped with referrals, and so forth. Physicians in the community reported greatly increased responsiveness of administrators to physicians' needs, and each hospital moved to develop a cadre of physicians who would not admit patients elsewhere either because of loyalty or economic connection. Such steps included engaging in joint hospital/physician ventures such as urgent care centers, and the development of office buildings. As a result most physicians in Coast Town developed clear primary loyalties to a particular hospital. A new cohesiveness has developed among the physicians that admit to each hospital, and the physicians have become willing to work together in the health maintenance organizations (HMOs) and preferred provider arrangements that were at an incipient stage. By contrast, in the other two communities studied, where competition among hospitals was less intense, physicians maintained their independence from individual hospitals and resisted efforts to form HMOs and preferred provider organizations.

Other responses to increased competition in the communities included vertical and horizontal diversification. After corporate restructuring, not-for-profit hospitals began to develop home care agencies, nursing homes, congregate housing facilities, and other health services. For-profit subsidiaries to sell such services as data management, consulting, and marketing were also developed. These initiatives represent attempts to sustain and enhance revenues in the face of erosion by decreased lengths of stay and competition from other hospitals and providers of out-of-hospital care.

In two of the communities, competition from out-of-hospital providers in facilities such as urgent care centers was causing hospitals (not-for-profit and investor-owned) to move to protect their market shares. Indeed these freestanding centers—the first ones being started as for-profit enterprises by physicians—were in some cases viewed as a much more serious threat to the not-for-profit hospitals than was the establishment of an investor-owned hospital. In an effort to retain their market share, several hospitals set up freestanding ambulatory care centers. However, it can be hazardous for a hospital to enter the freestanding ambulatory care market. In one community two major admitters to the investor-owned hospital opened an urgent care center. In an attempt to preserve the good will of these important physicians, the corporate owners of the hospital financed the new center's marketing campaign. Other physicians interpreted this as the hospital supporting an activity that was a direct threat to their office practices. Some outraged physicians stopped admitting patients to the investor-owned hospital and succeeded in having the administrator fired.

While increased competition among hospitals could be observed in communities after the entry of an investor-owned company, in no case had a not-for-profit hospital failed. In the short run, some not-for-profit hospitals had to make major strategic changes to recoup lost census. Others had to make more minor adjustments to compete with newly renovated and updated facilities by actively marketing to patients and physicians. In only one case does the longer run survival of a not-for-profit hospital appear doubtful. Although competition from the investor-owned hospital may contribute to this hospital's problems, it also appears to be suffering from poor administration that cannot move rapidly enough to cope with the fast-changing external environment.

Price increases also contributed to the survival of not-for-profit hospitals. The new investor-owners often priced services substantially above existing not-for-profit rates—possibly because substantial capital costs were involved in construction or renovation. Not-for-profit hospitals could, therefore, raise prices, increase their revenues, and still remain competitive.

In sum, the case studies indicate that whether the introduction of an investor-owned hospital has an immediate effect on the status of competition among hospitals depends to a great extent on whether demand for hospital services can absorb additional capacity or the upgrading of existing capacity. Two of the communities studied suffered from an economic recession some years after the advent of investor ownership. Demand for hospital care fell and all hospitals operated at low occupancy rates. When this occurred the competition from an investor-owned hospital, which had earlier been viewed by the administrators of not-for-profit hospitals as neutral or even as a positive stimulus to improve quality, was then viewed as more threatening. From this follows the question of whether all the hospitals in the communities studied can survive in an environment of increased competition, and whether an investor-owned hospital may cause existing hospitals to fail. Whether all the hospitals can continue to thrive as reimbursement gets tighter and competition stronger is unclear. If in the future some of the hospitals fail, it is likely to be for several reasons, of which increased competition from investor-owned hospitals is but one. Furthermore, if some hospitals in the communities studied are going to fail it is not at all certain that the investor-owned hospitals will not be counted among the failures.

## CARE FOR POOR PEOPLE

Two important questions have arisen in the context of investor ownership and people unable to pay for care. First, have investor-owned hospitals made it more difficult for not-for-profit or public hospitals to care for these people? Second, do investor-owned and not-for-profit hospitals provide similar amounts of uncompensated care relative to total care provided? The latter question is best answered by the national- and state-level data, as are discussed in the committee's report. Some observations regarding the former question were generated in the case studies.

Three factors appear to affect the way not-for-profit and for-profit hospitals approach the issue of providing uncompensated care and affect each other's provision of such care. First is the magnitude of the problem—whether a community includes such large numbers of people in need of free care that hospital administrators and trustees perceive demand to exceed the amount they are able to supply. Second is whether a public hospital is available where poor patients can seek care and to which they can be transferred by private hospitals. Third is the depth of the hospitals' commitment to providing uncompensated care.

The case studies provided examples of the importance and interactions of these factors. In a community where there existed a public hospital with sufficient subsidy and earned revenues to enable the hospital to satisfy most of the demand for uncompensated care, the investor-owned and private not-for-profit hospitals exhibited similar behavior. Uncompensated care represented between 2 and 3 percent of gross revenues in both hospitals. Both hospitals had similar policies for pre-admission deposits, credit checks on patients, and referring or transferring stable patients to the public hospital. The vast majority of people unable to pay for care went directly to the public hospital knowing that free care was available there. Moreover the private hospitals, especially the not-for-profit hospital, were less conveniently located for the central city population. The Catholic hospital administrators in this community spoke of a mission to provide care for people unable to pay. The corporate chief executive officer of the Catholic system spoke of uncompensated care as a necessary business practice to enhance image. The investor-owned hospital administrators spoke of admitting nonpaying patients as a service to physicians. Whatever the attitude, since the public hospital took care of most of the demand for uncompensated care, private hospitals could provide small amounts and the competitive balance between them was hardly affected.

In the two other communities, the situation was very different. In both communities providing care for medically indigent people was a serious problem. In one community there was no public hospital; in the other the public hospital had restricted access to become financially viable in the face of a reduced public subsidy. Thus, in both communities many people in need of care and with no source of payment were dependent on the willingness of the private hospitals to provide free care. In these two communities there were differences in the uncompensated care load of the not-for-profit and investor-owned hospitals. For example, in one community deductions from revenues for the not-for-profit hospitals ranged from 6 to 10 percent. For the investor-owned hospital that figure was 4 percent.

Although the issue of uncompensated care was of great moment in the two communities, the role of the investor-owned hospitals as a provider of uncompensated care scarcely entered the debate. There were several reasons for this. In one case the investor-owned hospital was not located in an area convenient for the city's poverty population. This hospital's proximity to a major highway may have given it more than its share of traffic accident victims, some of whom could not pay for their care, as well as some indigent patients from other communities. In the other community, the investor-owned hospital did not provide the services most likely to draw indigent patients—obstetrics, neonatal care, and trauma—and for many years did not operate an emergency room. The omission of these services came about because the physicians who established the hospital intended it as a place where they could admit patients needing routine elective surgery and uncomplicated medical care. The physicians also did not want to be on call for a third emergency room in the community.

An emergency room was eventually opened by the chief administrator with corporate support. The administrator believed that admission of additional paying patients through the emergency room would more than offset the amount of uncompensated care incurred. The private physicians who admitted patients to the hospital and who objected to having an emergency room were appeased by the hospital's contracting for physicians to staff the emergency room and by these physicians being able to admit the private physicians' patients in their absence. The emergency room, thus, became a convenience for physicians. Neither the investor-owned corporation nor the physicians at this hospital had any desire to admit nonpaying patients in significant numbers. Thus, for different reasons—location in one case, range of services and physician preference in another—the investor-owned hospitals were substantially insulated from the uncompensated care problem.

By contrast, the not-for-profit hospitals in these two communities were quite heavily involved in providing uncompensated care. While only one of the four not-for-profit hospitals in these two communities failed to produce positive margins (in two cases total net margins were in excess of 7 percent), the uncompensated care load was perceived as a problem by administrators at all the not-for-profit hospitals. The problem was most often couched in terms of maintaining solvency and distributing limited resources. The problem, however, was not always directly financial. One administrator observed that private patients disliked sharing the facility with patients who were obviously poor. In this community the two not-for-profit hospitals were negotiating to manage the public hospital, and it was widely assumed that their intent was to change the policies that had shifted more of the uncompensated care burden from the public hospital to the two not-for-profit hospitals.

In the communities studied it was clear that when publicly provided care was insufficient, the not-for-profit hospitals made significant contributions to the care of those unable to pay. It was also clear that the provision of uncompensated care was constrained by a regard for the financial health of the institution. In some Catholic hospitals, two mission-related

notions caused tension. On the one hand was the desire to care for those in need; on the other hand was the need to practice prudent stewardship. This latter function was described by one individual as not only conserving, but enhancing, the order's assets. The second requirement constrained the magnitude of the first requirement. Not-for-profit hospitals (like investor-owned hospitals) had mechanisms for deflecting some number of patients unable to pay for care. One not-for-profit hospital closed its maternity service when the financial drain became insupportable. It was acknowledged at several institutions that when it was possible, patients were transferred to public hospitals. Pre-admission financial screening was performed and deposits were generally required. Staff were alerted to frequent emergency room users who did not pay their bills. And legal action was taken to obtain payment of bills. Less directly, hospital administrators were active in the political arena trying to secure funding for the care of indigent patients.

Not-for-profit hospital administrators generally did not believe that the presence of an investor-owned hospital in their community had affected their provision of care for poor people. Rather, these administrators focused their attention on the provision of care by public hospitals and the need for the public sector to fund care for those unable to pay. However, looking toward the future, the erosion of revenues likely to be caused by increased outpatient services—often supplied on a for-profit basis—was seen in one community as likely to result in a reduction in uncompensated care. One administrator also noted that providing substantial uncompensated care would put his hospital at a competitive disadvantage with the investor-owned hospital—a disadvantage that would become important if health care purchasers became more price conscious.

Thus, the investor-owned hospitals in the communities studied made relatively small contributions to the provision of uncompensated care—because of decisions about location and range of services that ensured that the vast majority of people unable to pay for their care sought care elsewhere. Administrators of the not-for-profit and public hospitals that provided substantial amounts of uncompensated care did not feel that the presence of an investor-owned facility had reduced their ability to do so. The not-for-profit hospitals were able to provide varying and sometimes substantial amounts of uncompensated care while generally operating with healthy bottom lines.

Although there were differences in the relative amounts of uncompensated care provided by not-for-profit and investor-owned hospitals, there was great similarity in the methods used to assure payment (e.g., credit and insurance checks, deposits, litigation where necessary, and transfer of patients). The following description of emergency room procedures at an investor-owned hospital was typical of procedures at many of the hospitals visited. A triage nurse was the first person to see a patient. If she judged that a true emergency existed, the patient would be treated without evaluation of ability to pay. If the triage nurse did not view the case as an emergency, the patient would be interviewed by a business clerk. Should there be a problem with the patient's ability to pay, a physician would see the patient to make sure that he or she was not in peril. If not, the patient would be sent elsewhere. If the patient had a private physician, an effort would be made to contact the physician before the patient was sent away.

For the poor and uninsured people of the communities studied, the availability and location of hospital care was determined more by the existence and funding of a public hospital than the presence or absence of an investor-owned hospital. If there was a public hospital able to care for those in need, it was the locus of indigent care, and private hospitals provided minimal levels of uncompensated care. This situation pertained even when the subsidy to the public hospital was declining. The management contract at one (but not the other) public hospital specified that those in need of care must not be refused service. The corollary of this policy is that unless the public hospital generates sufficient revenue to subsidize free care, either the hospital will close or the county will have to continue financial support. By contrast, at another public hospital the management contract emphasized financial viability over service to those unable to pay. To deflect unsponsored patients, the emergency room was

closed, and patients presumably sought care at nearby not-for-profit hospitals. Thus, because of local governmental policies, the locus of much uncompensated care shifted to the private sector. And in the community without a public hospital, unsponsored patients either sought care in the not-for-profit hospitals, where they might or might not be admitted, or they traveled approximately 2 hours to the nearest public facility.

## MULTIHOSPITAL SYSTEMS

Also explored in the site visits was what it means for patients, physicians, board members, and administrators that their hospital is a member of a multihospital system. Are financial resources more readily available? Are administrators' areas of decision making more circumscribed? Are physicians less influential in hospital decision making? Is the board less influential in decision making? Does the home office provide valuable technical assistance? Responses to questions about the effect of system membership were varied. And just as the meaning and importance of membership in a system varied among hospitals, so did the systems vary in the extent and type of control they exercised over the hospitals they owned.

The three communities studied contained seven hospitals that were members of multihospital systems. The investor-owned systems appeared to have clear policies concerning the extent of centralized management; all three investor-owned hospitals functioned under well-established procedures that defined their relationship with the home office. Two Catholic hospitals were members of systems that appeared to be still unsure where to establish the boundaries for local autonomy in hospitals. These two systems were slowly increasing the amount of control that devolved to the central offices. Finally, two hospitals were members of not-for-profit systems that had few centralized functions, and few positive or negative aspects of system membership were noted. The systems can be grouped as follows: "nominal" not-for-profit systems without central management; centrally managed not-for-profit systems; and investor-owned systems.

An example of a nominal system was a hospital owned by a religious denomination that owned several hospitals in one state but that lacked any central organization to control or direct local operations. Membership in this system was of little direct importance to hospital operations. The hospital received $300,000 a year from the church and was required to adhere to certain rules relating to the composition of its board; physicians were excluded from board membership, and a certain number of ministers had to be included. Apart from those matters, the hospital functioned as an independent unit.

At the other end of the spectrum was a hospital owned by a highly centralized, investor-owned hospital company. Corporate oversight was apparent in almost every aspect of the operation of this hospital. Capital spending requests went through several layers of corporate review, depending on the size of the expenditure. Equipment was to be chosen from a list provided by the home office. Maintenance of equipment was often under a national contract negotiated by the home office. Detailed financial and operating goals were developed locally and negotiated with central management. Administrators' career advancement and compensation were linked to accomplishing these goals—and to achieve these goals, secondary goals that pertain to such details as staffing levels had to be met.

Although a not-for-profit "nominal" system was the most decentralized operation and an investor-owned system was the most centralized operation in the hospitals visited, an example was also seen of an investor-owned system that appeared to allow as much autonomy to individual hospitals as one of the not-for-profit systems with central management. No conclusion that one sector is always more or less highly centralized than the other could be supported from our visits.

## Not-for-profit Systems with Central Management

The following description is an amalgamation of elements from the two centrally managed not-for-profit systems that had not yet finalized the extent of home office control. The existing structure was developed because the organization recognized that the increasing complexity of health care demanded types of expertise that would be too costly to provide to hospitals unless they could be centralized in the home office. It was also recognized that a strategic planning approach was needed for the system as a whole, and that growth required capital that could be obtained more cheaply by a corporate system. The system floated a large bond issue in 1983.

Although recognizing both the necessity for and the benefits of some degree of centralization, corporate policy distinguished between what were described as strategic issues and operational issues. Strategic issues (e.g., future directions and financial goals) were defined as corporate responsibilities, as were functions that offer economies of scale such as purchasing, management development, and educational programs. Operational issues regarding how strategies or financial goals would be met were delegated to hospitals.

For individual hospitals, this meant that the administrator had considerable freedom within some overall constraints. Constraints included some powers that were reserved to the parent corporation—changing the hospitals' articles of incorporation; mortgaging, borrowing against, or selling property; adding or closing services; and entering a substantial association with another hospital. Capital expenditures over $30,000 and outside the budget required corporate approval, and employee benefits packages were determined and administered centrally. The corporation determined compensation for top-level hospital employees by use of a program developed by outside consultants. It offered slightly higher salaries than those at investor-owned facilities, to compensate, it was said, for lack of incentive bonuses. However, in the future, performance monitoring will be increased and local administrators given incentive compensation.

Although the centralized data system allowed the corporation to review detailed financial data from individual hospitals, the only financial goals specified by the corporate office were a net margin goal and a return-on-equity goal. Administrators, therefore, had almost complete discretion in how to attain the bottom line.

The flow of money between the corporation and individual hospitals in the not-for-profit systems was limited to the payment of a management fee based on a complex formula that relates mainly to operating cost and use of system resources. A payment in lieu of salaries for the nuns who worked in the hospital was made by the hospital to the religious order that provided support for the nuns.

## Investor-Owned Systems

It is more difficult to describe a typical investor-owned system because the extent of central control varied widely among the three we encountered. Common to each, however, were centralized financial data systems, capital budget processes that required higher levels of company approval for higher levels of expenditures, and reiterative or negotiated budget processes to develop annual financial goals which were translated into monthly goals and broken down to determine the contribution of operating units such as the emergency room, neonatal unit, radiology, and so forth. Some centralized purchasing occurred, and advice and consultation from the home office was available. There was a local advisory board composed largely of physicians but including business and other representation. Hospitals paid a corporate management fee.

## Advantages and Disadvantages of Ownership by a Centrally Managed System

Administrators in the hospitals belonging to centrally managed systems had different opinions about the pros and cons of multi-institutional membership. Their views appeared to be unrelated to whether the system was not-for-profit or investor-owned, and unrelated to the extent of oversight from central office. In one investor-owned hospital the chief administrator described the relationship with the home office as excellent and the corporate structure as providing some advantages. Other administrators there commented on the excellence of headquarters staff and easy availability of technical assistance. Also mentioned as advantages were the ability to compare the hospital's operating data with other hospitals in the system, and access to other administrators in the system with whom problems and solutions could be discussed. Similar com-

ments were heard in a not-for-profit system with central management.

In a not-for-profit system hospital, although access to other administrators in the system and the existence of a career ladder were viewed positively, there were complaints about time and energy spent on demands from the corporate level. For example, after plans for a home health agency had been approved by the local board, the administrator had to "sell it all over again" at the corporate level. Decision making at corporate level was described as slow and cumbersome. There was hope among hospital staff that some of the problems would be ironed out. Similar complaints came from medical staff in an investor-owned hospital which described the administrator as being hampered by corporate oversight.

Among physicians and board members there appeared to be no consensus on what belonging to a multi-institutional system meant. While one physician board member at a not-for-profit said, "We'd never know the hospital belongs to anyone," another member described the same board as "emasculated," and added, "All decisions are made at the corporate level; you can't initiate anything that goes against corporate policy." He also added that in the past the system had "never griped about spending money"—but this had resulted in what he considered to be waste in the use of supplies and in the purchase of excessive equipment, with the expense being passed on to patients—"We have laser equipment and no eye surgeon to use it." However, this physician described a changing attitude with a far greater emphasis on cost control, which he thinks the administrators can successfully carry through—"The administration is really good. They are not slowed down by the corporate office, and the hospital has always produced plenty of profit."

Despite differences of opinion about the advantages and disadvantages of being part of a hospital system, some themes emerged from our interviews. The most generally perceived benefit of system membership was access to capital. In all but the two hospitals in the "nominal" systems (where the hospitals themselves raise capital), administrators, physicians, and board members pointed to the advantages of the availability of corporate capital. Physicians indicated that their system made available all that is necessary to practice state-of-the-art medicine; administrators noted that available capital allowed them to respond to changes in their markets; board members felt that if they could justify capital spending decisions, implementation would follow because their hospital has access to capital acquired by the system. For an independent hospital visited, the lack of access to capital was described as a severe disadvantage in a highly competitive environment. This hospital joined a national alliance of not-for-profit hospitals whose capital-raising activities were described by the administrator as key to future survival.

Another advantage of system membership often commented on by hospital staff was the availability of consultation or expert help from corporate headquarters. This was most noticeable in implementing diagnosis-related group (DRG) systems. Almost all of the hospitals in centrally managed systems were presented with educational material for physicians and hospital staff (sometimes including computer programs, lectures, and films) and assistance with data systems. By contrast, at a "nominal" system hospital, three staff members had been given the responsibility of getting the hospital's DRG system up and working. The staff described how they had read everything useful they could obtain, had attended numerous professional meetings, and had generally gathered information wherever they could. They said that it had been a difficult and time-consuming process, and that they had lacked the support they felt they needed. They added that they were relying on the other community hospitals (members of centralized multihospital systems) to educate their physicians about DRGs.

Some systems have developed career ladders and staff development programs to help retain staff. Only one not-for-profit system had implemented a career development program that would allow staff movement among hospitals and between central office and hospitals. All three investor-owned systems had such programs. The benefit of the programs to individual hospitals was most clearly demonstrated when a new and experienced administrator arrived within a week after the chief administrator was fired. In another investor-owned hospital, the chief administrator had

previously been an assistant administrator at that hospital and had been moved to other hospitals in the system before eventually returning with much greater experience to go with his local knowledge. The management plans that hospital administrators in this system are required to prepare must include a description of a program to prepare promising lower-level administrators for advancement.

## PHYSICIAN INFLUENCE

It is well recognized that physicians rather than patients make many of the decisions concerning patients' hospitalization, and that in some circumstances physicians have the power to make or break a hospital. Recognizing this, the marketing activities of hospitals often focus directly on physicians. The case studies provide some rather dramatic illustrations of the influence of physicians in shaping the configuration of hospital services in communities. The studies also illustrate the augmentation of physician power that occurs when they act in groups.

The histories of the establishment of investor-owned hospitals in Coast Town and Center City illustrate how physicians can alter the configuration of hospital services. In both cities, physicians upset about what they saw as unaccommodating attitudes at the existing hospitals had negotiated with investor-owned corporations to build a new hospital. In Coast Town the physicians were in an existing group practice. In Center City a group of physicians came together for the sole purpose of bringing to the community a hospital more to their liking, and once they achieved this purpose, they no longer functioned as a group and did not confine their admissions to the new hospital. These two facts had important consequences. Since the existing hospitals in Center City continued to receive admissions from the physicians, the impact of the new hospital was much less strongly felt than in Coast Town. Furthermore, the new investor-owned hospital in Center City did not begin with, nor had it yet developed, the kind of assured patient base enjoyed by the investor-owned hospital in Coast Town. The Center City hospital, therefore, had to seek admissions from all community physicians (including the original physician investors) with whom hospital/corporate interests did not always coincide. This lack of accord was exemplified in the disagreement about whether the hospital should operate an emergency room, which was established despite physician objections. Because physicians had generally not aligned with any single hospital they had preserved the option of sending their patients elsewhere—an option that was used implicitly, if not explicitly, to influence decisions made at the hospital's home office. Clearly, even at a hospital operated by a well-capitalized and highly centralized investor-owned hospital company, the alienation of large numbers of physicians, able to control their admissions, can have a powerful economic impact on the hospital.

In Coast Town, a large multispecialty group of physicians committed its admissions to the new investor-owned hospital by building their office building on the hospital campus. A symbiotic relationship between the group and the hospital was reinforced by the alienation of many of the community's other physicians who would not admit patients to the new investor-owned hospital. This hospital's bylaws precluded physicians not in the multispecialty group from governing board membership. This investor-owned hospital, with the group's existing patient base, could locate in a growing part of town that was removed from downtown, from poor neighborhoods, and from the other hospitals. By contrast, in Center City the investor-owned hospital was located near existing hospitals because the physicians involved in its construction wanted to facilitate their seeing patients at all of the hospitals. In Coast Town, physicians who were not in the group practice became extremely valuable to the existing not-for-profit hospitals, and their influence increased as the census fell at those hospitals. At the time of our visit, the not-for-profit hospitals were acting to establish closer links with their staff physicians in ways (e.g., via an office building) that may eventually create a situation that is similar to the one at the investor-owned hospital.

It was generally difficult to see differences between investor-owned and not-for-profit hospitals in their responsiveness to physicians' needs, or in the influence of physicians in the hospitals. Rather, differences among hospitals related more to the level of competition in the community and to physicians' ability to have an economic impact on the hospital.

Important to the relationship between physicians and their hospitals was the degree of autonomy allowed to local administrators. The harmony of the triad of corporation/local administrator/physicians varied with the extent to which the three branches had common goals and with the extent to which corporate policy allowed the administrator the flexibility needed to reconcile conflicts. Physicians in two of the three investor-owned hospitals visited generally expressed satisfaction with the responsiveness of the corporation and administrators. In one hospital where corporate and local goals were to build census, establish a reputation for quality care, and carve out some specialty niches, the physicians' key role in those objectives was well understood by corporate staff who realized that good physician relationships were a priority for the local administrators.

In a second hospital, where almost all patients were admitted by a multispecialty group whose members had effectively cut themselves off from the other hospitals, there was a strong mutual dependence and unity of interest. In this most decentralized of the three investor-owned systems, both physicians and administrators commended the wide range of decisions that could be made locally without reference to corporate staff.

In the hospital belonging to the third, most centralized investor-owned system, the extreme control exercised by the corporate office together with occasional divergence of interests between physicians and corporate staff placed the hospital administrator in the extremely uncomfortable and ultimately untenable position of trying to balance conflicting corporate and physician demands with very little leeway for negotiation.

## SOME GENERAL CONCLUSIONS

Because of the importance of local circumstances in determining how other hospitals will fare after an investor-owned hospital enters the market, it is difficult to draw general conclusions about the impact of investor-owned hospitals from visits to three very different communities. Of particular importance were the circumstances of the entry of investor own-ership—whether at the behest of physicians, whether demand for hospital care was already being met, and whether physicians continued admitting to existing hospitals. Diverse sce-narios occurred because of the differences in local situations. In one community existing hospitals had to make strong efforts just to survive and eventually thrive in the highly competitive situation. In the two other com-munities, not-for-profit and investor-owned hospitals existed side-by-side and had only rel-atively minor impacts on each other until de-mand for care in the community lessened, causing the hospitals to try to secure their mar-kets in the face of increasing competition.

Regardless of whether the investor-owned hospital was newly built or an existing hospital that was bought and upgraded, competition among hospitals had become intense in all three communities. As a result some hospitals started to offer new services, upgrade existing ser-vices, and develop strengths in specialty ser-vices, and sought to increase their attractiveness to physicians and tie physicians to the hospi-tals. Whether such developments would oth-erwise have occurred in these communities is difficult to judge.

For patients, the choice of hospitals in-creased as a new or upgraded hospital was established, and many observers believed that greater competition had brought improve-ments in the quality of care available in the community. This was particularly noted in two communities. In Valleyville, an out-of-date, low-quality hospital was bought and upgraded by an investor-owned corporation. In Coast Town, the not-for-profit hospitals recruited to the community new and reputedly very good physicians and improved the quality of care in their hospitals. For physicians the advent of investor ownership often meant that the ex-isting hospitals became much more receptive to suggestions and more responsive to physi-cians' needs. In some circumstances physi-cians were able to increase their voice substantially in hospital policymaking. For payers, having an investor-owned hospital in the community appears to have brought in-creased duplication of services and price in-creases led by the investor-owned hospitals. These impacts can be traced to increased com-

petition and may not be effects of investor ownership per se.

Effects of investor ownership can be sought not only in accounts about communities before and after the coming of an investor-owned cor-poration, but also in examining the similarities and differences between the investor-owned and not-for-profit hospitals that were visited. Before discussing investor-owned and not-for-profit hospitals as groups, it should be noted that the hospitals within each group were quite diverse. In the investor-owned group, we saw a hospital containing an array of state-of-the-art, high-technology equipment, and one equipped at a much simpler level. We saw one hospital over which the home office exerted tight control, and one that functioned with rel-ative freedom from home office influence. We saw one hospital in which the relationship be-tween the physicians and administrators was one of mutual respect and cooperation. In an-other hospital the relationship was more con-flictual. The list could go on—and the group of not-for-profit hospitals represents a similarly diverse set of institutions.

The major difference observed between the not-for-profit and investor-owned hospitals was in the uncompensated care provided in the communities in which there was either no public hospital or more need for free care than the public hospital was willing to provide. The lesser amount provided by the investor-owned hos-pitals stemmed from their location and their having been established by physicians who wanted a particular type of hospital. The greater amount of uncompensated care in the not-for-profit hospitals appeared to flow in part from uncompensated care being seen as inherent in their mission. It also followed from their lo-cations, which sometimes came about because of the location of donated land. In some cases, when the hospitals were built, the area was more affluent. But regardless of reason, if a public hospital did not provide sufficient free care, people unable to pay for care were dis-proportionately cared for at the not-for-profit hospitals.

There were, however, striking similarities between the not-for-profit and investor-owned hospitals in some of the ways in which they sought to ensure payment for care. These in-cluded credit checking, triage in emergency rooms followed by referral to public providers when possible, litigation, and closing or not offering services likely to incur a burdensome uncompensated caseload.

Other similarities observed between the investor-owned and not-for-profit hospitals included some elements of the relationship between individual hospitals and the multihospital systems that own them. Almost all system hospitals were expected to meet financial goals—but these were often spelled out in greater detail by the investor-owned systems—and to submit budgets for approval to the central organization. To the extent that some investor-owned systems exercised more stringent control over the activities of the local administrators, some exacerbation was observed in local problems (e.g., in hospital-physician relationships) that were ignored by home office staff. Some not-for-profit systems appear to be moving towards oversight of more facets of hospital operations.

There was no important difference between the two sections in the strength of the voice of local boards. In some not-for-profit hospitals, the board appeared to be dominated by decisions made in the central office or by local administrators; in others they played a more major role. In the investor-owned hospitals, the local advisory boards included heavy physician representation, and the board's influence seemed to depend more on the history of the hospital than on corporate policy. Similarly, physician influence in the hospitals was dictated not so much by hospital or system policies as by organization of the physicians and their historical role in the hospital and the competitive environment.

Indeed, the competitive environment and the changes that are taking place in payment systems, location of services, and types of health care facilities are pushing all types of hospitals in new directions. If there is any one lesson for the future to be learned from the site visits, it is that the speed and sensitivity with which hospitals respond to change will be an important determinant of their future. Whether investor-owned or not-for-profit hospitals will perform better in the new environment was not clear. We saw not-for-profit hospitals respond rapidly and effectively to intensified competition. They made major changes in their internal organization, reached out to become attractive to physicians, and made investments that generated horizontal and vertical diversification.

However, one not-for-profit hospital that we visited had not responded sufficiently rapidly to the challenge of new freestanding providers and will likely increasingly lose segments of its markets to the new providers. The case studies also showed an example of investor-owned hospitals responding clumsily to competition of the new providers and alienating physicians, as well as examples of investor-owned hospitals engaging in joint ventures with physicians and new enterprises that may successfully protect their revenues.

*For-Profit Enterprise in Health Care.* 1986.
National Academy Press, Washington, D.C.

# Investor-Owned Multihospital Systems:
# A Synthesis of Research Findings

Dan Ermann and Jon Gabel

*The new medical-industrial complex is the most important recent development in American health care and it is in urgent need of study.*

—Arnold S. Relman[1]

## INTRODUCTION

In 1983, one of every seven U.S. hospitals with nearly 10 percent of the nation's hospital beds belonged to an investor-owned multihospital system, defined as three or more hospitals that are owned, managed, or leased by a single investor-owned organization.[2] Such systems account for approximately 42 percent of U.S. hospitals that belong to a multihospital system. Religious systems account for 35 percent with the remainder being voluntary and city hospital systems.[3]

In September 1984, there were 53 investor-owned systems operating. These range from the very small, such as Western Hospital Corporation, Inc., an Alameda, California chain that owns two hospitals and manages one other, to the very large. The four largest—Hospital Corporation of America (HCA), Humana, Inc., National Medical Enterprises, Inc. (NME), and American Medical International, Inc. (AMI)—own or manage 53 percent of investor-owned system hospitals and 75 percent of the hospital beds.[4] Some experts predict that within a few years, the four to five largest investor-owned systems will control over half the nation's hospitals.[5]

This paper examines investor-owned systems' growth patterns, the reasons why they have grown rapidly, and their effects on cost, access, and quality of care. To address these issues, this paper synthesizes more than 300 articles from the trade and academic literature through 1984, including 22 empirical studies. The next section describes the growth of investor-owned systems. The third section reviews the reasons for their growth. The fourth section presents findings about the effects of systems on the cost, quality, and access to care. We conclude with a summary of empirical findings and outline an agenda for future research.

## GROWTH OF INVESTOR-OWNED SYSTEMS

At the time of the enactment of Medicare and Medicaid legislation in 1965, there were no investor-owned hospital systems in the United States.[6] By 1970, 29 investor-owned systems had been formed which owned 207 hospitals.[7] The Federation of American Hospitals (FAH), the trade association representing independent and system investor-owned hospitals, reports that 1,234 hospitals were owned or managed by 53 investor-owned systems in 1984.[8]

Based on data from the FAH, Table 1 displays the annual growth of investor-owned system hospitals between 1977 and 1984. These figures include psychiatric and specialty hospitals, as well as community hospitals which grew at a considerably slower rate than psychiatric hospitals. For-profit independent hospitals managed by investor-owned systems are excluded. From 1977 to 1983 the number of hospitals owned by investor-owned systems increased at an average annual rate of 10.3 percent while the number of hospitals managed by such systems grew at a rate of 7.9 percent. By comparison, between 1977 and

---

Mr. Ermann is affiliated with the National Center for Health Services Research, U.S. Department of Health and Human Services, Rockville, Maryland. Mr. Gabel is with the Health Insurance Association of America.

**TABLE 1** Growth of Investor-Owned System Hospitals, 1977–1984

| Category | Number of Hospitals | | | | Annual Growth Rate, % | | |
|---|---|---|---|---|---|---|---|
| | 1977 | 1980 | 1983 | 1984 | 1977–1983 | 1983–1984 | 1977–1984 |
| Investor-owned system hospitals | 414 | 531 | 755 | 878 | 10.3 | 14.2 | 11.3 |
| Nonprofit hospitals managed by investor-owned systems | 179 | 264 | 282 | 325 | 7.9 | 13.2 | 8.9 |
| Total hospitals | 598 | 795 | 1,037 | 1,205 | 9.6 | 14.0 | 10.5 |

NOTE: These figures include community, psychiatric, and specialty hospitals.

SOURCES: Federation of American Hospitals, *Statistical Profile of the Investor-Owned Hospital Industry, 1982; Federation of American Hospitals, 1983 Annual Report;* Federation of American Hospitals, *1985 Directory: Investor-Owned Hospitals and Hospital Management Companies.*

1983, the number of independent investor-owned hospitals declined at an average annual rate of 7.0 percent per year,[9] while the total number of nonfederal hospitals declined at an average rate of 0.5 percent per year.[10]

Table 2 shows that the average annual growth in hospital beds for investor-owned system hospitals between 1977 and 1983 was 7.6 percent. Newly built or acquired hospitals tended to be smaller hospitals, whereas managed hospitals tended to be larger, often public hospitals. In contrast, independent investor-owned hospital beds declined at an annual rate of 7.3 percent,[11] while the total number of nonfederal hospital beds declined by 0.5 percent per annum during these years.[12]

These tables indicate that in 1984, the first year under Medicare's diagnosis-related group (DRG) payment for hospitals, the rate of growth for investor-owned systems was substantially greater than during the preceding years. In 1984 the number of investor-owned system hospitals increased by 14.0 percent, and the number of hospital beds increased by 12.5 percent. American Hospital Association (AHA) data for 1984 are not available presently. Therefore, it is not possible to compare investor-owned growth with other segments of the hospital industry.

Investor-owned systems have grown largely through the acquisition of financially troubled hospitals. Urban hospitals which have closed

**TABLE 2** Growth of Investor-Owned Hospital Industry by Beds, 1977–1984 (in thousands)

| Category | Number of Hospital Beds | | | | Average Annual Growth Rate, % | | |
|---|---|---|---|---|---|---|---|
| | 1977 | 1980 | 1983 | 1984 | 1977–1983 | 1983–1984 | 1977–1984 |
| Investor-owned system hospital beds | 58.2 | 74.0 | 90.3 | 100.1 | 7.6 | 11.5 | 10.0 |
| Not-for-profit hospital beds managed by investor-owned | 19.9 | 27.4 | 33.0 | 35.5 | 8.8 | 15.1 | 11.2 |
| Total beds | 78.1 | 101.4 | 123.3 | 135.6 | 7.9 | 12.5 | 10.3 |

NOTE: These figures include community, psychiatric, and specialty hospitals.

SOURCES: Federation of American Hospitals, *Statistical Profile of the Investor-Owned Hospital Industry, 1982; Federation of American Hospitals, 1983 Annual Report;* Federation of American Hospitals, *1985 Directory: Investor-Owned Hospital Management Companies.*

due to financial difficulties tend to be small nonprofit, inner city, voluntary hospitals serving many minority, uninsured, and Medicaid patients.[13] These, for the most part, are not the hospitals that investor-owned systems wish to acquire. Investor-owned systems generally seek to acquire poorly managed hospitals in communities with young, growing, well-insured populations. From 1980 to 1982, 43 percent of the growth in hospital beds of the six largest investor-owned systems resulted from the acquisition of other investor-owned hospitals. Newly constructed hospitals accounted for a third of the growth, with the remaining 24 percent emanating from the acquisition of government and nonprofit voluntary hospitals.[14] Investor-owned systems have located in high-income and high-population-growth, suburban Sunbelt areas with favorable regulatory environments and generous charge-paying Blue Cross plans.[15] Fifty-eight percent of the investor-owned system hospitals are found in five Sunbelt States—California, Texas, Florida, Tennessee, and Georgia. There are, in total, only nine investor-owned system hospitals in the four mandatory rate-setting states—Maryland, Massachusetts, New Jersey, and New York.[16]

Some analysts have interpreted the growth of investor-owned systems as evidence of a movement toward a vertically integrated health delivery system. Unfortunately, there are little historical data documenting the growth of nonhospital portfolios of investor-owned systems. The single exception is the annual survey of freestanding nursing homes and psychiatric hospitals by *Modern Healthcare*, a trade journal. *Modern Healthcare* figures indicate that from 1978 to 1983 investor-owned systems acquired and built nursing homes and psychiatric hospitals at a far more rapid rate than they acquired community hospitals. The growth rate for nursing homes exceeded 50 percent per year, while investor-owned systems increased their ownership of psychiatric hospitals at greater than 30 percent per year.[17]

In addition to psychiatric hospitals and nursing homes, investor-owned systems have entered such diverse health fields as alcohol and chemical dependency treatment, home health services, health maintenance organizations, preferred provider organizations, as well as ownership and management of hospitals in more than 20 foreign nations. In 1983, 6 percent of hospitals managed or owned by investor-owned systems were located in foreign nations.[18] These systems also operate nonhealth-related lines of business such as office building management, insurance company management, and real estate development.

Most investor-owned systems appear committed to diversification. For example, HCA, which doesn't consider itself highly diversified, runs more psychiatric facilities than any other U.S. hospital system. HCA owns 18 percent of Beverly Enterprises, the nation's largest nursing home chain, and operates the world's largest health maintenance organization (HMO) in Brazil.[19] In 1983, NME, a system known for its diversified business, operated 27 physician office buildings, 25 psychiatric hospitals, 249 long-term-care facilities, 13 home health care agencies, and a biomedical engineering and repair business. Forty-nine percent of NME's total revenues in 1983 were not from acute care hospital operations.[20]

Even more remarkable than the growth of investor-owned systems has been their financial performance. For 8 of the 10 years between 1971 and 1980, system net profits as a percentage of common equity increased. In 1980, net profits as a percentage of equity were 20.4 percent for the investor-owned systems, in contrast to an average of 14.9 percent for all industries.[21] Between 1975 and 1981, net revenues of the four major hospital companies grew at a compound rate of 36 percent, while earnings grew at a 46 percent growth rate.[22] America experienced its deepest recession since the Great Depression in 1982; yet, earnings grew 20 percent in the investor-owned hospital industry. In 1983, the industry's average return on equity of 18 percent far exceeded the average of 12.6 percent for other industries.[23] The average compensation for the chief executive officers in 1983 of the four leading systems was $854,000. When stock options are included, this figure triples.[24]

## WHY INVESTOR-OWNED MULTIHOSPITAL SYSTEMS GROW

There are three potential advantages of investor-owned systems over independent hospitals: (1) economic benefits, including improved access to capital, increased efficiency and economies of scale, and ability to diversify; (2) personnel and management benefits, such as improved recruiting and ability to develop and retain high-caliber staff; and (3) planning, program, and organizational benefits, which may lead to greater power to control environmental factors.[25]

Much of the literature does not distinguish between investor-owned and nonprofit systems in terms of their technical advantages. This section attempts to focus on advantages of investor-owned systems, although the literature does not always allow for this. Therefore, some of the discussion pertains to both nonprofit and investor-owned systems.

## Economic Benefits

Increasing financial pressure upon hospitals to remain solvent has stimulated the growth of multihospital systems.[26] In addition, some experts believe that an oversupply and maldistribution of hospital services has fostered the growth of systems.[27]

### Access to Capital

Hospitals require large sums of capital to replace, renovate, modernize, and expand. Estimates of their capital needs for the decade of the 1980s range from $49 billion to $231 billion.[28] With the reduction in private philanthropy and government grants-in-aid, such as the Hill-Burton Program, hospitals have turned increasingly to commercial borrowing to finance capital projects. In 1968, hospitals received, on average, 45 percent of their capital from philanthropy and government grants, and only 40 percent from debt. By 1981, hospitals received 8 percent from philanthropy and grants and 76 percent from debt capital.[29]

This growing dependency on debt capital between 1968 and 1981 is attributable to a number of factors. First, by covering patients that were previously uninsured, Medicare and Medicaid reduced the hospital's dependency on philanthropy. Second, Medicare and Medicaid provided stability in funding. This made the hospital a sounder credit risk and made hospital debt financing more accessible and

attractive. Third, increased use of cost-based reimbursement by Medicare, Medicaid, and Blue Cross reduced the hospital's incentive to control expenditures or finance capital in the least expensive manner, thereby further fostering debt financing. Fourth, the cost of debt capital was additionally reduced when revenue bonds were accorded tax-exempt status. This form of financing was used primarily by nonprofit hospitals.[30] Investor-owned hospitals can now only hold up to $40 million in tax-exempt bonds per corporation, virtually precluding their use by major investor-owned systems.[31]

The financial community provides more favorable borrowing conditions to systems than to independent hospitals. Systems (both tax-exempt and investor-owned) are perceived as sounder risks because of their larger revenue, asset and equity bases, and debt capacity.[32] This is further enhanced by increased recognition of systems in the capital markets. Systems are better able to time debt acquisitions to swings in the market, and to spread the risk of borrowing. They also face fewer constraints on growth than independent hospitals. Systems can more easily absorb new operating units without violating the terms of existing lending agreements, and without precipitously increasing the amount of financial leverage.[33] Investor-owned systems may, in addition, raise capital through the issuance of stock. In the bond market, $1 of hospital equity may raise $2, while in the equity (stock) market, $1 may raise $15 or $20. Investor-owned hospitals can choose between debt and equity approaches, depending on such factors as interest rates and stock prices,[34] giving them the option of using the leverage of their stocks to help finance capital projects.[35]

The types of debt financing generally used by investor-owned systems include taxable bonds, bank lines of credit, commercial paper, and convertible subordinated debentures drawing on both the domestic and foreign capital markets. The larger pool of outside investors available to investor-owned systems has been instrumental in their growth. Shareholders' equity in the largest four investor-owned multihospital systems nearly quadrupled from 1977 to 1981, from an aggregate of $461 million to $1.832 billion.[36]

There are a limited number of data-based

**TABLE 3**  Hospital Borrowers by Rating, 1978–1981 (percentage)

| Rating Category | Single Facility Provider | Multi-hospital Systems |
|---|---|---|
| Nonrated | 8 | 3 |
| BBB | 16 | 8 |
| A− | 23 | 5 |
| A | 35 | 23 |
| A+ | 16 | 38 |
| AA | 2 | 23 |

SOURCE: Kidder, Peabody and Company, Inc., Health Finance Group, Hospital Data Base.

studies that compare borrowing conditions for system and independent hospitals. These studies are based on national data sets, and in general, strongly support the proposition that systems operate at an advantage in the financial markets. Kidder, Peabody and Company reported that 61 percent of systems (investor-owned and nonprofit) debt borrowings between 1978 and 1981 were rated A+ or AA, whereas only 18 percent of independent hospitals were so rated (Table 3).[37] Bonds with full corporate pledges are rated considerably better than system issues with limited corporate pledges.[38] Hernandez and Howie reported that investor-owned systems have gained access to public capital markets that were previously denied to investor-owned independent hospitals.[39]

Investor-owned hospitals (both system and independent) have been able to raise more capital funds through operating margin, or profits, than nonprofit hospitals. This is due, in large part, to the return-on-equity payment that Medicare and some other third-party payers have provided to for-profit hospitals only. This feature is being reviewed in light of the Medicare prospective payment system with indications that return-on-equity payments may be eliminated in the near future.[40]

While there appears to be a consensus that systems enjoy an advantage in access to capital, no research has documented the extent that improved access translates into reduced cost of capital. Investor-owned systems' higher bond ratings may merely offset the tax advan-

tages of the nonprofit hospitals. Investor-owned systems may have lower unit costs of capital, but purchase greater quantities of capital, and thereby drive up operating costs.

### Increased Efficiency and Economies of Scale

The literature suggests that multihospital systems should realize certain economies of scale. These potential economies have been attributed to several factors. First, by securing discounts and obtaining superior price information, systems may realize savings through mass purchasing. Second, systems are believed to use capital facilities and equipment more efficiently than independent hospitals through sharing and specialization, in addition to central warehousing of inventories.[41] Third, systems are thought to use highly skilled personnel more efficiently than independent hospitals.[42] For example, five system hospitals may share the service of one reimbursement specialist at lower unit costs than if that specialist were employed by a single independent hospital.[43] Lastly, investor-owned systems are better able to control construction costs. Systems, because of their high use of construction firms, for example, may establish (less costly) ongoing relationships with design and construction concerns. They also use the same or modified designs and blueprints numerous times—further contributing to lower costs.[44] There is no research to support or refute these hypothesized efficiencies.

Empirical studies have focused on hospital-wide measures of efficiency, rather than economies associated with the aforementioned factors. Measures of efficiency include length of stay, admissions per bed, occupancy rate, and full-time equivalent staff per patient day. Between 1971 and 1984, nine studies examined efficiency in investor-owned system hospitals.[45] The only consensus appears to be that investor-owned system hospitals use fewer staff per bed than other system and nonsystem hospitals.

### System Diversification

In an earlier section it was noted that systems were committed to the ownership and management of nonhospital enterprises. Diversification is believed to provide systems with a number of technical advantages over independent hospitals.[46] First, profits from health and nonhealth lines of business provide a source of internal funds for financing new capital acquisitions. Second, diversification into nonhospital markets provides additional financial stability. Separate lines of business offer the potential of offsetting cash flow supply during the trough of the hospital's business cycle.[47] A recent General Accounting Office study suggests another possible advantage of diversification. System hospitals may purchase goods or services from affiliated entities or subsidiaries at inflated charges, thus increasing their revenues from cost-based insurers.[48] This may be contrary to reimbursement rules.

Fourth, diversification is a strategy for growth. Systems are increasingly entering nonhospital lines of business such as HMOs, preferred provider organizations, home health services, nursing homes, emergency centers, and surgery centers in order to increase revenues, control patient movement into and out of hospitals, and facilitate local market growth.[49] Management contracting, where one organization assumes responsibility for the management of another hospital or department, illustrates this point. In the short run, management contracting offers increased revenues and the opportunity to spread fixed costs over more units.[50] In the long run, management contracting may pave the way for future acquisition of the managed hospital.[51] In 1983, investor-owned systems managed 56 percent of the nation's contract-managed hospitals.[52]

The literature is rich with case studies and anecdotes describing diversification efforts of individual systems.[53] Absent from the literature are empirical studies of "economies of scope," i.e., whether the production of other products lowers unit costs for hospital services.

## Personnel Management

There is general agreement in the hospital trade and management literature that investor-owned and nonprofit systems attract and retain better trained management personnel than independent hospitals.[54] Attracting well-trained professionals is a serious problem for many rural hospitals. Empirical studies indicate that systems are better able to attract quality medical and administrative personnel in rural areas than independent hospitals.[55] There is insufficient empirical evidence to support or refute whether systems have an advantage in personnel management in urban areas.[56] Systems may, however, bring about a number of problems: medical staff objections to perceived corporate indifference, impersonal corporate attitudes toward employees and/or patients, replacement of older loyal employees with corporate personnel, and loss of local autonomy.[57]

## Planning and Organizational Benefits

Hospitals in underserved areas may benefit from improved linkages with other hospitals.[58] It is argued that investor-owned systems have the needed resources to maintain hospitals where none would have survived otherwise. It is also argued that systems have the resources to offer ambulatory services and primary care health centers, and, therefore, increase patient access to care.[59] They may, in addition, be able to experiment with new programs and services by trying them out selectively at different hospitals within the system before diffusing them to other hospitals as appropriate. In turn, system economic power can be converted into political power and used to influence local planning and state regulatory agencies, thereby enhancing the ability of systems to meet their goals.[60] Critics contend that there is a loss of local autonomy under systems, and that systems may not use their economic and political power in the public interest.[61] There are no data-based studies to support or refute these contentions.

## Why Investor-Owned Systems Grow: A Summary

The literature suggests a number of advantages that investor-owned systems might have over independent hospitals including economies of scale, improved access to capital, greater diversification, personnel, management advantages, and organizational benefits. Although there are few empirical studies to support or refute these claims, it appears that the principal advantage of systems is their favored status in the capital markets. Empirical studies indicate few differences in efficiency between system and independent hospitals, except that investor-owned systems appear to operate with fewer personnel per bed.

## INVESTOR-OWNED SYSTEMS AND THE COST OF HOSPITAL CARE

Twelve empirical studies (see Table 4) have examined the effect of investor-owned systems on the cost of care.[74] Each of these studies compares investor-owned system hospitals with a comparison group, usually nonprofit independent hospitals. Because our objective was to examine the impact of investor-owned systems, we have excluded studies that pool independent and system investor-owned hospitals, and studies that pool nonprofit systems with investor-owned systems. These exclusions reduced the number of relevant studies by almost one-half.

Seven of these 12 studies indicate that investor-owned systems increase the cost of care. Three studies show that costs are lower for system hospitals, and two studies indicate no difference. System hospitals appear to be more costly whether costs are measured as hospital expenses, revenues or charges, or on a per admission or per diem basis.

If investor-owned systems have some technical advantages over independent hospitals, particularly superior access to capital, how do they raise the cost of care? First, investor-owned systems provide more ancillary services.[75] Second, markups, the difference between hospital charges or revenues and hospital expenses, are greater, particularly for ancillary services.[76] Third, investor-owned system hospitals tend to be newer, thereby increasing capital costs.[77]

The conclusion that systems raise the cost of hospital care should be tempered by three considerations. First, existing research is based on the experience of the late 1960s through the early 1980s, a period when cost-reimbursement was the predominant reimbursement mechanism. Study findings may indicate how systems and independent hospitals responded to the existing incentive structure.

With the federal government's adoption of diagnosis-related group (DRG) payment for Medicare patients, hospitals are entering an era of prospective payment. Systems and independent nonprofit hospitals may behave in a radically different manner when they are rewarded rather than penalized for providing services at lower costs.

Second, when researchers fail to control for self-selection bias, study findings may be suspect. Systems expand by purchasing financially troubled independent hospitals. Cost differences between recently acquired system hospitals and independent hospitals may result from acquisition strategies of systems rather than from differences in the efficiency of system or independent hospitals. However, costs in system hospitals appear to rise quite rapidly in the first few years following a merger, a phenomenon inconsistent with the theory that higher system costs can be attributed to their former owners.

Third, previous studies have focused on costs for an individual hospital. With the exception of a few case studies,[78] the more global question, "What happens to area per capita medical care costs, as well as hospital costs, when an investor-owned system enters the market?" has not been addressed. One school of thought holds that investor-owned systems compete by limiting their clientele to the most profitable cases, so-called "cream-skimming." Nonprofit hospitals, which previously used the revenue from these cases to subsidize less profitable cases as well as certain community services (care of the indigent, teaching, and research) may respond to the entry of the investor-owned hospital by increasing prices for unprofitable cases, such as the severely ill, and reducing community services.[79] An opposing scenario views investor-owned hospitals as forcing efficiencies on other area hospitals. Community services that are no longer financed through patient cross-subsidies must be identified and supported directly, and this increases public awareness and improves social welfare.[80]

A case study by Lewin and Associates, Inc. suggests a third scenario—a market characterized by intense nonprice competition.[81] Investor-owned system hospitals were constructed in two market areas previously served by one nonprofit hospital each. Both nonprofit

**TABLE 4**  Empirical Studies on the Effect of Investor-Owned Systems on the Cost of Care

| Author | Sample | Findings |
|---|---|---|
| Ferber (1971)[62] | American Hospital Association (AHA) for 1969; 5,094 nonprofit hospitals and 157 for-profit chain hospitals | For bed sizes less than 200 beds, for-profit chain hospitals had greater per diem expenses<br>For hospitals greater than 200 beds, chain hospitals' per diem expenses were 29 percent less<br>Per admission expenses average 11 percent less for for-profit hospitals |
| Hill and Stewart (1971)[63] | California nonprofit independent hospitals, for-profit independents, and for-profit chains | For-profit chain hospitals had higher expenses than independent for-profits or independent nonprofit hospitals |
| Ruchlin et al. (1973)[64] | 56 for-profit chain hospitals matched with 11 independent local government hospitals and 45 independent voluntaries in 1970 | Revenue per adjusted day was 4 percent greater for the for-profit chain hospitals<br>Expense per adjusted day was equivalent |
| Lewin and Associates (1976)[65] | 345 hospitals from five Blue Cross Plan areas: 114 for-profit system hospitals, 90 independent for-profit hospitals, 141 independent nonprofit hospitals | Revenues per day were 29 percent greater for for-profit system hospitals than nonprofit hospitals<br>Charges for same diagnoses were 18 percent greater for the for-profit system hospitals<br>System expenses per day were 20 percent greater per adjusted day<br>System hospitals were newer; capital costs were nearly double those of nonprofits<br>Markups for for-profits were 20 percent more for lab and x-ray services than nonprofits<br>For most measures, acquired system hospitals were less expensive than system "indigenous hospitals" |
| Coyne (1978)[66] | Eight nonprofit systems; six investor-owned systems | Ownership had no effect on expenses per day<br>Centrally organized systems were found to be more efficient; geographically concentrated systems had higher occupancy rates |
| Bays (1979)[67] | 46 California hospitals including 12 for-profit chain hospitals | For-profit chain status reduced expense per case by 12 percent relative to nonprofit hospitals<br>For-profit chains' case mix was similar to nonprofits' case mix; this was not so for independent proprietaries |

**TABLE 4** *Continued*

| Author | Sample | Findings |
|---|---|---|
| Vraciu (1981)[68] | Florida, Texas, and Utah hospitals | Investor-owned hospitals in Florida had 7 to 21 percent lower revenue per patient day than other hospitals<br>Charges per admission were 4 to 9 percent lower in Utah, 5 percent lower in Texas |
| Lewin and Associates (1981)[69] | 53 matched pairs of for-profits and nonprofits; Florida, Texas, and California hospitals; 1978 data | Investor-owned hospitals' charges per inpatient day were 8 percent higher for routine charges and 36 percent higher for ancillary services per admission charges, 4 percent higher for routine and 26 percent higher for ancillary services<br>Expenses per day were 13 percent higher and 8 percent higher admission for investor-owned hospitals<br>Gross revenues per day were 18 percent higher per day and 12 percent higher per admission for investor-owned hospitals |
| Pattison and Katz (1982)[70] | 58 investor-owned chain and 217 nonchain investor-owned California hospitals in 1980; data are from the California Health Facilities Commission | For nearly all measures of cost, investor-owned chains were the most expensive group<br>Revenues per admission and per day were 10 percent higher for for-profit chains than voluntaries<br>Expenses per admission and day were 2 percent and 6 percent higher for for-profit chains than voluntaries<br>Ancillary revenues per admission and day were 29 percent and 38 percent greater for the chains than for the voluntaries<br>Daily service revenues were 7 percent and 11 percent higher per admission and day for the chain than for the voluntaries |
| Sloan and Vraciu (1983)[71] | Florida, nonteaching, short-term hospitals under 400 beds in 1980 | Net operating funds (operating revenues − taxes) per admission were identical<br>Net operating expenses per admission were 4.5 percent less for investor-owned chain hospitals<br>Investor-owned chain hospitals had 3.4 percent greater net operating funds per day and 2.7 percent less per per-diem net operating expenses |
| Coyne (1982)[72] | 91 system hospitals and 49 independent hospitals; data are from 1975 AHA survey | Religious, other nonprofit, and investor-owned system hospitals significantly raised the expense per case and per day, with investor-owned hospitals being the most expensive |
| Becker and Sloan (1984)[73] | 2,231 U.S. community hospitals in 1979 | Investor-owned chain hospitals that have joined chains in the last 4 years have per diem expenses 10 percent higher than independent nonprofits and per admission expenses 12 percent higher |

**TABLE 4** *Continued*

| Author | Sample | Findings |
|--------|--------|----------|
| Becker and Sloan (continued) | | Government chains formed in the past 6 years had per admission expenses 11 percent higher than independent voluntaries |
| | | Multihospital voluntaries were 2 percent more expensive than independent voluntaries |

NOTE: "Charges" refers to what the hospital bills the patient. "Revenues" refers to what the hospital collects from the patient, third-party payer, or other sources (e.g., government, philanthropy). "Expenses" refers to the total operating costs including payroll and nonpayroll costs.

hospitals responded to the entry of a system hospital by expanding services, renovating the hospital plant, constructing adjacent physician offices, and improving patient and physician relationships. The result was increased unit charges and expenses, markups, admissions, and hospital per capita expenditures.

## QUALITY AND ACCESS

Seven empirical studies have evaluated the effects of investor-owned systems on access, service availability, or quality.[82] Table 5 displays study findings.

Each of these studies potentially suffers from self-selection bias. Systems do not randomly choose where to locate, but self-select into favorable market areas. For example, investor-owned systems tend to locate in fast-growing, less regulated Sunbelt states and areas with lower Medicaid and indigent patient loads. Systems also purchase or build hospitals with certain services and size, generally avoiding large tertiary care hospitals with heavy research and teaching commitments. Studies which compare an experimental group (system hospitals) with a matched control group (independent hospitals) may find no differences simply because the matching process eliminated comparison of hospitals providing different services or teaching programs.

### Measures of Access

Seven studies compared investor-owned system hospitals with independent nonprofit hospitals. Measures of access included percentage of revenues from Medicare and Medicaid, availability of specific services, diagnostic case mix, and volume of charity care. Investor-owned system and independent hospitals treated equal percentages of Medicare as well as Medicaid patients.[86] Less research is reported on indigent or charity care. Two studies report no difference and one study reports that investor-owned systems provide less uncompensated care (charity care plus bad debt) than nonprofit control hospitals.[87]

There is anecdotal evidence of investor-owned hospitals providing less charity care than neighboring nonprofit facilities.[88] One difficulty in supporting these anecdotes is that ongoing data systems record who is admitted to a hospital, but not who is turned away or deterred from a hospital.

Service mix was studied using a number of proxy measures, including service profitability and scope of services offered. No significant differences were found between system and independent hospitals.[89]

The last measure of access to care tested was hospital case mix. Based on limited analysis of diagnostic case mix, no significant differences were found between investor-owned system and other hospitals.[90]

### Measures of Quality

Four studies compared the quality of care in investor-owned system hospitals with matched independent nonprofit hospitals. Researchers have focused on structural and pro-

**TABLE 5**   Empirical Studies on the Effect of Multihospital Systems on Quality of Care and Access

| Author | Sample | Findings |
|---|---|---|
| Ruchlin et al. (1973)[64] | 56 matched pairs of investor-owned chain hospitals and nonprofit voluntary or state and local government hospitals; data collected from interviews with hospital administrators | *Access* <br> For-profit chain facilities received about 35 percent of revenues from public third parties; nonprofits received about 60 percent from these payers <br> *Quality* <br> Gross death rates averaged 2.48 for nonprofits and 1.99 for for-profit chain hospitals; authors note these differences could be due to different patient case mixes <br> No discernible differences in educational residency and training programs, although for-profits had a lower percentage of residency positions filled (5 percent versus 13 percent) |
| Sloan et al. (1985)[83] | All hospitals responding to American Hospital Association (AHA) annual surveys of hospitals for 1978 through 1982 | *Access* <br> Investor-owned system hospitals provided 15 percent less uncompensated care (defined as bad debt or charity care) than other hospitals, other factors held constant |
| Lewin and Associates (1976)[65] | 345 system and independent for-profit and nonprofit hospitals located in five Blue Cross areas: Los Angeles, California; Florida; Texas; Kentucky; and Richmond, Virginia | *Access* <br> No significant differences in proportion of Medicare and Medicaid patient load <br> Scope and complexity of services offered (using a general service index) are similar between investor-owned system and nonprofits; independent investor-owned have somewhat lower index of services; investor-owned favor profitable services such as electrocardiograms, abortions, and full-time pharmacists <br> Little difference in case mix <br> *Quality* <br> Investor-owned system and nonprofits had comparable JCAH accreditation rates; independent investor-owned had considerably lower rates <br> No differences in malpractice convictions (limited data) <br> System investor-owned had a higher ratio of RNs to LPNs, but lower ratio of full-time to part-time nurses <br> System hospitals had few approved intern and residency programs and almost no medical school affiliations; system hospitals were more likely to offer nurse training programs than nonprofits |
| Biggs et al. (1980)[84] | 32 matched pairs of contract-managed and traditionally managed hospitals; hospitals under contract were nonprofit | *Access* <br> Both hospital groups had similar distributions of payers <br> Contract-managed hospitals tend to "offer a |

**TABLE 5** *Continued*

| Authors | Sample | Findings |
|---|---|---|
| Biggs et al. (continued) | and managed by 9 multifacility for-profit corporations in 18 states; hospitals paired on basis of number of beds, geographic location, population base, average per capita income, type of ownership and control, and presence of medical education programs | somewhat broader range of services" although not a statistically significant difference *Quality* No statistically significant difference between matched samples in terms of: percent board-certified staff physicians, extent to which hospitals provide full-time coverage in their emergency rooms, hospital accreditations, and hospital participation in a quality assurance program |
| Pattison and Katz (1983)[85] | Peer group of California urban/ suburban hospitals (excluding teaching, tertiary care, rural specialty, and HMO hospitals); 1980 data for 280 hospitals: 114 voluntary, 35 public, 79 independent investor-owned, and 53 chain-owned proprietaries | *Access* No significant difference between hospitals on treatment of Medicare patients Location, size, and type of hospital may be more significant than ownership in admission of Medicaid patients; however, public hospitals had highest Medicaid revenues, investor-owned chain lowest No significant difference in amount of charity care delivered *Quality* Investor-owned chain and nonchain performed no research activities; the rest of the peer group spent 0.4 percent on research Investor-owned chain spent 0.07 percent and nonchain spent 0.2 percent on teaching compared with 0.14 percent for the whole peer group and 0.81 percent for all California hospitals |
| Bays (1979)[67] | 46 short-term general California hospitals (18 for-profit and 28 nonprofit) for 1971 and 1972 | *Access* No significant differences in case mix between nonprofits and multihospital system for-profits |
| Sloan and Vraciu (1983)[71] | 112 Florida nonfederal, short-term, nonteaching hospitals under 400 beds (52 nonprofit, 45 investor-owned system, and 15 investor-owned independent) | *Access* No significant difference in Medicare and Medicaid utilization Except for cardiac care, no differences in services offered Investor-owned are more likely to offer emergency room services, but less likely to provide outpatient psychiatric care, although more offer clinical psychological services Nonprofits offer more "unprofitable" services as well as "profitable" services No differences in charity care or bad debt adjustments to revenue |

NOTE: "Charges" refers to what the hospital bills the patient. "Revenues" refers to what the hospital collects from the patient, third-party payer, or other sources (e.g., government, philanthropy). "Expenses" refers to the total operating costs, including payroll and nonpayroll costs.

cess measures of quality including staff physician qualifications, hospital accreditation, and educational and residency programs. No significant differences were found in staff qualifications (such as board certification), hospital accreditation, or gross mortality rates.[91] System hospitals performed no research activities and participated in fewer teaching and residency programs. However, the matched independent hospitals' commitment to research or teaching programs was also very limited.[92]

### CONCLUSION

This paper has addressed three questions: (1) What has been the extent and nature of the growth of investor-owned multihospital systems? (2) Why do they grow? (3) What are the effects of these systems on cost, quality, and access to care?

Investor-owned systems are growing in terms of hospitals and hospital beds at the rate of 10 percent a year. This growth has been achieved largely through the acquisition of independent investor-owned hospitals. Investor-owned systems are constructing and acquiring freestanding nursing homes and psychiatric hospitals at a rate more than three times that for community hospitals. The financial performance of investor-owned systems has been impressive. A dollar invested in an investor-owned system has returned nearly 40 percent more in earnings than the average for other industries in recent years.

The literature offers a number of reasons why investor-owned systems grow. The primary reasons are: economic benefits; personnel and management advantages; and planning, program, and organizational benefits. Claimed economic benefits were foremost in the literature and included increased efficiency, economies of scale, improved access to capital, and the ability to diversify. Empirical studies showed little difference between independent and investor-owned system hospitals in efficiency, with the exception that the investor-owned system hospitals use fewer personnel per bed. The major advantage of systems is their ability to finance capital purchases. Empirical evidence indicates strong preference for systems by the capital markets. Diversification

into nonhospital markets provides additional financial stability to systems; separate lines of business offer the potential of offsetting cash flow demands during the trough of the hospital's business cycle.

Twelve studies have investigated the effect of investor-owned systems on hospital costs. These studies do not address the question, "How does the entrance of a system hospital into a market area affect area per capita hospital and total medical care costs?" With this caveat in mind, the evidence indicates that the growth of systems results in higher hospital costs.

If systems hold certain technical advantages over independent hospitals, why don't they provide care more cheaply? First, investor-owned systems use their superior access into the capital markets to increase services, and provide more ancillary services per case. Second, markups, the difference between hospital unit expenses and charges, are greater for system hospitals. Third, available evidence indicates that system hospitals are newer, thereby increasing capital costs.

Some have alleged that investor-owned systems reduce access to care to the disadvantaged. Research on this issue is limited to seven studies. Findings may be artifacts of the matching process, where hospitals are matched on dependent variables, and consequently, no differences are found between experimental and control hospitals. Until recently, investor-owned systems have shunned large tertiary care teaching facilities and chosen to locate in growing middle-class markets. With this caveat in mind, study findings indicate little difference between system and control hospitals in access to care. System hospitals treat equivalent numbers of Medicare and Medicaid inpatients. No significant differences were found in the diagnostic case mix of system versus matched independent nonprofit hospitals. Two studies report that investor-owned system hospitals treat similar percentages of uncompensated care (defined as bad debt plus charity care) as do control hospitals, although neither system nor control hospital treated many.[93] One study found that investor-owned system hospitals provided a lower percentage of uncompensated care.[94]

Four studies examined differences in quality

of care between system and independent hospitals. Quality measures included physicians, qualifications, hospital accreditation, educational and residency programs, nursing staff composition, malpractice convictions, and gross mortality rates. In most cases, no differences were found between system and independent hospitals.

Our review of the literature identified a number of issues that empirical studies failed to answer. In concluding this paper with an agenda for future research, we urge researchers to focus on three methodological issues. First, future research should document market area spillover effects. To what extent are profits and savings from investor-owned systems the result of shifting undesirable services and patients to other hospitals? Conversely, do systems force efficiencies on other area hospitals? Small area case studies may be one method for addressing these issues. Second, researchers should more fully consider patterns of entry and exit in investor-owned system performance. System hospitals should be compared to contrasting, as well as similar, independent hospitals. Third, researchers should contrast the behavior of investor-owned system and independent hospitals under different incentive and reimbursement structures. The adoption by Medicare of DRG prospective hospital payment provides the opportunity to study a natural experiment.

## ACKNOWLEDGMENTS

The views expressed in this paper are those of the authors. No official endorsement by the National Center for Health Services Research or the Department of Health and Human Services is intended or should be inferred.

The authors wish to thank Fred Hellinger, Ira Raskin, Larry Rose, and Jackie Wallen for their helpful comments. We additionally thank Christine Mitchell and Eloise Van Riper for their secretarial support.

Many of the observations of this paper were presented in "Multihospital Systems: Issues and Empirical Findings," which appeared in the Spring 1984 edition of Health Affairs.

## NOTES

[1] Relman, A. (1980) The new medical-industrial complex, *The New England Journal of Medicine* 303(17):963.

[2] Cobbs, D. American Hospital Association, Center for Multi-Institutional Arrangements, personal communication; American Hospital Association, *Hospital Statistics: 1984 Edition*. Chicago, Illinois.

[3] Cobbs, D. American Hospital Association, Center for Multi-Institutional Arrangements, personal communication.

[4] Federation of American Hospitals (1985) *1985 Directory: Investor-Owned Hospitals and Hospital Management Companies.*

[5] Koenig, P. (1979) Skimming the profits off health care, *Nation* 229:619.

[6] Health Central System (1983) *Environmental Assessment: Health Care, New Dynamics, New Markets.*

[7] Steinwald, B., and D. Neuhauser (1970) The role of the proprietary hospital, *Law and Contemporary Problems* 35:817-838.

[8] Federation of American Hospitals, *1985 Directory: Investor-Owned Hospitals and Hospital Management Companies*. This figure includes 31 investor-owned independent hospitals managed by investor-owned systems.

[9] Ibid.

[10] American Hospital Association, *Hospital Statistics, 1984 Edition*. Data from the AHA's Center for Multi-Institutional Arrangements indicate that from 1979 to 1983, nonprofit system hospitals grew at an annual rate of 1.2 percent while investor-owned systems grew at 3.6 percent.

[11] Op. cit. American Hospital Association, *1984 Annual Report*. Data from the AHA's Center for Multi-Institutional Arrangements indicate that between 1979 and 1983 the number of hospital beds controlled by non-profit multihospital systems grew at an average annual rate of 0.4 percent while investor-owned systems grew at 5.2 percent.

[12] American Hospital Association, *Hospital Statistics, 1984 Edition.*

[13] Sager, A. (1983) Why urban voluntary hospitals close, *Health Services Research* 18(3):451-474.

[14] Federation of American Hospitals (1982) *Statistical Profile of the Investor-Owned Hospital Industry*, Washington, D.C.

[15] Mullner, R., and J. Hadley (1984) Interstate variations in the growth of chain-owned proprietary hospitals, 1973-1982, *Inquiry* 21:144-151; Mullner, R., C. Byrne, and J. Kubal (1981) Multihospital systems in the United States: A geographic overview, *Social Science and Medicine* 15:353-359.

[16] Federation of American Hospitals, *1985 Directory: Investor-Owned Hospitals and Investor-Owned Management Companies.*

[17] Franz, J. (1984) Hospitals turn from acquiring to

building new psychiatric units, *Modern Healthcare,* May 15; Ermann, D., and J. Gabel (1984) Multihospital systems: Issues and empirical findings, *Health Affairs* 3(1):54.

[18] Federation of American Hospitals, *1985 Directory: Investor-Owned Hospitals and Hospital Management Companies.*

[19] Hospital Corporation of America (1983) Form 10-K, Securities and Exchange Commission.

[20] National Medical Enterprises (1983) Form 10-K, Securities and Exchange Commission.

[21] Buchanan, R. (1982) The financial status of the new medical-industrial complex, *Inquiry* 19:308-316.

[22] Cohodes, D., and B. Kinkead (1984) *Hospital Capital Formation in the 1980s,* Johns Hopkins University Press, Baltimore, Md., p. 81.

[23] Greenberg, J. (1984) Investment Trends in the Hospital Industry, unpublished manuscript, Health Care Financing Administration, Washington, D.C.

[24] *Washington Health Cost Letter* (1984) special supplement, Washington Business Information, Inc., August 3. Estimates of the value of stock option benefits are based on Form 10-K for the four major investor-owned hospital management companies.

[25] Lewin and Associates, Inc. (1981) *Studies in the Comparative Performance of Investor-Owned and Not-for-Profit Hospitals,* Vol. I, Industry Analysis, Washington, D.C., pp. 8-9.

[26] Brown, M. (1979) An overview in *Multihospital Arrangements: Public Policy Implications,* S. Mason, ed., American Hospital Association; Barrett, D. (1980) *Multihospital Systems: The Process of Development,* Cambridge, Mass.: Oelgeschlager, Gunn and Hain, Publishers, Inc., p. 27; Zuckerman, H. (1979) *Multi-Institutional Hospital Systems,* L. Weeks, ed., Chicago, Ill.: Hospital Research and Educational Trust; and Hernandez, M., and C. G. Howie, Capital financing by multihospital systems in *Multihospital Arrangements: Public Policy Implications,* S. Mason, ed.

[27] Brown, M. (1979) Systems development trends, issues and implications, *Health Care Management Review* 4:23-32.

[28] Anderson, J., and P. Ginsberg (1984) Medicare payment and hospital capital, *Health Affairs,* 3(3):35-48.

[29] Mistarz, J. (1984) Capital: A crisis? *Hospitals,* January 1, pp. 70-74.

[30] Wilson, G., C. Sheps, and T. Oliver (1982) Effects of hospital revenue bonds on hospital planning and operations, *New England Journal of Medicine* 307(23):1426-1430; Kinkead, B. (1984) Medicare payment and hospital capital: The evolution of policy, *Health Affairs* 3(3):49-74.

[31] Telephone conversation with Jim Smith, Hospital Corporation of America, February 8, 1985.

[32] Toomey, R. E., and R. C. Toomey (1976) Political realities of capital formation and capital allocation, *Hos-*

*pital and Health Services Administration* 20:11-23; Regulation discouraging chains, shared services (1978) *Modern Healthcare* 8:9-10; Sloan, F., and R. Vraciu (1983) Investor-owned and not-for-profit hospitals: Addressing some issues, *Health Affairs* 2:25-37; Neuman, B. (1974) A financial analysis of a hospital merger: Samaritan Health Services, *Medical Care* 12:983-998; DiPaolo, V. (1980) Multi-units increasing municipal bond issues, *Modern Healthcare* 10:56-58; and Op. cit., Hernandez and Howie, Capital financing, pp. 37-47.

[33] Yanish, D. Leigh (1981) Pooled assets expand debt capacity, *Modern Healthcare* 11:86-88.

[34] Access to capital: Equity markets (1984) *Washington Report on Medicine and Health/Perspectives,* McGraw-Hill, Feb. 20.

[35] *Capital Development in the Hospital Industry* (1984) Health Policy Alternatives, Inc., Washington, D.C., June.

[36] Cohodes, D., and B. Kinkead (1984) Capital formation in hospital management companies in *Hospital Capital Formation in the 1980s,* Johns Hopkins University Press, Baltimore, Md., pp. 73-87.

[37] Op. cit., Hernandez and Howie, Capital financing, pp. 37-47.

[38] Ibid.

[39] Ibid.

[40] Op. cit., Health Policy Alternatives, Inc., 1984.

[41] Dorenfest, S. (1981) Hospital chains become important providers, *Modern Healthcare* 2:77-85; and Bennet and Ahrendt (1981) Achieving economies of scale through shared ancillary services, *Topics in Health Care Financing* 7(3):25-34.

[42] Steward, D. (1973) The history and status of proprietary hospitals, *Blue Cross Reports* 9:2-9; Hill, D., and D. Stewart (1973) Proprietary hospitals versus nonprofit hospitals: A matched sample analysis in California, *Blue Cross Reports* 9:10-16; and Steinwald, B., and D. Neuhauser (1970) The role of the proprietary hospital, *Law and Contemporary Problems in Health Care,* Vol. 37, Autumn. Duke University School of Law.

[43] Bennett, J., and K. Ahrendt (1981) Achieving economies of scale through shared ancillary and support services, *Topics in Health Care Financing: Managing in the Era of Limits* 7(3):25-34.

[44] Stevenson, G. (1978) Laws of motion in the for-profit health industry: A theory and three examples, *International Journal of Health Services* 8(2):234-256.

[45] Analyst gives AMI hospitals mixed reviews (1984) *Hospitals,* Jan. 1, p. 22; HCA hospitals' costs, efficiency studied (1984) *Hospitals,* Feb. 1, p. 21; Humana hospitals found more efficient, less costly than average U.S. hospital (1984) *Hospitals,* March 16, p. 22; NME hospitals expensive but efficient (1984) *Hospitals,* May 16, p. 21; Knowles, E. (1981) Distinguishing characteristics of institutions by ownership type within multihospital systems, graduate thesis, University of Min-

nesota, Jan. 30; Ferber, B. (1971) Analysis of chain-operated for-profit hospitals, *Health Services Research* 6:49-60; Treat, T. (1976) The performance of merging hospitals, *Medical Care* 14:199-209; Lewin, L., R. Derzon, and R. Margulies (1981) Investor-owned and non-profits differ in economic performance, *Hospitals* 55:52-58; Coyne, J. (1982) Hospital performance in multihospital systems: A comparative study of system and independent hospitals, *Health Services Research* 17:303-329.

[46]DiPaolo, V. (1980) American Medical International acquires Hyatt Medical for about $60 million, *Modern Healthcare* 10:12-13; DiPaolo, V. (1980) Highly diversified National Medical Enterprises show it's able to do it all, *Modern Healthcare* 10:58-60; Keenam, C. (1981) Not-for-profit systems position themselves to meet upcoming challenges, *Hospitals* 5:77-80; Op. cit., Longest, A conceptual framework; Toomey, R. E., and R. C. Toomey (1980) Political realities of capital formation and capital allocation in *Multi-Hospital Systems: Strategies for Organization and Management*, M. Brown and B. McCool, eds. Germantown, Md: Aspen Systems Corp.; Op. cit., Lewin and Associates, pp. 35-58.

[47]Woodford, B. G. (1981) Is diversification for you? *Topics in Health Care Financing* 7:32-43; Op. cit., Zuckerman, Multi-institutional hospital systems, pp. 4-8; Coyne, J. (1981) Networking and the future of not-for-profit hospitals, *Hospitals* 55:83-85; Mason, S. (1981) Hospital diversification as a competitive strategy, paper prepared for the Bureau of Health Planning, Health Resources Administration, U.S. Department of Health and Human Services, Washington, D.C., November, p. 4.

[48]General Accounting Office (1982) *Hospital Links with Related Firms Can Conceal Unreasonable Costs and Increase Administrative Burden, Thus Inflating Health Program Expenditures*, report to the Secretary of Health and Human Services, January 19.

[49]Seermon, L., M. Sachs, and K. Thompson (1984) Alternative services offer hospital systems local market control, *Modern Healthcare*, May 1, pp. 78-87; Tatge, M. (1984) Hospital systems race to form PPO networks to regain market share, *Modern Healthcare*, May 1, pp. 21, 24; Gabel, J., and D. Ermann (1985) Preferred provider organizations: Performance, problems and promise, *Health Affairs*, Spring; Punch, L. (1985) Humana money, name may cure financial woes of Doctors Officenters, *Modern Healthcare*, January 4, pp. 49, 52, 54, 56; Ermann, D., and J. Gabel (1985) The changing face of American health care: Multihospital systems, emergency centers and surgery centers, *Medical Care*, May.

[50]Wheeler, J., H. Zuckerman, and J. Aderholdt (1982) How management contracts can affect hospital finance, *Inquiry* 19:160-166; Op. cit., Lewin and Associates, *Studies in Comparative Performance*; DiPaolo, V. (1979) Chains grow with unbundled services, *Modern Health-*

*care* 9:54-56; Johnson, D., and V. DiPaolo (1981) Nonprofits compete effectively with investor-owned contract firms, *Modern Healthcare* 11:84-86; and Pattison, R., and H. Katz (1982) Investor-owned hospital management companies: Growth strategies and their implications, draft contract final report for Bureau of Health Facilities, Health Resources Administration, U.S. Department of Health and Human Services, June, p. 69.

[51]Op. cit., Pattison and Katz, Investor-owned hospital management companies.

[52]Cobbs, D. American Hospital Association, personal communication.

[53]Op. cit., DiPaolo, pp. 12-13; Op. cit., Johnson and DiPaolo; LaViolette, S. (1980) HCA builds white knight image in its quest for new markets, *Modern Healthcare* 11:56-60; Op. cit., Lewin and Associates, p. 58.

[54]Op. cit., Lewin and Associates, *Studies in Comparative Performance*, Vol. 99; Op. cit., Brown, An overview, Vol. 27.

[55]Treat, T. (1976) The performance of merging hospitals, *Medical Care* 14:199-209; Edwards, S. (1972) *Demonstration and Evaluation of Integrated Health Care Facilities*, Phoenix: Samaritan Health Services, Chicago: Health Services Research Center of the Hospital Research and Educational Trust, and Chicago: Northwestern University, June; Cooney, J., and T. Alexander (1975) *Multihospital Systems: An Evaluation, Parts I-IV*, Chicago: Health Services Research Center of the Hospital Research and Educational Trust and Northwestern University; Zuckerman, H. (1981) Multi-institutional systems: Adaptive strategy for growth, survival, *Hospital Progress* 62:43-45; Paulsen, R. (1981) The role of the multi-hospital system, *Texas Hospitals* 36:30-33; Money, W., D. Gilfillan, and R. Duncan (1976) A comparative study of the multi-unit health care organizations, in *Organizational Research in Hospitals*, S. Shortell and M. Brown, eds. Inquiry Book BCA, Invitational Forum, Northwestern University, May 12, 1975; Op. cit., Zuckerman, Multi-institutional hospital systems; Op. cit., Zuckerman, Presbyterian Hospital Center, Multi-institutional hospital systems, p. 150.

[56]Op. cit., Paulsen, Role of the multi-hospital system, p. 31.

[57]Op. cit., Money et al., p. 99.

[58]Op. cit., Milburn, pp. 95-96, and Shared management expertise spells survival for the small (1976) *Hospitals* 50:52-54; Friedrich, P., and A. Ross (1977) Consortium serves rural hospitals' educational needs, *Hospitals* 51:95-96; and Op. cit., Zuckerman, Presbyterian, p. 150.

[59]Studnicki, J. (1979) Multihospital systems: A research perspective, *Inquiry* 16:315-322; Mason, S. (1980) U.S. multihospital systems, *Public Health Reviews* 9:259.

[60]Op. cit., Mason, U.S. multihospital systems, p. 260; Foley, G. (1980) The ultimate shared service for hospitals: Political synergy, *Hospital and Health Services Administration* 25(Special II):35-42; Zuckerman

(1981) Multi-institutional systems: Adaptive strategy for growth, survival, *Hospital Progress* 62:43-45; and Simler, S. (1980) Multi-units threaten regulators' clout, *Modern Healthcare* 10:92.

[61]Starkweather, D. (1980) The pros and cons for multi-hospital systems, Technical Assistance Memo 57, San Francisco: Western Center for Health Planning, November 4, p. 4.

[62]Ferber, B. (1971) Analysis of chain-operated for-profit hospitals, *Health Services Research* 6:49-60.

[63]Hill, D., and D. Stewart (1971) Proprietary hospitals versus non-profit hospitals, *Blue Cross Hospitals*, March.

[64]Ruchlin, H., D. Pointer, and L. Cannedy (1973) Comparison of for-profit investor-owned chains and non-profit hospitals, *Inquiry* 10(December).

[65]Lewin and Associates, Inc. (1976) *A Study of Investor-Owned Hospitals*, Health Services Foundation, Chicago, Illinois.

[66]Coyne, J. (1978) A comparative study of the performance and characteristics of multihospital systems, Ph.D. dissertation, University of California, Berkeley.

[67]Bays, C. (1979) Cost comparisons of for-profit and non-profit hospitals. *Social Science and Medicine*, 13c:219-225.

[68]Vraciu, R. (1981) HCA hospitals cost less in three states, *Modern Healthcare* 11:70-72.

[69]Lewin and Associates, Inc. (1981) *Studies in the Comparative Performance of Investor-Owned and Not-For-Profit Hospitals*, Vol. 1, Industry Analysis, Washington, D.C., pp. 8-9.

[70]Pattison, R., and H. Katz (1982) Investor-owned hospital management companies: Growth strategies and their implications, draft contract final report for the Bureau of Health Facilities, Health Resources Administration, U.S. Department of Health and Human Services, June, p. 69.

[71]Sloan, F., and R. Vraciu (1983) Investor-owned and not-for-profit hospitals: Addressing some issues, *Health Affairs* 2:25-37.

[72]Coyne, J. (1982) Hospital performance in multi-hospital systems: A comparative study of systems and independent hospitals, *Health Services Research* 17:302-329.

[73]Becker, E., and F. Sloan (1984) Hospital ownership and performance, *Economic Inquiry*, 22, July.

[74]Hill, D., and D. Stewart (1971) Proprietary hospitals versus non-profit hospitals, *Blue Cross Hospitals*, March; Ferber, B., H. Ruchlin, D. Pointer, and L. Cannedy (1973) Comparison of for-profit investor-owned chain and non-profit hospitals, *Inquiry*, Dec.; Lewin and Associates (1976) *A Study of Investor-Owned Hospitals*, Chicago: Health Services Foundation; Bayes, C. (1979) Cost comparisons of for-profit and non-profit hospitals, *Social Science and Medicine* 13c:219-225; Vraciu, R. (1981) HCA hospitals cost less in three states, *Modern Healthcare*, pp. 70-72; Op. cit., Lewin and

Associates, 1981; Pattison, R., and H. Katz (1983) Investor-owned and not-for-profit hospitals: A comparison based on California data, *New England Journal of Medicine*, 309:347-353; Sloan, F., and R. Vraciu (1983) Investor-owned and not-for-profit hospitals: Addressing some issues, *Health Affairs* 2:25-37; Coyne, J. (1978) A comparative study of the performance and characteristics of multihospital systems, Ph.D. dissertation, University of California, Berkeley; Becker, E., and F. Sloan (1984) Hospital ownership and performance, *Economic Inquiry*, June; Op. cit., J. Coyne, Hospital performance in multi-hospital systems.

[75]Op. cit., Lewin and Associates, 1976; Op. cit., Lewin and Associates, 1981.

[76]Op. cit., Ruchlin et al.; Op cit., Lewin and Associates, *A Study of Investor-Owned Hospitals*; Op cit., Lewin and Associates, *Studies in Comparative Performance*; Op cit., Pattison and Katz, Comparison based on California data; Sloan and Vraciu, Investor-owned and not-for-profit hospitals.

[77]Op. cit., Sloan and Vraciu (1983); Kinkead, B. *Historical Trends in Hospital Capital Investment*, Urban Systems Research and Engineering, Inc., DHHS Contract No.: HHS-100-820038; F. Sloan, unpublished data, Vanderbilt University, personal communication.

[78]*New York Times* (January 25, 1985), Companies buy hospitals, treatment of poor is debated; Lewin and Associates (1981) *Studies in the Comparative Performance of Investor-Owned and Not-For-Profit Hospitals: Two Case Studies of Competition Between Hospitals*, Vol. 3; Kennedy, L. (1984) For-profit health care: Who shall pay? Unpublished paper presented at American Public Health Association meeting, Anaheim, California.

[79]White, W. (1979) Regulation and competition in a non-profit industry, *Inquiry* 16(2):50-61.

[80]Bayes, C. (1977) Case mix differences between for-profit and non-profit hospitals, *Inquiry* 14(1):19-23.

[81]Op. cit., Lewin and Associates (1981).

[82]Op. cit., Ruchlin et al., Comparison; Op. cit., Lewin and Associates, *Study of Investor-Owned Hospitals*; Op. cit., Bays, Cost comparisons; Op. cit., Sloan and Vraciu, Investor-owned and not-for-profit hospitals; Op. cit., Biggs, Kralewski, and Brown, Contract-managed and traditionally managed non-profit hospitals; Op. cit., Pattison and Katz, Comparison based on California data; Sloan, F., J. Blumstein, and J. Perrin (1986) *Uncompensated Hospital Care: Rights and Responsibilities*, Johns Hopkins University Press.

[83]Sloan, F., J. Blumstein, and J. Perrin (1985) *Uncompensated Hospital Care: Rights and Responsibilities*. Johns Hopkins University Press.

[84]Biggs, E. L., J. E. Kralewski, and G. D. Brown (1980) Contract-managed and traditionally managed non-profit hospitals, *Medical Care* 18:585-596.

[85]Pattison, R., and H. Katz (1983) Investor-owned and not-for-profit hospitals: A comparison based on Cal-

ifornia data, *New England Journal of Medicine* 309:347-353.

[86]Op. cit., Lewin and Associates, *Study of Investor-Owned Hospitals*; Op. cit., Sloan and Vraciu, Investor-owned and not-for-profit hospitals; Op. cit., Biggs, Kralewski, and Brown, Contract-managed and traditionally managed non-profit hospitals.

[87]Op. cit., Pattison and Katz, Comparison based on California data; Op. cit., Sloan and Vraciu, Investor-owned and not-for-profit hospitals; Op. cit., Sloan, Blumstein, and Perrin, *Uncompensated Hospital Care: Rights and Responsibilities.*

[88]Simler, S. (1984) Austin questions HCAs loyalty to town, *Modern Healthcare* 4:38; Dallek, G. (1983) For-profit hospitals and the poor, National Health Law Programs, Washington, D.C., October.

[89]Op. cit., Lewin and Associates, *Study of Investor-Owned Hospitals*; Op. cit., Sloan and Vraciu, Investor-owned and not-for-profit hospitals; Op. cit., Biggs, Kra-lewski, and Brown, Contract-managed and traditionally managed non-profit hospitals.

[90]Op. cit., Lewin and Associates, *Study of Investor-Owned Hospitals*; Op. cit., Bays, Cost comparisons.

[91]Op. cit., Lewin and Associates, *Study of Investor-Owned Hospitals*; Op. cit., Biggs, Kralewski, and Brown, Contract-managed and traditionally managed non-profit hospitals; Op. cit., Cooney and Alexander, Multihospital systems.

[92]Op. cit., Ruchlin, Pointer, and Cannedy, Comparison; Op. cit., Lewin and Associates, *Study of Investor-Owned Hospitals*; Op. cit., Pattison and Katz, Comparison based on California data.

[93]Op. cit., Pattison and Katz, Comparison based on California data; Op. cit., Sloan and Vraciu, Investor-owned and not-for-profit hospitals.

[94]Op. cit., Sloan, Blumstein, and Perrin, *Uncompensated Hospital Care: Rights and Responsibilities.*

*For-Profit Enterprise in Health Care.* 1986.
National Academy Press, Washington, D.C.

# The Changing Structure of the Nursing Home Industry and the Impact of Ownership on Quality, Cost, and Access

Catherine Hawes and Charles D. Phillips

## INTRODUCTION

Many observers view the increasing "corporatization" of American health care as the most significant development since the passage of Medicare and Medicaid. While there is general consensus about the trend toward corporatization, there is little agreement about the impact of this development on the cost, quality, and accessibility of American health care. Recently, the for-profit segment in the modern hospital sector has become prominent with the rapid growth of proprietary corporate chains. The nursing home sector has, however, been dominated by proprietary providers for decades, and publicly held corporations owning and operating nursing homes have been prevalent since the late 1960s.

Until fairly recently, nursing homes have not attracted substantial attention from researchers, except for studies on costs. Relatively few studies have focused on quality, and even fewer have investigated accessibility. Virtually none have focused on nursing home "chains," that is, corporations owning and operating nursing homes in a number of states. There are, however, a few empirical studies that address the impact of the type of ownership on nursing homes. They provide suggestive information about the incentive structure of these ownership forms and about what policymakers can expect if current trends continue.

This paper will explore what is known about the impact of ownership and the corporatization of health care in the nursing home industry. It will discuss the history of nursing homes, identify the current structure of the industry and the public policies that have contributed to this structure, and indicate potential results if current ownership trends persist. Finally, it will attempt to apply what is known about developments in nursing homes to the hospital sector.

Nursing home care is the third largest segment of the health care industry. It will continue to grow in prominence with increasing longevity, shifts in morbidity, and changing demographic, social, and economic patterns in the family. Given present demographic trends, (in particular, the dramatic growth of the 85 years of age and older segment of the population), the United States will need to increase its nursing home bed supply by an estimated 57 percent between 1980 and the year 1995 to keep pace with the current level of utilization (Harrington and Grant, 1985; Doty et al., 1985; Lane, 1984). Some experts predicted the need for an additional 1 million to 1.5 million beds by the year 2000, based on current utilization, prior rates of increase in utilization, and estimated rates of dependency among the elderly (Rice, 1984; Scanlon and Feder, 1984; U.S. DHHS, 1981b; Weissert, 1985). By 2040, 4.3 million elderly are expected to be institutionalized (Doty et al., 1985).

This apparent need for additional long-term care beds presents policymakers with an important opportunity to affect the future shape of the long-term care system. The debate about whether proprietary interests should be permitted to *remain* in the nursing home business, however, "is essentially moot" (Vladeck, 1980). For-profit interests own more than 75 percent of the nursing homes nationwide and are rapidly expanding in the home health and life care markets. Yet, today's public policy decisions on reimbursement, health planning,

Dr. Hawes is with the Research Triangle Institute, and Dr. Phillips is a member of the faculty of political science at the University of North Carolina at Chapel Hill.

licensure, and the use of low-interest bonds for new construction can affect the structure of tomorrow's industry. Thus, the possibility exists for public policies to significantly affect the structure of the health care sector.

Public policymakers have a clear stake in the emerging shape of the nursing home industry. First, government has a fundamental regulatory role as the primary purchaser of formal long-term care services. It dispenses more than half of the dollars spent for nursing home care and assists in paying for nearly 70 percent of all the patients in nursing homes.[1] As such, government has a responsibility to ensure that its funds are well spent.

Second, the regulatory system bears a significant responsibility for the quality of nursing home care because of the frailty of most consumers. Consumers needing long-term care generally suffer from a bewildering array of chronic physical, functional, or mental disabilities. In fact, studies indicate that the nursing home population is becoming even more aged and disabled, and this trend is likely to continue (GAO, 1982, 1983b; Manton, 1984). These consumers have only a limited ability to choose rationally among providers of long-term care. They have poor access to accurate information, limited ability to evaluate the information, and multiple disabilities that restrict their mobility and ability to switch easily from one provider to another. Thus, consumers have little to influence facilities' decisions and behavior.

Third, most nursing home patients lack advocates to represent their interests. An estimated 30 percent of the patients have no living immediate family members, and as many as half have no relatives nearby (Brody, 1977; U.S. Senate Special Committee on Aging, 1974). While physicians may recommend nursing home placement, they seldom choose the facility. Placement decisions for many individuals entering nursing homes are made by case workers and hospital discharge planners. These individuals may have the best interest of the patient at heart, but they labor under a set of incentives in which locating an empty bed—in any facility that will accept the patient—is a strong priority. Even when family members are present, they too labor under the burden of needing to locate an available

bed while lacking useful information on the comparative merits of different providers.

As a result, government's role in quality assurance is essential. Moreover, it is crucial. Despite considerable improvement in nursing homes since the inception of Medicare and Medicaid, substandard quality of patient care and quality of life remain serious problems nationwide. Inadequate nutrition, dehydration, overdrugging, excessive use of physical restraints, failure to provide prescribed therapies, inattention to the psychosocial needs of nursing home residents, and ineffective government regulatory activity are but a few of the problems commonly cited (Mech, 1980; Kane, 1983; Kane et al., 1979; Himmelstein et al., 1983; Zimmer, 1979; Ohio Nursing Home Commission, 1979; Virginia Joint Legislative Audit and Review Commission, 1978; Mendelson, 1974; Texas Nursing Home Task Force, 1978; AFL-CIO, 1977, 1983b; U.S. Senate Special Committee on Aging, 1974, 1975a,b; U.S. DHEW, 1975a; Ray et al., 1980; Ouslander et al., 1982; California Health Facilities Commission, 1982; California Commission on State Government Organization and Economy, 1983; Illinois Legislative Investigating Commission, 1983; Missouri State Senate, 1978; New Jersey State Nursing Home Commission, 1978).

Furthermore, nursing home costs have escalated at an even more dramatic rate than costs for hospital care. Discrimination against recipients of Medicaid and those individuals with heavy-care needs is widely acknowledged (Harrington and Grant, 1985; GAO, 1979, 1983a,b; Feder and Scanlon, 1981; Scanlon, 1980a,b; Vogel and Palmer, 1983). Given these problems in quality, cost, and accessibility of nursing home care, information about the impact of ownership is essential to rational policymaking in long-term care, particularly given the ability of public policies to restructure the industry.

## PUBLIC POLICY AND THE GROWTH OF NURSING HOMES

The nursing home industry is generally seen as an outgrowth of Medicare and Medicaid, but its roots are older and more complex. The industry is heir to both the almshouse and the hospital. Indeed, nursing home policy combines elements of health, welfare, and housing policy in a schizophrenic and nearly uncontrollable amalgam of increasing cost, substandard care, and discrimination against both those most in need of care and those least able to pay for such care. It has also produced a large new industry that grew and became profitable largely by providing services to the infirm and disabled poor.

Our current long-term care system is fundamentally a creature of government policy. Yet, nursing homes and now home health, retirement, and life care communities have rarely been directly addressed as policy issues of some consequence. As Vladeck (1980) observes,

> By and large, nursing home policy has been made not only with limited foresight, but largely by people who, at the time, were primarily concerned with doing something different. It has been an afterthought, a side effect of decisions directed at other problems.

The nursing home industry has grown as a result of a multiplicity of factors. It has thrived on the infusion of public dollars (through a variety of programs), a growth in need due to changes in demographics and shifts in morbidity patterns toward chronic diseases, and the interplay of policies aimed at other institutions (e.g., almshouses, mental institutions, and acute care hospitals). In the process of growing, the industry has also fundamentally changed. Some of the most profound changes include an increasingly medically oriented setting, a shift from smaller to larger facilities, a move away from government-owned and voluntary homes to proprietary ones. Most recently, the industry has witnessed a growing concentration of ownership in multifacility chains that are diversifying vertically as well as horizontally.

### Poor Laws and Poor Houses[2]

From colonial times to the Great Depression, public policy in the United States followed the tradition of the English poor laws, leaving care of the destitute to local governments and relying almost totally on "indoor relief" rather than direct income assistance. For the aged and infirm poor in America, this meant that the only form of public support was institutional, largely in almshouses and poor farms (Vladeck, 1980; Dunlop, 1979). There was, however, private support for the aged and infirm during this period. Approximately the same number of individuals resided in charitable private homes for the aged, sponsored largely by immigrant and religious groups, as lived in the poor homes.[3]

Taken together, the almshouses, poor farms, and charitable homes for the aged housed approximately 100,000 elderly Americans. Nearly as many aged individuals, an estimated 70,000, were inmates of mental hospitals (Vladeck, 1980; Dunlop, 1979; Markus, 1972; Waldman, 1983). Conditions in the mental institutions were undoubtedly wretched; however, it was the abominable conditions in almshouses and the destitution of 7 million aged Americans that commanded policymakers' attention during the 1920s and early 1930s. These concerns shaped the Social Security Act and helped frame the growth of what became the nursing home industry.

### Social Security and Old Age Assistance

The original entry of proprietary providers into the business of owning and operating nursing homes was an unforeseen and probably unintended consequence of the Social Security Act of 1935, which also established a federal grants-in-aid program to the states for old age assistance (OAA). OAA was a need-based (means-tested) cash grant program designed to provide income support to the elderly poor who would not yet draw sufficient benefits from the old age insurance (OAI) section of the act. Because of the scandals about almshouses and poor farms, however, the act prohibited payment of the cash grant to any "inmate of a public institution."

In effect, the framers of Social Security determined that OAA would not be used for the maintenance of almshouses. These restrictions enabled new OAA beneficiaries to turn elsewhere for care and assistance when they became incapable of caring for themselves (or being cared for) at home. Meager as most of the states' OAA payments were, they still provided the elderly with sufficient purchasing power to obtain institutional care without becoming wards of the cities or counties. The existing nonprofit institutions were accustomed to relying on payments from residents, supplemented by charitable contributions. As the Great Depression deepened, fewer residents and their families were capable of paying their share, and charitable contributions also began to dwindle. Nevertheless, voluntary organizations were slow to appreciate the opportunity that OAA provided. By the end of the 1930s, the total number of individuals these facilities served was nearly the same as before the onset of the depression (Vladeck, 1980; McClure, 1968; Thomas, 1969).

Private board and care homes for pensioners had existed for some years, but the Social Security Act's transfer of cash into the hands of the aged helped begin the transformation of this sector into a predominantly proprietary nursing home industry. The new flow of income to older people allowed private homes to provide some health services or supervision for those in need—rather than just board and care. In addition, the economic problems engendered by the depression encouraged many individuals—whose only resources were their labor and the possession of a house—to enter the business of providing "nursing" care in their homes.

While the business was tiny by comparison to today's industry, the combination of OAA payments with the growing proportion of the aged in the population spurred growth of the industry, particularly the proprietary "mom and pop" sector (U.S. Senate Committee on Labor and Public Welfare, 1960; McClure, 1968; Thomas, 1969).[4] As Table 1 indicates, the period between 1939 and 1950 was one of significant growth, a certain sign of the impact of increased purchasing power among the elderly as a result of Social Security and OAA.

### Post-World War II and the Eisenhower Era

After World War II, developments in the hospital sector affected nursing homes. Chronic disease hospitals began to upgrade their services to provide rehabilitative care. In addition, some acute care hospitals added beds to provide lower-cost care for patients needing subacute or extended recuperative care (Har-

rington and Grant, 1985). Although hospital-affiliated facilities did not capture a significant share of the market, they opened the way for the entrance of the medical profession into long-term care and for the eventual development of professional standards in what had primarily been a board and care industry (Lane, 1981, 1984; Dunlop, 1979).

This transformation of the nursing home industry was furthered by the extension of Hill-Burton grants to public and nonprofit organizations for the construction of nursing homes. Apart from minimal state licensing laws, there were no regulatory standards for what kind of care these nursing homes should provide. In administering Hill-Burton, the Public Health Service (PHS), formulated the first standards on physical plant design and construction as well as staffing patterns in nursing homes, further transforming these institutions into more medically oriented settings. They now belonged to health as well as welfare policy (Vladeck, 1980; Lane, 1984).

Two developments during the 1950s had a major impact on the growth and structure of the industry and attracted the first speculators to investment in nursing homes. The first was a vendor payment system, authorized under the 1950 amendments to the Social Security Act and expanded in 1956. This provided for federal matching funds to the states for *direct* payments to nursing homes (the "vendors") for care provided to OAA recipients. The second was increased availability of government-backed loans, through the Small Business Administration (SBA) and the Federal Housing Act (FHA), for nursing home construction and conversion (Markus, 1972).

The vendor payment system and increased government dollars available for nursing home care helped regularize payments, an attractive feature for businessmen. Perhaps most important for the long-run shape of the industry, it gave nursing home providers an identifiable political entity to be lobbied for rate increases and favorable regulations. The vendor payment program thus shaped a system in which the cost, quality, and level of services are decided in a transaction between vendors (providers) and the state, creating the politics of long-term care.

The availability of loans for nursing home

**TABLE 1**  Nursing Home Statistics by Year[a]

| Year | Number of Facilities[b] | Number of Beds[b] | Percentage Change from Prior Reported Year | Annual Compounded Rate of Change[c] | Number of Beds[d] | Persons in Nursing Home[e] | Average Facility Occupancy Rates[b] |
|---|---|---|---|---|---|---|---|
| 1939 | 1,200 | 25,000 | — | — | | | 35% |
| 1950 | 9,000[f] | 250,000[f] | 900 | — | | 296,783 | |
| 1961 | 9,900 | 510,180 | 104 | 14.7[g] | | 469,717 | 80 |
| 1963 | 12,800 | 568,560 | 11 | 5.6 | | | 90 |
| 1969 | 14,998 | 879,091 | 55 | 7.5 | | 972,514[h] | 91 |
| 1973 | 15,737 | 1,175,865 | 34 | 7.5 | | | 92 |
| 1976 | 16,426 | 1,317,909 | 12 | 3.9 | | | 93 |
| 1980 | 17,737 | 1,479,000[a] | 12 | 2.9 | 1,372,019[a] | 1,426,371 | 95 |
| 1982 | | 1,515,000 | 2.4 | 1.2 | 1,428,960[a] | | 95+ |
| 1983 | | | | | 1,450,413[a] | | 95+ |

[a]The discrepancies in the estimates are a result of several factors. For example, in many instances one nursing home that is certified to provide both skilled nursing care and intermediate care may be "double-counted." Also, some nursing homes also operate residential care beds, and these may sometimes be erroneously counted as nursing home beds. Thus, accurate estimates are difficult to achieve. The Aging Health Policy Center (AHPC) data were colllected directly from the state licensing agencies and may be the most accurate.

[b]Data from the National Center for Health Statistics (NCHS).

[c]Rate computed by Montgomery Securities (1983).

[d]Data compiled by the AHPC, University of California at San Francisco (Harrington and Grant, 1985).

[e]Data from U.S. Bureau of the Census, compiled by and reported in Scanlon and Feder (1984).

[f]Data from Dunlop (1979).

[g]Rate of increase from 1939 to 1961.

[h]Data from 1970.

construction and conversion through the SBA and FHA also had a major impact on the structure of the industry. Hill-Burton construction grants were only available for nonprofit providers, but SBA and FHA loans could be made to for-profit entities. Certainly these funds had an impact on the expansion of the proprietary sector, helping not only to increase bed supply but also to shift the facilities from converted homes with relatively few beds to the larger, more modern, single-purpose building that is the norm today. Additionally, it made builders and real estate speculators aware of a new and potentially very profitable market for investment—nursing homes. As Lane (1984) observes, "This capitalization of the profession by prudent real estate businessmen seeking a secured return on their investment helps to explain the proprietary nature of the industry."

Direct payment to vendors and construction loans attracted the first significant group of proprietary operators, many of whose names

eventually became synonymous with nursing home scandals—the Bergmans, Hollanders, Kosows, and the first rumored involvement of the Mafia in the industry (Mendelson, 1974). These public policies also resulted in significant increases in government spending and growth in the number of nursing home beds. In 1950, there were fewer than 9,000 nursing homes with approximately 250,000 beds (Dunlop, 1979). Total spending for nursing home care was just $187 million, or 1.5 percent of national health expenditures, and government paid only 10 percent of the nursing home expenditures (Gibson, 1979). By 1960, there had been a 181 percent increase in total national spending on nursing home care, and government was paying approximately 22 percent of that total.

Even with this expansion, the growth in beds was not sufficient to keep pace with the increasing numbers of elderly who needed long-term care. The U.S. General Accounting Office (GAO) estimated that by the early 1960s, the shortage of adequate nursing home beds was between 250,000 and 500,000 (Elliott, 1969; Spitz, 1976).[5] Thus, one of the major concerns in Congress with the passage of Medicare and Medicaid was the availability of funds for long-term care.

## The Development of Medicare and Medicaid

During the decade following the 1965 passage of Medicare and Medicaid, there was a dramatic expansion in the supply of nursing home beds and an even more dramatic escalation in costs. New facilities were built, and a more sophisticated set of owners emerged, including the multistate, multifacility systems or chains. These developments were largely a product of four factors: (1) the availability of funding; (2) the method of reimbursing facilities; (3) increasing demand; and (4) federal health and safety regulation.

### The Expansion of Coverage

The original framers of Medicare were well aware that the inclusion of nursing home services could destroy the fiscal viability of the system, particularly if it covered the kind of long-term custodial care most nursing homes were then providing. Despite this, substantial inflation in hospital rates during the 1950s and early 1960s made it desirable to have less costly alternatives than hospitals for patient convalescence (interview with Wilbur Cohen, personal communication, 1980; U.S. Senate Committee on Finance, 1970; Vladeck, 1980). Thus, as originally conceived, Medicare covered only hospital care, but was amended to add coverage for convalescing patients in "extended care facilities" (ECFs). With anticipated daily costs about half those of convalescent care in a hospital, ECFs were seen as a cost-efficient form of institutional care.

Although the extended care provision of Medicare was soon to haunt its framers, its impact pales beside that of another amendment to the Social Security Act, Title 19 or Medicaid. Medicaid attracted little attention from policymakers, and coverage of skilled nursing home care was included almost by default—again through vendor payments and

without much definition or a budgetary limit. This coverage (and the eventual extension to intermediate care as well) provided the financial fuel for the further growth of the nursing home industry.

With the passage of Medicare and Medicaid, sufficient funds were available to many of the elderly for much pent-up need to be translated into demand for and utilization of nursing home care. It was not, however, only the infirm aged residing in the community who came to demand nursing home care. Nursing home care also emerged as a substitute for housing (and some care or supervision) previously provided to many of the elderly in other settings, particularly mental institutions (Dunlop, 1979; Manard et al., 1975; Vladeck, 1980; Scanlon and Feder, 1984; Harrington and Grant, 1985). One observer estimated that 25 percent of the increase in nursing home utilization between 1960 and 1970 can be attributed to the deinstitutionalization or diversion of individuals from mental institutions into nursing homes (Morton Research Company, 1982).

Consumers of care and their families had a multitude of reasons for choosing nursing homes over other forms of institutional care. But it was also in the interest of the states and localities. In these other settings, most of the costs were borne by state and local governments, while transfer to a nursing home usually meant the state could collect the federal matching funds for the care of these individuals in nursing homes under the Medicaid program. As a result of these diverse factors, including reductions in hospital lengths of stay, the percentage of elderly persons in nursing homes rose 58 percent in the decade between 1950 and 1960 and 107 percent between 1960 and 1970.

A combination of factors, therefore, fueled the demand for and utilization of nursing home beds. Increased but unevenly distributed expenditures under Kerr-Mills led to significant growth, but it was the passage of Medicare and Medicaid in the mid-1970s, in conjunction with demographic trends, that led to substantially extended demand by the elderly for nursing home care. From the viewpoint of potential providers, expansion was a result not only of increased demand, but also the increased availability of public reimbursement and the attractiveness of the rates set up under these new programs, a result of the policy-makers' desire to assure substantial provider participation. While they expanded eligibility, Medicare and Medicaid could accomplish little if too few individuals and organizations were willing to provide services to program bene-ficiaries. To attract providers to the program—and increase the supply of nursing home beds—the federal government pursued two basic pol-icies, one related to reimbursement and an-other to regulation.

*Increased Reimbursement Rates.*    First, Medicare adopted a cost-based reimburse-ment policy very similar to that it employed for hospitals. Providers were basically reim-bursed for their reported costs. The formula placed no ceiling on reimbursement rates, and variations in reported costs between providers were ignored. In addition, the program pro-vided proprietary nursing homes a "profit" based on their net invested equity in the fa-cility. Finally, the American Hospital Associ-ation (AHA) lobbyed effectively for Medicare to reimburse hospitals for mortgage interest as well as depreciation of capital equipment, including the facility. This was extended to nursing home reimbursement. As a result, investors were virtually assured of covering their mortgage payments—and having a pos-itive cash flow (from depreciation) as well in the first years of the mortgage—through the Medicare program. They were also virtually assured of having their costs covered as well as receiving in effect a guaranteed profit (Shul-man and Galanter, 1976; Vladeck, 1980; Ohio Nursing Home Commission, 1979; Washing-ton Senate, 1978).

*Lenient Regulatory Posture.*    Medicare also adopted a policy of easing nursing homes' en-trance into the program. Although enacting mandatory minimum health and safety regu-lations for facilities participating in Medicare, the federal government estimated that few fa-cilities could actually meet even the minimum standards. Consequently, granted nursing homes were given participatory status in Med-icare and Medicaid if they were in "substan-tial" (rather than full) compliance with the new

federal minimum health and safety standards. The homes simply had to present to the survey and certification agency a plan for correcting their violations in order to be certified and receive payments.

This lenient regulatory posture, combined with open-ended, full-cost reimbursement, a guaranteed profit factor, and interest plus de-preciation for capital reimbursement in a pro-gram financially supported by the federal government, made investment in nursing homes very attractive. In addition, govern-ment funding and the aging of the population ensured the industry of a ready supply of cus-tomers. Thus, government policies eliminated much of the risk generally associated with most investments and nearly all new ventures—while promising substantial profits to those with the knowledge and ability to manipulate the sys-tem. As a result, in less than a decade the industry expanded its total supply of beds from approximately 460,000 (in 1965) to more than 1.1 million beds (by 1973) an increase of 139 percent in less than a decade.[6]

Expenditures grew even more rapidly. In 1950, total expenditures for nursing home care were less than $190 million, with government paying only 10 percent of that total. By 1960, government paid 22 percent of a total of $526 million. By 1965, just before the onset of Med-icare and Medicaid, expenditures totaled $1.328 billion, an increase in just 5 years of 153 per-cent. Between 1960 and 1974, expenditures on nursing home care grew approximately 1400 percent (U.S. Senate Special Committee on Aging, 1974). By 1978, the nation spent $15.8 billion on nursing homes, with government paying 53 percent of the total (Gibson, 1979). And by 1982, expenditures for nursing home care exceeded $27 billion annually with gov-ernment paying nearly 55 percent of the total (GAO, 1983b). In 1984, expenditures on nurs-ing home care exceeded $32 billion with gov-ernment paying 49 percent (Levit et al., 1985).

### The Emergence of Nursing Home Chains

At the same time that the industry was grow-ing and expenditures were skyrocketing, the pattern of ownership and control in the in-dustry was undergoing a significant change. Unlike the hospital sector, the proprietary nursing home firms industry has been prevalent and growing since the 1930s. The trend away from government and nonprofit facilities accelerated. In 1969, 64.5 percent of all nursing home beds were in proprietary facilities. By 1980, 81 percent of all the facilities and 69 percent of the beds were proprietary. During the same period, the proportion of beds in nonprofit facilities decreased from 25.8 percent to 22.7 percent, with government owning only 8 percent (U.S. National Center for Health Statistics, 1984). But the most significant development in the immediate post-Medicare period was the development of proprietary corporate nursing home chains. In 1966, only a handful of firms owning nursing homes were registered with the Securities and Exchange Commission (SEC). By 1969, that number had expanded to 58 and by 1970 had reached nearly 90 (Spitz, 1976).[7]

The post-Medicare need for capital was enormous because of the demand for new beds. New nursing home construction was needed to cope with existing bed shortages as well as to replace obsolete facilities that were often converted mansions, farmhouses, hotels, and motels. One way to secure capital for nursing home expansion was borrowing. Some owners calculated that once they had enough for a down payment on their first home (with interest and depreciation as part of the government reimbursement rate), government revenues could be expected to cover the cost of a first mortgage. The same was true for second-, third-, and even fourth-position mortgages. With few fiscal controls, the program provided virtually open-ended reimbursement for Medicare patients. Moreover, the owners could use the capital generated by these additional mortgages for whatever purposes they chose. Many used them to pyramid their nursing home holdings. With Medicaid, similar opportunities existed in the states through both reimbursement systems modeled on Medicare and through "flat-rate" systems. Under the latter methods, nursing home owners received a set fee for each Medicaid patient day—regardless of what they actually spent on patient care. Many owners used part of these funds to purchase new facilities, pyramiding their acquisitions on current holdings.

Publicly held nursing home chains had even more options for financing new growth. Going public with the sale of stock was an alternative to borrowing. In addition, a public market for a company's stock enhances its ability to attract borrowed funds, since the stock can be offered as collateral to secure loans. As it turned out, the stock market proved to be a very successful new source of capital for the nursing home industry. In 1969 alone, 40 nursing home corporations sold stock worth $340 million.

During the late 1960s, the "Fevered Fifty," corporations owning or planning to own nursing homes, emerged as the "hottest" stocks on the market. In a 1969 article in *Barron's*, J. Richard Elliott, Jr. (1969) explained the phenomenon:

Of late . . . [a] kind of frenzy seems to grip the stock market at the merest mention of those magic words: "convalescent care," "extended care," "continued care." All euphemisms for the services provided by nursing homes, they stand for the hottest investment around today. Companies never before near a hospital zone—from builders like ITT's Sheraton Corporation, National Environment, and Ramada Inns, to Sayre and Fisher . . . have been hanging on the industry's door. "Nobody, a new-issue underwriter said the other day, "can lose money in this business. There's just no way."

Even while the industry was telling state legislatures that it faced bankruptcy if Medicaid rates were not dramatically increased, some nursing home owners were promoting themselves on Wall Street as the most profitable investment around. According to stock prospectuses issued by some publicly held chains, the guaranteed government revenue and the growing number of elderly combined to produce an expected return on investment of at least 20 to 25 percent per year. These potential profits for the parent corporations were to be further augmented by the development of subsidiaries that would sell ancillary goods and services to the nursing homes—such as pharmaceuticals, food service, laundry, management, real estate development, and construction. The reported price/earnings ratios of the new nursing home chains were as much as 40 times that of blue chip stocks. For instance, in 1969 the price/earnings multiple for Bernard Bergman's Medic-Home chain was 179; for Unicare, another major nursing home chain, the multiple was 700 (Elliott, 1969).

The boom in nursing home stocks, however, was relatively brief, and the bust was spectacular. By 1971-1972, the stock prices had fallen far below their high marks of 1969. Medicenters of America, whose price per share had reached almost $60 during the late 1960s, was selling at less than $4 by the mid-1970s. And the same decline was true for all the chains. Four Seasons Nursing Centers, certainly the most publicized of the chains and the first to list its shares on a major exchange, started out as a housing construction company. Its stock ran up to nearly $100 per share in 1969. By 1970, when the SEC suspended trading, it was selling for 6¢ per share.

The bankruptcy of Four Seasons was a result of massive fraud, with the president, partners of the corporation's accounting firm, and two officers of a brokerage firm indicted for securities violations. This stock fraud was one factor in cooling off the market for nursing home stocks. Continuing scandals about poor care and patient abuse also dampened investors' enthusiasm. But perhaps the most important factor involved a serious miscalculation about the role of Medicare in paying for nursing home care.

A surprising number of the new nursing home entrepreneurs, like many of their investors and an unhappy number of Social Security recipients, initially assumed that Medicare and its unlimited, cost-plus reimbursement system would finance most of the nursing home care of the nation's elderly. In fact, given the original Medicare limitations and further restrictions on eligibility and coverage introduced during the Nixon administration, Medicare paid for relatively little of the nation's expenditures on nursing home care. Table 2 illustrates the actual funding pattern that has emerged.

The predominantly extended-care (or subacute care) market funded by Medicare, which was anticipated by the nursing home entrepreneurs, never materialized. The mainstay of the nursing home market proved to be the long-stay resident—an individual suffering from chronic rather than acute diseases and disabilities, unable to pay for her or his own care, and unable to qualify for Medicare coverage. And Medicaid was not as uniformly generous a payer as Medicare.[8]

Despite this, it was the Medicaid program

**TABLE 2** Nursing Home Expenditures by Payer (percentage)

| Payer | 1981 | 1982 | 1983 | 1984 |
|---|---|---|---|---|
| Medicare | 1.7 | 1.9 | 1.7 | 1.9 |
| Medicaid | 49.8 | 45.8 | 44.2 | 43.4 |
| Other government | 4.6 | 4.5 | 4.1 | 4.0 |
| Private insurance | 0.8 | 1.0 | 0.7 | 0.9 |
| Out-of-pocket | 43.2 | 46.0 | 48.3 | 49.4 |

SOURCE: Waldo and Gibson, 1982; Levit et al., 1985.

that removed the lid from expenditures on vendor payments to nursing homes. The initial legislation basically left the decision on how to reimburse nursing homes almost entirely to the states. Some provided generous rates under cost-based systems similar to the Medicare payment program; others provided a fixed (or "flat") rate for all facilities. Such fixed rates were independent of actual nursing homes' costs, differences in the severity of patient case mix, and quality of care. In general, however, Medicaid rates, tied to state welfare programs, were lower than Medicare rates. Yet Medicaid was an open-ended program, paying for the care of all eligible program beneficiaries, and its eligibility.

The limitations on Medicare coverage, retroactive claim denials, and payment and eligibility limitations imposed by most Medicaid programs made the nursing home industry less attractive financially. In addition, after the rapid expansion in bed supply during the initial investment euphoria, many nursing home beds were empty by the early 1970s, further contributing to some homes' financial difficulties. During this period, many nursing homes survived and prospered by either lowering expenditures (often by cutting back on food and staffing) or by engaging in real estate manipulations (see Ohio Nursing Home Commission, 1979; New York State Moreland Act Commission, 1975; and Shulman and Galanter, 1976).

The effects of this situation were varied. First, conditions in nursing homes continued to be a cause of concern for consumers and policymakers. Many attributed seriously substandard care not only to the failure of the regulatory system but also to the incentives inherent in many Medicaid reimbursement policies, particularly "flat-rate" systems (U.S. Senate Committee on Finance, 1972). Second, the trafficking in nursing home real estate—that is, the sale and resale of nursing homes—as well as inflated lease and rental charges artificially increased the cost of providing care. Nursing home chains slowed their rate of growth. From 1969 through the mid-1970s, the market share of the major multistate nursing home chains remained relatively stable. Policy changes in the 1970s, however, would significantly alter the structure of the industry.

In summary, four factors led to the creation of a nursing home sector and its expansion between 1930 and 1970: (1) increased demand resulting from shifts in mortality and morbidity, as well as the substitution of care in nursing homes for housing that had been provided to the elderly in other institutional settings, such as almshouses, poor farms, and mental hospitals); (2) increased funds available to pay for such care through government programs such as OAA and Social Security payments, Kerr-Mills, and finally Medicare and Medicaid; (3) favorable reimbursement rates and payments made directly to the vendors of nursing home services; and (4) a lenient regulatory posture toward nursing homes.

## PUBLIC POLICY CHANGES AND THE GROWTH OF NURSING HOME CHAINS: THE 1970s AND 1980s

The dominant trend in the nursing home industry during the 1970s and 1980s has been increasing concentration and corporatization of ownership. This transformation has been stimulated by changes in reimbursement and regulatory policy, health planning restrictions on bed supply, easier access for "chains" to expansion capital, and tax policies. Between 1982 and 1983, the 25-30 largest chains increased their control of total beds by another 15 percent. Although the holdings of chains remained relatively stable during the early 1970s, the late 1970s brought about a spate of merger and acquisition activities. Between 1972 and 1980, with most of the activity occurring

after 1976, the three leading chains dramatically increased their control of nursing home beds and facilities. Beverly Enterprises increased its facilities by 600 percent, ARA its holdings by approximately 250 percent, and Hillhaven by 200 percent. This growth pattern far outdistanced the growth rate in the total number of nursing home beds and facilities, which was only 18 percent during the same period. The *Modern Healthcare* annual surveys of multifacility systems show that between 1979 and 1982, the major investor-owned chains increased the proportion of all nursing home beds they controlled by 50 percent.

Some observers, including leaders of some of the major chains, predict that within the next 5 years, half of all nursing homes will be operated by proprietary chains, with the majority controlled by the 5 to 10 largest chains (LaViolette, 1983). Certainly, the growth rate of the largest chains has been spectacular (Tables 3 and 4). In 1973, the three largest chains owned only 2.2 percent of the beds. By 1980, the three largest chains controlled 6.4 percent of the beds nationwide, and by 1982, Beverly, ARA, and Hillhaven owned, leased, or managed 9.6 percent of all nursing home beds, a 2-year increase of 54 percent.

This picture of increased concentration, however, is somewhat misleading. The three largest chains have substantially increased their holdings largely through acquisition of small-to-medium chains, rather than through the purchase of individual facilities. Thus, this increased concentration does not represent a substantial increase in the control of total beds by the chains. It simply reflects the very largest chains' purchase of or merger with other large-to-medium multifacility systems. Despite the major increases in holdings by firms such as Beverly, the industry remains fairly fragmented, largely controlled by individual owners and small (5- to 20-facility) local and regional chains. Further, the rate of growth of the largest chains could be somewhat slowed as the number of medium-sized chains that can be efficiently acquired diminishes.[9]

Despite misperceptions about current levels of concentration, policymakers should focus attention on the industry's changing structure. Although the chains do not control an enormous proportion of nursing homes na-

**TABLE 3**   Nursing Home System Ownership, 1972

| Name of Chain | Number of Facilities | Number of Beds |
|---|---|---|
| National Health Enterprises | 79 | 10,551 |
| Unicare | 77 | 6,481 |
| First Healthcare Corporation[a] | 70 | 8,425 |
| Hillhaven[a] | 60 | 5,861 |
| Leisure Lodges[b] | 56 | 5,264 |
| Beverly Enterprises[b] | 47 | 5,670 |
| CENCO | 44 | 4,409 |
| American Medical International | 44 | 3,582 |
| National Living Centers[c] | 43 | 4,400 |
| Extendicare[d] | 41 | 5,045 |
| Geriatrics[c] | 41 | 4,394 |
| Americana[e] | 38 | 3,440 |
| Monterey Life Systems | 36 | 3,598 |
| Continental Care Centers | 30 | 3,286 |
| Medicenters[a] | 29 | 5,101 |
| Care Management | 28 | 1,690 |
| Anta/Four Seasons | 27 | 4,200 |
| Medic-Homes[f] | 26 | 3,105 |
| National Health Services | 23 | 2,590 |
| American Medical Affiliates | 20 | 1,979 |
| Aid, Inc. | 20 | 2,494 |
| Care Corp. | 20 | 2,494 |

[a]First Healthcare facilities were acquired by CNA and later sold to Hillhaven; Hillhaven also acquired Medicenters (1977).

[b]In 1976, Stephens Inc. became the sole owner of Leisure Lodges, and in 1977, through a complex series of exchanges, Stephens Inc. and Beverly facilities were merged.

[c]ARA owns both National Living Centers (1973) and Geriatrics (1974).

[d]Extendicare changed its name to Humana and sold its nursing homes to National Health Enterprises (1973).

[e]Americana was acquired by CENCO (1972–1973).

[f]Medic-Home was involved in violations of Securities and Exchange Commission regulations and was eventually split. Two of the main components of this chain were PMG and Liberty Nursing Homes.

tionwide, chains have achieved very significant market penetration in some areas of the country. In some regions of the country, the four largest nursing home operators already control between 60 and 100 percent of bed capacity. In Texas, for example, Beverly and ARA alone control nearly 25 percent of the beds, dominating many geographic areas of the state. The U.S. Department of Justice has been concerned about some of the merger and acquisition activity of the major chains. In January 1984, for example, it filed suit to block Beverly's plan to acquire Southern Medical Services, arguing that this acquisition would "substantially lessen" competition in four major markets in which Beverly would control between 29 and 48 percent of the total licensed nursing home bed capacity. Further, the major chains' predictions about their growth and increased concentration may well be accurate. The concerns many observers feel about such concentration is not only that it lessens competition but that it also substantially reduces the ability of the regulatory agencies to control the behavior of the highly concentrated providers.

Several factors have contributed to the concentration of nursing home ownership. First,

**TABLE 4**  Nursing Home System Ownership, 1983

| Name of Chain | Number of Facilities | Number of Beds |
|---|---|---|
| Beverly Enterprises | 810 | 90,670 |
| ARA | 260 | 30,197 |
| Hillhaven[a] | 253 | 30,978 |
| Manor Health Care[b] | 102 | 13,520 |
| Unicare[c] | 97 | 11,520 |
| Care Enterprises[d] | 79 | 8,234 |
| Angell Group | 76 | 8,129 |
| National Health Corporation[a] | 48 | 5,612 |
| Southern Medical Services | 43 | 5,016 |
| Care Corporation | 41 | 5,343 |
| ANTA/Four Seasons[b] | 40 | 5,249 |
| Health Care Retirement | 39 | 3,956 |
| Summit Care Corporation | 35 | 4,359 |
| Unifour Medical Management | 24 | 3,182 |
| Americare | 21 | 2,267 |
| Meridian Healthcare | 18 | 2,708 |
| American Medical Services | 17 | 2,748 |
| Vari-Care | 17 | 1,689 |
| National Health Care Affiliates | 14 | 2,064 |
| Convalescent Services | 14 | 1,737 |
| American Healthcare Systems | 12 | 1,416 |

[a]Hillhaven/NME acquires IDAK and 16.4 percent of National Health Corporation (during 1983-1984); Hillhaven plans to acquire at least 25 percent of National Health Corporation.

[b]Manor Health Care begins the acquisition of ANTA's subsidiary, Four Seasons Nursing Centers.

[c]Unicare merges with Extendicare, Ltd., which is then acquired by Crownx.

[d]Care Enterprises acquires North American. The holding company for Chase Manhattan Bank acquires 6.2 percent of Care Enterprises stock.

new and stricter licensing and certification standards put smaller, independent facilities out of business. Second, the increasing complexity of public reimbursement systems favors more sophisticated owners. In addition, capital reimbursement policies encouraged trafficking in nursing homes (the sale and resale of facilities) and other real estate manipulations that also favor more sophisticated operators. Third, there is a strong and increasing demand for nursing home and other forms of long-term care. Fourth, nursing home investment is profitable, making expansion an attractive alternative for investors. Fifth, attempts to contain spiraling nursing home costs, particularly in the Medicaid program, have led states to restrict the supply of beds, encouraging acquisitions rather than new construc-tion for firms that wish to expand. Sixth, acquisitions are easier for large, investor-owned firms, particularly the publicly held ones, because they have better access to financial markets. Seventh, tax policies adopted during the Reagan administration, as well as its position on anti-trust, have encouraged mergers.

### Changes in Regulatory Policy

During the early 1970s, the recurrent scandals about nursing home conditions and patient abuse that erupted periodically in newspapers and legislative committee hearings, combined with the too frequent tragedies of nursing home fires, led to some changes in regulatory and reimbursement policy, particularly in 1972 amendments to the Social Security Act. During the mid-to-late 1970s, states became more stringent about requiring nursing home compliance with federal standards, particularly the 1967 Life Safety Code (LSC), which in 1974 was extended to cover intermediate as well as skilled facilities.[10] Many states also went beyond the minimum federal standards by implementing stricter licensing requirements.

The imposition of strict building and fire safety code regulations—and the enforcement of these standards—meant the eventual demise of most of the "mom and pop" facilities that were still operating out of old converted homes, farm houses, motels, and hotels. By and large, these were relatively small facilities with fewer than 50 beds and usually fewer than 25 beds. The cost of converting such homes into the more modern, fire-resistant structures required by federal and often state laws was too high for many of these operators.

Many such homes went out of business or converted again (e.g., into boarding homes for the mentally retarded). For example, after a decade of leading the nation in nursing home fire deaths, Ohio adopted a sprinkler requirement as part of the state fire code for nursing homes. Largely as a result, 102 nursing homes went out of the business between January 1975 and March 1978. Of these homes, nearly 20 percent had fewer than 12 beds, and only 12 percent had more than 50 beds. These nursing home beds were replaced by newer and larger facilities, predominantly by homes that are part of chains (Ohio Nursing Home Commission, 1979). This was a pattern common to many states. For example, the Washington Senate Select Committee on Nursing Homes documented a 14 percent decline in the number of licensed facilities during the 1965-1975 period. However, the number of licensed nursing home *beds* increased by nearly 32 percent during this same period (Washington Senate, 1978).

This pattern of small, individually owned nursing homes closing was repeated throughout the nation. Between 1969 and 1980, the number of nursing home beds in the nation increased by more than 73 percent, but facilities with fewer than 50 beds declined by 27.7 percent. The growth was primarily in larger facilities, with 100 or more beds (Harrington and Grant, 1985). Over 6,000 nursing homes,

nearly 28 percent of the total facilities, closed between 1971 and 1976. During this same period, 4,800 new (and larger) nursing homes opened. As a result, the average size of nursing homes grew, from 54.5 to 68.9 beds (Sirrocco, 1983).

Through enforcement of building and fire safety standards, government policy contributed to the demise of the "mom and pop" nursing home. However, the nursing home chains, particularly those that sold stock on the open market, had entered the business with Medicare, and most of their facilities were newly built. So, enforcement of new building and fire safety code standards did not represent a serious problem for most of them. Indeed, enforcement of these standards helped the chains by eliminating some competitors (closing from 10 to 20 percent of the homes from state to state) and giving them an opportunity to construct new, larger facilities.

This regulatory strategy also relieved some of the pressure for regulatory reform and for enforcement of stronger health and welfare standards that might have been more troublesome to the chains. States tended to concentrate on the easily measured physical plant aspects of nursing home standards. The more subjective and difficult problem of assuring that the quality of care provided to patients was acceptable received much less attention. In short, the concentration of regulatory attention and efforts on the physical plant aspect of nursing homes focused regulatory energy largely on the "mom and pop" facilities, while the figures on nursing home closings gave the appearance that regulatory agencies were "cleaning up the mess" in long-term care. The more general problems of quality of life and care that existed in chain-owned and individually owned facilities, including the "mom and pop" operations, received relatively little regulatory attention. Thus, the nursing home chains, particularly those that were publicly held, suffered little from the new but limited regulatory stance of government.

### Changes in Reimbursement Policy

There were a variety of reimbursement systems in effect during the first 15 years of the Medicare and Medicaid programs, and few states had identical methodologies. Large chains became very skilled in manipulating each system so as to maximize their income and growth, but most independent owners lacked such sophistication. In addition, as noted, the chains concentrated their initial efforts on participation in Medicare, and they become especially skilled at manipulating Medicare's retrospective reimbursement system and state systems modeled on Medicare.

Medicare's reimbursement system, along with similar Medicaid reimbursement policies, paid nursing homes nearly all of the costs the homes reported they incurred in caring for program beneficiaries, plus a profit factor. At best, these systems gave operators few incentives to purchase efficiently. At worst, such systems encouraged fraud, abuse, and manipulation of loopholes that increased costs without necessarily improving patient care or quality of life. Since homes were guaranteed reimbursement of their costs, many saw the potential for making a profit off those costs by setting up subsidiaries that sold goods or services to the nursing homes. In this way, the parent company could make a profit from the sale to their nursing homes of goods and services that would be a reimbursable cost on the books of the nursing homes. Thus, many of the big chains diversified, forming subsidiaries that include real estate development, construction, management services, medical equipment, laundry, linen, food, and housekeeping services (information from 10K reports filed with the SEC by the corporations; Ohio Nursing Home Commission, 1979; Levinson, 1984; U.S. DHEW, 1978).

Both the inspector-general of the U.S. Department of Health, Education, and Welfare[11] (HEW) (1978) and the GAO (1979, 1983a) studied this vertical integration and concluded that such practices drove up costs significantly, without necessarily improving services. Moreover, they found that it was nearly impossible to enforce Medicare and Medicaid regulations that limited the price that owners could charge for goods and services sold to related nursing homes (non-arms-length transactions). It is particularly difficult to enforce such rules in multistate chains, where the home office is in a different state from the facilities being regulated and audited by the state Medicaid agen-

cies. Even the large insurance companies that are fiscal intermediaries for Medicare experienced significant problems in auditing chain home offices and subsidiaries to determine whether the prices charged to the nursing homes were reasonable (GAO, 1979; U.S. DHEW, 1978).

Chains that had diversified were also better prepared for the reimbursement policy changes that came with the 1972 amendments to the Social Security Act. Because of the record of seriously substandard care that was believed to result from the rather perverse incentives inherent in the "flat-rate" payment system used by many state Medicaid programs, Congress required that nursing homes participating in the Medicaid program be reimbursed by the states on a "reasonable cost-related" basis. While this did not mean that every home would receive reimbursement for *all* costs, it did require that homes report their costs to the state Medicaid agency. The Medicaid reimbursement rate would then be based on those reported costs considered "reasonable." Like Medicare's reimbursement system, this policy tended to favor the more sophisticated providers, the multistate chains and diversified firms.

The small "mom and pop" operations had grown up under state flat-rate systems and had had no need to understand refinements such as stock-swaps, debentures, sale, and leaseback arrangements, or intercompany loans. Profitmaking under a cost-related reimbursement system is a good deal more complicated. The new nursing home chains, with management skilled in the manipulation of Medicare's system, the intricacies of cost reporting, and the benefits of and organization to make purchases of ancillary goods and services from related suppliers, were perfectly positioned to take full advantage of these new Medicaid reimbursement policies.

Capital reimbursement policies under Medicare and most Medicaid programs also favored acquisition activity. First, Medicare and most of the state Medicaid programs reimbursed nursing homes for mortgage interest and depreciation.[12] This made many individual owners willing to sell and made it financially feasible for the chains to debt-finance many of their acquisitions. Second, tax policy favors sales and acquisitions. Owners experience declining tax deductions as their facilities age. In addition, capital gains (profits from the sale of buildings and equipment) are taxed at a lower rate than income from owning and operating the facility. Thus, individual owners are often willing to sell facilities. Finally, purchasers find acquisition attractive under many state plans and under Medicare reimbursement policies, since they can usually revalue the capital asset (basically the facility) following acquisition. This has meant that most reimbursement systems have treated the purchase price as the value of the facility and reimburses depreciation expenses accordingly. This, combined with full payment for the mortgage interest, makes government the primary payer for nursing home acquisitions and significantly reduces the risk for the acquirer.

Prospective payment systems, the most recent attempt to solve the continuing problem of escalating health care costs, remove many of the profitable features just discussed. Such systems do not eliminate the possibility of healthy profits, but they do require management skilled in planning and cost control. As Montgomery Securities observes, "Logic suggests that a prospective payment system should be favorable for efficient and large operators who benefit from economies of scale" (Montgomery Securities, 1983). In addition, chains that operate in several states often have the advantage of familiarity with such systems in one or more states and can efficiently adapt to its introduction in other states. Finally, while these policies may have achieved their purpose of containing (at least in part) escalating costs, any reduction of operating revenues available for direct patient care makes investment less attractive to nonprofits (Ohio Nursing Home Commission, 1979).

## Strong Demand for Long-Term Care

The strong and growing demand for long-term care services is also attracting corporate owners to the business of providing nursing home care. Several factors contribute to this: demographic trends; decreased availability of family support and a shift from private residences to nursing homes; and the substitution of nursing home care for acute care hospitals as a result of changes in Medicare policies. Each of these factors is expected to contribute significantly to a demand for nursing home expansion.

Although experts disagree about the magnitude of likely growth in the aged population, they agree that it will be significant during the next 50 years. Moreover, they agree that the growth rate will be most dramatic for age groups of 75 years and older, the segment of the population most likely to need nursing home care. Under current utilization patterns, 5 percent of the elderly reside in a nursing home on any given day, but at some time during their lives, 20 percent of the elderly will be in a nursing home (Palmore, 1976; Kastenbaum and Candy, 1973). If this utilization pattern continues, the aging of the population alone will result in significant additional demand (Manton, 1984; Weissert, 1985; Montgomery Securities, 1983).

Additional demand may also result from shifts in kinship patterns and familial relationships.[13] The number of widowed and single elderly is expected to increase within the next 15 years, and this has traditionally been a factor in increasing nursing home placements for the aged who have chronic physical and functional impairments (Weissert and Scanlon, 1983). Further, the increased involvement of women in the labor force, of elderly women with no living children, and of aged persons with fewer children may reduce the availability of children to care for elderly parents in their homes (GAO, 1983a,b; Manton, 1984). Montgomery Securities (1983), in advising potential nursing home investors, predicts that this combination may result in a net shift of 20 to 30 percent of the infirm elderly from private residences to institutional settings.

Changes in public policy may also increase the demand for nursing home care. In the past, to qualify for Medicare coverage of care in a skilled nursing facility (SNF), an individual had to have had at least a 3-day stay in an acute care hospital prior to the transfer to a nursing home. The Tax Equity and fiscal Responsibility Act of 1982 eliminated this requirement and some analysts predict that, if implemented by the U.S. Department of Health and Human Services (HHS), this could produce a 10 percent increase in demand for nursing home beds (Montgomery Securities, 1983).

A second policy change that may stimulate more use of nursing homes is Medicare's prospective payment system for hospitals, which seems to encourage hospitals to discharge Medicare patients as soon as medically feasible. As a result, elderly individuals requiring sub-acute or convalescent care are now more likely to be transferred to a nursing home when possible, rather than being left to convalesce in the hospital. Many analysts, such as Carl Sherman, a health care industry analyst with Oppenheimer and Company, believe that this shift in hospital payment policy will be a boon for the nursing home industry (Punch, 1984).

Taking all these factors into account, Montgomery Securities has developed "unit growth model" for nursing homes over the next 8 to 10 years. Changing demographics and shifts from private residences to nursing homes are expected to generate an average annual increase in demand for nursing home care of 7.6 percent. The shift of patients out of hospitals and into nursing homes would add an expected 1.4 percent annually to demand. The substitution of alternative sources of long-term care (e.g., home health and adult day care) could lead to an annual 3.1 percent reduction in demand. On the basis of these assumptions and estimates, Montgomery Securities expects an increased demand for nursing home beds of 5.9 percent annually between 1983 and 1990.

## Profitability

Investment analysts who are bullish on the market in "gray gold" expect continued growth in nursing home profit margins. Certainly, recent investment in nursing homes has paid handsomely. For instance, Beverly Enterprises experienced stock price gains around 700 percent between 1978 and 1981, and National Health Enterprises experienced an even more spectacular 900 percent increase (Blyskal, 1981). In fact, Beverly's growth in profits has far exceeded its growth in bed size. During 1981, its profits increased by 48 percent, and in 1982 by 38 percent. And Beverly was not alone. The major multistate chains responding to the survey by *Modern Healthcare* reported a 47.7 percent increase in profits between 1982 and 1983 (Punch, 1984). Even in "tight" reimbursement states such as Texas (see Table 5)

and California, returns on equity are impressive.[14] In California, 700 facilities had average annual returns on equity ranging from 58 percent to 154 percent in fiscal years 1983 and 1984 (U.S. Senate Special Committee on Aging, 1984).

## Health Planning and Limitations on Bed Supply

While the demand for long-term care services has been growing, the nursing home bed supply has not kept pace. Between 1963 and 1973, the supply of nursing home beds increased about 8 percent annually. But with the introduction of health planning and certificate-of-need (CON) legislation, that rate slowed. Between 1976 and 1980, the annual rate of growth in nursing home beds was only about 2.9 percent, and between 1981 and 1983, the growth rate was 1.75 percent per year. Nine states show slight losses in the total number of beds since 1981 (GAO, 1983b; Harrington and Grant, 1985). This decline in the growth of bed supply is primarily due to two factors: restrictive health planning requirements and high construction costs.[15]

As Table 1 shows, during the early and mid-1970s the supply of beds exceeded demand. As a result, many homes faced financial difficulties because of low occupancy rates, and the chains did not significantly expand. The imposition of health planning and CON requirements for new facility construction initially served the interests of the existing nursing home industry. As a result, these new measures were largely unopposed by this industry.

The initial goal of CON was cost containment, and state policies in the 1980s, which include strict CON requirements, explicit moratoria on nursing home bed construction, and refusal to certify new facilities for Medicaid participation, are designed to limit Medicaid expenditures. Without such limits, "the total costs of nursing home care for people eligible for Medicaid support (in a nursing home) would exceed what states are willing or able to pay" (Scanlon and Feder, 1984). However, these public policies also allow nursing home operators to increase revenues through higher charges to private patients, make discrimination against Medicaid patients possi-

**TABLE 5**   Industry Average Profits per Facility in Texas (percentage)

|                                     | 1978      | 1979   | 1980   | 1981   |
|-------------------------------------|-----------|--------|--------|--------|
| Before tax profit margins[a]        |           |        |        |        |
| All facilities                      | 5.3       | 6.5    | 7.6    | 5.8    |
| For-profits                         | 6.5       | 8.2    | 8.9    | 7.1    |
|                                     | (4.2)[b]  | (5.4)  | (5.8)  | (4.9)  |
| Not-for-profits                     | −0.6      | −3.3   | −0.2   | −1.8   |
| Return on equity                    |           |        |        |        |
| Before tax                          | 37.5      | 46.1   | 50.1   | 45.4   |
| All facilities                      | 25.0      | 28.2   | 34.1   | 28.8   |
| For-profits                         | 37.5      | 46.1   | 50.1   | 45.4   |
|                                     | (24.4)    | (30.0) | (32.6) | (31.8) |
| Not-for-profits                     | −1.6      | −6.4   | −0.4   | −3.8   |

[a] As a percent of total revenues.
[b] Figures in parentheses represent after-tax profits.

SOURCE: Moden, 1982.

ble, and encourage the concentration of ownership by creating incentives for firms to expand through acquisitions.

The average occupancy rate in nursing homes nationwide is at least 95 percent, and many facilities, particularly the better ones, have long waiting lists. This situation places the industry in a favorable position, given the limited availability of alternatives to nursing home care. First, occupancy rates are strongly and directly related to profitability. Second, tight supply allows nursing homes to select or "cream" from the queue of individuals seeking placement. By and large, facilities discriminate against "heavy-care" patients who require substantial hands-on care and against Medicaid patients in favor of the more lucrative private-pay patients (U.S. Senate Special Committee on Aging, 1984; Ohio Nursing Home Commission, 1979; Minnesota Senate and House, 1976). Engaging in these practices increases a home's likelihood of achieving substantial profits.

While these factors have made nursing home investment financially attractive, CON and similar regulations generally prevent new construction. Combined with high capital and construction costs, health planning policies thus encourage expansion through acquisition rather than new construction (Kuntz, 1981a; Punch, 1984). So, while several chains have plans to begin new construction, their rate of expansion through construction does not nearly approach their rate of growth through acquisition.

### Access to Capital

The scarcity of capital for expansion, improvement, or modernization makes it difficult for the small operator to compete with the larger chains and tends to encourage further consolidation of ownership. Single, independently owned facilities may continue to be absorbed by small chains—which may in turn be acquired by larger chains. The scale of operations, management sophistication, and ability to sell stock give the larger, multifacility chains a significant advantage in the capital market (LaViolette, 1982; Birney, 1981; Valiante, 1984).

Since significant expansion of the industry is predicted and will be needed by an aging population, the large, proprietary firms are in the best position to take advantage of these new opportunities and to expand their holdings. Without a significant change in public policies (such as restricting use of low-interest industrial revenue bonds), the predominant pattern is likely to be future expansion and increased acquisition by the leading chains.

## Tax Policies and a Loosening of Merger Rules

The structure and growth of the nursing home industry have also been affected by tax and anti-trust merger policies that were not specifically directed at nursing homes. Two significant sources of return to nursing home investors are largely dependent on the structure of the tax code. For example, there are tax savings resulting from rules on depreciation and after-tax capital gains. As real estate investments, nursing homes are not subject to the standard limitation on deductions, an advantage for a highly leveraged (low equity) industry like nursing homes. In addition, many nursing homes are organized as both an operating corporation and as a real estate partnership, with a lease or management contract between the two formal corporate entities (Shulman and Galanter, 1976; Baldwin and Bishop, 1983). This arrangement allows the partners to take depreciation and interest deductions against their personal income. Thus, there are substantial tax advantages to nursing home ownership.

These and other tax advantages accrue more to investors in high tax brackets than to nonprofit entities[16] or the original "mom and pop" investors. This influences who is most interested in purchasing any asset, including nursing homes. As Baldwin and Bishop (1983) observe,

To an investor whose marginal tax bracket (including federal and state taxes) is 50 percent or greater, a dollar of deduction is worth as much or more than a dollar of revenue. For tax-exempt investors . . . a dollar of revenue is worth a full dollar, but tax deductions are worthless.

Thus, the effect of such tax policies is to make nursing home investment more attractive to high-tax-bracket entities than to nonprofit firms and low-bracket investors. Baldwin and Bishop (1983) argue,

If the supply of investment opportunities is restricted, . . . then a natural "investor clientele" for nursing homes lies in the high tax brackets. It is not surprising, in light of these results, that "mom and pop" owner-operators of nursing homes have found any profitable opportunities for expansion of nursing home capacity snapped up by more wealthy corporate and private investors. In like manner, a nonprofit organization will find that, if a potential investment is worthwhile on a present value net flow equivalent basis . . . then it would be even more worthwhile to for-profit owners.

Several other tax policies contribute to the trend toward a new ownership structure. First, individuals or firms that have owned a nursing home for a long time find that the tax advantages of depreciation and the positive cash flow from Medicare and Medicaid reimbursement for depreciation have substantially declined, creating an incentive to sell. Thus, for long-time owners, such as the "mom and pop" operators, the incentive is to sell. In essence, as Baldwin and Bishop (1983) argue, public policy may also have had the unforeseen side effect of making ownership of homes attractive "only to certain high bracket individual and corporate investors."

Other policies, such as the investment tax credit (ITC) and the accelerated depreciation (ACRS) provisions of the Economic Recovery Tax Act (ERTA) of 1981, for instance, provided tax incentives for corporations to increase their investment in new plant and equipment and to increase productivity (*Congressional Quarterly Almanac*, 1981, pp. 92-93). However, in the nursing home sector (as in others) these provisions of the tax code seem also to have induced more economic concentration by making a firm worth more to an acquirer than to its stockholders (Trautman, 1984).[17] Certainly, there was a boom in nursing home mergers and acquisitions following passage of ERTA. For Beverly Enterprises, Unicare, Hillhaven, and ANTA, for instance, 1981-1982 was a time of substantial growth, and during that period, 11 of the 25 largest chains merged with or were acquired by other chains.[18]

While the federal tax code was encouraging mergers and acquisitions, the Department of Justice announced a liberalization of its regulations on mergers. It began to use a new method of measuring industrial concentration and developed more lenient rules regarding horizontal integration. In addition, Justice issued guidelines under which conglomerate mergers between companies with a customer-supplier relationship will have fewer problems. Thus, nursing home chains experienced fewer restrictions on either vertical or hori-

zontal growth and at the same time were beneficiaries of tax policy changes that encouraged
such growth.

## SUMMARY

Many factors, including a rapidly aging population and the availability of public assistance
in paying for such care, have contributed to
the growth of the nursing home sector. As
shown, Medicare and some Medicaid systems
seem to have provided nursing home investors
with overly generous compensation, especially
during the early years of these programs. At
the least, by paying for the cost of care, as well
as interest, depreciation, and an essentially
guaranteed return on equity, public reimbursement systems made nursing home investment extremely attractive. The result was
a rapid flow of capital into this sector.

Three public policy changes during the early
1970s helped eliminate the excess supply of
nursing home beds and make investment in
the nursing home sector even more attractive.
To a large degree these developments favored
the larger, multifacility proprietary firms—the
chains. The expansion of coverage to individuals needing intermediate care spurred increased demand.[19] At the same time the
extension of the LSC to those facilities providing intermediate care eliminated many of
the original "mom and pop" investors who
owned relatively small facilities that could not
be profitably operated if upgraded to meet LSC
requirements. In addition, many of these small
operators lacked the same kind of access to
capital for renovation or new construction as
publicly held and larger multifacility firms. Finally, the imposition of health planning, and
other limits on bed supply have encouraged
acquisitions rather than new construction for
investors that wish to expand their nursing
home holdings.

Medicaid (and to a lesser extent, Medicare)
reimbursement for interest and depreciation
made nursing home investment attractive from
a real estate viewpoint, and this was augmented by the tax advantages from depreciation and from capital gains rules. Thus, high
interest rates and construction costs, CON and
moratoriums on new nursing home construction, the availability of capital for the larger

operations (particularly the chains), and tax and
reimbursement policies were part of a con-
stellation of factors that contributed to a climate favoring mergers and acquisitions. As
Baldwin and Bishop (1983) argue,

It is no surprise that the new investors were not the
small owner-operators who had built nursing home
capacity and provided care since the mid-1930s; nor
were the owners of new capacity the charitable enterprises that had also been active in providing care
in the past. Instead, they were for-profit corporations and partnerships that could benefit from the
cash flow, tax savings, and capital gains on real estate
transactions.

## THE IMPACT OF OWNERSHIP ON COST, QUALITY, AND ACCESS

Nearly 20 years have passed since Medicare
and Medicaid began disgorging first millions
and now billions of dollars a year for nursing
home care. During that time, health and safety
regulations governing nursing homes have been
developed at both the state and federal level,
and the industry has become dominated by
investors who seem to be increasingly sophisticated businessmen. Despite these developments, quality of care and quality of life for
residents in the nation's nursing homes continue to be problems. Quality varies from excellent to seriously substandard. In addition,
long-term care is beset by escalating costs and
serious access problems for the elderly poor
and those who require a substantial amount of
exceptionally skilled care or extensive "hands-
on" care (U.S. Senate Special Committee on
Aging, 1984).

This section examines the various arguments, assertions, and hypotheses about the
impact of ownership type on cost, quality, and
access, using available empirical studies and
analyses of state regulatory agency reports to
examine the effect of ownership structure on
nursing home performance.

### The Impact of Ownership Type on Quality

Questions about the impact of nursing home
ownership on service delivery have provoked
considerable theoretical speculation as well as
some empirical research (e.g., Bishop, 1980;

Weisbrod and Schlesinger, 1983). In general, the view is that whether a nursing home is owned and operated by a proprietary or nonprofit organization will affect not only the cost and quality of care but also whether or not it is equally available to all persons needing such care. The issue has taken on new urgency in the minds of many observers and policymakers with the growth of the for-profit sector in long-term care, particularly with the emergence and growing presence of nursing home chains.

Debates about the impact of ownership type on the performance of nursing homes are often tied to arguments about the alleged benefits and shortcomings of private versus public ownership in health care generally. Critics of proprietary ownership generally speculate on the potential negative effects associated with the goal of profit maximization. They argue that a fundamental conflict may exist between the primary purpose of a proprietary business—to show a profit—and the provision of high-quality care. Since nursing home patients are typically so vulnerable physically and mentally and become impoverished in paying for nursing home care, most observers agree that patients are often unable to protect their own interests in the nursing home.[20] Thus, critics fear that in a conflict between achieving a profit and providing high-quality care, the care of the patient is likely to suffer (Butler, 1976; Fottler et al., 1981; Beattie and Bullock, 1964; AFL-CIO, 1977).

Many social theorists have argued that a community of nonprofit service providers is more desirable, given the history and orientation of voluntary organizations. These groups are rooted in the tradition of mutual benefit organizations, such as the religious and fraternal organizations, charitable groups, and labor unions that started old-age institutions for their members in the early part of this century. Their primary goal is seen as the provision of care and service, not achieving a profit (Vladeck, 1980; Weisbrod and Schlesinger, 1983; Harris, 1981; Lasch, 1979).[21]

This section reviews several types of information about the impact of ownership type on quality, including impressionistic findings; empirical analyses that use structural and resource input measures of quality; data from state licensure and certification agencies on violations (basically of structural or input measures of quality); complaints lodged by nursing home patients and their families; and an empirical analysis that uses process and outcome measures of quality. Some new data on the impact of chain ownership on quality are also presented.

### Impressionistic Evidence

Impressionistic findings suggest that nonprofit facilities tend to provide better quality of care and quality of life, but these findings are hardly conclusive. Brooks and Hoffman (1978) visited many intermediate care facilities (ICFs) in the Cleveland metropolitan area and concluded,

We . . . are impressed with the noticeable differences between the two types of ownership. In general, homes for the aged (nonprofits) appear to have a more "homey" atmosphere, to be more adequately staffed, to be kept in better repair, to be more closely linked to community organizations, and to have more patient activities than do proprietary intermediate care nursing homes.

Vladeck (1980) deals with this issue in his book, *Unloving Care*. On the basis of his observations and interviews, Vladeck concludes,

. . . on the average, voluntary facilities are somewhat better than proprietary ones. The worst nursing homes are almost exclusively proprietary. But in the middle ranges, there is substantial overlap. The best way to visualize the difference might be to conceive of the range of quality in each of the two types of nursing homes as a quasi-normal distribution . . . . The two distributions overlap markedly, with the mean for the voluntaries slightly higher than the mean for proprietaries, and with the voluntaries having a shorter low-quality tail.

Winn and McCaffree (1976) conducted a study of 282 nursing homes identified by state officials (in 16 states) as being high-quality homes and developed a different impression. (Their purpose was to study how the patterns of services received by patients in these excellent facilities differed from other facilities.) They observed that the proportion of nonprofit facilities identified as "high quality" did not differ from the proportion of nonprofit facilities in the population. However, without information about the distribution of the "adequate" and "seriously substandard" facilities, one cannot conclude that no difference exists.

The performance of nursing home chains is even more difficult to evaluate, even impressionistically, since it seems to vary significantly from chain to chain. In a study for a congressional committee, Richard Levinson (1984) and other staff interviewed state Medicaid and health department officials regarding the impact of chain ownership on quality. Most state officials lacked systematic information about quality of care, much less how it varies by type of ownership. Also, state officials often do not know which facilities are part of multifacility chains. However, while officials are concerned about the growing concentration of nursing home chains and the future implications of this trend, many currently view the chains in a fairly favorable light. Thus, Levinson notes, that though responses "are anecdotal and impressionistic, at best,"

. . . respondents from the state Medicaid administrations commonly report that the chains have been responsible for bringing a number of local privately owned facilities ("mom and pop" homes) which were substandard operations up to the minimum acceptable level. . . . The chains have the capital to upgrade institutions they purchase and are sometimes unwilling to jeopardize their name for deficiencies that can be remedied. Indeed, they indicated that some chains would not allow a facility they purchased to run under their name until it was brought up to—or close to—the minimum acceptable standard. It must be emphasized that these facilities are not necessarily viewed by state administrators as offering "good quality" care, but are just good enough to meet state standards. . . . Some credit the chains with helping them to remove the worst abuses in nursing home facilities.

In interviewing officials from several states, we heard much the same about the nursing home chains, but the view differed markedly depending on the chain under discussion. In four states where one chain operated, state officials cited it as the worst performer among all the chains—with quality of care a major problem in many of its facilities. Two other nursing home chains, however, were cited as making efforts to upgrade the facilities they purchased.[22]

Some state officials, like Governor John Carlin of Kansas, have expressed concern about the growing concentration of chain ownership, which they fear may lead to decreased competition and increased costs. Also corporations with facilities in one state and headquarters in another state are seen as more difficult to regulate. Several state officials expressed concern that large chains could exercise too much influence in state rate setting and regulatory issues with threats to withdraw from the Medicaid program. In addition, some state officials felt "outclassed" when regulatory actions involved legal proceedings because of the chains' high-priced and highly qualified legal representation, while state agencies typically must rely on relatively inexperienced lawyers.

Other state officials, however, felt that the chains were often more responsive to state Medicaid and survey agencies than were individual owners. Some cited the managerial ability of some chains in this regard. Others, like Dr. Janice Caldwell of the Texas Department of Human Resources, felt that a chain is more likely to take corrective action promptly when one of its facilities is cited for deficiencies because the parent corporation would be unwilling to jeopardize its relationship with state agencies and place all its facilities at risk of increased regulatory activity.[23]

Our impression, based on visits to more than 200 facilities and interviews with state officials, ombudsmen, and families of nursing home patients, is that nonprofit, church-affiliated homes tend to provide better quality of care and quality of life than proprietary facilities. Excellent facilities are found in each category, but truly wretched ones are almost always proprietary. However, one's evaluation of the performance of nursing homes may differ according to the dimension of quality under consideration. For example, Ms. Iris Freeman, head of the nursing home advocates program in Minnesota, observes that her office receives complaints about all types of facilities; complaints about quality of care tend to be about proprietary facilities, while complaints about violations of patients' rights (particularly about paternalism toward patients) tend to be lodged against nonprofits (Freeman, personal communication, 1985). Clearly, definitive conclusions about differences in quality are difficult to reach. However, most observers' general impressions seem to be that nonprofits, on the average, provide better quality as it is generally understood.

## Empirical Research: Variations in Input Measures of Quality

The findings of empirical studies on the relationship of ownership to resource input and structural measures of quality are occasionally inconsistent, although most have found significant differences between for-profit and nonprofit facilities in the amount of resources allocated to direct patient care. What these differences indicate, however, is a matter of substantial debate. The validity of resource inputs, such as nursing hours per patient or expenditures on raw food, as surrogates for quality has been questioned by critics who argue that such measures may bear little relationship to either quality of care or quality of life in a facility (O'Brien et al., 1983; Levey et al., 1973; Kane et al., 1983). Several studies have failed to find any statistically significant relationship between structural factors or resource inputs and process and outcome measures of quality (Lee, 1984; Kurowski and Breed, 1981).

Despite such criticisms of input measures of quality, their use can be supported on several grounds. First, the availability of resource inputs is clearly a precondition to their use in patient care (Kosberg and Tobin, 1972; Kosberg, 1973). Second, the lack of correlation between resource input or structural measures of quality and process or outcome measures may be due to the lack of variation in these independent variables in the homes studied (Linn et al., 1977; Kurowski and Breed, 1981). Third, some studies have found some resource inputs to be related to both process and outcome measures of quality of patient care (e.g., Kurowski and Breed, 1981; Shaughnessy et al., 1980). Linn et al. (1977) found that the number of registered nurse (RN) hours per patient day was positively associated with patient survival, improvement, and discharge from the nursing home. Raw expenditures on food and the availability of individual dietary planning were also associated significantly with two of the outcome measures of quality of care. In a 1977 study of homes rated as superior, the American Health Care Association found that these homes outscored other facilities in the

number of RN hours per patient day but were lower in licensed practical nurses (LPNs).[24]

Two state studies also examined the value of various resource inputs as indicators of quality. The Virginia Joint Legislative Audit and Review Commission (Virginia JLARC, 1978) identified facilities that state inspectors had found deficient in "meal menus, adequate food portions, or the quality of meals," and facilities that had "complaints about food." Raw food expenditure data were available for 9 of the 17 such nursing homes. JLARC found that

In all nine cases, the per day expenditure was below the state average. This supports the belief that low raw food costs and poor meal quality are related, and that food costs could serve as a measure of dietary adequacy.

The Ohio Nursing Home Commission (1979) studied differences between facilities rated as "high quality" and "low quality." On the basis of agreement from three sources (a reputational survey of nursing home ombudsmen, hospital discharge planners, and state inspection staff; licensure and federal certification survey reports; and inspections of facilities by commission staff), 60 nursing homes were identified as providing either high or low quality. Of these, 27 low-quality homes and 28 high-quality homes had current Medicaid cost reports on file with the Ohio Department of Public Welfare. A comparison of facilities' allocation of funds (Table 6) shows that "high-quality" homes have higher expenditures on direct patient care items, such as food, RNs, aides, medical and rehabilitative care, housekeeping, and laundry and linen.[25]

While the validity of resource inputs as indicators of quality is not definitively established, such studies support the utilization of resource input as at least partial indicators of quality of care. Several studies of for-profit and nonprofit facilities use such measures, and they yield fairly consistent findings about ownership. Two studies of resource inputs found no significant differences between for-profit and nonprofit facilities. Holmberg and Anderson (1968) interviewed administrators in 118 of the 392 nursing homes in Minnesota in 1967 and found several structural differences between for-profit and nonprofit homes.[26] Although average staffing patterns (RN hours per patient

**TABLE 6**   Spending Differences per Patient Day Between a Sample of High-Quality and Low-Quality Nursing Homes Participating in the Ohio Medicaid Program

| | Average per Patient per Day Expenditure, 1976[a] | | |
|---|---|---|---|
| Item | High-Quality Homes | Low-Quality Homes | Difference |
| Average total per diem | $26.27 | $21.12 | $5.15 (24%) |
| Raw food | 1.99 | 1.45 | 0.54 (37) |
| Registered nurses | 1.92 | 0.99 | 0.93 (94) |
| Aides and orderlies | 4.63 | 4.19 | 0.44 (11) |
| Total nursing staff | 7.53 | 6.63 | 0.90 (14) |
| Medical and rehabilitative care | 0.42 | 0.23 | 0.19 (83) |
| Housekeeping | 1.11 | 0.57 | 0.54 (95) |
| Laundry and linen | 0.73 | 0.54 | 0.19 (35) |
| Property cost[b] | 3.82 | 3.02 | 0.80 (27) |
| Licensed practical nurses | 0.98 | 1.45 | −0.47 (48) |
| Administrator salaries | 0.80 | 0.99 | −0.19 (24) |
| Motor vehicles | 0.04 | 0.14 | −0.10 (250) |
| Legal and accounting fees | 0.13 | 0.18 | −0.05 (39) |
| Profit factor | 0.78 | 0.78 | — |

[a]From a group of 28 high-quality facilities and 27 low-quality facilities of similar size (50 or more beds) and certification status (dually certified as SNF/ICF).

[b]This figure is based on the age, historical cost of the facility for depreciation and interest payments, or, if the facility is leased, the lease or rental payment. Observed differences in spending on ownership/property costs are probably associated with the age and size of the facilities.

SOURCE: Ohio Nursing Home Commission (1979).

day, average number of patient care staff) were very similar, nonprofits had significantly more physician hours per patient per week than the proprietaries, and the for-profits had more administrative hours per week.

However, Holmberg and Anderson (1968) concluded that most quality indicators were not significantly related to ownership type and that the differences between ownership types were less significant than the differences among facilities within each category. Levey et al. (1973) reached a similar conclusion. They studied 129 of 690 nursing homes in Massachusetts, using an index of nursing services, patient activities, and physical plant characteristics from survey and patient care reports. They found no significant differences in their quality index on the basis of facility ownership.

Some observers argue that the findings of Holmberg and Anderson (1968) and Levey et al. (1973) are not typical because Minnesota and Massachusetts are thought to have more-stringent regulatory policy and higher-quality

nursing homes than is average and the quality proxies used were based on resource inputs regulated by the state. A study by Gottesman (1974) supports these findings. Gottesman gathered data on 40 nursing homes and on the social, physical, and mental characteristics of 1,144 residents in those facilities. He also observed the activities of nursing home residents and staff during two 12-hour periods. Gottesman found better psychosocial activities and staff involvement in nonprofit homes and that "church-related facilities seem to have a strong sense of 'family' in their sponsorship." However, he argues that other factors, such as facility size, patient characteristics, and the mix of public and private-pay patients, may have more significance for these differences in quality than does ownership. For instance, of the proprietary facilities with high levels of public-pay patients, Gottesman argues,

These homes have a high proportion of socially marginal residents, fewer financial resources, and a resident group with many social disabilities and little community involvement. It should not be surprising that they come off most poorly with regard to basic medical and psychosocial activities as well as staff involvement.[27]

Other studies of resource inputs consistently find differences between for-profit and nonprofit nursing homes. For example, the concern about profit-taking at the expense of patient care has been heightened by a study (Fottler et al., 1981) that examined the relationship between profits and four measures of quality of patient care.[28] This study found that there is a consistently negative relationship between a nursing home's profitability and resource input measures of patient care quality. That is, the study found that quality decreases as profits increase. While reliance on structural/input measures of quality, like those employed in the Fottler study, may be subject to debate (O'Brien et al., 1983), few observers would argue that staffing is unrelated to quality. Most would agree that sufficient staffing is, at the least, a precondition to high quality of care. Moreover, the study's findings confirm the view of many long-time observers of the nursing home industry. As Vladeck (1980) observes,

The motivations, or actual behavior, of profit-seeking firms may run counter to the well-being of nursing home residents. Proprietary facilities tend to be physically smaller than voluntary ones, especially in the provision of public space. They have incentives to discriminate against Medicaid recipients and against admission of sicker patients. They are more likely to cut corners on supplies and staffing. And there can be no denying that most of the really scandalous conditions found in nursing home investigations have been in proprietary facilities.

Other studies find substantial differences between for-profit and nonprofit homes on resource inputs. The 1973 National Nursing Home Survey demonstrated that nonprofit homes had significantly more staff than for-profit facilities, with twice as many clerical, food service, housekeeping, and maintenance staff. Proprietary facilities had more administrative hours, as well as medical and therapeutic (e.g., physical therapy) staff hours. In both the 1973 and 1977 surveys, nonprofits had more RN hours (U.S. Department of Health, Education, and Welfare, 1975b, 1979).

Winn (1974) found similar differences in a study of a matched sample of 24 proprietary and 24 nonprofit nursing homes in Washington state. Nursing hours per patient day were slightly higher in nonprofit homes, and total employee hours per patient day were significantly higher in nonprofit facilities. The New York State Moreland Act Commission (1975) found that nonprofit facilities spent an average of $16.02 per patient per day on nursing, while for-profits spent only $12.78 per patient day. When the analysts controlled for facility size and location, however, much of the cost difference between for-profit and nonprofits was eliminated. In general, "ownership variables added only minor explanatory power," but it did account for some of the variation in spending on nursing staff.

The Minnesota Senate/House Select Committee on Nursing Homes also examined the spending patterns of nursing homes and found significant ownership differences in the distribution of expenditures (Minnesota Senate and House, 1976). Proprietaries spent nearly twice as much as nonprofits on cost of capital (property and related expenses), while nonprofits outspent the proprietaries on dietary, housekeeping, and plant operation (maintenance). In addition, the Minnesota study found

Proprietary SNFs incur 37.7% of their costs for care-related items and 20.8% for property-related items. For nonprofit SNFs, the percentages were 41% for care-related costs and 11.1% for property-related items. The differentials for ICFs were about the same.

The Virginia study (Virginia JLARC, 1978) also found substantial differences in the spending patterns of for-profit and nonprofit facilities, including that "profit status was found to have an effect on the distribution of nursing home expenditures but not on overall cost." Using data from facilities with the same average number of patient days, the Virginia study found striking differences, depicted in Table 7.

Caswell and Cleverley (1978) also found significant differences in both the costs and distribution of expenditures by different nursing home ownership types. They found that while for-profit facilities had lower overall costs, the savings were primarily in areas that may have

TABLE 7  Spending Patterns in Virginia Nursing Homes, 1977[a]

| Item | Proprietaries | Nonprofits |
|---|---|---|
| Nursing | $7.98 | $10.65 |
| Dietary | 3.58 | 4.51 |
| Administration | 3.97 | 3.00 |
| Property (depreciation, interest, rent) | 3.09 | 1.70 |

[a]Average per patient per day expenditures (Virginia JLARC, 1978).

direct or indirect effects on the quality of patient care: housekeeping, maintenance, nursing, and dietary. The for-profits, however, reported higher costs of property (interest, depreciation, and rent or lease payments). Caswell and Cleverley concluded that many proprietary facilities were probably staffed at lower levels than minimum health and safety standards required.

The Ohio Nursing Home Commission's analysis of 1977 costs reported by nursing homes to the state Medicaid agency revealed a similar pattern. On average, nonprofit facilities outspent proprietaries on raw food and dietary supplies ($4.67 per patient day versus $3.01), as well as on a composite of direct patient care items that includes nursing salaries, medical supplies and expenses, social services, and medical and rehabilitative salaries (Ohio Nursing Home Commission, 1979).[29]

Data from Texas (Moden, 1982) reveal similar differences in the distribution of spending. For instance, in 1978 the average for-profit facility had total net revenues 16.5 percent less than the average nonprofit. But the for-profits, on the average, spent 37 percent less on patient care (e.g., nursing staff) and 31 percent less on dietary than nonprofits. In 1980, the pattern was similar. Proprietary facilities had total net revenues (on the average) that were only 7.5 percent less than the average for nonprofit facilities, and spent 29 percent less on patient care items (e.g. nursing, medical, and rehabilitative care) and 27 percent less on food than the average nonprofit nursing home. Table 8 displays data on per diem expenditures broken out by cost category for 1981.

Elwell (1984) studied 424 skilled nursing

homes in New York State. His quality measures were "multiple scales of staffing and resource distribution" among the facilities. The distribution of resources was measured in terms of per diem expenditures on administration, medical, nursing, rehabilitation, social services, activities, nutrition, housekeeping, and other professional services. Staffing measures included RN, LPN, and aide hours per patient day, physician hours per patient week, and other professional staff hours per patient day. In addition, as a measure of quality of life (privacy and personal space), Elwell included the proportion of patients in multiple-bed rooms.

The proportion of Medicaid patients per facility, the proportion functionally impaired, and the size and location of facilities were included to help isolate the effect of ownership on the measures of quality. Even when controlling for these, in each patient service area Elwell measured, nonprofits spent more than the proprietaries.[30] He concludes that "the differences among ownership types were consistent with the hypothesis that . . . voluntary institutions are superior medical and personal care facilities" (Elwell, 1984). When controlling for location, Elwell found that

In each of the six regions, proprietary facilities spent significantly less than the regional mean for administration, nursing, nutrition, and housekeeping services. Proprietary facilities spent significantly less for medical services in five of the regions, for social and rehabilitation services in four of the regions. . . . In no region did proprietary facilities spend significantly more than the regional mean for any of the service areas measured.

He concluded,

The results of this analysis provide considerable confirmation for the hypothesis that government and voluntary facilities offer superior medical and personal care to their patients. The allocation of financial resources as well as the number of staff hours per patient day were all consistent with the hypothesis.

Data on the impact of for-profit nursing home chain ownership on quality of patient care are even more scant than that focusing on differences between for-profit and nonprofit facilities. Greene and Monahan (1981) analyzed data from 24 SNFs in the greater metropolitan area of Phoenix, Arizona. They felt that in the rel-

TABLE 8 Data on Revenues, Expenditures, and Spending Patterns[a] in Texas Nursing Homes, 1981

| Cost Area | Nonprofits | Proprietaries | Difference |
|---|---|---|---|
| Patient care | $18.19 | $12.30 | $5.89 (48%) |
| Dietary | 5.89 | 4.28 | 1.61 (38) |
| Facility (property) | 5.68 | 5.60 | .08 (1) |
| Administration | 3.15 | 2.97 | .18 (6) |
| Total expenditures | 32.91 | 25.15 | 7.76 (31) |
| Total revenues | 32.34 | 27.06 | 5.28 (20) |
| Difference between revenues and expenses | (−.57) | 1.91 | |

[a]Average per patient per day expenditures.

SOURCE: Data from Moden (1982) based on data reported to the Texas Department of Human Resources by nursing homes participating in the Medicaid program.

atively unregulated market of Arizona, which at the time had no state Medicaid program (and thus no federal health and safety standards or inspections), might make the orientation of nursing home owners more apparent. As a measure of quality, Greene and Monahan used a composite of facility spending on such items as RN hours, expenditures on RNs, and dietary expenditures. Greene and Monahan examined the behavior of nonprofit homes, individually owned or locally headquartered proprietaries, and for-profit nursing home chains. They found that "for-profit institutions give significantly lower levels of care, even with charges and other factors controlled," and that "distantly headquartered chain operations tend to provide lower levels of care than locally-owned facilities." However, since the number of homes in the Greene and Monahan study is small and the unregulated market of Arizona may not be typical, their findings cannot safely be generalized.

Data on Texas nursing home expenditures in fiscal year 1983, displayed in Table 9, further illuminate the relationship between ownership and allocation of funds to resources thought to affect quality of patient care. The nonprofit facilities outspend the for-profit facilities, on the average, in every category, including facility (property) and administrative costs. The differences in spending, however, are most notable in the patient care and dietary categories. Data on variations among the four

largest nursing home chains operating in Texas are shown in Table 10. In general, the differences are consistent with earlier findings. The statewide mean for spending on the patient care category is 44 percent of total expenditures. For proprietaries it averages 43 percent, while for chain-owned facilities, spending on patient care is 42 percent of total expenditures. The two largest chains in Texas both spend less than 39 percent of the total on patient care cost items. Nonprofit facilities spend an average of 47 percent of their total expenditures in the patient care category.

### Variations in Licensure and Certification Deficiencies and Complaints

Another source of data that can be used to evaluate the performance of different nursing homes is information on state licensure and federal certification reports regarding violations of minimum health and safety standards. These reports have often been justifiably criticized in terms of failing to reveal an accurate, multidimensional picture of the quality of care provided to patients in nursing homes, much less quality of life (e.g., Hawes, 1983; Ohio Nursing Home Commission, 1979; New Jersey State Nursing Home Commission, 1978; Missouri State Senate, 1978). Because inspections are usually announced or regularly scheduled, owners and administrators can anticipate the approximate date of inspections. In addition,

**TABLE 9**   Revenues, Expenditures, and Spending Patterns in Texas Nursing Homes, 1983[a]

| Cost Area | Statewide Mean | Nonprofits | Proprietaries | Difference Between Nonprofits and Proprietaries | |
|---|---|---|---|---|---|
| Patient care | $13.06 | $18.62 | $12.30 | $ 6.32 | (51%) |
| Dietary | 4.65 | 6.67 | 4.38 | 2.29 | (52) |
| Facility (property) | 6.70 | 7.60 | 6.58 | 1.02 | (16) |
| Administrative | 3.26 | 3.65 | 3.20 | .45 | (14) |
| Total expenditures | 29.80 | 39.76 | 28.44 | 11.32 | (40) |
| Total revenues | 31.16 | 36.64 | 30.41 | 6.23 | (21) |
| Net income | 1.36 | (3.12) | 1.98 | | |
| Occupancy (%) | 82.77 | 88.74 | 81.96 | | |
| Proportion private-pay (%) | | 41.96 | 26.27 | | |

[a]Data are per patient per day expenditures as reported to the Texas Department of Human Resources (1984) by the facilities participating in the Medicaid program.

the survey forms focus almost entirely on structural and input characteristics—on the capacity of the facility to provide care rather than on the condition and satisfaction of patients. For these reasons, critics argue that the inspection system—and the violation citations that emerge from this process—yields insufficient information about quality. On the other hand, there is no reason to expect that the deficiencies/violations do not accurately reflect failures by the facility to meet existing standards, nor to expect that the citation system is biased in favor of any particular ownership type. Thus, while they do not fully measure

quality, licensure and certification deficiencies may capture important aspects of quality of care.

Complaints reported by patients, family members, or others familiar with the facilities are another potential source of data about the performance of nursing homes. Many argue that complaints are especially valuable since they may reveal patients' and families' perceptions of quality and may reveal more than regulatory reports about quality of life, augmenting inspection reports (Weisbrod and Schlesinger, 1983). There is some concern that complaint data may be biased against higher

**TABLE 10**   Revenues, Expenditures, and Spending Patterns in Nursing Home Chains, Texas, 1983[a]

| Cost Area | All Chains | Beverly | ARA | ANTA/ Four Seasons | Hillhaven |
|---|---|---|---|---|---|
| Patient care | $12.51 | $11.38 | $10.65 | $14.72 | $15.73 |
| Dietary | 4.33 | 4.05 | 3.52 | 4.37 | 4.35 |
| Facility (property) | 7.29 | 7.40 | 6.64 | 6.35 | 9.34 |
| Administrative | 3.53 | 3.56 | 3.95 | 4.81 | 4.37 |
| Total expenditures | 29.79 | 29.98 | 27.11 | 32.53 | 36.75 |
| Total revenues | 30.83 | 30.65 | 29.73 | 33.43 | 32.92 |
| Net income | 1.05 | 1.66 | 2.13 | .90 | (3.83) |
| Occupancy (%) | 79.65 | 73.57 | 74.66 | 91.76 | 83.04 |
| Proportion private-pay (%) | 26.63 | 30.61 | 20.85 | 35.63 | 25.98 |

[a]Data are per patient per day expenditures as reported to the Texas Department of Human Resources (1984) by the facilities participating in the Medicaid program.

quality facilities, since in these homes patients and families may feel less fear of reprisal and less reluctance to complain. In addition, individuals may be more willing to lodge complaints when they feel most confident that corrective action will occur.

Existing studies and available data on regulatory violations and complaints indicate that nonprofit facilities offer higher quality of care and quality of life than proprietary ones. There are too few systematic data on the performance of nursing home chains—and too much apparent variation among different chains—to permit definitive conclusions.

The Minnesota Joint House/Senate Select Committee on Nursing Homes analyzed differences in complaints about poor quality of care (Minnesota Senate and House, 1976). The data from 1974 revealed that while only 39.1 percent of the licensed nursing homes in Minnesota were proprietary, 78.2 percent of the complaints filed with the state health department were lodged against for-profit homes. Of the 41 nursing homes that were the subject of three or more complaints during 1974, 39 (95 percent) were proprietary facilities.

The Ohio Nursing Home Commission (1979) analyzed characteristics of all (45) nursing homes that had such serious violations of health and safety standards that the Ohio Department of Health began proceedings to revoke their licenses in 1976. Only one (2 percent of the total) was a nonprofit facility, although nonprofit nursing homes constitute more than 20 percent of Ohio facilities.[31]

Koetting's study (1980) is perhaps the best-designed empirical study to date. Koetting selected a sample of 136 Illinois facilities divided into five ownership categories: (1) private nonprofits; (2) government-owned nonprofits; (3) proprietaries with working owners; (4) chain-owned proprietaries; and (5) other proprietaries. Quality-of-care measures were derived from licensure surveys and inspection-of-care reports. Using regression analysis to isolate the impact of ownership on these measures, and controlling for facility size, patient mix, and occupancy rate, Koetting concluded that nonprofit homes had superior quality.[32]

Riportella-Muller and Slesinger (1982) studied quality of care in 462 of 533 Wisconsin nursing homes. Measures of quality included

numbers of code violations and complaints. On the basis of the complaint data, the nonprofit homes provided better quality, but the data on violations yielded more complex findings. Small nonprofit homes had fewer violations than small proprietary homes, but large nonprofits (150 + beds) had more violations than similar proprietaries. Riportella-Muller and Slesinger concluded that although nonprofits performed somewhat better than proprietary nursing homes, the size and certification status of the facility were important mitigating factors and that simply eliminating for-profit entities would not necessarily significantly improve quality.

Weisbrod and Schlesinger (1983) also studied code violations and complaints filed against nursing homes in Wisconsin; however, their findings in favor of the nonprofits were much stronger than those of Riportella-Muller and Slesinger. Based on analysis of 431 nursing homes and data for 1976, Weisbrod and Schlesinger found that nonprofit homes had significantly fewer complaints than did proprietary firms. The picture for differences in ownership performance as measured by code violations was more complex. Nonprofit homes that were *not* church owned had significantly more regulatory violations than their for-profit counterparts of similar size. Church-owned nonprofits performed better on each measure (complaints and regulatory violations) than did for-profits.

States generally do not systematically report data on violations of state licensure and federal certification standards in a form that is useful to researchers. California, however, does assemble such data. The California Health Facilities Commission (1982) examined licensure citations to nursing homes that failed to meet minimum standard for the period 1977-1979. Proprietary firms generally performed worse than nonprofits. The average number of licensure citations per facility was 0.46 among church-related homes, 0.49 for other nonprofits, and 1.8 for proprietary homes[33] (see also AFL-CIO, 1983a,b).

Texas also systematically records serious violations on which the Department of Human Resources has taken action. We analyzed three types of increasingly severe punitive actions imposed by the department on long-term care facilities in Texas between January 1 and April 29, 1983. During that time, 181 compliance letters were issued, 35 vendor holds on Medicaid payments were imposed, and 42 facilities were terminated from the Medicaid program. Punitive actions were almost exclusively taken against proprietary facilities. For-profit homes (840 or 88 percent of facilities in the Medicaid program) received 169 (93.4 percent) of the compliance letters, 100 percent of the vendor hold actions, and between 90 and 100 percent of the 42 contract terminations.[34] Nonprofit nursing homes (115, or 12 percent of facilities in the Medicaid program) received 12 (6.6 percent) of the compliance letters, none of the vendor hold actions, and between 0 and 10 percent of the contract terminations.

In sum, in terms of code violations, nonprofit nursing homes perform much better than proprietaries. The relative performance of nursing home chains is more difficult to evaluate, although there are indications that chains may differ significantly from one another and that some chains do well in terms of violations of structural health and safety standards while others do quite poorly. For example, when we analyzed the 1983 Texas data on punitive actions, we found that

1. Beverly Enterprises owns/operates 121 or 12.7 percent of the facilities participating in the Texas Medicaid program; however, Beverly received 18.2 percent of all compliance letters, 17 percent of the vendor holds, and 14.3 percent of the contract terminations (decertification).

2. ARA owns 114 or 11.9 percent of the facilities and received 7.2 percent of the compliance letters, 14.3 percent of the vendor holds, and 2 percent of the contract terminations (decertification).

3. Hillhaven owns/operates 16 facilities (1.6 percent) and received 1.6 percent of the compliance letters and none of the vendor hold or decertification actions.

Thus, the chains varied in terms of violations cited and serious punitive actions instituted by the state. This suggests that nursing home chains are not a "monolith"—that is, each chain may have a slightly different orientation or organizational structure that affects its performance more than the mere structural characteristic of being a multifacility operation.

### Variations in Process and Outcome Measures of Quality

Only a few studies have attempted to measure variations in quality using process and outcome measures (Kane, 1983; Schlenker et al., 1983; Schlenker, 1984). One that directly addresses the impact of ownership on quality focused on nursing homes in Iowa where the state licensure agency developed an "outcome oriented" licensure survey for use in the annual inspection of nursing homes (Lee, 1984). The survey focuses not only on resource inputs but also on resident satisfaction (e.g., feelings of safety and security, enjoyment of food); professional health care (e.g., health care planning for individual residents); implementing the medication, treatment, and diet plans as prescribed by physicians; the quality of the living environment (e.g., cleanliness of rooms); room conditions; and food service (e.g., whether the food provides basic nutritional requirements and whether residents like the food). In analyzing the differences in Iowa facilities, Lee (1984) found not only that proprietary facilities had significantly fewer staff than similar nonprofits but also that nonprofits performed better on every outcome category: care planning, quarterly review of patients, room conditions, and quality of living environment.[35] The introduction of a "size" variable did not compromise the findings of the superiority of nonprofit facilities. Lee concluded that their findings are consistent with the Greene and Monahan study (1981) that "nonprofit(s) appear to provide consistently better quality of care when compared with the for-profit facilities" (Lee, 1984).

### Summary and Conclusions Regarding Quality

The preponderance of evidence from the relatively few studies that systematically address quality of care and ownership differences suggests the superiority of nonprofits—particularly of the church-related nonprofits. The data from the state surveys strongly support this finding. Studies using a variety of quality measures—resource inputs, licensure violations, complaints, and outcome-oriented measures of quality—are fairly uniform in finding nonprofit facilities superior in quality to for-profit nursing homes. The findings on the relative performance of the chains are less conclusive.

Because few studies have adequately controlled for the possible effects of differences in patient case mix, it is difficult to interpret data on resource inputs. Higher levels of staffing, for instance, may be a sign of higher quality of patient care, of a more intense case mix, or of inefficiency. Most studies have flaws, particularly in terms of the measures of quality (e.g., O'Brien et al., 1983). The nature and strength of the relationship between the proxies for quality and a patient-focused, multidimensional concept of quality have not been conclusively established. At best, such proxies as resource inputs are preconditions to, or partial indicators of, high quality of care. Until better measures are developed, tested, and used in studies, "knowledge" about the impact of ownership and other variables such as size is provisional.

Finally, researchers must use richer models of ownership. Lumping government-owned facilities with church-related homes and private nonprofits (that may be nonprofit in name only) into the same ownership category may obscure significant differences in performance. The same is true of the for-profits. A multibillion dollar multistate chain of 800 nursing homes, whose stock is publicly traded, is hardly the same organization as a 40-bed facility owned and operated by a practical nurse and her family. Yet, both are for-profits. Finally, there may be significant differences among various multifacility nursing home systems, and understanding the performance of chains may require analyses that distinguish among them.

### The Impact of Ownership on Cost

In general, empirical studies indicate that nonprofits report higher per patient per day costs than for-profit facilities. However, this finding requires qualification. First, most studies have employed inadequate measures of the severity of patient case mix and of qual-

ity of care. Thus, variations in cost may be due to differences in the facilities' mix of patients served or in the quality of patient care. Second, one of the most significant differences in costs is in the distribution of expenditures by different facilities, that is, in the way they allocate funds to various cost centers or items. This may have significant implications for quality and efficiency. Third, there is some indication that although certain types of facilities have lower costs, the actual price charged to patients varies relatively little.

### Cost Function Studies and Behavioral and Market Models

There have been a variety of studies that focus on nursing home costs. Many of the most useful studies utilize secondary data from one or more states and relate differences in costs to such factors as type of ownership, location, bed size, occupancy rate, mix by payee, and measures intended to capture differences in patient case mix and quality of care. Most studies have found the costs reported by nonprofit facilities to be higher than those of similar proprietary homes; however, proxies for such key factors as patient case mix and quality have varied and generally been inadequate. Thus, the results must be interpreted carefully.

Two studies found no significant variations in costs associated with ownership. The New York State Moreland Act Commission (1975) found that voluntary facilities reported significantly higher costs per patient day ($16.02) on the average in 1974 than proprietary facilities ($14.12). However, when the analysts controlled for the size of the facility and regional wage differences, "very little difference in cost was explained by the ownership factor alone."

The Virginia Joint Legislative Audit and Review Commission's (1978) analysis of reported nursing home costs also found little difference between nonprofit and proprietary facilities, although, as discussed earlier, the study found significant differences in the allocation of expenditures, among various cost centers, with "nonprofit facilities . . . [having] lower facility costs (interest, rent, and depreciation) and administrative expenses but . . . [spending] more for nursing care and dietary services."

A few other studies found only slight differences in costs between proprietary and nonprofit nursing homes. Levey et al. (1973) found that higher costs were associated with nonprofit ownership, but the difference was not statistically significant. Winn (1974), on the basis of data gathered from nursing home administrators, found per diem costs to be slightly higher among nonprofits—but not significantly so.

Two other studies reveal significant cost differences. Both Holmberg and Anderson (1968) and Koetting (1980) found that the costs reported by nonprofit facilities were, on average, significantly higher than those of for-profits. Koetting found that for-profit facilities could achieve the same level of quality (as measured by licensure code violations and deficiencies in individual patient medical reviews) at a lower cost than nonprofit nursing homes. Both studies, however, found little difference between the two types of facilities in actual charges to patients. Holmberg and Anderson found, in fact, that once the analysis of the proprietaries included their profit factor, then charges by nonprofit facilities were lower.

Other studies have consistently found nonprofits to have higher reported costs. Ruchlin and Levey (1972) studied 4 years of cost data (1965-1969) for 175 Massachusetts nursing homes and found nonprofit ownership generally had higher costs. Caswell and Cleverley (1978) in analyzing costs reported by Ohio nursing homes found that "proprietary homes do appear to be less costly than (nonprofit) . . . homes." Both noted that the allocation of expenditures within total spending differs, with the for-profits spending significantly more on property costs.

Birnbaum et al. (1981) analyzed data from several different data sets, including the National Nursing Home Survey and data on facilities participating in the Medicaid programs in New York, Massachusetts, and Indiana. They found nonprofit facilities (private and government-owned were both included) have higher costs than for-profit nursing homes. The analysis of each data set had some controls for variations in patient mix among the facilities, and in analyzing the New York data, Birnbaum et al. used inspection rating data as a proxy for quality. Even when these types of case mix

and quality measures were taken into account, the cost differentials between for-profit and nonprofit facilities persisted.

In her review of 12 major cost studies, Bishop (1980) concludes that for-profit facilities have lower per diem costs than nonprofit facilities, even when other factors associated with higher costs (such as location and the provision of skilled nursing care services) are held constant. Meiners (1982) also found that proprietary facilities had average costs that were significantly lower than nonprofit nursing homes, even when controlling for some measures of case mix, the range of therapeutic services available, and the type of staff coverage on daily shifts. Meiners also argued that whether a facility was part of a nursing home chain was not statistically significant in explaining variations in cost. Finally, Lee and Birnbaum (1983), Schlenker and Shaughnessy (1984), and Schlenker (1984) all report that nonprofit ownership is consistently related to higher costs.

Few available studies (e.g., Koetting, 1980; Lee et al., 1983; Meiners, 1982) directly address the impact of multistate chains on costs, and their data were from facility costs reported in the early 1970s. Further, we desired a more refined analysis of various ownership types. Thus, we undertook a new analysis of nursing home costs in Ohio. It examined variations among private nonprofit facilities (government-owned were excluded) and three types of proprietary facilities: (1) for-profit facilities owned by individuals who own and/or operate three or fewer facilities in Ohio; (2) intrastate chains, usually consisting of between four and ten facilities (all in Ohio) and owned by an individual, family, or partnership; and (3) multistate publicly held nursing home chains.[36]

Consistent with much previous research, our analysis found substantial cost differences between nonprofit facilities and those operating under the three proprietary forms. The average total costs per patient day in nonprofit homes were approximately $6.00 to $8.00 higher than average total costs in various proprietary facilities. The average total costs for individually owned homes and for those that are part of intrastate chains were almost identical, while the total costs for homes operated by multistate chains were approximately $1.50

higher than the other two proprietary forms. The same pattern holds for average operating costs per patient day. However, in our analysis we also examined differences in the allocation of expenditures and, using multiple regression techniques, were able to gain a clearer picture of cost differences and the factors that affect them.

Our new Ohio analysis shows expenditures on patient care to be much higher in nonprofit homes than proprietary ones. Nonprofits spent approximately 27 percent more per patient day on raw food than for-profit homes, from 30 to 100 percent more on medical and rehabilitative services, from 250 to 1300 percent more on social services, and from 25 to 32 percent more than the proprietaries on total nursing (which includes RNs, LPNs, and nurse's aides and orderlies). Individually owned and intrastate facilities spent more than the nonprofits on LPNs, in effect substituting one kind of professional nurse for another.

If, as we argue, these measures of resource inputs and service availability are valid proxies for quality of care, Ohio nonprofit facilities offer higher quality of care on the average than do the proprietary facilities. The findings, some of which are displayed in Table 11, also suggest that in Ohio, the multistate chains perform somewhat better than the other two proprietary categories. The intrastate chains commit the fewest resources to direct patient care and thus may provide the lowest quality of care.[37]

As noted, we found that the difference in costs between the nonprofit and the for-profit categories was between $6.00 and $8.00 per patient day. The regression analysis made it clear, however, that much of that difference derives from differential spending on patient care (quality) and from differences in facility

characteristics other than ownership (i.e., occupancy, admissions, patient mix by payer type, facility size, certification status, and location). The analysis also shows, however, that not all of the variation in costs between for-profit and nonprofit owners is related to these factors. The results indicate that controlling for different levels of patient care expenditures (our quality proxies) and different facility characteristics significantly reduced the cost difference; nevertheless, all three forms of proprietary facilities have total and operating costs that are still significantly lower than those found in the nonprofit facilities. For-profit facilities report costs per patient day that are approximately $2.50 lower than the nonprofits.

The analysis displayed in this section leads to several conclusions. First, nonprofit (nongovernment) facilities, on the average, report higher costs than the average for-profit facility. When we take into account factors other than ownership that might account for cost variations, the difference in costs between nonprofit and for-profit facilities is reduced, but even with these factors taken into account, there is still a significant cost difference between for-profit and nonprofit nursing homes in Ohio. Second, the differences between the various types of for-profits are quite interesting and may be missed by most analyses. When we used total or operating costs as the dependent variable, the three types of for-profit homes displayed little difference. Their behavior appeared quite similar. However, when we examine the for-profits' individual cost functions, their behavior differs; that is, the factors that are related to cost variations differ among the different ownership types. This is especially significant since it may indicate different re-

**TABLE 11** Comparison of Average Expenditures in Major Cost Centers, Ohio, 1977

| Cost Center | Type of Ownership | | | |
| --- | --- | --- | --- | --- |
| | Individual Ownership | Intrastate Chain | Multistate Chain | Nonprofit |
| General services costs | $2.47 | $2.44 | $2.04 | $3.27 |
| Ownership or rent | 3.12 | 3.12 | 3.10 | 2.69 |
| Patient care costs | 9.05 | 8.90 | 9.52 | 13.16 |
| Administrative costs | 2.73 | 2.90 | 2.53 | 3.17 |

sponses among the various ownership types to regulatory and reimbursement policies. This issue deserves further study to determine whether it is more broadly generalizable. Finally, the variations between the different ownership types in relation to the quality proxies are provocative. Like most other studies, our analysis shows significant differences between for-profit and nonprofit nursing homes in their expenditures on direct patient care and dietary items.

### The Impact of Chains and Chain Acquisition of Facilities

The best way to study the impact of multifacility chains may be to analyze facilities' performance before and after being acquired by a chain, and no empirical studies have systematically attempted this. Some evidence, however, suggests that chain acquisition may lead to higher costs, even when no improvement in the quality or level of services can be identified.

The facet of chain acquisition that has attracted the most attention is the impact on capital or property costs. The real estate advantages of nursing home investment have been discussed by several observers (e.g., Shulman and Galanter, 1976) and earlier in this paper. The Ohio Nursing Home Commission (1979) found that there were ownership changes in 20 to 25 percent of for-profit facilities annually—usually to take advantage of various tax and property cost reimbursement benefits. The result was that the private-pay patients and Medicaid program paid higher and higher costs for the same facility to provide essentially the same services it had before the ownership change. Vladeck (1980) argues that such turnover causes "a disproportionately high share of industry revenues . . . to [go to] depreciation, . . . interest premiums and personal profits" and may harm patient care. He argues

The high degree of leveraging also creates a kind of perpetual instability in the nursing home industry as a whole and within the life of any given institution. Nursing homes are always changing hands or changing financial structure; skimping and cornercutting fluctuate with financing cycles. . . . The one economic certainty in the typical nursing home is that the monthly mortgage payment must be met.

Expenditures on staff and supplies can wait, if necessary, but capital financing costs must be covered.

GAO (1983a,b) found that the acquisition of a hospital chain led to significantly higher property costs being charged to the Medicare program. This also occurs in nursing homes. The Kansas Division of Post Audits found that acquisitions and mergers led to higher property costs. The audit division estimated the takeover of 58 ICFs by a large, multistate chain after March 1982 added $650,000 to the Medicaid program's costs in 1983 alone (Levinson, 1984). Another example is Beverly Enterprises' acquisition of Provincial House nursing homes in Michigan. According to one analysis of Medicaid cost reports, the pre-sale interest expenses reported by Provincial House nursing homes in 1981 totaled $1,814,296. After the acquisition by Beverly, these same facilities reported an interest expense of $4,280,212 as a result of the debt financing of the purchase, a 1-year increase in interest expenses alone of 136 percent (AFL-CIO, 1983a).

Also troublesome is the possibility—suggested by the distribution of spending by the chains—that such increased costs may be covered by chains' reducing expenditures on patient care. The analysis of 1983 nursing home spending patterns in Texas demonstrates that the chains' *total* expenditures were almost identical to the statewide mean. However, they spend 9 percent more than the statewide mean on property costs and 8.2 percent more on administrative expenses, while spending 4.4 percent less on patient care and 7.4 percent less on dietary services (Texas Department of Human Resources, 1984; see also Table 10). Other data showing similar patterns (e.g., in Virginia) were reviewed earlier.

The large, multifacility chains have argued that their higher administrative costs contribute to improved administration and that their lower patient care costs and dietary expenditures are due to management and purchasing efficiencies. This is not supported by a variety of data discussed earlier, including the records of two chains operating in Texas that spend more than the statewide mean on administration, substantially less on patient care and dietary costs (Texas Department of Human Resources, 1984; see Table 10), and have received a high proportion of punitive actions for violations of minimum health and safety standards.

Two other studies also suggest that higher administrative costs among multifacility chains do not lead to greater operating efficiencies. A Virginia study (Virginia JLARC, 1978) found that homes that are subsidiaries of chains generally paid the home office management fees, which averaged $50,266 per facility in 1976 and added about $400 per year to the cost of each bed. However, these fees did not reduce overall administrative costs or produce savings in other cost categories. The study concluded, "It appears that chain ownership offers no substantial cost savings to either the patient or the Medicaid program." Similarly, the Ohio Nursing Home Commission (1979) found that facilities with management fees had higher "other" administrative costs.[38]

Although there may be circumstances in which acquisition activity does not lead to higher costs—for example, if payers will not pay for property costs following any sale—available evidence of such cost increases is persuasive. Whether the increased facility costs that result from the chains' acquisition and merger activities are justified by improved quality or more equitable access is difficult to determine since empirical studies have not adequately addressed this issue. Further, since it appears that chains vary among themselves in their total costs, the distribution of their expenditures, their performance in terms of regulatory standards, and their admission policies, more sophisticated analyses are required to address these issues.

## Summary and Conclusions Regarding Cost

Most studies find nonprofit homes to have higher reported costs than for-profit homes. Although controls for other factors that lead to higher costs reduce the magnitude of this difference in costs, they do not eliminate them. Even when proxies for quality are introduced, as well as measures of patient case mix intensity, the differences remain. Thus, some analysts, like Koetting (1980), argue that proprietaries are more efficient—that is, they can attain a given level of quality at lower cost than the nonprofits. Indeed, our analysis of

the Ohio nursing homes could be seen as supporting this proposition.

This conclusion may be premature. Many studies use inadequate measures of variations in patient case mix intensity. This is critical, since case mix differences between facilities have been found to be the best predictor of variations in costs (Schlenker, 1984) and since some evidence suggests nonprofit facilities typically have a more intense case mix. Thus, case mix may account for some of the cost differences between nonprofit and for-profit facilities (Stassen and Bishop, 1983b; Schlenker et al., 1983; Schlenker and Shaughnessy, 1984). Also nonprofit facilities tend to have a higher proportion of private-pay patients, who tend to be more functionally dependent than Medicaid patients (Liu and Mossey, 1980; Schlenker and Shaughnessy, 1984). Thus, to the extent that prior studies have not captured all relevant dimensions of case mix variation, they may overestimate the cost differential associated with ownership per se.

In addition, the proxies for quality used in cost studies are at best only partial measures of quality and, at worst, are unrelated to either quality of care or quality of life. Host studies use resource inputs as proxies for quality, although studies have found a weak relationship between inputs and process and outcome measures of quality. Even code violations, the majority of which are reflections of deficiencies in structural and input standards, are inadequate measures of quality. Thus, some variation in costs may be associated with unmeasured differences in quality.

Finally, the few analyses that focused on "charges" by facilities—rather than only their reported costs—found little or no differences between for-profit and nonprofit nursing homes. Once the analysis included the proprietary firms' profit factor and total charges, the differences between ownership types diminished. While these results may be an artifact of the states studied or the time period, they raise interesting issues that should be addressed in future research before firm conclusions are reached about the economic efficiency of different ownership forms.[39]

## The Problem of Access to Care

Much of the impetus for Medicare and Medicaid came from a growing commitment among policymakers to equality of access to health care. In this spirit, the Presidential Commission for the Study of Ethical Problems in Medicine and Biomedical and Behavioral Research concluded in 1983 that society has an ethical obligation to assure access to an "adequate level" of health care. Further, federal regulations make it clear that the Department of Health and Human Services and the state Medicaid agencies have an obligation to ensure that program beneficiaries have equitable access to care. Nevertheless, access remains a serious problem for many people who are eligible for Medicare and Medicaid and need nursing home care.

### Discriminatory Practices: Patient "Creaming"

Discrimination takes many forms. Many nursing homes maintain separate waiting lists for individuals seeking admission—one for private-paying patients and another for Medicaid recipients.[40] Other homes require as a condition of admission that the patient and/or his or her family sign a contract promising to pay the facility privately (at whatever rate the facility determines) for periods ranging from 6 months to 3 years before the facility will accept Medicaid as payment.[41] For instance, a New Jersey task force estimated that 80 percent of the state nursing homes require fixed periods of private pay for up to 3 years (U.S. Senate Special Committee on Aging, 1984). Other facilities "discharge" or evict individuals when they exhaust their private resources and become eligible for Medicaid. Nursing homes have also evicted Medicaid recipients when a private-paying patient has sought admission (Ohio Nursing Home Commission, 1979; U.S. Senate Special Committee on Aging, 1984). Finally, ombudsmen charge that nursing homes also discriminate against Medicaid recipients in room assignments and services (U.S. Senate Special Committee on Aging, 1984).

Access to nursing home services is a particular problem for two groups: Medicaid patients and those individuals with "heavy care

needs" (Greenless et al., 1982; Schlenker, 1984; Scanlon, 1980a,b; Feder and Scanlon, 1980, 1982; Cotterill, 1983; Institute of Medicine, 1981; U.S. Senate Special Committee on Aging, 1984). The National Summary of State Nursing Home Ombudsman Reports for the United States reported in fiscal year 1982 that discrimination against Medicaid recipients or potential Medicaid recipients was identified as a major problem in 21 states and was the fourth most frequently mentioned problem out of 74 problems cited by the ombudsman programs.

In addition to discrimination based on payment source, nursing homes often discriminate against those individuals most in need of nursing home care. The GAO (1983b) summarized 11 studies conducted since 1979 and concluded that severe access problems and discrimination were occurring on the basis of patient "handicap." Individuals who required especially heavy care or substantial "hands-on" care, such as those persons suffering from Alzheimer's Disease and other related disorders, were "backed-up" in hospitals awaiting nursing home placement—even when there were empty nursing home beds in the community.

Access problems are particularly severe for individuals with dementia. Because such individuals are often defined as not requiring rehabilitative therapies or daily care from an RN, they generally do not qualify for Medicare or for "skilled care," which is reimbursed at a higher level in many states. They do, however, require substantial care and assistance with activities of daily living. This hands-on care and frequent supervision is costly for nursing homes even if provided by aides. As a result, nursing homes have an incentive to select from their waiting lists individuals with the fewest functional disabilities and with the least mental impairment. This incentive is particularly strong under reimbursement systems that provide the same Medicaid rate for every patient—regardless of the degree of physical and mental impairment.

Access problems of Medicaid recipients and heavy-care patients may become quality of care problems after they find nursing home placement. On the basis of an analysis of national data for 1969 and 1973, Scanlon (1980b) posits a "dual" market in which private-pay patients receive desired care (at the market price) while public-pay patients will receive care only after the private demand has been satisfied. The result is not only a dual market in terms of demand but also a dual market in terms of supply, with Medicaid patients having access to those homes least able to compete successfully for private-pay patients. Thus, it is not surprising that, as Schlenker (1984) notes: "Several . . . studies found higher quality . . . associated with a lower Medicaid share and lower overall occupancy rate, both of which suggest access barriers for Medicaid recipients."

The finding that Medicaid utilization rates are associated with lower quality of care is fairly consistent (Bishop, 1980). The Ohio Nursing Home Commission (1979) found that 75 percent of the "low quality" homes had very high percentages (80 to 100 percent) of Medicaid patients, while only one (4 percent) of the "high quality" homes had such a high percentage of Medicaid patients. The commission reported that

Both the Commission and the Ombudsman have received many complaints from relatives, hospital social workers, county (welfare) personnel, etc., about the difficulty of placing Medicaid patients in homes offering high quality care. Sadly, the Commission's study of a sample of homes providing either very good or very poor care confirmed this testimony . . . . The Commission concludes that *Ohio is facing the development of a two-class system of long-term health care*, with Medicaid recipients having ready access to care in only a few of the best homes and thus being forced to become patients in the state's worst homes.

In effect, discrimination makes the operation of substandard homes financially viable. With severely limited choice, such patients often have no option but to enter whatever nursing home will accept them, even though it may provide undesirable quality of care, for as Beverly Enterprises noted in an annual report to the SEC, "There is little, if any, competition in price, services, or quality with respect to Medicare and Medicaid patients" (Beverly Enterprises, 1980).

### Reasons for Discrimination

Private-pay patients are much more lucrative for nursing home owners because of Med-icare and Medicaid payment limits. Some limits have to do with whether particular costs are allowable. In other cases, some states set "ceilings" on reimbursable costs or employ prospective or flat-rate systems to pay homes a set amount per patient day. Often that rate is based on some percentage of the average reported costs of similar facilities and is independent of any one facility's costs of providing care. A "reasonable" payment rate may be set, as in some states, at the 60th percentile or lower of average costs for all facilities in a "class." Thus, Medicare and Medicaid provide nursing homes with relatively little price flexibility, while nursing homes are able to charge much higher rates to private-pay patients (Montgomery Securities, 1983).

Health planning limitations and moratoria on new nursing home bed construction may also facilitate discrimination by contributing to very high occupancy rates in nursing homes in most parts of the country. Occupancy rates of better than 95 percent are the norm. In addition, there are few alternatives to nursing home care for those people who need long-term care on a daily basis. This combination of tight supply and a relatively inelastic demand gives nursing homes much flexibility in setting charges to private-pay patients and, for good quality homes, the ability to discriminate and still maintain high occupancy rates.

Price data for private-pay patients, as compared to Medicaid and Medicare patients, is difficult to determine (Lane, 1984). If charges reported on Medicare cost reports are indicative of private-pay rates, the differential may be between 13 and 18 percent, although some estimates of the differential are as high as 20 percent (Lane, 1984). Montgomery Securities, using more current data, estimates that private-pay rates, on average, range up to 30 percent above Medicaid and Medicare rates. Based on its survey of nursing homes, Montgomery Securities (1983) reports the 1982 rates as shown in Table 12.

The analysts conclude private-pay patients are central to a nursing home's profitability. Thus, nursing homes have a strong financial incentive to discriminate against Medicaid patients in favor of private-pay patients. The Montgomery Securities analysts comment

**TABLE 12**   Nursing Home Rates by Payee for 1982

|  | Bed Size | | |
| --- | --- | --- | --- |
| Payee | 1–59 | 60–299 | 300 + |
| Medicaid SNF | $39.46 | $39.22 | $50.87 |
| Medicaid ICF | 32.78 | 30.96 | 42.30 |
| Medicare | 52.00-55.00 | 52.00-55.00 | 52.00-55.00 |
| Private-pay | 46.00-112.00 | 46.00-109.00 | 50.00-54.00 |

SOURCE: Montgomery Securities (1983).

The higher the percentage load of private pay patients in the home's mix, the greater the nursing home's ability to cost and price shift, and the greater the prospects of increased profits (Montgomery Securities, 1983).

## Ownership and Discrimination

Evidence suggests that all nursing homes that can attract private-pay patients discriminate in their favor and against Medicaid patients. Nonprofit homes and facilities that are part of some of the major proprietary nursing home chains seem most successful in achieving a relatively high percentage of private-pay patients. Most empirical analyses have found that nonprofit facilities have a lower than average Medicaid utilization rate. While Winn (1974) found no significant relationship between type of ownership and rate of public assistance patients in Washington state nursing homes, most other analyses have found an association between nonprofit status and a lower Medicaid share. Gottesman (1974) found that proprietary facilities were more likely to serve Medicaid patients. Brooks and Hoffman (1978) found no difference in Medicaid utilization rates in SNFs based on ownership, but there was a significant difference in ICFs. Among the nonprofit ICFs in this study, the Medicaid utilization rate was 57 percent while in the proprietary homes the rate was 71 percent. Studies in Ohio (Ohio Nursing Home Commission, 1979) and California (Vladeck, 1980) show the proportion of Medicaid patients to be higher in for-profit than in nonprofit facilities. In Texas the pattern was the same, as Table 13 indicates.

Several of the major nursing home chains also have relatively low percentages of Med-

icaid recipients. For some, this is the product of a deliberate strategy. Care Enterprises (1984), for example, notes in its report to the SEC that

Care believes that rehabilitative services at its SNFs are relatively more profitable than other nursing services and have enhanced its ability to attract private and Medicare patients.

This chain reported that in 1982 the company was able to increase its revenues quite substantially over the prior year via increases in billing rates and changes in the mix of private, Medicare, and Medicaid patients. In 1982, Care Enterprises had an average Medicaid utilization rate of 60 percent, with 22 percent private pay and 16 percent Medicare.[42]

Care Enterprises is not alone in seeking to increase its private-pay patient load and decrease Medicaid utilization. Hillhaven/National Medical Enterprises is also concentrating on keeping a "favorable" mix of private-pay patients (Punch, 1984). However, the most aggressive large chain in this regard is Manor Care. In Ohio, Manor Care attempted to evict individuals whose care was paid for by Medicaid during the late 1970s (Ohio Nursing Home Commission, 1979). More recently Manor Care has "targeted" its acquisitions, purchasing facilities that already have high private-pay utilization rates and selling off homes with too many Medicaid patients. In 1982, for instance, Manor Care sold 14 facilities because they did not have sufficiently high ratios of private to Medicaid patients. As Manor Care (1981) noted in its report to the SEC, "As a general rule, the margin of profits is higher with private patients." The report continued,

Manor Care attempts to locate and operate its nursing centers in a manner designed to attract patients

TABLE 13 Average Percentage of Medicaid Days of Service by Owner Type, Texas (percentage)

| Type of Facility | 1978 | 1979 | 1980 | 1981 |
|---|---|---|---|---|
| All facilities | 77.7 | 79.1 | 78.5 | 77.1 |
| For-profit facilities | 80.0 | 80.6 | 80.6 | 79.3 |
| Nonprofit facilities | 64.7 | 68.0 | 65.4 | 61.9 |

SOURCE: Moden (1982).

who pay directly to the facilities for services without benefit of any government assistance program.

Evidence of its success in attracting private-pay patients and the greater price flexibility they have with these patients can be seen in the data displayed in Table 14.

### Summary and Conclusions Regarding Access

There is substantial evidence that Medicaid recipients—some two-thirds of all long-stay nursing home patients—and those with heavy care needs experience discrimination in access to nursing homes and that such discrimination places Medicaid patients disproportionately in homes that provide the lowest quality of care. The evidence is also clear that nonprofit homes provide the fewest beds on the average to Medicaid patients and that some nursing home chains systematically seek to reduce the proportion of Medicaid patients in their facilities.

Further, there is evidence that suggests discrimination and that a facility's patient mix has quality implications. Caswell and Cleverley (1978, 1983) argue that there is a differential effect of ownership control status on the relationship of Medicaid utilization to cost and quality. They found that, in general, increasing Medicaid utilization in a facility is associated with lower costs, particularly in patient care expenses. However, they found that for-profit facilities react more strongly than nonprofits to increasing Medicaid utilization. The nonprofits appear to reduce patient care expenditures far less than do for-profits as the proportion of Medicaid patients in the facility increases. Thus, while the evident discrimination is a matter of concern in terms of freedom of choice for consumers, it may also negatively affect the health, well-being, and quality of life of vast numbers of the aged and disabled.

### SUMMARY AND CONCLUSIONS

The nursing home industry's growth has resulted from a multiplicity of factors. The infusion of public dollars, a growth in need, and the interplay of policies aimed at other institutions have aided that growth. In the process of growing, the industry has also fundamentally changed. Some of the most profound changes include an increasingly medically oriented setting, a shift from smaller to larger facilities, a move away from government-owned and voluntary (not-for-profit) homes to pro-

TABLE 14 Proportion of Inpatient Days to Revenues by Payee—Manor Care (percentage)

| Type of Payer | 1980 | 1981 | 1982 |
|---|---|---|---|
| Private-pay patients | 60/66 | 61/65 | 54/61 |
| Medicaid patients | 32/23 | 30/25 | 36/26 |
| Medicare patients | 7/8 | 8/8 | 10/13 |

SOURCE: Manor Care 10K reports filed with the SEC for 1980, 1981, and 1982.

prietary ones, and a growing concentration of ownership in multifacility chains that are diversifying vertically and horizontally. Most recently, we see diversification of nursing homes into other areas of long-term care (e.g., retirement or life care community home health, durable medical equipment) and increasing participation of hospitals in the direct provision of long-term care ("swing beds" and certification of hospital wings as nursing homes). In many ways, these changes in the nursing home industry simply mirror developments in the wider health care sector. Throughout the American health care system, there is an increasing trend toward corporatization. The emergence of the large, multisystem corporate health care providers seems to herald a new era in American health care. These developments are altering not only the structure of decision making and locus of power, but perhaps the structure and performance of the health care system as well.

## Summary of the Findings on Quality, Cost, and Access

Perhaps the most consistent finding of empirical studies and analyses of state level data is that, on the average, nonprofit nursing homes provide better quality of care and quality of life to residents than do the for-profits. Certainly there are some qualifications to this conclusion. The size and patient composition of a nursing home, for instance, may influence the performance of the facility, independent of its ownership, in ways that affect quality. Further, the indicators most commonly used are generally viewed as inadequate measures of quality of care and life, although they do appear to capture some important dimensions of variations in quality. In addition, it is clearly true that many proprietary nursing homes provide excellent care, and that some nonprofit facilities provide poor care. Despite such qualifications, however, the evidence for the superiority of nonprofit owners seems conclusive.

The scant evidence about the relative performance of the nursing home chains, however, is more mixed. Studies using a national sample of facilities have generally found no differences between the chains' performance and that of other nursing homes. Data that

allow us to disaggregate the chains into large, multistate chains and individually owned, single state chains suggest that the multistate chains, at least in Ohio, perform more acceptably than either nonchain proprietaries or individually owned proprietary chains. Analysis of data from Texas, however, suggests that there may be significant differences in performance among the major multistate nursing home chains. Some large chains may provide very poor care, while others seem to provide acceptable, even very good care. This suggests that all nursing home chains do not pursue identical organizational goals and exhibit similar behaviors. Thus, the use of national or state level data that do not disaggregate the chains into more precise ownership forms, and even possibly individual corporate identities, may not yield useful information on the relative performance of various types of owners.

The evidence we do have about some of the nursing home chains—particularly the largest ones—does raise some serious concerns about cost, quality, and access. The evident ability and willingness of some major nursing home chains to finance their growth by increased allocation of funds to property costs and reduced expenditures on food, staffing, and social services is a cause for concern. The consistent pattern among many of the most rapidly expanding chains of spending proportionately less than the average (and less than nonprofits) on direct patient care and more on property and administration/home office fees raises the specter of growth and increased profitability occurring at the expense of the public purse and patient welfare. Further, the general pattern of differences among nonprofits and proprietary nursing homes, with the nonprofits consistently spending proportionately more on patient care and the for-profits spending more on property and administration, suggests that the cost of for-profit health care may be quite high, particularly for the most vulnerable members of our society—the infirm and disabled elderly.

While the findings about the impact of ownership on quality seem relatively clear, data about variations in cost and "efficiency" are more difficult to interpret. In general, empirical studies find that nonprofits are more costly. Controlling for other factors known to affect costs, such as size, location, and so on, reduces the magnitude of the difference in costs between nonprofits and proprietary nursing homes, but these other variables do not eliminate this difference. Even when proxies for quality and the patient case mix are introduced, some difference remains. Thus, some analysts argue that proprietary nursing homes are more efficient—that is, they can attain a given level of "quality" at a lower cost than the nonprofits.

These findings are subject to serious qualification. First, most of the studies use inadequate measures of patient case mix. In addition, the proxies for quality that have been used in these cost studies are at best only partial measures. Thus, some portion of the variation in costs between nonprofit facilities and for-profit nursing homes may be associated with unmeasured variations in case mix and quality. Finally, studies tend to focus on reported costs without including the profit factor or the charges to private-pay patients. Thus, the magnitude of the differences between the two ownership types is difficult to gauge accurately. These issues should be addressed in future research before firm conclusions are reached about the economic efficiency of different ownership forms.

The findings about accessibility for public-pay (Medicaid) and "heavy care" patients are uniformly disheartening. Available evidence suggests active discrimination by nearly all homes having a queue of individuals desiring admittance. Those homes that seem to practice discrimination most consistently are the nonprofits and some of the major proprietary corporate chains. Further, achieving a higher proportion of private-pay patients is the announced policy of most of the large, publicly held nursing home chains. To the degree that this is implemented and these chains expand their holdings, equity of access will become an even greater problem. What the nation faces is the entrenchment of a two-class system of long-term care, with the elderly who need the most care and those have become impoverished in paying for health care having ready access only to those facilities that provide the lowest quality of care.

## Implications for the Hospital Sector

The data presented in this paper suggest that the development of for-profit nursing homes and their dominance in this sector has gone far to meet demand that would not otherwise have been met. But, this emergence and expansion has had significant costs, particularly in terms of the quality of long-term care. In an arena of frequently low levels of payment, proprietary nursing homes have been profitable, but quality and access problems have been persistent.

In general, observers have felt that the problems of quality assurance and cost control in the nursing home sector were significantly different from those seen in the hospital sector. Quality control mechanisms that are thought to be effective in other health care sectors are largely absent in long-term care. First, long-term care patients are largely ineffective as consumers. They are disadvantaged in making informed initial choices, switching to other providers when dissatisfied, or using medical malpractice or consumer protection statutes to secure high quality of care. Moreover, most lack family who could serve as effective advocates in their stead.

Second, the usual professional checks on quality that are thought to exist in hospitals do not exist in nursing homes. Physicians are largely an absent or impotent force for quality control (U.S. Senate Special Committee on Aging, 1975a; N. Rango, personal communication, 1985). In addition, nursing homes have lower staff-to-patient ratios for direct-care staff than hospitals and place greater reliance on untrained aides and orderlies who provide 80 to 90 percent of all patient care. Many nursing homes do not have an RN on staff, and most have a single RN for only 40 hours per week (B. Cornelius, Office of Research and Demonstrations, Health Care Financing Review, U.S. Department of Health and Human Services, personal communication, 1985). Thus, trained and experienced health care professionals play a much less significant role in the control and daily operation of nursing homes than in hospitals. This difference in resource inputs has significant implications both for the provision of care and for the ability of nursing homes to develop and implement quality monitoring and assurance programs.

Third, there are significant structural differences between hospitals and nursing homes. Hospitals are still largely not-for-profit institutions and are presumed to operate under a set of professional and ethical norms that constrain their behavior to the benefit of patients. Nursing homes, however, are largely proprietary. As businesses, they must calculate the scope and quality of the services they provide with an eye constantly turned toward profitability goals.

Fourth, state and federal policies designed to contain long-term care costs may contain powerful incentives inimical to the provision of high quality care. These are primarily cost containment measures adopted in the last few years, such as prospective payment systems, reimbursement ceilings, and moratoria on new nursing home bed construction. For nursing homes with sizable populations of patients supported by Medicaid, such reimbursement policies contain incentives that tend to inhibit admission of those most in need of care and that may encourage reductions in staffing and food. Under prospective reimbursement systems that have been instituted in a number of states, payment rates are set in advance and homes are allowed to retain the difference between the rate and what they actually spend. Operating at the same level of quality but more efficiently is clearly the most socially desirable way of achieving profits in such a system; however, shifting to a less-costly-to-care-for patient mix is another way for facilities to achieve profits under such a system.[43] Reducing the scope and quality of services is a third way for homes to achieve profits. Reducing variable expenditures—such as staffing, activities, and food—is the simplest way for homes to hold their expenditures below prospective rates. Thus, discrimination and reductions in the level and quality of services are two ways in which homes may respond to these cost containment initiatives. The evidence on discrimination is clear, and there is some evidence that many nursing homes, the proprietaries in particular, may be reducing quality in response to severe reimbursement constraints (Schlenker, 1984; Birnbaum et al., 1979, 1981; Caswell and Cleverley, 1978; Holahan, 1984).

Finally, restrictive health planning and more stringent reimbursement policies have resulted in slowed construction of new nursing homes. In addition, there are few community-based services that can substitute for nursing home care. Because demand for long-term care exceeds supply, homes have little incentive to compete for Medicaid patients by offering higher quality. The only competition along quality lines occurs among homes that seek to maintain a high percentage of the more profitable private-paying patients. Thus, competition among providers is an unreliable mechanism for assuring quality in nursing homes.

Given changes in the structure of hospital ownership and in payment mechanisms, some of the apparent differences between the hospital and nursing home sectors may diminish. The emergence of a strong proprietary sector and of hospital chains that are growing vertically and horizontally represents a striking similarity to developments in the nursing home industry. Further, increasing concern with escalating hospital costs and the development of Medicare's prospective payment system are very similar to prior developments in the long-term care sector. This convergence of an emerging proprietary sector and tightened reimbursement policies could produce some of the negative consequences associated with the long-term care sector.

To a large extent, three factors are likely to determine the ultimate outcome of such developments: (1) the response of health professionals to a changing environment; (2) the response of patients and their willingness and ability to become more effective consumers; and (3) the ability of regulatory and peer review agencies to exert a strong influence for quality assurance. At the least, such developments suggest the need for more sophisticated and substantial quality assurance activities by public and private agencies to monitor accurately the effects on quality and access and to ensure that unacceptable reductions in quality and access do not occur.

**NOTES**

[1] Both Medicare- and Medicaid-eligible patients pay for part of their nursing home care; these individuals

must make copayments (Medicare) or devote nearly all of their income for care before Medicaid pays for the additional nursing home charges. In addition, private-pay patients tend to pay somewhat higher rates than Medicare and Medicaid patients. These two factors explain why half the dollars but a larger proportion of the patients are accounted for under government plans.

[2]This phrase is so apt that I've stolen it directly from Vladeck (1980).

[3]Indeed, these homes for the aged, dominated by immigrant and religious groups, are the forebears of the large, voluntary homes of today.

[4]Even in the 1930s, there was widespread concern and dissatisfaction with conditions in many proprietary nursing homes. The facilities were often aged and dilapidated houses, farms, or small motels that had been converted to use as a nursing home. Nursing and medical care were minimal at best, and reports of patient abuse were widespread. These prompted calls for reform—for state licensing and inspection. But the dilemma that still plagues the regulatory system arose then—with a shortage of facilities, the imposition of stricter standards would mean closing some, perhaps many, facilities, aggravating the bed shortage. Like modern regulatory officials, most states chose education and exhortation in an attempt to improve the facilities rather than development and enforcement of stricter standards of care (Vladeck, 1980; McClure, 1968; Thomas, 1969).

[5]One of the major forces contributing to the growth of nursing homes is the dramatic increase in the number and proportion of the population that is aged. The proportion of the U.S. population 65 years of age and older has increased from 4.4 percent in 1900 to 11.7 percent in 1983. Moreover, the projections are that by the end of the century, between 35 million and 37 million people, at least 13.1 percent of the population, will be aged. Moreover, the fastest growing cohort of the population is the very old—those most at risk in terms of needing long-term care services (Manton, 1984; Torrey, 1984; U.S. Bureau of the Census, 1983). Only with the availability of financial assistance, however, is this need translated into demand for nursing home care, since the majority of the aged who actually need long-term care cannot afford to pay for the care they require.

[6]Growth in bed supply has leveled off for a variety of reasons since the mid-1970s.

[7]For 1984, only 49 publicly held nursing home chains are listed with the SEC. An additional number of multifacility nursing home chains are owned and operated as subsidiaries of hospital chains.

[8]There are basically two types of nursing home residents—the "short-stay" patients whose average length of stay is less than 3 months, and the "long-stay" residents whose average LOS is more than 2.5 years (Liu and Mossey, 1980). While the short-stay residents constitute a sizeable proportion of admissions, on any given day the "long-stayers" are the majority of nursing home patients.

[9]In addition, ongoing debate and shifts in policy about whether public programs will reimburse higher capital or property costs that result from sales/purchases of nursing homes is also likely to affect the rate of chain growth.

[10]Active imposition of the LSC was delayed for several years in order to give facilities ample opportunity to come into compliance with what is fundamentally a federal fire safety code.

[11]HEW was renamed the U.S. Department of Health and Human Services (HHS) in 1981.

[12]During the early years of a mortgage, most of the payment is for interest on the loan; relatively little is applied to the principal. Depreciation payments by the state, however, are usually calculated on a 20- to 30-year life expectancy for a new nursing home and made on a straight-line basis. Thus, under most of the 1970s' cost-related systems, in the early years of a mortgage, the depreciation payment from the state to the facility exceeds the amount the facility actually has to pay the mortgage holder as the principal payment. (Interest is a direct pass-through.) The result is a positive cash flow to the facility during those years and an incentive to sell the facility as a depreciation payment from the state approaches the amount of the mortgage that is payment toward the principal (see Baldwin, 1980). Many states found nursing homes responding to this incentive, with proprietary facilities being sold as often as every three to four years, providing indirect profits to the facilities and increased costs (but not services) to the states (Ohio Nursing Home Commission, 1979; Washington Senate, 1978). This made many individual owners willing, even eager, to sell. Often owners would sell the facility to a chain and then lease it back to operate (see also Shulman and Galanter, 1976). For instance, in 1983, Beverly, the largest chain, leased more than half its facilities, and this is fairly common (Beverly Enterprises, 10K report filed with the SEC, 1983).

[13]One of the prevailing myths about long-term care is that the elderly are in nursing homes because their families have abandoned them. This is simply untrue—unless dying is viewed as abandonment. Long-term care is predominantly an issue involving widowed or single elderly women. Half of all nursing home residents have no immediate relatives living in close proximity. Those patients who do have relatives tend to be very functionally dependent (in terms of needing assistance in the activities of daily living, such as dressing, eating, walking, and toileting) and also mentally impaired (Barney, 1974; Liu and Mossey, 1980).

[14]For example, Beverly Enterprises' operation of 13 percent of the facilities in Texas (a low-rate, prospective reimbursement state) has average net revenues per patient day that are 2 percent lower than the average

for all Texas facilities but net income that is 22 percent higher.

[15]Some observers, such as Scanlon and Feder (1980) cite "inadequacy" of return as a potentially more important cause of declining growth. Data on the profitability of nursing homes, particularly the "chains" call this into question (U.S. Senate Special Committee on Aging, 1984).

[16]Many reimbursement systems exclude nonprofit owners from return on equity—a "profit" factor. Thus, nonprofit providers may receive less from Medicaid (and Medicare) programs than for-profit entities with comparable costs.

[17]The Tax Equity and Financial Responsibility Act of 1982 (TEFRA) eliminated some of the future benefits of ERTA.

[18]For instance, CENCO, one of the larger chains in 1979-1980, was the target of a major Wall Street battle and was eventually acquired by Manor Care. National Health Enterprises, the sixth largest nursing home chain in 1981 and Flagg Industries (number 20) were acquired by Hillhaven/National Medical Enterprises. Mediplex (number 8), Commercial Management (number 11), and Beacon Hill (number 21) have been acquired by or merged with Beverly Enterprises, which also acquired other small-to-medium size chains (e.g., P&H Enterprises, Inc.; Consolidated Liberty; PMG, Inc.).

[19]Demand is a function of need and ability and willingness to pay.

[20]Two-thirds of all middle-income patients in nursing homes spend their life savings within 2 years of admission and become Medicaid patients (U.S. Senate Special Committee on Aging, 1984).

[21]It is well to note, as Vladeck (1980) does, that these institutions do labor under some incentives that are similar to those of the for-profits. "The voluntaries may not be profit-maximizers, but they invariably operate under the constraint of trying at least to break even" (Vladeck, 1980). They may, however, select different methods than the for-profits to break even.

[22]Two such chains report (in their filings with the SEC) that the decision to expend funds upgrading newly purchased facilities is part of a corporate strategy aimed at attracting more private-pay and Medicare patients—who are more lucrative for the nursing home.

[23]Again, this may vary by chain. In addition, the record of Beverly Enterprises in Texas indicates that it has a disproportionate number of significant violations. Indeed, there is some evidence that Beverly does not promptly correct deficiencies when cited, since it has received a disproportionate share of punitive actions for failure to correct violations.

[24]Schlenker (1984), in reviewing studies on the relationship between costs, reimbursement policies and quality of care, argues that RN hours and dietary costs may be good indicators of quality. "A more intense

case mix and/or higher quality care should require some combination of more nursing hours per patient day, a greater ratio . . . RN or . . . LPN hours to aide hours, and possibly higher wage rates to reflect higher skill levels. . . . (Higher dietary costs may also be related) since nutritional adequacy is important to patients' overall health."

[25]While the high-quality homes outspent the low-quality homes on these items, the low-quality facilities had higher expenditures on administrator salaries, legal and accounting fees, and motor vehicles; they also seem to substitute LPNs for RNs.

[26]Nonprofits tended to have more beds, more buildings, and more floors in the building; they also tended to have more single rooms, more ward rooms (with five or more patients per room), and more bathrooms.

[27]An alternative explanation is that these facilities offer such low quality of care that they can attract only those individuals with no other choices, such as the elderly poor and disabled without family or other social supports (see Greene and Monahan, 1981; Ohio Nursing Home Commission, 1979).

[28]The Fottler et al. (1981) study used multiple regression analysis to study the relationship between profits per patient day (ppd) and four measures of quality: (1) skilled nursing hours ppd; (2) nonnursing hours ppd; (3) total nursing and nonnursing hours ppd, and (4) staffing ratios. They argue that these are useful surrogates for the quality of patient care and found that "profitability increases as the service intensity (quantity and quality of labor inputs) decreases." The study focused on 43 nursing homes in California.

[29]The commission also reported a strong correlation between the level of profitability and lower expenditures on food, dietary salaries, medical supplies, nurse's aides, medical and rehabilitative care, electricity, and housekeeping.

[30]Elwell notes that although some of the spending differences do not appear large, the figures represent per patient per day expenditures. He observes that reductions in such spending, even relatively small ones, can result in substantial savings for the facility. For instance, "by spending 35¢ less ppd for nursing, the average SNF (which in New York had 44,867 inpatient days in 1976) could save over $15,700 per year" (Elwell, 1984).

[31]Of those 45 facilities, 37 were earning profits on the Medicaid rate alone.

[32]Koetting also concluded that proprietary homes were more efficient—that is, they were able to attain a given level of quality at a lower cost than the nonprofit facilities. In addition, he found that cost and quality of care were only weakly related (Koetting, 1980).

[33]The performance of Beverly Enterprises, one of the major chains operating facilities in California, was particularly poor. According to an analysis of the California Health Facilities Commission data by the AFL-

CIO (1983a), "Beverly's . . . performance was abysmal. For 35 homes listed as belonging to Beverly, the average number of citations (per facility) came to 2.31, with 9 of the 35 exceeding the California standards . . . to rank among the worst homes in the state."

[34] The department does not maintain a listing by type of owner; therefore, the listing of facilities receiving some form of punitive action has to be matched against a separate ownership file. The control (ownership) type of four facilities terminated from the program could not be determined from these files.

[35] The study, however, did not find a relationship between staff ratios (resource inputs) and other quality of care measures. "The correlations are found all uniformly insignificant" (Lee, 1984).

[36] In Ohio, the multistate chains were Manor Care, Hillhaven, HCF (now Health Care and Retirement Fund, Inc.), Medicenters, and Americare. The data are derived from cost reports submitted to the Ohio Department of Public Welfare by 579 (77 percent) of the nursing homes participating in the Ohio Medicaid program in 1977. Eighty-five percent were for-profit facilities. Of these, 78 percent were operated by individual owners; 16 percent were owned by small, intrastate chains; and 8.5 percent (32 facilities) were part of large multistate nursing home chains.

[37] This seems to be borne out by anecdotal testimony and evidence presented to and gathered by the Ohio Nursing Home Commission. The major stockholder of the largest intrastate chain was indicted for Medicaid fraud and was the subject of several health department compliance actions. Two other intrastate chains had an unchallenged reputation for providing truly vile care.

[38] Management fees are significantly positively correlated with *increased* spending on other administrative salaries; office supplies and printing; communication; travel and other motor vehicle; advertising and public relations; legal and accounting fees; and other administrative . . . services" (Ohio Nursing Home Commission, 1979).

[39] Such studies should also take into account the variety of services that are provided under the daily rate and are incorporated in costs, as well as noting those services for which additional charges are billed to patients.

[40] Since Medicare pays for only about 2 percent of all expenditures on nursing home care, problems Medicare beneficiaries experience have not been as well-documented; moreover, they may be a result of the unwillingness of many homes to meet the higher certification and audit standards associated with Medicare rather than a result of the payment rate or disability of patients.

[41] ". . . two-thirds of all middle income patients in nursing homes spend their life savings within 2 years of admission and become Medicaid patients" (U.S. Senate Special Committee on Aging, 1984).

[42] The data are far from precise, but the average Medicaid utilization nationwide appears to be between 64 and 70 percent. In some states, of course, it is much higher, as in North Carolina where 89 percent of the patients receive assistance from Medicaid.

[43] One of the most common myths is that quality is low because profits are low or nonexistent. Research does not support this myth (Ohio Nursing Home Commission, 1979). Most for-profit homes earn healthy returns. It is the incentives inherent in reimbursment systems that seem to affect quality, not merely the rate, although clearly reimbursement rates must be sufficient to cover genuine, reasonable costs if quality of care is to be achieved (Schlenker, 1984).

## REFERENCES AND BIBLIOGRAPHY

AFL-CIO, Executive Council (1977) *Nursing Homes and the Nation's Elderly: America's Nursing Homes Profit in Human Misery.* Bal Harbour, Fla.: Statement and report adopted by the AFL-ClO.

AFL-CIO, Service Employees International Union (1983a) *Beverly Enterprises in Michigan: A Case Study of Corporate Takeover of Health Care Resources.* Washington, D.C.: The Food and Beverage Trades Department.

AFL-CIO, Service Employees International Union (1983b). *Beverly Enterprises Patient Care Record.* Washington, D.C.: The Food and Beverage Trades Department, AFL-CIO, January 27.

Aging Health Policy Center (1983) Unpublished Telephone Survey of States, Nursing Home Supply Data. San Francisco: The University of California.

American Association of Homes for the Aging (1981) *Factors Influencing the Provision of Non-institutional Long-Term Care by Homes for the Aging.* (Contract 18-p-976-24/3-01) Washington, D.C.: Health Care Financing Administration.

Arrow, K. J. (1979) The limitations of the profit motive. *Challenge* 22(Sept./Oct.):23-37.

Baldwin, C. Y. (1980) Nursing home finance: Capital incentives under Medicaid. Discussion paper, Brandeis University Health Policy Consortium, Waltham, Massachusetts.

Baldwin, C. Y., and C. E. Bishop (1983) Return to nursing home investment: Issues for public policy. A paper prepared at the Brandeis University Health Policy Consortium, Waltham, Massachusetts.

Barney, J. (1974) Community presence as a key to quality of care in nursing homes. *American Journal of Public Health* 64(3):265-268.

Beattie, W. M., and J. Bullock (1964) Evaluating services and personnel in facilities for the aged. In M. Leeds and H. Shore, eds., *Geriatric Institutional Management.* New York: Putnam.

Beverly Enterprises (1980) 10K Report to the Securities and Exchange Commission, Washington, D.C.

Birnbaum, H., C. Bishop, G. Jensen, A. J. Lee, and D. Wilson (1979) *Reimbursement Strategies for Nursing Home Care: Developmental Cost Studies.* Cambridge, Mass.: Abt Associates. (DHEW Contract No. 600-77-0068).

Birnbaum, H., C. Bishop, A. J. Lee, and G. Jensen (1981) Why do nursing home costs vary? The determinants of nursing home costs. *Medical Care* 19(11):1095-1107.

Birney, J. M. (1981) *The Growing Market in Long Term Care and Retirement Living.* New York: Furman, Selz, Mager, Dietz, and Birney.

Bisenius, M. F. (1984) *Quality of Health Care in Iowa Nursing Homes; Results from the ICF Outcome Oriented Survey, December 1, 1982-November 30, 1983.* Des Moines: Iowa State Department of Health, Division of Health Facilities.

Bishop, C. (1980) Nursing home behavior under cost-related reimbursement. Discussion paper (DP-9, revised), Brandeis University, University Health Policy Consortium, Waltham, Massachusetts.

Blyskal, J. (1981) Gray gold. *Forbes*, Nov. 23, pp. 80-81.

Brody, E. M. (1977) Environmental factors in dependency. In A. N. Exton-Smith and J. G. Evans, eds. *Care of the Elderly: Meeting the Challenge of Dependency.* New York: Grune and Stratton.

Brooks, C. H., and J. A. Hoffman (1978) Type of ownership and Medicaid use of nursing-care beds. *Journal of Community Health* 3(3):236-244.

Butler, R. N. (1976) We should end commercialization in the care of older people in the U.S.: Some thoughts. *International Journal of Aging and Human Development* 7:87-90.

California Commission on State Government Organization and Economy (1983) *The Bureaucracy of Care: Continuing Policy Issues for Nursing Home Services and Regulation.* Sacramento.

California Health Facilities Commission (1982) Economic criteria for health planning, FY 1981-1982/1982-1983. In *Long Term Care Facility Effectiveness Standards.* Sacramento.

Care Enterprises (1984) 10K Report to the Securities and Exchange Commission, Washington, D.C.

Caswell, J., and W. Cleverley (1978) *Final Report: Cost Analysis of Ohio Nursing Homes.* Columbus: Ohio Department of Health.

Caswell, R. J., and W. Cleverley (1983) Cost analysis of the Ohio nursing home industry. *Health Services Research* 18(Fall):359-382.

Cohen, J. (1983) *Public Programs Financing Long Term Care.* Washington, D.C.: National Governors Association.

Cotterill, P. G. (1983) Provider incentives under alternative reimbursement systems. In R. J. Vogel and H. C. Palmer, eds. *Long-Term Care: Perspectives from*

*Research and Demonstrations.* Washington, D.C.: Health Care Financing Administration.

Covaleski, M. A., and C. J. Davis (1981) Capital maintenance and equity erosion in the nursing home industry: A study in one state. *The Journal of Long-Term Care Administration* (Fall):11-24.

Cyr, A. B. (1983) Proxy case mix measures for nursing homes. *Inquiry* 20(Winter):350-360.

Doty, P., K. Liu, and J. Weiner (1985) An overview of long-term care. *Healthcare Financing Review* 6(3):69-78.

Dunlop, B. (1979) *The Growth of Nursing Home Care.* Lexington, Mass.: Lexington Books.

Elliott, J. R., Jr. (1969) No tired blood: Nursing home operators are long on enthusiasm, short on experience. *Barron's*, March 24.

Elwell, F. (1984) The effects of ownership on institutional services. Unpublished paper, Department of Sociology and Anthropology, Murray State University, Murray, Kentucky.

Etzioni, A., and P. Doty (1976) Profit in not-for-profit corporations: The example of health care. *Political Science Quarterly* 91(Fall):433-453.

Fackelmann, K. (1985) Manor Care chain's large profits a result of wooing wealthy patients. *Modern Healthcare* 15(February):146-148.

Feder, J., and W. Scanlon (1980) Regulating the nursing home bed supply. *Milbank Memorial Fund Quarterly Health and Society* 58(January):54-58.

Feder, J., and W. Scanlon (1981) *Medicare and Medicaid Patients' Access to Skilled Nursing Facilities.* A background report to the Health Care Financing Administration. Washington, D.C.: The Urban Institute. November.

Feder, J., and W. Scanlon (1982) The underused benefit: Medicare's coverage of nursing home care. *Milbank Memorial Fund Quarterly/Health and Society* 70:1152-1161.

Fottler, M. D., H. L. Smith, and W. L. James (1981) Profits and patient care quality in nursing homes: Are they compatible? *The Gerontologist* 21(5):532-538.

Fraundorf, K. (1977) Competition and public policy in the nursing home industry. *Journal of Economic Issues* 11(September):601-634.

GAO (U.S. General Accounting Office) (1979) *Problems in Auditing Medicaid Nursing Home Chains.* Washington, D.C.: U.S. Government Printing Office.

GAO (1982) *Preliminary Findings on Patient Characteristics and State Medicaid Expenditures for Nursing Home Care.* Washington, D.C.: U.S. Government Printing Office.

GAO (1983a) *Hospital Merger Increased Medicare and Medicaid Payments for Capital Costs.* Washington, D.C.: U.S. Government Printing Office.

GAO (1983b) *Medicaid and Nursing Home Care: Cost Increases and the Need for Services Are Creating Prob-*

*lems for the States and the Elderly.* Washington, D.C.: U.S. Government Printing Office.

Gettlin, R. (1984) Medicare, Medicaid to pay hospitals $218 million. *Durham Morning Herald*, March 21, p. 5B.

Gibson, R. M. (1979) National health expenditures, 1978. *Health Care Financing Review* 1-36.

Gottesman, L. E. (1974) Nursing home performance as related to resident traits, ownership, size, and source of payment. *American Journal of Public Health* 64:269-276.

Greene, V. L., and D. Monahan (1981) Structure and operational factors affecting quality of patient care in nursing homes. *Public Policy* 29:399-415.

Greenless, J. S., Marshall, J. M., and Yett, D. E. (1982) Nursing home admissions policies under reimbursement. *The Bell Journal of Economics* 13(Spring):93-106.

Greenwald, S., and M. W. Lin (1971) Intercorrelations of data on nursing homes. *The Gerontologist* 11:337-340.

Grimaldi, P. L. (1982) *Medicaid Reimbursement of Nursing Home Care.* Washington, D.C.: American Enterprise Institute for Public Policy Research.

Harel, Z. (1981) Quality of care, congruence and well-being among institutionalized aged. *The Gerontologist* 21(5):523-531.

Harrington, C. (1984) Public policy and the nursing home industry. *International Journal of Health Services* 14(3):481-490.

Harrington, C., and L. Grant (1985) *Nursing Home Bed Supply, Access and Quality of Care.* San Francisco: University of California at San Francisco, Aging Health Policy Center.

Harrington, C., and J. H. Swan (1984) Institutional long-term care services. In C. Harrington, R. J. Newcomer, and C. L. Estes, eds. *Long-Term Care of the Elderly: Public Policy Issues.*

Harrington, C., R. J. Newcomer, and C. L. Estes (1984) *Long-Term Care for the Elderly: Public Policy Issues.* Beverly Hills, Calif.: Sage Publications.

Harris, M. (1981) *American Now: The Anthropology of a Changing Culture.* New York: Simon and Schuster.

Hawes, C. (1976) Ownership and profits in the nursing home industry. Draft memo to Val Halamandaris, U.S. Senate Subcommittee on Long-Term Care.

Hawes, C. (1978) *Vertical and horizontal concentration of ownership and interlocking relationships among the major nursing home chains.* Memo and presentation to the Inspector-General, Department of Health, Education, and Welfare.

Hawes, C. (1983) Quality assurance in long-term care: Major problems and issues. A briefing paper prepared for the National Academy of Sciences Institute of Medicine Committee on Nursing Home Regulation (November).

Himmelstein, D. U., A. A. Jones, and S. Woolhandler (1983) Hypernatremic dehydration in nursing home patients: An indicator of neglect. *Journal of the American Geriatrics Society* (August).

Holahan, J. (1984) *Nursing Home Care Under Alternative Patient-Related Reimbursement Systems.* Washington, D.C.: The Urban Institute (September).

Holmberg, R. H., and N. A. Anderson (1968) Implications of ownership for nursing home care. *Medical Care* 6:300-307.

Illinois Legislative Investigating Commission (1983) *Regulation and Funding of Illinois Nursing Homes.* Springfield: Illinois Legislature.

Institute of Medicine (1981) *Health Care in a Context of Civil Rights.* Washington, D.C.: National Academy Press.

Jazwiecki, T. (1984) Medicaid systems for long-term care facility services. *Healthcare Financial Management* (April).

Jensen, G. (1979) Nursing home costs in Indiana. In Birnbaum et al. (1979), q.v.

Johnson, D. E. (1984) Survey plots 475 chains' growth. *Modern Healthcare* (May 15):65-84.

Kahn, K. A., W. Hines, A. S. Woodson, and G. Burkham-Armstrong (1977) A multidisciplinary approach to assessing the quality of long-term care facilities. *The Gerontologist* 17:61-65.

Kane, R. L. (1983) Predicting the outcomes of nursing home patients. *The Gerontologist* 23(2):200-206.

Kane, R. L., R. M. Bell, S. D. Hosek, S. Z. Riegler, and R. A. Kane (1983) Outcome-based reimbursement for nursing home care. A paper prepared for the National Center for Health Services Research. Santa Monica, Calif.: The Rand Corporation (December).

Kane, R., R. Kane, D. Keffel, R. Brook, C. Eby, G. Goldberg, L. Rubenstein, and J. Van Ryzin (1979) *The PSRO and the Nursing Home. Vol I, An Assessment of PSRO Long-Term Care Review.* Report submitted to Health Care Financing Administration (DHEW Contract no. 500-78-0040).

Kart, C., and B. Manard (1976) Quality of care in old age institutions. *The Gerontologist* 16:250-256.

Kastenbaum, R. J., and S. E. Candy (1973) The 4% fallacy: A methodological and empirical critique of extended care facility population statistics. *Journal of Aging and Human Development* 4(Winter):15-22.

Koetting, M. (1980) *Nursing Home Organization and Efficiency.* Lexington, Mass.: Lexington Books.

Kosberg, J. (1973) Differences in proprietary institutions caring for affluent and non-affluent elderly. *The Gerontologist* 13:229-304.

Kosberg, J., and S. Tobin (1972) Variability among nursing homes. *The Gerontologist* 12:214-219.

Kuntz, E. F. (1981a) Nursing home chains buy up smaller groups. *Modern Healthcare* (June):68-72.

Kuntz, E. F. (1981b) Retirement apartments promise big business for nursing home chains. *Modern Healthcare* (June):72-74.

Kuntz, E. F. (1982) Systems scoop up nursing homes. *Modern Healthcare* (May):102-104.

Kuntz, E. F. (1983) Firms converge on home care market. *Modern Healthcare* (May):142-143.

Kuntz, E. F. (1984) For-profits adding home health-care to aid bottom lines. *Modern Healthcare* (May 15).

Kurowski, B., and L. Breed (1981) *A Synthesis of Research on Client Needs Assessment and Quality Assurance Programs in Long-Term Care.* Denver: University of Colorado Health Services Research Center.

Lane, L. F. (1979) *Private Insurance for Long-Term Care: Availability Problems and Actions.* Washington, D.C.: American Health Care Association.

Lane, L. F. (1981) The nursing home: Weighing investment decisions. *Healthcare Financial Management* (May):30-45.

Lane, L. F. (1984) Developments in facility-based services. Paper prepared for the Institute of Medicine, National Academy of Sciences, Washington, D.C.

Lasch, C. (1979) *The Culture of Narcissism.* New York: Warner Books.

LaViolette, S. (1982) Nonprofits setting up for-profit divisions; may even sell stock. *Modern Healthcare* (May):98-100.

LaViolette, S. (1983) Nursing home chains scramble for more private paying patients. *Modern Healthcare* (May):130-138.

LeConey, M. (1979) *Institutional Report: Nursing Home Industry Review.* New York: Merrill, Lynch, Pierce, Fenner and Smith, Inc.

Lee, A. J., and H. Birnbaum (1983) The determinants of nursing home operating costs in New York State. *Health Services Research* 18(2):285-308.

Lee, A. J., H. Birnbaum, and C. Bishop (1983) How nursing homes behave: A multi-equation model of nursing home behavior. *Social Science and Medicine* 17(23):1897-1906.

Lee, Y. S. (1984) Nursing homes and quality of health care: The first year of result of an outcome-oriented survey. *Journal of Health and Human Resource Administration* 7(1):32-60.

Levey, S., H. S. Rucklin, B. A. Stotsky, D. R. Kinloch, and W. Oppenheim (1973) An appraisal of nursing home care. *Journal of Gerontology* 28:222-228.

Levinson, R. (1984) *Impact of Proprietary Chain Ownership in the Nursing Home Industry on Quality Access and the Cost of Care.* April 25 draft of a report to the U.S. House Subcommittee on Oversight and Investigations.

Levit, K. R., H. Lazenby, D. R. Walso, and L. M. Davidoff (1985) National health expenditures, 1984. *Health Care Financing Review* 7(Fall):1-35.

Lewin, L. S., P. A. Derzon, and R. Margulies (1981) Investor-owned and non-profits differ in economic performance. *Hospitals* 55(13):52-58.

Linn, M. W., L. Gurel, and B. S. Linn (1977) Patient outcome as a measure of quality of nursing home care. *American Journal of Public Health* (April):337-344.

Liu, K., and J. Mossey (1980) The role of payment source in differentiating nursing home residents, services, and payments. *Health Care Financing Review* 2(Summer):51-61.

Manard, B. B., C. S. Kirt, and D. van Gils (1975) *Old Age Institutions.* Lexington, Mass.: Lexington Books.

Manor Care (1981) 10K Report to the Securities and Exchange Commission, Washington, D.C.

Manton, K. (1984) Changing health status and need for institutional and noninstitutional long-term care services. Paper prepared for the Institute of Medicine Committee on Nursing Home Regulation. Durham, N.C.: Duke University, Center for Demographic Studies.

Markus, G. R. (1972) *Nursing Homes and the Congress: A Brief History of Developments and Issues.* Washington, D.C.: U.S. Library of Congress.

McClure, E. (1968) *More Than a Roof: The Development of Minnesota Poor Farms and Homes for the Aged.* St. Paul: Minnesota Historical Society.

Mech, A. B. (1980) Evaluating the process of nursing care in long-term care facilities. *Quality Review Bulletin* 6(March):24-30.

Meiners, M. (1982) An econometric analysis of the major determinants of nursing home costs in the United States. *Social Science and Medicine* 16:887-898.

Mendelson, M. A. (1974) *Tender Loving Greed.* New York: Alfred A. Knopf.

Mennemeyer, S. (1979) Long-term care costs in New York State. Discussion paper number 455, State University of New York at Buffalo, Department of Economics, New York.

Minnesota Senate and House, Select Committee on Nursing Homes (1976) *Final Report.* St. Paul: Minnesota State Legislature.

Missouri State Senate, Health Care Committee (1978) *Nursing and Boarding Home Licensing in Missouri,* Jefferson City, Missouri.

Moden, M. (1982) *Rate Setting—Texas Medicaid SNF/ICF Program.* Austin: Texas Department of Human Resources, Office of Programs, Budget and Statistics.

Montgomery Securities (1983) *The American Nursing Home Industry: Introduction to a Changing Industry.* An institutional report by W. R. Friedman, Jr., and A. Bergh, San Francisco, California.

Morton Research Company (1982) *The Cost of Operating Nursing Homes—An In-depth Financial Analysis of the Nursing Home Industry.* Merrick, N.Y.: Morton Research Company.

Moss, F., and V. Halamandaris (1978) *Too Old, Too Sick, Too Bad: Nursing Homes in America.* Germantown, Md.: Aspen Systems Corp.

New Jersey State Nursing Home Commission (1978)

*Report on Long-Term Care.* Trenton, N.J.: New Jersey State Nursing Home Commission.

New York State Moreland Act Commission (1975) *Reimbursing Operating Costs: Dollars Without Sense.* New York State Commission on Nursing Homes and Residential Facilities.

New York Temporary State Commission on Living Costs and the Economy (1975) *Report on Nursing Homes and Health Related Facilities in New York State.* Albany: New York Temporary Commission.

*New York Times* (March 29, 1983) U.S. sees family help on Medicaid costs.

O'Brien, J., B. O. Saxberg, and H. L. Smith (1983) For profit or not-for-profit nursing homes: Does it matter? *The Gerontologist* 23(4):341-348.

Ohio Nursing Home Commission (1979) *A Program in Crisis: Blueprint for Action.* Columbus: Ohio General Assembly.

Ouslander, J. G., R. L. Kane, and I. B. Abrass (1982) Urinary incontinence in elderly nursing home patients. *Journal of the American Medical Association* 248:1194.

Palmer, H. C., and R. J. Vogel (1983) Models of the nursing home. In R. J. Vogel and H. C. Palmer, eds. *Long-term Care: Perspectives from Research and Demonstrations.* Washington, D.C.: Health Care Financing Administration.

Palmore, E. (1976) Total chance of institutionalization among the aged. *The Gerontologist* 16:504-507.

Pechansky, R., and L. Taubenhaus (1976) Institutional factors affecting quality of care in nursing homes. *Geriatrics* 20:591-598.

Punch, L. (1982) For-profit nursing home systems consolidate; beds grow by 18%. *Modern Healthcare* (June):74-77.

Punch, L. (1984) Chains expand their operations, expecting prospective pay boon. *Modern Healthcare* (May):131-140.

Punch, L. (1985) Investor-owned chains lead increase in beds. *Modern Healthcare* (June):126-136.

Rango, N. (1982) Nursing home care in the United States: Prevailing conditions and policy implications. *The New England Journal of Medicine* 307(14):883-889.

Ray, W. A., C. F. Federspeil, and W. Schaffner (1980) A study of anti-psychotic drug use in nursing homes: Epidemiological evidence suggesting misuse. *American Journal of Public Health* 70:485-491.

Rice, D. (1984) The health care needs of the elderly. In C. Harrington et al., eds. *Long-Term Care for the Elderly: Public Policy Issues.* Beverly Hills, Calif.: Sage Publications.

Riportella-Muller, R., and D. P. Slesinger (1982) The relationship of ownership and size to quality of care in Wisconsin nursing homes. *The Gerontologist* 22:429-434.

Ruchlin, H., and S. Levey (1972) Nursing home cost analysis: a case study. *Inquiry* 9(3):3-15.

Scanlon, W. (1980a) Nursing home utilization patterns: Implications for policy. *Journal of Health Politics, Policy and Law* 4(4):619-641.

Scanlon, W. (1980b) A theory of the nursing home market. *Inquiry* 17(1):25-41.

Scanlon, W., and J. Feder (1984) The long-term care marketplace: An overview. *Healthcare Financial Management* (January).

Scanlon, W., and M. Sulvetta (1983) The supply of institutional long-term care: Descriptive analysis of its growth and current state. (Contract No. 100-80-0158). In *Project to Analyze Existing Long-Term Care Data.* Final Report, Vol. 5. Washington, D.C.: Department of Health and Human Services.

Schlenker, R. E. (1984) Nursing home reimbursement, quality, and access—a synthesis of research. Paper prepared for the Institute of Medicine Conference on Reimbursement, Anaheim, California.

Schlenker, R. E., and P. W. Shaughnessy (1984) Case mix, quality, and cost relationships in Colorado nursing homes. *Health Care Financing Review.*

Schlenker, R. E., P. W. Shaughnessy, and I. Yslas (1983) The effect of case mix and quality on cost differences between hospital-based and freestanding nursing homes. *Inquiry* 20(Winter):361-368.

Shaughnessy, P., E. Tynan, D. Landes, C. Huggs, D. T. Holub, and L. Breed (1980) *An Evaluation of Swing-Bed Experiments to Provide Long-Term Care in Rural Hospitals, Volume 2, Final Technical Report.* Denver, Colorado: Center for Health Services Research, University of Colorado Health Sciences Center.

Shulman, D., and R. Galanter (1976) Reorganizing the nursing home industry: A proposal. *Milbank Memorial Fund Quarterly/Health and Society* (Spring):129-143.

Silvers, J. B., and B. Spitz (1983) The nursing home: Capital formation and funding. In *Capital Management in Healthcare Organizations.* Healthcare Financial Management Association.

Sims, W. B. (1984) Financing strategies for long-term care facilities. *Healthcare Financial Management* (March).

Sirrocco, A. (1983) *An Overview of the 1980 National Master Facility Inventory Survey of Nursing and Related Care Homes.* Washington, D.C.: National Center for Health Statistics.

Smith, H. L., and M. D. Fottler (1981) Cost and cost containment in nursing homes. *Health Services Research* 16(1):17-41.

Spitz, B. (1976) Prospective reimbursement of nursing homes. A working paper. Washington, D.C.: The Urban Institute.

Stassen, M., and C. Bishop (1983a) Nursing home capacity in four states: Preliminary results. Draft report prepared for the Brandeis University Health Policy Consortium, Waltham, Massachusetts.

Stassen, M., and C. E. Bishop (1983b) *Incorporating Case Mix in Prospective Reimbursement for SNF Under Medicare: Critical Review of Relevant Research.* Waltham, Mass.: Brandeis University Center for Health Policy Analysis and Research.

Stevens, R., and R. Stevens (1974) *Welfare Medicine in America: A Case Study.* New York: The Free Press.

Texas Department of Human Resources (1984) "Peek '83—A Preliminary Look at 1983 Cost Reports, File NH 1983SE." A report prepared by the Office of Programs Budget, Rate Setting Operations. Austin, Texas.

Texas Nursing Home Task Force (1978) *Report on Texas Nursing Homes.* A report to John L. Hill, Attorney General. Austin, Texas.

Thomas, W. C., Jr. (1969) *Nursing Homes and Public Policy: Drift and Decision in New York State.* Ithaca, N.Y.: Cornell University Press.

Ting, H. (1984) New directions in nursing home and home healthcare marketing. Draft manuscript. National Medical Enterprises.

Torrey, B. B. (1984) The visible cost of the invisible aged: The fiscal implications of the growth in the very old. Paper presented at the American Association for the Advancement of Science Annual Meeting in New York City.

Trautman, W. B. (1984) *Economic Concentration and the Federal Tax Code.* Santa Monica, Calif.: The Rand Corporation (Rand Paper Series, P-6994).

U.S. Bureau of the Census (1983) America in transition: An aging society. *Current Population Reports.* Series P-23, No. 128. Washington, D.C.: U.S. Government Printing Office.

U.S. Congress, Senate Committee on Finance (1972) *The Social Security Amendments of 1972: Report to Accompany H.R. 1.* 92nd Congress, 2nd Session, S.R. 92-1230. Washington, D.C.: U.S. Government Printing Office.

U.S. Congress, Senate Committee on Labor and Public Welfare (1960) *The Condition of American Nursing Homes.* Washington, D.C.: U.S. Government Printing Office.

U.S. DHEW (Department of Health, Education, and Welfare) (1975a) *Long-Term Care Facility Improvement Study, Introductory Report.* Office of Nursing Home Affairs. Washington, D.C.: U.S. Government Printing Office.

U.S. DHEW (1975b) *Selected Operating and Financial Characteristics of Nursing Homes, United States: 1973-74 National Nursing Home Survey. Vital and Health Statistics,* Series 13, No. 12. DHEW Publication No. (HRA) 76-1773. Washington, D.C.: U.S. Government Printing Office.

U.S. DHEW (1978) Memo from the Audit Agency on multi-state chains to Tom Morris, inspector-general, HEW, Washington, D.C.

U.S. DHEW (1979) The national nursing home survey 1977 summary for the United States. *Vital and Health Statistics,* Series 13, No. 43. Washington, D.C.: U.S. Government Printing Office.

U.S. DHHS (Department of Health and Human Services) (1981a) *The Need for Long-Term Care.* Washington, D.C.: The Federal Council on Aging.

U.S. DHHS, Office of the Assistant Secretary for Planning and Evaluation (1981b) Working Papers on Long-Term Care Prepared for the 1980 Undersecretary's Task Force on Long-Term Care. Washington, D.C.: U.S. Department of Health and Human Services.

U.S. National Center for Health Statistics (1979) The national nursing survey 1977, summary for the United States. *Vital and Health Statistics,* Series 13, No. 43. Washington, D.C.: U.S. Government Printing Office.

U.S. National Center for Health Statistics (1984) Trends in nursing and related care homes and hospitals. *Vital and Health Statistics,* Series 14, No. 30. DHHS Pub. No. (PHS) 84-1825. Washington, D.C.: U.S. Government Printing Office.

U.S. Senate, Committee on Finance (1970) *Medicare and Medicaid: Problems, Issues and Alternatives.* 91st Congress, 2nd Session. Washington, D.C.: U.S. Government Printing Office.

U.S. Senate, Committee on Finance (1972) *The Social Security Act Amendments of 1972: Report to a Company H.R. 1.* 92nd Congress, 2nd Session. Washington, D.C.: U.S. Government Printing Office.

U.S. Senate, Committee on Labor and Public Welfare (1960) *The Condition of American Nursing Homes.* Washington, D.C.: U.S. Government Printing Office.

U.S. Senate, Special Committee on Aging (1984) *Discrimination Against the Poor and Disabled in Nursing Homes.* Senate Hearing 98-1091. Washington, D.C.: U.S. Government Printing Office.

U.S. Senate, Special Committee on Aging, Subcommittee on Long-Term Care (1974) *Nursing Home Care in the United States: Failure in Public Policy.* Washington, D.C.: U.S. Government Printing Office.

U.S. Senate, Special Committee on Aging, Subcommittee on Long-Term Care (1975a) Doctors in nursing homes: The shunned responsibility. Supporting paper No. 3. Washington, D.C.: U.S. Government Printing Office.

U.S. Senate, Special Committee on Aging, Subcommittee on Long-Term Care (1975b) Nurses in nursing homes: The heavy burden (the reliance on untrained and unlicensed personnel). Supporting paper No. 4. Washington, D.C.: U.S. Government Printing Office.

Valiante, J. (1984) Forecasting capital requirements: Potential trends. *Health Care Financial Management* (August):52-59.

Van Gelder, L. (1975) Stein for phasing out profit-making nursing homes. *New York Times,* February 27, p. 22.

Virginia Joint Legislative Audit and Review Commission (JLARC) (1978) *Long-Term Care in Virginia*. Richmond: The Virginia General Assembly.

Vladeck, B. (1980) *Unloving Care: The Nursing Home Tragedy*. New York: Basic Books.

Vogel, R. J. (1983) The industrial organization of the nursing home industry. In R. J. Vogel and H. C. Palmer, eds. *Long-term Care: Perspectives from Research and Demonstrations*. Washington, D.C.: Health Care Financing Administration.

Vogel, R. J., and H. C. Palmer, eds. (1983) *Long-term Care: Perspectives from Research and Demonstrations*. Washington, D.C.: Health Care Financing Administration.

Waldman, S. (1983) A legislative history of nursing home care. In R. J. Vogel and H. C. Palmer, eds. *Long-term Care: Perspectives from Research and Demonstrations*. Washington, D.C.: Health Care Financing Administration.

Waldo, D., and R. Gibson (1982) National health expenditures, 1981. *Health Care Financing Review* 4(1).

Wallack, S., and J. Greenberg (1984) Public financing of long-term care: Its relationship to delivery systems and private sector initiatives. *Healthcare Financial Management* (April).

Washington Senate, Select Committee on Nursing Homes (1978) *Report on the Current Rate-Setting and Cost Reimbursement System for Nursing Homes*. A report prepared for the State Senate by Touche Ross and Company.

Watkins, R., and W. Spicer (1984) Chains report big revenue gains. *Contemporary Administrator*.

Weisbrod, B. (1977) *The Voluntary Nonprofit Sector*. Lexington, Mass.: D.C. Heath.

Weisbrod, B. A., and M. Schlesinger (1983) Public, private, nonprofit ownership and the response to asymmetric information: The case of nursing homes. Discussion paper No. 209, Center for Health Economics and Law, University of Wisconsin at Madison.

Weissert, W. (1984) Home equity financing of long-term care. Presentation at the Heatlh Care Financing Administration Meeting on Long-Term Financing, January 24, Washington, D.C.

Weissert, W. G. (1985) Estimating the long-term care population: Prevalence rates and selected characteristics. *Health Care Financing Review* 6(4) (Fall).

Weissert, W., and W. Scanlon (1983) Determinants of institutionalization of the aged. In *Project to Analyze Existing Long-Term Care Data*. Final report, Vol. 111 (Contract No. 100-80-0158) Washington, D.C.: U.S. Department of Health and Human Services.

Weissert, W. G., and W. J. Scanlon (1985) Determinants of nursing home discharge status. *Medical Care* 23(April):333-343.

Winn, S. (1974) Analysis of selected characteristics of a matched sample of nonprofit and proprietary nursing homes in the State of Washington. *Medical Care* 12:221-228.

Winn, S. (1975) Assessment of cost related characteristics and conditions of long-term care patients. *Inquiry* 12:344-353.

Winn, S., and K. M. McCaffree (1976) Characteristics of nursing homes perceived to be effective and efficient. *The Gerontologist* 16:415-419.

Zimmer, J. G. (1975) Characteristics of patients and care provided in health-related and skilled nursing facilities. *Medical Care* 13(December):992-1010.

Zimmer, J. G. (1979) Medical care evaluation studies in long-term facilities. *Journal of the American Geriatrics Society* 27:62-72.

# Index

beds, 30, 32, 80, 475
capital costs, 80
capital raising by, 61
chief executive officer compensation, 476
closures by, 109-110
control of, 474
costs of care in, 480-483, 486
diversification by, 40, 476, 486
dividend yields, 72
drug and supply expenses, 80
economies of scale, 77, 80
effective tax rate, 53
expenses, 95
financial performance, 476, 486
flow-of-funds statement, 50, 52-54
freestanding facility operation by, 40
growth trends, 27-29, 108, 190, 250-259, 290,
    375, 474-480, 486
hospital size in, 30
information sources on, 250
lender preference for, 55, 60
lengths of stay in, 95
locational preferences, 29-30, 103-104, 105, 255
management of not-for-profit hospitals, 41
markup by, 480
medical staff size and composition, 431
number of hospitals, 30, 300, 474
occupancy rates, 94, 105
patient outcomes in, 367-368
physician compensation arrangements in, 430,
    432
physician exit and voice mechanisms in, 176
physician privileges in, 176, 431-432
price differentials between not-for-profit
    hospitals and, 80
pricing strategies, 294-296
profitability of, 290, 476
quality of care in, 367-368, 476, 483-486
revenue sources, 196
services offered by, 108-109, 480, 486
size, 29
staffing of, 176, 422-433
tax obligations and payments, 53-54, 62, 195
teaching hospitals, 143-149
uncompensated care by, 103, 486
vertical integration of services by, 40
local control in, 61, 467-470
medical staff sizes, 422-457
modeling of behavior of, 260-289
not-for-profit
    beds, 29, 30, 32
    capital raising by, 61
    corporate restructuring of, 42
    diversification by, 40
    formation of, 28-29
    geographic distribution of hospitals, 287
    government subsidy of, 62-63

investor-owned subsidiaries of, 42
management of for-profit hospitals by, 41
management of, 468-469
number of hospitals in, 29, 30
religious/secular breakdown, 29
vertical integration of services by, 40
occupancy rates, 39-40, 77, 95
personnel management by, 479
physician privileges, 422-457
planning by, 479
political power of, 479
pricing strategies, 277
quality of care in, 375-377, 483-487
revenue sources, 41
size, 29
types of health services, 26
vertical integration of services by, 39
*see also* Hospitals; Ownership/affiliation
    comparisons

## N

National Association of Private Psychiatric Hospitals,
    44
National Health Care Affiliates, 503
National Health Corporation, 503
National Health Enterprises, 502, 507
National Health Planning and Resources
    Development Act of 1974, 118
National Health Services, 502
National Medical Care, 38
National Medical Enterprises
    diversification by, 476
    educational endowments by, 148
    growth trends, 109-110, 250, 252-257
    home care enterprises, 35
    number of hospitals, 44, 250, 474
    nursing home operations, 33, 528
    psychiatric hospital ownership, 32, 44
    revenue sources, 40
    tax obligations and payments, 53, 114, 119
    teaching hospital construction, 144
    uncompensated care by, 114
    vertical integration of services by, 40
National Medical Home Care, Inc. 35
Netherlands, hospital ownership and financing in, 56
New Jersey
    College of Medicine and Dentistry of, 144
    investor-owned hospitals in, 476
    uncompensated care in, 119
New York
    investor-owned hospitals in, 476
    nursing home costs in, 522
North Carolina, financing uncompensated care in,
    119
Nurses per patient, 130, 131
Nursing homes
    access to care in, 110-111, 189, 526-531